D1474090

By James Robert Parish

AS AUTHOR

The Fox Girls*
The Paramount Pretties*
The Slapstick Queens
Good Dames
Hollywood's Great Love Teams*
Elvis!
The Great Movie Heroes
Great Child Stars
Film Directors Guide: Western Europe
Great Western Stars
The Jeanette MacDonald Story

AS CO-AUTHOR

The Emmy Awards: A Pictorial History
The Cinema of Edward G. Robinson
The MGM Stock Company: The Golden Era*
The Great Spy Pictures
The George Raft File
The Glamour Girls*
Vincent Price Unmasked
Liza!
The Debonairs*
The Swashbucklers*
The Great Gangster Pictures
The Great Western Pictures
Film Directors Guide: The U. S.
Hollywood Players: The Forties*

AS EDITOR

The Great Movie Series Actors Television Credits:
1950-72 & Supplement

AS ASSOCIATE EDITOR

The American Movies Reference Book:
The Sound Era TV Movies

Published by Arlington House

THE TOUGH GUYS

James Robert Parish

RESEARCH ASSOCIATES

GREGORY W. MANK ■ MICHAEL R. PITTS
DON E. STANKE ■ T. ALLAN TAYLOR
JOHN ROBERT COCCHI ■ FLORENCE SOLOMON

ARLINGTON HOUSE·PUBLISHERS
NEW ROCHELLE, NEW YORK

Copyright © 1976 by James Robert Parish

All rights reserved. No portion of this book may be reproduced
without written permission from the publisher except by a reviewer
who may quote brief passages in connection with a review.

Library of Congress Cataloging in Publication Data

Parish, James Robert.
  The tough guys.

  Includes index.
  CONTENTS: James Cagney.—Kirk Douglas.—Burt Lancaster.
[etc.]
  1. Moving-picture actors and actresses—United States—Biography. I. Title.
PN1998.A2P415   791.43'028'0922   [B]   76-16867
ISBN 0-87000-338-0

for

HUMPHREY BOGART

(1899-1957)

Table of Contents

Key to the Film Studios

AA	Allied Artists Picture Corporation
AIP	American International Pictures
AVCO/ EMB	Avco Embassy Pictures Corporation
BV	Buena Vista Distributions, Co., Inc.
CIN	Cinerama, Inc.
COL	Columbia Pictures Industries, Inc.
EL	Eagle Lion Films, Inc.
EMB	Embassy Pictures Corporation
FN	First National Pictures, Inc. (became part of Warner Bros.)
FOX	Fox Film Corporation (became part of Twentieth Century-Fox)
LIP	Lippert Pictures, Inc.
MGM	Metro-Goldwyn-Mayer, Inc.
MON	Monogram Pictures Corporation
PAR	Paramount Pictures Corporation
PRC	Producers Releasing Corporation
RKO	RKO Radio Pictures, Inc.
REP	Republic Pictures Corporation
20th	Twentieth Century-Fox Corporation
UA	United Artists Corporation
UNIV	Universal Pictures, Inc.
WB	Warner Bros., Inc.

Acknowledgments

RESEARCH MATERIAL CONSULTANT:
Doug McClelland
RESEARCH VERIFIER:
Earl Anderson

Richard Braff
Mrs. Loraine Burdick
Kingsley Canham
Cinemabilia (Ernest Burns)
Robert A. Evans
Morris Everett, Jr.
Filmfacts (Ernest Parmentier)
Film Fan Monthly
Films in Review
Focus on Film
Pierre Guinle

Mrs. R. F. Hastings
Richard Hudson
Ken D. Jones
Miles Kreuger
Jane Greer Lasker
William T. Leonard
Albert B. Manski
David McGillivray
Jim Meyer
Mrs. Earl Meisinger
Peter Migilierini
Norman Miller
Movie Poster Serive (Bob Smith)
Movie Star News (Paula Klaw)
Richard Picchiarini
Screen Facts (Alan G. Barbour)
Don Shay
Charles Smith
Mrs. Peter Smith
Roz Starr Service
Charles K. Stumpf
Views and Reviews

And special thanks to Paul Myers, curator of the Theatre Collection at the Lincoln Center Library for the Performing Arts (NYC) and his staff: Monty Arnold, David Bartholomew, Rod Bladel, Donald Fowle, Maxwell Silverman, Dorothy Swerdlove, Betty Wharton, and Don Madison of Photo Service.

Publicity pose for *White Heat* (WB, 1949)

James Cagney

5'6"
150 pounds
Red hair
Brown eyes
Cancer

Edward G. Robinson was once asked if there was anything he would have liked to have added to his many diversified professional credits. The star responded, "Yes, I would love to have been able to do a musical like *Yankee Doodle Dandy,* and do it just half as well as Jimmy Cagney did."

James Cagney, the cocky, shamrock-laden elitist of gangsterdom who never said, "You dirty rat," has enjoyed tributes like the one above throughout his screen career. Bette Davis dubbed her Warner Bros. confrere as the actor "who made the gangster artistic." The American Film Institute honored him with their second Life Achievement Award, sandwiching the star between the American screen's most honored director, John Ford, and its most original and erratic talent, Orson Welles. Despite his retirement, Cagney still is bombarded by lucrative offers from a Hollywood he has long since disowned.

The luck of the Irish has been a cornerstone in his career. Although he is remembered primarily as the screen's top thug, the diversity of roles that came his way is staggering. He shifted from early cinema gangsters to Bottom in *A Midsummer Night's Dream*; his ruthless dynamics would occasionally abate to make room for celluloid comedy; and his top triumph would be singing and dancing to frenzied flag-waving as George M. Cohan. Compared to such tough-guy contemporaries as Paul Muni and Edward G. Robinson, roles that did justice to his oversized talent came along very frequently and quite naturally. Seemingly, James' confident talent was a magnet for such challenges, allowing him to do three times as many pictures as Muni and outranking Robinson via quality of achievement if not in quantity of work.

Certainly, Cagney's personal lifestyle has made the public's instant acceptance of his image even more impressive. He is not a boisterous, multi-married ladies' man (he has been married to the same woman for over half a century). He hasn't been involved in political controversy. And the theme of his career has been "you-only-owe-the-public-a-good-performance." Whether it meant walking out of a studio or going into retirement, Cagney's focus was always on himself, always as a man who demanded and won what he wanted on his own terms.

Despite his abhorrence of and ban on public interviews in recent years, it is easy to understand why Cagney is still a popular household name. Few actors so personify a colorful era as does jut-chinned James. And few made oncamera mayhem so delightful a pleasure for audiences everywhere. Perhaps only feminists have a gripe against the ex-movie star. They may not be able to forgive him for pushing that trademark grapefruit into Mae Clarke's face some forty-five years ago.

James Francis Cagney, Jr. was born in New York City on July 17, 1899 (1904 would become the ritualized birth year given out by the studio). He was born above a saloon (his dad's) at the corner of Avenue D and 8th Street on the Lower East Side, an area known as the "gas house district." His father, James Francis Cagney, was descended from the O'Caignes of County Leitrim, Ireland, and his mother, nee Carolyn Nelson, was half-Irish, half-Norwegian. There were five children in the family; James, Jr. was number two.

Cagney, Sr. was a bartender. "He had a series of things he did every morning before leaving to go to work," recalled his famous son to newsmen years later. "He'd kiss mom good-bye; then he'd blow a kiss to us kids; put on his hat over his shock of heavy black hair; bless himself; run his hands over his trousers to make sure all his buttons were buttoned; and be off. As far as I know, he did that every morning of his married life." Once on the job, the bartender had a problem; he often drank more than the customers. "My father used to put it away, but he was a quiet drinker. You never knew he had it in him except by the angle of his hat. He would always tip his hat a little over one eye."

Due to the father's drinking problems, it fell on Mrs. Cagney to keep the family together, a task made none easier by her own ill health—she was regularly admitted to the local hospital for a gall bladder problem. And nothing was eased by the neighborhood to which the family moved when James was still very young; at that time, 96th Street, between 3rd and Lexington Avenues, was hardly an ideal area. Cagney would reminisce, "That always sticks in my memory as a street of stark tragedy, somehow. It seems, as I look back, that there was always crepe hanging on a door or two somewhere on the block. There was always the clanging of an ambulance bell. Patrol wagons came often. . . ." The ethnic makeup of the neighborhood was varied: it included a potpourri of immigrants of German, Hungarian, Italian, Irish, and Jewish origin. Cagney learned to speak fluent Yiddish very early. (In later years, Cagney would find himself in a Hollywood traffic jam directly across from fellow Yiddish-theatre-alumnus and Warner Bros. contractee Paul Muni, and the two passed the time swapping Yiddish insults.)

Mother Cagney insisted that all her children obtain a proper education. It would pay dividends: brothers Harry and Ed would become physicians; William would become an advertising executive-actor-movie producer and later James' mentor in films; and sister Jeanne would emerge as an actress of stage, screen, and television. To accomplish this mission required additional revenue in the Cagney household. So all the kids took on part-time jobs. Sometimes James juggled three at the same time. He was an office boy for the *New York Sun*, wrapped bundles for Wanamaker's Department Store, was a pool hall bouncer, sold tickets for the Hudson River Boat line, and even stacked books at the New York Public Library.

At one point, three of the Cagney boys worked as waiters in a restaurant on 114th Street, where James almost got a job for his mother as the cashier. But the manager discovered they were all related and fired the tribe in one fell swoop. Yet the assorted jobs provided the education, and Cagney was able to graduate from Stuyvesant High School and even to attend Columbia University for six months. (He kept tuition costs down by joining the Student Army Training Corps.)

When the Spanish influenza epidemic of 1918 swept through the city, it claimed Mr. Cagney's life before he was forty-two years old. "Near the end of his life, alcohol made him so sick," Jimmy would recall, "they'd wheel an ambulance up to the door and take him away to the hospital. It was rough to see that." It was so painful a lesson that Cagney, Jr. became a teetotaler permanently. Shortly after Cagney, Sr.'s demise, sister Jeanne was born, and Cagney, Jr. went back to work at Wanamaker's.

In the meantime, the ambitious Cagney boys had enrolled in a public speaking course at Lenox Hill Settlement House. The institution produced plays from time to time, and soon James replaced an indisposed Harry in a Chinese pantomime. Cagney was not very partial to the idea, as it took him away from his sports. But the actual performance captivated him. Soon he was seeking additional outlets for his dramatic interest. As a result, he appeared in a Settlement production of the musical comedy *What's For Why?*, as a Japanese emperor, played Pagliaccio in an Italian harlequinade written by a group member, starred in *The Lost Silk Hat*, and played a butler in the melodrama *The Two Orphans* at Hunter College. After returning to Wanamaker's, he also played in a Lenox Hill production of *The Faun*, in which he bounded across the stage in curly hair and a rather revealing goatskin costume.

While wrapping Wanamaker packages, a job whose dullness was matched only by the scant pay, Cagney confided about his money problems to a company salesman. The friend had heard that a show being produced at Keith's Eighth Street Theatre required a replacement for a cast member who had quit. Cagney jumped at the chance and reported to the theatre to audition.

When the over-anxious youth arrived, he could see why there was an opening. The show was *Every Sailor*, a wartime revue that refused to die. The available part required an actor to join some onstage servicemen as a female impersonator. The prospect of dressing up in the tackiest of 1919 female fashion did not appeal to Cagney at first. But the salary was twenty-five dollars a week, a lot better than the twelve dollars for a six-day work week he was earning at Wanamaker's. Cagney accepted.

On the first night he was with the show, his loyal family and friends arrived at the theatre. His entrance in drag with seven other beauties froze them into shock before his stoical mom gasped the command, "Applaud!" James capered in these distaff adornments for eight weeks. "It was a knockabout act, purely burlesque. We had a lot of fun and it never occurred to any of us to be ashamed of it. It might seem strange and unbelievable, taking into account my habitual desire to go unnoticed. But again, this illustrates what I mean when I say that I am not shy or self-conscious when I am on the stage or screen. For there I am not myself. I am not that fellow, Jim Cagney, at all. I certainly lost all consciousness of him when I put on skirts, wig, paint, powder, feathers, and spangles. Besides, that was the time, right after the war, when service actors were still fresh in mind, when female impersonators were the vogue."

Obviously, show business agreed with the resilient Cagney. Despite the pleas of his horrified mother, he decided to pursue it further. In the summer of 1920 he answered an open call audition for a new Broadway musical, *Pitter Patter*. It was based on the farce, *Caught in the Rain,* by William Collier and Grant Stewart, had a script by Will M. Hough, and music and lyrics composed by William B. Friedlander. William Kent was the star. James would later recall the important audition: "I didn't know the highland fling from a sailor's hornpipe and I couldn't even sing 'Sweet Adeline,' but I needed that job. Fifty applicants assembled. I watched the fellow's feet next to me and did what he did." The result was a chorus boy job with the show that paid $35 a week.

Pitter Patter debuted at the Longacre Theatre on September 29, 1920, and met with public endorsement. The *New York Times* recommended Kent's performance, noting: "a hard working, if not completely decorative chorus, took second ranking in the hearts of the audience." After three months, James was given a specialty number to perform and a fifteen-dollar weekly raise, which required that he serve as Kent's dresser. When pint-sized Ernest Truex replaced Kent, Cagney performed similar valet chores for him; when the show went on the road after 110 Manhattan performances, Cagney augmented his salary by carrying baggage.

Flanking James in the chorus of *Pitter Patter* were two people of whom he would see much in later years. One was Allen Jenkins, who would become a Warners' stock company player and a pal of Cagney's. (He was present at the Cagney Tribute in 1974, shortly before his death.) The other was an Iowa girl named Frances Willard Vernon, nicknamed "Billie." One night after a performance, her date stood her up. To cheer herself up, she asked Cagney to dinner. He did not have the spare cash, so she volunteered the funds. A romance developed. "While the rest of the cast was goofing off, Jimmy would either be studying, reading, or going over his routine," she recalled years later. "It seemed as though he just couldn't let go and have fun." His first impression of her, after their first dinner together, was "I just knew this was it." In 1921 they were wed and the actor's associates insist that she has always been the only woman in his life.

In 1921, *Pitter Patter* faded away. With Broadway prospects bleak, James and Billie tried vaudeville. The twenty-two-year-old chorus boy discovered he liked to dance. "I was always a hoofer," he informed *Newsweek* Magazine fifty-three years later. "Nobody taught me how. I'd watch a step, then steal it, change it, make it eccentric. I always thought it wasn't showy enough." But despite his ever-improving style, each new vaudeville act the couple devised failed to impress theatre managers or customers. One of the teamings, Parker, Rand, and Cagney, drew this comment from *Variety*: "One of the boys, James Cagney, can dance a bit. Small time is his only chance."

On occasion the Cagneys worked together. Alone, James played in *Dot's My Boy,* an act conceived by Hugh Herbert, and toured with the Ada Jaffee troupe. In the

14

meantime, Billie joined with Wynne Gibson (who was later to become a Paramount contract player specializing in roles as a tart), in a "sister" act that sometimes played in the same city and the same time as her husband (but also with some depressing near-misses). The engagements were always small time. The actor would later call the series of tank towns the "Cagney Circuit."

James and Billie did manage to appear together in *Lew Field's Ritz Girls of 1922,* a Shubert package that toured the country. The couple then traveled to Los Angeles, where James met his mother-in-law for the first time.

Attempts to win a movie contract proved fruitless. There was a brief try at organizing a dancing school, but that evaporated when Cagney discovered that most of his students knew more than he did. More small-time vaudeville followed. "Vernon and Nye," as the Cagneys now called themselves, appeared in Chicago in an act entitled "Out of Town Papers." James considered it a move upward when he appeared in a sketch in which he actually played a dramatic scene with Victor Kilian. Kilian, shortly afterward, defected to Broadway to play in Eugene O'Neill's *Desire under the Elms.* When the juvenile lead in that drama was being replaced, Kilian notified Cagney to audition. He did not win the part, but he did make an impression on the producer, who remembered him when he was casting a new play, *Outside Looking In.*

The play, by Maxwell Anderson, was based on Jim Tully's *Beggars of Life.* The theme was the life of the hobo. Charles Bickford was cast in the lead role of Oklahoma Red; James was the second lead, Little Red. It was a powerful drama, and Cagney's big moment came in the second act when he was tried by his fellow vagabonds in a kangaroo court, which was held in a boxcar, for eating in restaurants, saving a girl from a life of sin, sleeping in beds, and similar activities that conflicted with the hoboes' particular code of ethics.

When the play opened on September 7, 1925, at the Greenwich Village Theatre, its sardonic theme made the proper impact. "Never were there such ragamuffins on the stage," wrote the *New York Times,* adding that "James Cagney is sullen as Little Red and imaginative." Critic Burns Mantle *(New York Daily News)* was more ebullient in his praise, claiming that Bickford "and Mr. Cagney as his adversary, Little Red, do the most honest acting now to be seen in New York. I believe that Mr. Barrymore's effective performance of Hamlet would be a mere feat of eloquence if compared to the characterizations of either Mr. Bickford or Mr. Cagney, both of whom are unknowns." The show ran for 113 performances. By the time it closed, James Cagney was a recognizable, if not securely established, theatre name.

After the successful *Outside Looking In* closed, the Theatre Guild, the proving ground for Edward G. Robinson's acting talents, offered Cagney an opportunity with their highly lauded company. Cagney refused on the grounds that the money mentioned was not sufficient. At this point, producer Jed Harris, having witnessed Cagney's Little Red, offered him the leading role as the loquacious hoofer Roy Lane in the London-bound company of *Broadway,* then one of New York's hottest shows. (Lee Tracy was playing Roy Lane in the original cast.) It was a tremendous break, and to make matters ideal, his wife was granted a small role in the show. It was not until after two weeks of rehearsal, a smooth dress rehearsal, and putting his baggage on a ship, that Harris decided Cagney was not right in the role and fired him. (Reportedly, Cagney was dismissed because he refused to imitate Tracy's well-liked performance.) To avoid having to pay Cagney throughout the projected London run, a contingency provided for in the contract, Harris switched Cagney to a post as

Tracy's understudy in New York. James eventually replaced Roy R. Lloyd in the role of Mike in the Broadway version. Nevertheless, he was so upset by the change of events that he seriously pondered quitting the theatre.

Finding it difficult to visualize any other kind of living, Cagney accepted a none-too-good suitor's role in *Women Go On Forever,* a Daniel N. Rubin play examining life in a miserable boarding house. It debuted on September 7, 1927, at the Forrest Theatre. Brooks Atkinson *(New York Times)* penned a long-winded dismissal. Cagney had a more concise analysis to tell reporters about the less than pleasant results. "Mary Boland, who starred, had decided to abandon comic roles and return to serious dramas. On opening night, Mary's first word was 'jummph' and the audience broke up. That was the end of that play. We ran for 18 weeks, but it wasn't the same play we started out with."

While income from the play was steady, James opened The Cagneys' School of the Dance in Elizabeth, New Jersey, for professional dancers. Billie did most of the teaching, as Cagney was working quite steadily on Broadway now. The school supplied the couple with an assured income and also led to James' choreographing, dancing, and acting in *Grand Street Follies of 1928.* The satirical revue burlesqued such varied shows as *Romeo and Juliet, Dracula,* and *Porgy and Bess.* There were take-offs of such Broadway favorites as Laurette Taylor, Helen Hayes, and Lionel Atwill, and such national figures as Charles Lindbergh. Cagney's contributions were appreciated, but the show was carried mainly by Dorothy Sands who did a marvelous Mae West send-up, and by Albert Carroll, an adept female impersonator whose big moment was appearing onstage made-up on one side as Mrs. Fiske and on the other side as Ethel Barrymore. The show ran at the Booth Theatre for 144 performances and on May 1, 1929, a new version opened for 88 performances. *Grand Street Follies of 1929* used most of the same cast. Cagney's big moments in version number two were sketches called "The A.B.C. of Traffic" (as a dancing cop) and "I Need You So" (as a harlequin).

Ambitious James had little time and less inclination for frivolity during these days (he also filled in gaps between *Grand Street Follies* with stock in Cleveland, Ohio, and in Massachusetts as an actor-dancer), but he did form some lasting friendships. Pat O'Brien and Frank McHugh, both congenial Irish-Americans, and both winning attention on the Broadway stage, saw a good deal of the feisty Cagney. Often, the three would meet after performances at a local bar, although James steered clear of the booze.

Yet another sleazy boarding house drama followed. It was George Kelly's *Maggie the Magnificent,* which was unveiled at the Cort Theatre on October 21, 1929. Shirley Warde had the title role. Included in the cast was a young actress whom Cagney would be seeing a great deal of over the next few years. Her name was Joan Blondell. The *New York Times* had unkind words for the drama, but it did praise "the scape-grace son played with clarity and spirit by James Cagney, and the gum-chewing, posing, brazen jade played by Joan Blondell." The *New York World* also recommended "the perfect gas-house lingo of James Cagney," but was indifferent to the show itself. It closed after thirty-two performances.

The reviews garnered by Cagney and Miss Blondell (then a brunette) were too good to be ignored, and both quickly landed jobs after the demise of *Maggie the Magnificent.* They were teamed in *Penny Arcade* (Fulton Theatre: March 10, 1930), which was written by Marie Bauner and directed by William Keighley. It was a sordid story of carnival life, with James as a weakling who murders in self-defense and then tries to thrust the blame for the homicide onto his sister's lover. Blondell was a wise-cracking photographer's assistant. The play suffered by comparison with another carnie drama, *The Barker,* starring Claudette Colbert, that had opened on Broadway three years before. *Penny Arcade* only ran twenty-four performances, but again the scribes were kind to Cagney (the *New York Times* rated him "excellent"), and the play ran long enough for Cagney, Blondell, and Keighley to win attention. Al Jolson, who had helped to revolutionize the film industry with his part-talkie *The Jazz Singer* (Warner Bros., 1927), bought the film rights to *Penny Arcade.*

"Al Jolson bought it on spec and sold it to Warner Brothers," Cagney would recall in a later interview, "and then they shipped the body with it. Jolson suggested I play the part I had in the Broadway stage version." The Burbank studio offered James $450 a week with a three-week guarantee, plus train fare. Joan Blondell was similarly imported, and after each was introduced to the technicalities of screen acting, they began work on the film. Meanwhile, Warners had changed the story's title to *Sinners' Holiday* (1930), entrusted direction to John G. Adolfi, cast Grant Withers and Evalyn Knapp in the leading roles, and ordered that the production-line feature be completed as soon as possible. Cagney and Blondell were billed third and fourth respectively.

Miss Blondell recalls the results: "Jimmy and I did our scene together, and when the brass saw the rushes, saw how fast we talked and what we could do, they sent word to the backlot where we were shooting for us to come to the front office and they offered us five-year contracts."

So Cagney faced Jack L. Warner for the first of many contract negotiations. Warner ran a tight lot in those Depression months, cranking out seventy-six feature films in 1930 alone. Directors like Michael Curtiz, Mervyn LeRoy, Archie Mayo, and Roy Del Ruth were adept at churning out films under budget and on schedule, working their casts six days a week, usually fourteen hours a day. Sometimes the contract players would be shunted from one film's soundstage to another on the same day.

Warner Bros. had made screen history and boxoffice records with *The Jazz Singer,* had over-extended their budget to recruit the "world's greatest living actor," John Barrymore, as a studio property, and was currently brandishing monocled Mr. George Arliss (1929-1930 Oscar winner for Warners' *Disraeli*) as another asset in its company's store. Warner believed in retaining a strong stock company on constant call. Among those in the Warner Bros.-First National complex were: Joe E. Brown, Dorothy Mackaill, Loretta Young, Grant Withers, Douglas Fairbanks, Jr., Billie Dove, Mary Astor, Richard Barthelmess, Constance and Joan Bennett (for a time), and Rin Tin Tin. Like other studio moguls, Jack L. Warner was always seeking fresh faces who could bounce through the exhausting repertoire of celluloid fare pushed out by the studio. Warner viewed Cagney as one of those prospective new faces, not as the ulcer-inducer that Cagney would eventually become. Warner offered a three-year contract at $450 a week. When Cagney's agent advised his client that he could abrogate the agreement if the occasion warranted, he signed for what was pretty good money for a kid from 96th Street and Third Avenue.

Sinners' Holiday, all fifty-five minutes' worth, opened in late 1930. It was an unusual screen debut for Cagney. He was Harry Delano, a cheap carnival punk who frets, sweats, and repeatedly clutches his mother (Lucille LaVerne) with whining lines like: "I didn't mean to, Ma. Honest, I couldn't help it. Honest, I couldn't. Don't leave me. You've *got* to believe me. You've *got* to help me. I'm scared, Ma."

17

With Purnell Pratt, Grant Withers, Evalyn Knapp, and Beryl Mercer in *Sinner's Holiday* (WB, 1930)

The critics were impressed. One trade journal, *Exhibitor's Herald-World*, wrote: "Cagney has by no means an easy role in his portrayal of a highly nervous youth who by nature cannot go straight. It is the type of part which can be spoiled by the slightest shade of over-acting, but Cagney carries his characterization in each sequence just far enough." After Billie read her husband the *New York Times* comment that "the most impressive acting is done by James Cagney," the actor arranged for his wife to join him on the coast.

Cagney was assigned almost immediately to his next studio film, the Archie Mayo-directed *Doorway to Hell* (Warner Bros., 1930), one of the best of the early racketeer films. Unfortunately, it has never received the full credit it deserves. Lewis (Lew) Ayres, a major boxoffice attraction due to his recent triumph in Universal's *All Quiet on the Western Front*, played the leading role of a bootlegger attempting to go straight. James was billed sixth, as his chief lieutenant, Steve Mileway. Warners advertised the film as "the motion picture gangdom dared Hollywood to make."

William A. Wellman, the salty, flamboyant director, then cast Cagney in his railroad saga, *The Steel Highway*, eventually released as *Other Men's Women* (Warner Bros., 1931). Grant Withers starred, and second leads James Hall and Marian Nixon were replaced by Regis Toomey and Mary Astor. With all this swapping around, the result was a dull tale saved only by Wellman's flair for action sequences. Cagney was billed fourth, and Blondell, her exhaustive studio schedule in full swing, drew fifth, but neither had much of anything to do. Cagney was a gang worker on the railroad, Blondell was her usual saucy self, this time as a waitress named Marie.

Fortunately, Cagney won the attention of Mr. George Arliss, who shared the Warner star throne with John Barrymore. Appearing in an Arliss film was tanta-

With Lew Ayres and Robert Elliott in *Doorway to Hell* (WB, 1930)

mount to going to heaven—it was class with a capital C. Arliss was then preparing to star in *The Millionaire* (Warner Bros., 1931).

As he would detail in his autobiography, *My Ten Years in the Studios* (1940), Arliss recalled: "There was a small but important part in *The Millionaire*—the part of an insurance agent. . . . I saw several promising young men without being much impressed one way or the other; but there was one more waiting to be seen; he was a lithe, smallish man. I knew at once he was right; as I talked to him I was sure he could give me everything I wanted. He wasn't acting to me now; he wasn't trying to impress me; he was just being natural, and, I thought, a trifle independent for a bit actor; there was a suggestion of 'Here I am; take me or leave me; and hurry up.' As I came to my decision I remember saying, 'Let him come just as he is—those clothes —and no make-up stuff. Just as he is! The man was James Cagney. I was lucky!" When the film was released, James made a distinct impression with the public, even in the small assignment.

About the time that *The Millionaire* had gone into production, Cagney's career suffered a setback. *The Front Page,* a raucous newspaper story that on Broadway had starred Lee Tracy, was set for production by Howard Hughes. Lewis Milestone, about to direct the United Artists' release, recalled for the tabloids, "I originally wanted Jimmy Cagney to play Hildy Johnson. [Darryl F.] Zanuck [then production head of Warner Bros.] agreed, but Howard Hughes wouldn't accept him—he considered Cagney a 'little runt'; this was before Cagney had made his mark in *Public Enemy.*" James' friend Pat O'Brien won the Hildy Johnson role.

Then opportunity came again, but it almost did not happen. Two ex-Chicago newspaper reporters, Kuber Glasmon and John Bright, were trying to peddle a script entitled *Beer and Blood* to a Hollywood studio—any studio. They eventually

With George Arliss in *The Millionaire* (WB, 1931)

With Eddie Woods and Beryl Mercer in *The Public Enemy* (WB, 1931)

With Mae Clarke in *The Public Enemy*

21

made a solid contact at Warners, but Darryl F. Zanuck felt gangster films had run their course. (*Little Caesar* had only just been put into release by the studio.)

Warner Bros. director William A.Wellman disagreed. He sniffed simmering ingredients in the rough script that he hoped to bring to a full boil. Zanuck asked him for one good reason why this further variation of the underworld motif should be put onto film. Replied Wellman, "Because I'll make it the toughest one of them all!" Zanuck capitulated in the face of such strong conviction. Jack L. Warner gave the go-ahead and the studio began setting up the production that would become *The Public Enemy* (Warner Bros., 1931).

The Public Enemy dealt with one Tom Powers, a Chicago kid who grows up in the era of prohibition. He becomes associated with small time crooks, is eventually recruited by a big time bootlegging operation, becomes wealthy, estranges himself from his hard-working, honest, war-hero brother, kicks one moll out of his life for another one with more "class," throws punches and pumps bullets, and sees the "light" only after a barrage of machine guns makes him realize "I ain't so tough." But he never has the opportunity to go straight; rival gang members kidnap him from the hospital and deposit his corpse, trussed and bandaged, at his own front door. It was a dream part for any actor. The fortunate man to be cast in the role was Eddie Woods.

Who was Eddie Woods? He was a young actor on the rise in the film industry since he had become the fiancé of Louella O. Parsons' daughter. Pleasant, amiable, but not unique, was the verdict on Woods, but he got the part. To play Matt Doyle, Tom's lifelong friend who is his partner in crime but is basically a decent guy, the studio picked Cagney. It was a foil role designed more to shade Tom's animal brutality than anything else.

Wellman and the casting office stocked the cast with interesting faces. Beryl Mercer, so poignant as Lew Ayres' mother in *All Quiet on the Western Front,* became Powers' mother. She is the one individual in the film who regularly escapes her son's wrath. She actually rates his love, although he is never very demonstrative. Donald Cook played Mike, Tom's hard-working, "sucker," war-hero brother. (While quite an attraction on the stage, Cook somehow always drew level-headed, dull roles in the cinema.) Ubiquitous Joan Blondell and Mae Clarke joined the cast as Mamie and Kitty, respectively, floozies who become the mistresses of Matt and Tom. Jean Harlow, whose fair-haired beauty had just been showcased in *Hell's Angels* (United Artists, 1930), earned the role of Gwen Allen, a high-class hooker for whom Tom dumps Kitty. Murray Kinnell was Putty Nose, the crook who starts Matt and Tom on their criminal careers, Robert Emmett O'Connor played Paddy Ryan, the boys' later and more decent mentor, and Leslie Fenton played Nails Nathan, who brings the boys into the criminal big-time.

Cagney would not have long to play Matt Doyle. As Wellman once related: "I didn't see the rushes for three days because I was working late and said, 'Aw, to hell with them. I'll see them over the weekend.' When I looked at the rushes I said [to Zanuck], 'Look, there is a horrible mistake. We have the wrong guy in here. Cagney should be the lead.' Zanuck said, 'Well, you know who Eddie Woods is, don't you?' And I said, 'No, I don't. Who is he?' 'He's engaged to marry Louella Parson's daughter.' I said, 'Well, for Christ's sake, are you going to let some newspaperwoman run your business?' He said, 'Change them.' We changed them, and Cagney became a big star."

Surprisingly, Cagney was not pleased with the switch. He found the character of

Tom Powers offensive, and, like Edward G. Robinson with *Little Caesar* (First National, 1930), did not comprehend why anyone would be particularly interested in watching a full-length film about such a beast.

Nevertheless, it was a starring role. Cagney did his best to color it effectively. To individualize Tom Powers from the host of other screen gangsters who had so recently paraded before the public, James called on memories of his one-time East-Side companions. One denizen of his colorful area was a cherub-faced roughneck who always smiled: hence, the cocky, grinning nuance in *The Public Enemy*. Another local bad guy had a habit of baring his teeth like an animal whenever threatened: hence, that memorable close-up of Cagney walking alone in the night toward very probable extinction by the rival gang. A third characteristic, the gentle near-punch of a companion's chin, was a remembered gesture of his picturesque dad.

Wellman did all he could to keep his word to Zanuck about *The Public Enemy*. His direction is clever, fast-paced, and racy. Most of the murders are committed off-screen, a memorable exception being Matt Doyle's demise by being gunned down in the street. Some vivid examples of Wellman's directorial genius include the scene in which Cagney's Tom Powers and Woods' Matt Doyle follow Putty Nose home to avenge the bullying he gave them as kids. A cat runs before their path, setting the audience up for "bad luck" for the hoods in this endeavor. But bad luck does not come their way for a while. A few other memorable scenes: Tommy being fitted for more expensive clothes by a mincing, effeminate tailor; Tommy dancing with Harlow's Gwen Allen, with the camera single-mindedly following her shapely derriere; Cagney's Tommy rising in his pajamas for breakfast with Kitty, when we hear the giggling of Mamie in the next room, hinting at her and Matt's morning activity. And, of course, there is also their classic exchange in that particular scene:

> TOMMY (*Cagney*): *Got a drink in the house?*
> KITTY (*Clarke*): *Not before breakfast, dear.*
> TOMMY: *I didn't ask ya' for any lip I asked ya' if ya' had a drink!*
> KITTY: *I know, Tom, but . . . well, gee, I wish. . . .*
> TOMMY: *There ya' go with that wishin' stuff again! I wish you was a wishin' well—so that I could tie a bucket t'ya' and sink ya'!*
> KITTY: *Maybe you found someone you like better?*
> *At that, Cagney's Tommy takes half a grapefruit and grinds it into his mistress' face.*

The actor's recollection of this famous scene is, "We took it from a real life incident in which a gangster named Hymie Weiss hit his girl in the face with an omelet." Why was it changed from the original event? Director Wellman once gave his rationale:

"I was married then to a very beautiful girl who was an aviatrix . . . she was beautiful, and whenever we had an argument, she had a wonderful way of handling it. This wonderful, beautiful face became like a sculpture. There was no movement in it at all; it just was beautiful and dominant, just quiet. And it stayed that way for 2 or 3 days Well, that's a frightful thing to overcome, you know, you go absolutely crazy. And many a time when we had breakfast, and I used to have half a grapefruit, I wanted to take that grapefruit and mash it in her face. Just to make her change, and I had the grapefruit, I said, 'Oh baby, this is it! I can get rid of it here! I won't do something that will cost me money!' So I did it!"

Years later, Cagney was asked how many takes were shot before the scene was right. "Just one," he cracked. "Warners was never generous with props."

When the studio was ready to preview the film, they were concerned with the final scene. This was the vignette in which Tommy, kidnapped from the hospital by a rival gang, is delivered to his front door, a bandaged, roped, open-eyed corpse. When his brother, who, with the rest of Tommy's family, is expecting him home, opens the door, the corpse sways for a few moments, then falls into the house on its face. Wellman was especially proud of that scene, but, as he recalled later, this sequence resulted in a meeting of Jack L. Warner, Zanuck, the studio's reliable director, Michael Curtiz, and Wellman after the premier:

"It was a smash. But the last scene of Cagney being trussed up, you know, and Donald Cook opens the thing. Warner said, 'You gotta cut it out . . . it made me sick. It'll make *everybody* sick.' And Zanuck fought for it, and I fought for it, you know, but Zanuck was the one. . . . Zanuck was a tough little guy, don't kid yourself—and my fellow director was smoking a cigar, and Warner turned to him and said, 'Mike, don't you agree with me?' and Mike said, 'Yes.' Zanuck hauled off and knocked that cigar right down his throat! I'm not kidding you!" Then, "Wild Bill" Wellman added, *re* Curtiz' swallowed cigar, "*That's* what made pictures!"

Before *The Public Enemy* played New York City, Cagney wrote his mother a letter, warning her of the ghastly finish and reminding her that it would only be a movie and was nothing to upset her. The picture went into release in late April and met with immediate popularity. Wellman had delivered the formula well; the picture had enough comedy to keep the audiences amused and enough gunplay to keep them tense. As *Time* Magazine reported, "*The Public Enemy* is well-told and its intensity is relieved by scenes of the central characters slugging bartenders and slapping their women across the face. U.S. audiences, long trained by the press to glorify thugs, last week laughed loudly at such comedy and sat spellbound through the serious parts."

Yet, most critics compared *The Public Enemy* unfavorably to *Little Caesar,* released some four months earlier. One of the most repeated slurs at the picture accused it of "glamorizing" the gangster, which relates to the intrinsic ingredient which really sold the film—Cagney's performance. James made no effort to turn Tommy Powers into a sympathetic character. He found the figure detestable and hoped such a role would not come his way again. But he got so deeply into the character's psyche, so infected his part with what Edward G. Robinson called the actor's "curious quality of pugnaciousness," made his mayhem look like such fun, that hating him was virtually impossible. At the American Film Institute tribute forty-three years after the release of *The Public Enemy,* master of ceremonies Frank Sinatra touched on this point. He recalled that he once asked Cagney how he managed to be so cold-blooded, yet appealing. Cagney had responded, "Francis, always sprinkle the goodies along the way. Be as tough as you want but sprinkle the goodies for a laugh here and there. 'Cause anything they can laugh at they can't hate."

Such "goodies" are liberally sprinkled throughout *The Public Enemy.* There is the scene in which Tommy enters a store, timidly asks to see a pistol, inquires how the gun is loaded, and then holds up the storekeeper. Then there is the bit in which Tommy's promoter, Nails Nathan, is killed when his horse throws him. Cagney turns up at the stable, throws some money at the stable keeper, and righteously shoots the horse. These near-burlesque touches lighten Tommy's more unattractive moments, particularly the one in which he actually grins in "better you than me" relief after pal Matt Doyle is strafed in the street by rival thugs. When Tommy admits that, while bleeding from bullet wounds one rainy night, he ". . . ain't so tough," it is such a marvel that the cocksure punk has admitted weakness that further punishment seems superfluous.

The Public Enemy dates better today than *Little Caesar,* primarily because of the constant relief from violence and Cagney's timeless performance. In 1961, Dwight MacDonald reevaluated the motion picture and its actors in *Esquire* Magazine. He observed that Cagney's "Tom Powers is a human wolf, with the heartlessness and grace and innocence of an animal, as incapable of hypocrisy as of feeling; the smiling, unreflective delight with which he commits mayhem and murder makes Humphrey Bogart look like a conscience-stricken Hamlet."

Cagney's memories of the film, and the celebrated grapefruit business, have remained vivid. "The thing that the public remembers about *The Public Enemy* is the scene in which I shoved half a grapefruit into Mae's face. That half-grapefruit has become a piece of Americana. It was just about the first time, if not the very first, that a woman had been treated like a broad on the screen instead of like a delicate flower. . . . That bit of business became so identified with me that years afterward when I'd go into a restaurant, people would send me half-grapefruits with their compliments and I got so tired of that deal I began to duck eating in public. It was hard for me to get used to the idea that in *The Public Enemy* I had hit the jackpot overnight."

James had been cast in Wellman's next film, *Night Nurse* (Warner Bros., 1931) with Barbara Stanwyck, right after *The Public Enemy* was completed. But when Warner saw the rushes of the gangster film he withdrew Cagney from the film, wanting to put him in something better. His replacement was Clark Gable, the smirky gangster type from MGM. And Cagney was injected into *Smart Money* (Warner Bros., 1931), Edward G. Robinson's follow-up for *Little Caesar.* The gimmick was to boost the boxoffice receipts by offering Hollywood's two newest toughies on the same bill.

Cagney's role of Jack, Nick Venizelos' (Robinson) henchman, was obviously conceived *before* the scripters realized a new star would be enacting it. The film belongs to Robinson and a series of lethal blondes (Noel Francis, Margaret Livingston, and Evalyn Knapp) far more than to Cagney. In fact, it is Cagney's Jack whom Robinson kills accidentally when he tells Robinson, accurately, that his latest peroxide-tressed flame is working for the district attorney. Cagney's big moment in *Smart Money* is an eye-rolling pantomime he performs, trying to tell Robinson about a blonde visitor awaiting him. Strangely, the studio would never again star Cagney and Robinson in a film together, nor would the two compete with each other during their years on the Warner Bros. lot. Their approaches to acting were as different as their ethnic backgrounds. Thus, audiences would never be able to enjoy the shootouts between Cagney and Robinson that would erupt so splendidly between Cagney and Humphrey Bogart and Robinson and Bogie.

Then came *Larceny Lane* with Marian Marsh, who had just played Trilby to John Barrymore's *Svengali* at Warners. The title, for American release at any rate, was changed to *Blonde Crazy* (Warner Bros., 1931). The leading lady was Joan Blondell, (replacing Miss Marsh) who had long since become a blonde since her arrival on the Burbank lot. This time it was Cagney who was on the receiving end of the rough treatment as shapely Miss Blondell slaps him at regular intervals. ("I mustn't go before I tell you how much I care for you, Bert dear!" Slap!) She repeats the

25

In *Blonde Crazy* (WB, 1931)

attention-grabbing action whenever flirtatious Cagney tries to lure her into his train berth or hotel room. When James simply smiles at her and says, "I'd like to have you slap me like that every day," her response is another face swipe. Of course, Blondell emerges as Cagney's fiancée, but only after he has been carted off to jail and she has married and left a debonair bond salesman (played by Hollywood's new face, Raymond Milland).

Milland, in his recent memoirs, *Wide-Eyed in Babylon* (1974), remembers little of that film except a scene he played with Cagney "which was supposed to take 3 minutes to play. The way Cagney and I went through it, the scene was over in 26 seconds." Their timing in this scene led anguished director Roy Del Ruth to label the young actors "a couple of goddam woodpeckers."

The racy *Blonde Crazy* was another hit. But all was not well between the actor and the studio. The new star resented the authority that the lot held over him. He bridled when the company sent him on the road to promote pictures, not just his own, but those of other Warner Bros. stars, as well. Most of all, James wanted a raise. He felt the public response at the boxoffice and through the fan mail proved his point. Warner refused, and Cagney walked off the lot.

Vacating his Holloway Court apartment, Cagney and his wife returned to New York. Jack Warner was aghast. Cagney's original contract had been signed less than a year before. The studio boss felt that the new celebrity owed him gratitude, not a walkout, and attributed the move to egomania. As Warner described it in his memoirs, *My First 100 Years in Hollywood* (1964), Cagney "was another patient in ol' Doc Warner's clinic for inflated heads. In Jimmy's case, the tight-hat symptoms showed up at an early stage, shortly after he had taught frustrated lovers what to do with a grapefruit."

Nevertheless, Warner was anxious to keep and improve upon his stock company. After three months of negotiations, on October 13, 1931, Cagney re-signed with the studio. The new agreement tied Cagney to Warner Bros. for five years at a salary of one thousand dollars a week with "periodic reappraisals" of the star's worth.

It did not take long for Cagney to again wreak havoc with the powers-that-be once he returned to the lot. He began work on *Taxi* (Warner Bros., 1932), an assignment that initially went through four leading ladies: from Joan Blondell to Dorothy Mackaill to Nancy Carroll to Loretta Young. It required the thirty-two-year-old male lead to learn to drive. As Warner relates in his memoirs,

> *Director Roy Del Ruth phoned me in great agitation one morning.*
> *"Please come down to the* Taxi *set, Jack," he said. "Cagney is kicking up a fuss and won't do a scene."*
> *"What scene?"*
> *"Oh, there's nothing to it. He just goes through a door, but he won't shut it."*
> *I left my office and hurried across the lot to the stage. I knew what was in Cagney's mind. He could have shut the door if he had felt like it, but I had seen these tactics before when a rank beginner was beginning to feel his oats, and wanted out of a contract.*
> *When I got there Cagney had his chin out, a trick that was to be his trademark. He talked to me as though I was some flunky, in the mob.*
> *"Now look here, Jimmy," I said, "let's first establish who's running the studio, and there's no argument on that. Second—what's this I hear you can't close the door in this scene?"*

"I keep forgetting," he announced.

"All right, Jimmy. You've got a contract with us, and so let's live up to it and have no more of this nonsense."

He saw that I had him, and the next take was perfect. But it was not our last clash, and he later filed so many suits against us that our lawyers went out of their minds.

Taxi came in as planned. Del Ruth was one of the industry's quickest directors when it came to rushing a film into a can, and the resultant product was another breezy winner. George Raft had a bit in the picture, although studio reliables Guy Kibbee, David Landau, and George E. Stone had much more footage. The *New York Daily News,* after viewing the film, prognosticated, "We believe Cagney's popularity could equal or overtake that of Gable's this 1932. He has a grand sense of humor and he's one swell actor."

For a man who had just learned to drive, James got a strange challenge in his next picture, *The Crowd Roars* (Warner Bros., 1932). He was to play a reckless racing car driver. Howard Hawks supplied his usual rip-roaring directorial style, and Eric Linden was cast as Cagney's kid brother; Joan Blondell was at her eye-popping best as Linden's girl, and Ann Dvorak, Paul Muni's sister Cesca in *Scarface* (United Artists, 1932), was Cagney's dame. It was the first of Cagney's films with crony Frank McHugh, and also one of the star's less blatant early characterizations. In fact, one scene required James to fall, crying, into Miss Dvorak's arms, an acting touch that Cagney performs surprisingly well.

Winner Take All, his third and final 1932 Warner Bros. release, followed. Now that Cagney had learned to drive, he had to learn to box for the cameras. There followed three weeks of intensive training in Palm Springs, with instructions by

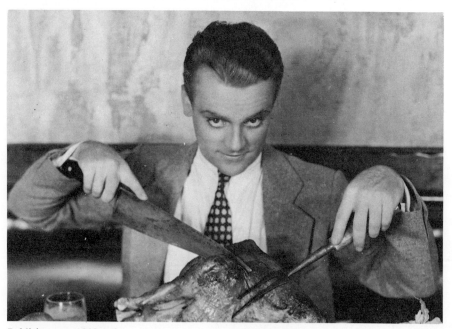

Publicity pose, 1932-style

With Mrs. Cagney at home (1932)

former fighter Harvey Perry, who also played a small role in the picture. Two leading ladies, Marian Nixon and Virginia Bruce (the latter, about to become Mrs. John Gilbert), surrounded the star, whose role as a jaunty boxer suited him admirably.

By the time *Winner Take All* was released, James and Warner were at it again. During the six-month period that Cagney had been back at the studio, his salary was nearly doubled; he was earning $1400 a week. But it was not enough; especially when he learned of the more lucrative deals given to William Powell, Kay Francis, and Ruth Chatterton, each of whom was managed by agent Myron Selznick and had been wooed away from Paramount to Warner Bros. Cagney asked the mogul for more money. Warner refused, and Cagney stayed away from the studio. As he told journalists, "A player should be in a position to demand what he is worth as long as he is worth it. When his box-office value drops, his earnings should be lopped off accordingly," claimed Cagney. (Implicit in his remarks was the fact that Powell and Miss Chatterton were then earning six thousand dollars per week.)

"J.L.," as Cagney called his boss, was mortified. The wisecracks about him and his studio hurt and embarrassed him. He was left with a fully prepared picture, *Blessed Event* (1932), that was suddenly without a star. Ironically, Lee Tracy, whom Cagney had refused to mimic for *Broadway* abroad, replaced him. The studio was also toying with the notion of starring Cagney in *I Am a Fugitive from a Chain Gang* (1933), and that leading role went to Paul Muni, whose performance as *Scarface* was then winning him cinema fame as well as a Warner Bros. contract. While Warner fumed, Cagney amused himself, filling the newspapers with explosive copy.

"I feel that I have given the best years of my life working for inadequate compen-

29

With Virginia Bruce in *Winner Take All* (WB, 1932)

sation. My employers can't see my way so I'm through. I have dispensed with my home here and next week I'm leaving for a tour of America and Europe. While abroad, I'll very probably accept vaudeville offers.

"Look, give me a break. I received honors, but I could not obey the studio code, so after my return to America I'll write a book called *Luck, Honor, and Obey*. I hope you'll like it. After that I'm turning seriously to the study of medicine. . . ."

James swore that he would enroll any day at Columbia University to follow his brothers, Harry and Ed, who were already doctors. He even offered the studio a "bargain," to ". . . work in 3 more pictures without a cent of salary, if, in return, the company would cancel the remainder of my 5-year contract." Mary Pickford announced that she wanted Cagney for her upcoming feature, *Shanty Town* (which was never made). Broadway rumored that the star might appear in the upcoming play *Little Ol' Boy*, and more than one studio attempted to purchase his contract. But Warner refused.

In retrospect, it is incredible that Warner's persistence weathered this barrage. The studio contract roster was shaping up nicely, with such popular faces as Kay Francis, George Brent, Edward G. Robinson, Douglas Fairbanks, Jr., Joan Blondell, Glenda Farrell, Loretta Young, Warren William, and Ruby Keeler beneath the Burbank banner. There was also a newcomer on the lot named Bette Davis, who would prove a distaff Cagney to the company where legal fees were concerned. Yet, with all this talent on tap, Warner still wanted Cagney. Obviously, Cagney knew it.

In September of 1932, Cagney finally agreed to confer with Warner and Zanuck, and the Academy of Motion Picture Arts and Sciences would supply Frank Capra as mediator. The result was a $3500 weekly contract with a boost to $4500, via stated

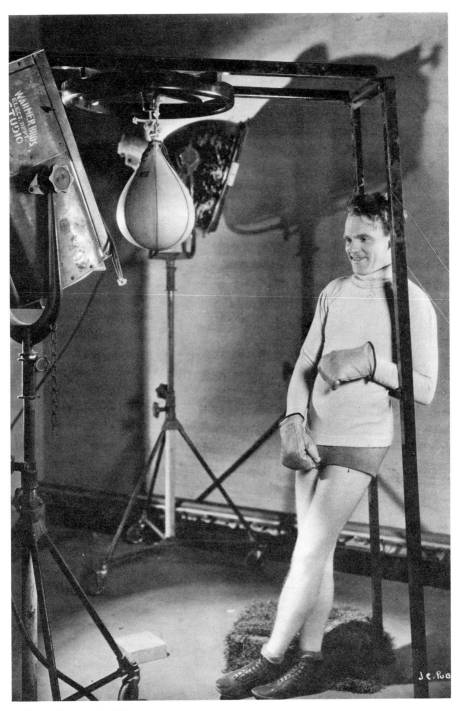

At the studio gym in 1932

raise intervals, by 1935. After the papers were signed and witnessed, Cagney figuratively spit in Warner's eye by laughingly admitting that his alleged medical plan was a big joke. Warner failed to see the humor. But he did savor one aspect of the new contract. In exchange for the demanded salary, Cagney had to promise to avoid giving out confidential information about the inside workings of the studio to sensation-seeking reporters. He also had to promise to avoid any more on-the-set dialogue blow-ups or soundstage disturbances of the kind that had blossomed during *Taxi* . Finally, he had to agree to be punctual and professional in all his studio commitments.

Photoplay Magazine, in its December, 1932 feature article entitled "Red-Headed Rebel," was typical of the fan publications intrigued by this one-man revolt against the system. "Jimmy's not the first lad to turn good because the Hollywood papas promised him an extra bite of plum pudding. Nor is he the first to kick and scream and run home to mother because he decided he wasn't being well-treated. . . . When he cools off from his Irish explosion, he's the gentlest kind of person."

The property waiting for Cagney when he returned to work after his six-month absence was *Bad Boy.* Warner Bros. was obviously trying to handle the Cagney problem with levity. Carole Lombard was originally scheduled to play opposite Cagney, but Paramount would not loan her. Mary Brian, in a blonde wig, filled her spot in what finally became *Hard to Handle* (1933). James played promoter Lefty Merrill who, among other things, handled grapefruits. Mervyn LeRoy directed the comedy in which Ruth Donnelly was especially praiseworthy for her characterization of Miss Brian's mother. It was also Cagney's first feature with Allen Jenkins, the ever-busy studio character player who had hoofed with Cagney in the chorus of *Pitter Patter.*

A succession of wise-cracking, big boxoffice films followed for Cagney. Perhaps the most engaging item of each of these features is the unpretentious quality of each of the storylines. *Picture Snatcher* (Warner Bros., 1933) saw him as a Sing Sing alumnus-turned-photographer. Lloyd Bacon directed this seventy-seven-minute entertainment, and Cagney met Ralph Bellamy on the set. The latter became one of his closest friends in Hollywood. *The Mayor of Hell* (Warner Bros., 1933) cast James as the superintendent of a boys' reform school. Madge Evans replaced Glenda Farrell, who had replaced Joan Blondell, as Cagney's sassy girlfriend, an ingredient no doubt added to her character so that the lobby ads could read, "With Jimmy setting new standards of male behavior, no maiden's jaw is safe. When he notices them, their hearts beat pitter-patter and their teeth rattle " Dudley Digges drew much acclaim as the rotten authority whom Cagney replaces. (When the studio remade the film as *Crime School* in 1938, Humphrey Bogart would inherit Cagney's role.)

Footlight Parade (Warner Bros., 1933) was something else: a cast including Ruby Keeler, Dick Powell, Joan Blondell, Frank McHugh, Guy Kibbee, Hugh Herbert; Lloyd Bacon's crisp direction; Busby Berkeley's kalaideoscopic choreography; songs by Sammy Fain-Irving Kahal and Harry Warren-Al Dubin; and myriads of full bosoms, shapely legs, and capped teeth of blonde chorines. It all welded together for one of the thirties' most memorable, if campy, films. Cagney dominated the raucous package of the backstage musical as a powerhouse director of movie theatre stage revues. His big number was with Ruby Keeler, and "Shanghai Lil' " is a gem. As the wide-eyed reviewer for the *New York Sun* wrote, "Anyone who can project the power of *The Public Enemy* and the humor of *Picture Snatcher* and *Taxi* and in addition can dance with the best of them, can do anything, probably, except play King Lear." Cagney's popularity soared even higher with this one.

There was no rest at Warner Bros. for the marquee lure that was Cagney's, and before 1933 was out James also starred in *Lady Killer*. Under Roy Del Ruth's direction it was a Hollywood spoof about a crook who becomes a movie star, only to have his old gang reappear and interest him in robbing celebrities' homes. Margaret Lindsay, new studio ingenue, was in the picture, as well as two graduates of *The Public Enemy*, Leslie Fenton and Mae Clarke. Miss Clarke was now on the receiving end of a new indelicacy. Within the story, Cagney drags her out of bed and across the room by her hair. Then he tosses her twelve feet down a hallway.

By this time, super-success Cagney was well settled in Hollywood. He purchased a home in Coldwater Canyon at 621 Hillcrest Road, complete with a swimming pool. His friends from Manhattan, Pat O'Brien and Frank McHugh, were on the studio payroll, and Frank Morgan, Spencer Tracy, and Lynne Overman would join their close circle. In 1933, James became one of the early members of the Screen Actors Guild, the "union" of performers. Years later, *Film* Magazine would report, "James Cagney, Gary Cooper, James Dunn, Otto Kruger, and Ann Harding joined on that memorable night, and no doubt the magic of their names had much to do with the fact that membership jumped from 81 to 4000 in 6 weeks."

Most of the time, however, the Cagneys were loners. The couple rarely joined in the forays of the Hollywood social set. Columnists were always amused to rediscover how reticent and mild he was offcamera. When one considers the outlet he found for his hostilities at Warner Bros. between his punch roles and contract battles, the quietness of his life away from the film lot should not have been surprising.

However, the seeming calm of Cagney's professional life was disrupted when

With Mae Clarke in *Lady Killer* (WB, 1933)

With Bette Davis, Allen Jenkins, and Alan Dinehart in *Jimmy the Gent* (WB, 1934)

he reported for work on *Jimmy the Gent* (Warner Bros., 1934). He reported to the soundstage with a severe, unflattering haircut. Director Michael Curtiz was aghast at the remodeled star, but production had to begin. Cagney's leading lady in this story of a con artist was Bette Davis, whose resentment of Jack Warner's autocratic power was building. She was not enthralled by this uninspired assignment, but she "greatly admired" Cagney. She cracked to her co-star, "You're the greatest chiseler since Michelangelo."

With his hair growing back, James again teamed with Joan Blondell for *He Was Her Man* (Warner Bros., 1934), in which she portrayed a prostitute named Rose Lawrence. The Lloyd Bacon-directed feature was offbeat and it was the first Cagney vehicle since *The Public Enemy* not to enjoy big business. Nevertheless, it prompted the *New York Herald-Tribune* to write prophetically: "More than any other screen actor today, Mr. Cagney is the exponent of the school of acting of which George M. Cohan is the brilliant dean." While Cagney performed in this picture with a full crop of hair, he reported for shooting wearing a moustache. It was grown for the same reason he had shorn his hair: he thought it would irk Jack Warner. It did.

He Was Her Man, with a rather explicit portrayal of the leading lady's trade, came in just before the Legion of Decency rose to power and Warner Bros. had to clean up its product, especially the Cagney films. Scenes with Cagney snapping molls' garters, or spouting lewd remarks with a knowing smirk, could no longer be permitted. The studio complied with the new rulings by placing their ace star in a gutsy service comedy, *Here Comes the Navy* (Warner Bros., 1934). Cagney was true to his cocksure form. However, the studio carefully flanked him with two men, Pat O'Brien and Frank McHugh, who would temper him on the set, and two actresses, Gloria Stuart and Dorothy Tree, who were considerably less brash than the celluloid ladies to whom Cagney was accustomed.

34

With Joan Bondell in *He Was Her Man* (WB, 1934)

Here Comes the Navy, his fourth of eight features directed by Lloyd Bacon, was shot almost entirely aboard the vessel *Arizona,* which would be sunk seven years later at Pearl Harbor. James and Pat O'Brien tore through the feature as brawling sailors who fight over girls and everything else, yet are good buddies under the rough-and-tumble veneer. The production clicked with the public and began what the *New York Times* would dub the "you-hit-me-and-I'll-hit you" type of film. Frank McHugh provided Cagney with a more comical sidekick. When McHugh receives orders that he has been transferred from the home ship, he exits turning to Cagney and sincerely blowing him a kiss. Cracks a nearby sailor, "Oh, Swifty . . . what are you two guys, a couple of violets?" The picture did well in distribution, and also won an Oscar nomination for Best Picture of 1934. (It lost to Columbia's *It Happened One Night.*)

In August of 1934, a few weeks after the release of *Here Comes the Navy,* James was back in the news—as a suspected Communist. The actor had become friends with author-lecturer Lincoln Steffens and his wife, Ella Winters. Winters, in turn, was a close associate of Caroline Decker, secretary of the Cannery and Industrial Workers Union and alleged "local Communist official." Detective Ray Kunz of the Los Angeles county police "Red" squad obtained some correspondence between Winters and Decker. The result was seventeen indictments issued against "suspected radicals" by district attorney Nick McAllister.

The letter from Miss Winters stated, "I have Cagney's money again. . . . Cagney was fine this time and is going to bring other stars up to talk to Stef about Communism." Of the star, she added impressively, "He wrote a piece for the Screen Actors Guild, which, as you know, is the employees rebellion against the producers, even though employees get $3500 a week [then Cagney's salary]." Another letter claimed James offered to provide Miss Decker with typewriter ribbons (!), stating, "If you

35

want them from him, his address is 621 Hillcrest Road, Beverly Hills. But don't give it to anyone else." It was all very mysterious and understandably so.

Although these missives never referred to Cagney by his whole name, detective Kunz assured the press: "We are satisfied that this is Cagney the motion picture star. There is no doubt in our minds. We have received information during our investigation to remove all doubt." On August 17, 1934, Cagney denied the charge, claiming that he "hardly could believe" Winters wrote the letters and attesting that she "had no right to do so." He admitted his friendship with Steffens but swore he had never given or offered any money to Communist-affiliated causes.

The next day Dolores Del Rio, Ramon Novarro, and Lupe Velez were similarly indicted (drawing a more volatile response from Lupe's husband of the moment, Johnny Weissmuller, than from the carefree Lupe herself). Cagney again defended himself, claiming, "I am against all isms but Americanism. . . . It appears to me that McAllister's actions are a bid for personal publicity at my expense." The whole mess washed away when Lincoln Steffens personally cleared Cagney, explaining: "Ella Winters reported the San Joaquin Valley cotton strike a year ago for a national magazine, and while she was there she saw a little baby die of starvation—turn black and die in the workers' district. When she told people, including Cagney, of the utter misery she had seen there, he gave some money to help. So did other people, who gave food or clothing or money for food or clothing when they heard those conditions described or saw them with their own eyes. That is all."

The entire matter was soon forgotten, and Cagney's popularity was not damaged a bit. In fact, his fame began to crest even higher.

It seemed only fitting that James then went into *The St. Louis Kid* (Warner Bros., 1934), in which he becomes embroiled in a dairy farmers' revolt. Originally, the scenario was a social comment on the Depression. However, by the time director Ray Enright added a shallow lustre to the proceedings, and Patricia Ellis provided a conventional blonde love interest, and Allen Jenkins did his comic thing, the message was pretty well concealed beneath a shellacking of studio varnish. Commented the *New York Times,* "It is still worth a filmgoer's time to watch Mr. Cagney hang one on somebody's button, but somehow the spectacle seems less than epic after you have watched the film pussyfoot around a dramatic subject." Warner would wait a few months and give Paul Muni's *Black Fury* (1935), the story of a coal strike, the full Depression social-relevance treatment.

In the meantime, Cagney's brother Bill had come to Hollywood, playing unmemorable roles in such films as *Palooka* (United Artists, 1934) and *Stolen Harmony* (Paramount, 1935). Eventually, and wisely so, Bill gave up acting to become an agent and his brother's mentor. He would even join with James to head their own production company. Bill would marry Boots Mallory, former "Wampas Baby Queen."

The year 1935 was one of James' most popular screen years. He began the professional season with another escapade with Pat O'Brien, this time in the sky. *Devil Dogs of the Air* (Warner Bros.) again finds O'Brien and Cagney brawling as Jimmy's conceit leaves no room for respect for the superior O'Brien. Again, they are competing for the same girl (Margaret Lindsay) in what was basically a rehash of *Here Comes the Navy.* Lloyd Bacon directed the formula as before. Some incredible stunt flying (particularly the sequence of Cagney's piloting of a burning craft) insured its boxoffice power. Frank McHugh, one of the studio's most overworked players, was his usual, giggly self.

36

Everyone was pleased with *Devil Dogs of the Air* except Cagney. He later claimed it was a picture "which had no reason to be filmed under any circumstances." Apparently, this remark came from his own restlessness, as the star was already seeking some reason, no matter how flimsy, to again tear up his hated contract. Meanwhile, he amused himself by hurling Yiddish profanities at Jack L. Warner whenever the two happened to cross paths.

Since Cagney's screen villains had become too likeable to the public for the studio to continue using the star in that type of role, Warner Bros., anxious for another gangster epic, simply switched their star to the other side of the law. The ensuing project was *G-Men* (1935). It proved to be one of the star's most popular vehicles of the decade as he brought his cockiness to the service of the F.B.I. within Seton I. Miller's screenplay. Based on Gregory Roger's *Public Enemy No. 1,* the picture had so much bloodshed and death that it was almost *The Public Enemy* all over again. Now, however, the violent temperament of Cagney's screen character was socially acceptable.

William Keighley, who had directed James on Broadway in *Penny Arcade,* was at the helm for this production. In the course of eighty-five minutes, Cagney's James "Brick" Davis survives a judo crunching, a slug in his chest, and a bullet-grazed scalp, in order to wipe out racketeer Barton MacLane's mob. The film took no chances in depicting its loyalty to the cause of justice. There were speeches urging the police to annihilate all hoods: "Give them handguns, shotguns, tear gas—this is war!"

As was the fashion at Warner Bros. in those days of the golden age of Hollywood, James had two leading ladies: Ann Dvorak, who sang through a nightclub number, "You Bother Me an Awful Lot," and Margaret Lindsay. In *G-Men,* Barton Mac-Lane, one of the studio's prime heavies, kills Miss Dvorak, his oncamera wife, after she tries to tip old flame Cagney to MacLane's activities. It provided the basis for a nice little death scene. "There isn't any rules that a G-Man can't kiss an old friend goodbye, is there?" she breathes to Cagney before she expires. Unspeakable Mac-Lane almost kills Miss Lindsay as well, snaring her as the law encircles him in a trap. "Come on, copper Are you going to let her have it—or am I?" But MacLane meets a bloody end. Cagney and Lindsay are free to face the future together, a romantic union of which even her screen brother (Robert Armstrong) approves.

"Yesterday: Public Enemy No. 1 in the never-to-be-forgotten Warner Brothers thriller *The Public Enemy.* Today: He's on Uncle Sam's side, staging his own private war with the public enemies of 1935!" hawked the posters for *G-Men.* "An enormously exciting topical melodrama," exclaimed *Time* Magazine, which reported, "[It had sufficient] bloodshed to cause cinema censors last week to consider banning the work from all Chicago theatres, on the ground that it might overstimulate small children." The well-attended feature would be re-released in 1949 to cash in on the twenty-fifth anniversary of the Federal Bureau of Investigation. A prologue would be added, with David Brian as "The Chief" and Douglas Kennedy as an F.B.I. agent.

A mild change of pace, *The Irish in Us* (Warner Bros., 1935) followed, with pals Cagney, O'Brien, and McHugh playing brothers. James was the lazy fight promoter Danny O'Hara; O'Brien, a cop; and McHugh, a fireman. The mother of this Hibernian brood was Mary Gordon (who later would play the part of Basil Rathbone's housekeeper, Mrs. Hudson, in Universal's *Sherlock Holmes* series). Allen Jenkins played a moronic boxer, and the girl who predictably turns from O'Brien to Cagney was Olivia de Havilland in her second film assignment. Lloyd Bacon directed the pleasant vehicle with little variation from the tried and true Cagney-O'Brien formula. It is doubtful whether the public would have tolerated much deviation.

One of Cagney's most unheralded film assignments came about by accident. One day, while sailing his yacht *Martha* near Catalina Island, James caught sight of the MGM company filming *Mutiny on the Bounty* (1935), starring Clark Gable, Charles Laughton, and Franchot Tone. He signaled the ship, which was actually a very small boat, came aboard, donned a navy dress uniform, and became an extra in a group scene being lensed that day. Nobody has yet reported being able to spot him in the released version of this outdoors epic.

A whole new acting experience opened up for Cagney in 1935. In Los Angeles, European impressario Max Reinhardt had staged a lavish tableau production of Shakespeare's *A Midsummer Night's Dream.* Jack Warner, who had brought the Bard to the screen in 1930's *The Show of Shows,* via John Barrymore's soliloqy from *Richard III*, decided to transfer Reinhardt's production to the screen. (It was his way of competing with MGM's long-planned version of *Romeo and Juliet* [1936] to star Norma Shearer.) The mogul ordered a big budget, elaborate costumes, and expensive special effects. He also cast some of his top contract players: Dick Powell as Lysander, Joe E. Brown as Flute, and Olivia de Havilland (who had won her Warner Bros. contract when the studio head saw her in Reinhardt's stage production) as Hermia. Mickey Rooney was assigned as Puck, with James Cagney top-billed as Bottom, a weaver who is transformed by the fairies into a donkey. The joke around Warner Bros. was that the executive had cast Cagney in the role just to exult in witnessing him scampering about in an ass's head.

With Joe E. Brown, Hugh Herbert, Dewey Robinson, Otis Harlan, Arthur Treacher, and Frank McHugh in *A Midsummer Night's Dream* (WB, 1935)

The big picture quickly was wrought with production problems. Continental Reinhardt had no conception of cinematic technique; William Dieterle had to co-direct the project. Perc Westmore lavished great attention on developing the fine makeup for the characters. Fred Jackson, Byron Haskin, and H. E. Koenekamp conjured up delightful special effects, and Erich Wolfgang Korngold delivered the first of his epic scores for the studio. The result was a 132-minute controversial feature that "has its fun and haunting beauty" (*New York Times*), on one hand, and "was more Barnum and Bailey than Shakespeare" (Don Miller in his 1958 career study of Cagney in *Films in Review*). On the other hand, while Joe E. Brown and Mickey Rooney were highly praised, Cagney's Bottom was panned. "[He] belabors the slapstick of his part beyond endurance" (*New York Times*), and "seemed to me to misconceive his character" (*London Times*). Considering its production costs, the paean to the Bard was not a profitable venture. Warner Bros. had to assess the experience as an important step in the art of the cinema, although some did not share the studio's view.

Of this unusual film venture, Cagney's most memorable public comment is: "I'm reasonably certain if the dramatist were alive today, movie producers would have asked Mr. Shakespeare to write in a scene in which I did physical violence to someone, for producers seem convinced that the public does not care for me if I don't deliver at least one punch per line."

In the summer of 1935, Warners had loaned Edward G. Robinson to United Artists for Sam Goldwyn's memorable *Barbary Coast,* a wild tale of San Francisco's gold rush days. When the film won such popularity, Warner Bros. apparently decided to prove that Goldwyn could be topped. Thus, *Frisco Kid* (1935) emerged,

With Joe Sawyer in *Frisco Kid* (WB, 1935)

with Cagney running that California city in the same arrogant style as the earringed Robinson had, and sharing the same doomed romance with Margaret Lindsay as "Little Caesar" had with Miriam Hopkins. The Warners version suffered greatly in comparison with the original treatment. The *New York Evening Post* called it a "carbon copy," though the supporting cast of Ricardo Cortez, Fred Kohler, and Lily Damita (then Mrs. Errol Flynn) was almost as enjoyable as Goldwyn's array of Walter Brennan, Frank Craven, and Brian Donlevy.

James grew back the moustache that Warner did not care for in approaching his next film, *Ceiling Zero* (Warner Bros., 1935), his fourth film with O'Brien. They were back in the sky, this time with the "Federal Air Lines." The treatment here was a bit deeper: Cagney's Dizzy Davis is busy dating June Travis, leaving Stuart Erwin (O'Brien) to fly his run, resulting in Erwin's death. Cagney's remorseful Davis then tests a de-icing device and dies a repentant hero in the process. Howard Hawks, who had taken over direction of *Barbary Coast,* contributed his usual exciting treatment and the film was another smash. "Both Cagney and O'Brien are profoundly moving," declared the *New York Daily Mirror.* "The 2 characters are so human, ring so true, that the tragedy of their association is doubly stirring." Cagney and O'Brien were achieving something unique at this time in the cinema, capturing the competitive affection that is the backbone of so many male friendships, oncamera and off. Warners looked forward to teaming them profitably over and over. Cagney and O'Brien did not.

O'Brien would later inform the press: "Jimmy's grand to work with. You couldn't ask for a better producer but there's a limit to that. I think one picture a year with Cagney would be fine. But, as it is, I've been with him in every uniform—the army, the navy, the police, the marines, the air corps—and it's always a case of me falling in love with his girl, or his falling in love with mine. It gets tiresome."

With James Bush and June Travis in *Ceiling Zero* (WB, 1935)

With brother William in March, 1936

Cagney reacted the same way. He was feeling his power again and refused to do his next assignment *(Over the Wall,* mixing prison and baseball). Also, he realized that in 1935 five pictures in which he starred were released. He recalled the agreement was for only four. That was the wedge he needed.

"It doesn't matter how competent an actor you may be, if the public doesn't want to see you anymore, you're all washed up," stated Cagney as he once more walked out of the studio. Warners was aghast as Cagney sued the studio to obtain the release of his contract. Pat O'Brien would recall it in his lively memoirs, *The Wind at My Back* (1967):

> I was often on Jack's carpet. Once he called me into his office and looked at me poker faced. "Jim Cagney has taken a powder, contractually speaking. He is on suspension."
>
> "I've been there myself."
>
> I didn't know what was on Jack's mind. One thing I was sure of, I knew he wasn't going to give me a raise.
>
> "Pat, you're pretty close to Cagney. I ask you as a favor—I want you to get him to come back."
>
> "Jack, I'm close to Jim, he's my pal and I love him, but . . ."
>
> "But what?"
>
> "I'd never make any overture like that to Jim. And Jack, you can't suspend me for that."
>
> "You're right—I can't."

When Cagney won his well-publicized law suit and was legally untangled from his contract, Warner was shocked. On top of this, Bette Davis grabbed headlines by

41

refusing to do Warner's bidding, and ran off to England. Warner followed her, and, through the courts, brought her back, complacent, to Burbank. He was not so fortunate with James Cagney, despite constant legal action to re-snare his red-headed terror. If the producer was sensitive about the headlines, and he was not an insensitive man, at least he was not alone. Eddie Cantor was at war with Goldwyn; Margaret Sullavan was raging at Universal; Carole Lombard was fighting Paramount; and Katharine Hepburn was in combat with RKO. It was a particularly feisty year in Hollywood.

Victorious Cagney surprised everybody by signing with Grand National, a new "bush-league" studio that was still in swaddling clothes. His union with them would produce only two pictures, both low-budget by big studio standards, but expensive by poverty row terms. Each picture relied almost solely on Cagney's presence to carry them at the boxoffice. *Great Guy,* released in December, 1936, reunited James with Mae Clarke in a gang-fighting epic, while *Something to Sing About* (1937), a musical centering around Hollywood, had the star doing some nifty dancing. He also sang "Any Love," backed up by a trio called The Three Shades. Evelyn Daw was the singing female lead, upstaged by delightful vamp Mona Barrie, who was seductively capped with a blonde wig in her part as a foreign film star. Cagney's hoofing was appreciated, but not praised; even the *Brooklyn Eagle* could only comment, "Though admittedly not a Fred Astaire, there is a certain grace and agility about the man."

Meanwhile, Warner Bros., whose veneer Grand National sorely lacked, built a storehouse of properties, hoping to lure back the dynamic Cagney. Among them were *Invisible Stripes* (eventually done with George Raft, William Holden, and Bogart); *John Dillinger, Outlaw* to star Bogart as the arch-criminal with Cagney as G-Man Melvin Purvis; *They Died with Their Boots On,* the story of General Custer, which was eventually re-tailored for Errol Flynn; *High Sierra,* which later passed from Muni to Raft to Bogart; and several others. They also dangled the stage musical *On Your Toes* as bait. The studio was indefatigable in its efforts to lure Cagney back to the lot. When the actor let it be known that he was interested in starring on Broadway in *Of Mice and Men,* Warners volunteered to purchase the screen rights and transform it into a starring vehicle for him.

Finally, Warner Bros. succeeded. They offered Cagney $150,000 per film against ten percent of the gross. Only Carole Lombard, at this time, was in a comparable position. Cagney accepted. In doing so, the star walked out on impoverished Grand National, where he had been the studio's great hope. Grand National was stuck with a picture in preparation. The property was *Angels with Dirty Faces.* The disheartened studio canceled production and waived the rights to the property. Warners quickly acquired the project.

Delighted to have Cagney back, Warner Bros. nevertheless selected a strange film for its welcome-home for James. This was *Boy Meets Girl* (1938), based on the Broadway hit by Bella and Sam Spewack. It was another behind-the-scenes Hollywood farce, originally done with Allyn Joslyn and Jerome Cowan onstage. Warners planned it as a Marion Davies vehicle, but when her union with the studio was terminated, the company offered the two male leads to Olsen and Johnson. When these two zany comedians were unavailable, the leads were passed to Cagney and O'Brien. It proved to be inspired casting.

Both male stars flung themselves wildly into the daffy roles, plunging into the world of screwball comedy with the same high-pressured performance they had

In *Great Guy* (Grand National, 1936)

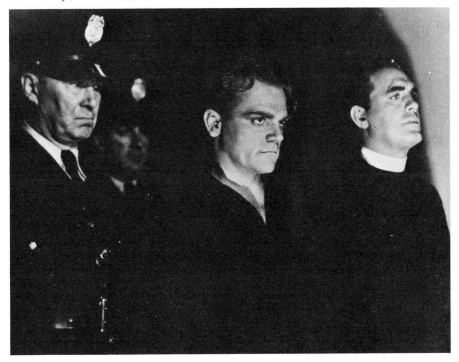

With Jack Perrin (second guard) and Pat O'Brien in *Angels with Dirty Faces* (WB, 1938)

43

given to more dramatic proceedings. Dick Foran was the egomaniacal cowboy star, and Marie Wilson, in the Marion Davies-intended role, was the pregnant commissary waitress whose child becomes a movie star at Foran's expense. Again, the resultant product was a big hit with the public, if not the fourth estate, who thought the format had been too diluted from the Broadway original. Again, however, Cagney stated that he wished he had not made the film. Perhaps his rationale was based on his self-appraisal of his appearance in a ridiculous garb of ascot, sunglasses, and a beret.

Then came Cagney's first Oscar nomination and one of his greatest performances, as Rocky Sullivan in *Angels with Dirty Faces* (Warner Bros., 1938). The picture had all the elements that made the Warner Bros. product of this period so unforgettable: expansive direction by slick Michael Curtiz, Pat O'Brien as a socially concerned priest, Ann "The Oomph Girl" Sheridan as Cagney's tough girl friend who has been hurt by her past marriage and has an attractive chip on her shoulder, Humphrey Bogart as a tough-lipped shyster lawyer, George Bancroft as a treacherous underworld boss, and the Dead End Kids, fresh from the 1937 United Artists feature that had given them their name. The latter were most believable as the gang of adolescent roughnecks who worship the toughness of Cagney, a product of their Lower East Side tenement arena. It is also the feature film that provided James' imitators with the familiar repertoire of mannerisms that the public seems never to tire of.

"New York's East Side was full of colorful characters," Cagney wrote for the *Saturday Evening Post* in 1956. "There was one guy, for example, who had a trick way of handling his body while he was engaged in sidewalk debate. He held his elbows against his sides as he argued, and he made his points by pointing his finger at you. When he met you, he never said, 'Hello, how are you?' He'd ask, 'What do you hear?' or 'What do you say?' In 1938 I dredged this character out of my past and used him in *Angels with Dirty Faces.*" Cagney also borrowed the neck-shoulder twitching and pants hitching of another East Side character in developing his Rocky portrayal.

There is no disputing Cagney's excellence in the film. Granted, subtlety and underplaying have never been part of the star's virtues, but in this film an inner warmth only previously hinted at was present. Perhaps the fine interplay of spunkiness and gentleness could be attributed to the reactions drawn from co-star Ann Sheridan, who had a way of drawing a better performance than usual out of her leading men. It is hard not to stand in awe of Cagney's closing scene in this film. He is in prison, sentenced to the electric chair. He vows to "spit in their eye," showing the authorities just how unafraid he is of dying (paralleling Clark Gable's role in the trend-setting *Manhattan Melodrama,* MGM's 1934 film which had such an influence on this production). But O'Brien visits his boyhood pal on death row and begs him to play a coward, to shatter the kids' idolatry of him. "They gotta despise your memory," explains O'Brien, who suggests that his friend must "straighten yourself out with God" before the end. Cagney refuses angrily, but later, as he enters the execution room after walking the last mile and O'Brien begins his prayers, the tough hood's crying and whining burst from the room. "Help me I don't wanna die " Director Curtiz only shows shadows and, at one point, Cagney's hand grasping a radiator to resist being dragged to the chair. It is enough that Rocky has "turned yellow"; the audience does not have to *see* it. The postscript scene finds O'Brien visiting the disillusioned gang and painfully assuring them that their idol died just

44

the way the reporters described it in the papers. Then he delivers the poignant famous closing line, which means nothing to the kids, but to the filmgoer recalls the earlier segment of the story where, as children, O'Brien and Cagney were pillaging a railway freight car. The cops arrived; O'Brien, swifter of foot, fled, but Cagney was caught and sent to reform school. Thus, as he marches up the steps of the kids' basement headquarters, a somber-faced O'Brien intones, "OK, boys—let's go say a prayer for a boy who couldn't run as fast as I could." An angelic chorus sings the film to a fine close.

"For Cagney, the picture is likely to bring added prestige, for the bantam rooster of a racketeer is just the kind of part he plays best," exclaimed *Variety*. For his Rocky Sullivan, Cagney won the New York Film Critics Award for Best Actor. (It took a reported seven ballots for his triumph, as he received only one vote on the first go-round.)

An Oscar nomination for Cagney as Best Actor also came via this standard-setting film. His competition included Charles Boyer for *Algiers* (United Artists), Robert Donat for *The Citadel* (MGM), Leslie Howard for *Pygmalion* (MGM), and Spencer Tracy for *Boys' Town* (MGM). It was pal Tracy who won, the man's second victory in a row, having won the 1937 Oscar for *Captains Courageous* (MGM). Cagney later commented that he convinced himself before the ceremony (each time he was nominated) that "the other fellow is going to get it. Spence won that particular little gilded mannikin, but I had such respect for him as an actor that losing it didn't hit me hard. In fact, I recall no particular disappointment."

There were three popular Cagney vehicles released in 1939, and *Photoplay* Magazine reflected his growing popularity with features like the one in their February, 1939 issue: "Like Ferdinand, He Loves to Smell Flowers." *Photoplay* assured its readers, "Jim Cagney is not the same Cagney when a plate of cookies comes within smelling distance. . . . He neither fought, stormed, nor schemed to get to the top." One can only wonder how Jack Warner reacted to that bit of insight.

The Oklahoma Kid (Warner Bros.) was his initial release that year. Cagney's hysterical performance of the title character ("I'm kinda handy at stoppin' stages"), in a ten-gallon hat, singing "I Don't Wanna Play in Your Yard" and "Rockabye Baby" in Spanish, is, for lack of a more appropriate word, unique. Nineteen hundred and thirty-nine was the season of the big Westerns (*Jesse James, Stagecoach, Union Pacific, Dodge City,* and the satirical genre piece, *Destry Rides Again*). But none of these superior vehicles had so incongruous a hero as Cagney. Humphrey Bogart, complete with an all-black outfit and a spit curl, was the villain Whip McCord. Both he and James obviously played the film while laughing up their expensive sleeves. Rosemary Lane was a demurely sweet leading lady, Donald Crisp was her kindly dad, and such hateful types as Ward Bond, Edward Pawley, and Lew Harvey backed up Bogart's rough interplay. *The Oklahoma Kid* is actually a richly entertaining film, though a late-show TV viewer might wonder as the closing credits appear if perhaps he had fallen asleep and dreamt the entire rowdy concoction.

Each Dawn I Die (Warner Bros., 1939), with George Raft, put Cagney back in jail. It was an unspoken fight to the finish between the two compactly built screen tough guys. Ex-Paramount star George Raft, anxious to outshine Cagney, Edward G. Robinson, and any other contender, was angling to take over the top tough-guy berth at Warners. As in past films, Raft would always work best when paired with a superior actor, as had been the case when he appeared with Gary Cooper in *Souls at Sea* (Paramount, 1937).

With Chuck Hamilton (second man) and Humphrey Bogart in *The Oklahoma Kid* (WB, 1939)

In this William Keighley-directed picture, James was a reporter who had been railroaded to prison for having uncovered corruption in the district attorney's office. Raft was Hood Stacey, the "lifer" who befriended him. Jane Bryan played Cagney's sweet, loyal girlfriend, with George Bancroft as the tough but understanding warden. The scenario included an exciting climactic break-out, complete with hand grenades.

Each Dawn I Die boosted Raft's stock with Warner Bros. and the public. He managed to make such potentially dumb lines as, "This is the last round-up for Stacey," carry conviction. As for Cagney, he got to spout one of his best celluloid speeches in this searing drama.

"When I first came here I believed in justice," he says while in prison. "I believed that some day I'd be released. Then I began to figure in weeks and months and now I hate the whole world and everybody in it for lettin' me in for this Buried in a black filthy hole because I was a good citizen, because I worked my head off to expose crime. And now I'm a convict! I act like a convict, smell like a convict! I think and hate like a convict! But I'll get out! I'll get out if I have to kill every screw in the joint!" It was a dynamite speech delivered by a top tactician of rapid-fire, high-voltage dialogue.

The words of this persuasive speech were scripted by Warren Duff, who also wrote *Frisco Kid* and *Angels with Dirty Faces.* He called Cagney "the perfect writer's actor. Every writer enjoys writing for an actor who will not just speak the lines but will bring the character to life. Cagney's almost intuitive understanding of the character he plays, plus his intelligent approach to creating it, guarantee the role's interpretation. This, of course, is gratifying to the writer."

46

Regarding *Each Dawn I Die,* the *Daily Worker,* a keen observer of the capitalistic Hollywood scene, wrote, "Warner Brothers, in teaming Cagney and Raft, have hit on a combination that will go far and win wide audiences." But the duo never teamed again. In fact, Raft's role was intended originally for John Garfield and then Fred MacMurray, while Jane Bryan had replaced Ann Sheridan.

The Roaring Twenties (Warner Bros., 1939) has everything a gangster film would require. Cagney runs a bootlegging racket, Bogart becomes his lethal rival, Gladys George is Cagney's appropriately tarnished moll, Frank McHugh is the loveable sidekick, and wholesome Priscilla Lane is the untouchable love interest who inadvertently brings about Cagney's downfall. Raoul Walsh, directing his first Cagney picture, captured all the heady decadence of that tinsel era. There were enough bullets, executions, thrills, and period nostalgia to satisfy the most demanding audience.

"A ROARING ERA becomes A ROARING HIT!" read the ads. "Here's more screen excitement than you've ever seen before! America at its maddest! America at its merriest . . . the land of the free gone wild! It's the heyday of the hotcha—the shock-crammed days G-Men took 10 whole years to lick! By far the biggest of all Jimmy's hits!"

Cagney was believable and entertaining as a returning war veteran who climbs to the top of the underworld, only to be wiped out by the stock market crash and tormented by his true love, Priscilla Lane. She has fallen in love with and married the crusading district attorney (handsome but bland Jeffrey Lynn). It was this devotion to Lane that sparked the third and final screen shootout between Cagney

With Frank McHugh in *The Roaring Twenties* (WB, 1939)

47

and Bogart. In the Mark Hellinger-derived story, Lynn is out to nab Bogart, the new crime kingpin of the city. Bogart, realizing Cagney's loyalty to Lane, orders his execution. This crackling dialogue is typical of the film:

> BOGART: *You're still in love with that girl and you'd do anything in the world to help her. You've got more on me than any guy in this town and I'll lay ya' odds that the minute you get outta here you're goin' straight to the cops and spill everything ya' know. Well, I'm just gonna beatcha to the finish. . . . Goodbye, Eddie, and . . . uh . . . happy New Year!*
>
> CAGNEY *(punching his way clear, now with a gun): Get 'em up George! So you thought I'd yell copper, huh? Well I never did that in my life and never will! I want anything done, I do it myself!*
>
> BOGART *(cowering): Yeah—you always was a fair guy, Eddie. I'll make a deal with you—we'll be partners again. . . . I'll take the heat off . . . I'll beat the rap some other way. . . . (Cagney shoots) Eddie! You're crazy! . . . Eddie . . . no . . . no . . . Eddie!*
>
> CAGNEY: *This is one rap you won't beat. . . .*

And for the third time onscreen, Bogart dies from Cagney's prop department bullets.

Of course, Cagney could not escape from Bogart's henchmen unscathed. *The Roaring Twenties* has *the* death scene everybody remembers; his dying on the steps of a church. Faithful dame Gladys George is there to speak the final words.

> COP: *Well, who is this guy?*
> GEORGE: *This is Eddie Bartlett.*
> COP: *Well, how are you hooked up with him?*
> GEORGE: *I'll never figure it out. . . .*
> COP: *What was his business?*
> GEORGE: *He used to be a big shot.*

"It has the glittery nervous journalistic quality, which distinguishes it from previous bootleg dramas," stated the *New York Daily Mirror*. Apparently, Warner Bros. thought this was the final word in gangster films as far as Cagney was concerned; he would not play another such part for ten years, when he would return to the lot for the classic *White Heat*.

Forty years old and still going strong, James Cagney began the new decade with *The Fighting 69th* (Warner Bros., 1940). It was an all-male, all-star show, featuring Pat O'Brien as Father Duffy, George Brent as Wild Bill Donovan, Jeffrey Lynn as poet Joyce Kilmer, and such studio contract players as Alan Hale, Frank McHugh, Dennis Morgan, and Dick Foran. (A role originally conceived for Priscilla Lane was scrapped when the studio decided to make the film a stag affair.) Cagney, top-billed as Jerry Plunkett, played a fictitious rebel punk (what else?) who turns yellow in the trenches. However, he redeems himself with a hero's death. The battle scenes, shot at the studio's Calabasas ranch, were most effective, as was the cast. The *New York World-Telegram* reconfirmed that Cagney and O'Brien were "two of the finest actors in movies." Unfortunately, the picture led to another lawsuit. As Jack Warner would recall in his autobiography,

> When *The Fighting 69th* was released, Cagney's contract specified that his name was to get top billing over Pat O'Brien, George Brent, Alan Hale, and

all others in the cast. I went to see the manager of the Warner Beverly Hills Theatre, where the premiere was scheduled, and warned him about the billing. I happened to be driving past the theatre a few days later and I flipped when I saw the marquee, with Pat O'Brien's name leading the list of stars.

"Dammit!" I snapped when I got the manager on the phone. "I told you about Cagney. Now get out there and change it before he blows a fuse!"

The man followed the order, but he was too late. Cagney had already seen the offending sign, and his lawyers had taken photographs of it. Shortly thereafter he filed suit, and we had no defense at all.

At least Cagney did not walk off the lot this time. However, he did grow *that* moustache back for *Torrid Zone* (Warner Bros., 1940), his last picture with O'Brien. This time it was breezy, confident Ann Sheridan who stole the limelight with her fast-paced, wisecracking "oomph." The story took place on a tropical plantation where no one was safe from her caustic tongue. For example, at one point, she tells O'Brien, "The stork that brought you must have been a vulture." Helen Vinson, her romantic rival in this entry, at one point earns a reprimand from Sheridan for not carefully disposing of her cigarette. After all, that is how the Chicago fire started, she reminds Vinson. "The Chicago fire was started by a cow," sneers Miss Helen. Sheridan's retort, "History repeats itself?" Sheridan's best lines are for Cagney, who asks her at one point, "Why don't you have that mind of yours sent out and dry cleaned?"

"What's the use?" deadpans the heroine. "Look at the company I'm in."

Cagney balked at uttering the film's closing line, "You and your 14 karat oomph," as he and Sheridan go into a fadeout clinch. But director William Keighley bet him that the line would receive the picture's biggest laugh. After the premiere, Cagney sent Keighley a one-hundred-dollar check.

His next screen work was *City for Conquest* (Warner Bros., 1940), one of his most dramatic entries. He plays a boxer who has been semi-blinded in the ring in his over-ambitious attempts to finance the musical education of his kid brother (Arthur Kennedy). It had a top cast (Ann Sheridan, Frank Craven, Donald Crisp, Frank McHugh, George Tobias, and Anthony Quinn), a Max Steiner score, and in-depth, if pretentious, direction by Anatole Litvak. The associate producer was William Cagney. The star's personal reviews for this message-laden drama were excellent. The *New York Morning Telegraph* insisted that he "stands forth in shining splendor," while the *New York Post* lauded his "stunning performance."

Elia Kazan, from whom the world of performing arts was to hear much in future years, was making his motion picture debut in *City for Conquest*. "I learned something from Jimmy Cagney," he later said to the press. "He taught me quite a lot about acting. Jimmy taught me some things about being honest and not overdoing it. He even affected my work with Brando a little bit. I mean, 'Don't show it, just do it.'"

Cagney, who already had been heard on *Lux Radio Theatre* (in 1936 in "Is Zat So" with sister-in-law Boots Mallory, in 1939 on the show's "Ceiling Zero" with Ralph Bellamy, and "Angels with Dirty Faces" with Pat O'Brien), returned to the medium in 1940 for a radio dramatization of Dalton Trumbo's *Johnny Got His Gun*. He portrayed an armless, legless, faceless veteran who understandably has an anti-war message to relate to anyone who will listen.

It was also the year that Cagney faced charges again of being a Communist. John

49

With Ann Sheridan in *City for Conquest* (WB, 1940)

R. Leech, allegedly the former "chief functionary" of Los Angeles' Communist party, named over twenty-five Hollywood figures, including Cagney, Bogart, and Fredric March, as Communists. In Cagney's case, he claimed that the 1934 imbroglio had resulted in such bad press that "any relation between Mr. Cagney and the Communist party would be conducted by the Central Committee of the Communist party. We were warned and advised that local interference would not be permitted." The accusations brought intense protests from the accused parties. March called Leech "an unmitigated liar." Bogart stated, "I dare the men who are attempting this investigation to call me to the stand." In addition, accused writer Sam Ornitz said of District Attorney Burton Fitts, "It is said he was elected to prey upon and slander innocent people just before the primary election, just because they oppose him."

Cagney was motoring in New England (he had bought a farm on Martha's Vineyard in 1936 for $85,000) when the news first broke. It made page one, column one, in the *New York Times*. Therefore, brother Bill made the initial publicized defense remarks. The next day Cagney commented that, as far as the investigation goes, "You can blame it on West Coast political aspirants." He appeared before the Dies Committee in San Francisco on August 20, 1940, and was vindicated, his "Communism" traced to his aid to the San Joaquin Valley cotton strikers, the Salinas Lettuce strikers, and his donation of an ambulance to the Abraham Lincoln Brigade of the Loyalists in the Spanish Civil War. Other people accused were similarly cleared. (Interestingly, Cagney's name would not come up later in the Hollywood red probes of the late forties and early fifties in which fellow tough guy Edward G. Robinson was wounded.)

The new year, 1941, saw James in two comedies. The first was *Strawberry Blonde*

50

With Olivia de Havilland in *The Strawberry Blonde* (WB, 1941)

With Bette Davis in *The Bride Came C.O.D.* (WB, 1941)

(Warner Bros.), Raoul Walsh's atmospherically directed period piece of 1910, which had been a Broadway play and a 1933 Paramount film with Gary Cooper. In the remake, Cagney plays Biff Grimes, an ambitious correspondence school dentist who is done dirt by Jack Carson. (Cagney later evens the score by pulling one of the latter's teeth without anaesthesia.) The star could not have asked for two better leading ladies. As *Time* Magazine would report: "Cagney makes the hero a tough but obviously peachy fellow. But the strawberry humdinger, Rita Hayworth, takes the picture away from him, and dark-eyed Olivia de Havilland, with her electric winks, each followed by a galvanizing 'Exactly!,' takes it away from both of them." The studio would remake the film yet again as a 1948 musical with Dennis Morgan, Janis Paige, and Dorothy Malone.

The Bride Came C.O.D. (Warner Bros., 1941) was a matching of the studio's two most mannered performers, Cagney and Bette Davis. It was the sappy story of a cocky pilot kidnapping a tycoon's self-willed daughter on the eve of her elopement, and then crashing in the desert in the bargain. As Miss Davis explains about this venture in her *The Lonely Life* (1962): "Next I made a picture with Jimmy Cagney. It was called a comedy. It had been decided that my work as a tragedian should be temporarily halted for a change of pace. Jimmy, who made the gangster artistic— Jimmy, who was one of the fine actors on my or any lot—Jimmy, with whom I'd always wanted to work in something fine, spent most of his time in the picture removing cactus quills from my behind. This was supposedly hilarious. We romped about the desert and I kept falling into cactus. We both reached bottom with this one." Audiences did not agree. The William Keighley-directed feature was a box-office hit.

Cagney's first 1942 release was *Captain of the Clouds* (Warner Bros.), a salute to the Canadians in training for the Air Corps Service. It was a northern version of Paramount's smash hit, *I Wanted Wings* (1941). It is mainly memorable because it was James' first Technicolor feature.

For several years up to this point, George M. Cohan had been negotiating with various studios to sell the screen rights to his colorful life story. Finally, Warner Bros. bid the highest price, paying the vaudevillian-playwright-composer-actor $50,000 and giving him cast and screenplay approval. Warner claimed in his memoirs that he immediately thought of Cagney for the role of bombastic Cohan. "When the time came to choose a star for *Yankee Doodle Dandy,* one of the finest pictures we ever made—it had Oscar written all over it—I knew that Cagney, despite the law suits and his Irish stubbornness, was the only man for the part." Cohan agreed. Cohan also gave his nod to the casting of Walter Huston as his father, Rosemary De Camp as his mother, and Cagney's sister Jeanne as sister Josie.

Cagney was delighted with the job prospect. "It was an exciting picture from an actor's point of view. I had knocked around in all kinds of shows and knew that every actor of Cohan's generation had been influenced by him. Cohan had unbounded energy and an interest in everything. He was bright as hell and had a drive second to none. Writing, dancing, and acting—he was a triple threat man. That's what made him interesting."

Nevertheless, the production had its share of strains. Cohan insisted that his approved script be followed to the letter. James thought the scenario was below par. The star insisted on a rewrite, and Warner's explanation of Cohan's veto power did not satisfy him. Consequently, the star once again threatened to go on suspension.

52

Only after brother Bill convinced him that the feature could do a lot for sister Jeanne, did Cagney reconsider.

Also, Cohan, married twice, refused to let there be any love scenes, lest his second wife be reminded of his previous domestic state. The studio circumvented this by incorporating wife number one and two into the pleasing form of "Mary" (which was not the name of either of Cohan's wives), played by that wholesome teenager Joan Leslie. Finally, after the lot lavished one and a half million dollars on the musical, Cohan entered the Burbank projection room to witness the finished product. Warner was in a state of nervous prostration, for the studio boss had learned that Cagney had surreptitiously had the scenario reworked on a day-to-day basis. Cohan's contract gave him the right to veto the film's release if he did not like it.

Cohan watched the picture with the mildest enthusiasm, while the studio brass tried to supply some positive audience response. The stage veteran did not seem to notice the changes, but he did withhold an immediate okay. His comment as the lights came up was, "I'd like Agnes to see it first. I'm not sure." Agnes (wife number two) was in a New York state convalescent home, situated in a town where there was not even a movie house. A print of the picture was flown there, the lady watched it in a fire house, and, with her approval, Warner Bros. could distribute its film. Cohan then sent Cagney a telegram: "Dear Jim: How's my double? Thanks for a wonderful job. George M. Cohan."

In May, 1942, *Yankee Doodle Dandy* had a gala Broadway opening, selling first night tickets for war bonds. The eighty-eight best seats sold for $25,000 each, and no seat sold for less than twenty-five dollars. As a result, $5,750,000 was garnered for the U.S. Treasury Department in that single night. The film was an immediate sensation. Songs like "Yankee Doodle Dandy," "Over There," and "You're a Grand

In *Yankee Doodle Dandy* (WB, 1942)

Old Flag" captivated audiences freshly immersed in war; and numbers like "45 Minutes from Broadway" and "Give My Regards to Broadway" took the viewers' minds off their troubles. Cagney's performance, with the direction of Michael Curtiz and the choreography of Leroy Prinz and Seymour Felix, became an instant classic. All the performances, from Walter Huston's tradition-steeped Jerry Cohan to Irene Manning's lilting Fay Templeton, had just the right touch of flamboyance and schmaltz.

"Mr. Cagney's most brilliant bit of make believe," declared the *New York Journal-American*. "It is a remarkable performance, possibly Cagney's best," judged *Time* Magazine. The *New York Times* penned, "As bold and respectable a performance as anyone could wish. But the truly remarkable nature of Mr. Cagney's accomplishment turns not so much on a literal imitation of Mr. Cohan, as it does on a shrewd and meticulous creation of a lusty, spontaneous character."

It was indeed Cagney's greatest professional triumph. In March, 1943, he found himself at the Academy Award ceremonies competing for Best Actor with Ronald Colman of *Random Harvest* (MGM), Gary Cooper of *Pride of the Yankees* (RKO), Walter Pidgeon of *Mrs. Miniver* (MGM), and Monty Woolley of *The Pied Piper* (Twentieth Century-Fox).

The Best Actor contestants had to squirm longer than usual that evening. Miss Greer Garson won the Best Actress statuette for *Mrs. Miniver* and her acceptance speech rambled on for over half an hour. It was the longest thank-you monologue in Academy history. Then Cagney's name was finally announced. He accepted by bounding onto the stage, grasping the microphone, and uttering, "An actor is only as good as people think he is and as bad as people think he is. I am glad so many thought I was so good."

By this time, Cagney was long gone from his home studio. *Dandy* had been the last film under his existing contract. In what must have been a truly painful experience for him, Jack Warner drafted a new agreement that would permit the Cagney brothers to produce features, with the studio backing and releasing them. Wielding the ultimate veto, the Cagneys refused this enviable offer and signed with United Artists, setting up their own Cagney Productions.

But first he went over to MGM for *You, John Jones,* a Mervyn LeRoy-directed short subject, which co-starred Ann Sothern and Margaret O'Brien. It was a hard-sell wartime bit of propaganda.

Back in 1936, after the star's worst brawl with Warner, he had toyed with the idea of establishing an acting troupe to offer Irish plays in cities of less than 100,000 population, and perhaps even to tour England and Ireland. Pat O'Brien, William Gargan, and Robert Montgomery were reportedly also interested. The idea did not materialize then, but it cropped up again after the termination of Cagney's Warner Bros. contract. However, by this time America was at war, traveling even in this country was under government regulation, and Cagney, who was too old to be called into military service, decided to best serve everyone's interests by continuing to make films.

The first production under the new Cagney brothers banner was *Johnny Come Lately* (United Artists, 1943), a too-leisurely story of a vagrant newspaperman. The plot concerned his help for the widow of a courageous news publisher in order to carry on her husband's activities against corrupt politicians and businessmen. William K. Howard directed this period piece. The Cagneys managed to recruit distinguished Grace George of the Broadway stage to play the elderly widow. Yet, the

With Marjorie Lord, Margaret Hamilton, George Cleveland, and Grace George in *Johnny Come Lately* (UA, 1943)

ninety-seven-minute result was unimpressive. "It is not dreadful," claimed the *New York Post.* "Cagney is still the unique Cagney—but it is far below his standards." Many thought that Marjorie Main as the colorful Gashouse Mary offered the film's most catchy performance. Boxoffice income on this entry sagged, forcing Cagney Productions to take their time before producing a new venture.

Cagney's extra-curricular activities kept him busy during the hectic war years. On September 28, 1942, he became president of the Screen Actors Guild. He became chairman of the Hollywood Victory Committee in 1943, touring with Bing Crosby, Pat O'Brien, Charles Boyer, Merle Oberon, Judy Garland, Dick Powell, Laurel and Hardy, and many others, in bond-raising tours. He performed at troop installations, lent the Coast Guard his yacht, turned his Martha's Vineyard estate over to the Army for maneuvers, and acted in several short subjects and recruiting trailers for the Allied war effort.

It was not until 1945 that another Cagney production, *Blood on the Sun* (United Artists), appeared. With Frank Lloyd directing, Cagney was again a newspaper editor, this time at war with unctuous Japanese militants in the 1930s Orient. Rosemary De Camp, his "mom" in *Yankee Doodle Dandy,* was in this one, as was Sylvia Sidney as a beautiful but mysterious half-Chinese lady. There was more action in this feature than in his last, including Cagney performing judo. It did much better business than *Johnny Come Lately,* even though by 1945 America and the world was tired of coping with the Japanese master plan.

From a practical point of view it was safer to work with another producing company's finances than his own, and so Cagney decided to be amenable to offers from outside filmmakers. He refused Twentieth Century-Fox's offer to star in *The Life of O. Henry,* but he did agree to accept the lead in *13 Rue Madeleine* (Twentieth Century-Fox, 1946), a role released by Rex Harrison. Henry Hathaway directed the

With Sylvia Sidney in *Blood on the Sun* (UA, 1945)

With Sam Jaffe in *13 Rue Madeleine* (20th, 1946)

With Gale Page and Reginald Beane (at piano) in *The Time of Your Life* (UA, 1948)

semi-documentary espionage caper dealing with the Gestapo. Location work was done in New England, particularly at Boston College. Now in his mid-forties, stocky Cagney was showing his age, and seemed a bit too mature for such action assignments. It was a part that was much better suited to the forties' favorite tough man, Alan Ladd.

Then came another William Cagney production, *The Time of Your Life* (United Artists, 1948). This was William Saroyan's Pulitzer prize-winning play, a very philosophical, yet flavorful, study. Cagney purchased the screen rights for $150,000, after Saroyan had turned down reportedly much larger offers from both Warner Bros. and MGM. The lead role of Joe, the cripple who observes life in a San Francisco saloon, was played by James. Among the others inhabiting the dive were Kitty Duvall (Jeanne Cagney), a cop (Broderick Crawford), a striker (Ward Bond), a dancer (Paul Draper), a bartender (Wayne Morris), a youngish man (Jimmy Lydon), and an old coot who thinks he is Kit Carson (James Barton). "As deft a compromise between stage and screen as you are likely to see," said *Time* Magazine. Even Saroyan was pleased, and sent Cagney a lengthy letter claiming that he got so involved in the film that "I was too busy enjoying it to care who wrote it."

White Heat (1949) followed. The script was so taut and in need of a much better production than their private company could provide, so that Cagney and his brother decided to agree to a shift of their base of operations back to Warner Bros. The year before, Edward G. Robinson had given a fresh slant to the gangster figure in *Key Largo* (Warner Bros.), which starred Humphrey Bogart as the top-billed war veteran hero. Undoubtedly, this helped to inspire Cagney to return to the genre which had so stereotyped him in the 30s.

Cagney's portrayal of Cody Jarrett, madman killer with a weakness for momma and a tendency toward epileptic fits, is one of his definitive screen performances. It started a new trend in cinema character development. Raoul Walsh was the director, and the film had a superior supporting cast that included Virginia Mayo as Cagney's cheap moll Verna, Edmond O'Brien as Hank Fallon, the G-Man who wins Cagney's confidence only to betray him, Steve Cochran as Cagney's intended usurper Big Ed, and Margaret Wycherly in the pivotal role of Ma Jarrett. The thriller was based on a story by Virginia Kellogg, and it was well scripted by Ivan Goff and Ben Roberts.

There are many famous scenes in *White Heat*. There is Cagney's initial epileptic fit in his mountain retreat, where his ma watches over him. "It's like having a red-hot buzz saw inside my head," he gasps as he recovers. He then sits on Ma's lap, thanking her devotion with, "Always thinking about your Cody, aren't ya'?" One of the movie's more unique executions follows when he locks a captive in a car trunk. The captive is not pleased. Cagney replies, "Oh. Stuffy, huh? I'll give ya' a little air." He then shoots his victim through the trunk lid. The sequence in the prison commissary, where Cagney learns that his ma (who has inspired him since childhood with her "top of the world, son") is dead, is one of the film's most vivid scenes. He goes into a rage, clambering over the tables and bleating insanely as he takes on a slew of guards.

And what a climax! High on top of a gasoline storage tank, Cagney is seen giggling wildly, combatting an army of heavy-armed police. The segment builds to a crescendo, as the hysterical Cagney screams, "Made it, Ma! Top of the world!" Just then a police bullet causes the tank to explode. "Cody Jarrett," eulogizes O'Brien, "finally got to the top of the world . . . and it blew right up in his face."

With Virginia Mayo and Margaret Wycherly in *White Heat*

Director Walsh publicly recalled Cagney as "a great man and a great actor. He was interested only in his picture. And he's a quiet sort of fella, and he would sit back and look at the scenes that I'd take with other people, and he'd say, 'That's great, skipper. . . .' We became very warm friends during all the years we met. I try to get him to come out, but he won't fly. It's the only thing I think he's afraid of—of anything in this world."

Many feel that Cagney deserved at least an Oscar nomination for his Cody Jarrett work, but one did not result. The performance was just too much for some reviewers to accept. As *Cue* Magazine wrote: "For 2 hours in *White Heat* you are subjected to an unending procession of what is probably the most gruesome aggregation of brutalities ever presented upon the motion picture screen under the guise of entertainment. James Cagney, heavier in voice, body, and jowl, plays a homicidal paranoiac with a mother fixation—a crazy killer who mixes train robbery with murder, bestiality with sadism, and tops the whole unsavory mess with a slobbering, shuddering series of epileptic fits the like of which I hope I may never again see in the fearful darkness of a movie theatre." Nevertheless, *White Heat* marks an important growth in maturity in the cinema's approach to the criminal mind: that the mentality of the individual himself, not society, is responsible for this most rabid of society's problems.

With the Cagneys back on the lot (but Edward G. Robinson gone and soon to be followed by Humphrey Bogart and Errol Flynn), the star went into *The West Point Story* (1950). It re-joined the star with Roy Del Ruth, director of many of Cagney's early Warner Bros. pictures, and featured Virginia Mayo of *White Heat*. Doris Day, Gordon MacRae, and Gene Nelson, the new breed on the lot, also contributed their musical talents. Despite songs by Jules Styne and Sammy Cahn, the whole thing

With Alan Hale, Jr. (center) in *The West Point Story* (WB, 1950)

misfired. *Time* Magazine branded it "a little monster of a flag-waving, hip-wagging movie." Virginia Mayo's legs got the best reviews.

Just as Joan Crawford was being typecast on the lot after her film *Flamingo Road* (Warner Bros., 1949) had established her new image, so Cagney was soon stuck in a rut of roles reminiscent of his early thirties' *Public Enemy* spin-offs. *Kiss Tomorrow Goodbye* (Warner Bros., 1950) saw James "bustin' out" of jail again. It was certainly brutal, and the state of Ohio banned the "sordid, sadistic presentation." Within the film he gets to rough up Barbara Payton as only he can. Bill Cagney appeared briefly onscreen as his brother.

On the other hand, there was *Come Fill the Cup* (Warner Bros., 1951), a well-received melodrama about alcohol. The film, though, did more for Gig Young as a drunk than it did for Cagney as a reformed boozer whose old girlfriend (Phyllis Thaxter) is now Young's wife. Young won an Oscar nomination for Best Supporting Actor. *Starlift* (Warner Bros., 1951) utilized most of the lot's remaining stars for boxoffice duty in a thin story about movie actors who entertain Korean-bound troops.

What Price Glory? (Twentieth Century-Fox, 1952) should have been a memorable major film and an exciting remake of the 1926 silent film which had starred Victor McLaglen and Edmund Lowe. But it was not. It was Cagney's first film with John Ford, whose World War I saga should have been much better. "The total result is deplorable," insisted the *New York Post,* "which is shocking when you see the name of John Ford as director." Cagney and Dan Dailey, neither young enough for the parts, had moments as Flagg and Quirt, and Corinne Calvet was certainly a pretty addition. However, the film was another in James' growing number of less-than-smash pictures.

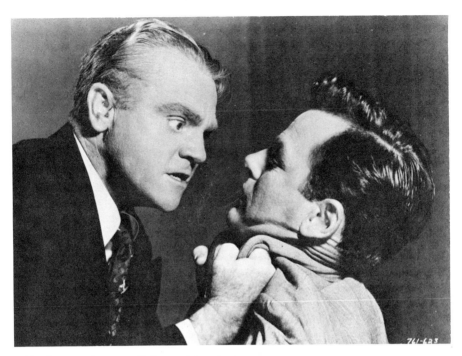

With Gig Young in *Come Fill the Cup* (WB, 1951)

In *What Price Glory?* (20th, 1952)

61

A Lion Is in the Streets (Warner Bros., 1953) was almost a family party for Cagney. He starred in it, brother Bill produced it, Jeanne played a feature role, brother Ed was story editor, and old buddy Frank McHugh was cast in a substantial supporting role. The star had been planning this Huey Long-like study for several years. He should have made the picture before the too similar *All the King's Men* (Columbia, 1949). Under Raoul Walsh's direction, Cagney portrayed Hank Martin, a successful backwoods politician dependent on his own trickery and practice of Bible-waving. *Variety* noted that Cagney's "portrayal has an occasional strength, but mostly is a styled performance done with an incongruous Southern dialect that rarely holds through a complete line of dialogue."

The star's cinema output had become so forgettable over the early fifties, that when some films were released with him in them in 1955, the press heralded them as a Cagney "comeback."

The first such release was *Run for Cover* (Paramount, 1955), a Western that had nice Technicolor and a good mixture of plot and action. More memorable was *Love Me or Leave Me* (MGM, 1955), in which James played Martin Snyder, more popularly known (and more unkindly) as "the Gimp." Doris Day, another ex-Warner Bros. star, was Ruth Etting, and the unusual co-starring bill worked out splendidly. Cagney discussed the character's limp with several doctors so as to gain an insight into his portrayal of the gangster. He decided the Gimp had been lame from birth. Miss Day's delivery of such period songs as "Mean to Me" and, particularly, "You Made Me Love You," were nicely received, as was the entire picture, which reaped Oscar nomination number three for Cagney. He lost to Ernest Borgnine's *Marty* (United Artists). However, an Oscar did go to Daniel Fuchs for his original story,

With Anne Francis and Barbara Hale in a publicity pose for *A Lion Is in the Streets* (WB, 1953)

With Mrs. Cagney and their children Casey and James, Jr. on the set of *Run for Cover* (Par., 1955)

With Doris Day in *Love Me or Leave Me* (MGM, 1955)

which angered the film's subject, Miss Etting. As she said in a recent interview with *Film Fan Monthly* about the musical film, "Oh, what a ——— mess that was . . . I was *never* at any time a dance hall girl. It was just a means of working in 'Ten Cents a Dance.' They took a lot of liberties with my life, but I guess they usually do with that kind of thing."

A more fortunate rendezvous with John Ford followed. *Mr. Roberts* (Warner Bros., 1955) was the cinema version of the successful Broadway play, with Henry Fonda repeating his stage role (thanks to Ford's insistence and support from the press, favoring him over first choices William Holden and Marlon Brando). Cagney played the ignorant Captain, injecting a lot of humor into the role, an ingredient not found in the original Broadway interpretation. Again, James had definite personality characteristics in mind while forming his character. "I asked myself, 'Who do I know who's like this skipper? How would he talk?' For a long time I'd been aping one of my best friends, the president of a Massachusetts bank. I'd been telling stories about him featuring his New England accent, so I stole the bank president pal's way of talking for my *Mr. Roberts'* role. This will probably come as news to him."

The film was shot on Midway Island and Hawaii on board the U.S.S. *Hewell,* a Navy cargo ship. The production was tragic. Fonda was extremely strong-minded about the way the film should be shot, and he sparred constantly with Ford. He felt the director was diluting the picture with slapstick, building up Ward Bond's role way out of proportion, reducing the crew members to chorus boys, etc. Finally, after a nasty incident that nobody on the film wants to discuss (but what has been reputed to be a physical brawl between Ford and Fonda), Ford left the picture. Conveniently, he had kidney trouble and the staff could inform the press that

With Henry Fonda in *Mister Roberts* (WB, 1955)

64

departure was due solely to ill health. Mervyn LeRoy was rushed in to complete the picture.

To anyone who remembers Cagney's movies, a favorite scene is the one in *Mr. Roberts* in which Fonda tosses Cagney's palm tree overboard on V.E. evening. Cagney then sounds the alarm, intoning his famous, "*Whooo* did it!" and then ultimately vomiting. Jack Lemmon would win a Best Supporting Actor Oscar for his hilarious performance of Ensign Pulver in this service story. But Lemmon's reminiscences about the film would cause the only sour note on Cagney's Life Achievement Award Evening some nineteen years later.

Also in 1955, James, as a favor to Bob Hope, appeared briefly as George M. Cohan once again onscreen. The comedian was making *The Seven Little Foys* (Paramount) and wanted Cagney to perform a cameo in the film. Thus the two did a brief dance together on a tabletop. Despite its brevity, it required three weeks of rehearsal. Cagney declined a fee for this appearance on the grounds that any Cohan part was worth the effort and time. Nevertheless, Hope and Paramount presented him with a red leather-lined horse trailer with the scroll, *Thanks for the trailer you did for us. Here's one for you.*

James Cagney's mid-fifties output was so impressive that many major magazines ran in-depth stories on him. In fact, he collaborated with Pete Martin in a three-part *Saturday Evening Post* installment, "How I Got This Way." In it, he commented about the idiosyncracies of the entertainment business. "Show business is as unpredictable as a bicycle in heavy traffic. A young kid comes along, does a few radio shows, works for a spell with a stock company, does a small bit on the stage. Then he gets a part with which he can do something, and away he goes.

"Everybody asks him: 'Where have you been?'

"To which he should reply: 'I've been in your casting offices, right under your noses, all the time, trying to make a lousy buck. Where have *you* been?' "

There were two almost forgettable James Cagney features in 1956. At MGM, he replaced Spencer Tracy in *Tribute to a Bad Man* when his friend was fired after some moody and troublesome behavior on location which was costing the studio thousands of dollars daily. *These Wilder Years*, at Metro, was a sugary mess that was more interesting for its off-set sidelines than for the action on the soundstages: Cagney and co-star Barbara Stanwyck would dance together between takes.

James made one film in 1957, *Man of a Thousand Faces* (Universal), the story of Lon Chaney, Sr. Chaney, Jr. later claimed that the studio had five writers reworking his father's story the day after he sold them the rights. Nevertheless, the results were most impressive, with Dorothy Malone excellent as Chaney's haunted first wife, and Jane Greer fine as the contrasting, understanding new woman in his life.

Chaney, Sr. had worked by the doctrine, "Unless I suffer, how can I expect people to believe me?" His makeups were exceedingly painful, utilizing such devices as fish hooks and straitjackets. Makeup men Bud Westmore and Jack Kevan had long since streamlined these makeups to a science of quickly applied procedures, using rubber pieces to mold their grotesques. Cagney was therefore transformed into re-creations of Chaney's Quasimodo (*The Hunchback of Notre Dame*, Universal, 1923), Erik (*The Phantom of the Opera*, Universal, 1925), the vampire of *London after Midnight*, (MGM, 1927), and more, effectively but not painfully. (He did, however, balk at using the special teeth Westmore designed for him; instead, he consulted his expensive Hollywood dentist to make the distorted teeth set that would not irritate his jaw and would allow him to speak. The bill for Universal was

With Bob Hope in *The Seven Little Foys* (Par., 1955)

On the set of *Man of a Thousand Faces* (Univ., 1957) with James Stewart and Orson Welles

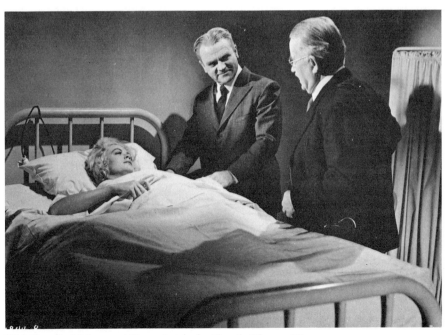

With Dorothy Malone and Harry Antrim in *Man of a Thousand Faces*

$1,400; the studio spent a total of $25,000 in makeup effects for Cagney.) *Life* Magazine hailed Cagney's "superb performance" and many thought he would surely be Oscar-nominated. But he was not. That was the year in which Alec Guiness won for *The Bridge on the River Kwai* (Columbia).

Meanwhile, Cagney had appeared on television, a medium he dislikes and for which he has done very little. On September 10, 1956, he was seen on an episode of "Robert Montgomery Presents" entitled *Soldiers from the War Returning*. Then he played on the "Christophers" program on June 30, 1957, and hosted an episode on "Navy Log" entitled *The Lonely Watch* (January 9, 1958). On June 20, 1955, he had appeared with Fonda on the "Ed Sullivan Show," re-enacting a scene from *Mr. Roberts*.

Cagney the individualist then directed a film for the first and last time. Friend A. C. Lyles arranged for him to helm *Short Cut to Hell* (Paramount, 1957), which was much better received in its original form as the Veronica Lake-Alan Ladd gangster melodrama, *This Gun for Hire* (Paramount, 1942). Cagney also appeared in the prologue. "Director James Cagney, in his first appearance behind the camera, manages to beauty-spot a few of the bare places with some characteristically Cagney touches," wrote an indifferent *Time* Magazine.

There would be only four more Cagney features. For Universal he starred with Shirley Jones in a lukewarm musical gangster drama about a crooked labor leader, *Never Steal Anything Small* (1959). *Shake Hands with the Devil* (United Artists, 1959) was somewhat better, but no more memorable. It was about the Black and Tans "troubles" in Ireland of the twenties. Don Murray, Dana Wynter, Glynis Johns, and Michael Redgrave were in the period piece, making for exciting viewing but, unfortunately, some inconsistency of dialect. *The Gallant Hours* (United Artists, 1960) starred Cagney as Admiral Halsey, and was a fine biography, produced and directed by former Navy man Robert Montgomery. Halsey visited the set and won the admiration of Cagney, who recalled, "After one big scene I walked over to him and asked him if it went the way he thought it should. He said, 'You would know that better than I would. You're the pro.'"

With Roger Smith, Cara Williams, and Robert Wilke in *Never Steal Anything Small* (Univ., 1959)

With Robert Montgomery, Jr., Robert Montgomery, and James Cagney, Jr. on location for
The Gallant Hours (UA, 1960)

"One of the quietest, most reflective, subtlest jobs that Mr. Cagney has ever
done," wrote the *New York Times*.

Although no one was really aware of it at the time, Billy Wilder's *One, Two, Three*
(United Artists, 1961) would be the star's cinema swan song. It was a frantic comedy
about a Coca-Cola salesman in West Berlin and his boss'· daffy daughter (Pamela
Tiffin) who falls for a Communist (Horst Buchholz). As he had with *The Public
Enemy* years before, Cagney gave the assignment his usual rat-a-tat-tat punchy
interpretation, making the usual Wilder mayhem even more exhilarating. "He
plays it fortissimo all the way, as is right, and his vulgar vitality is just what is
needed to keep the act from falling off the high wire," analyzed *Esquire* Magazine. Cagney was then nearly sixty-two years old.

The star would later recall: "While I was shooting *One, Two, Three,* I loaned my
boat to 3 of my pals and their wives for a cruise, and while they were out they had a
picture taken of the six of them standing on deck and toasting me. They sent me a
print of it and they wrote on it, 'Thank God you are gainfully employed.' And
didn't they look smug and happy. It showed up on a day when we were shooting
some last interiors at Goldwyn. And it was a beautiful day, a gorgeous day. I was
standing outside, catching the sun and the blue sky and the clouds, and the assistant
director came out and said, 'We're ready for you now, Mr. Cagney.' Well, I went
back inside that black cavern and right then I said to myself, 'That's it, baby,' and it
was. No more."

Bogart, Gable, and Cooper were dead, and now Cagney had retired. He did so
with no fancy good-byes, no statements at all. He just disappeared from the scene.
He certainly did not need to work. He was a reputed millionaire, and owned four
farms that paid for themselves: his Coldwater Canyon estate, a retreat in Twenty-
Nine Palms in the California desert, his Martha's Vineyard farm, and a farm near
Millbrook, New York, where he spends most of his time. He became very interested
in conservation, raised horses, painted, and ran and tap-danced to keep in shape.
When Jack L. Warner wanted him enough to offer a million dollars to play Doolittle
in *My Fair Lady* (Warner Bros., 1964), Cagney pondered the issue only briefly

69

With Hanns Lothar, Horst Buchholz, and Pamela Tiffin in *One, Two, Three* (UA, 1961)

before giving him a definite no. His interest in conservation resulted in his narrating a video special, *Smokey the Bear* (NBC-TV, November 23, 1966), and his friendship with A. C. Lyles led to his narration of *Arizona Bushwackers* (Paramount, 1968), a quickie Western with ex-boxoffice draws Howard Keel, Yvonne De Carlo, and Brian Donlevy.

Over the years, skeptics rumored that Cagney was gravely ill and/or unhealthily fat, which accounted for his going into seclusion. Actually, the truth was James Cagney was gloriously content and not the least bit interested in honoring any "responsibilities" which some claimed that the star had toward the public that had never tired of him.

Finally, thirteen years after his disappearing act, Cagney did agree to return to the public eye. In early 1974, the American Film Institute announced that Cagney was to be the second recipient of the Life Achievement Award. John Ford had received the first such tribute, five months prior to his death in 1973. Cagney dieted eighteen pounds from his frame in preparation for the ceremony. He revealed to the press after his arrival in Los Angeles that he still ran 350 yards uphill to his studio each day. With A. C. Lyles as mentor, Cagney arrived in Los Angeles and caught up with the interviewers who had missed him for so long.

Finally, the greatly heralded evening arrived. On Wednesday, March 13, 1974, over 1300 guests jammed into the ballroom at the Century Plaza Hotel in West Los Angeles. The occasion was roundly described as the most star-studded event in the social history of Hollywood. At a cocktail party which Cagney did not attend, but which launched the evening, scores of the cinema's new breed (Paul Newman, Clint Eastwood, Cicely Tyson) rubbed shoulders with such vintage faces as Loretta Young, Mae West, John Wayne, and, of course, Warner reliables such as Joan Blondell, Ruby Keeler, Brenda Marshall, Rosemary De Camp, Joan Leslie, and Mae Clarke. (Miss Clarke would present a delighted Cagney with a grapefruit tree.) Mervyn LeRoy and William A. Wellman were among the directors present, and Hal B. Wallis, with wife Martha Hyer, represented the Warners' hierarchy of Cagney's years there. (Some of the non-attendees were of note, including Jack L. Warner, who was in ill health, and Pat O'Brien, although his wife Eloise and son Terry were present.)

At about 8:15, James Cagney arrived at the hotel. The tables of honor assembled: Governor Ronald Reagan and wife Nancy, Los Angeles Mayor Tom Bradley and his wife, Mr. and Mrs. A. C. Lyles, Mr. and Mrs. Ralph Bellamy, Frank McHugh,

Mrs. Pat O'Brien, Jeanne Cagney, Cagney's son and daughter and their mates. The lights dimmed, and a voice intoned, "Ladies and Gentlemen, The American Film Institute is proud to welcome our guest of honor—James Cagney!" Nelson Riddle's Orchestra played "Yankee Doodle Dandy" and Cagney entered; he was polished, only slightly plump, and looking quite a figure for his seventy-five years. After a standing ovation, Mrs. Cagney joined her husband at the table and the show began.

Charlton Heston introduced the host of the evening, Frank Sinatra, who proceeded to comment on the career of James Cagney, interspersing his observations with clips from ten of the star's films. Among the actors who had comments to make on Cagney the performer were John Wayne ("You're a great actor, a great citizen . . . all of us, *all* of us, love you"), George C. Scott (who quoted from words written about General Lee relating to Cagney's qualities as a "wholly human gentleman"), and Bob Hope ("I know that everyone within the sound of my voice has his own special memories of you, Jim, whether as a co-worker or as a movie fan. So on behalf of them I take the privilege of saying to you: 'Jim, thanks for the memories' ").

Sinatra then made some special introductions, including Joan Blondell, Mae Clarke ("the citrus queen," cracked Sinatra), George Raft, and Allen Jenkins. Sinatra mentioned that Cagney's brother Bill, so active a part of his brother's career, was "indisposed" and could not be present.

While Doris Day's tribute to Cagney seemed to be performed nervously, it was genuine. What followed after a clip from *The Public Enemy* (the grapefruit scene, of course) was a mild disaster. Shirley MacLaine and Jack Lemmon took the stage. Mr. Lemmon began a long-winded speech that discoursed on his early years in television. Then he began to comment on *Mr. Roberts* and the fact that it was not until after beginning work with Cagney that he developed any respect for the performer. His circumlocutions apparently baffled even him, for he soon began to panic visibly at his *faux pas*. In the midst of Lemmon's fumblings, director Sam Peckinpah shocked the assemblage by rising from his table in the audience and screaming, "Come on, get to the Goddamn point and get the hell off the stage! You're becoming a big bore! We don't need you to tell us what a fine man Cagney is!" After some fumbled responses on the stage, Miss MacLaine grabbed the microphone and said a few closing remarks. "Jimmy . . . you're the best." "You're the best," chimed in Lemmon, and the two hustled into the safety of the wings. By the time the video editors were done condensing this segment of the tape for the planned television special of the evening, the Lemmon section was nearly deleted.

The next morning Lemmon phoned an apology to Cagney, the latter assuring him that all was okay. As it turned out, Lemmon had delayed a necessary hernia operation so he could attend the ceremony, doing so under medication. The afternoon following the ceremony, he was rushed to the hospital for an operation.

At any rate, the wind-up of the Cagney tribute evening moved along, with Frank Gorshin, who has made a name for himself imitating distinctive celebrities such as Cagney, saying, "I feel like the whole night's for me."

After tributes from Ronald Reagan, Mayor Thomas Bradley, and others, Sinatra offered his own tribute in the form of song. He sang a quite touching and clever accolade to the star to the tune of "My Way."

Finally Cagney took the center of stage, dancing a few steps to "Yankee Doodle Dandy." His initial remark was "I'm a wreck!" Then he related that A. C. Lyles had never really informed him what would be expected of him "About the award," he stated, "I'm very grateful for it. But why don't we just say for now that I'm merely

71

the custodian, holding it for all those wonderful guys and gals who worked over the years to bring about this night for me."

The honored guest read his favorite definition of art, taken from William Ernest Hocking's book, *Strength of Men and Nations.* "Art is life plus. Life plus caprice. Where the simple declarative sentence becomes a line of Shakespearean poetry. Where a number of musical notes strung together become a Beethoven sonata. Where a walk, done in cadence by a Freddie Astaire or Edward Vilella or Patricia Farrell, becomes an exciting dance. That's art." He added that art "affects our everyday lives," and that "if you look at it that way, you are holding the wonder that we are born with."

"Now I have a great many thanks to spread about this evening. We all know an event like this doesn't get itself on. It is the result of a lot of dedicated people working at peak pitch for a great many days. . . . Oh, Frankie [Gorshin], just in passing, I never said: 'Mmm, you dirty rat!' What I actually did say was: 'Judy! Judy! Judy!' And one more thing, Frankie Gorshin, that hitching of the trousers. I got that from a fellow who hung out on the corner of 78th Street and First Avenue. I was about twelve years old and he was most interesting to me. Because that's all he did [mimicking his famous trouser-hitching gesture] all day. When somebody would greet him, he didn't deign to say hello, he just stood back and did this [repeating the trouser-hitching]. Now let's face it, we are all indebted to that fellow. He was a type. And we had them—oh, how we did have them!"

He then proceeded to offer thanks to a series of confreres. He acknowledged among others, ". . . Harvey Perry, a stuntman who hung a cauliflower on my ear, on the first fight that I had in pictures. . . . I remember him well. And J. L., Jack Warner, who gave me a name I shall always cherish—affectionately, mind you— 'The Professional Againster.'

"But we're old now, and full of understanding, and that's all water over the dam. Am I right, Bill? My brother Bill. My sister Jeanne. [Here the star had to struggle to keep from crying] Gotta hang on, boy. . . . And all those Cagneys who over the years pulled their share of the burden—through those long and troubled years. There were many.

"And the names, the names, the names of my youth: Lager-head Quinlavan, Artie Klein, Peter Leyden, Jake Brodkin, Specks Torporcer, Brother O'Meara, Picky Houlihan! They were all part of a very stimulating early environment, which produced that unmistakable touch of the gutter without which this evening might never have happened at all. [Applause] I bless them. I bless Paul Keyes, and A. C. Lyles for their labors. And bless you!"

Cagney left the stage to an enormous ovation. Sinatra yielded the podium to Heston, and Heston concluded the evening by saying, "By being here with us tonight you helped create a moment in time that will last forever." During the course of the night's festivities, the actor had reaped ten standing ovations from the assemblage.

The day after the tribute, the American Film Institute board of directors hosted a lunch for James. The star was reportedly "still beaming" from the night before, and remarked about the tribute, "It worked. It really worked." Shortly thereafter, he and his wife packed up the award and returned to Martha's Vineyard. During the Hollywood sojourn he again had the pleasure of refusing a rash of new film offers, including the role of the coach in the movie version of *That Championship Season.*

While the lavish tribute did not launch any ideas for the star's comeback in the acting field, it did convince him (along with several unauthorized biographers) to

James Cagney in the Seventies

pen his memoirs. Early in 1975, Cagney obtained a temporary restraining order to fight American publication of *Cagney: A Biography* by English journalist Michael Freedland. Cagney claimed that he had made himself available for an interview with Freedland for one hour during his recent Hollywood stay. According to Cagney, the session was granted with the understanding that it would be used solely for the British Broadcasting Corporation radio network. When Freedland later used the interview in his book, James objected that the author gave the book "the ring of truth" by reference to the meeting thereby "leading the reader to believe I cooperated in the preparation of the book." In an affidavit accompanying his suit in New York State Supreme Court, James attested that he was ". . . very upset with the prospect of the bunk in [the] book moving toward publication as a purported factual review of my life," since the book was ". . . full of inaccuracies, falsities, and invented dialogue."

Cagney half-admitted that much of his action was due to his own book *Cagney by Cagney* due from Doubleday in the spring of 1976. The star lost his suit. The judge decided that Cagney's fame made such unauthorized biographies fair game, and Mr. Freedland's book found its projected U.S. publication.

As of this writing, James Cagney, the much honored actor, gentleman farmer, and life-long winner, is residing on Martha's Vineyard, enjoying the estate upon which nobody dares to trespass, tap-dancing, jogging, caring for his horses, avoiding his films on television, completing his memoirs. His sequestered existence reminds one of Orson Welles' Charles Foster Kane in his palatial Xanadu. But Cagney's life is much happier than that of the hapless Kane. And it is doubtful that Cagney ever ruminates, "I *might* have been a really great man."

73

JAMES CAGNEY

SINNERS' HOLIDAY *(Warner Bros., 1930), 55 min.*
Director, John G. Adolfi; based on the play *Penny Arcade* by Marie Baumer; screenplay, Harvey Thew, George Rosener; music director, Leo F. Forbstein; makeup, Perc Westmore; sound, Clare A. Riggs; camera, Ira Morgan; editor, James Gibbons.

Grant Withers (Angel Harrigan); Evalyn Knapp (Jennie Delano); James Cagney (Harry Delano); Joan Blondell (Myrtle); Lucille LaVerne (Ma Delano); Noel Madison (Buck); Otto Hoffman (George); Warren Hymer (Mitch McKane); Purnell B. Pratt (Sikes); Ray Gallagher (Joe Delano); Hank Mann (Happy).

DOORWAY TO HELL *(Warner Bros., 1930), 78 min.*
Director, Archie Mayo; based on the story *A Handful of Clouds* by Rowland Brown; screenplay, George Rosener; music director, Leo F. Forbstein; makeup, Perc Westmore; sound, David Forrest; camera, Barney McGill; editor, Robert Crandall.

Lew Ayres (Louis Ricarno); Dorothy Mathews (Doris); Leon Janney (Jackie Lamar); Robert Elliott (Captain O'Grady); James Cagney (Steve Mileway); Kenneth Thomson (Captain of Military Academy); Jerry Mandy (Joe); Noel Madison (Rocco); Bernard Granville (Man); Fred Argus (Machine Gunner); Dwight Frye, Tom Wilson, Al Hill (Gangsters); Ruth Hall (Girl).

OTHER MEN'S WOMEN *(Warner Bros., 1931), 70 min.*
Director, William A. Wellman; story, Maude Fulton; screenplay, William K. Wells; music director, Leo F. Forbstein; makeup, Perc Westmore; camera, Barney McGill; editor, Edward McDermott.

Grant Withers (Bill); Mary Astor (Lily); Regis Toomey (Jack); James Cagney (Ed); Joan Blondell (Marie); Fred Kohler (Haley); J. Farrell MacDonald (Pegleg); Lillian Worth (Waitress); Walter Long (Bixby); Bob Perry, Lee Moran, Pat Hartigan, Kewpie Morgan (Railroad Workers).

THE MILLIONAIRE *(Warner Bros., 1931), 80 min.*
Director, John G. Adolfi; based on the story *Idle Hands* by Earl Derr Biggers; screenplay, Julian Josephson, Maude T. Powell; dialogue, Booth Tarkington; music director, Leo F. Forbstein; makeup, Perc Westmore; camera, James Van Trees; editor, Owen Marks.

George Arliss (James Alden); Evalyn Knapp (Barbara Alden); David Manners (Bill Merrick); James Cagney (Schofield); Bramwell Fletcher (Carter Andrews); Florence Arliss (Mrs. Alden); Noah Beery (Peterson); Ivan Simpson (Dr. Harvey); Sam Hardy (McCoy); J. Farrell MacDonald (Sam Hardy); Tully Marshall (Briggs); J. C. Nugent (Physician).

THE PUBLIC ENEMY *(Warner Bros., 1931), 84 min.*
Director, William A. Wellman; based on the story *Beer and Blood* by John Bright; adaptor-dialogue, Harvey Thew; screenplay, Kubec Glasmon, Bright; art director, Max Parker; costumes, Earl Luick; makeup, Perc Westmore; music director, David Mendoza; camera, Dev Jennings; editor, Ed McCormick.

James Cagney (Tom Powers); Jean Harlow (Gwen Allen); Edward Woods (Matt Doyle); Joan Blondell (Mamie); Beryl Mercer (Ma Powers); Donald Cook (Mike Powers); Mae Clarke (Kitty); Mia Marvin (Jane); Leslie Fenton (Nails Nathan); Robert Emmett O'Connor (Paddy Ryan); Murray Kinnell (Putty Nose); Ben Hendricks, Jr. (Bugs Moran); Rita Flynn (Molly Doyle); Clark Burroughs (Dutch); Snitz Edwards (Hack); Adele Watson (Mrs. Doyle); Frank Coghlan, Jr. (Tommy as a Boy); Frankie Darro (Matt as a Boy); Robert E. Homans (Officer Pat Burke); Dorothy Gee (Nails' Girl); Purnell Pratt (Powers the Cop); Lee Phelps (Steve the Bartender); Helen Parrish, Dorothy Gray, Nanci Price (Little Girls); Ben Hendricks III (Bugs as a Boy); George Daly (Machine Gunner); Eddie Kane (Joe the Headwaiter); Sam McDaniel (Black Headwaiter); William Strauss (Pawnbroker); Douglas Gerrard (Assistant Tailor); Charles Sullivan (Mug).

SMART MONEY (Warner Bros., 1931), 90 min.

Director, Alfred E. Green; story, Lucien Hubbard, Joseph Jackson; screenplay, Kubec Glasmon, John Bright; additional dialogue, Hubbard, Jackson; music director, Leo F. Forbstein; makeup, Perc Westmore; camera, Robert Kurrle; editor, Jack Killifer.

Edward G. Robinson (Nick "The Barber" Venizelos); James Cagney (Jack); Evalyn Knapp (Irene Graham); Ralf Harolde (Sleepy Sam); Noel Francis (Marie); Margaret Livingston (District Attorney's Girl); Maurice Black (The Greek Barber); Boris Karloff (Sport Williams); Morgan Wallace (District Attorney Black); Billy House (Salesman-Gambler); Paul Porcasi (Alexander Amenoppopolus); Polly Walters (Lola); Gladys Lloyd (Cigar Stand Clerk); Clark Burroughs (Back-to-Back Schultz); Edwin Argus (Two-Time Phil); John Larkin (Snake Eyes); Walter Percival (Dealer Barnes); Mae Madison (Small Town Girl); Eulalie Jensen (Matron); Charles Lane (Desk Clerk); Edward Hearn (Reporter); Clinton Rosemond (George the Porter); John George (Dwarf on Train).

BLONDE CRAZY (Warner Bros., 1931), 74 min.

Director, Roy Del Ruth; story-screenplay, Kubec Glasmon, John Bright; music director, Leo F. Forbstein; songs, E. A. Swan; Gerald Marks and Buddy Fields; Roy Turk and Fred Ahlert; Sidney Mitchell, Archie Gottler, and George W. Meyer; makeup, Perc Westmore; camera, Sid Hickox; editor, Ralph Dawson.

James Cagney (Bert Harris); Joan Blondell (Ann Roberts); Louis Calhern (Dapper Dan Barker); Noel Francis (Helen Wilson); Guy Kibbee (A. Rupert Johnson, Jr.); Raymond Milland (Joe Reynolds); Polly Walters (Peggy); Charles Lane (Four-Eyes the Desk Clerk); William Burress (Colonel Bellock); Peter Erkelenz (Dutch); Maude Eburne (Mrs. Snyder); Walter Percival (Lee); Nat Pendleton (Hank); Russell Hopton (Jerry); Dick Cramer (Cabbie); Wade Boteler (Detective); Phil Sleeman (Conman); Ray Cooke, Edward Morgan (Bellhops).

TAXI (Warner Bros., 1932), 68 min.

Director, Roy Del Ruth; based on the play The Blind Spot by Kenyon Nicholson; screenplay, Kubec Glasmon, John Bright; art director, Esdras Hartley; music director, Leo F. Forbstein; assistant director, William Cannon; makeup, Perc Westmore; camera, James Van Trees; editor, James Gibbons.

James Cagney (Matt Nolan); Loretta Young (Sue Riley); George E. Stone (Skeets); Guy Kibbee (Pop Riley); David Landau (Buck Gerrard); Ray Cooke (Danny Nolan); Leila Bennett (Ruby); Dorothy Burgess (Marie Costa); Matt McHugh (Joe Silva); George MacFarlane (Father Nulty); Polly Walters (Polly); Nat Pendleton (Truck Driver); Berton Churchill (Judge);

Lee Phelps (Onlooker); George Raft (Willie Kenny); Harry Tenbrook (Cabby); Robert Emmett O'Connor (Cop with Jewish Man); Eddie Fetherstone (Judge); Ben Taggart (Cop); The Cotton Club Orchestra (Themselves); Hector V. Sarno (Monument Maker); Aggie Herring (Cleaning Woman).

THE CROWD ROARS *(Warner Bros., 1932), 85 min.*

Director, Howard Hawks; story, Hawks, Seton I. Miller; screenplay, Kubec Glasmon, John Bright, Niven Busch; art director, Jack Okey; assistant director, Dick Rossen; music director, Leo F. Forbstein; camera, Sid Hickox, John Stumar; editor, Thomas Pratt.

James Cagney (Joe Greer); Joan Blondell (Anne); Ann Dvorak (Lee); Eric Linden (Eddie Greer); Guy Kibbee (Dad Greer); Frank McHugh (Spud Connors); William Arnold (Bill Arnold); Leo Nomis (Jim); Charlotte Merriam (Mrs. Spud Connors); Regis Toomey (Dick Wilbur); Harry Hartz, Fred Guisso, Fred Frame, Jack Brisko, Ralph Hepburn, Phil Pardee, Spider Matlock, Lou Schneider, Bryan Salspaugh, Stubby Stubblefield, Shortly Cantlon, Wilbur Shaw, Mel Keneally (Drivers); James Burtis (Mechanic); Ralph Dunn (Official); Sam Hayes (Ascot Announcer); John Conte (Announcer); John Harron (Red—Eddie's Pitman); Robert McWade (Tom the Counterman).

WINNER TAKE ALL *(Warner Bros., 1932), 66 min.*

Director, Roy Del Ruth; based on the story *133 At 3* by Gerald Beaumont; screenplay, Wilson Mizner, Robert Lord; art director, Robert Haas; music, W. Franke Harling; music director, Leo F. Forbstein; costumes, Orry-Kelly; makeup, Perc Westmore; camera, Robert Kurrle; editor, Thomas Pratt.

James Cagney (Jim Kane); Marian Nixon (Peggy Harmon); Virginia Bruce (Joan Gibson); Guy Kibbee (Pop Slavin); Clarence Muse (Rosebud the Trainer); Dickie Moore (Dickie Harmon); Allan Lane (Monty); John Roche (Roger Elliott); Ralf Harolde (Legs Davis); Alan Mowbray (Forbes); Clarence Wilson (Ben Isaacs); Charles Coleman (Butler); Esther Howard (Ann); Renee Whitney (Lois); Harvey Parry (Al West); Julian Rivero (Pice); Selmer Jackson (Ring Announcer); Chris-Pin Martin (Manager); George Hayes (Interne); Bob Perry (Referee); Billy West (Second); Phil Tead (Reporter); Jay Eaton (Society Man); Charlotte Merriam (Blonde); Lee Phelps (Ring Announcer for Championship Bout); John Kelly (Boxing Spectator); Rolfe Sedan (Waiter).

HARD TO HANDLE *(Warner Bros., 1933), 81 min.*

Director, Mervyn LeRoy; story, Houston Branch; screenplay, Wilson Mizner, Robert Lord; art director, Robert Haas; music director, Leo F. Forbstein; costumes, Orry-Kelly; makeup, Perc Westmore; camera, Barney McGill; editor, William Holmes.

James Cagney (Lefty Merrill); Mary Brian (Ruth Waters); Ruth Donnelly (Lil Waters); Allen Jenkins (Radio Announcer); Claire Dodd (Marlene Reeves); Gavin Gordon (John Hayden); Emma Dunn (Mrs. Hawks the Landlady); Robert McWade (Charles Reeves); John Sheehan (Ed McGrath); Matt McHugh (Joe Goetz); Louise Mackintosh (Mrs. Weston Parks); William H. Strauss (Antique Dealer); Bess Flowers (Merrill's Secretary); Lew Kelly (Hash Slinger); Berton Churchill (Colonel Wells); Harry Holman (Colonel's Associate); Grace Hayle (Fat Lady with Vanishing Cream); George Pat Collins (Dance Judge); Douglass Dumbrille (District Attorney); Sterling Holloway (Andy); Charles Wilson (Jailer); and: Jack Crawford, Mary Doran, Stanley Smith, Walter Walker.

PICTURE SNATCHER *(Warner Bros., 1933), 77 min.*
Director, Lloyd Bacon; story, Danny Ahern; screenplay, Allen Rivkin, P. J. Wolfson; art director, Robert Haas; music director, Leo F. Forbstein; assistant director, Gordon Hollingshead; makeup, Perc Westmore; costumes, Orry-Kelly; camera, Sol Polito; editor, William Holmes.

James Cagney (Danny Kean); Ralph Bellany (McLean); Patricia Ellis (Patricia Nolan); Alice White (Allison); Ralf Harolde (Jerry); Robert Emmett O'Connor (Casey Nolan); Robert Barrat (Grover); George Pat Collins (Hennessy the Fireman); Tom Wilson (Leo); Barbara Rogers (Olive); Renee Whitney (Connie); Alice Jans (Colleen); Jill Bennett (Speakeasy Girl); Billy West, George Chandler (Reporters); George Daly (Machine Gunner); Arthur Vinton (Head Keeper); Stanley Blystone (Prison Guard); Don Brodie (Hood); Sterling Holloway (Journalism Student); Donald Kerr (Mike—Colleen's Boyfriend); Phil Tead (Reporter Strange); Charles King (Sick Reporter); Milton Kibbee (Reporter Outside Prison); Dick Elliott, Vaughn Taylor (Editors); Bob Perry (Bartender); Gino Corrado (Barber); Maurice Black (Speakeasy Proprietor); Selmer Jackson (*Record* Editor); Jack Grey (Police Officer); John Ince (Captain); Cora Sue Collins (Girl).

THE MAYOR OF HELL *(Warner Bros., 1933), 90 min.*
Director, Archie Mayo; story, Islin Auster; screenplay, Edward Chodorov; art director, Esdras Hartley; music director, Leo F. Forbstein; assistant director, Frank Shaw; makeup, Perc Westmore; costumes, Orry-Kelly; camera, Barney McGill; editor, Jack Killifer.

James Cagney (Patsy Gargan); Madge Evans (Dorothy Griffith); Allen Jenkins (Mike); Dudley Digges (Mr. Thompson); Frankie Darro (Jimmy Smith); Dorothy Peterson (Mrs. Smith); Farina (Smoke); John Marston (Hopkins); Charles Wilson (Guard); Hobart Cavanaugh (Tommy's Father); Raymond Borzage (Johnny Stone); Robert Barrat (Mr. Smith); George Pat Collins (Brandon); Mickey Bennett (Butch Kilgore); Arthur Byron (Judge Gilbert); Sheila Terry (The Girl); Harold Huber (Joe); Edwin Maxwell (Louis Johnston); William V. Mong (Walters); Sidney Miller (Izzy Horowitz); George Humbert (Tony's Father); George Offerman, Jr. (Charlie Burns); Charles Cane (Tommy Gorman); Wallace MacDonald (Johnson's Assistant); Adrian Morris (Car Owner); Snowflake (Hemingway); Bob Perry, Charles Sullivan (Collectors); Wilfred Lucas (Guard); Ben Taggart (Sheriff).

FOOTLIGHT PARADE *(Warner Bros., 1933), 104 min.*
Director, Lloyd Bacon; screenplay, Manuel Self, James Seymour; dialogue director, William Keighley; music director, Leo F. Forbstein; songs, Sammy Fain and Irving Kahal; Harry Warren and Al Dubin; costumes, Milo Anderson; dance numbers creator and stager, Busby Berkeley; makeup, Perc Westmore; art directors, Anton Grot, Jack Okey; camera, George Barnes; editor, George Amy.

James Cagney (Chester Kent); Joan Blondell (Nan Prescott); Ruby Keeler (Bea Thorn); Dick Powell (Scotty Blair); Guy Kibbee (Silas Gould); Ruth Donnelly (Harriet Bowers Gould); Hugh Herbert (Charlie Bowers); Frank McHugh (Francis); Arthur Hohl (Al Frazer); Gordon Westcott (Harry Thompson); Renee Whitney (Cynthia Kent); Philip Faversham (Joe Farrington); Juliet Ware (Miss Smythe); Herman Bing (Fralick the Music Director); Paul Porcasi (George Appolinaris); William Granger (Doorman); Charles C. Wilson (Cop); Barbara Rogers (Gracie); Billy Taft (Specialty Dancer); Marjean Rogers, Pat Wing, Donna Mae Roberts, Donna La Barr, Marlo Dwyer (Chorus Girls); Dave O'Brien (Chorus Boy); George Chandler (Drugstore Attendant); Hobart Cavanaugh (Title Thinker-upper); William V. Mong (Auditor); Lee Moran (Mac the Dance Director); Billy Barty (Mouse in "Sittin' on a Backyard Fence" Number); Harry Seymour (Desk Clerk in "Honeymoon Hotel" Number); Sam McDaniel (Porter); Fred Kelsey (House Detective); Jimmy Conlin (Uncle); Roger Gray (Sailor in "Shanghai Lil" Number); John Garfield (Sailor behind Table); Duke York (Sailor on Table); Harry Seymour (Joe the Assistant Dance Director).

LADY KILLER *(Warner Bros., 1933), 76 min.*

Production supervisor, Henry Blanke; director, Roy del Ruth; based on the story *The Finger Man* by Rosalind Keating Shaffer; adaptors, Ben Markson, Lillie Hayward; screenplay, Markson; assistant director, Chuck Hansen; costumes, Orry-Kelly; music director, Leo F. Forbstein; makeup, Perc Westmore; art director, Robert Haas; camera, Tony Gaudio; editor, George Amy.

James Cagney (Dan Quigley); Mae Clarke (Myra Gale); Leslie Fenton (Duke); Margaret Lindsay (Lois Underwood); Henry O'Neill (Ramick); Willard Robertson (Conroy); Douglas Cosgrove (Jones); Raymond Hatton (Pete); Russell Hopton (Smiley); William Davidson (Williams); Marjorie Gateson (Mrs. Wilbur Marley); Robert Elliott (Brannigan); John Marston (Kendall); Douglass Dumbrille (Spade Maddock); George Chandler (Thompson); George Blackwood (The Escort); Jack Don Wong (Oriental); Frank Sheridan (Los Angeles Police Chief); Edwin Maxwell (Jeffries the Theatre Manager); Phil Tead (Usher Sargeant Seymour); Dewey Robinson (The Movie Fan); H. C. Bradley (Man with Purse); Harry Holman (J. B. Roland); Harry Beresford (Dr. Crane); Olaf Hytten (Butler); Harry Strang (Ambulance Attendant); Al Hill (Casino Cashier); Dennis O'Keefe (Man in Casino); James Burke (Handout); Robert Homans (Jailer); Sam McDaniel (Porter); Herman Bing (Western Director); Spencer Charters (Los Angeles Cop); Luis Alberni (Director); Sam Ash (Hood); Ray Cooke (Property Man); Harold Waldridge (Letter Handler).

JIMMY THE GENT *(Warner Bros., 1934), 67 min.*

Executive producer, Jack L. Warner; director, Michael Curtiz; story, Laird Doyle, Ray Nazarro; screenplay, Bertram Milhauser; dialogue director, Daniel Reed; art director, Esdras Hartley; music director, Leo F. Forbstein; costumes, Orry-Kelly; makeup, Perc Westmore; camera, Ira Morgan; editor, Thomas Richards.

James Cagney (Jimmy Corrigan); Bette Davis (Joan Martin); Alice White (Mabel); Allen Jenkins (Louie); Arthur Hohl (Joe Rector [Monty Barton]); Alan Dinehart (James J. Wallingham); Philip Reed (Ronnie Gatston); Hobart Cavanaugh (The Imposter); Ralf Harolde (Hendrickson); Mayo Methot (Gladys Farrell); Joe Sawyer (Mike); Philip Faversham (Blair); Nora Lane (Posy Barton); Joseph Crehan (Judge); Robert Warwick (Civil Judge); Merna Kennedy (Jitters); Renee Whitney (Bessie); Monica Bannister (Tea Assistant); Dennis O'Keefe (Chester Coote); Don Douglas (Man Drinking Tea); Leonard Mudie (Man in Flower Shop); Harry Holman (Justice of the Peace); Camille Rovelle (File Clerk); Stanley Mack (Pete); Tom Costello (Grant); Ben Hendricks (Ferris); Billy West (Halley); Eddie Shubert (Tim); Lee Moran (Stew); Harry Wallace (Eddie); Robert Homans (Irish Cop); Milton Kibbee (Ambulance Driver); Howard Hickman (Doctor); Eula Guy (Nurse); Juliet Ware (Viola); Rickey Newell (Blonde); Lorena Layson (Brunette); Dick French, Jay Eaton (Young Men); Harold Entwistle (Reverend Amiel Bottsford); Charles Hickman (Bailiff); Leonard Mudie (Steamship Ticket Clerk); Olaf Hytten, Vesey O'Davoren (Stewards); Lester Dorr (Chalmers); Pat Wing (Secretary).

HE WAS HER MAN *(Warner Bros., 1934), 70 min.*

Director, Lloyd Bacon; story, Robert Lord; screenplay, Tom Buckingham, Niven Busch; art director, Anton Grot; music director, Leo F. Forbstein; song, Sidney Mitchell and Lew Pollack; costumes, Orry-Kelly; makeup, Perc Westmore; camera, George Barnes; editor, George Amy.

James Cagney (Flicker Hayes); Joan Blondell (Rose Lawrence); Victor Jory (Nick Gardella); Frank Craven (Pop Sims); Harold Huber (J. C. Ward); Russell Hopton (Monk); Sarah Padden (Mrs. Gardella); John Qualen (Dutch); Bradley Page (Dan Curly); Gino Corrado (Fisherman); James Eagles (Whitey); George Chandler (Waiter); Samuel S. Hinds (Gassy).

HERE COMES THE NAVY *(Warner Bros., 1934), 86 min.*
Director, Lloyd Bacon; story, Ben Markson; screenplay, Markson, Earl Baldwin; art director, Esdras Hartley; music director, Leo F. Forbstein; song, Irving Kahal and Sammy Fain; technical adviser, Commander Herbert A. Jones; makeup, Perc Westmore; costumes, Orry-Kelly; camera, Arthur Edeson; editor, George Amy.

James Cagney (Chesty O'Connor); Pat O'Brien (Biff Martin); Gloria Stuart (Dorothy Martin); Frank McHugh (Droopy); Dorothy Tree (Gladys); Robert Barrat (Commander Denny); Willard Robertson (Lieutenant Commander); Guinn Williams (Floor Manager); Maude Eburne (Droopy's Ma); Martha Merrill, Lorena Layson (Girls); Ida Darling (Aunt); Henry Otho (Riveter); Pauline True (Hat Check Girl); Sam McDaniel (Porter); Frank La Rue (Foreman); Joseph Crehan (Recruiting Officer); James Burtis (C.P.O.); Edward Chandler (Supply Sergeant); Leo White (Professor); Niles Welch (Officer); Fred "Snowflake" Toone (Sailor); Eddie Shubert (Skipper); George Irving (Admiral); Howard Hickman (Captain); Edward Earle (Navy Chaplain); Gordon "Bill" Elliott (Officer); John Swor (Attendant); Chuck Hamilton (Hood at Dance); Eddie Acuff (Marine Orderly); Nick Copeland (Workman); Eddie Fetherstone (Sailor).

THE ST. LOUIS KID *(Warner Bros., 1934), 67 min.*
Producer, Samuel Bischoff; director, Ray Enright; story, Frederick Hazlitt Brennan; screenplay, Warren Duff, Seton I. Miller; dialogue director, Stanley Logan; art director, Jack Okey; music director, Leo F. Forbstein; costumes, Orry-Kelly; makeup, Perc Westmore; camera, Sid Hickox; editor, Clarence Kolster.

James Cagney (Eddie Kennedy); Patricia Ellis (Ann Reid); Allen Jenkins (Buck Willett); Robert Barrat (Farmer Benson); Hobart Cavanaugh (Richardson); Spencer Charters (Merseldopp); Addison Richards (Brown); Dorothy Dare (Gracie); Arthur Aylesworth (Judge Jones); Charles Wilson (Harris); William Davidson (Joe Hunter); Harry Woods (Louie); Gertrude Short (The Girlfriend); Eddie Shubert (Pete); Russell Hicks (Gorman); Guy Usher (Sergeant); Cliff Saum, Bruce Mitchell (Cops); Mary Russell (Office Girl); Ben Hendricks (Motor Cop); Harry Tyler (Mike); Milton Kibbee (Paymaster); Tom Wilson (Cook); Alice Marr, Victoria Vinton (Secretaries); Lee Phelps (Farmer); Louise Seidel (Girl in Car); Mary Treen (Giddy Girl); Rosalie Roy, Nan Grey, Virginia Grey, Martha Merrill (Girls); Monte Vandergrift, Jack Cheatham (Deputies); Stanley Mack (Driver); Grover Liggen (Attendant); Frank Bull (Broadcast Officer); Wade Boteler (Sergeant); Frank Fanning, Gene Strong (Policemen); Clay Clement (Man); James Burtis (Detective); Joan Barclay, Eddie Fetherstone (Bits).

DEVIL DOGS OF THE AIR *(Warner Bros., 1935), 86 min.*
Producer, Lou Edelman; director, Lloyd Bacon; based on the story *Air Devils* by John Monk Saunders; screenplay, Malcolm Stuart Boylan, Earl Baldwin; art director, Arthur J. Kooken; music director, Leo F. Forbstein; assistant director, Eric Stacey; technical adviser, Major Ralph

J. Mitchell; costumes, Orry-Kelly; makeup, Perc Westmore; camera, Arthur Edeson; editor, William Clemens.

James Cagney (Tommy O'Toole); Pat O'Brien (Lieutenant William Brannigan); Margaret Lindsay (Betty Roberts); Frank McHugh (Crash Kelly); Helen Lowell (Ma Roberts); John Arledge (Mac); Robert Barrat (Commandant); Russell Hicks (Captain); William B. Davidson (Adjutant); Ward Bond (Senior Instructor); Samuel S. Hinds (Fleet Commander); Bill Beggs (Second Officer); Bob Spencer (Mate); Newton House, Ralph Nye, Harry Seymour (Officers); Selmer Jackson (Medical Officer); Gordon "Bill" Elliott (Instructor); Dennis O'Keefe, Don Turner, Dick French, Charles Sherlock (Students); Carlyle Blackwell, Jr. (Messenger); Martha Merrill (Girl); David Newell (Lieutenant Brown); Olive Jones (Mrs. Brown); Helen Flint (Mrs. Johnson); Joseph Crehan (Communications Officer).

G-MEN *(Warner Bros., 1935), 85 min.*
Director, William Keighley; based on the book *Public Enemy No. 1* by Gregory Rogers; screenplay, Seton I. Miller; art director, John J. Hughes; music director, Leo F. Forbstein; song, Sammy Fain and Irving Kahal; choreography, Bobby Connolly; costumes, Orry-Kelly; makeup, Perc Westmore; assistant director, William McGann; technical adviser, Frank Gompert; camera, Sol Polito; editor, Jack Killifer.

James Cagney (James "Brick" Davis); Ann Dvorak (Jean Morgan); Margaret Lindsay (Kay McCord); Robert Armstrong (Jeff McCord); Barton MacLane (Brad Collins); Lloyd Nolan (Hugh Farrell); William Harrigan (McKay); Edward Pawley (Danny Leggett); Russell Hopton (Gerard); Noel Madison (Durfee); Regis Toomey (Eddie Buchanan); Addison Richards (Bruce J. Gregory); Harold Huber (Venke); Raymond Hatton (The Man); Monte Blue (Analyst); Mary Treen (Secretary); Adrian Morris (Accomplice); Edwin Maxwell (Joseph Kratz); Emmett Vogan (Bill the Ballistics Expert); James Flavin (Agent); Stanley Blystone, Pat Flaherty (Cops); James T. Mack (Agent); Jonathan Hale (Congressman); Ed Keane (Bank Cashier); Charles Sherlock (Short Man); Wheeler Oakman (Henchman at Lodge); Eddie Dunn (Police Broadcaster); Gordon "Bill" Elliott (Interne); Perry Ivins (Doctor at Store); Frank Marlowe (Hood Shot at Lodge); Gertrude Short (Collins' Moll); Florence Dudley (Durfee's Moll); Frances Morris (Moll); Al Hill (Hood); Huey White (Gangster); Glen Cavender (Headwaiter); John Impolito (Tony); Bruce Mitchell (Sergeant); Monte Vandergrift (Deputy Sheriff); Frank Shannon (Chief); Frank Bull (Announcer); Gene Morgan (Lounger); Martha Merrill (Nurse); Joseph De Stefani (J. E. Blattner the Florist); Ward Bond, George Daly (Machine Gunners); Lee Phelps (McCord's Aide); Marc Lawrence (Hood at Lodge); Brooks Benedict (Man); Henry Hall (Police Driver); Tom Wilson (Prison Guard); David Brian (Chief —1949 Prologue).

THE IRISH IN US *(Warner Bros., 1935), 84 min.*
Producer, Samuel Bischoff; director, Lloyd Bacon; story, Frank Orsatti; screenplay, Earl Baldwin; art director, Esdras Hartley; music director, Leo F. Forbstein; costumes, Orry-Kelly; makeup, Perc Westmore; assistant director, Jack Sullivan; camera, George Barnes; editor, James Gibbons.

James Cagney (Danny O'Hara); Pat O'Brien (Pat O'Hara); Olivia de Havilland (Lucille Jackson); Frank McHugh (Mike O'Hara); Mary Gordon (Ma O'Hara); Allen Jenkins (Car Barn McCarthy); J. Farrell MacDonald (Captain Jackson); Thomas Jackson (Doc Mullins); Harvey Parry (Joe Delancy); Bess Flowers (Lady in Ring); Mabel Colcord (Neighbor); Edward Keans (Doctor); Herb Heywood (Cook); Lucille Collins (Girl); Harry Seymour (Announcer); Sailor Vincent (Chick); Mushy Callahan (Referee); Edward Gargan, Huntley Gordon, Emmett Vogan, Will Stanton (Men); Jack McHugh (Messenger Boy).

A MIDSUMMER NIGHT'S DREAM *(Warner Bros., 1935), 132 min.*

Producer, Jack L. Warner; production supervisor, Henry Blanke; directors, Max Reinhardt, William Dieterle; based on the play by William Shakespeare; screenplay, Charles Kenyon, Mary McCall; dialogue director, Stanley Logan; art director, Anton Grot; music, Felix Mendelssohn; music director, Leo F. Forbstein; music arranger, Erich Wolfgang Korngold; dance ensembles, Bronislava Nijinska, Nini Theilade; makeup, Perc Westmore; assistant director, Sherry Shourds; costumes, Max Ree; dialogue director, Stanley Logan; special camera effects, Fred Jackman, Byron Haskin, H. E. Koenekamp; camera, Hal Mohr; editor, Ralph Dawson.

James Cagney (Bottom); Dick Powell (Lysander); Joe E. Brown (Flute); Jean Muir (Helena); Hugh Herbert (Snout); Ian Hunter (Theseus); Frank McHugh (Quince); Victor Jory (Oberon); Olivia de Havilland (Hermia); Ross Alexander (Demetrius); Grant Mitchell (Egeus); Nini Theilade (Prima Ballerina-First Fairy); Verree Teasdale (Hippolyta, Queen of Amazons); Anita Louise (Titania); Mickey Rooney (Puck); Dewey Robinson (Snug); Hobart Cavanaugh (Philostrate); Otis Harlan (Starveling); Arthur Treacher (Ninny's Tomb); Katherine Frey (Pease-Blossom); Helen Westcott (Cobweb); Fred Sale (Moth); Billy Barty (Mustard Seed).

FRISCO KID *(Warner Bros., 1935), 77 min.*

Producer, Samuel Bischoff; director, Lloyd Bacon; story-screenplay, Warren Duff, Seton I. Miller; art director, John Hughes; music director, Leo F. Forbstein; costumes, Orry-Kelly; makeup, Perc Westmore; camera, Sol Polito; editor, Owen Marks.

James Cagney (Bat Morgan); Margaret Lindsay (Jean Barrat); Ricardo Cortez (Paul Morra); Lily Damita (Bella Morra); Donald Woods (Charles Ford); Barton MacLane (Spider Burke); George E. Stone (Solly); Addison Richards (William T. Coleman); Joseph King (James Daley); Robert McWade (Judge Crawford); Joseph Crehan (McClanahan); Robert Strange (Graber); Joseph Sawyer (Slugs Crippen); Fred Kohler (Shanghai Duck); Edward McWade (Tupper); Claudia Coleman (Jumping Whale); John Wray (The Weasel); Ivar McFadden, Lee Phelps (Lookouts); William Wagner (Evangelist); Don Barclay (Drunk); Jack Curtis (Captain); Milton Kibbee (Shop Man); Alan Davis (Young Drunk); Karl Hackett (Dealer); Wilfred Lucas, Jack Dillon (Policemen); James Farley, Edward Mortimer, William Holmes (Men); Charles Middleton (Speaker); Landers Stevens (Doctor); Frank Sheridan (Mulligan); Lew Harvey (Dealer); Edward Keane, Edward Le Saint (Contractors); Robert Dudley, Dick Rush (Vigilante Leaders); William Desmond (Vigilante Captain); Jessie Perry (Maid); Vera Stedman, Dick Kerr, Helene Chadwick, Bill Dale (Bits).

CEILING ZERO *(Warner Bros., 1935), 95 min.*

Producer, Harry Joe Brown; director, Howard Hawks; based on the play by Frank Wead; screenplay, Wead; art director, John Hughes; music director, Leo F. Forbstein; costumes, Orry-Kelly; makeup, Perc Westmore; assistant director, Les Selander; camera, Arthur Edeson; editor, William Holmes.

James Cagney (Dizzy Davis); Pat O'Brien (Jack Lee); June Travis (Tommy Thomas); Stuart Erwin (Texas Clark); Henry Wadsworth (Tay Lawson); Isabel Jewell (Lou Clark); Barton MacLane (Al Stone); Martha Tibbetts (Mary Lee); Craig Reynolds (Joe Allen); James Bush (Buzz Gordon); Robert Light (Les Bogan); Addison Richards (Fred Adams); Carlyle Moore, Jr. (Eddie Payson); Richard Purcell (Smiley Johnson); Gordon "Bill" Elliott (Transportation Agent); Pat West (Baldy Wright); Edward Gargan (Doc Wilson); Garry Owen (Mike Owens); Mathilde Comont (Mama Gini); Carol Hughes (Birdie); Frank Tomick, Paul Mantz (Stunt Fliers); Jerry Jerome (Mechanic); Jimmy Aye, Howard Allen, Mike Lally, Harold Miller (Pilots); Helene McAdoo, Gay Sheridan, Mary Lou Dix, Louise Seidel, Helen Erickson (Hostesses); Don Wayson, Dick Cherney, Jimmie Barnes, Frank McDonald (Office Workers); J. K. Kane (Teletype Operator); Jayne Manners (Tall Girl); Maryon Curtiz, Margaret Perry (Girls).

GREAT GUY *(Grand National, 1936), 75 min.*
  Presenter, Edward L. Alperson; producer, Douglas MacLean; director, John G. Blystone; based on *The Johnny Cave Stories* by James Edward Grant; screenplay, Henri McCarthy, Henry Johnson, Grant, Harry Ruskin; additional dialogue, Horace McCoy; art director, Ben Carre; music director, Marlin Skiles; costumes, Dorothy Beal; assistant director, John Sherwood; sound, Harold Bumbaugh; camera, Jack McKenzie; editor, Russel Schoengarth.

  James Cagney (Johnny Cave); Mae Clarke (Janet Henry); James Burke (Pat Haley); Edward Brophy (Pete Reilly); Henry Kolker (Conning); Bernadene Hayes (Hazel Scott); Edward J. McNamara (Captain Pat Hanlon); Robert Gleckler (Cavanaugh); Joe Sawyer (Joe Burton); Ed Gargan (Al); Matty Fain (Tim); Mary Gordon (Mrs. Ogilvie); Wallis Clark (Joel Green); Douglas Wood (The Mayor); Jeffrey Sayre (Clerk); Eddy Chandler (Meat Clerk); Henry Roquemore (Store Manager); Murdock MacQuarrie (Client); Kate Price (Woman at Accident); Arthur Hoyt (Furniture Salesman); Frank O'Connor (Detective); Jack Pennick (Truck Driver); Lynton Brent (Reporter); John Dilson (City Editor); Bud Geary, Dennis O'Keefe (Guests); Robert Lowery (Parker); Bobby Barber (Grocery Clerk); Ethelreda Leopold (Barton's Girl); Gertrude Green (Nurse); Bruce Mitchell (Cop at Accident); Lee Shumway (Mike the Cop); Harry Tenbrook (Receiving Clerk); James Ford, Frank Mills, Ben Hendricks, Jr. (Party Guests).

SOMETHING TO SING ABOUT *(Grand National, 1937), 84 min.*
  Producer, Zion Myers; director and story, Victor Schertzinger; art directors, Robert Lee, Paul Murphy; music director, C. Bakaleinikoff; choreography, Harlan Dixon; music arranger, Myrl Alderman; songs, Schertzinger; assistant director, John Sherwood; camera, John Stumar; editor, Gene Milford.

  James Cagney (Terry Rooney); Evelyn Daw (Rita Wyatt); William Frawley (Hank Meyers); Mona Barrie (Stephanie Hajos); Gene Lockhart (Bennett O. Regan); James Newill (Orchestra Soloist); Harry Barris (Pinky); Candy Candido (Candy); Cully Richards (Soloist); William B. Davidson (Cafe Manager); Richard Tucker (Blaine); Marek Windheim (Farney); Dwight Frye (Easton); John Arthur (Daviani); Philip Ahn (Ito); Kathleen Lockhart (Miss Robbins); Kenneth Harlan (Transportation Manager); Herbert Rawlinson (Studio Attorney); Ernest Wood (Edward Burns); Chick Collins (The Man Terry Fights); Duke Green (Other Man); Harlan Dixon, Johnny Boyle, Johnny "Skins" Miller, Pat Moran, Joe Bennett, Buck Mack, Eddie Allen (Dancers); Bill Carey (Singer); The Vagabonds (Specialty); Elinore Welz (Girl); Eddie Kane (San Francisco Theatre Manager); Edward Hearn (Studio Guard); Dottie Messmer, Virginia Lee Irwin, Dolly Waldorf (Three Shades of Blue); Robert McKenzie (Ship's Captain); Alphonse Martel (Headwaiter).

BOY MEETS GIRL *(Warner Bros. 1938), 80 min.*
  Producer, George Abbott; director, Lloyd Bacon; based on the play by Bella and Sam Spewack; screenplay, the Spewacks; music director, Leo F. Forbstein; song, Jack Scholl and M. K. Jerome; makeup, Perc Westmore; costumes, Milo Anderson; sound, Dolph Thomas; camera, Sol Polito; editor, William Holmes.

  James Cagney (Robert Law); Pat O'Brien (J. C. Benson); Marie Wilson (Susie); Ralph

Bellamy (C. Elliott Friday); Frank McHugh (Rossetti); Dick Foran (Larry Toms); Bruce Lester (Rodney Bevan); Ronald Reagan (Announcer); Paul Clark (Happy); Penny Singleton (Peggy); Dennie Moore (Miss Crews); Harry Seymour, Bert Hanlon (Songwriters); James Stephenson (Major Thompson); Pierre Watkin (B. K.); John Ridgely (Cutter); George Hickman (Office Boy); Cliff Saum (Smitty); Carole Landis (Commissary Cashier); Curt Bois (Dance Director); Otto Fries (Olaf); John Harron (Extra); Hal K. Dawson (Wardrobe Attendant); Dorothy Vaughan (Nurse); Bert Howland (Director); James Nolan (Young Man); Bill Telaak (Bruiser); Vera Lewis (Cleaning Woman); Jan Holm, Rosella Towne, Lois Cheaney (Nurses); Nanette Lafayette (Paris Operator); Peggy Moran (New York Operator); Eddy Conrad (Jascha); Sidney Bracy, William Haade, Clem Bevans (Bits).

ANGELS WITH DIRTY FACES *(Warner Bros., 1938), 97 min.*

Producer, Sam Bischoff; director, Michael Curtiz; story, Rowland Brown; screenplay, John Wexley, Warren Duff; art director, Robert Haas; music, Max Steiner; orchestrator, Hugo Friedhofer; song, Fred Fisher and Maurice Spitalny; assistant director, Sherry Shourds; sound, Everett A. Brown; camera, Sol Polito; editor, Owen Marks.

James Cagney (Rocky Sullivan); Pat O'Brien (Jerry Connelly); Humphrey Bogart (James Frazier); Ann Sheridan (Laury Martin); George Bancroft (MacKeefer); Billy Halop (Soapy); Bobby Jordan (Swing); Leo Gorcey (Bim); Bernard Punsley (Hunky); Gabriel Dell (Patsy); Huntz Hall (Crab); Frankie Burke (Rocky as a Boy); William Tracy (Jerry as a Boy); Marilyn Knowlden (Laury as a Girl); Joe Downing (Steve); Adrian Morris (Blackie); Oscar O'Shea (Guard Kennedy); Edward Pawley (Guard Edwards); William Pawley (Bugs the Gunman); John Hamilton (Police Captain); Earl Dwire (Priest); Jack Perrin (Death Row Guard); Mary Gordon (Mrs. Patrick); Vera Lewis (Soapy's Mother); William Worthington (Warden); James Farley (Railroad Yard Watchman); Chuck Stubbs (Red); Eddie Syracuse (Maggione's Boy); Robert Homans (Policeman); Harris Berger (Basketball Captain); Harry Hayden (Pharmacist); Dick Rich, Steven Darrell, Joe A. Devlin (Gangsters); William Edmunds (Italian Storekeeper); Frank Coghlan, Jr., David Durand (Boys in Poolroom); Bill Cohee, Lavel Lund, Norman Wallace, Gary Carthew, Bibby Mayer (Church Basketball Team); Billy McLean (Janitor); Wilbur Mack (Croupier); Poppy Wilde (Girl at Gaming Table); Ralph Sanford (City Editor at the *Press*); Wilfred Lucas (Police Officer); Lane Chandler (Guard).

THE OKLAHOMA KID *(Warner Bros., 1939), 85 min.*

Associate producer, Samuel Bischoff; director, Lloyd Bacon; story, Edward E. Paramore, Wally Klien; screenplay, Warren Duff, Robert Buckner, Paramore; art director, Esdras Hartley; music, Max Steiner; orchestrators, Hugo Friedhofer, Adolph Deutsch, George Parrish, Murray Cutter; costumes, Orry-Kelly; makeup, Perc Westmore; assistant director, Dick Mayberry; technical adviser, Al Jennings; sound, Stanley Jones; camera, James Wong Howe; editor, Owen Marks.

James Cagney (Jim Kincaid); Humphrey Bogart (Whip McCord); Rosemary Lane (Jane Hardwick); Donald Crisp (Judge Hardwick); Harvey Stephens (Ned Kincaid); Hugh Sothern (John Kincaid); Charles Middleton (Alec Martin); Edward Pawley (Doolin); Ward Bond (Wes Handley); Lew Harvey (Curley); Trevor Bardette (Indian Jack Pasco); John Miljan (Ringo); Arthur Aylesworth (Judge Morgan); Irving Bacon (Hotel Clerk); Joe Devlin (Keely); Wade Boteler (Sheriff Abe Collins); Whizzer (Kincaid's Horse); Dan Wolheim (Deputy); Ray Mayer (Professor); Bob Kortman (Juryman); Tex Cooper (Old Man in Bar); John Harron (Secretary); Stuart Holmes (President Cleveland); Jeffrey Sayre (*Times* Reporter); Frank Mayo (Land Agent); Jack Mower (Mail Clerk); Al Bridge (Settler); Don Barclay (Drunk); Horace

Murphy, Robert Homans, George Lloyd (Bartenders); Soledad Jiminez (Indian Woman); Clem Bevans (Postman); Ed Brady (Foreman); Tom Chatterton (Homesteader); Elliott Sullivan (Homesteader).

EACH DAWN I DIE *(Warner Bros., 1939), 92 min.*

Associate producer, David Lewis; director, William Keighley; based on the novel by Jerome Odlum; screenplay, Norman Reilly Raine, Warren Duff, Charles Perry; art director, Max Parker; music, Max Steiner; music director, Leo F. Forbstein; technical adviser, William Buckley; makeup, Perc Westmore; costumes, Howard Shoup; sound, E. A. Brown; camera, Arthur Edeson; editor, Thomas Richards.

James Cagney (Frank Ross); George Raft (Hood Stacey); Jane Bryan (Joyce Conover); George Bancroft (Warden John Armstrong); Maxie Rosenbloom (Fargo Red); Stanley Ridges (Mueller); Alan Baxter (Pole Cat Carlisle); Victor Jory (W. J. Grayce); John Wray (Pete Kassock); Edward Pawley (Dale); John Conte (Narrator); Willard Robertson (Lang); Emma Dunn (Mrs. Ross); Paul Hurst (Garsky); Louis Jean Heydt (Joe Lassiter); Joe Downing (Limpy Julien); Thurston Hall (D. A. Jesse Hanley); William Davidson (Bill Mason); Clay Clement (Stacey's Attorney); Charles Trowbridge (Judge); Harry Cording (Temple); John Harron (Lew Keller); John Ridgely (Jerry Poague); Selmer Jackson (Patterson); Robert Homans (Mac); Abner Biberman (Snake Edwards); Napoleon Simpson (Mose); Stuart Holmes (Accident Witness); Maris Wrixon (Girl in Car); Garland Smith, Arthur Gardner (Men in Car); James Flavin (Policeman); Walter Miller (Turnkey); Fred Graham (Guard in Cell); Wilfred Lucas (Bailiff); Vera Lewis (Jury Woman); Emmett Vogan (Prosecutor); Earl Dwire (Judge Crowder); Bob Perry (Bud); Al Hill (Johnny the Hood); Elliott Sullivan (Convict); Chuck Hamilton (Court Officer).

THE ROARING TWENTIES *(Warner Bros., 1939), 104 min.*

Producer, Hal B. Wallis; associate producer, Samuel Bischoff; director, Raoul Walsh; story, Mark Hellinger; screenplay, Jerry Wald, Richard Macaulay, Robert Rossen; art director, Max Parker; dialogue director, Hugh Cummings; assistant director, Dick Mayberry; music, Heinz Roemheld, Ray Heindorf; orchestrator, Heindorf; music director, Leo F. Forbstein; songs, Ernie Burnett and George A. Norton; Eubie Blake and Noble Sissle; Isham Jones and Gus Kahn; Jack Little, Joseph Young, and John Siras; montages, Don Siegel; costumes, Milo Anderson; makeup, Perc Westmore; sound, Everett A. Brown; special effects, Byron Haskin, Edwin A. Dupar; camera, Ernest Haller; editor, Jack Killifer.

James Cagney (Eddie Bartlett); Priscilla Lane (Jean Sherman); Humphrey Bogart (George Hally); Jeffrey Lynn (Lloyd Hart); Gladys George (Panama Smith); Frank McHugh (Danny Green); Paul Kelly (Nick Brown); Elisabeth Risdon (Mrs. Sherman); Ed Keane (Pete Henderson); Joe Sawyer (Sergeant Pete Jones); Abner Biberman (Lefty); George Humbert (Luigi the Proprietor); Clay Clement (Bramfield the Broker); Don Thaddeus Kerr (Bobby Hart); Ray Cooke (Orderly); Vera Lewis (Mrs. Gray); Murray Alper, Dick Wessel (Mechanics); Joseph Crehan (Fletcher the Foreman); Norman Willis (Bootlegger); Robert Elliott, Eddy Chandler (Officers); John Hamilton (Judge); Elliott Sullivan (Man in Jail); Pat O'Malley (Jailer); Arthur Loft (Still Proprietor); Al Hill, Raymond Bailey, Lew Harvey (Convicts); Joe Devlin, Jeffrey Sayre (Order Takers); Paul Phillips (Mike); George Meeker (Masters); Bert Hanlon (Piano Player); Fred Graham (Henchman); John Deering (Commentator); Lottie Williams, Harry C. Bradley (Couple in Restaurant); Lee Phelps (Bailiff); Nat Carr (Waiter); Wade Boteler (Policeman); Creighton Hale (Customer); Eddie Acuff, Milton Kibbee, John Ridgley (Cab Drivers); Ann Codee (Saleswoman).

THE FIGHTING 69th *(Warner Bros., 1940), 90 min.*

Executive producer, Jack L. Warner; producer, Hal B. Wallis; director, William Keighley; screenplay, Norman Reilly Raine, Fred Niblo, Jr., Dean Franklin; art director, Ted Smith; music, Adolph Deutsch; orchestrator, Hugo Friedhofer; music director, Leo F. Forbstein; assistant director, Frank Heath; technical advisers, Captain John T. Prout, Mark White; makeup, Perc Westmore; special effects, Byron Haskin, Rex Wimpy; camera, Tony Gaudio; editor, Owen Marks.

James Cagney (Jerry Plunkett); Pat O'Brien (Father Duffy); George Brent (Wild Bill Donovan); Jeffrey Lynn (Joyce Kilmer); Alan Hale (Sergeant Big Mike Wynn); Frank McHugh ("Crepe Hanger" Burke); Dennis Morgan (Lieutenant Ames); Dick Foran (Lieutenant Long John Wynn); William Lundigan (Timmy Wynn); Guinn "Big Boy" Williams (Paddy Dolan); Henry O'Neill (The Colonel); John Litel (Captain Mangan); Sammy Cohen (Mike Murphy); Harvey Stephens (Major Anderson); William Hopper (Private Turner); Tom Dugan (Private McManus); George Reeves (Jack O'Keefe); John Ridgely (Moran); Charles Trowbridge (Chaplain Holmes); Frank Wilcox (Lieutenant Norman); Herbert (Guy) Anderson (Casey); J. Anthony Hughes (Healey); Frank Mayo (Captain Bootz); John Harron (Carroll); George Kilgen (Ryan); Richard Clayton (Tierney); Edward Dew (Regan); Wilfred Lucas, Joseph Crehan, Emmett Vogan (Doctors); Frank Sully (Sergeant); James Flavin (Supply Sergeant); George O'Hanlon (Eddie); Jack Perrin (Major); Trevor Bardette, John Arledge, Frank Melton, Edmund Glover (Alabama Men); Edgar Edwards (Engineer Officer); Frank Faylen (Engineer Sergeant); Arno Frey, Roland Varno (German Officers); Robert Layne Ireland (Hefferman); Elmo Murray (O'Brien); Jacques Lory (Waiter); Jack Boyle, Jr. (Chuck); Creighton Hale, Eddie Acuff (Bits).

TORRID ZONE *(Warner Bros., 1940), 88 min.*

Producer, Mark Hellinger; director, William Keighley; screenplay, Richard Macaulay, Jerry Wald; art director, Ted Smith; set decorator, Edward Thorne; music, Adolph Deutsch; music director, Leo F. Forbstein; song, M. K. Jerome and Jack Scholl; costumes, Howard Shoup; technical adviser, John Mari; makeup, Perc Westmore; sound, Oliver S. Garretson; camera, James Wong Howe; editor, Jack Killifer.

James Cagney (Nick Butler); Pat O'Brien (Steve Case); Ann Sheridan (Lee Donley); Andy Devine (Wally Davis); Helen Vinson (Gloria Anderson); Jerome Cowan (Bob Anderson); George Tobias (Rosario); George Reeves (Sancho); Victor Kilian (Carlos); Frank Puglia (Rodriquez); John Ridgely (Gardner); Grady Sutton (Sam); Paul Porcasi (Garcia); Frank Yaconelli (Lopez); Jack Mower (McNama); Paul Hurst (Daniels); George Regas (Police Sergeant); Elvira Sanchez (Rita); George Humbert (Hotel Manager); Trevor Bardette, Ernesto Piedra (Policemen); Manuel Lopez (Chico); Tony Paton (Charley); Max Blum, Betty Sanko (Bits).

CITY FOR CONQUEST *(Warner Bros., 1940), 101 min.*

Producer, Anatole Litvak; associate producer, William Cagney; director, Litvak; based on the novel by Aben Kandel; screenplay, John Wexley; art director, Robert Haas; dialogue director, Irving Rapper; music director, Leo F. Forbstein; music, Max Steiner; orchestrator, Hugo Friedhofer; choreography, Robert Vreeland; costumes, Howard Shoup; assistant director, Chuck Hansen; makeup, Perc Westmore; sound, E. A. Brown; special effects, Byron Haskin, Rex Wimpy; camera, Sol Polito, James Wong Howe; editor, William Holmes.

James Cagney (Danny Kenny); Ann Sheridan (Peggy Nash); Frank Craven (Old Timer); Donald Crisp (Scotty McPherson); Arthur Kennedy (Eddie Kenny); Frank McHugh (Mutt);

George Tobias (Pinky); Jerome Cowan (Dutch Schultz); Anthony Quinn (Murray Burns); Lee Patrick (Gladys); Blanche Yurka (Mrs. Nash); Elia Kazan (Googi);, George Lloyd (Goldie); Joyce Compton (Lilly); Thurston Hall (Max Leonard); Ben Welden (Cobb); John Arledge (Salesman); Ed Keane (Gaul); Selmer Jackson, Joseph Crehan (Doctors); Bob Steele (Callahan); Billy Wayne (Henchman); Pat Flaherty (Floor Guard); Sidney Miller (M.C.); Ethelreda Leopold (Dressingroom Blonde); and: Lee Phelps, Howard Hickman, Ed Gargan, Murray Alper, William Newell, Margaret Hayes, Lucia Carroll, Bernice Pilot, Ed Pawley.

THE STRAWBERRY BLONDE (Warner Bros., 1941), 97 min.

Producer, Jack L. Warner; associate producer, William Cagney; director, Raoul Walsh; based on the play *One Sunday Afternoon* by James Hagan; screenplay, Julius J. Epstein, Philip G. Epstein; art director, Robert Haas; music, Heinz Roemheld; orchestrator, Ray Heindorf; costumes, Orry-Kelly; assistant director, Russ Saunders; sound, Robert E. Lee; camera, James Wong Howe; editor, William Holmes.

James Cagney (Biff Grimes); Olivia de Havilland (Amy Lind); Rita Hayworth (Virginia Brush); Alan Hale (Old Man Grimes); George Tobias (Nick Pappalas); Jack Carson (Hugo Barnstead); Una O'Connor (Mrs. Mulcahey); George Reeves (Harold); Lucile Fairbanks (Harold's Girl); Edward McNamara (Big Joe); Herbert Heywood (Toby); Helen Lynd (Josephine); Roy Gordon (Bank President); Tim Ryan (Street Cleaner Foreman); Addison Richards (Official); Frank Mayo (Policeman); Jack Daley (Bartender); Susan Peters, Peggy Diggins, Ann Edmonds (Girls); Frank Orth (Baxter); James Flavin (Inspector); George Campeau (Sailor); Abe Dinovitch (Singer); George Humbert (Guiseppi); Creighton Hale (Secretary); Russell Hicks (Treadway); Wade Boteler (Warden); Peter Ashley (Young Man); Roy Gordon (Bank President); Max Hoffman, Jr., Pat Flaherty (Policemen); Bob Perry (Hanger-On); Dorothy Vaughan (Woman); Richard Clayton (Dandy); Lucia Carroll (Nurse).

THE BRIDE CAME C.O.D. (Warner Bros., 1941), 92 min.

Executive producer, Hal B. Wallis; associate producer, William Cagney; director, William Keighley; story, Kenneth Earl, M. M. Musselman; screenplay, Julius J. Epstein, Philip G. Epstein; music director, Leo F. Forbstein; music, Max Steiner; orchestrator, Hugo Friedhofer; costumes, Orry-Kelly; makeup, Perc Westmore; assistant director, Frank Heath; sound, Robert E. Lee; special effects, Byron Haskin, Rex Wimpy; camera, Ernest Haller; editor, Thomas Richards.

James Cagney (Steve Collins); Bette Davis (Joan Winfield); Stuart Erwin (Tommy Keenan); Jack Carson (Allen Brice); George Tobias (Peewee); Eugene Pallette (Lucius K. Winfield); Harry Davenport (Pop Tolliver); William Frawley (Sheriff McGee); Edward Brophy (Hinkle); Harry Holman (Judge Sobler); Chick Chandler, Herbert Anderson, Douglas Kennedy (Reporters); William Hopper (Keenan's Pilot); Charles Sullivan (Ambulance Driver); Eddy Chandler, Tony Hughes, Lee Phelps (Policemen); Jean Ames (Mabel); Alphonse Martel (Headwaiter); The Rogers Dancers (Dance Trio); Peggy Diggins, Mary Brodel (Operators); James Flavin (Detective); Sam Hayes (Announcer); Richard Travis (Airline Dispatcher); Lester Towne, Richard Clayton, Garland Smith, Claude Wisberg (Newsboys); Saul Gorss, Creighton Hale, Jack Mower, John Ridgely (Bits).

CAPTAINS OF THE CLOUDS (Warner Bros., 1942), C-113 min.

Producer, Hal B. Wallis; associate producer, William Cagney; director, Michael Curtiz; story, Arthur T. Horman, Roland Gillett; screenplay, Horman, Richard Macaulay, Norman Reilly Raine; art director, Ted Smith; music, Max Steiner; music director, Leo F. Forbstein;

song, Harold Arlen and Johnny Mercer; makeup, Perc Westmore; Technicolor consultants, Natalie Kalmus, Henri Jaffa; technical adviser, Squadron Leader O. Cathcart-Jones; dialogue director, Hugh MacMullan; sound, C. A. Riggs; special effects, Byron Haskin, Rex Wimpy; camera, Sol Polito, Wilfred M. Cline; aerial camera, Elmer Dyer, Charles Marshall, Winton C. Hoch; editor, George Amy.

James Cagney (Brian MacLean); Dennis Morgan (Johnny Dutton); Brenda Marshall (Emily Foster); Alan Hale (Tiny Murphy); George Tobias (Blimp Lebec); Reginald Gardiner (Scrounger Harris); Air Marshal W. A. Bishop (Himself); Reginald Denny (Commanding Officer); Russell Arms (Prentiss); Paul Cavanagh (Group Captain); Clem Bevans (Store Teeth Morrison); J. M. Kerrigan (Foster); J. Farrell MacDonald (Dr. Neville); Patrick O'Moore (Fyffo); Morton Lowry (Carmichael); O. Cathcart-Jones (Chief Instructor); Frederic Worlock (President of Court Martial); Roland Drew (Officer); Lucia Carroll (Blonde); George Meeker (Playboy); Benny Baker (Popcorn Kearns); Hardie Albright (Kingsley); Roy Walker (Mason); Charles Halton (Nolan); Louis Jean Heydt (Provost Marshal); Gig Young, Tod Andrews (Student Pilots); Willie Fung (Willie); Frank Lackteen, James Stevens, Bill Wilkerson (Indians); Emmett Vogan (Clerk); Miles Mander (Churchill's Voice); Larry Williams (Duty Officer); Tom Dugan (Bartender).

YANKEE DOODLE DANDY *(Warner Bros., 1942), 126 min.*

Executive producer, Jack L. Warner; producer, Hal B. Wallis; associate producer, William Cagney; story, Robert Buckner; screenplay, Buckner, Edmund Joseph; dialogue director, Hugh MacMullan; art director, Carl Jules Weyl; music director, Leo F. Forbstein; orchestrator, Ray Heindorf; music adaptor, Heinz Roemheld; choreographer, Leroy Prinz, Seymour Felix; makeup, Perc Westmore; Mr. Cagney's dance staged by John Boyle; technical adviser, William Collier, Sr.; costumes, Milo Anderson; montages, Don Siegel; sound, Everett A. Brown; camera, James Wong Howe; editor, George Amy.

James Cagney (George M. Cohan); Joan Leslie (Mary); Walter Huston (Jerry Cohan); Richard Whorf (Sam Harris); George Tobias (Dietz); Irene Manning (Fay Templeton); Rosemary De Camp (Nellie Cohan); Jeanne Cagney (Josie Cohan); S. Z. Sakall (Schwab); George Barbier (Erlanger); Walter Catlett (Manager); Frances Langford (Nora Bayes); Minor Watson (Ed Albee); Eddie Foy, Jr. (Eddie Foy); Chester Clute (Harold Goff); Douglas Croft (George M. Cohan at Age Thirteen); Patsy Lee Parsons (Josie at Age Twelve); Captain Jack Young (Franklin D. Roosevelt); Audrey Long (Receptionist); Odette Myrtil (Madame Bartholdi); Clinton Rosemond (White House Butler); Spencer Charters (Stage Manager in Providence); Dorothy Kelly, Marijo James (Sister Act); Henry Blair (George at Age Seven); Jo Ann Marlow (Josie at Age Six); Thomas Jackson (Stage Manager); Leon Belasco (Magician); Syd Saylor (Star Boarder); William B. Davidson (New York Stage Manager); Harry Hayden (Dr. Lewellyn); Francis Pierlot (Dr. Anderson); Charles Smith, Joyce Reynolds, Dick Chandlee, Joyce Horne (Teenagers); Frank Faylen (Sergeant); Wallis Clark (Theodore Roosevelt); Georgia Carroll (Betsy Ross); Joan Winfield (Sally); Dick Wessel, James Flavin (Union Army Veterans); Sailor Vincent (Schultz in *Peck's Bad Boy*); Fred Kelsey (Irish Cop in *Peck's Bad Boy*); Tom Dugan (Actor at Railway Station); Garry Owen (Army Clerk); Murray Alper (Wise Guy); Creighton Hale (Telegraph Operator); Ruth Robinson (Nurse); Eddie Acuff, Walter Brooke, Bill Edwards, William Hopper (Reporters); William Forrest, Ed Keane (Critics); Dolores Moran (Girl); Poppy Wilde, Leslie Brooks (Chorus Girls in "Little Johnny Jones" number).

JOHNNY COME LATELY *(United Artists, 1943), 97 min.*

Producer, William Cagney; director, William K. Howard; based on the novel *McLeod's Folly* by Louis Bromfield; screenplay, John Van Druten; art director, Jack Okey; set decorator, Julie Heron; music director, Leigh Harline; assistant director, Lowell Farrell; sound, Benjamin Winkler; camera, Theodor Sparkuhl; editor, George Arthur.

James Cagney (Tom Richards); Grace George (Vinnie McLeod); Marjorie Main (Gashouse Mary); Marjorie Lord (Jane); Hattie McDaniel (Aida); Edward McNamara (W. W. Dougherty); Bill Henry (Pete Dougherty); Robert Barrat (Bill Swain); George Cleveland (Willie Ferguson); Margaret Hamilton (Myrtle Ferguson); Lucien Littlefield (Blaker); Edwin Stanley (Winterbottom); Irving Bacon (Chief of Police); Tom Dugan, Charles Irwin, John Sheehan (Cops); Clarence Muse (Butler); John Miller, Arthur Hunnicutt (Tramps); Victor Kilian (Tramp in Box Car); Wee Willie Davis (Bouncer); Henry Hall (Old Timer).

BLOOD ON THE SUN (United Artists, 1945), 98 min.

Producer, William Cagney; director, Frank Lloyd; story, Garrett Fort; screenplay, Lester Cole; additional scenes, Nathaniel Curtis; art director, Wiard Ihnen; set director, A. Roland Fields; music, Miklos Rozsa; costumes, Robert Martien; makeup, Ernest Westmore, Josef Norin; assistant director, Harvey Dwight; technical adviser, Alice Barlow; sound, Richard De Wesse; camera, Theodor Sparkuhl; editors, Truman K. Wood, Walter Hanneman.

James Cagney (Nick Condon); Sylvia Sidney (Iris Hilliard); Wallace Ford (Ollie Miller); Rosemary De Camp (Edith Miller); Robert Armstrong (Colonel Tojo); John Emery (Premier Tanaka); Leonard Strong (Hijikata); Frank Puglia (Prince Tatsugi); Jack Halloran (Captain Oshima); Hugh Ho (Kajioka); Philip Ahn (Yomamoto); Joseph Kim (Hayoshi); Marvin Miller (Yamada); Rhys Williams (Joseph Cassell); Porter Hall (Arthur Bickett); James Bell (Charley Sprague); Grace Lem (Amah); Oy Chan (Chinese Servant); George Paris (Hotel Manager); Hugh Beaumont (Johnny Clarke); Gregory Gay, Arthur Loft, Emmett Vogan, Charlie Wayne (American Newspapermen in Tokyo).

13 RUE MADELEINE (Twentieth Century-Fox, 1946), 95 min.

Producer, Louis De Rochemont; director, Henry Hathaway; screenplay, John Monks, Jr., Sy Bartlett; art directors, James Basevi, Maurice Ransford; set decorator, Thomas Little; music, Alfred Newman; music director, David Buttolph; orchestrators, Edward Powell, Sidney Cutner, Leo Shuken; costumes, Rene Hubert; makeup, Ben Nye; assistant director, Abe Steinberg; sound, W. D. Flick, Harry M. Leonard; special effects, Fred Sersen; camera, Norbert Brodine; editor, Harmon Jones.

James Cagney (Bob Sharkey); Annabella (Suzanne de Bouchard); Richard Conte (Bill O'Connell); Frank Latimore (Jeff Lassiter); Walter Abel (Charles Gibson); Melville Cooper (Pappy Simpson); Sam Jaffe (Mayor Galimard); Marcel Rousseau (Duclois); Richard Gordon (Psychiatrist); Everett G. Marshall (Emile); Blanche Yurka (Madame Thillot); Peter Von Zerneck (Karl); Alfred Linder (Hans Feinkl); Ben Low (Hotel Clerk); James Craven (R.A.F. Officer); Roland Belanger (Joseph); Horace McMahon (Burglary Instructor); Alexander Kirkland (Briefing Officer); Donald Randolph (La Rockhe); Judith Lowry (Peasant Lady); Red Buttons (Dispatcher); Otto Simanek (German Staff Officer); Walter Greaza (Psychiatrist); Roland Winters (Van Duyval); Harold Young (Tailor); Sally McMarrow (Chief Operator); Coby Neal, Karl Malden (Flyers); Jean Del Val (French Peasant); Reed Hadley (Narrator).

THE TIME OF YOUR LIFE (United Artists, 1948), 109 min.

Producer, William Cagney; director, H. C. Potter; based on the play by William Saroyan; screenplay, Nathaniel Curtis; production designer, Wiard Ihnen; set decorator, A. Roland Fields; assistant director, Harvey Dwight; music, Carmen Dragon; makeup, Otis Malcolm;

sound, Earl Sitar; camera, James Wong Howe; editors, Walter Hanneman, Truman K. Wood.

James Cagney (Joe); William Bendix (Nick); Wayne Morris (Tom); Jeanne Cagney (Kitty Duval); Broderick Crawford (Policeman); Ward Bond (McCarthy); James Barton (Kit Carson); Paul Draper (Harry); Gale Page (Mary L.); James Lydon (Dudley); Richard Erdman (Willie); Pedro De Cordoba (Arab); Reginald Beane (Wesley); Tom Powers (Blick); John "Skins" Miller (A Drunk); Natalie Schafer (Society Lady); Howard Freeman (Society Gentleman); Renie Riano (Blind Date); Lanny Rees (Newsboy); Nanette Parks (Girl in Love); Grazia Narciso (Nick's Mother); Clarie Carleton ("Killer"); Moy Ming (Cook); Gladys Blake (Sidekick); Marlene Ames (Nick's Daughter); Donald Kerr (Bookie); Ann Cameron (B Girl); Floyd Walters (Sailor); Eddie Borden, Rena Case (Salvation Army Workers).

WHITE HEAT (Warner Bros., 1949), 114 min.
Producer, Louis F. Edelman; director, Raoul Walsh; story, Virginia Kellogg; screenplay, Ivan Goff, Ben Roberts; music, Max Steiner; orchestrator, Murray Cutter; assistant director, Russell Saunders; makeup, Perc Westmore, Eddie Allen; costumes, Leah Rhodes; art director, Fred M. MacLean; sound, Leslie Hewitt; special effects, Roy Davidson, H. F. Koenekamp; camera, Sid Hickox; editor, Owen Marks.

James Cagney (Cody Jarrett); Virginia Mayo (Verna Jarrett); Edmond O'Brien (Hank Fallon [Vic Pardo]); Margaret Wycherly (Ma Jarrett); Steve Cochran ("Big Ed" Somers); John Archer (Phillip Evans); Wally Cassell (Cotton Valetti); Mickey Knox (Het Kohler); Fred Clark (The Trader); G. Pat Collins (The Reader); Paul Guilfoyle (Roy Parker); Fred Coby (Happy Taylor); Ford Rainey (Zuckie Hommell); Robert Osterloh (Tommy Ryley); Ian MacDonald (Bo Creel); Marshall Bradford (Chief of Police); Ray Montgomery (Ernie Trent); George Taylor (Police Surgeon); Milton Parsons (Willie Rolf); Claudia Barrett (Cashier); Buddy Gorman (Popcorn Vendor); De Forrest Lawrence (Jim Donovan); Garrett Craig (Ted Clark); George Spaulding (Judge); Sherry Hall (Clerk); Harry Strang, Jack Worth (Guards); Sid Melton (Russell Hughes); Fern Eggen (Margaret Baxter); Eddie Foster (Nat Lefeld); Lee Phelps (Tower Guard); Jim Thorpe (Big Con).

THE WEST POINT STORY (Warner Bros., 1950), 107 min.
Producer, Louis F. Edelman; director, Roy Del Ruth; story, Irving Wallace; screenplay, John Monks, Jr., Charles Hoffman, Wallace; art director, Charles H. Clarke; set decorator, Armor E. Marlowe; music director, Ray Heindorf; choreography, LeRoy Prinz; dance stagers, Eddie Prinz, Al White; Mr. Cagney's dances created by Johnny Boyle, Jr.; songs, Jules Styne and Sammy Cahn; vocal arranger, Hugh Martin; orchestrator, Frank Perkins; makeup, Otis Malcolm; costumes, Milo Anderson, Marjorie Best; assistant director, Mel Deller; sound, Francis J. Scheid; special effects, Edwin Dupar; camera, Sid Hickox; editor, Owen Marks.

James Cagney (Elwin Bixby); Virginia Mayo (Eve Dillon); Doris Day (Jan Wilson); Gordon MacRae (Tom Fletcher); Gene Nelson (Hal Courtland); Alan Hale, Jr. (Bull Gilbert); Roland Winters (Harry Eberhart); Raymond Roe (Bixby's "Wife"); Wilton Graff (Lieutenant Colonel Martin); Jerome Cowan (Jocelyn); Frank Ferguson (Commandant); Russ Saunders (Acrobat); Jack Kelly (Officer-in-Charge); Glen Turnbull (Hoofer); Walter Ruick (Piano Player); Lute Crockett (Senator); James Dobson, Joel Marston, Bob Hayden, De Wit Bishop (Cadets).

KISS TOMORROW GOODBYE (Warner Bros., 1950), 102 min.
Producer, William Cagney; director, Gordon Douglas; based on the novel by Horace McCoy; screenplay, Harry Brown; art director, Wiard Ihnen; set decorator, Joe Kish; music, Carmen Dragon; makeup, Otis Malcolm; assistant director, William Kissell; sound, William

Lynch; special effects, Paul Eagler; camera, Peverell Marley; editors, Truman K. Wood, Walter Hannemann.

James Cagney (Ralph Cotter); Barbara Payton (Holiday); Ward Bond (Inspector Weber); Luther Adler (Mandon); Helena Carter (Margaret Dobson); Steve Brodie (Jinx); Rhys Williams (Vic Mason); Barton MacLane (Reece); Herbert Heyes (Ezra Dobson); Frank Reicher (Doc Green); John Litel (Tolgate); Dan Riss (District Attorney); John Halloran (Cobbett); William Frawley (Byers); Robert Karnes (Detective Gray); Kenneth Tobey (Detective Fowler); Neville Brand (Carleton); William Cagney (Ralph's Brother); George Spaulding (Judge); Mark Strong (Bailiff); Matt McHugh (Satterfield); Georgia Caine (Julia); King Donovan (Driver); Frank Wilcox (Doctor); Gordon Richards (Butler).

COME FILL THE CUP *(Warner Bros., 1951), 113 min.*
Producer, Henry Blanke; director, Gordon Douglas; based on the novel by Harlan Ware; screenplay, Ivan Goff, Ben Roberts; art director, Leo F. Kuter; set decorator, William K. Kuehl; music, Ray Heindorf; costumes, Leah Rhodes; assistant director, Frank Mattison; makeup, Gordon Bau; sound, Stanley Jones; camera, Robert Burks; editor, Alan Crosland, Jr.

James Cagney (Lew Marsh); Phyllis Thaxter (Paula Copeland); Raymond Massey (John Ives); James Gleason (Charley Dolan); Gig Young (Boyd Copeland); Selena Royle (Dolly Copeland); Larry Keating (Julian Cuscaden); Charlita (Maria Diego); Sheldon Leonard (Lennie Carr); Douglas Spencer (Ike Bashaw); John Kellogg (Don Bell); William Bakewell (Hal Ortman); John Alvin (Travis Ashbourne II); King Donovan (Kip Zunches); James Flavin (Homicide Captain); Torben Mayer (Welder); Norma Jean Macias (Ora); Elizabeth Flourney (Lila); Henry Blair (Bobby).

STARLIFT *(Warner Bros., 1951), 103 min.*
Producer, Robert Arthur; director, Roy Del Ruth; story, John Klorer; screenplay, Klorer, Karl Kamb; art director, Charles H. Clarke; set decorator, G. W. Berntsen; technical advisers, Major James G. Smith USAF, MATS, Major George E. Andrews, USAF, SAC.; assistant director, Mel Dellar; songs: Ira Gershwin, George Gershwin, Cole Porter, Joe Young and Jimmy Monaco, Edward Heyman and Dand Suesse, Sammy Cahn and Jules Styne, Irving Kahal and Sammy Fain, Harry Ruskin and Henry Sullivan, Ruby Ralesin and Phil Harris, Percy Faith; music director, Ray Heindorf; choreography, LeRoy Prinz; costumes, Leah Rhodes; makeup, Gordon Bau; sound, Francis J. Scheid; camera, Ted McCord; editor, William Ziegler.

Doris Day, Gordon MacRae, Virginia Mayo, Gene Nelson, Ruth Roman (Themselves); James Cagney, Gary Cooper, Virginia Gibson, Phil Harris, Frank Lovejoy, Lucille Norman, Louella O. Parsons, Randolph Scott, Jane Wyman, Patrice Wymore (Guest Stars); Janice Rule (Nell Wayne); Dick Wesson (Sergeant Mike Nolan); Ron Hagerthy (Rick Williams); Richard Webb (Colonel Callan); Hayden Rorke (Chaplain); Howard St. John (Steve Rogers); Ann Doran (Mrs. Callan); Tommy Farrell (Turner); John Maxwell (George Norris); Don Beddoe (Bob Wayne); Mary Adams (Sue Wayne); Bigelowe Sayre (Dr. Williams); Eleanor Audley (Mrs. Williams); Pat Henry (Theatre Manager); Gordon Polk (Chief Usher); Robert Hammack (Piano Player); Ray Montgomery (Captain Nelson); Bill Neff (Co-Pilot); Stan Holbrook (Ground Officer); Jill Richards (Flight Nurse); Joe Turkel (Littler Case); Rush Williams (Virginia Boy); Brian McKay (Pete); Jack Larson (Will); Lyle Clark (Nebraska Boy); Dorothy Kennedy, Jean Dean, Dolores Castle (Nurses); William Hunt (Boy with Cane); Elizabeth Flournoy (Army Nurse); Walter Brennan, Jr. (Driver); Robert Karnes, John Hedloe (Lieutenants); Steve Gregory (Boy with Camera); Richard Monohan (Morgan); Joe Recht, Herb Latimer (Soldiers in Bed); Dick Ryan (Doctor); Bill Hudson (Crew Chief); Sarah Spencer (Miss Parsons' Assistant); James Brown (Non-Com); Ezelle Poule (Waitress).

WHAT PRICE GLORY? *(Twentieth Century-Fox, 1952), C-111 min.*
Producer, Sol C. Siegel; director, John Ford; based on the play by Maxwell Anderson, Laurence Stallings; screenplay, Phoebe Ephron, Henry Ephron; art director, Lyle R. Wheeler; set decorators, George W. Davids, Thomas Little, Stuart A. Reiss; music, Alfred Newman; orchestrator, Edward Powell; songs, Jay Livingston and Ray Evans; Technicolor consultant, Leonard Doss; sound, Winston Leverett, Roger Heman; camera, Joseph MacDonald; editor, Dorothy Spencer.

James Cagney (Captain Flagg); Corinne Calvet (Charmaine); Dan Dailey (Sergeant Quirt); William Demarest (Corporal Kiper); Craig Hill (Lieutenant Aldrich); Robert Wagner (Lewisohn); Marisa Pavan (Nicole Bouchard); Casey Adams (Lieutenant Moore); James Gleason (General Cokely); Wally Vernon (Lipinsky); Henry Letondal (Cognac Pete); Fred Libby (Lieutenant Schmidt); Ray Hyke (Mulcahy); Paul Fix (Gowdy); James Lilburn (Young Soldier); Henry Morgan (Morgan); Dan Borzage (Gilbert); Bill Henry (Holsen); Henry Kulky (Company Cook); Jack Pennick (Ferguson); Ann Codee (Nun); Stanley Johnson (Lieutenant Cunningham); Luis Alberni (The Great Uncle); Barry Norton (Priest); Torben Meyer (Mayor); Alfred Zeisler (English Colonel); George Bruggeman (English Lieutenant); Sean McClory (Lieutenant Austin); Scott Forbes (Lieutenant Bennett); Charles Fitzsimons (Captain Wickham); Louis Mercier (Bouchard); Mickey Simpson (M.P.).

A LION IS IN THE STREETS *(Warner Bros., 1953), C-88 min.*
Producer, William Cagney; director, Raoul Walsh; based on the novel by Adria Locke Langley; screenplay, Luther Davis; production designer, Wiard Ihnen; set decorator, Fred M. MacLean; music, Franz Waxman; makeup, Otis Malcolm; assistant director, William Kissel; Technicolor consultant, Monroe W. Burbank; sound, John Kean; camera, Harry Stradling; editor, George Amy.

James Cagney (Hank Martin); Barbara Hale (Verity Wade); Anne Francis (Flamingo); Warner Anderson (Jules Bolduc); John McIntyre (Jeb Brown); Jeanne Cagney (Jeannie Brown); Lon Chaney, Jr. (Spurge); Frank McHugh (Rector); Larry Keating (Robert J. Castelberry); Onslow Stevens (Guy Polli); James Millican (Mr. Beach); Mickey Simpson (Tim Beck); Sara Haden (Lula May); Ellen Corby (Singing Woman); Roland Winters (Prosecutor); Burt Mustin (Smith); Irene Tedrow (Sophy); Sarah Selby (Townswoman).

RUN FOR COVER *(Paramount, 1955), C-93 min.*
Producer, William H. Pine; director, Nicholas Ray; story, Harriet Frank, Jr., Irving Ravetch; screenplay, William C. Thomas; art directors, Hal Pereira, Henry Bumstead; set decorators, Sam Comer, Frank McKelvy; assistant director, Francisco Day; music director, Howard Jackson; song, Jackson and Jack Brooks; Technicolor consultant, Richard Mueller; costumes, Edith Head; makeup, Wally Westmore; sound, Gene Merritt, John Cope; special effects, John P. Fulton; special camera effects, Farciot Edouart; camera, Daniel Fapp; editor, Howard Smith.

James Cagney (Mat Dow); Viveca Lindfors (Helga Swenson); John Derek (Davey Bishop); Jean Hersholt (Mr. Swenson); Grant Withers (Gentry); Jack Lambert (Larsen); Ernest Borgnine (Morgan); Ray Teal (Sheriff); Irving Bacon (Scotty); Trevor Bardette (Paulsen); John Miljan (Mayor Walsh); Gus Schilling (Doc Ridgeway); Emerson Treacy (Bank Manager); Denver Pyle (Harvey); Henry Wills (Townsman).

LOVE ME OR LEAVE ME *(MGM, 1955), C-122 min.*
Producer, Joe Pasternak; director, Charles Vidor; story, Daniel Fuchs; screenplay, Fuchs,

Isobel Lennart; art directors, Cedric Gibbons, Urie McCleary; costumes, Helen Rose; music adviser, Irving Aaronson; music director, George Stoll; Miss Day's music, Percy Faith; songs, Ted Koehler and Rube Bloom; Joe McCarthy and James Monaco; Jack Palmer and Spencer Williams; Walter Donaldson; B. G. DeSylva, Lew Brown, and Ray Henderson; Gus Kahn and Donaldson; Roy Turk and Fred Ahlert; Richard Rodgers and Lorenz Hart; Irving Berlin; Chilton Price; Nicholas Brodzky and Sammy Cahn; choreography, Alex Romero; sound, Wesley C. Miller; camera, Arthur E. Arling; editor, Ralph E. Winters.

Doris Day (Ruth Etting); James Cagney (Martin "The Gimp" Snyder); Cameron Mitchell (Johnny Alderman); Robert Keith (Bernard V. Loomis); Tom Tully (Frobisher); Harry Bellaver (Georgie); Richard Gaines (Paul Hunter); Peter Leeds (Fred Taylor); Claude Stroud (Eddie Fulton); Audrey Young (Jingle Girl); John Harding (Greg Trent); Dorothy Abbott (Dancer); Phil Schumacher, Otto Reichow, Henry Kulky (Bouncers); Jay Adler (Orry); Mauritz Hugo (Irate Customer); Veda Ann Borg (Hostess); Claire Carleton (Claire); Benny Burt (Stage Manager); Robert B. Carson (Mr. Brelston the Radio Station Manager); James Drury, Michael Kostrick (Assistant Directors); Richard Simmons (Dance Director); Roy Engle, John Damler (Reporters); Genevieve Aumont (Woman); Roy Engel (Propman); Dale Van Sickel, Johnny Day (Stagehands); Jimmy Criss, Henry Randolph (Photographers); Chet Brandenberg (Chauffeur); Robert Malcolm (Doorman); Robert Stephenson (Waiter); Larri Thomas, Patti Nestor, Winona Smith, Shirley Wilson (Chorus Girls).

MISTER ROBERTS *(Warner Bros., 1955), C-123 min.*
Producer, Leland Hayward; directors, John Ford, Mervyn LeRoy; based on the play by Joshua Logan, Thomas Heggen and the novel by Heggen; screenplay, Frank Nugent, Logan; art director, Art Loel; set decorator, William L. Kuehl; music, Franz Waxman; orchestrator, Leonid Raab; makeup, Gordon Bau; assistant director, Wingate Smith; technical advisers, Admiral John Dale Price, USN, Commander Merle MacBain, USN; sound, Earl N. Crain; camera, Winton C. Hoch; editor, Jack Murray.

Henry Fonda (Lieutenant "J. G." Roberts); James Cagney (Captain); Jack Lemmon (Ensign Frank Thurlowe Pulver); William Powell (Doc); Ward Bond (C.P.O. Dowdy); Betsy Palmer (Lieutenant Ann Girard); Phil Carey (Mannion); Nick Adams (Reber); Harry Carey, Jr. (Stefanowski); Ken Curtis (Dolan); Frank Aletter (Gerhart); Fritz Ford (Lidstrom); Buck Kartalian (Mason); William Henry (Lieutenant Billings); William Hudson (Olson); Stubby Kruger (Schlemmer); Harry Tenbrook (Cookie); Perry Lopez (Rodrigues); Robert Roark (Insignia); Pat Wayne (Bookser); Tige Andrews (Wiley); Jim Moloney (Kennedy); Denny Niles (Gilbert); Francis Conner (Johnson); Shug Fisher (Cochran); Danny Borzage (Jonesy); Jim Murphy (Taylor); Kathleen O'Malley, Maura Murphy, Mimi Doyle, Jeanne Murray-Vanderbilt, Lonnie Pierce (Nurses); Martin Milner (Shore Patrol Officer); Gregory Walcott (Shore Patrolman); James Flavin (M. P.); Jack Pennick (Marine Sergeant); Duke Kahanamoku (Native Chief); Carolyn Tong (Chinese Girl Who Kisses Bookser); George Brangier (French Colonel); Clarence E. Frank (Naval Officer).

THE SEVEN LITTLE FOYS *(Paramount, 1955), C-95 min.*
Producer, Jack Rose; director, Melville Shavelson; screenplay, Shavelson, Jack Rose; art directors, Hal Pereira, John Goodman; music director, Joseph J. Lilley; choreography, Nick Castle; technical adviser, Charley Foy; camera, John F. Warren; editor, Ellsworth Hoagland.

Bob Hope (Eddie Foy); Milly Vitale (Madeleine Morando); George Tobias (Barney Green); Angela Clarke (Clara); Herbert Heyes (Judge); Richard Snannon (Stage Manager); Eddie Foy, Jr. (Narrator); Billy Gray (Brynie); Lee Erickson (Charley); Paul De Rolf (Richard Foy); Lydia Reed (Mary Foy); Linda Bennett (Madeleine Foy); Jimmy Baird (Eddie, Jr.); James Cagney (George M. Cohan); Tommy Duran (Irving); Lester Matthews (Father O'Casey); Joe Evans, George Boyce (Elephant Act); Oliver Blake (Santa Claus); Milton Frome (Driscoll);

King Donovan (Harrison); Jimmy Conlin (Stage Doorman); Marian Carr (Soubrette); Harry Cheshire (Stage Doorman at Iroquois); Renata Vanni (Italian Ballerina Mistress); Betty Uitti (Dance Specialty Double); Noel Drayton; Joe Flynn (Priest); Jack Pepper (Theatre Manager); Dabbs Greer (Tutor); Billy Nelson (Customs Inspector); Jerry Mathers (Brynie at Age Five); Lewis Martin (Presbyterian Minister).

TRIBUTE TO A BAD MAN *(MGM, 1956), C-95 min.*
Producer, Sam Zimbalist; director, Robert Wise; based on the short story by Jack Schaeffer; screenplay, Michael Blankfort; art directors, Cedric Gibbons, Paul Broesse; set decorators, Edwin B. Willis, Fred MacLean; music, Miklos Rozsa; costumes, Walter Plunkett; assistant director, Arvid Griffin; makeup, William Tuttle; color consultant, Charles K. Hagedon; sound, Dr. Wesley C. Miller; camera, Robert Surtees; editor, Ralph E. Winters.

James Cagney (Jeremy Rodock); Don Dubbins (Steve Miller); Stephen McNally (McNulty); Irene Papas (Jocasta Constantine); Vic Morrow (Lars Peterson); James Griffith (Barjak); Onslow Stevens (Hearn); James Bell (L. A. Peterson); Jeanette Nolan (Mrs. L. A. Peterson); Chubby Johnson (Baldy); Royal Dano (Abe); Lee Van Cleef (Fat Jones); Peter Chong (Cooky); James McCallion (Shorty); Clint Sharp (Red); Tony Hughes, Roy Engel (Buyers); Carl Pitti (Tom); Bud Osborne, John Halloran, Tom London, Dennis Moore, Buddy Roosevelt, Billy Dix (Cowboys).

THESE WILDER YEARS *(MGM, 1956), 91 min.*
Producer, Jules Schermer; director, Roy Rowland; story, Ralph Wheelwright; screenplay, Frank Fenton; art directors, Cedric Gibbons, Preston Ames; set decorators, Edwin B. Willis, Edward G. Boyle; Miss Stanwyck's costumes, Helen Rose; makeup, William Tuttle; assistant director, Al Jennings; sound, Dr. Wesley C. Miller; camera, George J. Folsey; editor, Ben Lewis.

James Cagney (Steve Bradford); Barbara Stanwyck (Ann Dempster); Walter Pidgeon (James Rayburn); Betty Lou Keim (Suzie Keller); Don Dubbins (Mark); Edward Andrews (Mr. Spottsford); Basil Ruysdael (Judge); Grandon Rhodes (Roy Oliphant); Will Wright (Old Cab Driver); Lewis Martin (Dr. Miller); Dorothy Adams (Aunt Martha); Dean Jones (Hardware Clerk); Herb Vigran (Traffic Cop); Ruth Lee (Miss Finch); Matt Moore (Gateman); Jack Kenny (Chauffeur); Harry Tyler (Doorman); Luana Lee (Stenographer); William Forrest, John Maxwell, Emmett Vogan, Charles Evans (Board of Directors); Michael Landon (Boy in Pool Room); Jimmy Ogg (Ad Lib Boy); Elizabeth Flournoy (Spottsford's Secretary); Kathleen Mulqueen (Prim Lady); Russ Whitney (Hotel Clerk); Lillian Powell (Proprietress).

SHORT CUT TO HELL *(Paramount, 1957), 87 min.*
Producer, A. C. Lyles; director, James Cagney; based on the screenplay for *This Gun for Hire* by W. R. Burnett, from the novel *A Gun for Sale* by Graham Greene; screenplay, Ted Berkman, Raphael Blau; assistant director, Richard Caffey; costumes, Edith Head; art directors, Hal Pereira, Roland Anderson; music director, Irvin Talbot; special camera effects, John P. Fulton; camera, Haskell Boggs; editor, Tom McAdoo.

Robert Ivers (Kyle); Georgann Johnson (Glory Hamilton); William Bishop (Stan); Jacques Aubuchon (Bahrwell); Peter Baldwin (Adams); Yvette Vickers (Daisy); Murvyn Vye (Nichols); Milton Frome (Los Angeles Police Captain); Jacqueline Beer (Waitress); Gail Land (Girl); Dennis McMullen (Los Angeles Policeman); William Newell (Hotel Manager); Sarah Selby (Adams' Secretary); Mike Ross (Inspector Ross); Douglas Spencer (Conductor); Danny Lewis (Piano Player); Richard Hale (A. T.); Douglas Evans (Mr. Henry); Hugh Lawrence, Joe Bassett (Patrolmen); Roscoe Ates (Extension Road Driver); John Halloran (Guard); Joe Forte (Ticket Seller); Russell Trent (Trainman); William Pullen (Used Car Lot Manager); James Cagney (Prologue).

MAN OF A THOUSAND FACES *(Universal, 1957), 122 min.*
Producer, Robert Arthur; director, Joseph Pevney; story, Ralph Wheelwright; screenplay, R. Wright Campbell, Ivan Goff, Ben Roberts; art directors, Alexander Golitzen, Eric Orbom; music, Frank Skinner; orchestrator, Joseph Gershenson; costumes, Bill Thomas; makeup, Bud Westmore, Jack Kevan; assistant director, Phil Bowles; sound, Leslie I. Carey, Robert Pritchard; special effects, Clifford Stine; camera, Russell Metty; editor, Ted J. Kent.

James Cagney (Lon Chaney); Dorothy Malone (Cleva Creighton Chaney); Jane Greer (Hazel Bennett); Marjorie Rambeau (Gert); Jim Backus (Clarence Locan); Robert J. Evans (Irving Thalberg); Celia Lovsky (Mrs. Chaney); Jeanne Cagney (Carrie Chaney); Jack Albertson (Dr. J. Wilson Shields); Nolan Leary (Pa Chaney); Roger Smith (Creighton Chaney at Twenty-One); Robert Lyden (Creighton at Thirteen); Rickie Sorensen (Creighton at Eight); Dennis Rush (Creighton at Four); Simon Scott (Carl Hastings); Clarence Kolb (Himself); Danny Beck (Max Dill); Phil Van Zandt (George Loane Tucker); Hank Mann, Snub Pollard (Comedy Waiters).

NEVER STEAL ANYTHING SMALL *(Universal, 1959), C-94 min.*
Producer, Aaron Rosenberg; director, Charles Lederer; based on the play *Devil's Hornpipe* by Maxwell Anderson, Rouben Mamoulian; screenplay, Charles Lederer; art director, Alexander Golitzen; set decorators, Russell A. Gausman, Ollie Emert; music, Allie Wrubel; music supervisor, Joseph Gershenson; songs, Wrubel and Anderson; choreography, Hermes Pan; costumes, Bill Thomas; makeup, Bud Westmore; assistant directors, Dave Silver, Ray De Camp; sound, Leslie I. Carey, Robert Pritchard; camera, Harold Lipstein; editor, Russ Schoengarth.

James Cagney (Jake MacIllaney); Shirley Jones (Linda Cabot); Roger Smith (Dan Cabot); Cara Williams (Winnipeg); Nehemiah Persoff (Pinelli); Royal Dano (Words Cannon); Anthony Caruso (Lieutenant Tevis); Horace McMahon (O. K. Merritt); Virginia Vincent (Ginger); Jack Albertson (Sleep-Out Charlie); Robert J. Wilke (Lennie); Herbie Faye (Hymie); Billy Greene (Ed); John Duke (Ward); Jack Orrison (Osborne); Roland Winters (Doctor); Ingrid Goude (Model); Sanford Seegar (Fats Ranny); Ed "Skipper" McNally (Thomas); Gregg Barton (Deputy Warden); Edwin Parker (Cop); Jay Jostyn (Judge); John Halloran, Harvey Parry (Detectives); Rebecca Sand (Coffee Vendor); Phyllis Kennedy (Waitress).

SHAKE HANDS WITH THE DEVIL *(United Artists, 1959), 100 min.*
Executive producers, George Glass, Walter Seltzer; producer-director, Michael Anderson; based on the novel by Reardon Conner; adaptor, Marian Thompson; screenplay, Ivan Goff, Ben Roberts; production designer, Tom Morahan; set decorator, Josie Macavin; music, William Alwyn; music director, Muir Mathieson; ladies' costumes, Irene Gilbert; wardrobe supervisor; Tony Sforzini; assistant director, Chris Sutton; special military adviser, Lieutenant Colonel William O'Kelly; sound, William Bulkley; camera, Erwin Hillier; second unit camera, Eric Besche; editor, Ronald Coppleman.

James Cagney (Sean Lenihan); Don Murray (Kerry O'Shea); Dana Wynter (Jennifer Curtis); Glynis Johns (Kitty); Michael Redgrave (General); Sybil Thorndike (Lady Fitzhugh); Cyril Cusack (Chris); John Breslin (McGrath); Harry Brogan (Cassidy); Robert Brown (Sergeant); Marianne Benet (Mary Madigan); Lewis Carson (The Judge); John Cairney (Mike O'Callaghan); Harry Corbett (Clancy); Eileen Crowe (Mrs. Madigan); Alan Cuthbertson, Peter Reynolds (Captains—Black and Tans); Donal Donnelly (Willie Cafferty); Wilfred Dawning (Tommy Connor); Eithne Dunne (Eileen O'Leary); Paul Farrell (Doyle); Richard Harris (Terence O'Brien); William Hartnell (Sergeant Jenkins); John Le Mesurier (British General); Niall MacGinnis (Michael O'Leary); Patrick McAllinney (Donovan); Ray McAnally (Paddy Nolan); Clive Morton (Sir Arnold Fielding); Christopher Rhodes (Colonel Smithson); Alan White (Captain Fleming); Ronald Walsh (Sergeant—Black and Tans).

THE GALLANT HOURS *(United Artists, 1960), 111 min.*

Producer-director, Robert Montgomery; screenplay, Beirne Lay, Jr., Frank D. Gilroy; art director, Wiard Ihnen; set decorator, Frank McKelvey; music, Roger Wagner; music editor, Alfred Perry· costumes, Jack Martell; makeup, Lorand Cosand; assistant director, Joseph C. Behm; technical supervisor, Captain Idris B. Monahan, USN; technical consultant, Captain Joseph U. Lademan, USN; Japanese naval technical adviser, James T. Goto; camera, Joe MacDonald; editor, Frederick Y. Smith.

James Cagney (Fleet Admiral William F. Halsey, Jr.); Dennis Weaver (Lieutenant Commander Andy Lowe); Ward Costello (Captain Harry Black); Richard Jaeckel (Lieutenant Commander Roy Webb); Les Tremayne (Captain Frank Enright); Robert Burton (Major General Roy Geiger); Raymond Bailey (Major General Archie Vandergrift); Carl Benton Reid (Vice Admiral Robert Ghormley); Walter Sande (Captain Horace Keys); Karl Swenson (Captain Bill Bailey); Vaughan Taylor (Commander Mike Pulaski); Harry Landers (Captain Joe Foss); Richard Carlyle (Father Gehring); Leon Lontoc (Manuel); James T. Goto (Admiral Isoroku Hamanoto); James Yagi (Rear Admiral Jiri Kobe); John McKee (Lieutenant Harrison Ludlum); John Zaremba (Major General Harmon); Carleton Young (Colonel Evans Carlson); William Schallert (Captain Tom Lamphier); Nelson Leigh (Admiral Callaghan); Sydney Smith (Admiral Scott); Herbert Lytton (Admiral Murray); Selmer Jackson (Admiral Chester Nimitz); Tyler McVey (Admiral Ernest J. King); Maggie Magennis (Red Cross Girl); James Cagney, Jr., Robert Montgomery, Robert Montgomery, Jr. (Bits); Art Gilmore (Narrator of Japanese Sequences).

ONE, TWO, THREE *(United Artists, 1961), 108 min.*

Producer, Billy Wilder; associate producers, I. A. L. Diamond, Doane Harrison; director, Wilder; based on a play by Ferenc Molnar; screenplay, Wilder, Diamond; art director, Alexander Trauner; music, Andre Previn; second unit director, Andre Smagghe; assistant director, Tom Pevsner; sound, Basil Fenton-Smith; special effects, Milton Rice; camera, Daniel Fapp; editor, Daniel Mandell.

James Cagney (C. P. MacNamara); Horst Buchholz (Otto Ludwig Piffl); Pamela Tiffin (Scarlett); Arlene Francis (Mrs. MacNamara); Lilo Pulver (Ingeborg); Howard St. John (Hazeltine); Hanns Lothar (Schlemmer); Leon Askin (Peripetchikoff); Peter Capell (Mishkin); Ralf Wolter (Borodenko); Karl Lieffen (Fritz); Henning Scluter (Dr. Bauer); Hubert Von Meyerinck (Count Von Droste-Schattenburg); Lois Bollton (Mrs. Hazeltine); Tile Kiwe (Newspaperman); Karl Ludwig Lindt (Zeidlitz); Red Buttons (Military Police Sergeant); John Allen (Tommy MacNamara); Christine Allen (Cindy MacNamara); Rose Renee Roth (Bertha); Ivan Arnold (Police Corporal); Helmud Schmid (East German Police Corporal); Otto Friebel (East German Interrogator); Werner Buttler (East German Police Sergeant); Klaus Becker, Siegfried Dornbusch (Policemen); Paul Bos (Krause); Max Buschbaum (Tailor); Jaspar Von Oertzen (Haberdasher); Inga De Toro (Stewardess); Werner Hassenland (Shoeman); Jacques Chevalier (Pierre).

ARIZONA BUSHWHACKERS *(Paramount, 1968), C-87 min.*

Producer, A. C. Lyles; director, Lesley Selander; story, Steve Fisher, Andrew Craddock; screenplay, Fisher; art directors, Hal Pereira, Al Roelofs; set decorators, Robert Benton, Jerry Welch; makeup, Wally Westmore; music, Jimmie Haskell; assistant director, Dale Hutchinson; special camera effects, Paul K. Lerpae; camera, Lester Shorr; editor, John F. Schreyer.

Howard Keel (Lee Travis); Yvonne De Carlo (Jill Wyler); John Ireland (Dan Shelby); Marilyn Maxwell (Molly); Scott Brady (Tom Rile); Brian Donlevy (Mayor Joe Smith); Barton MacLane (Sheriff Lloyd Grover); James Craig (Ike Clanton); Roy Rogers, Jr. (Roy); Reg Parton (Curly); Montie Montana (Stage Driver); Eric Cody (Bushwhacker); James Cagney (Narrator).

Publicity pose for *Spartacus* (Univ., 1960)

2

Kirk Douglas

6'
170 pounds
Blond hair
Green eyes
Sagittarius

Dimpled, grinning Kirk Douglas has been starring in motion pictures for over thirty years. He has often teamed and co-produced with fellow performer Burt Lancaster, a man he has much admired and envied. The public has on occasion confused the two distinctly different performers. However, industry observers have generally been aware that Lancaster was and is the more popular figure both on and off the screen.

The gutsy intensity of both Douglas and Lancaster represented the new movie star ideal of the post-World War II era. Throughout the fifties Kirk traded on this prominence with a vitality of drive that was not always matched by credibility of performance. Columnist Sheilah Graham once observed of Douglas: "His personality has no elasticity. He is at his best as a driving egotist, propelled on some inner motor."

On or off the soundstage, Douglas never seems to relax. Whether producing, directing, and/or starring in films, he is a frenetic force. For the average person this compulsion is baffling, but it has made Kirk an intense, intrepid performer, one who is always interesting to observe, if not always to appreciate.

The only son of seven children was born to Herschel (Harry) and Bryna (Sanglel) Danielovitch of Amsterdam, New York, on Saturday, December 9, 1916. The boy, who would grow up to be known as Kirk Douglas and who, fifty-eight years later, would be described as "one of the most masculine film stars . . . he exudes an air of life and vitality,"[1] had green eyes, blond hair, a strong chin with a deep cleft, and destitute parents.

His father and mother, poor Russian Jews, had immigrated to New York by steamship steerage in 1910 from Mogoloskova Burnya, a town south of Moscow. Failing to find the prophesied gold in the streets of New York City, the still optimistic couple moved upstate to Amsterdam, thirty miles from Albany, in the Mohawk Valley. There, Harry, unskilled but physically powerful, acquired a horse-drawn wagon from which he peddled fruit, delivered wood, and collected junk. Of his father, the son, in 1957, would say, "The business of earning a living in his adopted country baffled him. Sometimes he just sat there, looking bewildered, wondering how other men managed to buy low and sell high."

Three daughters were born to the poor immigrants in rapid succession, followed by the son who was named Issur. Three more girls came along, and in 1921, Harry found that he could not cope with the problems of providing for eight dependents. He deserted his brood.

Before his departure, he had changed the family's surname to Demsky. But regardless of what they were called, there was little food, warmth, or clothing in the humble household. Bryna supported her offspring as best she could, with the three oldest girls forced to go to work. Issur, now sporting the nickname Izzy, sold soda pop and candy to the factory workers at Amsterdam's two leading rug-carpet mills, Mohawk and Sanford. "Sometimes I made enough to buy a couple of boxes of corn flakes and two quarts of milk," he later confided to Pete Martin of *The Saturday Evening Post* (June, 1957). (In those days, milk sold for seven cents a quart and bread was five cents a loaf.)

Despite the deprivation of the Demskys, Bryna, who could neither read nor write, insisted that her children attend public school. "Ma told all seven of us kids that the opportunity to acquire knowledge was the 'gold in the streets' an immigrant could find in America."

Izzy worked hard at any job he could obtain: selling paper, washing dishes, operating a punch press, acting as a lifeguard at the town swimming pool or protecting a mill at night. His very existence became devoted to dreaming of the day when he might have the wherewithal to escape the pauper's life. Whenever possible, he hoarded away a few coins toward his college fund. This seemingly impossible goal was encouraged by a teacher named Louise Livingston, who introduced him to poetry, drama, and literature. She often called on him to read poems aloud in her classroom and she became the adult to whom he confessed some of his dreams for a future. Through their friendship, he decided that he wanted to become a poet.

While Izzy was in junior high school, a Mr. Sanford, the town's philanthropist, established a fund to provide an annual medal to be given to the boy or girl who would excel in public speaking. Even though Izzy, at thirteen, was busy being a stock clerk at Goldmeer's Wholesale Company on weekday afternoons and on Saturdays, he was determined to win the Sanford trophy. With a ten-minute recitation of the poem "Across the Border," which was about a wounded soldier hovering between life and death, he was pronounced the contest winner. It was an honor he would never forget. Mr. Goldmeer was so impressed by his stock clerk's oratory that he later asked him to repeat his recitation in front of a Saturday morning gathering

[1]Attributed to Elaine Kaufman, owner of "Elaine's," one of Manhattan's more famous show business restaurants.

of employees. In competition with the noise of Chuctanunda Creek which roared past the building, along with persistently ringing telephones, it was a tribute to Izzy's fortitude that he got through the "show." The future star would later recall, "Since then I've given performances under difficult conditions, but that morning in Mr. Goldmeer's office still ranks with me as tops in rough going."

Through his various jobs, the youth was able to save $350 toward college. But by the time he was mid-way through high school, the sum had been handed over to his mother to supplement the depleted household funds. At Wilbur Lynch High School, he performed in a few plays and participated on the debate team, but one of his most remembered experiences was a trip to Albany with his English class to watch Katharine Cornell perform in *The Barretts of Wimpole Street*. He was intrigued with the stage, but eliminated from his mind any notion of becoming an actor, chiefly because it would not seem a manly pursuit to his group of friends.

On graduation from high school in 1933, he postponed his plans to attend college and would have forsaken them completely had it not been for his former teacher. It was Miss Livingston who "convinced me that college was worth working for; worth waiting for." For a year he was employed as a clerk-window washer at Lurie's Department Store during which time he managed to save $163. The sum was hardly enough to finance his way through college. But another friend, Pete Riccio, a student at St. Lawrence University, was to supply the advice that would set him on his way. Riccio suggested that he accompany him to the University at Canton, New York and ask the dean if he would qualify for admission in spite of his meagre funds. "The worst they can say is 'No,' " Riccio added wisely. With assurance from his sisters that they would take care of his mother, Izzy took to the highways with his friend to hitchhike to Canton, some 140 miles to the north.

The final twenty miles were spent riding on top of a truck loaded with fertilizer. There is no doubt but that the dean was duly impressed with Izzy, not only because of his brashness at asking to be admitted purely on the basis of high school credentials and $163 in cash, but because of the air about him which carried the smell of cow dung. Perhaps because of both, the man said, "We'll take a chance on you." The eighteen-year-old boy from Amsterdam was granted a loan from the college, to be reimbursed by part-time campus gardening at thirty cents an hour. Within no time at all he lost that job and became a part-time janitor. Since he could not afford to reside in a dormitory, he slept and studied in the janitor's room.

The college employees were not allowed to eat in the campus cafeteria (not that Izzy had the money anyway), so classmates sneaked food to him. He selected English literature as his major curriculum, with a minor in German, because he still thought of becoming a poet. "I used to wear my shirt open down the front," he told *Redbook* Magazine readers in 1966, "and write a lot of poetry. And it was a shocking day when I suddenly realized that all the poetry I ever wrote was rather mediocre. And if there's anything I hate, it's mediocrity."

By the time he had become a college junior, he reached the decision, with the encouragement of teachers and classmates, to become an actor. He hitchhiked to New York City where he approached the secretary of The American Academy of Dramatic Arts with the statement, "When I'm done at St. Lawrence I'm coming here." The secretary pointed out that the Academy offered no scholarships, but he did allow the eager young man to read for him from a script. The employer must have been favorably impressed when he said, "If you still want to come here when you graduate, we'll try to get you in."

Back at the university, Izzy participated in plays and onstage debates, and was accepted as a member of the varsity wrestling team. Although too poor to join a fraternity, he was chosen top-man-on-campus with his election as president of the student body in his senior year and was awarded a special plaque as the school's only undefeated wrestler. He also played the lead in the university's production of *Death Takes a Holiday* after being voted president of "The Mummers," the student dramatic club. Along the way he learned a drastic lesson in economics by losing his "small fund of cash" in a poker game with the boys. He later earned a bit of spending money when he worked for a carnival that passed through town. Izzy worked as a "volunteer" from the audience who wrestled with the show's muscle man. Other scholastic honors included the vice-presidency of the German Club and head of the Middle Atlantic Region of the National Student Federation.

In June, 1939, he packed his plaque and Bachelor of Arts diploma in a battered suitcase, along with an overcoat salvaged from a fellow student who had no further use for such a relic, and hitchhiked to Manhattan. The secretary of the American Academy of Dramatic Arts greeted him with the good news that an exception would be made on his behalf with the establishment of a special scholarship.

Izzy was overjoyed, naturally, but his next task was to find a job that would provide him with sufficient cash for a room and food. He obtained a post at the Greenwich Settlement House teaching drama to kids, and "that way I earned enough to rent an attic room and eat two cheap meals a day, breakfast and dinner. I skipped lunch." Additionally, he accepted odd jobs as they could be found, such as a bell hop, an usher, a soda jerk, etc. He spent the following summer earning while learning in summer stock in Speculator, New York. But the money he saved was soon depleted, and at Thanksgiving time in his second year at the AADA, he was down to thirty cents. He has recounted standing in line at the Bowery's Salvation Army haven to buy a twenty-five-cent turkey feast, "but when I reached the head of the line the food had run out." Instead of turkey that Thanksgiving Day, 1940, he was forced to spend twenty cents at a lunch wagon for a bowl of stew.

Among his classmates at the Academy was a girl named Betty Persky (later to become known as Lauren Bacall), who liked him to the point of worrying about him in his oversized, second-hand overcoat—the previous owner stood four inches taller than Izzy's six feet. Betty persuaded an uncle to give him a new coat that fit. Another AADA classmate was an attractive blonde from Bermuda named Diana Dill in whom he took more than a casual interest.

A director in summer stock helped him settle on a stage name more suitable to his career than either Issur Danielovitch or Izzy Demsky. "I chose the name Douglas," he has publicly said. "I can't remember why. Perhaps if a psychiatrist drained my mind he would find the name Douglas Fairbanks floating in the sludge. Anyhow, I remember that we decided to put Kirk in front of the Douglas because it would sound *Snazzy*."

But Kirk Douglas, drama student, still had several months of hard study ahead of him before graduation, so he got a job waiting on tables from nine P.M. until one A.M. at Schrafft's Restaurant, where the pay was fifteen dollars a week, plus tips, and an occasional stolen sandwich.

After graduating from the Academy in 1941, he spent another summer in stock at Nuangola, Pennsylvania, where he once more hoarded his earnings toward what might prove to be a long, payless quest for work. Again, he was fortunate. He obtained an interview with producer Guthrie McClintic, who asked him if he could

100

sing "Yankee Doodle," and project it loud. Slack-jawed, Kirk responded that he guessed he could, and he was hired as a singing Western Union boy who had one scene at the end of the second act of *Spring Again*. His legitimate acting debut occurred on Monday, November 10, 1941, at the Henry Miller Theatre, in the company of the show's two distinguished stars, C. Aubrey Smith and Grace George.

For Thanksgiving dinner that year, he was among those invited to observe the event at the home of Katharine Cornell and Guthrie McClintic, quite in contrast to his solitary lunch wagon experience of the previous year.

Spring Again lasted for 241 performances. When it closed, Kirk went through some weeks at liberty before his next stage job, in Miss Cornell's revival production of *The Three Sisters* at the Ethel Barrymore Theatre. The show opened on December 21, 1942. Kirk had several very brief bits to perform in the drama. At one point he was the servant who silently sets a samovar on a birthday lunch table before Miss Cornell, Judith Anderson, and Ruth Gordon. In the third act, he was heard but not seen as a soldier-actor on his way to war, shouting, "Yo-ho," as a kind of farewell. Kirk provided the echo of the man's voice as it resounded through the make-believe forest. With so little to do, he was happy to work also as assistant stage manager and understudy. However, he left the show before its closing (April 3, 1943) and enlisted in the United States Navy.

After boot camp training, he attended midshipman school at Notre Dame University, and earned the rank of ensign. He was assigned as a communications officer aboard an anti-submarine patrol boat in the Pacific. In 1943, while his craft was escorting a large ship to Pearl Harbor, a Japanese submarine appeared on the scene and the patrol boat's crew ejected depth charges from its fantail. One charge exploded too close to the small vessel, resulting in internal injuries to Ensign Douglas. These injuries, later complicated by amoebic dysentery, put him in sick bay at Balboa Hospital at the San Diego, California Naval Station, where he was to spend several months recuperating. While convalescing, he was married to his former classmate, Diana Dill, on November 2, 1943.

After receiving a medical discharge from the service in 1944, he returned to Manhattan to resume a marriage and a career. To gain added acting experience, he became employed as a radio performer in continuing roles in about a dozen daytime soap operas. On September 25, 1944, Diana Dill Douglas gave birth to a son who was named Michael Kirk, and, late in 1944,[2] Kirk was back on a Broadway stage.

At the Biltmore Theatre, he replaced Richard Widmark as Army lieutenant Lenny Archer of the original cast of *Kiss and Tell*. He and Joan Caulfield provided the comedy's juvenile love interest in a cast headed by Jessie Royce Landis and Robert Keith. Next, as though he were deliberately following Widmark, he replaced him in *Trio* at the Belasco Theatre in January, 1945. In this play, he was involved in a strange triangle affair with Lydia St. Clair and Lois Wheeler. Perhaps he foretold the production's fate[3] by withdrawing to go into another play, *Alice in Arms* at the

---

[2]Kirk was among those who auditioned for a role in the musical *On the Town* (Adelphi Theatre; December 28, 1944, 463 performances), and was requested to sing a song about a lady, "Louie the Lou." However, Douglas developed a case of laryngitis and was dropped from the show's lineup.

[3]*Trio* was shut down by Paul Moss, New York City License Commissioner because of the play's lesbian theme. Moss gave the Belasco management the option of either canceling the production or losing their theatre license.

Kirk Douglas as a baby   As a Navy midshipman

With wife Diana Dill in 1945

National Theatre. The latter was a bad choice, for it lasted only five performances after its January 31, 1945 opening.

In the meantime, his friend from the AADA, now re-christened Lauren Bacall, had created a smash on film with her first appearance in Warner Bros.' *To Have and Have Not* (1944). She happened to be on the same eastbound train from Los Angeles as producer Hal B. Wallis. Since Wallis had a reputation for seeking new talent for motion pictures, Miss Bacall recommended that he get in touch with a stage newcomer named Kirk Douglas. Wallis did just that and offered a screen test.

Kirk, however, was in rehearsals for a new play, and "my dream had always been to be a star on the Broadway stage. Now, with opportunity knocking on my door like a mad woodpecker, I was frightened. I called Wallis to say I was sorry, but I was going to stick with the show."

The show was Ralph Nelson's *The Wind Is Ninety*, starring Bert Lytell, Blanche Yurka, and Wendell Corey. It opened at the Booth Theatre on June 21, 1945, and survived 108 performances. The play was a fantasy about a fighter pilot (Corey) who is killed over Germany, and whose ghost returns home, hoping to soften the blow to his family, when they get the telegram. In his role of the Unknown Soldier who guides Corey back home, Kirk had some sharp lines of dialogue and earned critical praise. John Chapman (*New York Daily News*) insisted that he was "nothing short of superb," while Howard Barnes (*New York Herald-Tribune*) reported that Kirk played the role "with a jaunty grace that endows it with dignity and feeling."

Despite his reviews, the downbeat show did not attract the ticket-buying public, and its closing left Kirk in a depressed state about his future on the stage. He was financially incapable—so it seemed—of supporting himself, let alone a wife, who still wanted a career of her own, and an infant son. He visited Hal Wallis at his New York offices and later recalled saying, "If you're still interested in having me make a picture, I'll try." Wallis had not lost interest, and a deal was negotiated for Kirk to go to California for a screen test.

The test resulted in Kirk obtaining the fourth-billed role of Walter O'Neil in the Lewis Milestone-directed *The Strange Love of Martha Ivers* (Paramount, 1946). It was a bizarre film, to say the least. Within the Robert Rossen screenplay, the teenaged Walter (Mickey Kuhn) witnesses the murder of wealthy Mrs. Ivers (Judith Anderson) by her granddaughter, Martha (Janis Wilson) because she is prevented from running away with her beau, Sam Masterson (Darryl Hickman). Rather than admitting what he has seen, Walter permits an innocent man to take the rap. Years later (via one of those Hollywood montage jumps), the principals grow up to become the adult Martha (Barbara Stanwyck), Walter (Kirk), and Sam (Van Heflin).

Martha has married Walter to keep him quiet and has set him up as the town district attorney. While he weakly indulges in alcoholic shame, she spreads her favors among several admirers, until Sam, now a gambler, returns to Iverstown. She and Walter presume that Sam is there to blackmail them, and they make the mistake of having him beaten up. It is then that he pieces together the bits of the mystery to come up with the right answer. But he has now fallen for Martha, who tries to get him to murder Walter. Murder is not in the gambler's makeup, however, and he resists. In a drunken stupor, Walter confesses his grizzly past and is then killed as he falls down a staircase. Fearing reprisals, the suddenly conscience-stricken Martha commits suicide, leaving Sam free to leave Iverstown forever (and to make a new life for himself with luscious ex-convict Lizabeth Scott). In the *New York World-Telegram*, William Hawkins wrote that Kirk, "in his first picture, gives

103

With Van Heflin and Barbara Stanwyck in *The Strange Love of Martha Ivers* (Par., 1946)

the weakling Walter a convincingly sustained color." Hal Wallis was sufficiently impressed to sign him to a five-picture contract.

While awaiting the movie-going public's reaction to his first screen performance, Kirk received permission from Wallis to make another attempt at Broadway. On April 17, 1946, he opened in Bella and Sam Spewack's comedy *Woman Bites Dog* at the Belasco Theatre. The show, starring Taylor Holmes, dealt with the arena of newspaper publishers. It turned out to be yet another flop ("It is as uneven as a piece of splintered wood," said Howard Barnes of the *New York Herald-Tribune*). Kirk, as the veteran who takes a big publisher over the ropes, was rated "attractively brazen" (Barnes of the *Herald-Tribune*) and a "likeable lad with a pleasing personality" (*Brooklyn Citizen News*). But good notices in a show that closes after five performances are only of academic interest. So, with his pregnant wife and son in tow, he returned to Hollywood to pick up a career in films. But since Wallis had nothing on tap for him, he spent several months setting up living quarters and enjoying the sunshine of California. He consulted a plastic surgeon about the possibility of removing the cleft in his chin, but was advised to leave well enough alone. On January 23, 1947, a second son was born to the Douglases, and he was named Joel.

Ever anxious to earn some financial return on his personal players, Wallis loaned Kirk to RKO for the somber *Mourning Becomes Electra* (1947), from Eugene O'-Neill's play, in a relatively undemanding minor role (sixth billing). The film, completed in seventy-seven days, underwent considerable editing and re-editing and was released on November 19, 1947 to unreceptive audiences.[4] ("Word-of-mouth

[4]In an attempt to instill some prestige into this "arty" production, RKO arranged a distribution tie-in with the Theatre Guild, for road-showing the feature in some twenty cities on a two-

With Rosalind Russell, Nancy Coleman, and Michael Redgrave in *Mourning Becomes Electra* (RKO, 1947)

won't be of any help in attracting the average layman.") Talky, monotonous, and downright dull, the film is laid in Massachusetts and concerns the Mannon family, whose members distrust each other. Lavinia Mannon (Rosalind Russell), on learning that her mother (Katina Paxinou—complete with incongruous accent) has murdered her father (Raymond Massey), also discovers that the man she loves (Leo Genn) is her mother's lover. She persuades her dreamy brother (Michael Redgrave), who has a suspicious fascination with mama, to help do away with the lover, thus leading to the matriarch's suicide. In the course of this high-class soap opera, ex-Union army officer Peter Niles (Kirk) believes he is in love with Lavinia, but his romantic notion is soon dissipated, what with all the unhappiness surrounding him, much of which has been instigated by the warped, hateful Lavinia. For her heavy-handed efforts, Miss Russell (more safely comedic than tragic as here) was Oscar-nominated as Best Actress of 1947, but lost to Loretta Young of *The Farmer's Daughter* (RKO). Kirk made little impression in this tragedy.

RKO also utilized Kirk's services, on loan, for *Out of the Past* (1947), officially released one day after *Electra*. The "past" of the title belongs to Robert Mitchum, the film's star, who thinks he has quit the business of private investigating. In flashback, it is revealed that he was hired by a hoodlum (Kirk) to find his mistress (Jane Greer), who shot him before leaving the country with $40,000. Mitchum finds her down in Mexico, but falls in love with the sultry lady. He refuses to report back to his client, Douglas. It is not long before Mitchum discovers that she is a murder-

a-day basis. Then, with a shotgun approach of attracting some, or any patrons, the studio advertised the feature with the campaign, "Mother and daughter . . . loving the same man . . . hating each other."

With Robert Mitchum in *Out of the Past* (RKO, 1947)

ess, whose darkest traits soon come to the fore. He leaves her. The story then jumps back to the present where Douglas, ensconced in a Lake Tahoe lodge, figures he is owed a debt by trench-coated Mitchum and orders him to steal some financial records that could prove the former's participation in income tax evasion. This present-day action presents plot number two. Eventually, everyone of importance in the storyline is killed off, with only Mitchum's loyal if drab girl (Virginia Huston) remaining. *The Nation's* James Agee claimed that Kirk was "wasted as usual" in the "medium-grade thriller."

Although he was far from "wasted" in his next effort, now for Wallis, Kirk was vociferous in his desire to avoid type-casting in gangster roles, a rut to which he was fast being relegated. Furthermore, he and Burt Lancaster (another Wallis find),[5] with whom he acted in *I Walk Alone* (Paramount, 1947), demanded higher salaries of Wallis. It was a move that, for Kirk, would mean the termination of his pact with his movie benefactor.

Ably directed by Byron Haskins, with a fine score by Victor Young, *I Walk Alone* cast Kirk as Noll Turner, a rich, clever racketeer who has become successful while his partner (Lancaster) sweats out four years in prison. The latter, on his release, wants to cash in on the success, but Kirk's modern, corrupt business system baffles the ex-convict and he finds that he is alone in the world except for a nightclub thrush (Lizabeth Scott), who has switched her allegiance from Kirk to him. The corporation's bookkeeper (Wendell Corey) is murdered by Kirk's men as he pre-

[5]Other Wallis contractees at the time were Lizabeth Scott, Wendell Corey, and Kristine Miller, who were all cast in this packaged deal.

pares to desert the rackets to aid Burt. Lancaster is suspected by the police as the murderer. A trap is set by Lancaster at Kirk's office when the two shoot it out in the dark, with Lizabeth at Burt's side. Actually, the only honest character in the film is the nightclub singer (and her oncamera singing voice is dubbed), but her feeling for Lancaster makes him seem to be an okay guy. In third billing, Kirk stole the acting honors with his by now customary flashy intensity, bristling walk, toothy smile, penetrating eyes, and a cold, sharp voice.

Having arranged for the cutting of his contractual ties to Wallis, Kirk set out on a freelance course, a tricky bit of business in the studio-controlled days of the late 1940s. At Twentieth Century-Fox, he took on a more sympathetic role (fourth billing) in *The Walls of Jericho* (1948), directed by John B. Stahl. He is a newspaper publisher in 1908 Jericho, Kansas, whose uncontrollable wife (Linda Darnell) persuades him to discredit in print his one-time best friend (Cornel Wilde) after Wilde has turned away from her physical advances. Darnell's oncamera virulence is boundless. Kirk weakly takes his cues from her, to the point of publicly ridiculing Wilde, who has become enamored of a law school graduate (Anne Baxter) although he is married to dipsomaniac Ann Dvorak. Later in the plot, Kirk wins a political election and goes to Washington, but his wife remains in Jericho to further spin her evil web, which includes persuading Dvorak to shoot Wilde during a jealous tantrum. The costume drama concludes with Kirk ridding himself of the troublesome wife and with Baxter and Wilde exchanging knowing looks at the hospital (Wilde is recovering from Dvorak's powder blasts).

After five too heavily dramatic films, Kirk, who already had an insatiable need to become an established star, yearned to try something different. He latched onto the

With Ann Dvorak, Cornel Wilde, and Linda Darnell in *The Walls of Jericho* (20th, 1948)

With Keenan Wynn, Helen Walker, Laraine Day, and Rudy Vallee in *My Dear Secretary* (UA, 1948)

With Ann Sothern in *A Letter to Three Wives* (20th, 1948)

108

role of Owen Waterbury in the Harry Popkin production, *My Dear Secretary* (United Artists, 1948), a comedy by Charles Martin. It was a mistake for him, as it was for co-star Laraine Day, the latter having adopted a rather unbecoming blonde coiffure. In the film he is a fun-loving writer whose string of secretaries provide his sexual amusement until Miss Day comes along, with whom he genuinely falls in love. They marry and she also turns to writing, creating a triumph with her first novel. He is jealous of her and they separate, but reunite because . . . because they truly love each other. As Howard Barnes (*New York Herald-Tribune*) accurately pointed out about Kirk and Miss Day, "They both lack the full-spirited ease for this type of fast-moving screwballism." Kirk has even admitted to reporters, "I tried to be a sort of Cary Grant character, and I just was terrible in it. I saw it only in a rough cut. I'd never see it again."

Next, however, in Twentieth Century-Fox's comedy-drama *A Letter to Three Wives* (1948), he came through much better under the subtle, sophisticated direction of Joseph L. Mankiewicz, who also was responsible for the screenplay. In this classic celluloid story of three marriages that have good reason for breaking up, Kirk (again fourth billed) is a teacher of English literature whose attractive wife (Ann Sothern) is a radio soap opera script writer, or, as he puts it, "a fearful, sniveling writer of drooling pap." As the three spouses (Sothern, Linda Darnell, Jeanne Crain) board a riverboat for a day's cruise, chaperoning kids, each is handed, in turn, a letter from the town vamp (never seen, but heard through the narrative voice of Celeste Holm), declaring that she intends to steal one of their husbands. The agonizing boat trip is then devoted to flashbacks while each distraught wife analyzes her marriage. Supporting actresses, Connie Gilchrist and Thelma Ritter as two old beer-guzzling dames, stole each of the scenes in which they appeared.

At MGM, Kirk was all but poised to sign for the third-billed (above the title) role in *The Great Sinner* (1949) when a bid came from a then unknown producer, Stanley Kramer, to star in his proposed production of a Ring Lardner short story called *Champion*. This account of a prizefighter who ruthlessly forces his way to the top appealed to Kirk more than anything that had ever come his way. "The rock-hard fighter I was to play was so off-beat to me," he said, "that I couldn't wait to begin."

Against the advice of agent and friends, he turned his back on the fifty-thousand-dollar offer from MGM (the role would be played by another Douglas—Melvyn) and accepted Kramer's deal for a fifteen-thousand-dollar salary plus a percentage of profits. In persuading a group of hesitant bankers to finance the necessary capital for the venture, Kramer first put Kirk's muscular torso on display and then personally vouched for his acting abilities. While Carl Foreman was honing the Lardner story into script form, Kirk took boxing lessons from a retired fighter, Mushy Callahan.

With *Champion* (United Artists, 1949), Kirk Douglas established himself as one of the toughest, meanest guys on the American screen. As Midge Kelly, he is almost demonically hateful as he stomps on his manager (Paul Stewart), his crippled brother (Arthur Kennedy), a nice girl (Ruth Roman), and a married woman (Lola Albright) in his determination to achieve the position of king in the fight ring.

Told in flashback, the story unrolls as the two brothers arrive in California to claim a restaurant inheritance which turns out to be non-existent. Midge is forced to marry Emma (Roman), a sincere young woman who is too good for him, when her father (Harry Shannon) finds them together. However, he quickly deserts her when

With Ruth Roman in *Champion* (UA, 1949)

the two brothers go to Los Angeles, where Midge enters the boxing profession. As a boxer, he meets Grace Diamond (Marilyn Maxwell), a smart girl involved with the fight ring syndicate. Although he refuses to throw a fight, she intercedes on his behalf to allow him to continue fighting. She is never intimidated by him, but because of her help he is on the way upward.

In pursuit of fame, he dumps his loyal manager (Stewart) and takes on a replacement (Luis Van Rooten), whose comely wife (Albright) he finds more appealing. The new manager pays him to stay away from Albright, which puts an end to that affair. But when Midge learns that Emma intends to divorce him so she may marry his brother, Midge spitefully makes another play for her. The angry brother clobbers him with his cane, but Midge floors him with his fists in a powerful scene that clearly delineates the fighter's unswervingly selfish nature. By now, Midge has become the champ, and in a contest against Johnny Drew (John Day), he receives the beating of his life (a sequence admirably filmed by cinematographer Franz Planer). Despite the walloping he is taking, Midge will not concede defeat in the ring. With a last, strong punch Midge knocks the contender unconscious, but during the fight he had suffered a brain concussion. As he enters the locker room, it is evident that Midge is losing his mind. He brutally smashes his fist into a locker, and later he dies. Of this final scene, Kirk was to say, "It was perfect."

The Mark Robson-directed film became one of Hollywood's biggest hits of 1949, in spite of its being beaten into release by RKO's *The Set-Up* (1949), a film with a similar theme, which starred Robert Ryan. Of the dynamic *Champion*, *Time* Magazine assessed, "[It] is a brilliant example of the kind of punch a small studio can pack, if it has an intelligent script and a smart director."

After three years of filmmaking, Kirk was now one of the hottest boxoffice attractions in Hollywood, known by *his* name and no longer to be confused with Melvyn or Paul Douglas. Critics such as Alton Cook of the *New York World-Telegram* found him to be one of the screen's "most accomplished actors, full of the charm of a leading man, a charm that can become an obvious veneer when he chooses, with a few slight gestures, to hint at the depth of a seething deviltry that lies just beneath."[6]

Eight years after the release of *Champion*, Kirk would confess to Pete Martin of *The Saturday Evening Post:* "When I think of *Champion*, I think about a guy who put all his money on the long shot in a horse race and won. *Champion* made me very lucky. But when it was all done and Stanley [Kramer] held a preview, I still didn't know whether it was good or bad. There were two clues: When I walked outside, people began to ask for my autograph. And, my agent suddenly became very considerate and charming, and asked me to his house for dinner." Not everyone in town was as kind, though, and soon after the impetus of the film's success, columnist Sheilah Graham told him, "You know, Kirk Douglas, you've changed. This *Champion* has really gone to your head, you know. You're such a son-of-a-bitch now." Kirk replied, "You're mistaken. I was a son-of-a-bitch *before Champion*, but you never noticed."

With his cinema career on the upswing, it was ironic but predictable that his domestic life was deteriorating. He and Diana separated in 1949, presumably because of her desire to also pursue an active life of her own in films.[7] Kirk took time to go home to Amsterdam where he visited his family, including his returned father. The latter took advantage of the occasion to introduce his famous son to boilermakers made up of Scotch and beer. Kirk later drove down to New York City for several television and radio appearances on behalf of *Champion*, the film that had cost $600,000 to make and was now such a money winner.

Offers came from every Hollywood studio after *Champion*, but the most enticing one was from Warner Bros. He returned to California to sign a seven-year pact which called for nine pictures and which permitted him to make one film a year for other companies.[8] The package assured his future to the financial tune of one million dollars. (It was all a far cry from the not-so-long-ago days when he was receiving $500 a week under his Hal B. Wallis contract.) Douglas telephoned his mother with the exciting news, saying, "Ma, I'm calling you from California! Listen, I just signed a million-dollar contract." Her concerned reaction was, "That's nice, son, but is it steady?" *Photoplay* Magazine certainly hoped to make it steady by naming him the Number One star of 1949. He upstaged stalwarts Cary Grant and Bob Hope in the magazine's published consideration.

While Twentieth Century-Fox wanted Kirk for a projected feature on the famed German General Rommel, he remained on his new home lot to make *Young Man with a Horn* (Warner Bros., 1950), taken from Dorothy Baker's novelette. Written for the screen by Carl Foreman and Edmund H. North, the film is a highly glossed

[6]Other scribes were equally laudatory in their comments. John Rosenfield of the *Dallas Morning News* decided *Champion* was "a thespic knock-out for 33-year-old Kirk Douglas who has the body for a middle-weight champion and the intuitions of a top theatrical performer." *Time* Magazine reasoned that the film's "final wallop it owes to Kirk Douglas, who fills out every corner of Kelly's unattractive pug with bulging assurance and conviction."

[7]Using the name of Diana Douglas, she cut a narrow swath with minor roles in *The Sign of the Ram* (Columbia, 1948), *House of Strangers* (Twentieth Century-Fox, 1949), *The Whistle at Eaton Falls* (Columbia, 1951), etc.

[8]He had a commitment to do a film per year for Screen Play, Inc., the company which had produced *Champion*.

biography of jazz trumpeter Bix Beiderbecke (1903-1931). Prior to filming, Kirk worked daily for three months with Harry James[9] in order to get the proper feel of handling a trumpet and to insure proper breath control. Compulsive, determined, dedicated, Kirk concluded his music sessions as a fairly competent horn blower. Lauren Bacall, his discoverer, was cast in second billing, and Doris Day found herself in the role of a band singer.

Young Man with a Horn, as whipped into celluloid shape by director Michael Curtiz, begins in flashback as lonely, ten-year-old Rick Martin (Orley Lindgren) finds that he loves the music played by Art Hazzard's (Juano Hernandez) jazz band on Chicago's skid row. He saves enough money to buy a used trumpet of his own and Hazzard teaches him all he knows about music—which, we are to presume, is a great deal. Ten years[10] pass and we now find Rick salaried and performing with a dance band in which pert Jo Jordan (Day)[11] and Smoke Willoughby (Hoagy Carmichael) are members. When Rick and Smoke are fired for attempting to introduce jazz into their playing, Rick heads for New York, where Jo introduces him to Amy North (Bacall), a bored society dame. Amy and Rick fall in love and marry. His music takes a back seat to his attempts at pacifying and keeping up with her socializing, and he soon hits the bottle because of his feelings of artistic unfulfillment.

Later, on learning that Hazzard has died, he attends the funeral, and afterward has a brawl with Amy, who wrecks his collection of phonograph records. He fails to put his life in order and becomes a drinking member of skid row. Jo finds him in a hospital for alcoholics, where he daydreams of hitting an impossibly high note. When he suddenly hears the wail of an ambulance he sits up and whispers, "They told me there was no such note." The last thing we see in this one-hundred-eleven-minute chronicle is a pleasing finale of Rick blowing his horn and sounding just like that ambulance siren.

[9]It was also James' trumpeting that was heard on the soundtrack.
[10]Kirk, at thirty-four, did *not* look twenty.
[11]In Dorothy Baker's story, both Jo and Smoke are black, and they are sister and brother.

With Doris Day in *Young Man with a Horn* (WB, 1950)

Almost needless to say, *Young Man with a Horn* displeased a lot of thinking people. *Time* Magazine offered a quiet critique: "[The film], which starts out to adapt the bestselling story of a jazz musician's integrity, winds up badly in need of some integrity of its own." As for Kirk, *Time* reported: "Actor Douglas gives plenty of vitality to the central role, but he is called on to repeat a good deal of what he did in *Champion*; one scene, in which he bangs a trumpet to pieces and breaks into sobs, is almost a remake of the climax of his earlier film. Having discovered what Actor Douglas does best, Hollywood apparently is determined to work him to death at it." Perhaps *Motion Picture* Magazine summed up the film best when it declared that the story, as compared to the book, was "thoroughly loused up."

But regardless of the feature's artistic integrity or lack of it, *Young Man with a Horn* was a big picture and gave prestige to Kirk's burgeoning screen career. "Today, the movie world is absolutely Kirk's oyster," Hedda Hopper wrote in *Photoplay* of February, 1950. In picking the five actors who would shine as stars in 1950, she named him first, with, "Kirk hasn't a pebble in his path to the all-time Hollywood greatest I predict he'll reach in 1950. The only puff in his sky is a mixed-up marriage, and, in 1950, he just might straighten that out, too."

A few days after the release of *Young Man with a Horn,* the nominations were revealed for the 1949 Academy Award contention. Kirk was in the sweepstakes for the Best Actor Oscar, while Arthur Kennedy was nominated in the Best Supporting Actor category. But both failed to win on the night of March 23, 1950, at the RKO Pantages Theatre. The statuette for Best Actor went to Broderick Crawford of *All the King's Men* (Columbia), while the Best Supporting Actor accolade went to Dean Jagger of *Twelve O'Clock High* (Twentieth Century-Fox).

After the two similar characterizations of doomed men in search of a viable identity, Kirk's next Warners assignment was that of the gentleman caller (Jim)[12] in the Jerry Wald-Charles K. Feldman production of Tennessee Williams' *The Glass Menagerie* (1950). The character of Jim is a man whose brief visit to a St. Louis home unintentionally changes the lives of its inhabitants. The role, although small in comparison to the rest of the cast, is the pivotal one, in that he brings a sense of reality into the lives of the Wingfields, who, heretofore, spent most of their time fantasizing.[13]

The mother, Amanda (Gertrude Lawrence, in a rare screen appearance), dwells in the past, when she was a belle of true southern aristocracy. In the present she causes her shy, lame daughter Laura (Jane Wyman) to withdraw into herself. The retiring girl finds solace in her collection of small glass animals, each as fragile as her timid self. The woman's son, Tom (Arthur Kennedy), has longed to go to sea but has not had the nerve to leave, since his father, a telephone repair man "who fell in love with long distance," had also deserted the family some years before. Amanda consistently begs Tom to bring home an eligible man to meet Laura. He finally invites Jim O'Connor for dinner, not knowing that his acquaintance is already engaged to another girl.

Jim talks with bashful Laura and nicknames her "Blue Roses." They dance together in the parlor where he accidentally brushes against the precious glass figurines. A unicorn is knocked to the floor and loses its horn, but Laura is surprisingly calm over the mishap. Jim takes her dancing at a dancehall down the street and

[12]Originated by Anthony Ross on Broadway in 1945, and played by Sam Waterston in the Katharine Hepburn video version (ABC-TV, December 16, 1973).
[13]"It gives me a chance at a comedy character," he told Hedda Hopper.

gives her her first kiss. Guessing that he might have gone too far for the sheltered girl, he reveals his engagement to a girl named Betty. After he leaves, Amanda is furious, but Laura suddenly realizes that her lameness has been more a result of her shyness than the consequence of physical problems. She becomes a more secure person. Tom bids his family a hasty farewell and goes to sea, leaving them behind to await future gentlemen callers. In his restrained, modified role, Kirk did not have an opportunity to display his usual robust vitality. Thus confined, his performance seemed forced and unfulfilled. As it was, the film was not a commercial success with the general public, who did not cotton to a tale revolving around such generally untypical American folk.

The lofty Cecil B. DeMille considered Kirk, among others, for either of the two male leads for his Technicolor spectacular, *The Greatest Show on Earth* (Paramount, 1952), but settled on Cornel Wilde as the aerialist and Charlton Heston as the circus manager. Instead, Warners cast an already rebellious Kirk in his first Western, *Along the Great Divide* (1951). Described by *Variety* as "just fair entertainment," the tale has him as a U.S. marshal with an unshakable belief that it was he who had been responsible for his own father's death. Kirk enthusiastically devoted himself to learning to ride a horse and to handle pistols.

Most of the outdoor film's action occurs on the trail to Santa Loma, the town where the marshal intends to place his prisoner (Walter Brennan) on trial for murder. On the trip, the group (including deputies John Agar and Ray Teal) meet up with Brennan's feisty, blonde daughter (Virginia Mayo), who tries but fails to rescue her father, and the man who is the actual murderer (James Anderson). At script's end, Brennan is vindicated of all suspicions, while Kirk and Virginia ride off together into the morning sun. The *New York Times'* Bosley Crowther observed that Kirk as a cowpoke "is just a little shy of absurd." The less said about Douglas' singing of the folk song "Down in the Valley" (the theme song here), the better.

Bridling at his lucrative but artistically confining Warner Bros. agreement, Kirk managed two loan-outs in succession, first to Billy Wilder for *Ace in the Hole* (Paramount, 1951), in which he played a cynical, heartless newsman. It was the kind of opportunist role that had won him his screen plaudits in the late forties. To "make sure I wouldn't goof as a screen reporter once I was before a camera," Kirk arranged for a few days' on-the-job-training with the *Los Angeles Herald and Express* as a rewrite man, and wound up with a byline story about a boy who accidentally swallowed poison.

In the black-and-white film, he is Charles Tatum, in need of one journalistic triumph to put himself back on top of the heap. While on his way to cover a snake hunt, accompanied by novice reporter Robert Arthur, he discovers a man (Richard Benedict) who is buried by a cave-in while digging for Indian artifacts. Tatum persuades the sheriff (Ray Teal) to keep the trapped man a secret from other members of the press while he finds a way to dig through to the man. He figures this method will add dramatic impetus to his story. He dissuades rescuers from bracing the tunnel with props in order to get the man out, and talks them into drilling to the man from overhead. This job takes nearly a week, during which time word leaks out of the incident and the area becomes a regular sideshow for sight-seers—ferris wheels, concessions, and even a song written for the doomed man. Tatum seeks out the victim's wife (Jan Sterling), who could not be less concerned, but gets her picture on the front page of his paper accompanying his running saga. When the drilling ends, the man is found dead and Tatum is uncharacteristically

With Jan Sterling in *Ace in the Hole* (Par., 1951)

sorry, but it is too late. He has made a charade of the entire situation, and is stabbed by the man's widow in an unbelievable ending.

Newspapers of America gave little critical support to the film because of its slant on reporters, and it was not a financial success. Later, it was re-released as *The Big Carnival* but the title change deceived few viewers; it remained a boxoffice dud. The film—under both titles—goes down in cinematic history as Wilder's folly. Years later, iconoclastic Wilder was to pat Kirk on the back by saying, "Kirk gives you all he's got. His chest begins to heave even before a director snaps his fingers. He doesn't need violins playing in a corner to put him in the right mood."

William Wyler did better by Kirk in *Detective Story* (1951), distributed by Paramount. Before the filming began, though, Kirk sojourned in New York City for several late nights of involvement at the Sixteenth Precinct stationhouse.[14] Then, back in Hollywood he asked associate producer William Schorr to assemble a stage company so "I could give the role a flesh-and-blood run-through before tangling with the celluloid version." Schorr complied with the request, signing a cast of thirty-five actors to perform the Sidney Kingsley play at the Sombrero Theatre in Phoenix, Arizona, where it was scheduled to open on June 23, 1951.

[14]Douglas likes to recall an episode that occurred during his on-the-job training at the Manhattan precinct. "Late one night I was behind the desk doing the sergeant's job when the cops brought in a petty crook. He had just been caught breaking into a house. . . . I was fingerprinting him, and he kept staring at me. Finally, he said—'You're Kirk Douglas!' And I said, 'If I was Kirk Douglas, with all his money, would I be here taking your fingerprints?' And he said, 'Of course not.'"

Prior to that date, Kirk developed a gigantic case of stage fright. His nervousness at facing a live audience again, after five years of making movies, was compounded by severe laryngitis. Another actor was called in to replace him, but, "I didn't like it at all. I didn't like anyone else playing my part I didn't like sitting on the sidelines." He rallied 'round, and by opening night was in good shape and went on stage as Detective James McLeod of the New York Police Department. "I had been scared," he says. "I never met an actor who didn't have stage fright. Jimmy Cagney calls it 'Flop Sweat.' There's only one cure for Flop Sweat—the fear you may lose the part." The production played the Sombrero Theatre for one week.

Many film enthusiasts credit *Detective Story* as Kirk's "finest hour," although he has said, "The truth is, I'd like to forget that picture. It's a sore point with me." This is said because Hollywood folk informed him, "You're sure to get an Oscar out of this," and, "I didn't even get nominated." The acceptance speech he had prematurely written had to be tossed away.

Within the one-hundred-five-minute feature, which took only five weeks to film (thanks to the extensive rehearsal periods), Kirk's James McLeod[15] is a tough detective. He hates crime and criminals, which, it develops, stems from his mixed respect and disgust for his father who was not altogether an honest man. Kirk is ruthless in his endeavors to the point of beating confessions out of suspects. His loyal wife (Eleanor Parker) complicates matters for him when it is discovered that she had once undergone an abortion, an act he cannot condone.[16] His lack of understanding is further enforced because she had been operated on by a man he detests (George Macready). Kirk's law enforcer cannot forgive or forget, and he sacrifices himself to the bullet of a hoodlum burglar (Joseph Wiseman) as he attempts to escape from the police station. Critics were unanimous in their praise for Kirk's tough acting ("Superb," *New York Times;* "Never before so convincing," *New Yorker;* "A picture of fire and zeal," *New York Herald-Tribune*). Kirk received a Laurel Award from the motion picture exhibitors for his gutsy performance.

In 1951, Diana Douglas obtained a divorce from the man who was now one of Hollywood's most sought-after actors.[17] Their breakup was amenable, with each calling the other "a friend." Kirk once said, "I constantly run into people who think it is vaguely immoral for me to talk about my first wife with respect and admiration. The simple truth is, she deserves it." At the time of the divorce, *Motion Picture* Magazine declared, "Neither has ever discussed the reasons, and the reasons are, of course, their very own. But the timing is a la Hollywood."

By the end of 1951, Kirk wanted out of his Warner Bros. contract. He once confessed, "I had had insurance against insecurity of a sort, but I had made a disturbing discovery; there was nothing in my contract that insured me against getting bad roles." He had turned down several studio projects, including *Fort Worth* (1951), in which he was replaced by Randolph Scott; *Tomorrow Is Another Day* (1951), replaced by Steve Cochran; and *Retreat, Hell!* (1952) replaced by Frank

---

[15]Performed by Ralph Bellamy in the Broadway production of 1949.

[16]At one point in the film, Kirk's character grills his wife about her former men friends. "Seven isn't a few. Did they give you money . . . did they give you presents . . . expensive ones? I'd rather go to jail for twenty years than find out my wife was a tramp."

[17]Interestingly, Kirk was *not* among the top ten money-making stars of 1951 (or any other year) in the Quigley Publications' *Motion Picture Herald*-Fame poll. The top ten in 1952 were John Wayne, Dean Martin & Jerry Lewis, Betty Grable, Bud Abbott & Lou Costello, Bing Crosby, Bob Hope, Randolph Scott, Gary Cooper, Doris Day, and Spencer Tracy.

Lovejoy. However, he finally offered to do *The Big Trees* (1952) without salary, providing Warners would release him from their deal. The studio agreed.

The "trees" in the film's title refer to California's mammoth redwoods, from which fortunes were made in the early 1900s. The scenario, by John Twist and James R. Webb, was ambiguous as to whether Kirk's character was a heel or a hero. He is unscrupulous but rather likeable as the former, but when, in the last thirty minutes, he changes coats and helps the underdog regain his rightful lumber lands, he becomes downright dull. Neither Kirk nor Warners could have chosen a less memorable film (despite the color photography) for his contractual swan song.

According to Kirk, his acting in *The Big Trees* for free was the "sanest thing I've ever done. Since then I've free-lanced and . . . I've been kept busy all the time and I've been able to pick my own stories. Of course, I've made mistakes, in accepting some of the parts I've played, but they've been my own mistakes, and I'd rather have it that way."

His first venture as a free agent was not a mistake insofar as his characterization was concerned, but *The Big Sky* (RKO, 1952) did not make an impressive dent on boxoffice receipts. Produced and directed by Howard Hawks, and based on A. B. Guthrie's novel (scripted by Dudley Nichols), the black-and-white feature is about thirty minutes too long. With screen newcomers Dewey Martin and Elizabeth Coyotte Threatt, Kirk is the sole star. He and Martin are fun-loving, close buddies in nineteenth-century Kentucky who decide to go west for the adventure of finding the latter's Uncle Zeb (Arthur Hunnicutt). They locate him in a St. Louis jail. Afterward, the trio join a fur-trading expedition, whose destination is some thousand miles away. With them is an Indian princess (Threatt) who eventually stirs the interest of both Douglas and Martin, with the woman finally choosing the latter. The zesty role of Deakins was tailor-made for Kirk's vibrant personality.

With Alan Hale, Jr. in *The Big Trees* (WB, 1952)

117

With Barbara Billingsley, Lana Turner, and Marietta Canty in *The Bad and the Beautiful* (MGM, 1952)

In 1952, with an estimated annual income of $300,000, Kirk formed his own production organization, known as Bryna Productions, named in honor of his mother. He talked of putting Ben Hecht's melodrama *The Shadow* on film, but none of his plans for Bryna Productions were to materialize for three years. Instead, he went to MGM for John Houseman's lavish production of *The Bad and the Beautiful* (1952), taken from a story by George Bradshaw and directed by Vincente Minnelli.

In this movie about Hollywood and, specifically, a movie producer, Kirk received second billing as the heel, Jonathan Shields, who molds successful careers for certain individuals but makes enemies of these same people after they have served him. The film opens at the point when he is teetering at the edge of his own washed-up career. He is calling on several people (through his only friend, studio executive Walter Pidgeon) to join forces with him for a blockbusting production. From there, the fascinating story is told in flashback, detailing how he brought fame and high finance to, first, director Fred Amiel (Barry Sullivan), before double-crossing him; second, actress Georgia Lorrison (Lana Turner), whom he raised from alcoholic obscurity to stardom; third, writer James Lee Bartlow (Dick Powell), whose wife (Gloria Grahame) was accidentally killed when sent on a trip by Jonathan to get her out of the way. The trio are invited to Pidgeon's office where they decline unanimously to indulge in any further dealings with Shields. As they pass through an adjoining office, the actress picks up an extension phone and the three huddle close to listen in on the conversation. Although no change of heart takes place oncamera, the audience is left with the assumption that Shields finally will be helped by his three one-time associates.

The Bad and the Beautiful, which cost one and a half million dollars to produce, is a film which should be seen at least twice, because much of the swift dialogue and behind-the-scenes insight into moviemaking is easily missed the first time around. *Motion Picture* Magazine predicted that the film is "so powerful, so wonderful, it's headed for the year's ten best list,"[18] and classified Kirk's performance as a "knockout." Bosley Crowther's remarks in the *New York Times* included the following: "Kirk Douglas plays . . . with all that arrogance in the eyes and jaw that suggests a ruthless disposition covering up for a hurt and a bitter soul."

Kirk's next film, also at MGM, was *The Story of Three Loves* (1953), in which he is a trapeze artist. As is customary with the athletic actor, "I trained for that, too, until I could do some real 'flying.' " The three separate stories are told in flashback, with *Equilibrium* as the title of Kirk's portion. It is the third segment in which he is a famed circus flier whose partner has been killed. He finds a replacement in the person of Pier Angeli, a girl he saves from suicide and whom he suspects will be a good trainee since she has little connection with reality. They fall in love and the film ends as he quits his hazardous profession in order to spend the rest of his life with her, with both feet on the ground.

Offscreen, too, it seemed as though Kirk and Miss Angeli were considering a marital liaison as they began an around-Hollywood romance, but there was not much time to devote to their relationship, since Kirk had been commissioned by Stanley Kramer to portray *The Juggler* (Columbia, 1953) on location in Israel. It almost seemed that Kirk insisted upon portraying men of unusual professions so that he could channel his enormous energies into learning the appropriate physical dexterity required for the role, rather than becoming a bundle of raw nerves anxious to chomp into a new celluloid role.

[18]Regarding Kirk's role in *The Bad and the Beautiful, Variety* observed that he "scores as the ruthless individual out to prove he is the best when it comes to making pictures."

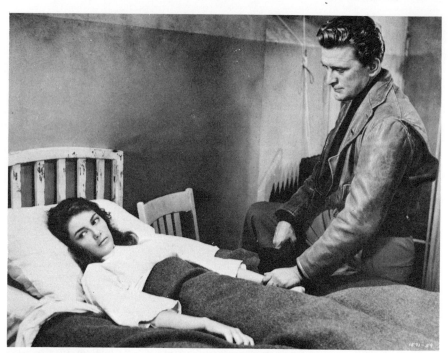

With Pier Angeli in *The Story of Three Loves* (MGM, 1953)

With Marthe Mercadier in *Act of Love* (UA, 1953)

Douglas trained with a professional juggler for several weeks for his role of Hans Muller, a German-Jewish circus performer who has survived a Nazi concentration camp, but suffers from hallucinatory images. He flees from Germany to Israel, where he runs away from the immigration camp because he is reminded of his camp life. In his later flight (he thinks he has killed a policeman), he is befriended in a kibbutz by a boy (Joey Walsh) and by an attractive woman (Milly Vitale). He regains self-confidence by performing his old juggling tricks while dressed as a tramp in white face. At last, he is ready to admit that he requires psychiatric help. Underrated and undersold, *The Juggler* contains some of Kirk's best acting.[19]

From Israel, the dynamic performer went to France for Anatole Litvak's production, *Act of Love* (United Artists, 1953). It was there, in mid-January, 1953, that he met Belgian-born Anne Mars Buydens, blonde, beautiful, poised, divorced, and fluent in four languages. She had been hired by Litvak to handle the chores of publicity because she was acquainted with the motion picture business, having worked as production cordinator with John Huston on *Moulin Rouge* (United Artists, 1952).

Act of Love is another film told by the flashback method: the story of an American soldier who returns to France after the war and reminisces, alone, in the Riviera sunshine. Back in 1944 he had been a clerk with the Allied Liberation Army at the military replacement center in Paris. He had met a French girl (Dany Robin) with whom he had set up housekeeping on the pretense of marriage, because a couple could find housing easier than single people. When the girl is unable to produce identification papers or a marriage certificate, she is listed by the authorities as a prostitute. The soldier's requests for permission to marry her are repeatedly turned down because of the horrendous number of pleas from others who want to marry European girls, which the commanding officer (George Mathews) considers a mistake. The girl kills herself by leaping into the Seine. Having relived his wartime love idyl-tragedy, Douglas' thoughts return to the Hotel Belle Rive at Villafranche, where Kirk's Robert Teller must cope with the present day. The "weak, attenuated script" (*Saturday Review*) received most of the blame for the film's flabby performance.

While Kirk worked in Europe, his peers in Hollywood nominated him a second time as Best Actor in the Oscar race, this time for his stellar performance in *The Bad and the Beautiful*. The leading contender was sentimental favorite Gary Cooper, who had performed so effectively in *High Noon* (United Artists). Cooper won the coveted prize on March 19, 1953, the first televised Oscar show.

In August, 1953, columnist Sidney Skolsky mused, "I wonder if Kirk Douglas is anxious to get back to the U.S. now that the eighteen months tax deal isn't working." But Kirk's mute response was in the form of a shift of scenery to Rome, where he starred as Ulysses in the film of the same name (Paramount, 1954), produced by Dino De Laurentiis and Carlo Ponti and based on Homer's *Odyssey*. "Before playing the title role in *Ulysses*," he was to say later, "I did my best to find out what kind of man he was. After reading the *Odyssey* through twice, I decided that its hero was shrewd, calculating and a warrior who was always on the muscle. The way I saw him, he wasn't unhappy staying away from his wife for such a long time. He was having a ball, roaming and fighting, so he took his time getting home." Anne

[19]Kramer was to later say of his star of *Champion* and *The Juggler*, "Kirk uses his chin the way Marilyn Monroe uses her walk. He thrusts it forward to register masculinity; then pulls it back to indicate tenderness."

In *Ulysses* (Par., 1954)

Buydens also handled the publicity for *Ulysses,* and during the seven months required for filming she and Kirk discovered each other's charms, although he was also still interested in Pier Angeli.

On December 7, 1953, Mrs. Estelle Auguste, the widow of financier Harmon Spencer Auguste and a friend of Kirk's, announced in New York City that she had broken her five-day engagement to Jack Dempsey because of his objection to her friendship with Kirk. Meanwhile, having completed the Italian *Ulysses,* Kirk spent a short vacation in Switzerland with Anne Buydens. From there he went to Jamaica for *20,000 Leagues Under the Sea* (Buena Vista, 1954) for Walt Disney while Anne returned to the Riviera to work with Italian producer Marcello Girosi on *The Monte Carlo Story* (United Artists, 1957).

In the screen adaptation by Earl Fenton of Jules Verne's *20,000 Leagues Under the Sea* (released in the U.S. prior to *Ulysses*), Kirk is Ned Land, a roguish harpoonist who, with Professor Aronnax (Paul Lukas) and Conseil (Peter Lorre), is taken hostage by the fiendish yet ingenious Captain Nemo (James Mason) aboard his 1868 submersible craft. The professor and Conseil are intrigued by their captor and his vessel, but Land encloses messages inside various bottles which he sends above to float on the water in the hope that he will be rescued. Nemo and his crew are dedicated to destroying the world, but turn about to negotiate peace when the *Nautilus* is cornered at its harbor at Vulcania by warships of the upper world, led there by Land's messages. The three captives escape the ship, but Nemo, determined that he will share his secrets with no one, blows up the island, the ship, and

With Peter Lorre and Paul Lukas in *20,000 Leagues Under the Sea* (BV, 1954)

With Anne Buydens on their wedding day (May 29, 1954) in Las Vegas

In *The Racers* (20th, 1955)

himself by means of an enormous time bomb. Interiors and much of the underwater work was accomplished at Disney's Burbank studios where a large tank was constructed to accommodate the two-hundred-foot-long *Nautilus*. This five-million-dollar feature,[20] in which Kirk strummed a guitar and sang "A Whale of a Tale," gained him fans he had never before had—the juvenile generation.

In the spring of 1954, Sheilah Graham observed in her syndicated column, "Pier Angeli expected to be Mrs. Kirk Douglas by the time you read this—but she'll be a very sad little miss. . . ." Miss Graham's remarks referred to the fact that Anne Buydens had joined Kirk in Hollywood. The couple surprised no one by flying to Las Vegas during a lull in the filming of *20,000 Leagues* where they were married on May 29, 1954. She was thirty-one; Kirk was thirty-seven. Eight years later, Mrs. Douglas was to write in *The Saturday Evening Post*, "I was so bewildered and excited I didn't understand everything he [the wedding official] said, so when he said 'lawful wedded husband,' I said 'awful wedded husband.' " The bride's malapropism is evidently something she has never been able to cast aside. Also in 1954, Kirk's father, Harry Danielovitch died in Amsterdam, New York, without ever finding his pot of American gold.

Not one to remain cinematically inactive for very long, Kirk was next seen in *The Racers* (Twentieth Century-Fox, 1955), filmed in Rome, Paris, and around the French Riviera. Aside from its scenery and exciting racing shots which looked superb in CinemaScope and color, the film had little to offer (besides providing a miniature showcase for studio head Darryl F. Zanuck's protegee, Bella Darvi). Kirk performs *a la* Midge Kelly as a man intent on bettering his social and financial levels. Miss Darvi is on hand as a ballet dancer who provides romance and money to the speed demon. The *Saturday Review*, which dismissed the film (quite properly),

[20]The film was awarded Oscars for art direction, set decoration, and special effects.

125

said of the co-stars that they "do not manage to suggest the slightly mad dedication to the world of speed which is the central drama of the film." It would be a later, less noisy, but far more viable racing drama, *Winning* (Universal, 1969), that would demonstrate that the backdrop of this dangerous sport could provide the basis for decent screen fare.

But the film that followed, *Man without a Star* (Universal, 1955)[21] is one of Kirk's best. It is the type of film, obviously a Western from its title, that he rebelled against while under contract at Warners. However, this one cast him as a sexually oriented cowpoke with a sense of humor. He is muscular and robust in his portrayal of Dempsey Rae, a man destined to continually roam the range because he is without benefit of a guiding star. Under the direction of King Vidor, the character emerges as a real being rather than the typically wooden, banal hero of Western films.

As Dempsey Rae, Kirk again sings to his own accompaniment on guitar (the song: "And the Moon Grew Brighter and Brighter"). The man makes pals with a farm boy (William Campbell), in whom he finds a willing student of gunplay and the art of wooing a pretty lady. His sound advice includes, "A stranger doesn't dismount before a ranch house until he's invited to step down," and puts it to use as they stop at the property owned by Reed Bowman (Jeanne Crain was miscast in this role) to seek jobs. They stick around long enough to learn that Reed is an avaricious lovely who wants the entire range land and is disdainful of the small rancher. Dempsey later throws in his lot with the underdog. He is befriended by the town madam

[21]Remade as *A Man Called Gannon* (Universal, 1969) with Tony Franciosa, Michael Sarrazin, and Susan Oliver.

With William Campbell and Jeanne Crain in *Man without a Star* (Univ., 1955)

(Claire Trevor) and roughed up by his job replacement (Richard Boone), and finally gets tough. He leaves town alone (his protégé has been killed) after squaring things with the badmen.

The *New York Times* accoladed Kirk for having "hit a properly satisfactory if not a high note." From his energetic performance, it was impossible to tell that Kirk had broken four ribs during the filming when he fell off a train, causing director Vidor to comment, "Kirk is a tireless worker and a first-rate performer." Mr. Vidor also revealed, "I felt that Kirk was working himself up to being a director and couldn't help in studying a scene the night before, figuring out the way he would do it if he were directing." The director has not stated that this type of practice caused friction between them, but Kirk's reputation for aggressiveness included complaints from co-workers that he was not an easy one with whom to work. In his own defense of such accusations, Kirk has stated simply, "I work hard, I expect everybody else to work hard."

Decca Records produced a forty-five r.p.m. disc of Kirk singing "A Whale of a Tale," from the *20,000 Leagues Under the Sea* soundtrack; the B-side featured his song from *The Man without a Star,* and "my first royalty check came to $1,000." He told Peter Martin of *The Saturday Evening Post,* "My ma keeps harping on what a wonderful country this is, and she's right. I have more nerve than voice, and if a guy like me can collect for a couple of recordings, this is quite a country."

After performing well at European boxoffices (with Kirk's voice dubbed for Continental audiences), *Ulysses* enjoyed a successful British release, although one English scribe put it down because Kirk "plays Ulysses with an American accent." The film reached U.S. audiences on June 29, 1955, when Jack Moffitt of *The Hollywood Reporter* claimed that Kirk "achieves full maturity as an actor. He reaches moments in it he's never reached before." Unfortunately, most critics in America did not agree, nor did its audiences.

On November 23, 1955, a third son was born to Kirk, his first child by Anne. The newest addition to the Douglas line was named Peter.

Bryna Productions finally came forth. Its initial vehicle set out to capitalize on the popularity of the Western film of the fifties with its *The Indian Fighter* (United Artists, 1955). Kirk starred, of course, as a virile frontier scout, Johnny Hawks, hired by the U.S. Army to escort a wagon train of settlers to Oregon when it is stopped by the Sioux. The Indians are not scalp-happy; their chief (Eduard Franz) wants peace, but they will not permit the wagons to pass because of recent trouble caused by white traders who are after the gold that the Indians have hidden away in a mine. Hawks arranges for the signing of a peace treaty which is all but ruined when an Indian is killed by two white men (Walter Matthau and Lon Chaney, Jr.). During the action, Hawks is smitten with love for an Indian girl (played by Italian Elsa Martinelli), romantically pursued by a zealous widow (his real-life ex-spouse, Diana Douglas), and is the victor in a fight with the Indian chief's brother (Harry Landers). Douglas kills Chaney, turns Matthau over to the Indian chief, and marries the Indian girl while the wagon train rolls toward Oregon. Filmed in color in Oregon by director Andre de Toth, Kirk claims to have broken his nose during this one when he fell from a horse.

Vincente Minnelli selected Kirk to portray Vincent Van Gogh (1853-1890) in his directorial assignment at MGM, *Lust for Life* (1956), based on Irving Stone's bestselling biographical novel of 1934. Minnelli was to remember, "Once we received the green light to proceed with the picture, there was no question that Kirk would play

127

In *Lust for Life* (MGM, 1956)

Van Gogh. No other actor was ever considered for the part. Backed by a team of experts,[22] the company went to Europe for authentic Van Gogh backdrops. In addition to letting his beard grow (the hair on his head was lightened, but his beard grew naturally to the desired color to match Van Gogh's), Kirk hired a French artist to teach him to paint crows. "The director had told me that he wanted me to add crows to a painting of a wheatfield [oncamera]—crows in the manner of Van Gogh. In practice sessions I painted more than 800 crows. I am not one of the art world's immortals, but at least I can now catch a crow in flight." Anne Douglas, in her article in *The Saturday Evening Post,* wrote of this period, "Kirk always brings his roles home with him. . . . He came home in that red beard of Van Gogh's wearing those big boots, stomping around the house—it was frightening."

In recreating the Dutch-born artist's adult life, from the film's beginning when he arrives in a Belgian mining town (in 1878) as a man of God to give spiritual aid to the poor, until the last scene when he dies of a self-inflicted gunshot wound in that wheatfield he had captured on canvas, Kirk gave the stellar performance of his acting life to date. His mad scenes were completely realistic, aided by the Miklos Rozsa musical score, and the fact that, facially, Kirk resembled Van Gogh, helped immeasurably. Of course, there is the vivid scene where he mutilates his left ear during an epileptic seizure, a sequence which prompted *Time* Magazine's critic to write, "Because the Hollywood story builds relentlessly to Van Gogh's ear-slicing for its climax, *Lust for Life* falls midway between being a first-rate art film and high-pitched melodrama." Years later (in 1974) Kirk would say, "I've always considered

[22]Photographers Freddie Young and Russell Harlan; art directors Cedric Gibbons, Hans Peters, and Preston Ames.

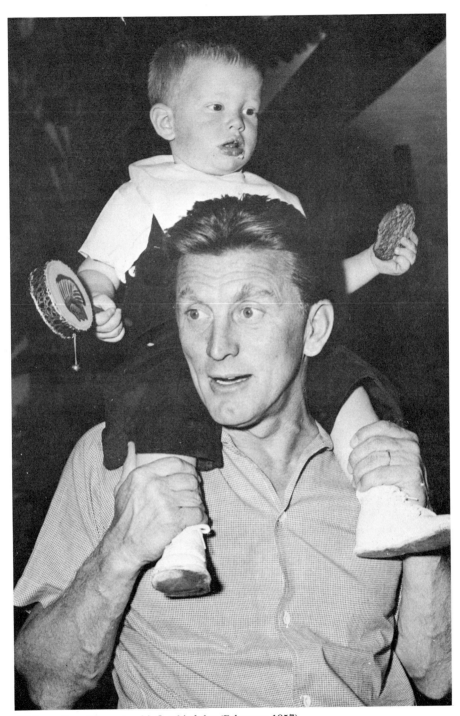

With son Peter Vincent on his first birthday (February, 1957)

myself a character actor," and this statement could not have applied more adequately than to his Van Gogh representation. As Gordon Gow observed in *Hollywood in the Fifties* (1971), "The craggy face of Douglas, beneath the broad-brimmed straw hat, caught the very essence of the artist in decline."

After many months in France, the Douglases returned to Hollywood, where, on August 1, 1956, Kirk filed a $415,000 invasion-of-privacy suit against his former friend, Walt Disney, and the ABC-TV network. He charged that movies of him and his family shot during a social visit to Disney's home had been used on Disney's video program. The suit was eventually settled out of court.

While the New York Film Critics and The Foreign Press named Kirk the best actor of 1956 for his Van Gogh interpretation, he was seen in a comedy taken from a John P. Marquand novel which Warner Bros. had bought originally as a starring vehicle for Humphrey Bogart and Lauren Bacall. Bogart's illness prevented the studio from pursuing its intentions and Kirk was called in to play the leading part in *Melville Goodwin, USA,* which was ultimately changed to *Top Secret Affair* (1957). His co-star was the very beautiful, very high-powered Susan Hayward, who definitely proved that she should have stuck to her forte of screen drama. She is Dottie Peale, a powerful magazine publisher intent on discrediting Major General Goodwin because he was given a top government job for which she considers him unfit. During the course of the publisher's mean campaign her hatred turns to love. The stars look good together, causing the viewer to wonder if they got along offcamera as well as they did while on, since both had well-earned reputations as perfectionists.

In February, 1957, when the Academy Award nominations were published, it came as no surprise to find Kirk Douglas' name on the Best Actor list for *Lust for Life.* Trade magazine advertisements touting his performance had appeared frequently prior to the nominations, but such ads were then seen almost daily through March 27, 1957, the day of the televised Award Show. These costly ads, together with Kirk's sudden guest appearances on the fast-rising coast-to-coast TV talk shows (those of Jack Paar and Mike Wallace), failed to make him a winner, although for many he had seemed a sure bet. Yul Brynner won the Oscar that night at the Pantages Theatre for his re-creation of the monarch's role in the musical *The King and I.* (*Lust for Life* won only one Academy Award: Anthony Quinn was named Best Supporting Actor for his portrayal of Paul Gauguin.)

John Wayne had told Kirk, after seeing *Lust for Life,* "Jeez, Kirk, why in hell did you play this pantywaist? Guys like us, we should play the heroes." As though in proof to people like Wayne that he could still be tough and heroic, Kirk chose as his next role the impersonation of Doc Holliday in *Gunfight at the O.K. Corral* (Paramount, 1957). He and Burt Lancaster revisited the producing facilities of Hal B. Wallis for this fictionalized version of the Earp Brothers and Holliday in the big shoot-out (October 26, 1881) with the dastardly Clantons. As William K. Zinsser (*New York Herald-Tribune*) observed, "No single event in the movie will surprise anybody. But everything is done with an extra degree of quality." Hollis Alpert (*Saturday Review*) added, "Not only has the movie been based on a good deal of fact, but it is far more relaxed than most movies of the type." Concerning this successful genre piece, Alpert also added, "Perhaps we can credit television with helping to return the barroom Western to the state of popularity it generally enjoyed in movie theatres before *High Noon.*" The *Christian Science Monitor* was a little more restrained about this motion picture, which grossed $4.7 million in distributors' do-

THE STRANGEST ALLIANCE
THE SIDE OF HEAVEN OR HELL

...Between the most famed lawman
and the most feared gambler-badman
reached its climax
that deadly day in Tombstone!

BURT   KIRK   HAL   GUNFIGHT AT
LANCASTER · DOUGLAS WALLIS' THE O.K. CORRAL

RHONDA FLEMING · JO VAN FLEET · JOHN IRELAND · Directed by JOHN STURGES   Screenplay by LEON URIS · Music Composed and Conducted by Dimitri Tiomkin · A Paramount Picture

Advertisement for *Gunfight at the O.K. Corral* (Par., 1957)

mestic rental, "In the manner of the latter-day super-Western, *Gunfight at the O.K. Corral* commences atmospherically, lasts for more than 2 hours, and moves portentously to its noisily exciting climax."

Kirk was presented with the Man-of-the-Year Award in 1957 from the Beverly Hills Jewish Council, and during the same year received the Distinguished Contribution Award from the American Labor Council and a Special Award of Merit from the George Washington Carver Memorial Fund. Also in 1957, as he later recalled, "I found a young guy, Stanley Kubrick. He had a script that he was trying to get made called *Paths of Glory*. It was based on a true historical court martial. He couldn't get it made, so with my company, I helped put it together. I thought it was a wonderful picture. I loved it. It never made a nickel."

Filmed in Germany at a cost of $900,000 ($300,000 of which represented Kirk's salary) it is a bleak recording of neurosis and egomania among the French army officers of World War I. Topnotch cinematography by George Krause, whose camera caught the exact look of death in the trenches, was instrumental in making the feature an unforgettable one.

In the eighty-six-minute storyline, the French soldiers are ordered to attack the German forces on Ant Hill, an action that is both ridiculous and foredoomed in that the French are greatly outnumbered both in men and equipment. They make little progress against the superior enemy forces and must remain in their trenches. French General Mireau (George Macready) orders his own artillery to open fire on his Infantry countrymen, but the artillery commander refuses. In a rage, the general orders a retreat and places the entire regiment under arrest. As Colonel Dax, the regimental commander, Kirk is unable to reason with either Mireau or his associate, General Broulard (Adolphe Menjou), who treat the foot soldiers like

131

In *Paths of Glory* (UA, 1957)

pawns in an evening chess game. Dax talks the generals out of court-martialing a section of each of the three companies for cowardice and mutiny and they settle for the trial of one man from each company. Dax, a peacetime lawyer, acts as defense counsel for his men, who are doomed for execution from the beginning because the generals need retribution to cover their own lack of judgment in ordering the attack.

Paths of Glory (United Artists, 1957) is an unusually effective film because the viewer finds himself hating the unjust system; the picture's running time passes very quickly.[23] The production was officially released on November 19 that year, for consideration in the annual Oscar race. The prediction was that Kirk would be again Oscar-nominated, but such was not to be the case. At the ceremonies held on March 26, 1958, at the Pantages Theatre, Kirk joined with Burt Lancaster and others to sing a parody on nominee jitters, entitled "It's Great Not to be Nominated." A few minutes later, the Best Actor Award was extended to Alec Guinness for *The Bridge on the River Kwai* (Columbia).

The Vikings was a 1952 bestselling novel by Edison Marshall about the violent, crafty Norsemen who ruled the seas through the eighth to tenth centuries. On behalf of Bryna Productions, Kirk bought the screen rights and, in June, 1957, flew to Norway with cast and crew. The screen adaptation by Dale Wasserman and Calder Willingham had an original estimated budget of two and a half million dollars, which later rose to $3.7 million. Before the production was completed, however, more than five million dollars were spent on the picture. Rights to the use of a fjord were leased, an area which included an uninhabited rock. On this mammoth stone was constructed a Viking village. Next, a fleet of Viking ships were built, copied from genuine vessels on display in the Oslo Ship Museum. Three of the copies cost $60,000.

Since there were no living quarters for the six hundred people involved with *The Vikings,* Kirk placed them on two vessels (one was a former yacht of Barbara Hutton's) anchored in a cove. Two ferry lines (consisting of seventeen P.T. boats) were then established to transport everyone from the ships to the island, as well as to the nearest town, some nine miles away. Of the sixty days spent in Norway, forty-nine were dark and rainy.[24] At a cost of $45,000 a day, the producers could not afford to wait for sunshine, so cinematographer Jack Cardiff created a special waterproof attachment and the camera rolled. Kirk later said, "The rain scenes have a black, brooding quality that go with the Viking character and the shots of the long ships sailing into the fog are the most beautiful [in Technicolor] I've ever seen on the screen."

The Vikings company later moved to France, where a castle was rented to represent just such a structure in the England of that era, and studio space was taken over in West Germany for interior shots. With regards to costs, Kirk later admitted to Louella O. Parsons, "I started from the bottom before, so if I lose everything I'll just start from the bottom again."

One million dollars was spent publicizing the film with the warning, "The Vikings Are Coming " Newspaper and magazine reviewers throughout the U.S. were sent a

---

[23]The film, as was to be expected, was banned in France in the late 1950s. It was not until October, 1974, when French president Valery Giscard d'Estaing eased the lid on political censorship, that an attempt was made to release *Paths of Glory* in France.

[24]As reported by *Newsweek* Magazine, producer Jerry Bresler inquired of a Norwegian extra, "Does it always rain here?" The boy replied, "I don't know, I'm only eighteen years old."

With Tony Curtis in *The Vikings* (UA, 1958)

plastic Viking ship and a letter opener in the form of a Viking dagger. Seven Norwegian seamen were hired to sail one of the long ships across the Atlantic to New York harbor where they were met in triumph by television cameramen and news reporters.

On June 11, 1958, the film premiered at two major Manhattan movie palaces, the Victoria and the Astor. "I remember driving through Times Square in a big limousine with my mother beside me," Kirk told Katie Kelly of Andy Warhol's *Interview* in February, 1974. "And there was *The Vikings* in lights covering an entire block, with her name, Bryna Productions." On premiere day, Kirk swung off the roof of the Hotel Astor in a bosun's chair and christened an immense sign of a Viking ship with a bottle of fjord water.

The film, hugely popular with the action and kiddie crowds, tells of the rivalry between the sons of Ragnar, the Viking chief (Ernest Borgnine). The son Einar (Kirk) is the heir apparent to the throne that is surrounded by bearded musclemen, while the son Eric (Tony Curtis) is a bastard, the result of Ragnar's ravaging of Northumbria and its queen. Twenty-five years pass, with Eric being brought to Norway as a slave. He and Einar instantly hate each other, although they do not yet know they are half brothers. In one of the gory film's bloodier scenes, Kirk's Einar loses his left eye to the claws of Eric's hawk. In reprisal, Eric is chained in a tidal pool to be eaten by crabs, but his god of war, Odin, saves him. When a Welsh princess (Janet Leigh) is captured and taken to Norway, all the Vikings crave her, but Einar wants her the most of all. The girl, in spite of herself, falls in love with Eric and they

134

escape to England with the Norwegians in pursuit. Eric loses his left hand to the sword of the English king and Einar and Eric later engage in a vicious battle with swords. The former, who now knows that Eric is his brother, cannot bring himself to kill him and, in hesitating, is himself killed. He is given a magnificent Viking funeral. At the film's end, with Ragnar having been tossed into a wolf's pit, "everybody seems to go positively berserk with happiness—except possibly the adult members of the audience" (*Time* Magazine).

The Vikings did not win any Oscars, but it grossed over six million dollars in distributors' domestic rentals.[25] A good degree of the film's popularity must be attributed to the smart casting of the real life husband-and-wife team of Tony Curtis and Janet Leigh in such prominent roles. Above all, such casting proved that when it came to showmanship and the hopes of squeezing out a few more boxoffice dollars, Douglas was not above sacrificing some of the screen limelight.

On June 21, 1958, forty-one-year-old Kirk became the father of a fourth son when Eric Anthony was born in Los Angeles.

In throwing himself vigorously into the business of creating yet another role, Kirk fractured his right arm when he fell over a bar stool in the making of *Last Train from Gun Hill* (Paramount, 1959). Hal B. Wallis had recruited him once again for this John Sturges-directed Western[26] that has him as the Pauley, Oklahoma, marshal whose wife (Ziva Rodann) is raped and murdered by two rowdies (Earl Holliman and Brian Hutton). Then, Bryna Productions paired with Hecht-Hill-Lancaster on *The Devil's Disciple* (United Artists, 1959), one of George Bernard Shaw's plays that the author himself did not like. Kirk and Burt Lancaster are

[25]Kirk talked of a video series of *The Vikings,* in which he intended to use miscellaneous footage of the on-location landscape, etc., but these plans did not materialize.

[26]It was billed as "the most important outdoor drama ever made at Paramount!" The *New Yorker* insisted of Kirk's performance here, that he was "extravagantly dimple-chinned."

With Laurence Olivier, Janette Scott, and Harry Andrews in *The Devil's Disciple* (UA, 1959)

135

reunited as the bumptious, rebellious American colonist[27] and the thelogian-turned-fighter, respectively. Kirk is nothing short of excellent in his portrayal of the early American, but the meat of the film belongs to Laurence Olivier as British General Burgoyne. A talky film, loaded with philosophies, it has never been a popular boxoffice attraction.

In 1960, when adultery-in-the-suburbs and Kim Novak were a few of the more newsworthy items, Bryna and Richard Quine packaged a film version of Evan Hunter's novel, *Strangers When We Meet* (Columbia). Kirk starred as architect Larry Coe who builds "oddball houses" and is verbally abused by his attractive wife (Barbara Rush). Miss Novak co-starred as Maggie Gault, who is beautiful, but sexually neglected by her husband (John Bryant). She and Kirk conduct an affair in motels, at cocktail lounges, at coastside hideaways, and within the unfinished house[28] he is building for a writer (Ernie Kovacs). Unhappy as they allegedly are with their mates, they decide to relinquish their hold on one another when faced with a decision. Each returns to his/her respective spouse.

Strangers When We Meet is lavishly soapy, but has a polish that is enhanced by its capable cast. In one scene, Kirk's character is asked to explain how he manages the shaving technique of his dimpled chin, of which *Newsweek* Magazine asked its readers, "Who else could have handled that one?" Offscreen, it soon became common knowledge that a high degree of rancor existed between Kirk and Kim, which

[27]The role, originated on the New York stage by Richard Mansfield in 1900, was played by Basil Sydney in a 1923 revival and in 1950 by Maurice Evans. In 1933 RKO Radio Pictures shelved plans to film the property with John Barrymore as its star.

[28]Located in Bel Air Canyon, the house, costing $250,000, was later given to Quine as a possible honeymoon site for him and Miss Novak. Their anticipated marriage, however, did not take place.

With Kim Novak in *Strangers When We Meet* (Col., 1960)

prompted Mike Connolly of The *Hollywood Reporter* to suggest a film title switch to *Stranglers When We Meet.*[29]

In January, 1958, Kirk had read a book about the slave rebellion in early Rome, called *Spartacus,* written by Howard Fast. He liked the story and later bought the screen rights for Bryna Productions. Initially set at a budget of six million dollars, it emerged as an even costlier (twelve-million-dollar) venture than *The Vikings,* had an all-star cast and consumed 190 minutes of screen time.

Of the herculean production, Kirk was quoted as saying, "It scares hell out of me, but it's fun." When asked what scared him the most about it, he answered, "When I came on the set before shooting began and saw the row of dressing rooms marked 'Sir Laurence Olivier,' 'Peter Ustinov,' and 'Charles Laughton.' Holy smoke, I thought! Is someone kidding? It's a dream come true. A dream, that's what it is. I don't dare look at it realistically. I mean, if I did I'd get really scared and run away."

His dream took him to Spain where most of the exterior battle scenes were shot, but the remainder of the film was done at Universal Studios and adjoining lots. Because of the California environment, two outdoor scenes had to be re-photographed, once when a plane's vapor trail showed up in the supposed 73 B.C. sky and again when the camera exposed a portion of the busy Hollywood Freeway. In

[29]There had also been a good deal of problems on the sets of *The Devil's Disciple.* Alexander MacKendrick, the film's original director, "walked out" on the production in August, 1958, when he insisted that the venture should not be turned into a sexy adventure yarn. He was replaced by Guy Hamilton. When *The Devil's Disciple* had been reactivated in 1957, Kirk had not been part of the package. The cast then was to consist of Lancaster, Olivier, Montgomery Clift, and Carroll Baker.

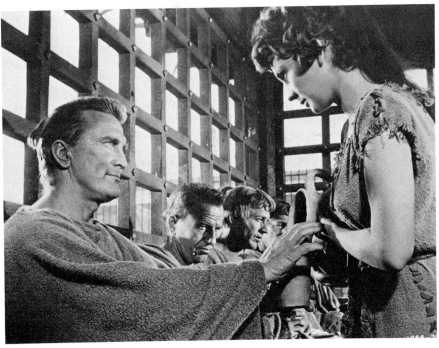

With Jean Simmons in *Spartacus*

addition to the impressive casting mentioned above, there were Jean Simmons, John Gavin, and Nina Foch, plus Tony Curtis (Kirk's buddy) as a handsome Roman slave, a part that was written into Dalton Trumbo's adaptation.

The hero, Spartacus, played by Kirk, is a Tracian slave who escapes from a gladiator training school, 193 miles from Rome. He then frees 90,000 other slaves and spends two years leading them in revolt against Roman control. They defeat nine Roman armies, but meet their match in the battle against the main body of the Roman army under the command of Crassus (Olivier). The rebels are thereafter crucified along the Appian Way.[30]

In this intelligent, Stanley Kubrick-directed epic, Laughton is a Roman senator (described by one critic as "hilarious and frightening as Khruchshev in a bed sheet"); Ustinov is the owner of a slave gladiator school;[31] Gavin is a young, handsome Julius Caesar; and Simmons is a slave girl in love with Spartacus. Permitted to decorate the proceedings with a helping of British cheesecake, the latter is photographed in her bath with the proper amount of propriety for American audiences. For the European viewer, however, Miss Simmons did not object to playing stripped to the waist when Kirk ordered the shooting of a second version of the scene.

While *Motion Picture Herald* credited Kirk with offering "the finest performance of his very active and diversified screen career," *Time* Magazine, however, avowed that the film's success was due to director Kubrick, under whose scrutiny "even wooden-faced Hero Douglas is inspired . . . to achieve a certain consistency of obviousness that, without actual characterization, nevertheless suggests a character." Regardless of which critical faction was correct, *Spartacus* (1960) went on to gross $14.6 million in distributors' domestic rentals.

Kirk then turned to a pair of melodramas, both of which contained a suicide. For Bryna's *The Last Sunset* (Universal, 1961), he led the company to Mexico where the temperature averaged 110 degrees, where baby tornadoes plagued daily filming, and where the non-natives suffered from intestinal infection. In spite of such adversities, they managed to make a film in which Kirk (in second billing—following Rock Hudson) is a murderer pursued by a marshal (Hudson). He visits his former lady love Belle (Dorothy Malone), whom he has not seen in sixteen years, and falls in love with her pert daughter, Missy (Carol Lynley). In the course of the chase, the marshal learns to respect Kirk as they become involved with cattle drives and Indian attacks. As Douglas prepares to run away with the daughter, Belle warns him that it is impossible because he is actually the girl's father. Insisting on a showdown with the marshal, Kirk is killed; it is then discovered that he had intentionally walked into the duel with an empty gun. Robert Aldrich directed this solid, if too glamorous, genre piece.

Germany was the locale of *Town without Pity* (United Artists, 1961), with Kirk again playing a lawyer. He defends four G.I.s (Richard Jaeckel, Robert Blake, Frank Sutton, and Mal Sondock) accused of raping a sixteen-year-old German girl (Christine Kaufmann). The girl had a reputation for being a tease with all the

[30]Kirk has frequently recalled one oncamera episode during the filming. "I got crucified at the end—strung up on a cross. It was the dramatic highlight of the whole picture. But do you know that while this great, emotional, and moving scene was being shot, an extra turned on his transistor radio full blast so he could listen to a baseball game between the Mets and the Dodgers."

[31]Ustinov won a Best Supporting Actor Oscar for his role in *Spartacus*.

With Dorothy Malone in *The Last Sunset* (Univ., 1961)

With Gena Rowlands in *Lonely Are the Brave* (Univ., 1962)

139

fellows, which Kirk uses as his prime weapon in reducing the girl on the witness stand. She collapses and is unable to complete her testimony. The soldiers are given prison sentences. Kirk is not happy with the course of events, but prepares to leave town when he learns that the girl has killed herself rather than face the townspeople.

It was no accident that Kirk continued to become involved with such message films as *Town without Pity*. To a greater degree than friend and frequent co-worker Burt Lancaster, Douglas had a driving need to preach to moviegoers while entertaining them. It was an inner push that often led him into involvement with uncommercial film ventures.

One of Kirk's favorite films is *Lonely Are the Brave* (Universal, 1962), produced by Joel Productions, an offspring of Bryna, named for his second son. He told *Redbook Magazine* in 1966, "I love that picture," and added facetiously, "I think I'm just *wonderful* in it." The whole venture resulted from Douglas having read a paperback novel called *Brave Cowboy*, by Edward Abbey. For three years he tried to arouse Universal's interest, without success, because of the story's social nature, of a man "trying to achieve freedom and how impossible it is." Finally, the studio agreed to do it, with Kirk supplying the completion money and his services as the star. He played a cowboy in modern New Mexico who rebels against the system of society, but who is ultimately destroyed by it when he is killed on a freeway. As Jack Burns, he is the cowboy who is born one hundred years too late, a man who would have thrived on the uncluttered prairie. Although the lovely (and underrated) Gena Rowlands had the feminine lead, there is no romance in the cowboy's life. Dalton Trumbo, of "Hollywood Ten" fame, who had created the anti-establishment scenario for *Spartacus*, was responsible for the screenplay for *Lonely Are the Brave*.

Then, at MGM, the team[32] that had done so well with *The Bad and the Beautiful* ten years earlier tried it again with the screen version of the Irwin Shaw novel, *Two Weeks in Another Town* (1962). Anyone who had read the book was hard pressed to recognize much of the story (not one of Shaw's best); many of the characters reached the screen with altered names.

It is another tale of moviemaking, this time in Italy, and it even went so far as to utilize footage from the 1952 project. Kirk is Jack Andrus, a former film star who has turned to alcohol, largely because of Carlotta Lee (Cyd Charisse), his ex-wife. He is called to Rome by a director friend, Maurice Kruger (Edward G. Robinson), to assist in dubbing a lousy film already in production. When Kruger has a heart attack, Andrus takes over as director and improves many of the scenes and re-shoots several of those that were previously done. Later, he is rebuffed by Kruger, who refuses to acknowledge any improvement in the finished product, and Andrus decides to accept only those offers in the future which are meaningful to him. During the dreary proceedings, he tells a young associate, "You don't need anyone but yourself," which, coming from actor Douglas, seems to epitomize his own convictions.

In 1962, Anne Douglas, in a *Saturday Evening Post* article said, "Living with my husband is like sitting in a beautiful garden right next to a volcano that may erupt at any moment." Mrs. Douglas stated that her spouse's energies were boundless: after working all day, he would come home and change clothes for a quick swim, then

[32]Producer John Houseman, director Minnelli, star Douglas, scripter Charles Schnee, composer David Raksin.

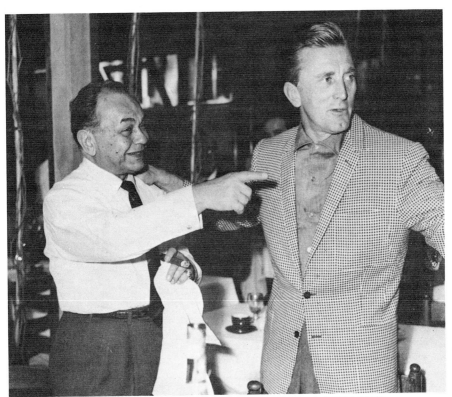

With Edward G. Robinson on the set of *Two Weeks in Another Town* (MGM, 1962)

play tennis, take her for a walk, and make numerous phone calls. He would read a script or view a movie, read the trade papers, and then go to bed. Often during the night, he would awaken with ideas which he jotted down on a bedside pad. She claimed that their marriage lasted because she was not in the acting profession and was, therefore, better able to understand him. They lived in a Beverly Hills home with sons Eric and Peter. Kirk's older children spent their summers with them. Anne was known as one of filmdom's best-dressed ladies who devoted much of her free time to charities.

Kirk's next film, *The Hook* (MGM, 1963), is a talky endeavor which, said the *New Yorker* Magazine, "would certainly have failed if it had tried to come to grips with nobility; in fact, it never catches sight of it, being satisfied to fail through a laborious iteration of the much humbler theme that a man can be taught to behave well by having someone set him a good example." Directed by George Seaton, it is a grainy study in morals, as two soldiers (Robert Walker, Jr. and Nick Adams) and their tough sergeant (Kirk), the only survivors of a bombing attack in Korean waters, rescue a North Korean airman (Enrique Magalona) from the ocean. When they are picked up by a Finnish freighter, the sergeant receives radio orders to execute the "gook" prisoner.

During the boat trip the soldiers and their prisoner are forced to share quarters, with the Korean tied to his bunk. The sergeant, as tough as he is, cannot shoot the

141

With Robert Walker, Jr. in *The Hook* (MGM, 1963)

With George C. Scott in *The List of Adrian Messenger* (Univ., 1963)

man but threatens his countrymen with court-martial when they attempt to help him escape by lifeboat. At the point where the sergeant is exposed as a lonely man facing retirement after twenty years in the military, the word is received of an armistice in the Korean conflict. By this time, the prisoner has cut his bonds and is hiding in the ship's engine room, where the three Americans try to tell him that the fighting is over. He does not understand English and is accidentally killed. As the Korean's draped body is about to be buried at sea, an almost benevolent sergeant says almost softly, "He couldn't understand our words; I hope he'll understand our silence." Of Kirk's performance, *Newsweek* Magazine judged "Douglas, is, as usual, more than competent." The film itself passed into oblivion rather quickly.

If the studios or other producers were not as anxious as they had been in previous years to hire Douglas' expensive services, he was still able to initiate a wide variety of film projects for himself. Kirk's Joel Productions, which owned the murder tale *The List of Adrian Messenger* (Universal, 1963), placed the story (written for the screen by Anthony Veiller and directed by John Huston) before the cameras in England and Ireland. It is a gimmicky photoplay inasmuch as disguise is the key to the whole thing and, to add to the fun, guest stars Tony Curtis,[33] Frank Sinatra, Robert Mitchum, and Burt Lancaster were seen incognito in several scenes. The entire celluloid affair revolved around a complex plot involving a wartime informer (Kirk) and his obsession for gaining control of wealthy British relatives' money (he is Canadian). He kills his eleven buddies from the war (the names on Messenger's list), who could identify him, and then proceeds to do away with each member of the wealthy family.

This film was not successful, nor was Kirk's next effort for Universal, *For Love or Money* (1963), a cute comedy attempt, his first since 1948. He should have known better and stepped aside to allow an actor more proficient at laugh-getting to frolic

[33]On February 8, 1963, at the Riviera Hotel in Las Vegas, Kirk and Anne Douglas stood as witnesses at the marriage of their friend Tony Curtis to Kirk's former co-star, Christine Kaufmann.

With Gig Young and Julie Newmar in *For the Love of Money* (Univ., 1963)

with the likes of Mitzi Gaynor, Gig Young, and Thelma Ritter. Kirk is a glib lawyer who is hired by a rich matron (Ritter) to match her three daughters (Gaynor, Leslie Parrish and Julie Newmar) with suitable husbands, and to manage their financial affairs.

Evidently sensing that he was coming to a crossroads in his professional career, Kirk decided to return to his acting origins, the Broadway stage. On November 13, 1963, he opened at the Cort Theatre in Dale Wasserman's adaptation of *One Flew Over the Cuckoo's Nest*. Douglas appeared as Randle F. McMurphy, a chronic drifter who shoulders his way into a mental ward where he comes into conflict with the head nurse (Joan Tetzel). The glib, vivacious "hero" manages to change several inmates' way of thinking before his adversary (Tetzel) condemns him to a prefrontal lobotomy. He is then smothered to death by a friend who refuses to see the once-lively man continue living as a vegetable. Others in the cast were Gene Wilder and Ed Ames.

The play itself was not greeted with much enthusiasm "[It] is not a sturdy play, nor a comforting play and many will be appalled by it for a variety of reasons. . . ." (Whitney Bolton of *The New York Morning Telegraph*), although Kirk received some fine notices. "I thought Mr. Douglas was just great and he may be able to carry the show" (John McClain, *New York Journal American*). "Douglas deftly keeps him from being too good to be true" (Norman Nadel, *New York World-Telegram*). Even the usually iconoclastic *Village Voice* had to admit, "He [Douglas] really tries. He is warm, likable, and a rather competent actor." However, the sombre play folded after eighty-two performances. A rather bitter Kirk told the press later "Broadway was dead and I didn't know it. There was *Mary, Mary*, a hit, a piece of crap."

Chagrined by this succession of non-boxoffice films and his Broadway failure, Kirk needed a career bolster. He found it in a dramatization of Fletcher Knebel's and Charles W. Bailey II's co-authored novel of political maneuvering, *Seven Days in May* (Paramount, 1964). The screen rights were purchased on behalf of Joel Productions, and, with a screenplay by Rod Serling, the property was produced in conjunction with Seven Arts. Exteriors were filmed in the nation's capital with the full cooperation of President Kennedy and Pierre Salinger, the president's press secretary. John Frankenheimer[34] directed. For the fourth time, Kirk was co-starred[35] with Burt Lancaster.[36] Fredric March was cast as President Jordan Lyman, and Ava Gardner as the former mistress of General Lancaster.

In sharp, adult terms, the story deals with a military plot, headed by General James M. Scott (Lancaster), the chairman of the Joint Chiefs of Staff, to overthrow the U.S. Government when President Lyman signs a nuclear treaty with Russia. As Colonel "Jiggs" Casey, Kirk is General Scott's aide, who, because of his patriotic image, is not included among those service staff men who know of the pending plot.

[34]Frankenheimer and Douglas did not see "eye to eye on the production." As the director has stated, "I had my problems with Ava [Gardner] and, also, with Kirk Douglas. He was jealous of Burt Lancaster. He felt he was playing a secondary role to him. . . . I told him before he went in, he would be. He wanted to be Burt Lancaster. He's wanted to be Burt Lancaster all his life. In the end it came to sitting down with Douglas, saying, 'Look, you prick, if you don't like it, get the hell out.'"

[35]It is interesting to note that Kirk never played opposite any one actress more than once; this can be said of few of Hollywood's male stars.

[36]This would be the last time that Kirk and Lancaster co-starred. Douglas would later say, "I've finally got away from Burt Lancaster. My luck has changed for the better. I've got nice-looking girls in my films now."

With Fredric March and Martin Balsam in *Seven Days in May* (Par., 1964)

145

He is a smart guy, though, and suspects dirty work. He informs the president of his suspicions. At first, the man is disbelieving, but too many puzzling facts are unaccounted for, and the plot is soon exposed, with the help of the president's loyal friend, Alabama Senator Raymond Clark (Edmond O'Brien). "Jiggs" borrows a pack of incriminating love letters from their addressee (Gardner), written to her by Scott. However, these are not required to bring Scott under containment. On television the president asks for and receives the resignations of the chiefs of staff, leaving Scott alone in his defeated plans to become the first American dictator.

Perhaps Mike McGrady (*Newsday*) best summed up the inherent problems of *Seven Days in May*, which, like the similar doomsday story *Fail-Safe* (Columbia, 1964), endured stiff boxoffice resistance. "[*Seven Days*], both as a novel and a movie, is the damnedest story anyone ever heard. And there's a good chance that even a dazzling display of dramatic fireworks won't keep the viewer distracted from reality for two hours." The *Sunday London Times* exclaimed of the film, "It makes the mistake of confusing seriousness with solemnity."

As for Kirk's performance in this heady political melodrama, *Time* Magazine described him as "loyal [cleft chin], but uncertain [tiny eyes]," while the *New York Times'* Bosley Crowther found him "sturdy and valiant." Dwight MacDonald (*Esquire* Magazine) took the opportunity to poke a few jabs at the Douglas image: "Kirk Douglas, togged out in a sharpie uniform that broadens his shoulders and narrows his waist—from the back he looks like Jayne Mansfield—resembles a Broadway tailor's dummy and is sometimes almost as animated."

Seven Days in May, his forty-first film, proved yet another dividing point in Kirk's career. Not only did it conclude his professional relationship with Lancaster,[37] but it also ended another business association, that of producing partner Edward Lewis (who went on to join with John Frankenheimer in a producing company venture). For many people in the industry, it now seemed that Kirk, who had reached his boxoffice peak in the fifties, was losing ground in the sixties, where younger stars (Paul Newman, Jack Lemmon, Richard Burton, Elvis Presley, and Rock Hudson) or much slicker veterans (Cary Grant and John Wayne) were getting and maintaining the public's attention.

Never one to conceal his preference for the Democratic party, Kirk had toured South America as an agent of good will ("It hasn't always been an easy task. But it has been one of the most rewarding experiences of my life.") For President Kennedy in 1963, he talked to students, primarily, for thirty minutes, after which he held a question-and-answer session. In 1964 he traveled to Yugoslavia, Greece, and Turkey in an equal capacity. "I don't go as a salesman trying to sell a picture," he said. "I got there as an American. I *happen* to be a movie star, but I am an American. . . . The whole idea of it is to have a contact—is to communicate."

In 1965, Kirk's eldest son, Michael, a student at the University of California at Santa Barbara, lived off campus in a commune. On visiting his son in the house he shared with other students, Kirk said, "I worked all my life to prevent this kind of misery, and here you are proud of living in this dreadful dump. My God!" His parting verbal salvo to his son was, "I'm not going to give you money to lead the kind of life you have in this pad." Michael was on his own. The twenty-year-old boy

[37]Often compared to Burt Lancaster, sometimes not too favorably, especially by Sheilah Graham, Kirk has stated that he and Burt have always gotten along well, but that there was no conscious or subconscious desire on his part to emulate his friend. "I have enough trouble just being Kirk Douglas."

quit college temporarily and took odd jobs in San Francisco and Hawaii before returning to Santa Barbara to study dramatics.

"It looks like a gut-bustin', mother-lovin' Navy war," Commander Paul Eddington (Kirk) exclaims to Captain Rockwell Torrey. "It does seem to shape up that way, doesn't it?" replies the big captain with the weathered face (John Wayne). These non-shattering remarks are, of course, exchanged after the Japanese have attacked Pearl Harbor and the U.S. Navy is placed *In Harm's Way* (Paramount, 1965). Wendell Mayes' screenplay (from James Bassett's novel) contains many lines similar to the above, and some are even less erudite. Otto Preminger's direction[38] of the film is patterned on those productions of World War II, perhaps intentionally, to cash in on the war nostalgia craze that existed in the mid-1960s. Even many screen personalities popular during the war era were taken from moth balls and placed in supporting roles (Dana Andrews, Franchot Tone, Burgess Meredith, Bruce Cabot, Slim Pickens, with Henry Fonda in a role of cameo proportions).

In Harm's Way, which grossed $4.25 million in distributors' domestic rentals, deals with war and its effects on people, with Kirk as Wayne's flinty sidekick. He is obsessed with bitterness about his young, unfaithful wife being killed in the initial Japanese attack, and he sacrifices his life, later, by flying above the enemy ships to

[38]The usually unenthusiastic Preminger was quite pleased by the cooperation he received from his co-stars in this large-scale production. He said, "What good troopers John Wayne and Kirk Douglas are! I did not even show them the script, just told them the story and they came [to the location site at Ilikai, Waikiki Beach, Honolulu]." As if answering the about-to-be-asked question of whether Douglas showed his usual inclination to take control, Preminger added, "I don't welcome advice from actors; they are here to act."

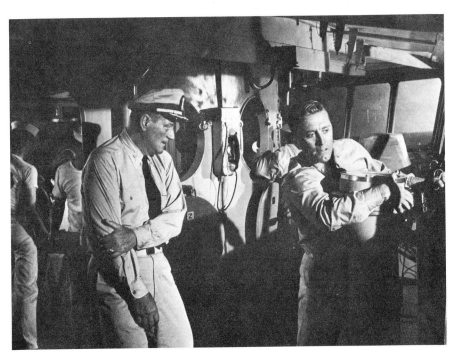

With John Wayne in *In Harm's Way* (Par., 1965)

147

radio report their location. When not distracted by the mawkish soap opera subplots of the film, most audience attention focused on "Duke" Wayne and Patricia Neal, who were being reunited for the first time since *Operation Pacific* (Warner Bros., 1951). Critical reaction to Kirk's bizarre character was mixed. *Variety* reasoned, "He comes through rousingly in a broad and aggressive performance that gives off sparks." Bosley Crowther (*New York Times*), on the other hand, wrote, "Kirk Douglas is awfully shallow, too—just a noisy and naughty tin-can sailor who comes to shameful but sacrificial end." The latter, unfortunately, was closer to the truth in this macabre sentimentalization of the Second World War.

Also, in 1965, Kirk starred with Richard Harris in *The Heroes of Telemark* (Columbia). If even a fraction of the rumors and reports can be accepted as the truth, the greatest friction occurred not oncamera between the opposing war forces, but between the two co-stars each of whom had a definite image of his own importance and just how to project that vision for public consumption. Kirk was cast by director Anthony Mann as Dr. Rolf Pedersen, a Norwegian scientist who thwarts the German endeavor to create the atomic bomb in 1943. Harris was on hand as the tough underground leader. The film was partially shot in Norway during the winter of 1964-1965 in sub-zero weather, according the cameras extensive and beautiful coverage of snow-covered mountain sides. Although a well-devised, suspenseful venture, the film was not a winner, because audiences, fickle as always, seemed then to be weary of grim recounts of World War II.

Kirk might have finally won that elusive Academy Award, had he not rejected the role of the drunken gunfighter in Columbia's *Cat Ballou* (1965). He claims his agent badgered him out of accepting the role, and "it would have been a perfect part for me." It seems odd that a man as strong-willed as Kirk would have permitted an agent to talk him out of something he considered right for himself, but, be that as it may, Lee Marvin took the role which gained him the Best Actor Award for 1965.

Instead, Kirk trekked back to Israel for *Cast a Giant Shadow* (United Artists, 1966), as the American Army officer David "Mickey" Marcus, who, in 1947, was asked by the Israelis to organize an army to defend their country against the Arabs. Within this true story, guest appearances were made by John Wayne (the film was co-produced by Wayne's son Michael), Yul Brynner, and Frank Sinatra, none of whom added much substance to the initially serious venture. After all of Colonel Marcus' heroics in the course of the hundred-forty-one-minute color feature, he is killed by one of his own Israeli sentries because, by not learning the Hebrew language, he could not respond to the sentry's command. Of Douglas' performance in this modestly successful, oversized feature, the British had quite a few perspicacious observations to make. In *Films and Filming*, Allen Eyles noted, "Kirk Douglas is an engaging actor, I find, but it's not until the end of the film that you realise what engaged him about the part . . . which ends in the same way as about every other straight part Douglas has played." The *Monthly Film Bulletin* observed that, although Kirk played his part with "tight-lipped efficiency, [it] never emerges as what it should be—the cornerstone of the film."

Next in Kirk's hyperactive career came *Is Paris Burning?* (Paramount, 1966), an overly ambitious production with fifteen international screen stars in what amounted to cameo roles. Based on the book by Larry Collins and Dominique Lapierre, the film relates the final days of the Nazi occupation of Paris and the Nazi commandant's (Gert Frobe) unhurried obeisance to Hitler's frantic order to burn the city before the Allied Armies' take-over. Filmed in the Paris of 1965 and utiliz-

With Senta Berger and Rina Ganor on the set of *Cast a Giant Shadow* (UA, 1966)

149

ing left-over war equipment, the chronicle is told from the viewpoints of the French, the German and the allied liberators. Kirk appears briefly as General George Patton (giving nowhere near the bite to the iconoclastic general that George C. Scott did in his Oscar-winning performance of *Patton* [Twentieth Century-Fox, 1970]). The over-all effect of *Is Paris Burning?* is one of utter confusion. It is often impossible for the viewer to decide if the characters oncamera are the good French or the Communist collaborators. The editing of the film, even in the original release version, is often incoherent.

"I've done a few cowboys," Kirk has said. "I've done a different one every time." In *The Way West* (United Artists, 1967) he is something of a dandy, a U.S. Senator with a vision of establishing civilization in the Oregon territory of 1843. After organizing the Oregon Liberty Company, he inspires a group of malcontents to leave Missouri via wagon train to help him build cities in the far west. The trip is filled with people with problems, including Robert Mitchum, miscast as a scout. Richard Widmark is on hand with a pretty wife (Lola Albright), whom the widowed Douglas seems to covet. When Kirk's young son (Stefan Arngrim) is killed in a buffalo stampede, the senator asks his black slave to whip him as punishment for not having treated the boy more kindly. Afterward, he becomes even more of a demagogue until the company revolts against him and Widmark takes over as their leader. Finally, when the senator is killed while descending a gorge, the wagon train continues westward to fulfill his original dream. The long (one hundred twenty-two minutes) feature turned out to be a tedious melange.

In his eleventh Western, *The War Wagon* (Universal, 1967), Kirk is a hired gun-slinger commissioned by badman Bruce Cabot to rid the world of big John Wayne. Instead of killing Wayne, he becomes his partner in an often comic attempt to steal

With Stefan Arngrim in *The Way West* (UA, 1967)

150

With John Wayne in *The War Wagon* (Univ., 1967)

Cabot's tank-like wagon filled with gold bullion. It is a rapid-paced, shoot-'em-up production, with the weird casting of Howard Keel as an Indian. Although Kirk appears to leap agilely onto a horse oncamera without difficulty, in truth he uséd a springboard that was hidden from the camera. Also, during the course of filming, he fractured the little finger of his right hand while drawing his gun (his fourth career accident to result in a broken bone). For the record, *The War Wagon*, which top-cast Wayne, provided fifty-one-year-old Kirk with his first nude scene oncamera. In one lighthearted bit it is revealed that Kirk's character may wear his holstered six-shooters to bed, but beyond that, he sleeps in the raw.

"I think Frank Gorshin is brilliant," Kirk has said of the man who impersonates him so well. "I've talked with comedians and apparently I'm not easy to imitate. But he—as a matter of fact, he can be more me than I am." Along with his imitation of Kirk, Gorshin has mastered the art of impersonating Cagney, Lancaster, and Widmark, among others, not only in their voices but in their facial gestures, as well. All of this just goes to prove the point that by the mid-sixties Kirk was an American institution. How well revered this living landmark was, and still is, remains a moot question.

Kirk's only celluloid outing of 1968 was *A Lovely Way to Die* (Universal), in which he is a policeman forced into resignation because of his tough treatment of crooks. Reminiscent of his McLeod role in *Detective Story*, his character says, "I just can't get used to coddling criminals." He is hired by a lawyer (Eli Wallach) as a bodyguard to his client (Sylvia Koscina), who is charged with the murder of her husband (William Roerick). In the scheme of things, Kirk falls for the lady who is proved innocent of the charges against her. The film was all done in an unimpressive manner which would have made the project more viable as a run-of-the-mill telefeature.

151

With Sylva Koscina in *A Lovely Way to Die* (Univ., 1968)

With Susan Strasberg, Luther Adler, Alex Cord, Connie Scott, and Irene Papas in *The Brotherhood* (Par., 1969)

In the year that Mario Puzo's *The Godfather* was attracting millions of book readers, Kirk produced and starred in his own tale of Mafia leadership squabbles, *The Brotherhood* (Paramount, 1969). With a moustache and dyed hair he is Frank Ginetta, a middle-aged syndicate board member who opposes expansion into areas that might cause intervention by the Federal government. When his young brother (Alex Cord) is discharged from the army and decides to join the organization, Frank says, "You don't know how long I've been waiting to hear you say that. Ginetta Brothers—what's better than that?" But, when Frank continually refuses to agree to involvement with the electronic unions, the other board members threaten to replace him with his brother. Meanwhile, deposed Mafia leader Don Peppino (Eduardo Ciannelli) informs Frank that his fellow board member Dominick Bertolo (Luther Adler), years ago, had betrayed forty loyal Mafia members who were later massacred by the new regime. Since one of the forty had been Frank's and Vince's father, Frank is compelled by tradition to avenge the murder. He kills Bertolo brutally and flees to Sicily with his wife (Irene Papas). Vince is then ordered to go to Sicily and "hit" his brother or suffer the consequences of losing his wife (Susan Strasberg). Frank quickly guesses why Vince has come to see him, and after telling his wife good-bye, takes him into an almond orchard where he hands him their father's rifle and tells him that he must shoot. After exchanging the kiss of death, Vince, knowing that he has no other viable alternative, kills his brother. Despite the fault that the film takes itself too seriously, especially given the rather specious presentation, it deserved a much kinder box office fate than it received. *Variety* thoughtfully acknowledged of Kirk that "after treading water, although quite competently, for the past several years in starring roles, Kirk Douglas forges ahead with an outstanding role and an outstanding personal production."

His next film was anything but outstanding. With *The Arrangement* (Warner Bros., 1969), Kirk hit an all-time low due to the poorly directed, badly produced and scripted Elia Kazan venture. Marlon Brando had been set for the lead role in early 1968, but then walked out on the project. After some delay, Kirk was chosen as a suitable replacement. Douglas appears as Eddie Anderson, a successful advertising executive who outwardly has everything life can provide. His assets include a comely wife (Deborah Kerr) and an attractive mistress (Faye Dunaway), but he is disenchanted with life and falls into an emotional abyss. He attempts suicide, burns down his father's (Richard Boone) house, and is later shot by Dunaway. He survives these many crises to permit his incarceration in a mental institution, in which he obviously should have been put from the start. Eddie Anderson turns out to be a character whom audiences did not care about one way or another. Just as the ambiguously promoted "Kiss of Death" aspect of *The Brotherhood* had received the most attention from the public, so Deborah Kerr's nude scenes in *The Arrangement* demanded most of the moviegoers' otherwise vague interest. It seemed that the time of Kirk Douglas' audience hold was diminishing rapidly.

In *There Was a Crooked Man* (Warner Bros.-Seven Arts, 1970), Kirk has the title role of a thoroughly dishonest man who robs a rancher of $500,000, hides the cache in a rattlesnake pit, and is sent to prison[39] for his deed. The remainder of the wry film deals with his plot to escape, which he does, only to die by a rattlesnake bite in his neck as he reaches into the desert pit for the money. His pursuer, Henry Fonda as the prison warden, then returns Kirk's body to prison, but trails off to Mexico

[39] A walled prison was especially built for the production in the desert of California's Joshua Tree National Monument, at a cost of $300,000.

153

With Deborah Kerr in *The Arrangement* (WB-7 Arts, 1969)

On the set of *Hail, Hero* (National General, 1969) with son Michael.

With Michael Blodgett and Warren Oates in *There Was a Crooked Man* (WB-7 Arts, 1970)

155

with the loot. It all proved director-producer Joseph L. Mankiewicz's proposition that "there's a little bad in every good man." For this undeservedly overlooked Western gem, Kirk dyed his hair red and wore glasses.

Then, in *A Gunfight* (MGM, 1971), he and Johnny Cash are a pair of legendary gunmen who stage an arena-style gunfight with paid admissions. Kirk, as Will Tenneray, is the town's favorite, but he is not quick enough for the lightning-fast draw of his opponent and dies in the bullring. It is a strange commentary on man's quest for a quick buck and the public's urging for any type of thrill (here, a gladiator-style duel). Filmed in New Mexico, the low-keyed feature was financed by the Jicarilia Apache Indian tribe of that state.

Already in his mid-fifties, Kirk no longer could hope to portray convincingly the still-youthful, if middle-aged, hero, and thus he turned to character leads as a new avenue of continuing his already lengthy career. The subtle switching of type parts began with *The Light at the Edge of the World* (National General, 1971) which derived from a Jules Verne novel of 1865. It dealt with a lighthouse at the southernmost tip of South America, at Cape Horn. (The film was actually shot in Spain, where the ocean waters were less perilous.) The lighthouse in question is staffed by three men (Kirk, Fernando Rey, and Massino Ranieri), two of whom are murdered by pirates led by bloodthirsty Yul Brynner. Kirk escapes, is captured, and escapes a second time. Eventually, he blows the pirate ship to smithereens, killing the nasty pirate, who by this time has ordered the slaughter of countless passengers and crews of ships he has lured to the lighthouse. Unlike *20,000 Leagues Under the Sea,* which had grossed a hefty $11 million in distributors' domestic rentals, *Lighthouse,* which was never geared for any one particular market (adult, action, kiddie, or television), was not among the top boxoffice attractions of its year.

In 1971, for the first time, Kirk produced a film (*Summertree* [Columbia]) without appearing in it. Instead, his son Michael had the lead part in this study of the generation gap. On the other hand, it might have been better if Kirk had not been involved in any way or shape with *Catch Me a Spy* (J. Arthur Rank, 1971), a very lacklustre entry in the spy film genre. The thin plotline revolves around the heroine (Marlene Jobert) who romantically snags herself a spy (Kirk) after attempting to trade him off to the Russians in exchange for her husband's (Patrick Mower) release.

Before 1973, Kirk's television acting had been limited to the narration on ABC of the Christmas special, *The Legend of Silent Night* (December 25, 1968). His on-tube acting debut occurred on March 7, 1973, when he was seen in the title role(s) of *Dr. Jekyll and Mr. Hyde,*[40] set to music! Filmed in England and presented by Timex, in color on the NBC network, Kirk did his best, but it was not enough to save the very stagey presentation from being a consummate bore. As *Variety* analyzed it, "Problem is that almost anything can be forgiven in a rehash of Jekyll-Hyde except a lack of dramatic fun and gusto."

Almost all of the Douglas family, including their Labrador retriever, "Shaft," went on location to Yugoslavia for the Bryna Production of *Scalawag* (Paramount, 1973), directed by and starring Kirk, with Anne Douglas serving as producer. From

[40]Portrayed on film by John Barrymore in 1920 (Paramount), Fredric March in 1932 (Paramount), Spencer Tracy in 1941 (MGM), and caricatured by Jerry Lewis in 1963's *The Nutty Professor* (Paramount) and by Ralph Bates and Martine Beswick, respectively, in *Dr. Jekyll and Sister Hyde* in American International's 1973 release. On television, Jack Palance, in the 1973 Canadian-shot television special, tackled the Stevenson classic.

In *Scalawag* (Par., 1973)

a Robert Louis Stevenson story of a one-legged rogue named Peg (Kirk), who leads a group of cutthroats on a California treasure hunt in the 1840s, the film was still-photographed by son Peter and assistant-produced by son Eric. The project was premiered in fifty major U.S. and Canadian cities in October, 1973, to benefit The Big Brothers of America movement. "I tried to make a family film and, by golly, I've done it," Kirk told Radie Harris of *The Hollywood Reporter.* "I designed it as entertainment for parents as well as for kids." It might have been nice for Kirk's declining boxoffice standing, if he had designed a moneymaker. (The film had cost two million dollars, with the Douglases supplying half of the financing.)

My Father Gave Me America, a documentary, was seen on WNEW-TV, New York, on New Year's Eve, 1973. The sixty-minute tribute to the millions of immigrants who have come to the U.S. in search of their dreams was hosted by Kirk, who was also given the opportunity to speak of his own parents. Greer Garson and Ossie Davis were others who helped to relate the history of early Americans. "All in all," said *Variety,* "it was a contemporary update of the 'immigrant dream'—and still a source of inspiration."

Next, Kirk starred in a Saturday night ABC-TV "Suspense Movie" on March 9, 1974, called *Mousey.* Directed by Daniel Petrie and filmed in Montreal, the thriller was made by the newly-formed RSO (Robert Stigwood Organization), in association with Universal, and was slated for theatrical release outside the United States. Kirk is George Anderson, a timid man who teaches high school biology and is called "Mousey" by his students. His ten-year marriage has ended in an ugly divorce, with his ex-wife, Laura (Jean Seberg), taking custody of the child she bore to his name, although he was not the father. In the divorce court, she made public the information that he was incapable of fathering a child and then took the son to the home of

With Jean Seberg in *Mousey* (ABC-TV, 1974)

158

her boyfriend (John Vernon). When Laura refuses to let the youngster retain the Anderson name, George plots her death.

Wearing horn-rimmed glasses and a greasy hat, Kirk looked anything but the hero of such epics as *The Vikings*, or *Spartacus*. "I was always the toughest, meanest hell," he told syndicated writer Bart Mills. "My image, or whatever you call it, was bigger than life. But what was I trying to prove? I don't always have to play Spartacus." When asked if he was using his name to cash in on the "horror quickie" film genre, he replied, "That's a lot of dung. I'll act as long as I want to, as long as I'm believable. There's no age limit."

Also in March, 1974, he prepared for a public service film concerned with energy conservation, and he co-hosted (with Jack Benny and Gloria Swanson), *Paramount Presents*, a tribute to that company's sixty-second anniversary celebration on ABC-TV's "ABC Wide World of Entertainment." Then, in May of 1974, Warner Bros. quietly tossed into release *The Master Touch*.[41] One critic called the Italian-West German production, "[an] imported and dreary safe cracking meller. . . . Little domestic potential." Kirk is the safecracker, fresh out of jail, who arranges a million-dollar insurance company theft which backfires. He loses his long-suffering wife (Florinda Balkan) and gets tossed back into prison. Ironically, on May 2, 1974, while he was in Miami promoting the film, Kirk's suite at the Palm Bay Club was robbed of five hundred dollars, according to news reports. Kirk later said of the robber, "That guy was sharp—he should've played the role in the movie."

One wonders when Kirk and Anne Douglas find sufficient time to enjoy their two homes—one, at Palm Springs and the other, an estate in Beverly Hills (their neigh-

[41]Originally a National General picture, it was included in the library picked up by Warner Bros. as a part of its First Artists acquisitions.

In *The Master Touch* (WB, 1974)

159

With Alexis Smith in *Jacqueline Susann's Once Is Not Enough* (Par., 1975)

bors are Rosalind Russell and Rona Barrett). In the summer of 1974, they were off to Spain, New York, Switzerland, and back to Los Angeles, where Kirk took on a starring role in Paramount's *Jacqueline Susann's Once Is Not Enough* (1975). Kirk is the protagonist named Mike Wayne, suspiciously akin to Mike Todd. Douglas was not British director Guy Green's choice for the role; he wanted Dick Van Dyke. Green further made himself unpopular with Douglas when it was suggested that he permit his chin dimple to be filled in with makeup, which Green felt would give Kirk a needed new image. Douglas' retort was, "You hired me, you know what I look like. How dare you suggest that I change my looks." For the prestigious production, Kirk dieted to the point where he weighed in at 175 pounds, only two pounds above his weight in 1949 when he played in *Champion*. The ostensible reason for losing weight was that he had a semi-nude scene in the picture.

By the time the film opened in mid-1975, the famed Miss Susann had succumbed to cancer. It was just as well the publicity-conscious authoress was not around to witness the botch made of her sizzling novel. As *Time* magazine lambasted: "There is something exhilarating about inadvertent comedy. Few things are as bracing as the spectacle of a lot of people spending good money trying to be serious and making fools of themselves. . . . As for the actors, they are all worthy of every moment of this film, which is both the most and least that can be said of them."

It was a toss-up which were the more offensive and embarrassing moments in the picture. There is the interchange between Deborah Raffin and David Janssen:

> RAFFIN: *We had something special once, didn't we?*
> JANSSEN: *Yeah.*
> RAFFIN: *But once is not enough!*

For most it was the self-conscious lesbian love scenes between Alexis Smith and Melina Mercouri.

160

Reportedly, three different endings for the confused melodrama were lensed, the producers baffled at how to conclude the lugubrious soap opera. The finale chosen (Raffin pondering the death of Douglas and her lost love with Janssen) did little to endear the film with the cynical public.

More substantial but less commercial was Kirk's Bryna Production of *Posse* (Paramount, 1975) shot in Tucson, Arizona in September-October, 1974. Directed by Kirk, who had a secondary part (to that of Bruce Dern), the film marked the return to the screen of James Stacy, who had lost an arm and a leg in a 1973 motorcycle accident. Kirk was the first producer to come forth with a definite, humane offer for the one-time leading man. Despite public apathy, the film received some sterling reviews. As the British *Monthly Film Bulletin* offered, "That rarity of recent years—a taut, well-made Western that delivers its message about the dangers of political machines and the ambition that drives them with a welcome lack of visual or verbal rhetoric. The connections with recent American history—from Vietnam to Watergate—are there for the asking, but it is to the film's credit that it is not begging for them to be made."

In his *Hollywood Reporter* review of *Posse,* critic Arthur offered a brief editorial. "After at least two dozen Westerns, Douglas has announced that *Posse* will be his last. 'After the 1890s,' he has said, 'you jump into the Twentieth Century where the West, except for myth, disappears.' Perhaps so, but that's no reason for not going back farther in time and re-evaluating the myths of the past. As an actor, Kirk Douglas has always been particularly at home on the range. Now, as a director, he seems even more so. It would be a shame if he were to let this very special talent languish." (Kirk reportedly later agreed to make *Una Desperado* in Italy with Lee Van Cleef.)

In *Posse* (Par., 1975)

Kirk traveled throughout Western Europe promoting his two 1975 Paramount releases. In early July, 1975, he was at the Berlin Film Festival where *Posse*, according to *Variety's* reporter, was greeted with "thunderous applause." He delivered a "crowd-pleasing presentation speech—entirely in German, to warm response."

Kirk's son Michael, after a few television stints, hit pay dirt with the teleseries, "The Streets of San Francisco," and in late 1974 made the filmed production of *One Flew Over the Cuckoo's Nest*, with Jack Nicholson in Kirk's Broadway lead role. Michael's co-producer was brother Joel. The film opened in late 1975 to phenomenal reviews and box-office response. Peter Douglas is currently a freelance photographer and has said, "I want to be known as Peter Douglas rather than Kirk's son."

Meanwhile, the symbol of ruggedness that is Kirk Douglas seems to know no bounds. Recently he was signed to star in a four-hour TV version of Arthur Hailey's best-seller, *The Moneychangers*. The NBC-TV mini-series is to be directed by Boris Sagal, produced by Ross Hunter and Jacques Mapes, and to co-star Christopher Plummer.

Kirk Douglas is a man who has admitted about his offscreen personality: "I'm not a very good actor because I can't fake it. If I don't like someone that person knows at once how I feel. It's really hard for me to mask my feelings. I'm often accused of being too direct, too frank, even when I guard my speech." As for the movie industry: "A film-maker's principal responsibility is to entertain. Many highfalutin' directors are ashamed if their films are unabashedly commercial. I'm proud when mine are seen by lots of people who get totally lost in the story." As for his future: "I've been reported to be thinking about retirement. Well, I've thought of it, indeed. But I don't think I can manage it. My wife would never agree. Maybe she doesn't want me hanging around the house."

Kirk claims to have only ambition left in life: "I would like to write just one book. I have already put down about 1,000 pages of my autobiography. There is no final title yet, but I was thinking of calling it, *My Life Is a B-Script*."

KIRK DOUGLAS

THE STRANGE LOVE OF MARTHA IVERS *(Paramount, 1946), 117 min.*

Producer, Hal B. Wallis; director, Lewis Milestone; story, Jack Patrick; screenplay, Robert Rossen; art directors, Hans Dreier, John Meehan; set decorators, Sam Comer, Jerry Welch; music, Miklos Rozsa; assistant director, Robert Aldrich; sound, Harold Lewis, Walter Oberst; process camera, Farciot Edouart; camera, Victor Milner; editor, Archie Marshek.

Barbara Stanwyck (Martha Ivers); Van Heflin (Sam Masterson); Lizabeth Scott (Toni Marachek); Kirk Douglas (Walter O'Neil); Judith Anderson (Mrs. Ivers); Roman Bohnen (Mr. O'Neil); Darryl Hickman (Sam as a Boy); Janis Wilson (Martha as a Girl); Ann Doran (Secretary); Frank Orth (Hotel Clerk); James Flavin, Max Wagner (Detectives); Mickey Kuhn (Walter as a Boy); Charles D. Brown (Special Investigator); Matt McHugh (Bus Driver); Walter Baldwin (Dempsey the Garage Owner); Catherine Craig (French Maid); Sayre Dearing, Harry Leonard (Crap Shooters); William Duray (Waiter); Payne B. Johnson (Bellboy); Tom Fadden (Taxi Driver); Blake Edwards (Sailor); Betty Hill (Waitress); Tom Schamp, Robert Homans, Kernan Cripps (Cops); Thomas Louden (Lynch the Butler); Kay Deslys (Jail Matron); John Kellogg, Tom Dillon (Plainclothesmen); Bob Perry (Bartender); Olin Howlin (Newspaper Clerk).

MOURNING BECOMES ELECTRA *(RKO, 1947), 173 min.*

Producer, Dudley Nichols; associate producer, Edward Donahue; director, Nichols; based on the play by Eugene O'Neill; screenplay, Nichols; assistant director, Harry Mancke; art director, Albert S. D'Agostino; set decorators, Darrell Silvera, Maurice Yates; music, Richard Hageman; orchestrator, Lucien Calliet; music director, C. Bakaleinikoff; dialogue director, Jack Gage; sound, Earl Wolcott, Clem Portman; special effects, Vernon L. Walker, Russell Cully; camera, George Barnes; editors, Roland Gross, Chandler House.

Rosalind Russell (Lavinia Mannon); Michael Redgrave (Orin Mannon); Raymond Massey (Ezra Mannon); Katina Paxinou (Christine Mannon); Leo Genn (Adam Brant); Kirk Douglas (Peter Niles); Nancy Coleman (Hazel Niles); Henry Hull (Seth Beckwith); Sara Allgood (Landlady); Thurston Hall (Dr. Blake); Walter Baldwin (Amos Ames); Elisabeth Risdon (Mrs. Hills); Erskine Sanford (Josiah Borden); Jimmy Conlin (Abner Small); Lee Baker (Reverend Hills); Tito Vuolo (Joe Silva); Emma Dunn (Mrs. Borden); Nora Cecil (Louise Ames); Marie Blake (Minnie Ames); Clem Bevans (Ira Mackel); Jean Clarenden (Eben Nobel); Andre Charlot (Dr. Hamil); Robert Dudley (Chemist); Colin Kenny (Policeman); Marjorie Eaton (Woman at Home); Hans Hopf, Gordon Warren (One-legged Soldiers); Broderick O'Farrell (Station Master).

OUT OF THE PAST *(RKO, 1947), 97 min.*

Executive producer, Robert Sparks; producer, Warren Duff; director, Jacques Tourneur; based on the novel *Build My Gallows High* by Geoffrey Homes; screenplay, Homes; music, Roy Webb; music director, C. Bakaleinikoff; assistant director, Harry Mancke; art directors, Albert S. D'Agostino, Jack Okey; set decorator, Darrell Silvera; sound, Francis M. Sarver, Clem Portman; special effects, Russell A. Cully; camera, Nicholas Musuraca; editor, Samuel E. Beetley.

Robert Mitchum (Jeff Bailey); Jane Greer (Kathie Moffatt); Kirk Douglas (Whit); Rhonda Fleming (Meta Carson); Richard Webb (Jim); Steve Brodie (Fisher); Virginia Huston (Ann); Paul Valentine (Joe); Dickie Moore (The Kid); Ken Niles (Eels); Lee Elson (Cop); Frank Wilcox (Sheriff Douglas); Jose Portugal, Euminio Blanco, Vic Romito (Mexican Waiters); Jess Escobar (Mexican Doorman); Primo Lopez (Mexican Bellhop); Tony Roux (Joe Rodriguez); Sam Warren (Waiter at Harlem Club); Mildred Boyd, Ted Collins (People at Harlem Club); Caleb Peterson (Man with Eunice); Theresa Harris (Eunice); James Bush (Doorman); John Kellogg (Baylord); Oliver Blake (Tillotson); Wallace Scott (Petey); Michael Branden (Rafferty); William Van Vleck (Cigar Store Clerk); Phillip Morris (Porter); Charles Regan (Mystery Man); Harry Hayden (Canby Miller); Adda Gleason (Mrs. Miller); Manuel Paris (Croupier).

I WALK ALONE *(Paramount, 1947), 98 min.*

Producer, Hal B. Wallis; director, Byron Haskin; based on the play *Beggars Are Coming to Town* by Theodore Reeves; adaptors, Robert Smith, John Bright; screenplay, Charles Schnee; art directors, Hans Dreier, Franz Bachelin; set decorators, Sam Comer, Patrick Delany; music, Victor Young; song, Ned Washington and Allie Wrubel; dialogue director, Joan Hathaway; assistant director, Richard McWhorter; sound, Harry Lindgren, Walter Oberst; process camera, Farciot Edouart; camera, Leo Tover; editor, Arthur Schmidt.

Burt Lancaster (Frankie Madison); Lizabeth Scott (Kay Lawrence); Kirk Douglas (Noll Turner); Wendell Corey (Dave); Kristine Miller (Mrs. Richardson); George Rigaud (Maurice); Marc Lawrence (Nick Palestro); Mike Mazurki (Dan); Mickey Knox (Skinner); Roger Neury (Felix).

THE WALLS OF JERICHO *(Twentieth Century-Fox, 1948), 106 min.*
Producer, Lamar Trotti; director, John M. Stahl; based on the novel by Paul Wellman; screenplay, Trotti; art directors, Lyle Wheeler, Maurice Ransford; set decorators, Thomas Little, Paul S. Fox; music, Cyril Mockridge; orchestrators, Herbert Spencer, Maurice De Packh; music director, Lionel Newman; assistant director, Arthur Jacobson; costumes, Kay Nelson; makeup, Ben Nye; sound, Alfred Bruzlin, Roger Heman; special effects, Fred Sersen; camera, Arthur Miller; editor, James B. Clark.

Cornel Wilde (Dave Connors); Linda Darnell (Algeria Wedge); Anne Baxter (Julia Norman); Kirk Douglas (Tucker Wedge); Ann Dvorak (Belle); Marjorie Rambeau (Mrs. Dunham); Henry Hull (Jefferson Norman); Colleen Townsend (Marjorie Ransome); Barton Mac-Lane (Gotch McCurdy); Griff Barnett (Judge Hutto); William Tracy (Cully Caxton); Art Baker (Peddigrew); Frank Ferguson (Tom Ransome); Ann Morrison (Nellie); Hope Landin (Mrs. Hutto); Helen Brown (Mrs. Ransome); Norman Leavitt (Adam McAdam); Whitford Kane (Judge Foster); J. Farrell MacDonald (Bailiff); Dick Rich (Mulliken); Will Wright (Dr. Patterson); Daniel White (Loafer); Les Clark (Photographer); William Sheehan (Reporter); Gene Nelson, Jack Gargan (Assistant Prosecutors); James Metcalfe (Court Clerk); Douglas Carter (Interne); Paul Palmer (Policeman); Oliver Hartwell (Bootblack); Edward Clark (Barber); Joe Forte, Charles Marsh, Lou Mason, Ralph Littlefield, William H. Gould (Politicians); Dorothy Granger, Ann Doran (Gossips); Cecil Weston (Head Nurse); Gene Collins (Harmonica Player); Patricia Morison (Mrs. Landon); Brick Sullivan (Iceman); David Hammond (Messenger Boy); Guy Beach (Hack Driver); Robert Filmer, Wallace Scott, Herbert Heywood, Fred Graff (Toughs); Morgan Farley (Proprietor); Kay Riley (Woman).

MY DEAR SECRETARY *(United Artists, 1948), 83 min.*
Executive producer, Harry Popkin; producer, Leo C. Popkin; associate producer, Joe Nadel; director and screenplay, Charles Martin; art director, Rudi Feld; set decorator, Raymond Boltz, Jr.; music director, Edward Kay; assistant director, Melville Shyer; sound, L. J. Myers; camera, Jackson Rose; editor, William Austin.

Laraine Day (Stephanie Gaylord); Kirk Douglas (Owen Waterbury); Keenan Wynn (Ronnie Hastings); Helen Walker (Elsie); Rudy Vallee (Charles Harris); Florence Bates (Mrs. Reeves); Alan Mowbray (Deveny); Grady Sutton (Sylvan Scott); Irene Ryan (Mary); Gale Robbins (Dawn O'Malley); Virginia Hewitt (Felicia Adams); Abe Reynolds (Bill the Taxi Driver); Jody Gilbert (Hilda Sneebacher); Helene Stanley (Miss Pidgeon); Joe Kirk (Process Server); Russell Hicks (Dick Fulton); Gertrude Astor (Miss Gee); Marten Lamont (Simpson the Secretary); Ben Welden (Bookie); Charles Halton (Mr. Kilbride); Stanley Andrews (McNally); Dorothy Vaughan (Mrs. Hastings); Dewey Robinson (Croupier).

A LETTER TO THREE WIVES *(Twentieth Century-Fox, 1948), 103 min.*
Producer, Sol C. Siegel; director, Joseph L. Mankiewicz; based on the novel *A Letter to Five Wives* by John Klempner; adaptor, Vera Caspary; screenplay, Mankiewicz; art directors, Lyle Wheeler, J. Russell Spencer; set decorators, Thomas Little, Walter M. Scott; music, Alfred Newman; orchestrator, Edward Powell; assistant director, Gaston Glass; makeup, Ben Nye; costumes, Kay Nelson; sound, Arthur L. Kirbach, Roger Heman; camera, Arthur Miller; editor, J. Watson Webb, Jr.

Jeanne Crain (Deborah Bishop); Linda Darnell (Lora May Hollingsway); Ann Sothern (Rita Phipps); Kirk Douglas (George Phipps); Paul Douglas (Porter Hollingsway); Barbara Lawrence (Babe); Jeffrey Lynn (Brad Bishop); Connie Gilchrist (Mrs. Finney); Florence Bates (Mrs. Manleigh); Hobart Cavanaugh (Mr. Manleigh); Patti Brady (Kathleen); Ruth Vivian (Miss Hawkins); Thelma Ritter (Sadie); Stuart Holmes (Old Man); George Offerman, Jr.

(Nick); Ralph Brooks (Character); Joe Bautista (Thomasino); James Adamson (Butler); John Davidson, Sammy Finn (Waiters); Mae Marsh (Woman); Carl Switzer, John Venn (Messengers); Celeste Holm (Voice of Addie).

CHAMPION *(United Artists, 1949), 99 min.*

Producer, Stanley Kramer; associate producer, Robert Stillman; director, Mark Robson; based on the story by Ring Lardner; screenplay, Carl Foreman; production designer, Rudolph Sternad; set decorator, Edward G. Boule; music and music director, Dmitri Tiomkin; assistant director, Ivan Volkman; makeup, Gus Norin; costumes, Adele Parmenter; sound, Jean Speak; camera, Franz Planer; editor, Harry Gerstad.

Kirk Douglas (Midge Kelly); Marilyn Maxwell (Grace Diamond); Arthur Kennedy (Connie Kelly); Paul Stewart (Tommy Haley); Ruth Roman (Emma Bryce); Lola Albright (Mrs. Harris [Palmer]); Luis Van Rooten (Jerome Harris); John Day (Johnny Dunne); Harry Shannon (Lew Bryce).

YOUNG MAN WITH A HORN *(Warner Bros., 1950), 111 min.*

Producer, Jerry Wald; director, Michael Curtiz; based on the novel by Dorothy Baker; screenplay, Carl Foreman, Edmund H. North; art director, Edward Carrere; music director, Ray Heindorf; music advisor, Harry James; camera, Ted McCord; editor, Alan Crosland, Jr.

Kirk Douglas (Rick Martin); Lauren Bacall (Amy North); Doris Day (Jo Jordan); Hoagy Carmichael (Smoke Willoughby); Harry James (Offcamera Trumpeter); Juano Hernandez (Art Hazzard); Jerome Cowan (Phil Morrison); Mary Beth Hughes (Marge Martin); Nestor Paiva (Louis Galba); Orley Lindgren (Rick as a Boy); Walter Reed (Jack Chandler); Jack Kruschen (Cab Driver); Alex Gerry (Dr. Weaver); Jack Shea (Male Nurse); James Griffith (Walt); Dean Reisner (Joe); Everett Glass (Man Leading Song); Dave Dunbar (Alcoholic Bum); Robert O'Neill (Bum); Paul E. Burns (Pawnbroker); Julius Wechter (Boy Drummer); Ivor James (Boy Banjoist); Larry Rio (Owner); Hugh Charles, Sid Kane (Men); Vivian Mallah, Lorna Jordan, Lewell Enge (Molls); Bridget Brown (Girl); Dan Seymour (Mike); Paul Dubov (Maxie); Keye Luke (Ramundo); Frank Cady (Hotel Clerk); Murray Leonard (Bartender); Hugh Murray (Doctor); Dick Cogan (Interne); Katharine Kurasch (Miss Carson); Burk Symon (Pawnbroker).

THE GLASS MENAGERIE *(Warner Bros., 1950), 106 min.*

Producers, Jerry Wald, Charles K. Feldman; director, Irving Rapper; based on the play by Tennessee Williams; screenplay, Williams, Peter Berneis; art director, Robert Haas; music, Max Steiner; camera, Robert Burks; editor, David Weisbart.

Jane Wyman (Laura Wingfield); Kirk Douglas (Jim O'Connor); Gertrude Lawrence (Amanda Wingfield); Arthur Kennedy (Tom Wingfield); Ralph Sanford (Mendoza); Gertrude Graner (Woman Instructor); Cris Alcaide (Paul); John Compton (Young Man); Ann Tyrell (Department Store Clerk); Dick Bartell (Barman); Sarah Edwards (Mrs. Miller);Victor Desney, Peter Camlin, Philip Ahn (Sailors); Louise Lorrimer (Miss Porter); Perdita Chandler (Girl in Bar); Marshall Romer, James Horn (Callers); Sean McClory (Richard).

ALONG THE GREAT DIVIDE *(Warner Bros., 1951), 88 min.*

Producer, Anthony Veiller; director, Raoul Walsh; story, Walter Doniger; screenplay, Doniger, Lewis Meltzer; art director, Edward Carrere; music, David Buttolph; camera, Sid Hickox; editor, Thomas Reilly.

Kirk Douglas (U.S. Marshal Clint Merrick); Virginia Mayo (Ann Keith); John Agar (Billy Shear); Walter Brennan (Pop [Tim] Keith); Ray Teal (Deputy Lou Gray); Hugh Sanders (Sam Weaver); Morris Ankrum (Ned Hoden); James Anderson (Dan Hoden); Charles Meredith (The Judge); Lane Chandler (Sheriff); Kenneth MacDonald (Crowley the Rancher); Steve Clark (Witness); Carl Harbaugh (Jerome); Zon Murray (Wilson the Witness); Sam Ash (Defense Counsel); Steve Darrell (Prosecutor); Al Ferguson (Bailiff); Guy Wilkerson (Jury Foreman).

ACE IN THE HOLE (a.k.a., THE BIG CARNIVAL, *Paramount, 1952), 111 min.*

Producer, Billy Wilder; associate producer, William Schorr; director, Wilder; screenplay, Wilder, Lesser Samuels, Walter Newman; assistant director, C. C. Coleman, Jr.; art directors, Hal Pereira, Earl Hedrick; music, Hugo Friedhofer; song, Ray Evans and Jay Livingston; technical advisors, Agnes Underwood, Harold Hubbard, Wayne Scott, Dan Burroughs, Will Harrison; sound, Harold Lewis, John Cope; camera, Charles Lang, Jr.; editors, Doane Harrison, Arthur Schmidt.

Kirk Douglas (Charles Tatum); Jan Sterling (Lorraine Minosa); Bob Arthur (Herbie Cook); Porter Hall (Jacob Q. Boot); Frank Cady (Mr. Federber); Richard Benedict (Leo Minosa); Ray Teal (Sheriff); Lewis Martin (McCardle); John Berkes (Papa Minosa); Frances Dominguez (Mama Minosa); Gene Evans (Deputy Sheriff); Frank Jaquet (Smollett); Harry Harvey (Dr. Hilton); Bob Bumpas (Radio Announcer); Geraldine Hall (Mrs. Federber); Tim Carey (Construction Worker); Bob Kortman (Digger); Edith Evanson (Miss Deverich); Ralph Moody (Kusac the Miner); Claire Dubrey (Spinster); William Fawcett (Sad-Faced Man); Larry Hogan (Television Announcer); John Bud Sweeney, Stanley McKay, Bert Stevens, Frank Parker (Reporters); Lester Dorr (Priest); Martha Maryman (Woman); William N. Peters, Chico Day (Photographers); Roy Regnier (Nagel); Oscar Belinda (Barker); Iron Eyes Cody (Indian Copy Boy); Charles Griffin (Newspaper Man); Ken Christy (Jessop); Bert Moorhouse (Morgan); Basil Chester (Indian); Frank Keith (Fireman).

DETECTIVE STORY *(Paramount, 1951), 105 min.*

Producer, William Wyler; associate producer, William Schorr; director, Wyler; based on the play by Sidney Kingsley; screenplay, Philip Yordan, Robert Wyler; art directors, Hal Pereira, Earl Hedrick; camera, Lee Garmes; editor, Robert Swink.

Kirk Douglas (Jim McLeod); Eleanor Parker (Mary McLeod); William Bendix (Lou Brody); Cathy O'Donnell (Susan); George Macready (Karl Schneider); Horace McMahon (Lieutenant Monahan); Gladys George (Miss Hatch); Joseph Wiseman (Burglar); Lee Grant (Shoplifter); Gerald Mohr (Tami Giacoppetti); Frank Faylen (Gallagher); Craig Hill (Arthur); Michael Strong (Lewis Abbott); Luis Van Rooten (Joe Feinson); Bert Freed (Dakis); Warner Anderson (Sims); Grandon Rhodes (O'Brien); William "Bill" Phillips (Callahan); Russell Evans (Barnes); Edmund Cobb (Detective Ed); Burt Mustin (Willie the Janitor); James Maloney (Mr. Pritchett); Howard Joslin (Gus Keogh); Lee Miller (Policeman); Mike Mahoney (Coleman); Catherine Doucet (Mrs. Farragut); Ann Codee (Frenchwoman); Ralph Montgomery (Finney); Pat Flaherty, Jack Shea (Desk Sergeants); Bob Scott (Mulvey); Harper Goff (Gallantz); Charles D. Campbell (Newspaper Photographer); Donald Kerr (Taxi Driver); Kay Wiley (Hysterical Woman).

THE BIG TREES *(Warner Bros., 1952), C-89 min.*

Producer, Louis F. Edelman; director, Felix Feist; story, Kenneth Earl; screenplay, John Twist, James R. Webb; art director, Edward Carrere; music, Heinz Roemheld; assistant director, Frank Mattison; camera, Bert Glennon; editor, Clarence Kolster.

Kirk Douglas (Jim Fallon); Eve Miller (Alicia Chadwick); Patrice Wymore (Daisy Fisher); Edgar Buchanan (Yukon Burns); John Archer (Frenchy LeCroix); Alan Hale, Jr. (Tiny); Roy Roberts (Judge Crenshaw); Charles Meredith (Elder Bixby); Harry Cording (Cleve Gregg); Ellen Corby (Mrs. Blackburn); William Challee (Brother Williams); Lester Sharp (Gray); Mel Archer (Ole); Billy McLean (Ivan); Elizabeth Slifer (Mrs. Wallace); Duke Watson (Murdock); Michael McHale (Accountant); Lillian Bond, Vickie Raaf, Kay Marlow (Daisy's Girls); Sue Casey, Ann Stuart (Young Ladies); Art Millan (Charlie); Iris Adrian (Girl in Bar); William Vedder (Man).

THE BIG SKY *(RKO, 1952), 140 min.*

Producer-director, Howard Hawks; based on the novel by A. B. Guthrie, Jr.; screenplay, Dudley Nichols; assistant director, Arthur Rosson; art directors, Albert S. D'Agostino, Perry Ferguson; set decorators, Darrell Silvera, William Stevens; assistant director, William McGarry; costumes, Dorothy Jeakins; makeup, Mel Berns, Don Ash; sound, Phil Brigandi, Clem Portman; special effects, Donald Steward; camera, Russell Harlan; editor, Christina Nyby.

Kirk Douglas (Deakins); Dewey Martin (Boone); Elizabeth Threatt (Teal Eye); Arthur Hunnicutt (Zeb); Buddy Baer (Romaine); Steven Geray (Jourdonnais); Hank Worden (Poordevil); Jim Davis (Streak); Henri Letondal (Labadie); Robert Hunter (Chouquette); Booth Colman (Pascal); Paul Frees (MacMasters); Frank de Kova (Moleface); Guy Wilkerson (Longface); Cliff Clark (Jailer); Fred Graham (Eggleston); George Wallace, Max Wagner, Charles Regan (Friends); Sam Ash, Abe Dinovitch (Singers); Don Beddoe (Horse Trader); Jim Hayward, Anthony Jochim (Trappers); Nolan Leary (Store Keeper); Frank Lackteen (Indian); Sherman Sanders (Dance Caller); Ray Hyke (Bartender); Eugene Borden (Tavern Proprietor); Veola Vonn (Bar Maid); Cactus Mack (Streak Man); Theodore Last Star (Chief Red Horse); Crane Whitley (Henchman).

THE BAD AND THE BEAUTIFUL *(MGM, 1952), 118 min.*

Producer, John Houseman; director, Vincente Minnelli; story, George Bradshaw; screenplay, Charles Schnee; art directors, Cedric Gibbons, Edward Carfagno; music, David Raksin; camera, Robert Surtees; editor, Conrad A. Nervig.

Lana Turner (Georgia Lorrison); Kirk Douglas (Jonathan Shields); Walter Pidgeon (Harry Pebbel); Dick Powell (James Lee Bartlow); Barry Sullivan (Fred Amiel); Gloria Grahame (Rosemary Bartlow); Gilbert Roland (Victor "Gaucho" Ribera); Leo G. Carroll, (Henry Whitfield); Vanessa Brown (Kay Amiel); Paul Stewart (Syd Murphy); Sammy White (Gus); Elaine Stewart (Lila); Jonathan Cott (Assistant Director); Ivan Triesault (Von Ellstein); Kathleen Freeman (Miss March); Marietta Canty (Ida); Lucille Knoch (Blonde); Steve Forrest (Leading Man); Perry Sheehan (Secretary); Robert Burton (McDill); Francis X. Bushman (Eulogist); Harold Miller (Man); Ned Glass (Wardrobe Man); Sandy Descher (Little Girl); George Lewis (Lionel Donovan); Dee Turnell (Linda Ronley); George Sherwood (Cameraman); Bob Carson (Casting Director); Barbara Billingsley (Lucien); Alex Davidoff (Priest); Madge Blake (Mrs. Rosser); Lillian Culver (Real Estate Woman); William Tannen, Dabbs Greer, Frank Scannell, Sara Spencer (Reporters); Stanley Andrews (Sheriff); John Bishop (Ferraday); William E. Green (Hugo Shields); Phil Dunham (Pawn Broker); Marshall Bradford, Pat O'Malley (Men Outside Club); Harte Wayne (Judge); Paul Power (Theatre Manager); Karen Verne (Rosa); Eric Alden (Stunt Man); Dorothy Patrick (Arlene); Stuart Holmes, Reginald Simpson, Larry Williams (Poker Players); Roger Moore (Cigar Clerk); Peggy King (Singer); Bess Flowers (Joe's Friend at the Party); Major Sam Harris (Party Guest); A. Cameron Grant (Assistant Director).

167

THE STORY OF THREE LOVES *(MGM, 1953), 122 min.*
Producer, Sidney Franklin; music, Miklos Rozsa; choreography, Frederick Ashton; art directors, Cedric Gibbons, Preston Ames, Edward Carfagno, Gabriel Scognamillo; camera, Charles Rosher, Harold Rosson; editor, Ralph E. Winters.

The Jealous Lover: director, Gottfried Reinhardt; screenplay, John Collier; camera, Charles Rosher.

Moira Shearer (Paul Woodward); James Mason (Charles Coudray); Agnes Moorehead (Aunt Lydia); Jacob Gimpel (Pianist); Miklos Rozsa (Conductor); John Lupton (Studious Young Man); Jack Raine (Doctor); Lysa Baugher (Ballerina); Flo Wix, Towyna Dally, Colin Kenny, Major Sam Harris (Ad Libs); Ottola Newsmith (Usher); Bruce Lansbury, Bruce Edwards, Ivan Hayes (Chorus Boys); Anne Howard, Paula Allen (Chorus Girls); Reginald Sheffield (Production Manager).

Mademoiselle: director, Vincente Minnelli; story, Arnold Phillips; screenplay, Jan Lustig, George Froeschel; camera, Harold Rosson.

Farley Granger (Thomas Campbell, Jr.); Leslie Caron (Mademoiselle); Ethel Barrymore (Mrs. Pennicott); Ricky Nelson (Tommy); Zsa Zsa Gabor (Girl Flirt); Paula Raymond (Mrs. Campbell); Hayden Rorke (Mr. Rorke); Larry Olsen (Terry); Robert Horton (Young Man on Boat); Manuel Paris (Mr. Carlos); Alberto Morin (Mr. Sandes); Andre Simeon (Waiter); Z. Yacconelli (Bellhop); Peter Brocco (Bartender); Phyllis Graffeo (Italian Girl); Argentina Brunetti (Saleswoman); Nick Thompson (Coachman) Tom Quinn (American Man in Bar); Rudy Lee (Little Boy); Noreen Corcoran (Little Girl); Ernesto Morelli (Railway Porter); Ed Agresti (Railway Conductor); Victory Desny (Italian Air Force Officer).

Equilibrium: director, Reinhardt; based on a story by Ladislas Vajda; adaptors, Lustig, Froeschel; screenplay, Collier; camera, Rosher.

Pier Angeli (Nina); Kirk Douglas (Pierre Narval); Richard Anderson (Marcel); Steven Geray (Legay); Alix Talton (Rose); Karen Verne (Mdme. Legay); Torben Meyer (Man); Ken Anderson (Jacques); Peter Norman (Rudolph Kramer); Jack Tesler (Bartender); Joan Miller (Woman on Bridge); Paul Bryar (River Policeman); Kay English (Nurse); Elizabeth Slifer (Concierge); Christofer Appel (Boy); Bertha Feducha (Woman Vendor); Frank Scannell (Master of Ceremonies); Paul Maxey (Bill Cyrus); Leo Mostovoy (Stranger in Cafe); Frank Wilcox, John Pickard (Ship's Officers).

THE JUGGLER *(Columbia, 1953), 84 min.*
Producer, Stanley Kramer; director, Edward Dmytryk; based on the novel by Michael Blankfort; screenplay, Blankfort; art director, Robert Peterson; music, George Antheil; camera, Roy Hunt; editor, Aaron Stell.

Kirk Douglas (Hans Muller); Milly Vitale (Ya'El); Paul Stewart (Detective Karni); Joey Walsh (Yehoshua Bresler); Alf Kjellin (Daniel); Beverly Washburn (Susy); John Banner (Emile Halevy); Charles Lane (Rosenberg); Richard Benedict (Kogan); Oscar Karlweis (Willy Schmidt); John Bleifer (Mordecai); Greta Grandstedt (Sarah); Jay Adler (Papa Sander); Shep Menken (Dr. Traube); Gabriel Curtiz (Dr. Sklar); Teddy Infuhr (Avran); Marlene Ames (Hannah); Leah (Thomas) Farah (Shirah); Carlo Tricoli, Michael Mark, Leo Mostovoy (Old Men); Esther Michelson, Eloise Hardt (Women); Al Eben (Policeman); Harlan Warde (Shaul); Ralph Moody (Mukhtar); Jack Mannick (Tower Man); Carol Heath, Donna Boyce (Daughters); Erno Verebes, John Maxwell (Officials); Hanne Axman (Telephone Girl).

ACT OF LOVE *(United Artists, 1953), 108 min.*

Producer, Anatole Litvak; associate producer, Georges Maurer; director, Litvak; based on the novel *The Girl on the Via Flaminia* by Alfred Hayes; screenplay, Irwin Shaw; music, Michel Emer, Joe Hajos; set designer, Alexandre Trauner; makeup, Roger Chanteau; sound, Joseph de Bretagne; camera, Armand Thirard; editor, William Hornbeck.

Kirk Douglas (Robert Teller); Dany Robin (Lisa); Barbara Laage (Nina); Robert Strauss (Blackwood); Gabrielle Dorziat (Adele); Gregoire Aslan (Commissaire); Marthe Mercadier (Young Woman); Fernand Ledoux (Fernand); Serge Reggiani (Claude); Brigitte Bardot (Mimi); Gilberte Geniat (Mme. Henderson); George Mathews (Henderson); Leslie Dwyer (English Sergeant); Richard Benedict (Pete).

20,000 LEAGUES UNDER THE SEA *(Buena Vista, 1954), C-120 min.*

Director, Richard Fleischer; based on the novel by Jules Verne; screenplay, Earl Fenton; art director, John Meehan; music, Paul Smith; special effects camera, Ralph Hammeras; camera, Franz Planer; editor, Elmo Williams.

Kirk Douglas (Ned Land); James Mason (Captain Nemo); Paul Lukas (Professor Aronnax); Peter Lorre (Conseil); Robert J. Wilke (Mate on *Nautilus*); Carleton Young (John Howard); Ted de Corsia (Captain Farragut); Percy Helton (Diver); Ted Cooper (Mate on *Lincoln*); Edward Marr (Shipping Agent); Fred Graham (Casey Moore); J. M. Kerrigan (Billy).

ULYSSES *(Paramount, 1954), 104 min.*

Producers, Dino De Laurentiis, Carlo Ponti, in association with William Schorr; director, Mario Camerini; based on *The Odyssey* by Homer; screenplay, Franco Brusati, Camerini, Ennio de Conscini, Hugh Gray, Ben Hecht, Ivo Perilli, Irwin Shaw; music, Alessandro Cicognini; costumes, Giulio Coltellacci, Madame Gres; naval assistant, Giuseppe Barbaro; architect, Flavio Mogherini; sets, Andrea Tommasi; makeup, Eugene Schuftan; sound, Mario Morigi; camera, Harold Rosson; editor, Leo Cattozzo.

Kirk Douglas (Ulysses); Silvana Mangano (Penelope/Circe); Anthony Quinn (Antinous); Rossana Podesta (Nausicaa); Sylvie (Euriclea); Daniel Ivernel (Euriloco); Jacques Dumesnil (Alcinous); and: Franco Interlenghi, Elena Zareschi, Evi Maltagliati, Ludmilla Dudarova, Tania Weber, Piero Lulli, Umberto Silvestri, Gualtiero Tumiati, Teresa Pellati, Mario Feliciani, Michele Riccardini.

THE RACERS *(Twentieth Century-Fox, 1955), C-112 min.*

Producer, Julian Blaustein; director, Henry Hathaway; based on the novel by Hans Ruesch; screenplay, Charles Kaufman; art directors, Lyle Wheeler, George Patric; set decorators, Walter M. Scott, Stuart Reiss; music, Alex North; song, Jack Brooks and North; orchestrator, Edward B. Powell; wardrobe designer, Charles Le Maire; costumes, Kay Nelson; technical advisers, John Fitch, Phil Hill, E. de Graffenried; makeup, Ben Nye; special camera effects, Ray Kellogg; camera, Joe MacDonald; editor, James B. Clark.

Kirk Douglas (Gino); Bella Darvi (Nicole); Gilbert Roland (Dell 'Oro); Cesar Romero (Carlos); Lee J. Cobb (Maglio); Katy Jurado (Maria); Charles Goldner (Piero); John Hudson (Michel Caron); George Dolenz (Count Salom); Agnes Laury (Toni); John Wengraf (Dr. Taber); Richard Allan (Pilar); Norbert Schiller (Dahlgren); Mel Welles (Fiori); Gene D'Arcy (Rousillon); Mike Dengate (Dell 'Oro's Mechanic); Peter Brocco (Gatti); Stephen Bekassy (Race Official); Ina Anders (Janka); Gladys Holland (Nurse); Ben Wright (Dr. Segar); Chris

Randall (Teenage Mechanic); Joe Vitale (Dr. Bocci); George Givot (Baron); George Crisnas (Taxi Driver); Jack del Rio (Race Official); Diane Dubois, Ernesto Morelli (Couple at Bar); Renate Nuy (Girl with Michele); Paul Cesari (Barman); Nino Marcell (Italian Autograph Hound).

MAN WITHOUT A STAR *(Universal, 1955), C-89 min.*
Producer, Aaron Rosenberg; director, King Vidor; based on the novel by Dee Linford; screenplay, Borden Chase, D. D. Beauchamp; art directors, Alexander Golitzen, Richard H. Riede; assistant directors, Frank Shaw, George Lollier; costumes, Rosemary Odell; camera, Russell Metty; editor, Virgil Vogel.

Kirk Douglas (Dempsey Rae); Jeanne Crain (Reed Bowman); Claire Trevor (Idonee); William Campbell (Jeff Jimson); Richard Boone (Steve Miles); Jay C. Flippen (Strap Davis); Myrna Hansen (Tess Cassidy); Mara Corday (Moccasin Mary); Eddy C. Waller (Tom Cassidy); Sheb Wooley (Latigo); George Wallace (Tom Carter); Roy Barcroft (Sheriff Olson); James Hayward (Duckbill); Paul Birch (Mark Tolliver); Malcolm Atterbury (Fancy Joe Toole); William Challee (Brick Gooder); William Phillips (Cookie); Ewing Mitchell (Ben Johnson); Mil Patrick (Boxcar Alice); Mark Hanna (Concho Joe); Frank Chase (Little Waco); Casey Macgregor (Hammer); Jack Ingram (Jessup); Carl Andre (Texas Gang Member); Jack Elam (The Drifter); Myron Healey (Mogollon); Lee Roberts (The Brakeman).

THE INDIAN FIGHTER *(United Artists, 1955), C-88 min.*
Producer, William Schorr; associate producer, Samuel P. Norton; director, Andre de Toth; story, Ben Kadish; screenplay, Frank Davis, Ben Hecht; art director, Wiard Ihnen; music, Franz Waxman; songs, Irving Gordon; assistant director, Tom Connors, Jr., Jack Voglin; camera, Wilfrid M. Cline; editor, Richard Cahoon.

Kirk Douglas (Johnny Hawks); Elsa Martinelli (Onahti); Walter Abel (Captain Trask); Walter Matthau (Wes Todd); Diana Douglas (Susan Rogers); Eduard Franz (Red Cloud); Lon Chaney (Chivington); Alan Hale, Jr. (Will Crabtree); Elisha Cook (Briggs); Michael Winkelman (Tommy Rogers); Harry Landers (Grey Wolf); William Phipps (Lieutenant Blake); Buzz Henry (Lieutenant Schaeffer); Ray Teal (Morgan); Frank Cady (Trader Joe); Hank Worden (Crazy Bear); Lane Chandler (Head Settler).

LUST FOR LIFE *(MGM, 1956), C-122 min.*
Producer, John Houseman; director, Vincente Minnelli; based on the novel by Irving Stone; screenplay, Norman Corwin; art directors, Cedric Gibbons, Hans Peters, Preston Ames; music, Miklos Rozsa; camera, Freddie Young, Russell Harlan; editor, Adrienne Fazan.

Kirk Douglas (Vincent Van Gogh); Anthony Quinn (Paul Gauguin); James Donald (Theo Van Gogh); Pamela Brown (Christine); Everett Sloane (Dr. Gachet); Niall MacGinnis (Roulin); Noel Purcell (Anton Mauve); Henry Daniell (Theodorus Van Gogh); Madge Kennedy (Anna Cornelia Van Gogh); Jill Bennett (Willemien); Lionel Jeffries (Dr. Peyron); Laurence Naismith (Dr. Bosman); Eric Pohlmann (Colbert); Jeanette Sterke (Kay); Toni Gerry (Johanna); Wilton Graff (Reverend Stricker); Isobel Elsom (Mrs. Stricker); David Horne (Reverend Peeters); Noel Howlett (Commissioner Van Den Berghe); Ronald Adam (Commissioner De Smet); John Ruddock (Ducrucq); Julie Robinson (Rachel); David Leonard (Camille Pissarro); William Phipps (Emile Bernard); David Bond (Seurat); Frank Peris (Pere Tanguy); Jay Adler (Waiter); Laurence Badie (Adeline Ravoux); Mitzi Blake (Elizabeth); Anthony Sydes (Cor); Anthony Eustrel (Tersteeg); Ernestine Barrier (Jet); Jerry Bergen (Lautrec); Belle Mitchell (Mme. Tanguy); Alec Mango (Dr. Rey); Fred Johnson (Cordan); Norman MacCowan (Pier);

170

Mickey Maga (Jan); Betty Sinclair (Maid); Karen Scott (Girl); Al Haskell (Concertina Player); Henry Corden (Waiter); Gordon Richards (Customer) Helen Van Tuyl (Elderly Customer); Marc Snow (Landlord); George Lewis (Gendarme); Paul Bryar (Inspector); Rex Evans (Durand-Ruel); Roy Gordon (Elderly Gentleman); Len Lesser (Cartoonist); Betty Blythe (Dowager); Delia Salvi, Lynne Millan (Girls).

TOP SECRET AFFAIR *(Warner Bros., 1957), 100 min.*

Producers, Milton Sperling, Martin Rackin; director, H. C. Potter; based on characters from the novel *Melville Goodwin, U.S.A.* by John P. Marquand; screenplay, Roland Kibbee, Allan Scott; art director, Malcolm Bert; music, Roy Webb; camera, Stanley Cortez; editor, Folmar Blangsted.

Kirk Douglas (Major General Melville Goodwin); Susan Hayward (Dottie Peale); Paul Stewart (Phil Bentley); Jim Backus (Colonel Gooch); John Cromwell (General Grimshaw); Roland Winters (Senator Burwick); A. E. Gould-Porter (Butler); Michael Fox (Lotzie); Frank Gerstle (Sergeant Kruger); Charles Lane (Bill Hadley); Edna Holland (Myra Maynard); Ivan Triessault (German Field Marshal); Lee Choon Wha (Korean Dignitary); Franco Corsaro (Armande); Lyn Osborn (Stumpy); Patti Gallagher (Girl); Sid Chatton (Drunk-at-Table); Jonathan Hole (Mr. Jones); Charles Meredith (Personage); James Flavin (Man); Louis Quinn (TV Announcer); Tom Coleman (Houseman); Hal Dawson, Hugh Lawrence, Richard Cutting (Reporters).

GUNFIGHT AT THE O.K. CORRAL *(Paramount, 1957), C-122 min.*

Producer, Hal B. Wallis; associate producer, Paul Nathan; director, John Sturges; suggested by the article by George Scullin; screenplay, Leon Uris; assistant director, Michael D. Moore; costumes, Edith Head; music, Dmitri Tiomkin; song, Tiomkin and Ned Washington; art directors, Hal Pereira, Walter Tyler; camera, Charles Lang, Jr.; editor, Warren Low.

Burt Lancaster (Wyatt Earp); Kirk Douglas (Doc Holliday); Rhonda Fleming (Laura Denbow); Jo Van Fleet (Kate Fisher); John Ireland (Ringo); Lyle Bettger (Ike Clanton); Frank Faylen (Cotton Wilson); Earl Holliman (Charles Bassett); Ted De Corsia (Shanghai Pierce); Dennis Hopper (Billy Clanton); Whit Bissell (John P. Clum); George Mathews (John Shanssey); John Hudson (Virgil Earp); DeForrest Kelley (Morgan Earp); Martin Milner (James Earp); Kenneth Tobey (Bat Masterson); Lee Van Cleef (Ed Bailey); Joan Camden (Betty Earp); Olive Carey (Mrs. Clanton); Brian Hutton (Rick); Nelson Leigh (Major Kelley); Jack Elam (Tom McLowery); Don Castle (Drunken Cowboy); Dennis Moore, Gregg Martell (Cowboys); Roger Creed, Morgan Lane, Paul Gary (Killers); Dorothy Abbott (Girl); Ethan Laidlaw (Bartender); William Norton Bailey (Merchant); Trude Wyler (Social Hall Guest); Tony Merrill (Barber); Harry Mendoza (Cockeyed Frank Loving); Roger Creed (Deputy); James Davis, Joe Forte, Max Power, Courtland Shepard (Card Players).

PATHS OF GLORY *(United Artists, 1957), 86 min.*

Producer, James B. Harris; director, Stanley Kubrick; based on the novel by Humphrey Cobb; screenplay, Kubrick, Calder Willingham, Jim Thompson; art director, Ludwig Reiber; music, Gerald Fried; camera, George Krause; editor, Eva Kroll.

Kirk Douglas (Colonel Dax); Ralph Meeker (Corporal Paris); Adolphe Menjou (General Broulard); George Macready (General Milreau); Wayne Morris (Lieutenant Roget); Richard Anderson (Major Saint-Auban); Joseph Turkel (Private Arnaud); Timothy Carey (Private Ferol); Peter Capell (Colonel Judge); Susanne Christian (German Girl); Bert Freed (Sergeant Boulanger); Emile Meyer (Priest); John Stein (Captain Rousseau).

171

THE VIKINGS *(United Artists, 1958), C-114 min.*

Producer, Jerry Bresler; director, Richard Fleischer; based on the novel *The Vikings* by Edison Marshall; screenplay, Calder Willingham; adaptor, Dale Wasserman; music-music arranger, Mario Nascimbene; music conductor, Franco Ferrara; production designer, Julien Derode; assistant director, Andre Smagghe; makeup, John O'Gorman, Neville Smallwood; second unit director, Elmo Williams; camera, Jack Cardiff; second unit camera, Walter Wottitz; editorial supervisor, Williams.

Kirk Douglas (Einer); Tony Curtis (Eric); Ernest Borgnine (Ragnar); Janet Leigh (Morgana); James Donald (Egbert); Alexander Knox (Father Godwin); Frank Thring (Aella); Maxine Audley (Enid); Eileen Way (Kitale); Edric Connor (Sandpiper); Dandy Nichols (Bridget); Per Buckhoj Bjorn); Almut Berg (Pigtails).

LAST TRAIN FROM GUN HILL *(Paramount, 1959), C-94 min.*

Producer, Hal B. Wallis; associate producer, Paul Nathan; director, John Sturges; based on the story *Showdown* by Les Crutchfield; screenplay, James Poe; art director, Walter Tyler; assistant directors, Michael D. Moore, Danny McCauley; music, Dmitri Tiomkin; camera, Charles Lang, Jr.; editor, Warren Low.

Kirk Douglas (Matt Morgan); Anthony Quinn (Craig Belden); Carolyn Jones (Linda); Earl Holliman (Rick Belden); Brad Dexter (Beero); Brian Hutton (Lee); Ziva Rodann (Catherine Morgan); Bing Russell (Skag); Val Avery (Bartender); Walter Sande (Sheriff Bartlett); Lars Henderson (Petey Morgan); John P. Anderson (Salesman at Horseshoe Bar); Lee Hendry (Man in Lobby); William Newell (Hotel Clerk); Kym Leslie (Townswoman); Sid Tomack (Roomer); Charles Stevens (Keno); Julius Tannen (Cleaning Man); Ken Becker, Courtland Shepard, Ty Hardin (Cowboys); Glenn Strange (Saloon Bouncer); Jack Lomas (Charlie); Tony Russo (Pinto); Rickey William Kelman (Boy); Walter "Tony" Merrill (Conductor); Michael Bachus, Dick Haynes (Townsmen); Hank Mann (Storekeeper); Frank Carter (Cowboy on Train); William Benedict (Small Man).

THE DEVIL'S DISCIPLE *(United Artists, 1959), 82 min.*

Producer, Harold Hecht; director, Guy Hamilton; based on the play by George Bernard Shaw; screenplay, John Dighton, Roland Kibbee; art directors, Terence Verity, Edward Carrere; set decorator, Scott Slimon; makeup, Paul Habiger; technical adviser, Alan Binns; music, Richard Rodney Bennett; music conductor, John Hollingsworth; assistant director, Adrian Pryce-Jones; sound, Leslie Hammond; camera, Jack Hildyard; editor, Alan Osbiston.

Burt Lancaster (Anthony Anderson); Kirk Douglas (Richard Dudgeon); Laurence Olivier (General Burgoyne); Janette Scott (Judith Anderson); Eva LeGallienne (Mrs. Dudgeon); Harry Andrews (Major Swindon); Basil Sydney (Lawyer Hawkins); George Rose (British Sergeant); Neil McCallum (Christopher Dudgeon); Mervyn Johns (Reverend Maindeck Parshotter); David Horne (William); Jenny Jones (Essie); Erik Chitty (Titus).

STRANGERS WHEN WE MEET *(Columbia, 1960), C-117 min.*

Producer-director, Richard Quine; based on the novel by Evan Hunter; screenplay, Hunter; art director, Ross Bellah; set decorator, Louis Diage; music, George Duning; orchestrator, Arthur Morton; music supervisor, Morris Stoloff; assistant director, Carter DeHaven; gowns, Jean Louis; makeup, Ben Lane; sound, Charles J. Rice, Lambert Day; camera, Charles Lang, Jr.; editor, Charles Nelson.

Kirk Douglas (Larry Coe); Kim Novak (Maggie Gault); Ernie Kovacs (Roger Altar); Barbara Rush (Eve Coe); Walter Matthau (Felix Anders); Virginia Bruce (Mrs. Wagner); Kent Smith (Stanley Baxter); Helen Gallagher (Betty Anders); John Bryant (Ken Gault); Roberta Shore (Linda Harder); Nancy Kovack (Marcia); Carol Douglas (Honey Blonde); Paul Picerni (Gerandi); Ernest Sarracino (Di Labbia); Harry Jackson (Bud Ramsey); Bart Patton (Hank); Robert Sampson (Bucky); Ray Ferrell (David Coe); Douglas Holmes (Peter Coe); Timmy Molina (Patrick Gault); Betsy Jones Moreland (Mrs. Gerandi); Audrey Swanson (Mrs. Baxter); Cynthia Leighton (Mrs. Ramsey); Judy Lang (Ad Lib Girl); Charles Victor, Joe Palma, Tom Anthony, Sheryl Ellison, Mark Beckstrom (Bits); Sue Ane Langdon (Daphne); Sharyn Gibbs (Girl at Beach); Lorraine Crawford (Redhead); Dick Crockett (Charlie); Ruth Batchelor (Waitress).

SPARTACUS (*Universal, 1960*), *C-190 min.*

Executive producer, Kirk Douglas; producer, Edward Lewis; director, Stanley Kubrick; based on the novel by Howard Fast; screenplay, Dalton Trumbo; music and music director, Alex North; production designer, Alexander Golitzen; art director, Eric Orbom; set decorators, Russell A. Gausman, Julia Heron; main titles-design consultant, Saul Bass; historical-technical adviser, Vittorio Nino Novarese; wardrobe, Peruzzi; Miss Simmons' costumes, Bill Thomas; assistant director, Marshall Green; sound, Waldon O. Watson, Joe Lapis, Murray Spivack, Ronald Pierce; camera, Russell Metty; additional camera, Clifford Stine; editor, Robert Lawrence; assistant editors, Robert Schulte, Fred Chutlak.

Kirk Douglas (Spartacus); Laurence Olivier (Marcus Crassus); Jean Simmons (Varinia); Tony Curtis (Antoninus); Charles Laughton (Gracchus); Peter Ustinov (Batiatus); John Gavin (Julius Caesar); Herbert Lom (Tigranes); Nina Foch (Helena Glabrus); John Ireland (Crixus); John Dall (Glabrus); Charles McGraw (Marcellus); Joanna Barnes (Claudia Marius); Harold J. Stone (David); Woody Strode (Draba); Peter Brocco (Ramon): Paul Lambert (Gannicus); Robert J. Wilke (Guard Captain); Nick Dennis (Dionynius); John Hoyt (Caius); Frederic Worlock (Laelius); Saul Gorss, Charles Horvath, Gil Perkins (Slave Leaders); John Daheim (Capua Guard); Dayton Lummis (Symmachus); Lili Valenty (Old Crone); Jill Jarmyn (Julia); Jo Summers, Autumn Russell, Kay Stewart, Lynda Lee Williams, Louise Vincent (Slave Girls); Joe Haworth (Otho); Anthony Jochim (Petitioner); Dale Van Sickel, Marvin Goux (Trainers); Rod Normond, Larry Perron (Guards); Ted De Corsia, Arthur Batanides, Robert Stevenson (Legionaires); Edwin Parker (Middle Aged Slave); Otto Malde (Roman General); Tom Steele, Aaron Saxon, Wally Rose (Gladiators); Wayne Van Horn, Brad Harris, Cliff Lyons, Buff Brady, Jerry Brown (Soldiers).

THE LAST SUNSET (*Universal, 1961*), *C-112 min.*

Producers, Eugene Frenke, Edward Lewis; director, Robert Aldrich; based on the novel *Sundown at Crazy Horse* by Howard Rigby; screenplay, Dalton Trumbo; music, Ernest Gold; music conductor, Joseph Gershenson; song, Dmitri Tiomkin and Ned Washington; art directors, Alexander Golitzen, Al Sweeney; set decorators, Oliver Emert; costumes, Norma Koch; assistant director, Thomas J. Connors, Jr.; sound, Waldon O. Watson, Donald Cunliffe; camera, Ernest Laszlo; editor, Edward Mann.

Rock Hudson (Dana Stribling); Kirk Douglas (Brendan O'Malley); Dorothy Malone (Belle Breckenridge); Joseph Cotten (John Breckenridge); Carol Lynley (Missy Breckenridge); Neville Brand (Frank Hobbs); Regis Toomey (Milton Wing); Rad Fulton (Julesberg Kid); Adam Williams (Bowman); Jack Elam (Ed Hobbs); John Shay (Calverton); Margarito De Luna (Jose); Jose Torvay (Rosario); Chihauhau (Chihauhau); Jose Frowe, Manuel Vergara (Men at Cock Fight); Peter Virgo (Man); George Trevino (Manuel).

TOWN WITHOUT PITY *(United Artists, 1961), 105 min.*

Producer-director, Gottfried Reinhardt; based on the novel *The Verdict* by Manfred Gregor; adaptor, Jan Lustig; screenplay, Silvia Reinhardt, George Hurdalek; music-song, Dmitri Tiomkin; art director, Rolf Zehetbauer; assistant director, Eva-Ruth Ebner; wardrobe, Lilo Hagen, Anton Lanner; sound, Helmut Ransch; camera, Kurt Hasse; editor, Hermann Haller.

Kirk Douglas (Major Steve Garrett); Christine Kaufmann (Karin Steinhof); E. G. Marshall (Major Jerome Pakenham); Robert Blake (Jim); Richard Jaeckel (Bidie); Frank Sutton (Chuck); Mal Sondock (Joey); Barbara Ruetting (Inge); Hans Nielsen (Herr Steinhof); Karin Hardt (Frau Steinhof); Ingrid Van Bergen (Trude); Gerhart Lippert (Frank Borgmann); Eleanore Van Hoogstraten (His Mother); Max Haufler (Dr. Urban); Siegried Schurenberg (Burgemeister); Rose Renee Roth (Frau Kulig); Alan Gifford (General Stafford).

LONELY ARE THE BRAVE *(Universal, 1962), 107 min.*

Producer, Edward Lewis; director, David Miller; based on the novel *Brave Cowboy* by Edward Abbey; screenplay, Dalton Trumbo; music, Jerry Goldsmith; assistant directors, Tom Shaw, Dave Silver; art directors, Alexander Golitzen, Robert E. Smith; set decorators, George Milo; makeup, Bud Westmore; sound, Waldon O. Watson, Frank Wilkinson; camera, Phil Lathrop; editor, Leon Barsha.

Kirk Douglas (Jack Burns); Gena Rowlands (Jerri Bondi); Walter Matthau (Sheriff Johnson); Michael Kane (Paul Bondi); Carroll O'Connor (Hinton); William Schallert (Harry); Karl Swenson (Reverend Hoskins); George Kennedy (Gutierrez); Dan Sheridan (Deputy Glynn); Bill Raisch ("One Arm"); William Mims (Deputy in Bar); Martin Garralaga (Old Man); Lalo Rios (Prisoner).

TWO WEEKS IN ANOTHER TOWN *(MGM, 1962), C-107 min.*

Producer, John Houseman; associate producer, Ethel Winant; director, Vincente Minnelli; based on the novel by Irwin Shaw; screenplay, Charles Schnee; music, David Raksin; assistant director, Erich Von Stroheim, Jr.; art directors, George W. Davis, Urie McCleary; set decorators, Henry Grace, Keogh Gleason; color consultant, Charles K. Hagedon; Miss Charisse's gowns, Pierre Balmain; wardrobe, Walter Plunkett; makeup, William Tuttle; sound, Franklin Milton; special visual effects, Robert R. Hoag; camera, Milton Krasner; editors, Adrienne Fazan, Robert J. Kern.

Kirk Douglas (Jack Andrus); Edward G. Robinson (Maurice Kruger); Cyd Charisse (Carlotta); George Hamilton (David Drew); Dahlia Lavi (Veronica); Claire Trevor (Clara Kruger); Rosanna Schiaffino (Barzelli); James Gregory (Brad Byrd); Joanna Roos (Janet Bark); George Macready (Lew Jordan); Mino Doro (Tucino); Stefan Schnabel (Zeno); Vito Scotti (Assistant Director); Tom Palmer (Dr. Cold Eyes); Erich Von Stroheim, Jr. (Ravinski); Leslie Uggams (Chanteuse).

THE HOOK *(MGM, 1963), 98 min.*

Producer, William Perlberg; director, George Seaton; based on the novel *L'Hamecon* by Vahe Katcha; screenplay, Henry Denker; music, Larry Adler; art directors, George W. Davis, Hans Peters; set decorators, Henry Grace, Keogh Gleason; assistant director, Donald Roberts; makeup, William Tuttle; sound, Franklin Milton; camera, Joseph Ruttenberg; editor, Robert J. Kern, Jr.

Kirk Douglas (First Sergeant P. J. Briscoe); Robert Walker, Jr. (Private O. A. Dennison); Nick Adams (P.F.C. V. R. "Hack" Hackett); Enrique Magalona (Gook [Kim]); Nehemiah

Persoff (Captain Van Ryn); John Bleifer (Steward); Mark Miller (Lieutenant D. D. Troy); Bert Freed (Svenson); Anders Andelius (Winkler); Frank Richards (Cascavage); William Challee (Schmidt); Barnaby Hale, John Gilgreen (Seamen); Ralph Ahn (Major Chun); Dallas Mitchell (Radio Sergeant).

FOR LOVE OR MONEY *Universal, (1963), C-108 min.*
Producer, Robert Arthur; director, Michael Gordon; screenplay, Larry Markes, Michael Morris; music, Frank De Vol; music supervisor, Joseph Gershenson; art directors, Alexander Golitzen, Malcolm Brown; set decorator, Ruby Levitt; gowns, Jean Louis; makeup, Bud Westmore; assistant director, Joseph Kenny; sound, Waldon O. Watson, Corson Jowett; camera, Clifford Stine; editor, Alma Macrorie.

Kirk Douglas (Deke Gentry); Mitzi Gaynor (Kate Brasher); Gig Young (Sonny Smith); Thelma Ritter (Chloe Brasher); Leslie Parrish (Jan Brasher); Julie Newmar (Bonnie Brasher); William Bendix (Joe Fogel); Richard Sargent (Harvey Wofford); William Windom (Sam Travis); Elizabeth MacRae (Marsha); Willard Sage (Orson Roark); Ina Victor (Nurse); Alvy Moore (George); Jose Gonzales Gonzales (Jaime); Don Megowan (Gregor); Billy Halop (Elevator Operator); Joey Faye (Shopper); Theodore Marcuse (Artist); Frank Mahony (Red Beard); Alberton Morin (Maitre d'); Don Beddoe (Nilo); Nydia Westman (Martha); Karen Norris (Pat); Charlene Holt (Ava); Sean MacGregor (Seymour); Shelia Rogers (Blinking Shopper); Paul Potash (Gas Station Attendant); Edy Williams (Girl); Seaman Glass, Harry Raven, Charles Cirillo, Ralph Neff (Seamen); Oliver Cross (Bewildered Man); Bess Flowers (Bewildered Woman); George Simmons, Betty Raskoff (Ad Libs); John Indrisano, Ted Fish (Pugs).

THE LIST OF ADRIAN MESSENGER *(Universal, 1963), 98 min.*
Producer, Edward Lewis; director, John Huston; based on the novel by Philip MacDonald; screenplay, Anthony Veiller; music, Jerry Goldsmith; music supervisor, Joseph Gershenson; assistant directors, Tom Shaw, Terry Morse, Jr.; art directors, Stephen Grimes, George Webb; set decorator, Oliver Emert; second unit director, Ted Scaife; makeup, Bud Westmore; camera, Joseph MacDonald; editors, Terry Morse, Hugh Fowler.

George C. Scott (Anthony Gethryn); Dana Wynter (Lady Jocelyn Bruttenholm); Clive Brook (Marquis of Gleneyre); Herbert Marshall (Sir Wilfred Lucas); Jacques Roux (Raoul Le Borg); Bernard Archard (Inspector Pike); Gladys Cooper (Mrs. Karoudjian); Walter Anthony Huston (Derek); John Merivale (Adrian Messenger); Marcel Dalio (Anton Karoudjian); Anita Sharpe-Bolster (Shopkeeper); Noel Purcell (Farmer); John Huston (Lord Aston the Fox Hunter); Tony Curtis (Harlan); Kirk Douglas (George Brougham); Burt Lancaster (Woman); Robert Mitchum (Jim Slattery); Frank Sinatra (Gypsy Stableman); Joe Lynch (Cyclist); Mona Lilian (Proprietress); Tim Dunant (Hunt Secretary); Richard Peel (Sergeant Flood); Stacy Morgan (Whip Man); Anna Van Der Heide (Stewardess); Roland Long (Carstairs); Bernard Fox (Lynce); Barbara Morrison (Nurse); Jennifer Raine (Student Nurse).

SEVEN DAYS IN MAY *(Paramount, 1964), 120 min.*
Producer, Edward Lewis; director, John Frankenheimer; based on the novel by Fletcher Knebel, Charles W. Bailey; screenplay, Rod Serling; art director, Cary Odell; set decorator, Edward Boyle; music, Jerry Goldsmith; assistant director, Hal Polaire; sound, Joe Edmondson; camera, Ellsworth Frederick; editor, Ferris Webster.

Burt Lancaster (General James M. Scott); Kirk Douglas (Colonel Martin "Jiggs" Casey); Fredric March (President Jordan Lyman); Ava Gardner (Eleanor Holbrook); Edmond O'Brien (Senator Raymond Clark); Martin Balsam (Paul Girard); George Macready (Christopher Todd); Whit Bissell (Senator Prentice); Hugh Marlowe (Harold McPherson); Bart Burns (Arthur Corwin); Richard Anderson (Colonel Murdock); Mack Mullaney (Lieutenant Hough); Andrew Duggan (Colonel "Mutt" Henderson); John Larkin (Colonel Broderick); Malcolm Atterbury (Physician); Helen Kleeb (Esther Townsend); John Houseman (Admiral Barnswell); Colette Jackson (Bar Girl).

IN HARM'S WAY *(Paramount, 1965), 165 min.*

Producer-director, Otto Preminger; based on the novel by James Bassett; screenplay, Wendell Mayes; art director, Al Roelofs; music, Jerry Goldsmith; assistant director, Danny McCauley; camera, Loyal Griggs; editors, George Tomasini, Hugh S. Fowler.

John Wayne (Captain Rockwell Torrey); Kirk Douglas (Commander Paul Eddington); Patricia Neal (Lieutenant Maggie Haynes); Tom Tryon (Lieutenant J.G. William McConnel); Paula Prentiss (Bev McConnel); Brandon De Wilde (Ensign Jeremiah Torrey); Jill Haworth (Ensign Annalee Dorne); Doana Andrews (Admiral Broderick); Stanley Holloway (Clayton Canfil); Burgess Meredith (Commander Powell); Franchot Tone (CINCPAC I Admiral); Patrick O'Neal (Commander Neal O'Wynn); Carroll O'Connor (Lieutenant Commander Burke); Slim Pickens (CPO Culpepper); James Mitchum (Ensign Griggs); George Kennedy (Colonel Gregory); Bruce Cabot (Quartermaster Quoddy); Barbara Bouchet (Liz Eddington); Tod Andrews (Captain Tuthill); Larry Hagman (Lieutenant Cline); Stewart Moss (Ensign Balch); Richard Le Pore (Lieutenant Tom Agar); Chet Stratton (Ship's Doctor); Soo Young (Tearful Woman); Dort Clark (Boston); Phil Mattingly (P-T Boat Skipper); Henry Fonda (CINCPAC Admiral).

THE HEROES OF TELEMARK *(Columbia, 1965), C-131 min.*

Producer, S. Benjamin Fisz; director, Anthony Mann; based on *Skis Against the Atom* by Knut Haukelid and *But For These Men* by John Drummond; screenplay, Ivan Moffat, Ben Barzman; music and music conductor, Malcolm Arnold; assistant directors, John Quested, Derek Cracknell; art director, Tony Masters; set decorators, Bob Cartwright, Ted Clements; wardrobe, Elsa Fennell; stunt supervisor, Jerry Crampton; makeup, Neville Smallwood; sound, Ted Mason, Bill Daniels, Gordon McCallum; special effects, John P. Fulton; camera, Robert Krasker; editor, Bert Bates.

Kirk Douglas (Dr. Rolf Pedersen); Richard Harris (Knut Straud); Ulla Jacobsson (Anna); Michael Redgrave (Uncle); David Weston (Ame); Anton Diffring (Major Frick); Eric Porter (Terboven); Mervyn Johns (Colonel Wilkinson); Jennifer Hilary (Sigrid); Roy Dotrice (Jensen the Mysterious Stranger); Barry Jones (Professor Logan); Ralph Michael (Nilssen); Geoffrey Keen (General Bolts); Maurice Denham (Doctor at Hospital); Wolf Frees (Knippelberg); Robert Ayres (General Courts); Sebastian Breaks (Gunnar); John Golightly (Freddy); Alan Howard (Oli); Patrick Jordan (Henrik); William Marlowe (Claus); Brook Williams (Einar); David Davies (Captain of the *Galtesund*); Karel Stepanek (Hartmuller); Faith Brook (Woman on Bus); Elvi Hale (Mrs. Sandersen); Gerard Heinz (Erhardt); Victor Beaumont (German Ski Sergeant); Philo Hauser (Businessman); George Murcell (Sturmfuhrer); Russell Waters (Mr. Sandersen); Jan Conrad (Factory Watchman); Alf Joint (German Guard on Ferry); Paul Hansard (German Official); Pamela Conway (Girl in Barroom); Annette Andre (Girl Student); Terry Plummer, Joe Powell (Quislings); Grace Arnold, Howard Douglas (*Galtesund* Passengers).

CAST A GIANT SHADOW *(United Artists, 1966), C-141 min.*

Producer, Melville Shavelson; co-producer, Michael Wayne; director, Shavelson; based on

176

the book by Ted Berkman; screenplay, Shavelson; second unit director, Jack Reddish; assistant directors, Charles Scott, Jr., Tim Zinnemann; music, Elmer Bernstein; orchestrators, Leo Shuken, Jack Hayes; production designer, Michael Stringer; art director, Arrigo Equini; makeup, David Grayson, Euclide Santoli; costumes, Margaret Furse; sound, David Bowen, Chuck Overhulser; special effects, Sass Bedig; camera, Aldo Tonti; second unit camera, Marco Yakovlevich; editors, Bert Bates, Gene Ruggiero.

Kirk Douglas (David "Mickey" Marcus); Senta Berger (Magda Simon); Angie Dickinson (Emma Marcus); Stathis Giallelis (Ram Oren); Luther Adler (Jacob Zion); Gary Merrill (Pentagon Chief of Staff); Haym Topol (Abou Ibn Kader); Ruth White (Mrs. Chalson); Gordon Jackson (James MacAfee); *Guest Appearances:* Frank Sinatra (Vince); Yul Brynner (Commander Asher Gonen); John Wayne (General Mike Randolph); and: Michael Hordern (British Ambassador); Allan Cuthbertson (British Immigration Officer); Jeremy Kemp, Sean Barrett (British Officers on the Beach); Michael Shillo (Magda's Husband); Rina Ganor (Rona); Roland Barthrop (Bert Harrison); Vera Dolen (Mrs. Martinson); Robert Gardett (General Walsh); Michael Ballston, Claude Aliotti (Sentries in Israel); Samra Dedes (Belly Dancer); Michael Shagrir (Truck Driver); Frank Lattimore, Ken Buckle (U.N. Officers); Rodd Dana, Robert Ross (Aides); Arthur Hansell (Pentagon Officer); Don Sturke (Parachute Jump Sergeant); Hillel Rave (Yaskov); Shlomo Hermon (Yussuff).

PARIS BRULE-T-IL? (a.k.a., IS PARIS BURNING?, *Paramount, 1966), 173 min.*

Producer, Paul Graetz; director, Rene Clement; based on the book by Larry Collins, Dominique Lapierre; screenplay, Gore Vidal, Francis Ford Coppola, Jean Aurenche, Pierre Bost, Claude Brule; additional dialogue, Marcel Moussy; second unit director, Andre Smagghe; assistant directors, Yves Boisset, Michel Wyn; music, Maurice Jarre; art director, Willy Holt; set decorator, Roger Volper; costumes, Jean Zay, Pierre Nourry; makeup, Michel Deruelle, Aida Carange; sound, William R. Sivel, Antoine Petit John; special effects, Robert MacDonald, Paul Pollard; camera, Marcel Grignon; second unit camera, Jean Tournier; editor, Robert Lawrence.

Jean-Paul Belmondo (Morandat); Leslie Caron (Francoise Labe); George Chakiris (G. I. in Tank); Alain Delon (Jacques Chaban-Delmas); Glenn Ford (General Omar Bradley); Daniel Gelin (Yves Bayet); Yves Montand (Marcel Bizien); Claude Rich (General Jacques Leclerc); Robert Stack (General Edwin Sibert); Pierre Vaneck (Major Roger Gallois); Skip Ward (G. I. with Warren); Charles Boyer (Charles Monod); Jean-Pierre Cassel (Lieutenant Henri Karcher); Claude Dauphin (Lebel); Kirk Douglas (General George Patton); Gert Frobe (General Dietrich von Choltitz); E. G. Marshall (Intelligence Officer Powell); Anthony Perkins (Sergeant Warren); Simone Signoret (Cafe Proprietress); Jean-Louis Trintignant (Serge); Marie Versini (Claire); Orson Welles (Consul Raoul Nordling); Bruno Cremer (Colonel Rol); Suzy Delair (A Parisienne); Pierre Dux (Parodi); Billy Frick (Hitler); Michel Piccoli (Pisani); Sacha Pitoeff (Joliot-Curie); Wolfgang Priess (Ebernach); Michel Berger (Chief of Explosives); Germaine De France (Old Woman); Pascal Fardoulis (Gilet); Bernard Fresson (Liaison Agent); Jean-Pierre Honore (Alain Perpezat); Peter Jakob (General Burgfofff); Paloma Matta (The Bride); Jean Negroni (Villon); Jean Valmont (Bazooka); Jo Warfield (U.S. Major); Joachim Westhoss (German Officer); Jean-Pierre Zola (Corporal Mayer); Billy Kearns (Aide to Patton).

*Re-edited to 135 min.

THE WAY WEST (*United Artists, 1967), C-122 min.*

Producer, Harold Hecht; director, Andrew V. McLaglen; based on the novel by A. B. Guthrie, Jr.; screenplay, Ben Maddow, Mitch Lindemann; music, Bronislau Kaper; music conductor, Andre Previn; title song, Kaper and Mack David; art director, Ted Haworth; set decorator, Robert Priestley; costumes, Norma Koch; makeup, Frank McCoy; assistant directors, Terry Morse, Newt Arnold, Tim Zinnemann; sound, Jack Solomon; special effects, Danny Hays; camera, William H. Clothier; editor, Otho Lovering.

Kirk Douglas (Senator William J. Tadlock); Robert Mitchum (Dick Summers); Richard Widmark (Lije Evans); Lola Albright (Rebecca Evans); Michael Witney (Johnnie Mack); Sally Field (Mercy McBee); Katherine Justice (Amanda Mack); Stubby Kaye (Sam Fairman); William Lundigan (Michael Moynihan); Paul Lukather (Turley); Roy Barcroft (Masters); Jack Elam (Weatherby); Patric Knowles (Colonel Grant); Ken Murray (Hank); John Mitchum (Little Henry); Nick Cravat (Calvelli); Harry Carey, Jr. (Mr. McBee); Roy Glenn (Saunders); Connie Sawyer (Mrs. McBee); Anne Barton (Mrs. Moynihan); Eve McVeagh (Mrs. Masters); Peggy Stewart (Mrs. Turley); Stefan Arngrim (Tadlock, Jr.) Hal Lynch (Big Henry); Gary Morris (Paw-Kee-Mah); Eddie Little Sky, Michael Keep (Sioux Braves); Michael Lane (Sioux Chief); Mitchell Schollars (Indian Boy); Jack Coffer, Everett Creach, Jim Burk, Gary McLarty (Four Drovers).

THE WAR WAGON *(Universal, 1967), C-101 min.*
Producer, Marvin Schwartz; director, Burt Kennedy; based on the novel *Badman* by Clair Huffaker; screenplay, Huffaker; second unit director, Cliff Lyons; assistant directors, Al Jennings, H. A. Silverman; music, Dmitri Tiomkin; title song, Tiomkin and Ned Washington; art director, Alfred Sweeney; wardrobe, Robert Chiniquy, Donald Wolz; makeup, Bud Westmore; sound, Waldon O. Watson; camera, William H. Clothier; editor, Harry Gerstad.

John Wayne (Taw Jackson); Kirk Douglas (Lomax); Howard Keel (Levi Walking Bear); Robert Walker (Billy Hyatt); Keenan Wynn (Wes Catlin); Bruce Cabot (Pierce); Valora Noland (Kate); Gene Evans (Hoag); Joanna Barnes (Lola); Bruce Dern (Hammond); Terry Wilson (Strike); Don Collier (Shack); Sheb Wooley (Snyder); Ann McCrea (Felicia); Emilio Fernandez (Calita); Frank McGrath (Bartender); Red Morgan (Early); Chuck Roberson (Brown); Hal Needham (Hite); Marco Antonio Arzate (Wild Horse); Perla Walter (Rosita).

A LOVELY WAY TO DIE *(Universal, 1968), C-103 min.*
Producer, Richard Lewis; director, David Lowell Rich; screenplay, A. J. Russell; music, Kenyon Hopkins; title song, Hopkins and Judy Spencer; art director, Willard Levitas; set decorators, John McCarthy, John Ward; costumes, Mary Merrill; makeup, Martin Bell; assistant directors, Pete Scoppa, John Corless; sound, Dennis Maitland; camera, Morris Hartzband; editor, Sidney Katz.

Kirk Douglas (Jim Schuyler); Sylva Koscina (Rena Westabrook); Eli Wallach (Tennessee Fredericks); Kenneth Haigh (Jonathan Fleming); Martyn Green (Finchley); Sharon Farrell (Carol); Ruth White (Cook); Doris Roberts (Feeney); Carey Nairnes (Harris); John Rogers (Cooper); Philip Bosco (Fuller); Ralph Waite (Sean Magruder); Meg Myles (Mrs. Magruder); Gordon Peters (Eric); William Roberts (Loren Westabrook); Dana Elcar (Laydon); Dee Victor (Mrs. Gordon); Dolph Sweet (Haver); Lincoln Kilpatrick (Daley); Alex Stevens (Lumson); Conrad Bain (James Lawrence); Robert Gerringer (Connor); John Ryan (Harry Samson); Jay Barney (The Real Finchley); Marty Glickman (Racetrack Announcer).

THE BROTHERHOOD *(Paramount, 1969), C-96 min.*
Producer, Kirk Douglas; director, Martin Ritt; screenplay, Lewis John Carlino; second unit director, Francesco Cinieri; art director, Tambi Larsen; second unit art director, Toni Sarzi-Braga; set decorator, Robert Drumheller; second unit set decorator, Giorgio Postiglione; scenic artist, Murray Stern; technical supervisor, Carlino; costumes, Ruth Morley; makeup,

Martin Bell; assistant director, Peter Scoppa; second unit assistant director, Giorgio Gentili; music, Lalo Schifrin; sound, Jack C. Jacobsen; camera, Boris Kaufman; second unit camera, Americo Gengarelli; editor, Frank Bracht.

Kirk Douglas (Frank Ginetta); Alex Cord (Vince Ginetta); Irene Papas (Ida Ginetta); Luther Adler (Dominick Bertolo); Susan Strasberg (Emma Ginetta); Murray Hamilton (Jim Egan); Eduardo Ciannelli (Don Peppino); Joe De Santis (Pietro Rizzi); Connie Scott (Carmela Ginetta); Val Avery (Jake Rotherman); Val Bisoglio (Checch); Alan Hewitt (Sol Levin); Barry Primus (Vido); Michele Cimarosa (Toto); Louis Badolati (Don Turridu).

THE ARRANGEMENT *(Warner Bros., 1969), C-125 min.*
Producer, Elia Kazan; associate producer, Charles Maguire; director, Kazan; based on the novel by Kazan; screenplay, Kazan; assistant director, Burt Harris; production designer, Gene Callahan; art director, Malcolm C. Bert; set decorator, Audrey Blasdel; music and music director, David Amram; sound, Larry Jost; camera, Robert Surtees; editor, Stefan Arnsten.

Kirk Douglas (Eddie Anderson); Faye Dunaway (Gwen); Deborah Kerr (Florence Anderson); Richard Boone (Sam Anderson); Hume Cronyn (Arthur); Michael Higgins (Michael); John Randolph Jones (Charles); Carol Rossen (Gloria); Anne Hegira (Thomna); Dianne Hull (Ellen); William Hansen (Dr. Weeks); Charles Drake (Finnegan); Harold Gould (Dr. Liebman); E. J. Andre (Uncle Joe); Michael Murphy (Father Draddy); Philip Bourneuf (Judge Morris); Clinton Kimbrough (Ben); Ann Doran (Nurse Costello).

THERE WAS A CROOKED MAN *(Warner Bros.-Seven Arts, 1970), C-126 min.*
Executive producer, C. O. Erickson; producer-director, Joseph L. Mankiewicz; screenplay, David Newman, Robert Benton; assistant director, Don Kranze; art director, Edward Carrere; music, Charles Strouse; titles, Wayne Fitzgerald; sound, Al Overton, Jr.; camera, Harry Stradling, Jr.; editor, Gene Milford.

Kirk Douglas (Paris Pitman, Jr.); Henry Fonda (Woodward Lopeman); Hume Cronyn (Dudley Whinner); Warren Oates (Floyd Moon); Burgess Meredith (The Missouri Kid); John Randolph (Cyrus McNutt); Arthur O'Connell (Mr. Lomax); Martin Gabel (Warden Le Goff); Michael Blodgett (Coy Cavendish); Claudia McNeil (Madam); Alan Hale (Tobaccy); Victor French (Whiskey); Lee Grant (Mrs. Bullard); C. K. Yang (Ah-Ping); Pamela Hensley (Edwina); Bert Freed (Skinner); Barbara Rhoades (Miss Jessie Brundidge); J. Edward McKinley (The Governor); Gene Evans (Colonel Wolff); Jeanne Cooper (Prostitute).

A GUNFIGHT *(Paramount, 1971), C-90 min.*
Producers, A. Ronald Lubin, Harold Jack Bloom; associate producer, Saul Holiff; director, Lamont Johnson; screenplay, Bloom; music, Laurence Rosenthal; title song, Johnny Cash; production designer, Tambi Larsen; set decorator, Darrell Silvera; costumes, Mickey Sherard; makeup, Otis Malcolm, Jack Young; assistant directors, William Green, William Sheehan; sound, Jack Solomon; camera, David Walsh; editor, Bill Mosher.

Kirk Douglas (Will Tenneray); Johnny Cash (Abe Cross); Jane Alexander (Nora Tenneray); Raf Vallone (Francisco Alvarez); Karen Black (Jenny Simms); Eric Douglas (Bud Tenneray); Phillip L. Mead (Kyle); John Wallwork (Toby); Dana Elcar (Marv Green); Robert J. Wilke (Cater); George Le Bow (Dekker); James D. Cavasos (Newt Hale); Keith Carradine (Cowboy); Paul Lambert (Ed Fleury); Neil Davis (Canberry); David Burleson, Dick O'Shea (Poker Players); Douglas Doran (Teller); John Gill (Foreman); Timothy Tuinstra (Joey); R. C. Bishop (MacIntyre); Donna and Paula Dillenschneider (Saloon Hostesses).

THE LIGHT AT THE EDGE OF THE WORLD *(National General, 1971), C-101 min.*
Presenter, Alexandre Salkind; executive producer, Alfredo Matas; producer, Kirk Douglas; associate producer, Ilya Salkind; director, Kevin Billington; based on the novel by Jules Verne; screenplay, Tom Rowe; dialogues, Rachel Billington; additional ideas, Bertha Dominiguez; second unit script, Paquita Vilanova; assistant director, Julio Sempere; second unit director, Juan Estelrich; music, Piero Piccioni; art director, Enrique Alarcon; costumes, Deirdre Clancy, Manuel Mampaso; makeup, Jose Antonio Sanchez, Ramon De Diego; sound, A. J. Willis, Wally Milner, Enrique Molinero; special effects, Antonio Molina, Richard M. Parker; camera, Henri Decae; second unit camera, Cecilio Paniagua; editor, Bert Bates.

Kirk Douglas (Denton); Yul Brynner (Kongre); Samantha Eggar (Arabella); Jean-Claude Drouot (Virgilio); Fernando Rey (Captain Moriz); Renato Salvatori (Montefiore); Massimo Ranieri (Felipe); Aldo Sambrell (Tarcante); Tito Garcia (Emilio); Victor Israel (Das Mortes); Tony Skios (Santos); Luis Barbo (Calso Largo); Tony Cyrus (Valgolyo); Raul Castro (Malapinha); Oscar Davis (Amador); Alejandro De Enciso (Morabbito); Martin Uvince (Balduino); John Clark (Matt); Maria Borge (Emily Jane); Juan Cazalilla (Captain Lafayette).

CATCH ME A SPY *J. Arthur Rank, 1971), C-94 min.*
Producers, Steven Pallos, Pierre Braunberger; associate producer, Ian La Frenais; director, Dick Clement; based on the novel by George Marton, Tibor Meray; screenplay, Clement, La Frenais; assistant director, Kip Gowans; art director, Carmen Dillon; music, Claude Bolling; music director, Anthony Bowles; sound, Derek Ball, Gerry Humphreys; camera, Christopher Challis; editor, John Bloom.

Kirk Douglas (Andre); Marlen Jobert (Gabienne); Trevor Howard (Sir Trevor Dawson); Tom Courtenay (Baxter Clarke); Patrick Mower (John Fenton); Bernadette Lafont (Simone); Bernard Blier (Webb); Sacha Pitoeff (Stefan); Richard Pearson (Haldane); Garfield Morgan (Jealous Husband); Angharad Rees (Victoria), Isabel Dean (Celia); Robin Parkinson (British Officer); Jonathan Cecil (British Attache); Robert Raglan (Ambassador); Jean Gilpin (Ground Stewardess); Bridget Turner (Woman on Plane); Trevor Peacock (Man on Plane); Clive Cazes (Rumanian on Plane); Ashley Trevor, Philip Da Costa (Schoolboys); Robert Gillespie (Man in Elevator); Sheila Steafel (Woman in Elevator); Bunny May (Elevator Operator) Fiona Moore, Bernice Stegers (Russian Girls); Dinny Powell, Del Baker (Heavies).

SCALAWAG *(Paramount, 1973), C-93 min.*
Producer, Anne Douglas; associate producer, Eric Douglas; director, Kirk Douglas; based on the story by Robert Louis Stevenson; screenplay, Albert Maltz, Sid Fleishman; assistant director, Bata Maricic; art director, Sjelko Senecic; music, John Cameron; camera, Jack Cardiff; editor, John Howard.

Kirk Douglas (Peg); Mark Lester (Jamie); Neville Brand (Brimstone/Mudhook); George Eastman (Don Aragon); Don Stroud (Velvet); Lesley Anne Down (Lucy-Ann); Danny DeVito (Fly Speck); Mel Blanc (Barfly the Parrot); Phil Brown (Sandy); Davor Antolic (Rooster); Stole Arandjelovic (Beanbelly); Fabijan Sovagovic (Blackfoot); Shaft Douglas (Beau).

UN UOMO DA RISPETTARE (a.k.a., THE MASTER TOUCH, *Warner Bros., 1974), C-96 min.*
Executive producer, Manolo Bolognini; producer, Marina Cicogna; director, Michele Lupo; screenplay, Mino Roli, Franco Burcerci, Roberto Leoni, Lupo; music, Ennio Morricone; art director, Francesco Bronzi; camera, Tonino Delli Colli; editor, Antonietta Zitta.

Kirk Douglas (Wallace); Florinda Balkan (Anna); Giuliano Gemma (Marco); Rene Koldehoff (Detective); Wolfgang Preiss (Miller).

MOUSEY *(ABC-TV, 1974), C-90 min.*

Executive producer, Beryl Vertue; producer, Aida Young; director, Daniel Petrie; screenplay, John Peacock; music and music conductor, Ron Grainer; art director, Roy Stannard; assistant director, David Tringham; costumes, Emma Porteous; sound, Kevin Sutton, Mike Le Mare, Ken Scrivener; camera, Jack Hildyard; editor, John Trumper.

Kirk Douglas (George Anderson); Jean Seberg (Laura Anderson); John Vernon (David Richardson); Sam Wanamaker (Detective Inspector); James Bradford (Private Detective); Bessie Love (Mrs. Richardson); Beth Porter (Sandra); Suzanne Lloyd (Nancy); Bob Sherman (Barman); James Berwick (Headmaster); Valerie Colgan (Miss Wainwright); Margo Alexis (Miss Carter); Robert Henderson (Attorney); Louis Negin (Couturier); Stuart Chandler (Simon); Jennifer Watts (Party Guest); Tony Sibbald (Workman); Don Fellow (Foreman); Francis Napier (Engineer); Roy Stephens (Hotel Receptionist); Elsa Pickthorney (Concierge).

JACQUELINE SUSANN'S ONCE IS NOT ENOUGH *(Paramount, 1975), C-122 min.*

Executive producer, Irving Mansfield; producer, Howard W. Koch; director, Guy Green; based on the novel by Jacqueline Susann; screenplay, Julius J. Epstein; production designer, John DeCuir; art director, David Marshall; set decorator, Ruby Levitt; music, Henry Mancini; songs, Mancini and Larry Kusik; titles, Dan Perri; sound, Larry Jost; camera, John A. Alonzo; editor, Rita Roland.

Kirk Douglas (Mike Wayne); Alexis Smith (Deidre Milford Granger); David Janssen (Tom Colt); George Hamilton (David Milford); Melina Mercouri (Karla); Gary Conway (Hugh Robertson); Brenda Vaccaro (Linda Riggs); Deborah Raffin (January Wayne); Lillian Randolph (Mabel); Renata Vanni (Maria); Mark Roberts (Rheingold); John Roper (Franco); Leonard Sachs (Dr. Peterson); Jim Boles (Scotty); Ann Marie Moelders (Girl at El Morocco); Trudi Marshall (Myrna); Eddie Garrett (Maitre d' in Polo Lounge); Sid Frohlich (Waiter); Kelly Lange (Weather Lady); Maureen McCluskey, Harley Farber, Michael Millius, and Tony Ferrara (Beautiful People).

POSSE *(Paramount, 1975), C-93 min.*

Executive producer, Phil Feldman; producer/director, Kirk Douglas; story, Christopher Knopf; screenplay, William Roberts, Knopf; production designer, Lyle Wheeler; set decorator, Fred Price; music/music director, Maurice Jarre; titles, Wayne Fitzgerald, assistant directors, Jack Roe, Pat Kehoe; camera, Fred Koenekamp, Jules Brenner; editor, John W. Wheeler.

Kirk Douglas (Howard Nightingale); Bruce Dern (Jack Strawhorn); Bo Hopkins (Wesley); James Stacy (Hellman); Luke Askew (Krag); David Canary (Pensteman); Alfonso Arau (Pepe); Katharine Woodville (Mrs. Cooper); Mark Roberts (Mr. Cooper); Beth Brickell (Mrs. Ross); Dick O'Neill (Wiley); Bill Burton (McCanless); Louie Elias (Rains); Gus Greymountain (Reyno); Allan Warnick (Telegrapher); Roger Behrstock (Sheriff Buwalda); Jess Riggle (Hunsinger); Stephanie Steele (Amie); Melody Thomas (Laurie); Dick Armstrong, Larry Finley, and Pat Tobin (Shanty Outlaws).

Publicity pose for *The Crimson Pirate* (WB, 1952)

Burt Lancaster

6'2"
185 pounds
Light brown hair
Blue eyes
Scorpio

In his cinema fledgling days, Burt Lancaster played a succession of robust, taciturn gangsters. Brutality was the keynote of his presence. He soon learned that Neanderthal heroics were career limiting and that he must do more than look tough.

Before he became a cerebral performer, however, he enjoyed a career phase as a swashbuckler. To the pleasant surprise of all (surely including himself) he was amazingly felicitous as the grinning, toothy hero of costume yarns. With his athletic physique and acrobatic training, he was wonderfully adept at performing stunts that had long been the special domain of Douglas Fairbanks (Sr. and Jr.) and Errol Flynn.

In later years, producer-director-star Burt Lancaster became a post-Method actor. Winning an Oscar for his dynamic *Elmer Gantry* (United Artists, 1960) convinced him that he was on the right professional path. Since then the variety of his performances has been in name only. He always seems to be the resolute, t-h-i-n-k-i-n-g player, bent on motivation of character rather than the audience's entertainment. Nevertheless, he has endured through four decades of screen stardom, a testament to his iron will.

Burt Lancaster's family claims to have been descended from the English House of Lancaster, but Burton Stephen Lancaster was born in the barrio section of New

183

York City on Friday, November 2, 1913. His family resided at 209 East 106th Street, in a poor but respectable part of the metropolis which housed Puerto Rican immigrants. His father, James H. Lancaster, worked as a clerk in the Madison Square Garden branch of the New York City Post Office. Burton was the youngest of five children.[1]

Years later, with an understandable touch of nostalgia, Lancaster would recollect for the press about his childhood:

> They tell me that, as a young man, Dad was the handsomest thing on the East Side and my mother, even in her 40s, was so beautiful, guys whistled at her in the streets. She was the landlord's daughter. When my father married her, he was a postal clerk. He went smack to the top in civil service, all the way up to $48 a week.
>
> When my mother's father died, she inherited the house where we lived. Actually it was a series of flats with a common toilet on each floor, out in the hall. Like our neighbors, we Lancasters just squeaked by, yet it was a rich life. My mother used to say to us three boys and my sister, "If you want to know about love, stay in the house. If you want to know about life, go out in the streets." Bums were forever knocking at our door for handouts. First my mother would bawl them out. Then she'd feed them. And what tact she had! She used to talk broken English to the neighbors, because they talked broken English. She always said to us, "You are your own slum area. You can make it as mean or as meaningful as you wish."
>
> The life of the steps had warmth in my childhood. My Dad had an old guitar and on summer nights he'd sit out on the steps and sing in his clear Irish voice. We were the only Irish family in the block. All around us were Italians. They would listen and applaud Dad. One night I joined in his singing. He dropped out, just playing the accompaniment. That way I rated the applause. It was my first applause. I thoroughly enjoyed it.
>
> We boys had the run of all N.Y.C. and it was all exciting. Sure, we ran in gangs, but we fought only with our fists or stones and sticks. There were kind people all around us. At 14, I learned my first respect for stern, Jewish morality because I had fallen in love with a Jewish girl. I first knew there was something called Art from David Morrison who taught in our neighborhood. Another good man was Harry Ely Adrians. The richest churches were after him, but he refused them to preach in our slums.

As a youth, Burt attended P.S. 83 and then DeWitt Clinton High School. At an early age he became interested in reading and became a regular visitor to the neighborhood public library. He also began to attend the Union Settlement House where he discovered his athletic abilities. In later life he would comment that these two institutions kept him from becoming a full-fledged juvenile delinquent. Due to his energetic workouts at the settlement house, Burt became a good athlete in high school, excelling in basketball, and he won an athletic scholarship to New York University. (When he became famous, Lancaster would remember the Union Settlement House with large yearly donations.)

While participating in the activities at the Settlement House, Burt met Nick Cravat. The two boys practiced stunt gymnastics and were later taught acrobatics by former circus performer Curley Brent. From Brent, the youths developed a love

[1]When an infant sister died, Lancaster became the "youngest" child. His oldest brother, William, died in 1955; another brother, James, became a New York City policeman; and sister Jane was a schoolteacher.

for the big top life. However, realistic Burt gave up the dream of a circus life to attend New York University. He planned to become a physical education teacher and an athletic coach. While he was at the university he played basketball, baseball, and football, and took part in boxing, track, and gymnastics. Burt spent two years in college. However, by 1931, with the Depression well underway, the young man became annoyed with formal education, especially because his classmates were more interested in football than studying. Then too, Burt had not been able to conquer his love of the circus. While sitting in class one day he made up his mind about the future: "I walked out of that class and never went back."

He re-teamed with Cravat, and for ninety dollars the two men purchased a used car. They drove to Petersburg, Virginia, where they were hired for a bar act by the Kay Brothers Circus. They were billed as Lang and Cravat and they were paid the hardly munificent sum of three dollars per week, plus board. They remained with the Kay Circus for thirty weeks, then left to join another, bigger show. For nearly a decade they performed in small-time tent shows and in vaudeville, with occasional brief forays into such big-time shows as the Ringling Brothers Circus. They also worked carnivals.

In 1935, Lancaster married June Ernst, a circus aerialist, "the only woman in America who could do horizontal bar tricks." They were divorced almost immediately, although for the next few years Burt worked in a show act that starred his ex-mother-in-law, who was an accomplished trapeze artist.

In the late thirties, Burt tired of circus life and briefly left the sawdust work to join the Federal Theatre Project, part of the Work Projects Administration (WPA). The WPA had been set up to aid the unemployed and to develop new theatrical talent. Lancaster's work with the WPA in Manhattan found him being trained by people who had studied with Richard Boleslawski. It was here that Burt learned to act in the form that was basically a precursor of "The Method."

Still entranced by the world of the circus, Burt later returned to that entertainment sphere. But in 1939, while he was in a circus act in St. Louis, he developed a serious finger infection after ripping open his hand during a workout. Doctors advised him that amputation would be necessary if he did not quit the act. He took inventory of his career stock and found that he had little to show for his years in the circus. Unsure of his future professional direction, he went to Chicago, where a circus family, the Smiletas, took him in while he sought employment. For the next three years he was employed in a variety of jobs: as a floorwalker in the lingerie department at Marshall Field's, as a furniture, and then a haberdashery, salesman, as a firemen, and then as an engineer for a meatpacking firm. At one point he was also servicing home refrigerators.

In 1942 he learned of an opening with the Community Concerts Bureau, operated by CBS in New York City. He applied for the post and was accepted. He was trained for traveling as an advance man, promoting the shows being sponsored by the Bureau. But before he ever became accustomed to the new job, he was drafted.

Thanks to his years in the circus, Burt was placed in the Special Services Division of the Fifth Army as an entertainer. He toured Europe, performing for servicemen in Austria, Italy, and North Africa in a show entitled *Stars and Gripes*. It was while he was on this tour that he met a girl with the USO named Norma Anderson. She had seen him on stage and arranged for an introduction.

After three years in the military service, Lancaster returned to New York in 1945, where Norma Anderson was then employed as a secretary to a radio producer. One

Publicity pose (1946)

day, as he was about to take her out for lunch, he noticed he was being observed by a stranger. The man turned out to be Jack Mahlor, an associate of Irving Jacobs, who was producing a new show on Broadway, *A Sound of Hunting*. Mahlor introduced himself and stated he was impressed by Burt's manner and appearance. He asked him if he wanted to audition for a role in the play which dealt with American soldiers on the Italian front during World War II. Feeling that he had nothing to lose by accepting, Lancaster decided to bluff his way through the interview. Nevertheless, he was surprised to learn that he had won the part of Sergeant Joseph Mooney in the Harry Brown play.

Directed by Anthony Brown, *A Sound of Hunting* opened at the Lyceum Theatre on November 21, 1945. It told of a group of G.I.s at Cassino who want to go to the front when one of their number is caught between the German-U.S. lines. They fail to rescue the man, but a soldier (Sam Levene) with a reputation for cowardice is encouraged to attack an enemy machine-gun nest. The sought-after confederate is later found dead. The troops then return to Naples.

Of his Broadway debut, Lancaster later recalled. "I wasn't nervous at all. 'What can happen to me?' I said to myself. 'I can miss a line, but I can't get hurt.'"

Most critics were disappointed by the production, although they admitted it was a valiant attempt at something different.[2] It lasted only twenty-three performances. The cast, besides Levene and Burt, included Frank Lovejoy, William Beal, and Stacy Harris. Billed as Burton Lancaster, the newcomer received some kind notices. *PM* found his performance "attractive," while Robert Garland (*New York Journal-American*) stated, "Burton Lancaster, as Mooney, is the non-com every private prays for."

While *A Sound of Hunting* was a failure, it did serve to bring Burt to the attention of several Hollywood producers. Fellow actor Sam Levene advised Burt to obtain the services of an agent. He introduced the fledgling actor to Harold Hecht, who was a one-time dancer, and who had once worked with Martha Graham. Lancaster found Hecht to be "honest and outspoken" and felt that these traits were "impressive." He gave Hecht the authority to investigate the various Hollywood offers which were touted as the road to Lancaster's glory. Lancaster accepted the bid from producer Hal B. Wallis, the astute filmmaker who had recently contracted such other newcomers as Kirk Douglas and Lizabeth Scott. The deal called for Lancaster to perform in two pictures a year for Wallis, with the option to make one outside production per year.[3]

In Hollywood, the new contractee quickly made four features, *Desert Fury, Variety Girl, The Killers,* and *Brute Force.* The first two were delayed in release, so *The Killers* was his first picture in distribution, and the fourth film coming third in distribution.

Lancaster had made a test for *Desert Fury* for Wallis, and New York columnist Mark Hellinger, about to make his producer's debut with *The Killers* (Universal, 1946), saw it. Hellinger had initially thought of having Wayne Morris star in his film, but, when the star of *Kid Galahad* (Warner Bros., 1937) was not available, he agreed to use Burt as a substitute. Lancaster later commented of his role in this Ernest Hemingway-derived feature, "In *The Killers* I was a big, dumb Swede. I could be very simple in the part; there was no need to be highly ostentatious or

[2]In 1952 the play would be translated into the film *Eight Iron Men* (Columbia), with Lee Marvin in Lancaster's old role.

[3]The special option clause was the persuading factor in making Lancaster sign with Wallis instead of one of the major studios.

theatrical. For a new actor this is much easier than something histrionic. There's no question about the good fortune of being ushered into films in that kind of role."

According to the future star, he had "always been a Hemingway aficionado. I'd read everything he'd ever written. I remember Mark Hellinger asking me what I thought about the script, and I said, 'Well, the first sixteen pages is Hemingway verbatim, and after that you have a rather interesting whodunit film, but nothing comparable to Hemingway.' He said, 'Well, you're not really a dumb Swede after all.' And I said I didn't think I was." Lancaster found director Robert Siodmak not only inventive with the camera, but "particularly well fitted to directing it [*The Killers*]; a charming, engaging man ... strong, dramatic films were his *metier*."

Told in flashback, *The Killers* was the violent account of a fighter (Burt) on the skids who had been double-crossed by underworld hoodlums and his tramp girl-friend (Ava Gardner). As he awaits death, he recalls the course of events leading up to his plight. Ironically, in the lunch room below the fighter's apartment are the two hit men (Charles McGraw and William Conrad) who have been hired to liquidate him.

The Killers turned out to be one of the big hits of the 1946 season. It made Lancaster and Ava Gardner stars and launched a rash of features about good, but not too bright men, who are done in by siren types. (Such a vogue had been popular a decade before in Europe, mainly through the French films of Jean Gabin).

Burt fared quite well in his screen bow. Otis L. Guernsey, Jr. (*New York Herald-Tribune*) recorded that he "portrays a likeable fall guy in a most promising screen debut." *Variety* agreed that "he does a strong job." When Donald Siegel directed a new version of *The Killers* (Universal) in 1964, John Cassavetes would assume Lancaster's former role.

With Jeff Corey, Albert Dekker, and Ava Gardner in *The Killers* (Univ., 1946)

With Norma Anderson on their wedding day (December 28, 1946) in Yuma, Arizona

As a sign of growing status, Lancaster, along with several other Wallis contractees, appeared in the 1947 Paramount all-star revue show, *Variety Girl*. Burt was paired with Lizabeth Scott. He was the cowboy assigned to shoot a cigarette out of the actress' languid mouth. After the shot is fired, a puff of smoke materializes. Then complacent Lancaster is seen arranging a sign, "Girl Wanted." Finish of the blackout sketch.

Following the success of *The Killers*, Burt's role in *Desert Fury* (Paramount, 1947) was expanded again. "The part I was to play in *Desert Fury* as it was originally set up was a good one, but very definitely a secondary kind of role; and if I had done it before, it's impossible to say how long it would have been before I'd have been given anything that would have captured the public's fancy. Hal Wallis re-wrote all of *Desert Fury* to enlarge my role because suddenly he decided he had a star on his hands."

While *Desert Fury* was reshaped to the producer's specifications, Burt was allowed to re-join producer Mark Hellinger at Universal for *Brute Force* (*Desert Fury* and *Variety Girl* constituted his two Wallis-Paramount releases for 1947). This new film turned into a brooding, but heavy-handed prison melodrama as directed by Jules Dassin. First-billed Burt played Joe Collins, one of a number of jailbirds whose unfortunate backgrounds are related via flashbacks. Lancaster's role called for him to take part in an attempted prison break in order to go home to be with the girl (Ann Blyth) he loves while she undergoes a cancer operation. A dark, awesome feature, *Brute Force* focused on the terrible ways in which prisoners were forced to live. Hume Cronyn as Captain Munsey stole top acting honors as the sadistic prison authority. For boxoffice allure Universal guest-starred four of its top newcomer-leading ladies (Yvonne De Carlo, Blyth, Ella Raines, and Anita Colby) and promi-

189

nently featured an alluring picture of Miss De Carlo on the film's advertising. The accompanying blurb read, "This kind of woman drives men to prison—and then drives them *crazy to get out!*" Perhaps the most interesting parts of the hard-hitting film were the flashbacks with the four girls.

The powerful *Brute Force* did a lot to consolidate Burt's screen reputation. As the *New York Herald-Tribune* acknowledged, "Jules Dassin's staging has called for a great many closeups of Lancaster looking steely-eyed and unshaven; but these do not become monotonous within Lancaster's brooding effective performance." The film has always remained a favorite with Lancaster. "It was a very potent, and I think for those particular days—the middle of the 1940s—it was a larger-than-life approach to things. The characters were all very strong, and very romantically written—as opposed to the documentary approach to that kind of film."

Regarding the gratuitous use of the women in the film, Burt acknowledged to journalists: "No doubt about it. But this was all part of Hollywood then. The emphasis was always with the love story. A film could be about Gable or Tracy, but the conflict was always with a woman who loved Gable or Tracy. The feeling was that people always wanted to see some sort of love story; and the truth is that this still prevails today in the so-called popular film. Or even in a deeper sense, we often say that no story's worth telling unless it's a love story. We don't mean now that no story's worth telling unless it's a love story. We don't mean now that it has to be a boy-girl or man-woman love story. It can be something about the love of an idea or a cause, or the hatred of an establishment which means therefore the love of humanity. But in those days they made films for very safe reasons. They believed that what was known to work well at the box office should not be tampered with. So in *Brute Force* the men in jail had to have love interests on the outside, to create a sympathetic link. If one of the girls didn't really love the man but was just using him, that made you feel sorry for him—and so on.

"The character I played in *Brute Force* was different from The Swede. The Swede was confused and lacked sophistication so when his love affair with the glamorous Ava Gardner went to pieces he literally didn't care to live anymore, which is some indication of his limits if you like. But for Collins in *Brute Force,* it was another matter. He wasn't stupid. Of course, he had a very sticky, sentimental relationship with Ann Blyth as a little crippled girl. But there was one prevailing thing: Collins, in his own uneducated way, was a strong and shrewd man with a growing desire to be free. No prison should hold anybody—that's the way he felt. It's a concept that was thought of as romantic in those days, but now we recognize the fallibility of the penal system, and its inability to do any good. Societies are at last having to face the idea that just putting people in jail doesn't do any good anymore, and that maybe society itself has to come up with a new concept of how to deal with people who break its laws."

Desert Fury was finally released in the fall of 1947. Despite the Wallis rewrite, Burt's role was still a secondary one, although he was given major billing. By anyone's standards it was a rather strange story. Lizabeth Scott appeared as the refined nineteen-year-old daughter of brothel-cum-casino operator Mary Astor. Scott falls for killer John Hodiak, who is on the run and stops at Miss Astor's establishment. Burt was cast as the backward local sheriff who secretly loves Scott but does not win her heart until the end of the movie when Hodiak has been killed. Wendell Corey made his screen debut in this fracas, appearing as Hodiak's overprotective gunsel.

In his ambiguous part, Burt had to be alternatively burly and brusque or husky and meek. In one scene he has a run-in with snide Hodiak:

LANCASTER: *You know . . . funny thing . . . I keep wishing for something to happen and it does.*
HODIAK: *Like what?*
LANCASTER: *Like bustin' you in the nose.*

Later on, Burt quietly rebukes willful Scott.

LANCASTER: *I always thought the best way to gentle a colt was to put a rope around it. But I'm beginning to have my doubts.*

The *New York Times* found the color film's only fury in the musical score. As for Burt, the *New York Herald-Tribune* decided, "Lancaster is merely a romantic prop."

If Burt's film career was not progressing on a steady, upward curve, his personal life seemed to be smooth enough. On December 28, 1946, he had wed Norma Anderson. Soon their entire household—her son by a previous marriage, Burt's widowed father (who had become his manager), and Lancaster's widowed sister-in-law—were living at a surfside home at Malibu Beach.

Ever anxious to make full use of his stock company, Wallis cast Burt with Lizabeth Scott, Kirk Douglas, Wendell Corey, and Kristine Miller in *I Walk Alone* (Paramount), the first of his four starring pictures for the 1948 season. The publicity for this sticky thriller read, "He fell for the oldest trick in the world. . . . If you want to pump a guy—send a dame." The dame in question was moist-lipped Miss Scott, who was teamed with Burt for the third and last time.

I Walk Alone was made in the same vein as *The Killers* with Burt as an ex-bootlegger who has just been released from prison after fourteen years behind bars. He has trouble adjusting to outside life and becomes bitter, wanting revenge against the smart-mouthed hoodlum (Douglas), who had framed him, causing him to go to jail. At Kirk's club he falls for the local thrush (Scott), who happened to be Douglas' mistress. The conflict over the girl and the prior double-cross lead the two men to a final showdown.

The film, produced on a tight budget, was successful, but did little for Burt's career. Bosley Crowther (*New York Times*) noted that he played the role of Frankie Madison "with the blank-faced aplomb of Tarzan." As with *Brute Force,* critics were beginning to comment on the "expressionless" attitude of Lancaster in his film roles. Some insisted that the only acting he did was by changing the style of his haircut. Lancaster later described both *Desert Fury* and *I Walk Alone* as "lightweight in their value."[4]

Burt took a large salary cut to return to Universal to work for producer Chester Erskine in his adaptation of Arthur Miller's Broadway play *All My Sons* (1948). Burt was given second-billing as Chris Keller, the son of a factory owner (Edward G. Robinson) in a small town. Robinson once stood trial for selling defective parts to the government which caused the death of twenty-one flyers. Chris is quite loyal to his dad, but he also loves Louisa Horton, the daughter of Frank Conroy, Robinson's ex-partner who went to jail due to the scandal. Howard Duff, the girl's brother,

[4]On May 24, 1948, Lancaster made his radio debut with Miss Scott and Kirk Douglas as the trio repeated their roles from *I Walk Alone* on "Lux Radio Theatre."

191

Publicity pose for *I Walk Alone* (Par., 1947)

With Barbara Stanwyck and Ann Richards in *Sorry, Wrong Number* (Par., 1948)

urges her not to marry Chris because his father was actually guilty, not their own father, and because she also loved Chris' brother (who was one of the flyers killed). Lancaster's Chris learns that his dad, having been set free on a technicality, is actually the culprit. Later, Lancaster discovers a letter from his brother who said he went on the suicide mission as retribution for his father's act. He reads the letter to Robinson, who later commits suicide. Then Chris and the girl leave to get married.

Critical reaction to *All My Sons* was decided mixed, due primarily to the confusing plot rather than the performances. Said Howard Barnes (*New York Herald-Tribune*), "While there are scenes of fine indignation in the motion picture, realized to the full by Edward G. Robinson, Burt Lancaster, Mady Christians, and Frank Conroy, they do not off-set fabricated situations and blurred characterizations." Robinson and Lancaster repeated their roles on radio on NBC's "Camel Screen Guild Players" production of the film on November 11, 1948.

Next, the actor "prevailed upon Hal Wallis to put me into *Sorry, Wrong Number*. I was out fishing with him one day and we got to talking about the film, which of its kind was rather good. The part I played was originally intended, as Wallis explained to me, for someone like the actor Lee Bowman, who tended to play characters who were rather weak. But Bowman himself was not going to be in it. They were searching for someone. I said, 'Why don't you let me play it?' And Wallis said, 'You're too strong for it.' Those were his exact words. And I said, 'But that's the whole idea: a strong-looking boy on the threshold of life allows a woman to buy him and then suffers for it, and all of his character has been drained out of him. And at the beginning of the film they'll believe I'm strong, and the contrast will make for real dramatic excitement.' Well, he talked about it to Anatole Litvak, who was to direct it; and Litvak liked the idea. So I did that."

Sorry, Wrong Number (Paramount, 1948) was adapted to the screen by Lucille Fletcher from her famed radio script; originally, the melodrama was a solo character outing which was made famous in the audio medium by Agnes Moorehead. On celluloid the basic idea was expanded and it now concerned a wealthy, but greedy woman (Barbara Stanwyck) who is bedridden in her large mansion, alone except for a telephone. She accidentally overhears plans on the phone to kill her and she spends the remainder of the eighty-nine minute feature trying desperately to convince first the police and then anyone whom she could get to listen to her that she has been marked for murder. Lancaster had the decidedly secondary role of her young husband who has hired an assassin to kill her so he may collect her fortune and pay off his mounting gambling debts. An added plotline was his battle with himself on whether or not to allow the killing to take place. By the time he convinces himself to stop the slaughter, it is too late.

A taut melodrama, *Sorry, Wrong Number* won Barbara Stanwyck an Academy Award nomination, and it did nothing to hurt Burt's ever-rising career. "Burt Lancaster continues his steady advance from muscleman to accomplished actor," claimed *Look* Magazine. Howard Barnes (*New York Herald-Tribune*) acknowledged, "Lancaster is grimly persuasive as the homicidal husband who gets caught in mesh of telephone calls." By this point, filmmakers estimated that Burt's name on a picture meant a minimum gross of one million dollars. Clearly, he had kept abreast of such other cinema toughs as established John Garfield and newcomer Kirk Douglas.

Since Lancaster meant so much boxoffice power for studios, he and Harold Hecht decided to form a production company to take advantage of his profitable allure. They formed Hecht-Norma Productions, Inc., named after Harold and Lancaster's wife. Their first film, however, was hardly a forecast of the artistic films they would create over the next decade. The initial venture was *Kiss the Blood Off My Hands* (Universal, 1948), taken from Gerald Butler's novel. It was directed by ex-actor Norman Foster. Lancaster and Hecht borrowed the needed funds and managed to bring in the project only three days over the planned forty-five-day shooting schedule. The fledgling producers surmounted a wild array of production problems, including inclement weather which delayed the outdoor shooting, star Joan Fontaine's pregnancy, and troubles with co-lead Robert Newton who found it difficult to adjust to sudden changes in the shooting schedule.

Kiss the Blood Off My Hands has a captivating opening sequence: running Lancaster is being chased by an unknown person. The foreword announces, "War brings ruin to men and cities, and cities are easier to rebuild." It turns out Burt is a young Canadian merchant marine who is subject to fits of uncontrolled rage. While drinking in a London pub one night, he is accosted by a drunk whom he stabs. A black marketeer barfly (Newton) observes the killing and blackmails the frightened young man who had spent years in a Nazi concentration camp. Newton demands that Lancaster participate in a hijacking venture. While being hounded by Newton, Burt meets young, aristocratic nurse Joan Fontaine and they fall in love ("You're everything that's bad—but I've never loved any man like this," proclaimed the ads). She is dragged into Lancaster's problems, and eventually the good girl stabs and kills Newton when he tries to put additional pressure on her new lover. The couple then

194

With Joan Fontaine in *Kiss the Blood Off My Hands* (Univ., 1948)

make a dash for freedom, but in the unsatisfying finale, they change their minds, and decide to turn themselves over to the police.[5]

With such an exploitable title plus the contrast of such diversified lead players, it was almost impossible for *Kiss the Blood Off My Hands* not to do well in distribution. Best of all, it demonstrated that producer Lancaster knew how to showcase Lancaster the star actor. Even the *New York Herald-Tribune*'s Joe Pihodna had to admit, "[He] walks off with the acting honors even with stiff competition from Joan Fontaine." On the other hand, Thomas M. Pryor (*New York Times*) made his review of the melodrama into a short essay on Lancaster the performer. In a piece captioned "Lancaster Fights the World Again," Pryor said: "The process of humanizing Burt Lancaster obviously is not going to be easy and it is going to take time. Mr. Lancaster is handy with his fists and speaks most eloquently when using them. But to develop fully as an actor and to come over to the right side of society he will have to make a break someday, for there are only so many variations on the theme of being misunderstood and Mr. Lancaster has just about exhausted them."

Not content with turning out four major films for 1948 release, Burt found time to join with his old pal Nick Cravat in a circus act which they performed on a personal appearance tour (Chicago, Milwaukee, and New York City) in November, 1948. The act received a ten-thousand-dollar weekly salary.

Burt was very conscious of his tough man image, a stereotype which he found hard to shake. The clichéd image persisted despite such folksy publicity pieces as

[5]In the novel, the heroine and her beau end up outside of England, but her face is scarred beyond recognition.

the following from *Movie Pix*: "It may come as a surprise to a lot of people that Burt Lancaster has a charming smile, but he has. . . . The down-at-the-spirit roles he has been playing ever since *The Killers* have not given him much opportunity to smile on the screen. Fans have not complained, for in a lad [he was thirty-six at the time!] like Lancaster, the rugged qualities they adore do not necessarily include a flashing set of white teeth."

Nineteen-hundred-forty-nine was a year of variety for Burt. He and Cravat returned to their old employers, the Cole Brothers Circus, to perform their acrobatic act, but this time they were paid a weekly salary of $11,000. Having proved that he was now in the big league, Burt's name was frequently mentioned for this or that major project. At one point, he was considered as a replacement for a recalcitrant John Garfield in *The Breaking Point* (Warner Bros., 1950), but Garfield eventually agreed to the project. Through his production unit, Lancaster hoped to film *The Naked and the Dead,* with Mark Robson directing, and to do a version of Theodore Dreiser's *St. Columba and the River,* neither of which projects materialized for the star. One idea which tremendously appealed to Lancaster, especially after his Cole Bros. stint, was *Advance Man,* which dealt with a circus press agent. At the time he assured everyone who would listen that it would in no way compete with the pending Cecil B. DeMille epic, *The Greatest Show on Earth* (Paramount, 1952). With his Wallis agreement subject to renegotiation, Burt was able to wangle a contract with Warner Bros. which provided that he would, via his Norma Productions, make three films for the Burbank studio over the next three years. It put Lancaster in the same category as that veteran tough-guy star James Cagney who, with his brother William, had just signed a similar advantageous producing pact with Warner Bros. Under the revised agreement with Wallis, Lancaster owed the studio at least three more feature film appearances.

Burt's first film foray in 1949 was *Criss Cross* (Universal). "There are a lot of behind-the-scenes things that people just don't know," Lancaster later explained. "In the case of *Criss Cross,* Mark Hellinger had an original idea about the holding up of a race track, and he had gone into an enormous amount of study as to how this would be done: things to do with the guards, and the handling of the trucks that come, and the switching back and forth of millions of dollars from the bank. He had an exciting *Rififi* approach to the whole thing. But at this time Hellinger died. Now, apart from my Wallis contract, I had a contract with Hellinger for three pictures. I had made two, *The Killers* and *Brute Force.* Then this half-finished version of *Criss Cross* was part of Hellinger's estate, which under his contract with Universal reverted to the studio. And I was obliged to do it. But they really didn't have a script. So they came up with a kind of a rehashed-chow of a script. Siodmak was in a similar position to me: he was obligated to do that film as part of his deal with the Hellinger estate. So we backed into a picture that nobody really wanted to do, and the end result was a poor one."

Actually, Burt's dislike of the film may be due more to the fact that he took a decided second place to Yvonne De Carlo and Dan Duryea in the proceedings than to the quality of the picture. Siodmak effectively used his equipment to draw a tight picture of a dark, brooding underworld where men are manipulated for desire of money. Also following a subplot from *The Killers,* the film pointed out how a seductive woman (De Carlo) can use and break men at her will. The film also had a most uncompromising finale. Today it holds up very well. Thomas M. Pryor (*New York Times*) took another crack at the star. In his newspaper review headlined,

"Burt Lancaster Same Old Guy," he labeled the film "A tough, mildly exciting melodrama." He then burst out with, "Burt Lancaster eventually gets around to being the same old tough guy of yore. It should not be surprising that his performance is competent for he has been working at the same type of role for some time." James S. Barstow, Jr. (*New York Herald-Tribune*) echoed this opinion: "Lancaster is almost forced into a near-by parody of his previous dumb brute portrayals. . . . He is given the thankless job of holding down a responsible job as an armored car policeman and at the same time appearing stupid enough to be led by the nose by a floozie to an improbable group of criminals and his death after a payroll holdup."

Lancaster's next film, *Rope of Sand* (Paramount, 1949), was a steamy melodrama which, by reteaming Paul Henreid, Claude Rains, and Peter Lorre, hoped to create some of the magic of their last joint outing, *Casablanca* (Warner Bros.). However, Corinne Calvet, in her American film debut, was no Ingrid Bergman, Burt Lancaster did not have Humphrey Bogart's charisma, and *Rope of Sand,* as directed by William Dieterle, was pretty flimsy going. Set in the diamond fields of South Africa, it cast taciturn Lancaster as a big game hunter who returns to the town of Diamondstad to hand out revenge on an old enemy, vicious police commandant Henreid, as well as to abscond with a few diamonds. There he meets sultry Miss Calvet as well as the urbane chief of a local mining company (Rains).

However, some of the film's dialogue was more priceless for its silliness than the gems in question:

> RAINS: *How did you get in?*
> LANCASTER: *The door was open.*
> (Or later:)
> CALVET: *What's going to happen when someone unties the knot that holds you together?*
> LANCASTER: *Maybe you'll be around to pick up the pieces.*
> (But it is Rains who has the most engaging line to speak [to Calvet]: *How do I know I can trust you? I can't compete with love.*

Rope of Sand can be said to close Burt's fledgling period in Hollywood. No longer under the direct aegis of Wallis (although the director would still be a great influence on the star), Burt had risen from vagabond to a top flight screen star, equaling in popularity Kirk Douglas, Robert Mitchum, and others of the new breed. Having specialized in the tough, inwardly tormented soul, in the new decade, Burt would try to break into new acting paths. Ironically, the fifties would be ruled by the antiheroes, Marlon Brando and James Dean. The latter died at the peak of his fame in the middle of the decade, and the former might never have gotten his big movie break, if it had not been for Lancaster.

During Burt's early years in Hollywood, Elia Kazan, and Tennessee Williams in New York City, wanted him to star in the role of Stanley Kowalski for the original Broadway production of *A Streetcar Named Desire*. Due to his film obligations, however, he had to reject the part that eventually went to Brando. "I don't say that I would have done it as well as Brando, but I do think I would have been very good for that particular role, but I never got the chance to do it."

For his first co-production with Warner Bros., Burt teamed with Harold Hecht and Frank Ross to produce and appear in the tongue-in-cheek swashbuckler, *The Flame and the Arrow* (1950). Smoothly directed by Jacques Tourneur, this colorful

With Nick Cravat and Robin Hughes in *The Flâme and the Arrow* (WB, 1950)

medieval thriller cast Lancaster as a daredevil in Lombardy who aids a fair damsel (Virginia Mayo) and, with his mute pal (Nick Cravat),[6] succeeds in eliminating German invaders, led by Robert Douglas, from the Italian city.

The Flame and the Arrow gave Lancaster and Cravat full opportunity to resume their acrobatics. The picture is full of pole-climbing, chandelier-swinging, and leaps, along with sword fights and bow and arrow tournaments. Burt refused the use of a stuntman and did all of his own stunts in the film. Later, he went on tour to promote the motion picture and did many of the gymnastics he had performed oncamera in person. Asked why he did so, he replied, "I've got a couple of thousand bucks in that picture. What's a neck?"

Most critics applauded this swashbuckling spoof and took occasion to compare Burt favorably with established legends in the genre like Douglas Fairbanks (Sr. and Jr.) and Errol Flynn. Stripped to his waist on several onscreen occasions here, Burt was, as the *New York Herald-Tribune* admitted, "a sight to behold."

Originally, Hal B. Wallis had scheduled Burt to star in *Dark City* (Paramount, 1950) with Lizabeth Scott, but then there arose two loan-out deals which would have been too lucrative for the producer to turn down. While Lancaster was shipped off to Twentieth Century-Fox and to MGM, Wallis' new contractee, Charlton Heston,

[6]Born in 1911, Nick Cravat made his film debut in *The Flame and the Arrow* and later appeared with former circus partner Lancaster in *The Crimson Pirate* (1952), *Run Silent, Run Deep* (1958), *The Scalphunter* (1968), *Airport* (1970), and *The Midnight Man* (1974). Among his other films were *Veils of Bagdad* (1953), *Three Ring Circus* (1954), *King Richard and the Crusaders* (1954), *Davy Crockett—King of the Wild Frontier* (1955), *Kiss Me Deadly* (1955), *The Story of Mankind* (1957), and *The Way West* (1967).

made his major film debut in *Dark City*. (Nine years later, Lancaster would turn down an offer to star in *Ben Hur* for MGM, and Heston would take that role, too.)

Being a "movie star" did not exempt an individual from undergoing the usual complexities of home life. Burt Lancaster was no exception. There were now three children[7] in the Lancaster household: James, William (born November 17, 1947), and Susan (born July 5, 1949). In 1950 son Billy contracted a mild case of poliomyelitis. Fortunately, the illness did not last very long, and the boy would grow up to appear in some of his father's films.

For his second feature of 1950, Burt went to Fox for *Mister 880*, a lighthearted little film in which he played a U.S. Treasury agent on the trail of the title character (Edmund Gwenn). Old man Gwenn made counterfeit one-dollar bills and had eluded the law for a decade. Along the way the agent becomes romantically entangled with a United Nations translator (Dorothy McGuire). While he did his best to add a sense of *joie de vivre* to the proceedings, Burt's flashy, toothy smile was far overshadowed by the deftness of Gwenn's crafty performance.

Plans for Burt to star in the life story of William Lurye, the International Ladies Garment Workers Union official who died a violent death at the hands of hoodlums, fell through when Warners Bros. decided that this semi-documentary project was not "viable" entertainment. But Lancaster did decamp to Culver City to make his first Western, *Vengeance Valley* (1951). This lusty drama, which utilized location filming in the Rocky Mountains of Colorado, benefitted from Richard Thorpe's direction which added a tough quality to the feature. Many critics hailed its very authentic cattle roundup scenes. Lancaster was cast as no-good Robert Walker's foster brother, who continually takes the blame for Walker's wrong-doings. The final breaking point comes when Walker fathers a son by a local waitress and then

[7]Daughter Joanne would be born on July 2, 1951, and daughter Sighle-Ann on July 3, 1954.

With Sally Forrest in *Vengeance Valley* (MGM, 1951)

With Phyllis Thaxter in *Jim Thorpe—All American* (WB, 1951)

tries to foist off the child as Burt's so he will not lose his good wife. Eventually, Lancaster turns on Walker and they have a fatal showdown. In the first of what would be many shoot-em-up adventures, Lancaster proved a natural for the genre.

With his athletic prowess, it seemed a natural for Burt to star in *Jim Thorpe—All American* (Warner Bros., 1951). As helmed by facile Michael Curtiz, the feature retold the famed athlete's life, from his poor beginnings to his winning contests at the 1912 Olympics, in which he was later disqualified. Again calling for a lot of physical action on the part of the star, the film unfortunately had too many talky interludes. To the film's credit, the romantic scenes with Phyllis Thaxter were well handled, as were the segments in which Thorpe wins the friendship of a previously hostile college mate (Steve Cochran).

Although the film remains one of Lancaster's favorites—in it, he began to preach for the cause of the American Indian—the film glossed over too many of the unpleasant real events in Thorpe's life. In the last years of his life (he died on March 28, 1953) Thorpe was reduced to accepting bit parts in films, usually playing the stereotyped Indian in ever-increasing cheaper and more witless productions. Hollywood could jab itself in the ribs with tongue-in-cheek comedies or sentimental glamour dramas like *Sunset Boulevard* (Paramount, 1950), but hard-hearted films about people like Thorpe who were often abused by the movie industry were *verboten* at this time.

Then, for Hecht-Norma Productions, Lancaster went over to Columbia for the mindless diversion, *Ten Tall Men* (1951). Conceived as pure escapist fare, this desert drama presented Burt as Sarge, the leader of the Foreign Legionnaires of the title who battle the Riffs in the Sahara Desert while they kidnap a sheik's daughter. The whole affair, if unmemorable, was at least action-filled and fun.

As part of the package for *Ten Tall Men* at Columbia, Harry Cohn's studio agreed to release Hecht-Norma Productions' *The First Time* (1951). Harold Hecht was listed as the sole producer of this weak farce in which an infant narrates his trials and tribulations with his parents (Barbara Hale and Robert Cummings) as they attempt to care for their prima-donna child.

About this time, Burt, who still had contractual obligations to Hal B. Wallis, agreed to appear on television with Wallis' *wunderkind*, Dean Martin and Jerry Lewis, on their NBC-TV hosted show, "The Colgate Comedy Hour." The usually serious Lancaster took part in a comedy skit with the mayhem duo.

Very mindful of the terrific response to Burt's appearance in *The Flame and the Arrow*, Hecht-Norma and Warner Bros. were eager to offer the star in another swashbuckling epic for public consumption and profit. As in the former entry, pal Nick Cravat again played Lancaster's onscreen henchman in this heavily tongue-in-cheek satire on the genre, *The Crimson Pirate* (Warner Bros. 1952). Here, Lancaster's Vallo abandons his profession as a pirate to join with a South American revolution against Spain in the buccaneer days in order to win the heart of exotic Conseulo (Eva Bartok). The film was full of action and comedy, leading many critics to endorse it as the best satire ever made on the Douglas Fairbanks-Errol Flynn type of cinema fare.

The Crimson Pirate was shot on location in England and on the Mediterranean Sea, although the locale for this sixteenth-century story was the Caribbean. The actor later commented, "I designed all the action sequences for *The Crimson Pirate*, all the comedy stuff, I worked with a comedy writer as well as with [director Robert] Siodmak himself. And as a matter of fact, the whole last part of the film, the fight on the ship, which runs eighteen minutes of screentime, with all the gags and jokes, was shot by a writer and myself while Siodmak was in London shooting interiors for another part of the film."

After viewing *The Crimson Pirate,* critic Alton Cook called Lancaster "one of our most amiable and strenuous comedians" and many critics began to comment that he was the perfect successor to Errol Flynn in action films. Never wanting to be type-cast, Lancaster only re-entered the swashbuckler field once more.

By this time, Burt realized an actor had to be astute in the choice of roles he accepted in motion pictures. "An actor has got to have certain things going for him, if he's a truly great actor. I could describe the quality as something innate in him, something that in a sense has nothing to do with any qualification or experience he might have: it's just a God-given talent. On the other hand, a very good actor has to be intelligent, has to be sensitive, and has to have some kind of strength. That applies to women, too. A good actress has 'balls' in addition to heart and mind. As for myself, I had a pretty varied background. I was an avid reader. I was a music buff: I lived at the opera and at concerts. I wasn't the little boy coming to town from some place in South Dakota, who looked as if he'd just walked off the farm. I was born in New York and I'd spent all my life there, and it's a very sophisticated city. I had a reasonable knowledge of the political aspect of things, too. So, with these qualities, I was able to look at a script and see the values in it."

Naturally, Lancaster's desire for responsible cinema was made manifest in his own productions. "I felt [when starting Hecht-Norma] that Hollywood couldn't go on doing a lot of what was pure pap, as well as a lot of good films that were purely entertaining. People had to be given some of the realities of life. And, of course, in the years following the war, the USA was going through an enormous catharsis at all levels, and the country today finds itself in a very unpleasant position as a result of the evolution of those years. Films in their own way are history-making. Like all good art they illuminate something.

"This doesn't mean that all films should be very serious things. There's a great deal of room for the pleasant fun film. But people also need to be aware—because what's going on in the world is in some way affecting the way they're living, and how they're going to live in the future. In the final analysis, the direction life takes will fall into their own hands. They will have to make decisions as to how they want their own societies to move. So all art must take that into consideration—and film can be one of the great art forms."

Long before he became a star, Lancaster had learned to discount the myths of Hollywood and its way of life. "When I was a kid I was aware that fine films were coming from abroad. Some of the early French and English films had a great deal to say. They were not necessarily popular in the USA. You'd see them in New York in small theatres: it's ironic that a film like *La Grande Illusion* should only play at a small theatre, but it did. The feeling of exhibitors was that people wouldn't be interested. Even later on, I can remember the first time I saw *Great Expectations* I thought, 'Gee, that's a marvelous film.' But it wasn't a successful film in the USA. Yet on every level it was superb. Now when people see it on TV, they think, 'My, what a marvelous film.' But at the time when it was new the theatres were reluctant to show English films because they thought that Americans wouldn't know what the actors were saying. The reactions were terribly basic. But all that's changed now. The world of film is international now."

Although a deal could not be worked out for Burt's services to be loaned to Cecil

B. DeMille for *The Greatest Show on Earth* (Paramount, 1952), Hal B. Wallis utilized the star's talents for *Come Back, Little Sheba* (Paramount, 1952). William Inge's touching play had been produced on Broadway with Shirley Booth and Sidney Blackmer to great acclaim. When Wallis announced his plans to film the project with Miss Booth recreating her stage part, Burt requested the role of the husband, Doc Delaney. "I guess I wanted to play [the part] more than any other I ever got close to. Doc Delaney is the most human, if imperfect, kind of guy ever written into a play or script. I purposely didn't see the play because I had my own ideas of how Doc should be portrayed."

Come Back, Little Sheba was the melancholy account of a quiet-living middle-aged couple. Lola Delaney (Booth) is the slatternly wife, a woman who had once been beautiful but who has faded with each year. Burt's Doc is an alcoholic on the wagon. He had had to leave medical school to marry Booth, although their child died in infancy. Then he became a chiropractor, but in the ensuing years he began to drink. As the story opens he has reformed and is working again. His wife listens intently to soap operas and makes a general nuisance of herself. The stimulus of a young girl boarder (Terry Moore) in the house reminds Doc of his squandered life, and he goes back to the bottle, then attempts to kill his wife. He is yanked off to a hospital for therapy and alcohol withdrawal, and eventually returns to his wife. As they reconcile, the slightly wiser woman admits that her precious little dog, Sheba, who has been missing for weeks, is probably gone forever. She now realizes that Doc must be her full-time interest.

Miss Booth received an Academy Award for her performance, but most critics found Lancaster too young and inexperienced for the part of her drunken husband.[8] Said Lindsay Anderson in *Sight and Sound*, "Lancaster is an actor of instinctive sensitivity, whose playing has always a certain gentleness and sensibility. But his range is limited, and this difficult part goes beyond it. In the simple matter of age he is quite wrong, and the heavy lines of make-up and the whitened hair do not convince."

But the venture was not a loss, as far as Burt was concerned: "I got extraordinarily interesting reviews for the first time. The tendency of a reviewer is to regard you in the image you have had before. In other words I was the leading man or the swashbuckler, blah-blah-blah. And suddenly they began to think of me as a serious actor. So that was a progression in my career."

To help finish out his Warner Bros. obligations, Lancaster made *South Sea Woman* (1953) which was produced "very quickly." In it, he played a Marine sergeant in pre-World War II Honolulu who tries to save a buddy (Chuck Connors) from a tart (Virginia Mayo), but quickly becomes enamored of her himself. Arthur Lubin, a veteran at this type of fare, handled it well, but the picture was termed "a terrible lot of nonsense" by Bosley Crowther (*New York Times*).

While making this low-budget vehicle, Lancaster agreed to perform a cameo in Warner Bros.' *Three Sailors and a Girl* (1953), and he even wore his uniform from *South Sea Woman* in his brief unbilled appearance. The film was an old-fashioned Gordon MacRae-Jane Powell musical. At the finale, Burt appears backstage and says to Sam Levene, "You'll never make it in show business, kid."

Burt's next 1953 appearance, filmed before *Come Back, Little Sheba*, was *From Here to Eternity* (Columbia). It contains what is most likely Lancaster's finest screen

[8]Miss Booth counseled Lancaster, "Burt, once in a while you hit a note of truth and you can hear a bell ring. But most of the time I can see the wheels turning and your brain working."

In *Come Back, Little Sheba* (Par., 1952)

With Virginia Mayo and Chuck Connors in *South Sea Woman* (WB, 1953)

With Montgomery Clift and Frank Sinatra in *From Here to Eternity* (Col., 1953)

performance, and for it he received his first Academy Award nomination. Taken from James Jones' bestseller and directed by Fred Zinnemann, the feature won eight Academy Awards, including Best Picture of the Year. Despite the fact that Lancaster and co-star Montgomery Clift both lost out in the Oscar's Best Actor sweepstakes to William Holden (of *Stalag 17*), Burt did win the New York Film Critics' Award for Best Actor that year. He had finally arrived as an actor of both commercial success and artistic rank in the movie colony.

Harry Cohn had wanted Lancaster for the leading role of the tough Marine sergeant in *From Here to Eternity,* but to do so Columbia had to pay Hal B. Wallis $150,000 for a commitment the actor had to that producer. Lancaster in turn received $120,000 of that money, while Wallis earned an extra $40,000 by demanding that, as part of the package of borrowing Lancaster's services, Columbia agree to film *Bad for Each Other* (1953) with Lizabeth Scott and Charlton Heston.

In *From Here to Eternity,* Burt had the most substantial role, that of a professional Marine in Hawaii just prior to Pearl Harbor. He is a straight-laced career leather-neck who falls in love with a commissioned officer's wife (Deborah Kerr). The scene in which Lancaster and Kerr make love on the beach wearing only their swimsuits caused quite a stir at the time due to its blatant sexuality.

This seething melodrama with its pointed attack on the abuses of U.S. military life was a financial blockbuster, garnering $12.2 million in distributors' domestic rentals. As the focal point of this virile film study, Burt was now more concretely established as a top star. A. H. Weiler (*New York Times*) analyzed. "In Burt Lancaster, the producer has got a top kick to the manner born, a man whose capabilities are obvious and whose code is hard and strange, but never questionable.... His view of officers leaves him only with hatred of caste, although he could easily achieve rank, which would solve his romantic problem. But he is honest enough to eschew it and lose the only love he has known."

Following his work in *Come Back, Little Sheba,* Lancaster informed writer Erskine Johnson, "I'll go on making swashbucklers for my own company. But in my outside pictures, I want to do things that will help me as an actor against the time when I have to give up all the jumping around."

Apparently, Burt was not yet ready to give up "all the jumping around," because he returned to the sword-and-cloak genre for another time in *His Majesty O'Keefe* (Warner Bros., 1953). It was to be his final foray into the genre, his last commitment to Warner Bros., and the end of the production company called Hecht-Norma. Thereafter, Burt's independent firm would bear the name Hecht-Lancaster, until it was even later altered to Hecht-Hill-Lancaster.

The thin story behind *His Majesty O'Keefe* cast Burt as a South Seas vagabond in the 1870s who is cast off his ship by a mutinous crew and is washed ashore on the isle of Viti Levu, where he is attracted to a local girl (Joan Rice) and teaches the natives to mine copra. He becomes rich as the island's new ruler. Location filming was accomplished on the South Seas island of Fiji.

For his last two ventures of 1954 and his first two productions[9] under the Hecht-Lancaster banner, the star employed director Robert Aldrich for *Apache* and *Vera Cruz,* each released by United Artists. Later, Aldrich said he found Lancaster "not

[9]Hecht-Lancaster acquired the screen rights to *Operation Heartbreak* by the late Viscount Norwich, Sir Alfred Duff Cooper, the First Lord of the Admiralty (1937-1938). The production firm hoped to star Alec Guinness in the screen rendition of the property, but the project never materialized.

With Benson Fong in *His Majesty O'Keefe* (WB, 1953)

an easy man to get along with but quite responsive." *Apache* was a colorful and well-intentioned Western that "gives onetime Circus-Acrobat Lancaster plenty of opportunities to leap daringly from crag to crag, horse to horse, and frying pan to fire" (*Time* Magazine). The color production left behind the usual Indian stereotypes in relating the account of a brave named Massai who attempts to improve the lot of his people by conducting a one-man war against the United States Army in the 1880s. Jean Peters as his squaw and Lancaster made an "outstanding" team (*Variety*). The film opened with a touching performance by Monte Blue, in his final picture role, as the dying Geronimo.

The chief fault with *Apache*, which was not a crowd-pleaser, was cited by the British *Monthly Film Bulletin:* "We remain conscious that these are two actors [Lancaster and Peters] doing a very decent best in an impossible task. The strangeness is missing: Indians are not just white Americans with a different-colored skin and a simplified vocabulary." Another failing of the project was the finale. Onscreen the surrounded loner, Massai, hears the cry of his new-born child, and feeling there is now something to live for, gives up to the advancing whites. This unconvincing finish to the plotline was brought about at the demands of the front office, whereas Hecht-Lancaster had originally planned a tragic ending to the rebel Indian who escaped from the deportation train taking him to exile in Florida.

Although Burt had made several male camaraderie films already, *Vera Cruz* was the first to team him with a top-notch boxoffice attraction. Hecht-Lancaster obtained the services of Gary Cooper, who took first billing as Lancaster's co-star. Filmed in SuperScope and Technicolor in Mexico, this actioner was set in 1866 during the Mexican Revolution, with Cooper and Lancaster cast as two U.S. sol-

In *Apache* (UA, 1954)

dlers-of-fortune who become mercenaries. Sarita Montiel falls for Cooper and asks him to fight for the rebels under Juarez, while an aide (Cesar Romero) to Emperor Maximilian asks them to fight for the government. At a ball, the duo meet a countess (Denise Darcel) and they agree to escort her to Vera Cruz. Along the way she tells them that she has gold for the Emperor's cause and suggests they "steal" the precious metal and split the proceeds among themselves. Romero, however, learns of the plans, absconds with the money, and leads Cooper and Lancaster (and their contingent) to storm the enemy fortress. Although Lancaster gains possession of the gold, Montiel convinces Cooper that the money belongs to the rebels. Cooper trails Lancaster and is forced to kill the latter when he refuses to relinquish the loot.

The *New York Times* observed of this action film, "Guns are more important in this shambles than Mr. Cooper or Mr. Lancaster. In short, there is nothing to redeem this film—not even the spirit of the season. Some Christmas show, indeed." If people wondered about Lancaster's generosity at handing Cooper the supposed fattest role in the picture, any of their speculation about his charity was dispelled by the final results (and all to the detriment of the feature). Said Rene Jordan in *Gary Cooper* (1974): "*Vera Cruz*, for what little it is worth, belongs to Burt Lancaster, who seduces Denise Darcel and performs many an acrobatic feat with a glittering, malevolent grin, as if his very teeth were high on adrenalin. It is a divertingly hammy performance that Aldrich tried vainly to control: co-producer Lancaster was on his way to directing himself as *The Kentuckian* [1955] and was trying his new britches on for size all over the location."

With Gary Cooper, Sarita Montiel, and Denise Darcel on the set of *Vera Cruz* (UA, 1954)

Vera Cruz did, however, provide Lancaster with his first decidedly villainous role and it was somewhat chancy on his part to abandon his painstakingly acquired hero image on film to portray a bad guy. Unfortunately, Burt would not frequently play a villain onscreen, usually preferring the good man mold. Had he lent his ability to playing psychotics and other decidedly villainous characters more often, as Robert Mitchum and especially Robert Ryan did, he might well have emerged from his "expressionless" mold that his usual run of films have permitted.

It seems almost inevitable that multi-talented people such as Lancaster would be drawn into the same pitfall as would an opposing screen type, Jerry Lewis, by directing his own pictures. *The Kentuckian* (United Artists, 1955) could not be faulted for its photography, nor for its lively musical score by Bernard Herrmann. Moreover, it had an excellent array of performers of both sexes. But the hundred-four-minute project was badly paced and limped along with little action or interest until the bullwhip sequence between Burt and Walter Matthau some eighty minutes into the production.

Lancaster starred as Big Eli, a pioneer widower, who, with his young son (Donald MacDonald), intends to leave Kentucky for the Texas frontier. However, they get sidetracked by a servant girl (Dianne Foster), a schoolmarm (Diana Lynn), and a town bully (Matthau). The *New York Times* thought this historical re-creation had "no sense of dramatic focus or control," and *Variety* insisted that Burt's acting job was "a bit too self-conscious, as though the director and the actor couldn't quite agree." On the small plus side, the picture did contain some nice cameos, especially by Una Merkel and John Carradine, the latter as a none-too-honest peddler.

The Kentuckian was a failure critically and did only mediocre boxoffice business.

With Donald MacDonald and Dianna Foster in *The Kentuckian* (UA, 1955)

210

Following its release, Lancaster told the press, "Long ago I learned it's no trick to be a director. The tough job is being a good director. . . . I probably will never again act in a picture I also direct. [It was a promise he forgot, unfortunately, some nineteen years later.] Much as I've enjoyed working as an actor in the past, it's possible I may quit that phase of show business and concentrate on being a director. That's been my real ambition ever since starring in motion pictures."

Following the grim results of *The Kentuckian*, Lancaster returned to work for Hal B. Wallis in Paramount's film version of Tennessee Williams' touching but rather uncommercial *The Rose Tattoo* (1955). The playwright had originally written the vehicle for Anna Magnani (who eventually starred in the film), but the actress had language problems and the Broadway role went to Maureen Stapleton. For box-office insurance, Burt was cast as Alvara Mangiacavallo, a visceral Italian truck driver who comes into the life of a woman who has lived with the memory of her dead husband for many years. Upon meeting Lancaster, who physically reminds the Sicilian woman of her late spouse, and finding that her dead true love had been unfaithful to her, the widow takes Lancaster in as a physical replacement for the man she once loved.

Like most Williams' works, the play had some nice dialogue and a rather engaging situation, but it was Magnani as the earthy and sexy Serafina who gave the film its life, and, for her efforts, she won an Academy Award. Lancaster, who did not appear oncamera until the film was nearly half over, emerged a decidedly second best. Said Arthur Knight (*Saturday Review*) of this Daniel Mann-directed picture, "He [Lancaster] attacks the part with zest and intelligence. . . . But one is always aware that he is acting, that he is playing a part that fits him physically, but is beyond

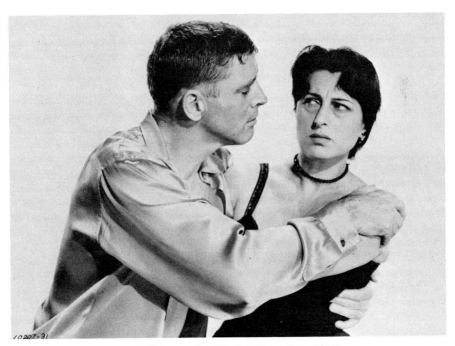

With Anna Magnani in a publicity pose for *The Rose Tattoo* (Par., 1955)

With his children (c. 1955)

his emotional depth." By way of consolation, the vulnerable star could point to the review of the *New York Times* which suggested that Lancaster "superbly" matched Magnani's performance.

Although the year 1955 was none too great from an acting point of view for Lancaster, his production company turned out the "sleeper" hit of the year in *Marty*, which Delbert Mann directed for United Artists. Ernest Borgnine starred in the Paddy Chayefsky screenplay (based on the playwright's effective earlier teleplay), and the film won four Academy Awards, including Best Picture of the Year.

Burt Lancaster has been an actor who keeps his private life very private. Despite his years as a star, he has rarely been involved in any gossip. However, in 1955, like many celebrities, he came under attack from *Confidential* Magazine. In a May issue story by Charles A. Wright, it was alleged that the actor had physically abused a number of women, including Francesca de Scaffa (Mrs. Bruce Cabot) when she came to his Santa Monica studio to test for a role in *Vera Cruz*, and playgirl Zina Rachevasky, daughter of the head of the Strauss banking concern.

The smutty story claimed that Burt had been physically abusive since he was a young boy and that he had "been handing out lumps ever since. Not a few of these have been collected by some of the world's best-known beauties." Like most of the magazine's fare, the story had no credibility or factual substance.

In 1956, Lancaster appeared in two money-makers, *Trapeze* and *The Rainmaker*, and in both he was liked by the critics. *Trapeze* was directed by Britisher Carol Reed

In *Trapeze* (UA, 1956)

With Katharine Hepburn in a publicity pose for *The Rainmaker* (Par., 1956)

for United Artists. It featured Burt as a faded, crippled ex-high-wire artist who is persuaded by a young circus performer (Tony Curtis)[10] to forget his bitterness and return to the high wire with him in a new act. The older performer teaches the younger one the tricks of the craft, until shapely aerialist Gina Lollobrigida arrives on the scene and quickly shifts her affections from Curtis to Lancaster, causing the expected emotional problems.

Trapeze was lensed in and about Paris' famed Cirque d'Hiver and the three stars did most of their own aerial work, which garnered a tremendous amount of publicity for the film. While some critics would carp at the clichéd storyline, few could discount the aerial thrills. At age forty-three, Lancaster showed that he had lost none of the agility he had enjoyed two decades before when he and Nick Cravat had performed their act in various circuses, carnivals, vaudeville houses, and nightclubs.

Switching back to Paramount and to the aegis of Hal B. Wallis, Lancaster, replacing William Holden, co-starred with aging Katharine Hepburn in N. Richard Nash's adaptation of his own stage play, *The Rainmaker*,[11] which Joseph Anthony directed. Set in the rural and drought-ridden Southwest, Burt played a jack-of-all-trades who masquerades as a "rainmaker" and comes to the small town all set to bring rain to the locals, for a price. He stays only long enough to romance spinster Hepburn. The film is talky and colorful and a fanciful attempt at an almost fairy-tale-like love affair between two lost and misguided souls.

Lancaster's burly, vital character is a brash, footloose man who is used to having his way with the ladies until he meets leathery Hepburn, a frail desert flower who helps the man turn his thoughts away from his inward self to the outside world. In turn, he convinces her that she is indeed a beautiful person and one worthy of any man. Hepburn and Lancaster's comprehension of their sensitive roles gave the film far more entertainment value than it might have had in lesser hands. Cameron Prud'Homme was on hand to provide a realistic portrayal as Hepburn's farmer father.

There is a point within *The Rainmaker* in which Lancaster's character says to the heroine, "Once in a life you've got to take a chance on a con man." Many insiders in the Hollywood community felt that Hepburn took that chance when she agreed to co-star with scene-stealing, "mugging" Lancaster. That she was Oscar-nominated for the role, said her defenders, was a tribute to her artistic ability. On the other hand, supporters of Lancaster insisted that without his flamboyant presence, the film would have died in the can.

Early in 1957, Hecht-Lancaster Productions made *The Bachelor Party* (United Artists), which, like *Marty*, was directed by Delbert Mann from a teleplay by Paddy Chayefsky. Without a real boxoffice-oriented cast (which included Don Murray, E. G. Marshall, and Carolyn Jones), the film still did good business and won fine reviews.

[10]Curtis had made his film debut in an earlier Lancaster picture, *Criss Cross*. The two cinema leads got along so well in *Trapeze* that they announced that they would jointly appear in a film version of *The Ballad of Cat Ballou*, taken from Roy Chanslor's novel. When the book was finally turned into a movie vehicle, it would be for Columbia in 1965 with Lee Marvin in an Oscar-winning performance and Michael Callan cast as his sidekick.

[11]Nash's drama was originally seen on CBS-TV's "Philco Playhouse" (August 16, 1953), with Darren McGavin in the title role. It opened on Broadway on October 28, 1954, with McGavin again playing the lead role (and Geraldine Page as his vis-a-vis). The play was eventually turned into a musical in 1964, as *110 in the Shade,* with Robert Horton in the male lead.

With Kirk Douglas at a London benefit show (July, 1958)

Lancaster appeared in two features that year, *Gunfight at the O.K. Corral* (Paramount), his final assignment for Hal B. Wallis, and *The Sweet Smell of Success*, the latter produced by his company now called Hecht-Hill-Lancaster Productions (James Hill had joined the corporation that year).

Scripted by Leon Uris and directed by John Sturges, *Gunfight at the O.K. Corral* told the events leading up to the famous gun battle between Wyatt Earp (Burt) and his friend Doc Holliday (Kirk Douglas) and the Clanton Brothers. From the beginning credits, with Frankie Laine singing the rousing title theme, throughout the colorful Western, the movie gave only a glossy reproduction of the famous gun battle. It made very little effort to stay close to the facts. Little of the true characters of Earl Holliday, and the Clantons were brought out in the adventure film. In fact, screenwriter Uris included a lady gambler (Rhonda Fleming) and a madame (Jo Van Fleet) to give the proceedings some added "dimension."

Thanks to the marquee value of Lancaster and Douglas in tandem, and the well-staged climactic gunfight, *Gunfight at the O.K. Corral*[12] did exceptionally well with the public, luring into theatres viewers who normally would have watched oaters for free on home TV.

It is interesting to note that this film re-united Burt and his old pal Kirk Douglas, the duo who starred together in *I Walk Alone* (1948) for producer Wallis. As contractees to that mogul, the two had joined together for many arguments with the producer over salaries and roles in the late forties and had developed a comradeship both personally and professionally. Some insisted that Douglas was guilty of a Burt Lancaster complex, that his chief ambition was to emulate his co-worker and to top him as a performer and producer.

Lancaster next starred for his company in *Sweet Smell of Success* (United Artists, 1957), which Clifford Odets and Ernest Lehman adapted from Lehman's novel and Britisher Alexander MacKendrick directed. For the first time he appeared for his firm in a feature that might have had dubious wide appeal had it not re-united Burt and Tony Curtis in the focal roles. The star delivered a cunning performance as a slick, bespectacled Broadway columnist who hires an equally devious young publicist (Curtis) to carry out his dirty work. The film was a cutting exposé of the viciousness of the hack journalist who has achieved wide acclaim and power through the gossip medium. A subplot found Lancaster's J. J. Hunsecker trying to use his power to control the life of his sister (Susan Harrison).

The *New York Times* judged the film "meanness . . . rendered fascinating," and *Variety* reported that it was "a remarkable change of pace for Lancaster, who appears . . . quiet but smoldering with malice and menace." In short, the finished product offered a new variation on the typical Lancasterian performance; here the inbred, inner turmoil and excess energy were channeled, not toward self-destruction or frivolous physical exertion, but toward self-aggrandizing viciousness.

In 1957 Burt was asked by *Dance* Magazine, "What does dance mean to you?" In most instances the actor would probably have ignored the question, but, being aesthetically inclined, he supplied a rather cerebral response to the monthly journal. "What particularly excites me about all art is the revelation of an individual. In dance, because of its enormous physical expenditure, which is a springboard to true

---

[12]In 1967, also for United Artists release, director John Sturges in *Hour of the Gun* would create a sequel to *Gunfight*. In the follow-up, James Garner was Wyatt Earp, Jason Robards appeared as Doc Holliday, with Robert Ryan as Ike Clanton.

With Tony Curtis, Jay Adler, and William Forrest (right) in *The Sweet Smell of Success* (UA, 1957)

psychological release, the human personality is revealed in all its nakedness." This was hardly the reply the general public would have expected from the dumb Swede of *The Killers.*

Believing that no one could protect his career interests better than himself, Burt's company produced both of his 1958 film appearances. *Run Silent, Run Deep* (United Artists) was under the strong direction of Robert Wise.[13] Remembering the box-office bonanza created by teaming Lancaster and Gary Cooper in *Vera Cruz,* the company sought the services of Clark Gable to co-star with Burt in this manly underwater tale.

Run Silent, Run Deep takes place during World War II and tells of a submarine commander (Gable) who assumes a new post after his previous sub has been sunk. His orders are to leave Pearl Harbor and overtake and destroy an enemy vessel. But he is opposed at all turns by his crew and his troubled executive officer (Burt), who in reality wants to have Gable's job. Before the finale, however, the captain earns the respect of his men and successfully carries out his mission before dying a hero's death.

This film defied the dogma that all male service pictures (especially those set in

[13]In an interview with Rui Nogueira for *Focus on Films* (1973), Wise recollected: "We had a lot of problems with the script before we started—getting something we could all agree on. Then as we were shooting, there was a lot of behind the scenes fighting and pulling going on between the three partners in the company. . . .

"[Gable] started to sense half, two-thirds of the way through the film what was going on with the script and, since it was Lancaster's company, he started to be concerned about what was going to happen to him. So he started to raise a little fuss about wanting to know what the end of the script was going to be."

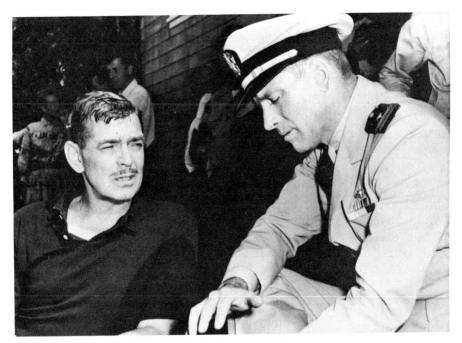

On the set of *Run Silent, Run Deep* (UA, 1958) with Clark Gable

the briny deep) would be boxoffice bombs. The tandem performances of Gable and Lancaster reminded many viewers of the Gable-Spencer Tracy teaming of years before. Critically, the venture earned some plaudits, with Bosley Crowther (*New York Times*) declaring, "A better film about guys in the 'silent service' has not been made." Of course, in financial returns, this project came nowhere near to matching the success of another masculine-oriented service venture, the comedy *Operation Petticoat* (Universal, 1959) which starred Cary Grant and Tony Curtis. It seemed the public was always more willing to respond to a laugh than to a bit of oncamera dramatic tension.

Since *Come Back, Little Sheba,* Lancaster had carefully avoided screen roles which were obviously beyond his abilities or which would lead audiences to perceive his limitations as an actor. In 1958, however, his company bought the screen rights to Terence Rattigan's two-act play, *Separate Tables,* in which Burt would play one of the leading roles with Sir Laurence Olivier set to direct the proceedings, while Vivien Leigh would star. The play had been presented on Broadway in 1956, with Margaret Leighton and Eric Portman of the London cast re-creating their original roles (each playing the two leads in the two playlets). For the film version, it was decided to enhance the boxoffice appeal by separating the cast into four major parts. After viewing Burt's "try-out" for the project, Olivier withdrew, both as actor and director, because he felt he could not properly direct the actor. He was re-placed by director Delbert Mann and by actor David Niven. Miss Leigh also withdrew from the production and was replaced by Rita Hayworth. As the fourth starring figure, Deborah Kerr was re-united with her *From Here to Eternity* co-star.

Filmed in black-and-white, the drama told the melancholy story of several people who reside at a seaside hotel in Bournemouth, England. There is Major Pollock

(Niven), who delights in spouting his war record; the timid Sibyl Railton-Bell (Kerr), who is ruled by her social snob mother (Gladys Cooper), an alcoholic American writer (Burt), who is carrying on an affair with the matronly hotel owner (Wendy Hiller). Others at the sterile hotel include two elderly ladies, a female racing buff, two unmarried lovers, and a lonely professor.

The crux of the plot breaks into two almost simultaneous events: the arrival of a newspaper with the story that the major has been convicted of lewd activities in a moviehouse, and the arrival of Lancaster's ex-wife (Rita Hayworth), an aging socialite, who wants to reclaim her lost love.

Separate Tables was nominated for Best Picture of the Year but lost to *Gigi,* while Niven won a Best Actor Oscar and Wendy Hiller was named the Best Supporting Actress. Deborah Kerr was given her fourth Oscar bid, although she lost that year to Susan Hayward (*I Want to Live*). Of the lead performers, it was Burt who came off the worst in the proceedings. His role of the defeated writer was a well-constructed character, but he did very little with it. Beyond rustling his hair, looking tired, and adopting dated stage dramatics to indicate his indecision at whether he should accept Hiller's or Hayworth's love, he did little with the part. Perhaps Laurence Olivier knew of the future when he withdrew from the project rather than try to tame the producer-star.

If *Separate Tables* was an acting defeat for Burt, it wasn't a financial one. Not only was that venture financially positive, but Hecht-Hill-Lancaster had just negotiated a twenty-six-million-dollar deal with United Artists that called for six upcoming[14] productions from the independent firm.

For his sole 1959 starter, Lancaster and company joined with Kirk Douglas' Bryna Production Company[15] to spin out a screen version of George Bernard Shaw's 1897 play *The Devil's Disciple.* The third co-star of the venture was none other than Sir Laurence Olivier who had mended his differences with Lancaster. An added attraction for the more cultured filmgoer was the return to the cinema of one of the greatest actresses of the stage, Eva LeGallienne.

The Devil's Disciple was made in Great Britain and underwent a good deal of production problems[16] before completing its lensing on a forty-eight-day schedule. It told the story of a minister (Burt) who abandons religious pacifism to join in the American Revolution. Douglas played the scoffer Richard Dundegon and Laurence Olivier capped the acting honors with his fine underplaying as the dapper British commander, General Burgoyne. The black-and-white film, unfortunately, lacked the biting satire of Shaw's original and bogged down in long stretches of uninspired diatribe. Lancaster earned some unpleasant reviews. *Time* Magazine recorded, "Lancaster glooms away Shaw's most romantic scenes as if he were lost on a Bronte moor."

[14]Among the projects was *The Way West,* which would finally be made in 1967 for United Artists with Kirk Douglas, Robert Mitchum, and Richard Widmark.

[15]Montgomery Clift had originally been signed for Douglas's role.

[16]Lancaster would later recall about the firing of director Alexander MacKendrick (who was replaced by Guy Hamilton), "A very clever director, and a very nice guy. But he took one helluva lot of time. He would get hold of a scene that was five and a half pages long and attempt to do it in one take by moving the dolly around and through his characters—an incredibly difficult task. We would arrive on the set ready to go at nine in the morning and we'd be hanging around till three in the afternoon rehearsing the moves we had to make. Then we'd shoot, and sometimes he'd say, 'No, I don't like that much. Let's do it a different way.'"

With Basil Sydney in *The Devil's Disciple* (UA, 1959)

After the failure of *The Devil's Disciple*, Hecht-Hill-Lancaster Productions came to an end in 1959 with their final venture, *Take a Giant Step*, which was released through United Artists. It starred Johnny Nash (today a popular singing star) as the young black boy who endures various trials and tribulations, including adjusting to racial prejudice and adolescent sexual urges. The *New York Times* said the film was "like a cross between a social justice brochure and a Negro Andy Hardy Film."

With two flops in a row, Lancaster's firm dissolved after nearly a decade of production. The star later noted, "We had built up an organization that was too big for the things we wanted to do. We had taken on some of the overhead-aches of a major studio, and could no longer afford to operate the way we wanted to. You can't spend two or three years preparing for a film that will have limited appeal when your overhead is the size of ours."

Extricating himself from the producing firm was no easy task and Burt was required to participate in some other ventures with his partners. James Hill produced *The Unforgiven* (United Artists, 1960), which was shot on location in the old mining town of Durango, Mexico, by director John Huston. Both Lancaster and Audrey Hepburn received $300,000 each for their work in the feature, which cost more than five million dollars to produce. Part of the enormous expense was due to delays entailed when Miss Hepburn fell off a horse while on the set, which resulted in her breaking her back. Although a colorful, actionful, and at times meaningful Western, *The Unforgiven* barely recouped its costs.

In the film, elfin Hepburn had the pivotal role as the daughter of a pioneer family; she turns out to be a half-breed and the bone of contention between the settlers and the Kiowa Indians. Burt played Ben Zachary, her foster brother, who

221

With Doug McClure in *The Unforgiven* (UA, 1960)

In *Elmer Gantry* (UA, 1960)

defends her from both sides, and who, after the climactic battle between the whites and Indians, marries her. The film contains a downbeat ending with Burt and Hepburn winning out over the "savages" but still faced with prejudice and hatred from the local settlers.

Religion in the cinema usually has been treated with kid gloves. Occasionally, however, a film would appear that questioned the more fringe type of religious zealot. One of the groups to be most consistently assaulted by the cinema has been the hell fire-and-damnation preachers of the South. For Lancaster's second 1960 film he was cast in the title role of Sinclair Lewis' 1927 novel, *Elmer Gantry* (filmed by United Artists), which Richard Brooks adapted and directed. The feature won Lancaster an Academy Award as Best Actor of the Year and his second Best Actor Award from the New York Film Critics.

Brooks had been peddling his adaption of the Lewis novel to studios since the late 1940s. In 1947, when he and Lancaster were working together on *Brute Force,* he had tried to interest the actor in playing the lead role, but at that time he could not obtain any studio backing. Brooks described the film: "*Elmer Gantry* is the story of a man who wants what everyone is supposed to want—money, sex, religion. He's the All-American boy."

Elmer Gantry centers on a Southern traveling salesman and ex-divinity student (Burt) who peddles his con game through the rural areas of the South in the 1920s. (He has been expelled from his theology work after seducing a deacon's daughter.) He arrives in a small community where he witnesses a revival meeting held by Sister Sharon Falconer (Jean Simmons) and he becomes a member of her congregation. Soon, through the uses of his studies and his culpability, he rises to become one of the most powerful people in her organization. He romances the troubled Sister, whom he loves in his own way, but he also takes up with a prostitute (Shirley Jones).

By 1960, Lewis' originally explosive, iconoclastic story would not have shocked too much of America, nor have engendered terrific boxoffice response on its own. But thanks to the revisions created by Brooks and the spellbinding performance of Burt in the title role, the film took on a cogency and drive that was unrelenting and captivating. As A. H. Weiler (*New York Times*) viewed it, "He is . . . Elmer Gantry who would have delighted the cold, inquiring eye and crusading soul of Sinclair Lewis."

Regarding the part which brought him his greatest critical acclaim, Burt has said, "Some parts you fall into like an old glove. Elmer really wasn't acting. It was me." Wrote Gordon Gow in *Films and Filming,* "There are . . . those winning occasions when a Lancaster performance, in quite a serious film, will recall just a slight and very discreet flavor of the old circus flourish, a little something he has doubtless retained from the time when he gave a grand air to the finish of an acrobatic feat or when he verbalized elaborately in the capacity of M.C. This element was needed, and handsomely provided, for the guy with the evangelistic kick in . . . *Elmer Gantry*."

Like a new Ph.D. graduate, Oscar-winner Burt Lancaster thought he knew best in his chosen field. Time would prove him quite wrong. He followed his sterling work in *Elmer Gantry* with a mundane melodrama, *The Young Savages* (United Artists, 1961). One could readily comprehend why Evan Hunter's novel (*A Matter of Conviction*) would appeal to the social conscience in a person like Burt. Realistically filmed in Spanish Harlem and lower Manhattan, the film starred Lancaster as a politically ambitious assistant district attorney who slowly gives up his social climbing activities.

223

With Shirley Jones in *Elmer Gantry*

With Greer Garson, accepting his *Elmer Gantry* Oscar (1961)

When he begins an investigation into an alleged murder by a young Puerto Rican boy he nearly causes his own demise as well as that of his blue-blood wife (Dina Merrill). Eventually he comes to believe the boy is innocent and tries to prove this contention, with almost tragic results.

Time Magazine thought the film "at its best when at its ugliest," and that it attempted to present a searing and realistic profile of juvenile delinquency in Spanish Harlem. The motion picture did contain a good performance by often unmanageable Shelley Winters as the delinquent's mother who is none too law-abiding herself. Most realistic of all were the sequences of street brutality. However, nearing forty-eight years of age, Burt was too old to be playing a rising assistant district attorney. Then, too, in many respects, the black-and-white feature was nothing more than a reworked update of Evan Hunter's more successful *The Blackboard Jungle,* which had been brought to the screen earlier (MGM, 1955) and was far more commercially successful.

For his second 1961 film appearance,[17] Burt was one of a number of stars to appear in *Judgment at Nuremberg* (United Artists), taking second-billing behind Spencer Tracy. Lancaster was a last-minute replacement for the originally signed Laurence Olivier. Produced and directed by Stanley Kramer, the road show film was shot on location in West Germany with interiors lensed in Hollywood. It was written by Abby Mann, who expanded the screenplay from his 1959 teleplay which had been presented on "Playhouse 90." During the shooting, there was much leaked-out publicity of the on-the-set conflicts between Burt and co-star Maximilian Schell. The latter would win an Academy Award for his role as the defense attorney in the film.

Judgment at Nuremberg was a long (one hundred eighty-nine minutes) and drawn-out affair in which Tracy portrayed a retired U.S. judge who is appointed to an American court which is to try four Nazi jurists (Burt, Werner Klemperer, Torben Meyer, and Martin Brenast) on charges of perverting justice. Richard Widmark is the prosecutor and Schell is his opposite number. After a long trial the defendants are sentenced to ninety-nine-year jail terms, with the tacit understanding that they will not serve very long actual sentences.

Burt was featured as Ernst Janning, a wartime scholar and law interpreter whose long monologue[18] defending his World War II activities is the crux of the defense case. For many, the highlights of the feature were not the heavy dramatic scenes, but the cameo appearances by Marlene Dietrich as a sophisticated widow of a German army officer, and by plump Judy Garland as a distraught victim of the Third Reich.

Variety penetrated to the heart of Burt's acting problem in *Judgment at Nuremberg*: "Lancaster's role presents the actor with a taxing assignment in which he must overcome the discrepancy of his own virile identity with that of the character. This he manages to do with an earnest performance, but he never quite attains a cold, superior intensity."

Although the moralistic and quite theatrical *Judgment at Nuremberg* earned far less

[17]Burt was to have co-starred with Rita Hayworth in a film version of the play *The Summer of the 17th Doll.* But when it was filmed in Australia as *Season of Passion* (United Artists, 1961), Anne Baxter, Ernest Borgnine, Angela Lansbury, and John Mills had the leads.

[18]This monologue (running eight minutes, eleven seconds) is included as part of the film's soundtrack album which was issued on United Artists Records.

than some of Burt's other starring vehicles,[19] the five million dollar take in distributor domestic rentals for the film were enough to assure the star eleventh place in the *Motion Picture Herald-Fame* poll of the top money-making performers of 1961.

Burt's sole 1962 film appearance in *Birdman of Alcatraz* (United Artists)[20] won him his third Academy Award nomination and his last critically acclaimed performance to date. Charles Crichton started directing this film but was replaced by John Frankenheimer.[21] The project was sponsored by the revived Norma Productions, its last film to date.

[19] *From Here to Eternity* earned $12.2 million; *Trapeze*, $7.5 million; *Elmer Gantry*, $5.2 million (all in distributors' domestic rentals).

[20] *Birdman of Alcatraz* was actually shot before *Judgment at Nuremberg*, but, due to lengthy revisions and reshootings, was not released until later.

[21] In *The Cinema of John Frankenheimer* (1969), Frankenheimer, who has directed Lancaster in five films, would tell author Gerald Pratley:

> I think he is one of the most hard-working individuals I've ever met. He's a true professional. He cares deeply about what he does. He's very considerate of other actors. I think he's one of the few men, one of the few actors that I've met who really knows something about production. He knows something about cutting, about the problems of making a film. . . . I find it very easy to work with him. When he's correctly cast, there is nobody better. . . . I directed his . . . film, Birdman of Alcatraz, because he owned the script. It was up to him to approve the director. He was really not ideal casting, but he was very, very good and I don't know who could have played it better. Whenever I think of this film, I think of Burt, how he really applied himself to that role. He loved doing it, and in my opinion, he did a beautiful job. Strangely enough it was a much more difficult part for him to play than the one in Elmer Gantry.

On the set of *Birdman of Alcatraz* (UA, 1962) with Ben Hecht

227

In *Birdman of Alcatraz*

Birdman presented the story of seventy-three-year-old criminal Robert Stroud, a two-time murderer who has learned to spend his time in solitary confinement studying ornithology and doing detailed research. The film vividly depicted the despair of a person in such a situation—a man who has been denied twenty-four applications for parole. (There are those who insist that the film glossed over the actual facts in the Stroud case, being too intent on proselytizing for Stroud's release.)

Although he lost the Academy Award for *Birdman of Alcatraz*, (Gregory Peck won for *To Kill a Mockingbird*), Lancaster did win the Venice Film Festival Award for Best Actor. Even hard-to-please *Time* Magazine had to admit that he gave the part "a firm restraint that never conceals a deep-felt conviction that Stroud should not be in stir at all." Stanley Kaufmann (*The New Republic*) penned, "The pleasantest report about the film is that Burt Lancaster gives one of his few good performances." Thanks to the attention garnered by this project, Burt placed number ten in the *Motion Picture Herald-Fame* players' poll for 1962.

Years later, Burt would reflect on this plum role. "I'd never met this man Robert Stroud, . . . but I felt I knew him intimately. I would actually begin to weep during some of the scenes. I've never been so personally involved in a part before or since. The film wasn't a great success, but now people constantly talk to me about it. It proves something, but I don't know what. If I could prepare myself as thoroughly for every part as I did for that, I'd be happy."

One of Burt's most dramatic performances won no awards. On April 24, 1962, he was a guest on Mike Wallace's "PM" video talk show. During the taping, the host, who had promised the previously concerned subject that he would stick to an announced scope of questions, persisted in delving into Burt's so-called temperament and his alleged inability to get along with co-players. Wallace needled Lancaster by inquiring into the well-publicized altercations on the sets of *Judgment at Nuremberg*.

A miffed Lancaster glared at Wallace, saying, "There's no reason to talk about it. . . . My temper belongs to me."

Wallace retorted that he was merely trying to be honest.

A fuming Lancaster responded, "I am suggesting you are not. . . . I think this line of questioning is unreasonable."

Then Wallace chirped out that Lancaster was the guest on the show and had no choice but to be responsive to the host's questions.

Burt popped up with, "I say you won't have the advantage long if we keep going on." Soon afterward, the star rose from his seat and walked out of the television studio.

In 1963, Lancaster appeared in three theatrical releases, none of which was very commercial. Their combined grosses only placed him as number eighteen in the *Motion Picture Herald-Fame* poll for the year. It was the last time he would be listed in that survey. This trio of pictures was the obvious beginnings of the erosion of his screen popularity. It was the same career decline as his contemporary, Kirk Douglas, was experiencing.

A Child Is Waiting (United Artists, 1963) was produced by Stanley Kramer, directed by John Cassavetes, and offered Judy Garland another cinema comeback. Filmed with actual patients at the Pacific State Hospital in Pomona, California, the stark proceedings was a moving narrative of the lives of mentally retarded children. Lancaster had the role of ultra-concerned Dr. Matthew Clark, the superintendent-doctor of the state institution, and Garland was co-starred as a new member of the staff who becomes too emotionally involved with a borderline child. The crux of the story, however, centered around the boy (Bruce Ritchey) and his emotionally unstable parents (Gena Rowlands and Steven Hill). Critical reaction was mixed to this bleak bit of "entertainment."

For the second time in his career, Burt agreed to perform a cameo assignment. This time he joined with Tony Curtis, Kirk Douglas, Robert Mitchum, and Frank Sinatra in heavily made-up guest appearances in *The List of Adrian Messenger* (Universal, 1963). Burt, of all things, was an old woman!

Of his next film, Burt had the following to say: "Once the public decides what you are, you might as well give up trying to be anything else. One of the most unusual and valuable experiences of my life was working with [Luchino] Visconti in *The Leopard*. But I remember a lot of my fans couldn't understand why I'd made it.

"I'll tell . . . how I got that part. [Goffredo] Lombardo, the producer, came to L. A. to talk about an adventure story. But somehow, we got around to *The Leopard* and I told him what a wonderful book it was and how much I'd like to do the film. He went back to Visconti, who said, 'No, that's ridiculous. He's a cowboy . . . a gangster.' After he couldn't get the Russian actor he wanted for the part, he signed Olivier, though he wasn't available at the right time because of his commitments in England and it just happened that Visconti saw *Judgment at Nuremberg*. That did it. He phoned me, and I said yes.

"I worked on the screenplay with him, too. He imparted this tremendous confidence, and you couldn't but share it with him. But everything had to be exactly as he wanted in other departments. He wouldn't work unless it was so."

With Judy Garland in *A Child Is Waiting* (UA, 1963)

230

On the set of *The Leopard* (20th, 1963) with his son Billy

With Claudia Cardinale in *The Leopard*

The Leopard, based on Giuseppe Di Lampedusa's acclaimed novel, was adapted for the screen by five writers, including Visconti. It was the complex story of Don Fabrizio Salinas (Burt), a Sicilian aristocrat, who lives through many political changes, including the 1860 unification of Italy by Garibaldi. It became a long, leisurely, pictorially resplendent picture filmed in a variety of languages (and partially redubbed for the appropriate country of distribution). It was a critical success and it did big business in Italy, France, and other areas of Europe. When the originally two-hundred-five-minute feature was issued in an English-speaking version, however, it was clipped to a hundred sixty-five minutes and the footage made little sense. Even with the marquee lure of Lancaster, Alain Delon, and Claudia Cardinale—not to mention the importance of it being a Visconti production—the film failed to make an impact with American audiences.

As the moustached, white-haired prince, Burt was a model of restraint, leading *Time* Magazine to enthuse, "Lancaster, within definite limits, is superb." *Variety* recorded, "In the final reels, it is again Lancaster who gives the picture some of its deeply moving moments as he moves, a sad, lonely and aging figure no longer his own."

Regarding his interpretation of the essentially alien role, Burt elaborated: "But as far as my acting was concerned, Visconti gave me complete freedom regarding the way I wanted to move, the whole acting aspect of it. There was only one time on the set when we had a long talk—about three hours—about the approach to one scene. And the ideas he wanted me to get across were brilliant. They were far superior to anything I had in mind. But in the main, if he thinks you're a good and thorough professional and you know what you're doing, then he'll let you go straight ahead

232

and do whatever you want to do. And after that, you see, he'll refine the things you've done. I was very happy with *The Leopard*. I think it was some of my best work."

Burt's first attempt to repair his tattered boxoffice status came in the politically oriented melodrama, *Seven Days in May* (Paramount, 1964). The film proved to be the fifth and final joint acting venture between Lancaster and Kirk Douglas, the latter having a particularly tough time coping with pro-Lancaster director John Frankenheimer.

In those naive, pre-Watergate days, the public, as with *Fail-Safe* (Columbia, 1964), was not in a receptive mood to buy a heavy dose of conscience entertainment. As *Time* Magazine indicated, the film suffered from self-seriousness. ("The movie is least successful when it tries to sound significant.") Judith Crist, writing in the *New York Herald-Tribune*, offered, "Burt Lancaster combines a finely controlled fanaticism with innate conviction."

"Burt Lancaster! Before he can pick up an ashtray, he discusses his motivation for an hour or two. You want to say just pick up the ashtray and shut up." So spoke France's answer to Bette Davis, Jeanne Moreau, who co-starred with Burt in *The Train* (United Artists, 1965). From many points of view, the film, with its hazardous on-location shooting, was a debacle. A few weeks into production, director Arthur Penn was relieved of his post. Associate producer Bernard Farrell took over the reins on the elaborate project for a time, and then Lancaster induced his good friend John Frankenheimer[22] to take over control of the feature which was running amok.

[22]Frankenheimer would later admit to cinema historian Gerald Pratley: "If Burt Lancaster and I had that film to do over again, we would both do it differently. . . . Once Burt became involved he began to live the film so intently that he said to me, 'My God, if only we had started this together, I would have played it with a French accent. Then we wouldn't have had to dub the other actors into that hoarse, American-English, and the entire film would have been more convincing.' "

With Mrs. Lancaster (*c.* 1964)

233

With Albert Remy in *The Train* (UA, 1965)

Adapted from Rose Valand's book *Le Font de L'Art,* it was a stark study of the Germans taking the Gallic art treasures to their Nazi homeland, with a French railroad official (Burt) joining a desperate underground plot to stop the proceedings, all in the name of restoring French patriotism. If the plot threads were a bit vapid, the film did conclude with a well-staged (by Lee Zavitz) train wreck. However, at a hundred four minutes, the picture was too long to maintain sufficient audience attention.

Far more than when he had portrayed the Sicilian prince in *The Leopard,* Burt subjected himself to a battery of abuse from the critics. They felt he had badly overreached himself in his attempt to capture the essence of his Continental character. In contrast to Paul Scofield's fine portrayal of the Nazi general intent on kidnapping the art treasures of France, Burt's Americanism was out of context. "Not for a moment does he [Lancaster] seem to be a French patriot," decried *Time* Magazine. Granted, *The Train* did provide the fifty-ish star with an athletic part which permitted him to scale walls, slide down embankments, and leap on and off the train of the title. But such a workout was at odds with the cerebral purpose of the zealots' drama. ("Lancaster lacks the grace that derives from true sophistication and his heedless acrobatics have a derailing effect. . . ." *Films in Review.*)

Just as Kirk Douglas was never at ease in comedy (e.g., *For Love or Money* [Universal, 1963]), Burt should have learned to avoid farce like the plague. However, he agreed to star in *The Hallelujah Trail* (United Artists, 1965). John Sturges directed this flimsy, too-long (a hundred sixty-two minutes) Western. Its slight plotline dealt with an army officer who was to take a shipment of whiskey to Denver, a city suffering a liquor shortage in the winter of 1867. Along the way, he and his convoy are harassed by Indians (who want the firewater), miners, road agents, and a bevy

234

of female temperance zealots, led by flirtatious Lee Remick. Burt was cast as Colonel Thadeus Gearhart. Unlike *Cat Ballou* (Columbia, 1965), which knew when to end its satire, or *Blazing Saddles* (Warner Bros., 1974), which Mel Brooks pushed to the nth degree, *The Hallelujah Trail* was neither one thing nor the other. Its attempts at satire were fitful, its humor too heavy-handed to arouse any major guffaws. And it proved once again that Burt Lancaster was no comedian.

Richard Brooks who had resurrected Burt's career with *Elmer Gantry*, came to the rescue again, this time with *The Professionals* (Columbia, 1966), which grossed $8.8 million in distributors' domestic rentals. The film placed Burt back in the strong silent he-man role that he could still handle so efficiently. It also teamed him with a variety of tough guys, ranging from agile Robert Ryan to blatant Jack Palance, crude Lee Marvin, and muscled Woody Strode. Lancaster responded to the ambiance of such sturdy masculine performers, and came forth with a cohesive performance.

Shot in Panavision and Technicolor, Burt starred as Delworth, one of four mercenaries (along with Ryan, Marvin, Strode). The four are hired by a wealthy man (Ralph Bellamy) to retrieve his young wife (Claudia Cardinale) from the Mexican bandit (Palance) who had kidnapped her and whose company she seemingly prefers. Arch Lancaster-supporter Judith Crist (*New York Journal-Tribune*) would say of *The Professionals*, "Burt Lancaster has never been more athletically suave. . . ."

Although now in his mid-fifties, Lancaster would not agree that he had passed his prime or that he could not rise to new heights as a performer. "As an actor I know I can still improve. Oh God, yes. We've all got to keep trying to reach new horizons." But on other occasions, he would rehash his goal of abandoning the performing

With Claudia Cardinale in *The Professionals* (Col., 1968)

With Nancy Cushman and House Jameson in *The Swimmer* (Col., 1966)

profession. "Some actors go on for ever, into the grave. Not me. I don't want to be like that. I want to get away from acting altogether."

But wishes and reality often do not coincide, and Burt continued in the field. He would be off the screen for the next two years, not because of any lack of projects, but because of production problems with *The Swimmer* (Columbia, 1968). After that trouble-plagued venture, he made *The Scalphunters* (United Artists, 1968), which would be pushed into distribution before the arty, unsatisfactory *The Swimmer*.

The Scalphunters was filmed in Mexico, but rumors filtered back to Hollywood that star and director (Sydney Pollack) were having a *very* difficult time on the set together. As fur trapper Joe Bass, Burt teams with a slave (Ossie Davis) on the run to track a pack of scalphunters, led by Telly Savalas and his cigar-smoking mistress (Shelley Winters), who have stolen Lancaster's annual yield of furs. Along the way they are beset by warring Kiowa Indians. The finale finds Savalas and his crew liquidated by the redskins, Lancaster and Davis going their way, and rough-and-tumble Winters rather willingly going off with the Kiowas. It was all a lot more fun than Lancaster's earlier *The Hallelujah Trail*.

Although Lancaster believed his work in *The Swimmer* was far more valid than his role in *The Scalphunters* had been, the feature was distinctly much less of a success commercially. Columbia acknowledged it was a dud, no matter how they tried to sell it to an unbuying public. Shot in 1966, largely in Connecticut, by producers Frank and Eleanor Perry, the picture went through various stages of re-editing, and finally the Perrys hired Sydney Pollack to reshoot one whole sequence in which Barbara Loden was replaced by Janice Rule.

The Swimmer is an allegorical study which takes place "on one of those mid-

236

summer Sundays when everyone sits around saying, 'I drank too much last night.' "
Burt played Ned Merrill, a suburbanite who finds himself alone in all senses of the
word. He decides to swim home, more than eight miles, via his neighbors' swimming pools. Along the way he recounts his life, which is told in semi-flashbacks,
including his loves, his failures, and his fears. At the climax he reaches his home
and is seen pounding at the door as he stands in the rain—the house is vacant.

There was no doubt that in his several nude scenes (never frontal) Burt presented
a fine figure of masculinity, but there was heated dispute as to the calibre of the
star's performance. Hollis Alpert (*Saturday Review*) termed him "lacklustre," while
Judith Crist (*New York* Magazine) championed that it was "perhaps the best [acting]
of his career." Too few filmgoers ventured into theatres showing this film to make
the argument anything but academic.

Castle Keep (Columbia, 1969) was Burt's first R-rated film. It was a financial
failure. Despite past differences with Sydney Pollack, Burt teamed with the director
again for this adaptation of William Eastlake's novel. The resulting film was a
sometimes comical, sometimes brutal (and often fantasy-prone) World War II
chronicle that became "hard-hitting . . . once the shooting starts" (*Variety*). Filmed in
Yugoslavia, *Castle Keep* offered Burt as one-eyed Major Abraham Falconer who sets
up his headquarters in an old castle in the Ardennes Forest where he agrees to
father a son by the young wife of the impotent count (Jean-Pierre Aumont) who
owns the fortress, so the man will have the desired heir. When the Germans advance on the area and the Allies order a full retreat, Lancaster remains behind to
defend the castle. The building is destroyed by the Axis in a torrent of bombs.

While *Castle Keep* had few merchandizing points, *The Gypsy Moths* (MGM, 1969)
had the selling virtues of reuniting Deborah Kerr and Burt, as well as the highly
promoted nude scenes of Miss Kerr (and the often deleted topless dance by performer Sheree North). The project was Burt's fifth and final (to date) joint association with director John Frankenheimer, the man who seemed most capable of
drawing a controlled performance from the star. Burt was top-cast as Mike Rettig,
one of a trio (with Gene Hackman and Scott Wilson) of sky divers who come to a
small Kansas town. Their arrival has a profound effect on the populace, including
that of married Kerr. During one of the crowd-pleasing aerial dives, Lancaster
plunges to his death. It remains unsettled whether he took his own life, for he had
indicated earlier that a man should choose the manner and time of his own end.

This study in "existential pessimism" failed to garner much boxoffice attention.
Even the usually generous *Variety* labeled it "a poor skydiver yarn." Richard
Shickel, writing in *Life* Magazine, said: "One is uncomfortably reminded of the
romance these two [Burt and Kerr] enacted in *From Here to Eternity*—and of the
passage of time since. . . . As he has grown older, Mr. Lancaster has developed a
capacity, unique in established stars to 'give away' scenes that his status in the movie
pecking order entitles him to dominate. He did it in *Castle Keep*, he does it again in
The Gypsy Moths and he deserves full credit for its shrewd selflessness." However,
most of the acclaim (whatever there was) for the film derived from its stunningly
conceived aerial diving sequences, which were executed by Carl Boenisch.

As if auguring the great changes that were occurring in his professional career as
he approached a new decade, Burt's private life took a sudden turn in 1969. After
over twenty-two years of marriage to Norma Anderson, she sued him for divorce in
July, 1969. She was granted her suit in a Santa Monica court. They divided at least
$2 million and Norma received custody of the three under-age children: Susan,

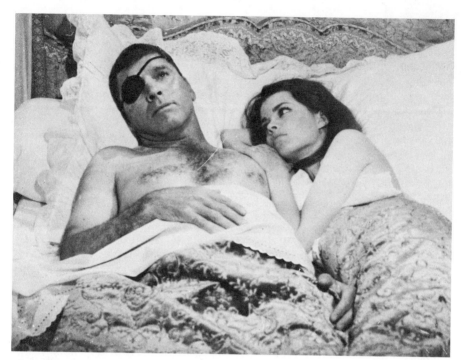

With Astrid Heeren in *Castle Keep* (Col., 1969)

With Deborah Kerr in *The Gypsy Moths* (MGM, 1969)

Joanne, and Sighle-Ann. Three years earlier, their son Bill had married Kippie Kovacs, the daughter of the late comic Ernie Kovacs. Today, Lancaster has several grandchildren.

Bachelor Lancaster's boxoffice stature was suddenly rescued when he appeared in the blockbuster[23] *Airport* (Universal, 1970). The entertaining disaster film contained an all-star cast,[24] but it was the overall film set aboard a giant 747 craft which made the picture such a winner. George Seaton directed this film version of Arthur Hailey's book, which had been on the bestseller list for some sixty-five weeks. In true glossy soap-opera fashion, according to the dictates of producer Ross Hunter, the movie concentrated on the lives of several people at the airport of the title. Burt played an aging airport manager who, in one snowy night, is faced with a number of problems, ranging from dealing with a deranged bomber (Van Heflin) aboard a trans-oceanic flight, to deciding if he prefers his selfish, cold wife (Dana Wynter) to the fetching airport public relations miss (Jean Seberg). With its star-studded cast —Helen Hayes won an Academy Award for her old lady Ada Quonsett performance—it was hard for film viewers not to find each and every section of the narrative engaging if not captivating. As if to beat the more aesthetic-minded critics to the punch, Burt admitted of the project, "[It's] the biggest piece of junk ever made."

While in Europe making *Castle Keep*, Lancaster had flown back to the U.S. for a day to take part in Martin Luther King's freedom march on Washington, D.C. His second 1970 film release was a documentary about that fateful procession. Burt was

[23]The film grossed $45.3 million distributors' domestic rentals.
[24]Second-billed Dean Martin commanded a salary plus ten percent of the film's gross after the break-even point.

With George Kennedy in *Airport* (Univ., 1970)

seen in the documentary footage, along with other Hollywood players such as Paul Newman. The hundred-fifty-three-minute documentary was titled *King: A Filmed Record . . . Montgomery to Memphis.* An extended five-and-one-half-hour version was distributed to college campuses.

In 1971, Burt returned to the stage for the first time since his Broadway bow in *A Sound of Hunting,* to star in Kurt Weill and Maxwell Anderson's musical, *Knickerbocker Holiday.*[25] Lancaster assumed the role of Peter Stuyvesant, the ruler of New York City in the days when it was controlled by the Dutch. In a part that required both singing and dancing, he played the one-legged leader who slyly romanced and won the heart of a young girl. Burt took a large salary cut (he claimed at the time to be making $750,000 per film plus a percentage of the proceeds) to do the play.

The show opened in San Francisco on May 11, 1971 for a seven-week run and then moved to the Dorothy Chandler Pavilion in Los Angeles for an eight-week engagement. Lancaster termed it "the most challenging [role] of my career." The critics were less kind. Dan Sullivan of the *Los Angeles Times* reported, "Oddly enough, his singing isn't at all bad. It's the acting side of the role that gives him trouble. To begin with, he is no more comfortable in period dress on the stage than he is on the screen. Secondly, he has to hop around on a silver peg-leg that gives him much too much to think about. Finally, he is simply not at home in sly, twinkling, mock-ferocious comedy. Lines that ought to come out with deft irony sound like heavy camp, as if the actor were doing a parody guest shot [on TV]. It's an

[25]Walter Huston had starred in the Broadway edition (1938), introducing the song "September Song." Nelson Eddy headed the cast of the 1944 United Artists' film version.

In *Knickerbocker Holiday* (1971), as Peter Stuyvesant

240

uphill fight all the way, and the applause at the end is more for effort than achievement." The show never made it East to Broadway.

Although he conquered the heart of the young lass in *Knickerbocker Holiday,* Burt confessed to the press that he was now getting "too old to get the girl anymore" oncamera. In an interview with *The National Enquirer,* he admitted, "Filmgoers these days aren't about to accept me winning the girl in movies, although I've been doing it pretty well for more than twenty-five years. For me romance is out. Soon I'll be pushing sixty, so I can't go chasing some young woman. I can still play leading men. But guys with more character than sex appeal."

Perhaps Lancaster knew whereof he spoke, for in *Valdez Is Coming* (United Artists, 1971) he had a "brief fling with Susan Clark, but not like the old days where it all ends sweetly." In this Edwin Sherrin-directed feature, he is Mexican-American lawman Bob Valdez, who is forced to kill a man in self-defense and then is hunted by a band of gunfighters. To protect himself, he begins a one-man war against the so-called posse.

Much more effective (and more commercial) than *Valdez* was *Lawman* (United Artists, 1971),[26] produced and directed by the well-regarded Britisher Michael Winner. As Marshal Jered Maddox, Burt rides into a small Western town to arrest a wealthy rancher (Lee J. Cobb) for the accidental murder of an elderly man. Lancaster wins the support of the community's weak-willed sheriff (Robert Ryan), but the townfolk dislike the cold stranger with his vicious methods. He is soon at odds with them, as well as with Cobb's array of hired men who try to ambush him.

On the small screen, Burt made one of his rare video appearances on the Public Broadcasting Corporation's children's program, "Sesame Street." He performed a pre-filmed bit on an episode, reciting the alphabet from A through Z. This particular segment has been constantly re-run as part of the educational series.

The actor's sole 1972 feature, *Ulzana's Raid* (Universal), is his last Western at this writing. The project re-united Lancaster with director Robert Aldrich. The film was given an R rating and it contains a great deal of violence. Opening in an Army fort in the old West, it soon develops into a chase film with an aging Indian fighter (Burt), a young cavalry lieutenant (Bruce Davison), and an Indian scout (Jorge Luke) tracking down a group of Apache Indians who are rampaging against the whites in the area. Reminiscent of the Lancaster-Aldrich *Apache* of two decades before, the film indulges in some moralizing on the racial issue. At one point, Lancaster's McIntosh tells young officer Davison, "What bothers you, Lieutenant, is that you don't like to think of white men behaving like Indians. It kinds of confuses the issue." In another scene he tells the inexperienced solder, "Hating Apaches would be like hating the desert because there ain't no water on it." Despite the studied artiness and excessive gore, *Ulzana's Raid* bears careful study, providing a showcase for the latter-day histrionics of mannered but agile Burt Lancaster.

Having fared so well with Michael Winner in *Lawman,* Burt was quite willing to join with the director in *Scorpio* (United Artists, 1973). As added boxoffice insurance, this cold-war spy film offered Alain Delon in a co-starring role, with Paul Scofield in a top featured role. Unfortunately, this entry came along too late in the espionage picture cycle to hit financial paydirt. *Variety* explained, "Despite its anachronistic emulation of mid-1960s' cynical spy mellers, *Scorpio* might have been an acceptable action programmer if its narrative were clearer, its dialog less 'cultured'

[26]Filmed on location in Durango, Mexico.

In *Scorpio* (UA, 1973)

and its visuals more straightforward." Burt, moving stiff-limbed, but proudly and methodically, was seen as Cross the veteran secret agent involved in the assassination of an Arab government official. Lancaster is also a U.S. agent who just might be a Soviet double operative. Another C.I.A. worker, Delon, who had been trained in the field by Lancaster, is ordered by the C.I.A. to liquidate Burt, a job the younger man accepts only after being blackmailed by his employers. The cat-and-mouse game shifts from Paris to Washington, D.C. to Vienna and then back to Paris. In some rather amateurish theatrics, Lancaster performs his death scene. Upon being confronted in a garage basement by gun-toting Delon he urges his assailant to shoot him, weary of his precarious existence. He sinks to the ground in a spasm of death throes.

Unlike *Scorpio*, Lancaster's second 1973 feature, *Executive Action* (National General), did make money, more than $2.5 million in distributors' domestic rentals. The film had a blitzkrieg-style advertising campaign and a natural plotline for exploitation: the theory that a conspiracy was behind the killing of President John F. Kennedy.

Executive Action was produced by Edward Lewis (the former partner of Kirk Douglas and the producer of *Seven Days in May*) and scripted by Dalton Trumbo, a long-time Leftist in Hollywood circles. Lancaster was seen as a professional spy and a thinly veiled C. I. A. agent who is hired by two wealthy Texans (Robert Ryan and Will Geer) to kill Kennedy after the president has announced his plans to aid the civil rights movement and withdraw troops from Vietnam. The ninety-one-minute semi-documentary feature is mainly concerned with the actual scheme to kill the U.S. leader, which includes hiring a man (a Lee Harvey Oswald look-alike) to be

With Robert Ryan in *Executive Action* (National General, 1973)

With Susan Clark in *The Midnight Man* (Univ., 1974)

used as the scapegoat for the assassination. Actual newsreel footage of the November 22, 1963 tragedy was incorporated into the proceedings to prove that Kennedy was killed by this group of right-wing Americans.

Needless to say the film was quite controversial and in some areas of the U.S. was not widely screened. Some television stations on both coasts refused to carry commercials for the film, claiming the teaser ads were "overly violent and violated standards of taste." Lancaster came to the defense of the project, stating, "I have made many films much more violent than this one and the commercials for them, none of which was ever censored or refused, were more violent than these." Interestingly enough, another film, *The Second Gun*, which was an exposé of the assassination plot, was completely suppressed after one New York run.

Burt's only 1974 film was *The Midnight Man* (Universal), which he co-wrote, co-produced, and co-directed with Roland Kibbee (who co-adapted *The Devil's Disciple*). *New York Times'* critic Vincent Canby dubbed it "the second worst film of 1974."

The carefully budgeted feature was made on location in South Carolina. In it, Burt starred as Jim Slade, an ex-policeman who had spent time in jail for shooting at his wife's lover and who now lives with friends (Cameron Mitchell and Joan Lorring) in a small town, working as a night security officer for a college. When a young coed is murdered, the local sheriff tries to pin the rap on an oddball religious fanatic, but Lancaster believes there is more to the crime than meets the eye. He begins a personal, intense investigation that leads to beatings, blackmail, attempted rape, and murders.

In reviewing Lancaster's appearance in this cluttered, non-money-maker, Vincent Canby of the *New York Times* declared: "Mr. Lancaster is an intelligent actor. He thinks about his characterizations. He makes choices. He moves through *The Midnight Man* with studied humility, saying 'yes, sir,' and 'no, sir' more often than is always necessary, listening attentively when spoken to. The mannerisms don't suggest a middle-aged parolee, uncertain of his future, as often as they suggest a reformed alcoholic trying desperately to succeed as a liveried chauffeur." For the record, it was Burt's son William who played the murdered girl's boyfriend, and even Nick Cravat popped up in a bit part. After this second unsuccessful foray behind the camera, it is doubtful that Burt will ever again be found financing such a gambit.

In the summer of 1973, Burt traveled to Israel to begin work in his first teleseries, *Moses—The Lawgiver*, a series of six major one-hour dramas based on the Book of Exodus. The project was filmed on location in Jerusalem and other Middle Eastern areas and was co-produced by RAI Television of Italy and Associated Television Corp., Ltd. of London, with scheduled showings in the U.S. over CBS. At the time of the filming, the star enthused, "Moses will be very different from the version put on the screen by Cecil B. DeMille. None of that larger-than-life stuff. My Moses will be a real man. Not a hero, not a leader, but a man who is aware of his own and other people's failings." Lancaster's son William was hired to play the young Moses, in contrast to his dad's Moses at age 120.

The show would be aired in six parts on American TV in mid-summer 1975 and received less than enthusiastic reception from the critics or the public. As *Variety* summarized it, "Makes stab at realism through location sites but generally skims over religious-historical aspects as digest of Exodus. Figures lack genuine depth thanks to episodic approach. As drama, film fails to generate dramatic values or,

In *Moses—The Lawgiver* (CBS-TV, 1975)

most important, involvement." The *New York Times* was a little kinder to Burt Lancaster's interpretation: "As an actor, Mr. Lancaster is not great but, given favorable circumstances, he can be good. As Moses, he would appear to be extremely good—restrained, intense and, for a man somewhere about age 60, in superb physical condition. He and most of the other principals are rewardingly, even surprisingly, effective." In 1976 the footage was re-edited and released theatrically by Avco-Embassy.

Meanwhile, Burt returned to Europe to star in two films, *1900* and *Conversation Piece.* The former was shot in Italy, entirely in the Po Valley basin. As directed by Bernardo Bertolucci, the motion picture covers life in this century as seen through the eyes of two children born on the same day in 1900, who remain friends through the years despite social differences. Lancaster and Sterling Hayden appear in the first section of the film, portraying the grandfathers of the two boys.

Conversation Piece, which re-united the actor with director Luchino Visconti, was also filmed in Italy. It concerns an aging remote art historian (Lancaster) who takes on as lodgers a family of unique eccentrics. It develops into a conflict between two different worlds: the professor with his solitary life and the newcomers who are exploding with too much life. Visconti, who was recovering from a stroke at the time of making this project, directed *Conversation Piece* from a wheelchair.

To say that *Conversation Piece* is overly verbose is an understatement. When it had its American debut as the opening selection of the 13th New York Film Festival (September 24, 1975) it "laid a mighty egg" (*Variety*). The *New York Times* branded the film a "disaster." *Time* Magazine analyzed: "Visconti forsakes the wit of the opening for a kind of tongue-tied general valedictory. He is interested not so much in exposing his characters as having the Professor embrace all of them, opening his arms to their indulgences and sanctioning their moral impotence." For moviegoers who remembered Burt Lancaster in earlier, virile days, it was sad to hear him mouthing such dialogue as "I'm an old man, neurotic and slightly hysterical!"

The distributors yanked *Conversation Piece* from its projected American release to

246

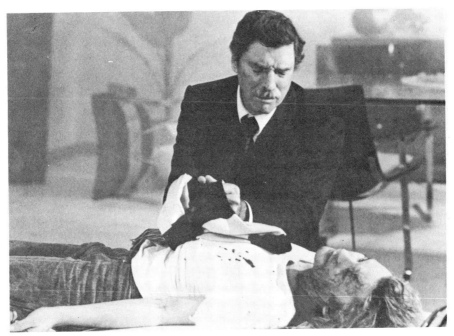

With Helmut Berger in *Conversation Piece* (1975)

re-edit the picture severely, hoping to diminish its dullness and incredible plotting by greatly shortening it. The film, which Lancaster hoped to add as a prestige credit to his roster, has proved a major embarrassment to him.

Back in the United States Lancaster moved into the swank Century Towers Apartments in Century City, California, where his neighbors include Gig Young, George Raft, and David Janssen. He also maintains a home at Malibu Beach for more casual living. He insisted to the press, at that time, that his alleged "secret marriage," to long-time companion Jackie Bone, was really an "arrangement." "No, I'm not married and I probably never will be again. There's no point in matrimony unless a couple plan to have children. And at my age raising another family is not exactly uppermost in my thoughts. The relationship between Jackie and me is great. There is no ownership between us. We aren't possessive."

Although he claims he wants to ease out of acting, he still accepts new assignments. He spent approximately one week working for Robert Altman in *Buffalo Bill and the Indians* (United Artists, 1976). He played Ned Buntline, the "conscience of Bill" (Paul Newman). Then he flew to Italy to join Ava Gardner and others in Carlo Ponti's *Cassandra Crossing*, another disaster genre picture. Still later in 1976, the work-anxious Lancaster joined the cast of Robert Aldrich's *Twilight Last Gleaming*, a Germany-located feature co-starring Burt with Roscoe Lee Brown, Joseph Cotten, and Melvyn Douglas.

As for the future, Lancaster is unspecific about total retirement. He does admit, "I've been a star for most of my years in movies. I'm glad I've been able to stay alive in this business, but let's face it, I'm [over sixty-two years] old now. All I can do are character parts. So I'm trying to back slowly out of the business."

247

BURT LANCASTER

THE KILLERS *(Universal, 1946), 105 min.*
  Producer, Mark Hellinger; director, Robert Siodmak; based on the story by Ernest Hemingway; screenplay, Anthony Veiller; art directors, Jack Otterson, Martin Obzina; set decorators, Russell A. Gausman, E. R. Robinson; music, Miklos Rosza; assistant director, Melville Shyer; sound, Bernard B. Brown, William Hedgcock; special camera, D. S. Horsley; camera, Woody Bredell; editor, Arthur Hilton.

  Burt Lancaster (Swede); Edmond O'Brien (Riordan); Ava Gardner (Kitty Collins); Albert Dekker (Colfax); Sam Levene (Lubinsky); John Miljan (Jake); Virginia Christine (Lilly); Vince Barnett (Charleston); Charles D. Brown (Packy); Donald MacBride (Kenyon); Phil Brown (Nick); Charles McGraw (Al); William Conrad (Max); Queenie Smith (Queenie); Garry Owen (Joe); Harry Hayden (George); Bill Walker (Sam); Jack Lambert (Dum Dum); Jeff Corey (Blinky); Wally Scott (Charlie); Gabrielle Windsor (Ginny); Rex Dale (Man); Harry Brown (Paymaster); Beatrice Roberts (Nurse); Howard Freeman (Police Chief); John Berkes (Plunther); John Sheehan (Doctor); Charles Middleton (Farmer Brown); Al Hill (Customer); Noel Cravat (Lou Tingle); Reverend Neal Dodd (Minister); George Anderson (Doctor); Vera Lewis (Mrs. Hirsch); Howard Negley, Perc Launders, Geoffrey Ingham (Policemen); Ann Staunton (Stella); William Ruhl (Motorman); Therese Lyon (Housekeeper); Ernie Adams (Little Man); Jack Cheatham (Police Driver); Ethan Laidlaw (Conductor); Michael Hale (Pete); Wally Rose (Bartender); Audley Anderson (Assistant Paymaster); Mike Donovan (Timekeeper); Nolan Leary, John Trebach, Milton Wallace (Waiters).

VARIETY GIRL *(Paramount, 1947), 83 min.*
  Producer, Daniel Dare; director, George Marshall; screenplay, Edmund Hartman, Frank Tashlin, Robert Welch, Monte Brice; art directors, Hans Dreier, Robert Clatworthy; set decorators, Sam Comer, Ross Dowd; Puppetoon sequence, George Pal; music, Joseph J. Lilley; music associate, Troy Sanders; orchestrator. N. Van Cleave; music for Puppetoon sequence, Edward Plumb; songs, Frank Loesser; assistant director, George Templeton; sound, Gene Merritt, John Cope; special effects, Gordon Jennings; process camera, Farciot Edouart; camera, Lionel Lindon, Stuart Thompson; editor, LeRoy Stone.

  Mary Hatcher (Catherine Brown); Olga San Juan (Amber La Vonne); De Forest Kelley (Bob Kirby); Bing Crosby, Bob Hope, Gary Cooper, Ray Milland, Alan Ladd, Barbara Stanwyck, Paulette Goddard, Dorothy Lamour, Veronica Lake, Sonny Tufts, Joan Caulfield, William Holden, Lizabeth Scott, Burt Lancaster, Gail Russell, Diana Lynn, Sterling Hayden, Robert Preston, John Lund, William Bendix, Barry Fitzgerald, Cass Daley, Howard da Silva, Billy De Wolfe, MacDonald Carey, Patric Knowles, Mona Freeman, Virginia Field, Richard Webb (Themselves); William Demarest (Barker); Frank Faylen (Stage Manager); Frank Ferguson (J. R. O'Connell); Cecil B. DeMille, Mitchell Leisen, Frank Butler, George Marshall (Themselves); Roger Dann (French Number); Pearl Bailey (Specialty); Jim and Mildred Mulcay, Spike Jones and His City Slickers (Themselves); Glen Tryon (Bill Farris); Barney Dean (Himself); Jack Norton (Busboy at Brown Derby); Torben Meyer (Andre the Headwaiter at Brown Derby); Nella Walker (Mrs. Webster); Elaine Riley (Cashier); Charles Victor (Assistant to Mr. O'Connell); Gus Taute (Assistant to Assistant); Harry Hayden (Stage Manager at Grauman's Chinese Theatre); Janet Thomas, Roberta Jonay (Girls); Wallace Earl (Girl with Sheep Dog); Dick Keene (Dog Trainer); Ann Doran (Hairdresser); Jerry James (Assistant Director); Eric Alden (Makeup Man); Frank Mayo (Director); Mary Edwards, Virginia Welles (Themselves); Lucille Barkley, Carolyn Butler (Secretaries); Pinto Colvig (Special Voice Impersonation); Edgar Dearing (Cop); Russell Hicks, Crane Whitley, Charles Coleman, Hal K.

Dawson, Eddie Fetherston, Len Hendry, Lorin L. Raker (Men at Steam Bath); Sammy Stein (Masseur); Douglas Regan, Warren Joslin (Boys); Sally Rawlinson (Herself); John Stanley, Joel Friend, Al Ruiz (Specialty Dancers); Pat Templeton, Larry Badagaliacca (Boys at Grauman's Theatre); Bob Alden (Autograph Seeker); Pat Moran (Drunken Tumbling Act); Lee Emery, Marilyn Gray, Renee Randall (Usherettes); Audrey Saunders, Ray Saunders, Russ Saunders, Ted DeWayne, William Snyder, Fay Alexander (Six DeWaynes); Raymond Largay (Director of Variety Club); Alma Macrorie (Proprietress); Duke Johnson (Juggler).

BRUTE FORCE *(Universal, 1947), 98 min.*

Producer, Mark Hellinger; associate producer, Jules Buck; director, Jules Dassin; story, Robert Patterson; screenplay, Richard Brooks; art directors, Bernard Herzbrun, John F. De Cuir; set decorators, Russell A. Gausman, Charles Wyrick; music, Miklos Rosza; assistant director, Fred Frank; sound, Charles Felstead, Robert Pritchard; special camera, David S. Horsley; camera, William Daniels; editor, Edward Curtiss.

Burt Lancaster (Joe Collins); Hume Cronyn (Captain Munsey); Charles Bickford (Gallagher); Yvonne De Carlo (Gina); Ann Blyth (Ruth); Ella Raines (Cora); Anita Colby (Flossie); Sam Levene (Louie); Howard Duff (Soldier); Art Smith (Dr. Walters); Roman Bohnen (Warden Barnes); John Hoyt (Spencer); Richard Gaines (McCollum); Frank Puglia (Ferrara); Jeff Corey (Freshman); Vince Barnett (Muggsy); James Bell (Crenshaw); Jack Overman (Kid Coy); Whit Bissell (Tom Lister); Sir Lancelot (Calypso); Ray Teal (Jackson); Jay C. Flippen (Hodges); James O'Rear (Wilson); Howland Chamberlain (Gaines); Kenneth Patterson (Bronski); Crane Whitley (Armed Guard in Drain Pipe); Charles McGraw (Andy); John Harmon (Roberts); Gene Stutenroth (Hoffman); Wally Rose (Peary); Carl Rhodes (Strella); Guy Beach (Convict Foreman); Edmund Cobb (Bradley); Tom Steele (Machine Gunner); Alex Frazer (Chaplain); Will Lee (Kincaid); Ruth Sanderson (Miss Lawrence); Francis McDonald (Regan); Jack S. Lee (Sergeant); Virginia Farmer (Saide); Billy Wayne (Prisoner); Paul Bryar (Harry); Glenn Strange (Tompkins); Al Hill (Plonski); Peter Virgo, Eddy Chandler, Kenneth MacDonald (Guards); Herbert Heywood (Chef); Rex Lease (Hearse Driver); William Cozzo, Frank Marlo, Rex Dale (Prisoners); Kippee Valez (Visitor).

DESERT FURY *(Paramount, 1947), C-97 min.*

Producer, Hal B. Wallis; director, Lewis Allen; based on the novel by Ramona Stewart; screenplay, Robert Rossen; art director, Perry Ferguson; set decorators, Sam Comer, Syd Moore; music, Miklos Rosza; assistant director, Dick McWhorter; Technicolor consultants, Natalie Kalmus, Francis Cugat; sound, Harry Lindgren, Walter Oberst; camera, Charles Lang, Edward Cronjager; editor, Warren Low.

John Hodiak (Eddie Bendix); Lizabeth Scott (Paula Haller); Burt Lancaster (Tom Hanson); Mary Astor (Fritzi Haller); Kristine Miller (Claire Lindquist); Wendell Corey (Johnny Ryan); William Harrigan (Judge Berle Lindquist); James Flavin (Sheriff Pat Johnson); Jane Novak (Mrs. Lindquist); Ana Camargo (Rosa the Mexican Maid); Milton Kibbee (Mike the Bartender); Ralph Peters (Pete the Cafe Owner); John Farrell (Drunk in Jail); Ray Teal (Bus Driver); Harland Tucker (Chuck the Crap Dealer); Lew Harvey (Doorman); Tom Schamp (Dan the Sheriff's Deputy); Ed Randolph, Mike Lally (Dealers).

I WALK ALONE *(Paramount, 1948), 98 min.*

Producer, Hal B. Wallis; director, Byron Haskin; based on the play *Beggars Are Coming to Town* by Theodore Reeves; adaptors, Robert Smith, John Bright; screenplay, Charles Schnee; art directors, Hans Dreier, Franz Bachelin; set decorators, Sam Comer, Patrick Delany; music,

Victor Young; song, Ned Washington and Allie Wrubel; dialogue director, Joan Hathaway; assistant director, Richard McWhorter; sound, Harry Lindgren, Walter Oberst; process camera, Farciot Edouart; camera, Leo Tover; editor, Arthur Schmidt.

Burt Lancaster (Frankie Madison); Lizabeth Scott (Kay Lawrence); Kirk Douglas (Noll Turner); Wendell Corey (Dave); Kristine Miller (Mrs. Richardson); George Rigaud (Maurice); Marc Lawrence (Nick Palestro); Mike Mazurki (Dan); Mickey Knox (Skinner); Roger Neury (Felix).

ALL MY SONS *(Universal, 1948), 94 min.*

Producer, Chester Erskine; director, Irving Reis; based on the play by Arthur Miller; screenplay, Erskine; assistant director, Frank Shaw; art directors, Bernard Herzbrun, Hilyard Brown; set decorators, Russell A. Gausman, Al Fields; music, Leith Stevens; orchestrator, David Tamkin; makeup, Bud Westmore; costumes, Grace Houston; sound, Leslie I. Carey, Corson Jowett; special effects, David S. Horsley; camera, Russell Metty; editor, Ralph Dawson.

Edward G. Robinson (Joe Keller); Burt Lancaster (Chris Keller); Mady Christians (Kate Keller); Louisa Horton (Ann Deever); Howard Duff (George Deever); Frank Conroy (Herbert Deever); Lloyd Gough (Jim Bayliss); Arlene Francis (Sue Bayliss); Henry "Harry" Morgan (Frank Lubey); Elisabeth Fraser (Lydia Lubey); Walter Soderling (Charlie); Therese Lyon (Minnie); Charles Meredith (Ellsworth); William Johnstone (Attorney); Herbert Vigran (Wertheimer); Harry Harvey (Judge); Pat Flaherty (Bartender); George Sorel (Headwaiter); Helen Brown (Mrs. Hamilton); Joseph Kerr (Norton); Walter Bonn (Jorgenson); Victor Zimmerman, George Slocum (Attendants).

SORRY, WRONG NUMBER *(Paramount, 1948), 89 min.*

Producers, Hal B. Wallis, Anatole Litvak; director, Litvak; based on the radio play by Lucille Fletcher; screenplay, Fletcher; art directors, Hans Dreier, Earl Hedrick; set decorators, Sam Comer, Bertram Granger; music, Franz Waxman; assistant director, Richard McWhorter; costumes, Edith Head; makeup, Wally Westmore; sound, Gene Merritt, Walter Oberst; special effects, Gordon Jennings; process camera, Farciot Edouart; camera, Sol Polito; editor, Warren Low.

Barbara Stanwyck (Leona Stevenson); Burt Lancaster (Henry Stevenson); Ann Richards (Sally Lord Dodge); Wendell Corey (Dr. Alexander); Harold Vermilyea (Waldo Evans); Ed Begley (James Cotterell); Leif Erickson (Fred Lord); William Conrad (Morano); John Bromfield (Joe the Detective); Jimmy Hunt (Peter Lord); Dorothy Neumann (Miss Jennings); Paul Fierro (Harpootlian); Kristine Miller (Dolly, Dr. Alexander's Girl Friend); Suzanne Dalbert (Cigarette Girl); George Stern (Proprietor of Drug Store); Joyce Compton (Blonde); Tito Vuolo (Albert the Waiter); Garry Owen (Bingo Caller); Holmes Herbert (Wilkins the Butler); Neal Dodd (Minister); Louise Lorimer (Nurse); Yola D'Avril (Marie the French Maid); Pepito Perez (Boat Operator); Ashley Cowan (Clam Digger); Igor Dega, Grace Poggi (Dance Team); Cliff Clark (Sergeant Duffy).

KISS THE BLOOD OFF MY HANDS *(Universal, 1948), 79 min.*

Executive producer, Harold Hecht; producer, Richard Vernon; associate producer, Norman Deming; director, Norman Foster; based on the novel by Gerald Butler; adaptors, Ben Maddow, Walter Bernstein; screenplay, Leonardo Bercovici; art directors, Bernard Herzbrun, Nathan Juran; set decorators, Russell A. Gausman, Ruby R. Levitt; music, Miklos Rosza; assistant director, Jack Voglin; makeup, Bud Westmore; sound, Leslie I. Carey, Corson Jowett; special effects, David S. Horsley; camera, Russell Metty; editor, Milton Carruth.

Joan Fontaine (Jane Wharton); Burt Lancaster (Bill Saunders); Robert Newton (Harry Carter); Lewis L. Russell (Tom Widgery); Aminta Dyne (Landlady); Grizelda Hervey (Mrs. Faton); Jay Novello (Sea Captain); Colin Keith-Johnston (Judge); Reginald Sheffield (Superintendent); Campbell Copelin (Publican); Leyland Hodgson (Tipster); Peter Hobbes (Young Father); Thomas P. Dillon (Welshman); Joseph Granby (Theatre Manager); Robin Hughes (Policeman); Harry Allen (Drunk); Valerie Cardew (Change Girl); Ben Wright (Cockney Tout); Wally Scott (Hanger-on); Harold Goodwin (Whipper); Keith Hitchcock (Official); Alec Harford (Doctor); Lora Lee Michel (Little Girl); Jimmy Aubrey (Taxi Driver); Leslie Denison (Constable); Arthur Gould-Porter (Bookie); Charles McNaughton (Telescope Man); Harry Cording, Art Foster (Policemen); Felippa Rock (Woman); Timothy Bruce, Anne Whitfield, Suzanne Kerr (Children); Frank Hagney, James Logan, David McMahon (Seamen); Ola Lorraine (Donald's Mother); Colin Kenny (Proprietor); Al Ferguson (Marker); Tommy Hughes (Bookie); James Fowler, Robert Hale, Fred Fox (Tipsters); Harry Wilson (Man in Pub); Duke Green, Wesley Hopper (Men); Marilyn Williams (Barmaid).

CRISS CROSS (Universal, 1949), 87 min.

Producer, Michel Kraike; director, Robert Siodmak; based on the novel by Don Tracy; screenplay, Daniel Fuchs; art directors, Bernard Herzbrun, Boris Leven; set decorators, Russell A. Gausman, Oliver Emert; music, Miklos Rosza; assistant director, Fred Frank; makeup, Bud Westmore; costumes, Yvonne Wood; sound, Leslie I. Carey, Richard DeWeese; special effects, David S. Horsley; camera, Frank Palmer; editor, Ted J. Kent.

Burt Lancaster (Steve Thompson); Yvonne De Carlo (Anna); Dan Duryea (Slim Dundee); Stephen McNally (Pete Ramirez); Richard Long (Slade Thompson); Esy Morales (Orchestra Leader); Tom Pedi (Vincent); Percy Helton (Frank); Alan Napier (Finchley); Griff Barnett (Pop); Meg Randall (Helen); Joan Miller (The Lush); Edna M. Holland (Mrs. Thompson); John Doucette (Walt); Marc Krah (Mort); James O'Rear (Waxie); John "Skins" Miller (Midget); Robert Osterloh (Mr. Nelson); Vincent Renno (Headwaiter); Charles Wagenheim (Waiter); Tony Curtis (Gigolo); Beatrice Roberts, Isabel Randolph (Nurses); Stephen Roberts (Doctor); Garry Owen (Johnny); Kenneth Patterson (Bently the Guard); Gene Evans (O'Hearn the Guard); George Lynn (Andy); Michael Cisney (Chester); Robert Winkler (Clark); Lee Tung Foo (Chinese Cook); Ann Staunton, Dolores Castle, Jeraldine Jordan, Kippee Valez (Girlfriends); Diane Stewart (Girl); John Roy (Bartender); Vito Scotti (Track Usher).

ROPE OF SAND (Paramount, 1949), 104 min.

Producer, Hal B. Wallis; director, William Dieterle; screenplay, Walter Doniger; additional dialogue, John Paxton; art directors, Hans Dreier, Franz Bachelin; set decorators, Sam Comer, Grace Gregory; music, Franz Waxman; songs, Josef Marais; assistant director, Richard McWhorter; makeup, C. Silvera; sound, Harold Lewis, Walter Oberst; special effects, Gordon Jennings; process camera, Farciot Edouart; camera, Charles B. Lang, Jr.; editor, Warren Low.

Burt Lancaster (Mike Davis); Paul Henreid (Commandant Paul Vogel); Claude Rains (Arthur Martingale); Peter Lorre (Toady); Corinne Calvet (Suzanne Renaud); Sam Jaffe (Dr. Francis Hunter); John Bromfield (Thompson); Mike Mazurki (Pierson); Kenny Washington (John); Josef Marais, Miranda (South African Veldt Singers); Edmond Breon (Chairman); Hayden Rorke (Ingram); David Hoffman (Waiter); Carl Harbord (Operator of Perseus Club); Georges Renavent (Jacques the Headwaiter); Ida Moore (Woman); David Thursby (Henry the Bartender); Trevor Ward (Switchboard Operator); Martin Wilkins, Everett G. Brown, Darby Jones (Batsuma Chiefs); Byron Ellis (Callboy); James R. Scott (Clerk); Blackie Whiteford, Harry Cording, Art Foster (Guards).

THE FLAME AND THE ARROW *(Warner Bros., 1950), C-89 min.*
Producers, Harold Hecht, Frank Ross; director, Jacques Tourneur; story-screenplay, Waldo Salt; art director, Edward Carrere; music, Max Steiner; camera, Ernest Haller; editor, Alan Crosland, Jr.

Burt Lancaster (Bardo); Virginia Mayo (Anne); Robert Douglas (Alessandro); Aline Mac-Mahon (Nonna Batoli); Frank Allenby (Ulrich); Nick Cravat (Piccolo); Lynne Baggett (Francesca); Gordon Gebert (Rudi); Norman Lloyd (Troubadour); Victor Kilian (Apothecary); Francis Pierlot (Papa Pietro); Robin Hughes (Skinner).

MISTER 880 *(Twentieth Century-Fox, 1950), 90 min.*
Producer, Julian Blaustein; director, Edmund Goulding; based on the article *Old Eight Eighty* by St. Clair McKelway; screenplay, Robert Riskin; art directors, Lyle Wheeler, George W. Davis; music director, Lionel Newman; camera, Joseph LaShelle; editor, Robert Fritch.

Burt Lancaster (Steve Buchanan); Dorothy McGuire (Ann Winslow); Edmund Gwenn (Skipper); Millard Mitchell (Mac); Minor Watson (Judge O'Neil); Howard St. John (Chief); Hugh Sanders (Thad Mitchell); James Millican (Olie Johnson); Howland Chamberlin (Duff); Larry Keating (Lee); Kathleen Hughes (Secretary); Geraldine Wall (Miss Gallagher); Marvin Williams (U.S. Attorney); Norman Field (Bailiff); Helen Hatch (Maggie); Robert B. Williams (Sergeant); Ed Max (Mousie); Frank Wilcox (Mr. Beddington); George Adrian (Carlos); Michael Lally (George); Joe McTurk (Gus); Minerva Urecal (Rosie); George Gastine (Waiter); Ray De Ravenne, Paul Bradley, Arthur Dulac (Men); Curt Furberg (German); Joan Valerie (Cashier); Jack Daly (Court Clerk); Dick Ryan (U.S. Marshal); William J. O'Leary (Junk Man); Billy Gray (Mickey); Billy Nelson (Taxi Driver); Bill McKenzie (Jimmy); Herbert Vigran (Barker); Mischa Novy (Violinist); Erik Neilsen, Michael Little, Patrick Miller, Whitey Haupt, Timmie Hawkins, Tommie Mann Menzies, Gary Pagett, Peter Roman (Boys); Ronnie Ralph (High School Boy); Rico Alaniz (Spanish Interpreter); Eddie Lee, George Lee (Chinese Interpreters); Victor Desny (Russian Interpreter); Sherry Hall (Clerk in Cigar Store); John Hiestand (Narrator); Bessie Wade, Polly Bailey (Women); Robert Boon, Dr. D. W. De Roos (Dutchmen).

VENGEANCE VALLEY *(MGM, 1951), C-83 min.*
Producer, Nicholas Nayfack; director, Richard Thorpe; story, Luke Short; screenplay, Irving Ravetch; art directors, Cedric Gibbons, Malcolm Brown; music, Rudolph Kopp; camera, George J. Folsey; editor, Conrad A. Nervig.

Burt Lancaster (Owen Daybright); Robert Walker (Lee Strobie); Joanne Dru (Jen Strobie); Sally Forrest (Lily); John Ireland (Hub Fasken); Carleton Carpenter (Hewie); Ray Collins (Arch Strobie); Ted de Corsia (Herb Backett); Hugh O'Brian (Dick Fasken); Will Wright (Mr. Willoughby); Grace Mills (Mrs. Burke); James Hayward (Sheriff Con Alvis); James Harrison (Orv Esterly); Stanley Andrews (Mead Calhoun); Glenn Strange (Dave Allard); Paul E. Burns (Dr. Irwin); Robert E. Griffin (Cal); Harvey Dunn (Dealer); John McKee (Player); Tom Fadden (Obie Rune); Monte Montague, Al Ferguson, Roy Butler (Men); Margaret Bert (Mrs. Calhoun); Norman Leavitt, Dan White, Bob Wilke, Louis Nicoletti (Cowhands).

JIM THORPE—ALL AMERICAN *(Warner Bros., 1951), 107 min.*
Producer, Everett Freeman; director, Michael Curtiz; based on the biography by Russell J. Birdwell, Jim Thorpe; story, Douglas Morrow, Francis X. Flaherty; screenplay, Morrow, Everett Freeman; art director, Edward Carrere; technical adviser, Thorpe; music, Max Steiner; camera, Ernest Haller; editor, Folmer Blangsted.

Burt Lancaster (Jim Thorpe); Charles Bickford (Pop Warner); Steve Cochran (Peter Allendine); Phyllis Thaxter (Margaret Miller); Dick Wesson (Ed Guyac); Jack Bighead (Little Boy); Suni Warcloud (Wally Denny); Al Mejia (Louis Tewanema); Hubie Kerns (Ashenbrunner); Nestor Paiva (Hiram Thorpe); Jimmy Moss (Jim Thorpe, Jr.); Billy Gray (Jim Thorpe As a Boy); Nick Rodman (Frant Mr. Pleasant); Eula Morgan (Charlotte Thorpe); Bob Williams (Lafayette Coach); Sarah Selby (Miss Benton); Jack Baston (King Gustav); Frank McFarland (Chairman); Joseph Kerr, Phil Tead (Board Members); Roy Gordon (Coach McGraw); Ralph Montgomery, Tim Graham (Photographers); Norman Phillips (Reporter); Mary Alan Hokanson (Operator); Robert Harrison (Locker Room Boy); Hal Baylor, Charles Horvath, Chester Hayes, John Close (Players); Tom Greenway (Coach Howard); Max Terhune (Farmer); George Spalding (Doctor); Chris Munson (Indian Athlete); Dewey Robinson (Bartender); Jack Perrin, Joe Gilbert, Buddy Thaw (Spectators); Dale Van Sickel (Cop); Charles O'Brien (Owner).

TEN TALL MEN *(Columbia, 1951), C-97 min.*

Producer, Harold Hecht; director, Willis Goldbeck; story, James Warner Bellah, Goldbeck; screenplay, Roland Kibbee, Frank Davis; art director, Carl Anderson; music director, Morris Stoloff; camera, William Snyder; editor, William Lyon.

Burt Lancaster (Sergeant Mike Kincaid); Jody Lawrence (Mahla); Gilbert Roland (Corporal Luis Delgado); Kieron Moore (Corporal Pierre Molier); George Tobias (Londos); John Dehner (Jardine); Nick Dennis (Mouse); Mike Mazurki (Roshko); Gerald Mohr (Caid Hussin); Ian MacDonald (Lustig); Mari Blanchard (Marie DeLatour); Donald Randolph (Yussif); Robert Clary (Mossul); Henry Rowland (Kurt); Michael Pate (Browning); Stephen Bekassy (Lieutenant Kruger); Raymond Greenleaf (Sheik Ban Allal); Paul Marion (Iejah); Henri Letondal (Administrator); Philip Van Zandt (Henri); Joy Windsor, JoAnn Arnold, Edith Sheets, Diana Dawson, Gwen Caldwell, Helen Reichman (Ladies in Waiting); George Khoury (Aide); Nick Cravat, Shimen Ruskin (Disgruntled Riffs); Carlo Tricoli (Holy Man); Tom Conroy (Chanter, Hussin's Aide); Alan Ray, Frank Arnold, Ralph Volkie (Riffs); Mickey Simpson (Giant Riff); Charlita, Rita Conde (Belles); Benny Burt (Beggar).

THE CRIMSON PIRATE *(Warner Bros., 1952), C-104 min.*

Producer, Harold Hecht; director, Robert Siodmak; screenplay, Roland Kibbee; art director, Paul Sheriff; music, William Alwyn; music director, Muir Mathieson; camera, Otto Heller; editor, Jack Harris.

Burt Lancaster (Vallo); Nick Cravat (Ojo); Eva Bartok (Consuelo); Torin Thatcher (Humble Bellows); James Hayter (Prudence); Leslie Bradley (Baron Gruda); Margot Grahame (Bianca); Noel Purcell (Pablo Murphy); Frederick Leicester (El Libre); Eliot Makeham (Governor); Frank Pettingell (Colonel); Dagmar Wynter (La Signorita); Christopher Lee (Attache).

COME BACK, LITTLE SHEBA *(Paramount, 1952), 99 min.*

Producer, Hal B. Wallis; director, Daniel Mann; based on the play by William Inge; screenplay, Ketti Frings; art directors, Hal Pereira, Henry Bumstead; set decorators, Sam Comer, Russ Dowd; music, Franz Waxman; sound, Walter Oberst, Don McKay; camera, James Wong Howe; editor, Warren Low.

Burt Lancaster (Doc Delaney); Shirley Booth (Lola Delaney); Terry Moore (Marie Loring); Richard Jaeckel (Turk Fisher); Philip Ober (Ed Anderson); Edwin Max (Elmo Huston); Lisa Golm (Mrs. Coffman); Walter Kelley (Bruce); Paul McVey (Postman); Peter Leeds (Milkman);

Anthony Joachim (Mr. Cruthers); Kitty McHugh (Pearl Stinson); Ned Glass (Parent of Child); Susan Odin (Girl); Henry Blair (Western Union Boy); Virginia Mullen (Henrietta); James Davies (Man); Virginia Hall (Blonde); Beverly Mock (Judy Coffman); William Haade (Interne).

SOUTH SEA WOMAN *(Warner Bros., 1953), 99 min.*

Producer, Sam Bischoff; director, Arthur Lubin; based on the play *General Court-Martial* by William M. Rankin; adaptors, Earl Baldwin, Stanley Shapiro; screenplay, Edwin Blum; art director, Edward Carrere; set decorator, William L. Keuhl; assistant director, Frank Mattison; wardrobe, Moss Mabry; dialogue director, Herschel Daugherty; music, David Buttolph; choreography, Lester Horton; orchestrator, Maurice de Packh; makeup, Gordon Bau; sound, Francis J. Scheid; special camera effects, H. F. Koenekamp; camera, Ted McCord; editor, Clarence Kolster.

Burt Lancaster (Sergeant James O'Hearn); Virginia Mayo (Ginger Martin); Chuck Connors (Davey White); Barry Kelley (Colonel Hickman); Hayden Rorke (Lieutenant Fears); Leon Askin (Marchand); Veola Vonn (Madame Duval); Raymond Greenleaf (Captain Peabody); Robert Sweeney (Lieutenant Miller); Paul Burke (Ensign Hoyt); Cliff Clark (Lieutenant Colonel Parker); John Alderson (Fitzroy); Rudolph Anders (Van Dorck); Henri Letondal (Alphonse); Georges Saurel (Jacques); Arthur Shields (Jimmylegs Donovan); William O'Leary (Mr. Smith); John Damler (Lieutenant Kellogg); Alena Awes (Mimi); Jacqueline Duval (Julie); Violet Daniels (Suzette); Paul Bryar (Captain of the Gendarmes); Anthony Radecki (Military Policeman); Tony Garsen (Orderly); Guy de Vestal, Gregory Gay (Free French); Strother Martin (Young Marine); Jim Hayward (Masterson); Peter Chong (Woo Ching); Grace Lem (Mama Ching); Danny Chang (Wong); Paul Liu (Ho); Noel Cravat (Fatso); Gisele Verlaine (Olga); Al Hill, Jack Kenney (Bartenders); Keye-Luke, Frank Kumagai, Edo Mita, Robert Kino, Rollin Moriyama (Jap Officers).

FROM HERE TO ETERNITY *(Columbia, 1953), 118 min.*

Producer, Buddy Adler; director, Fred Zinnemann; based on the novel by James Jones; screenplay, Daniel Taradash; music supervisor-conductor, Morris Stoloff; background music, George Duning; orchestrator, Arthur Morton; song, Jones, Fred Karger, and Robert Wells; art director, Cary Odell; set decorator, Frank Tuttle; gowns, Jean Louis; assistant director, Earl Bellamy; technical adviser, Brigadier General Kendall J. Fielder, U.S.A., Ret.; makeup, Clay Campbell; sound, Lodge Cunningham; camera, Burnett Guffey; editor, William Lyon.

Burt Lancaster (Sergeant Milton Warden); Montgomery Clift (Robert E. Lee Prewitt); Deborah Kerr (Karen Holmes); Donna Reed (Lorene); Frank Sinatra (Angelo Maggio); Philip Ober (Captain Dana Holmes); Mickey Shaughnessy (Sergeant Leva); Harry Bellaver (Mazzioli); Ernest Borgnine (Sergeant "Fatso" Judson); Jack Warden (Corporal Buckley); John Dennis (Sergeant Ike Galovitch); Merle Travis (Sal Anderson); Tim Ryan (Sergeant Pete Karelsen); Arthur Keegan (Treadwell); Barbara Morrison (Mrs. Kipfer); Jean Willes (Annette); Claude Akins (Sergeant Baldy Dhom); Robert Karnes (Sergeant Turp Thornhill); Robert Wilke (Sergeant Henderson); Douglas Henderson (Corporal Champ Wilson); George Reeves (Sergeant Maylon Stark); Don Dubbins (Friday Clark); John Cason (Corporal Paluso); Kristine Miller (Georgette); John Bryant (Captain Ross); Joan Shawlee (Sandra); Angela Stevens (Jean); Mary Carver (Nancy); Vicki Bakken (Suzanne); Margaret Barstow (Roxanne); Delia Salvi (Billie); Willis Bouchey (Lieutenant Colonel); Al Sargent (Nair); William Lundmark (Bill); Robert Healy, Patrick Miller, Norman Wayne, Joe Sargent, Mack Chandler, Edward Laguna, John Veitch, John Davis, Carey Leverette (Soldiers); Brick Sullivan (Military Guard); Tyler McVey (Major Stern); Weaver Levy (Bartender); Louise Saraydar, Joe Roach

(Bits); Carleton Young (Colonel Ayres); Fay Roope (General Slater); Moana Gleason (Rose); Freeman Lusk (Colonel Wood); Robert Pike (Major Bonds).

THREE SAILORS AND A GIRL *(Warner Bros., 1953), C-95 min.*

Producer, Sammy Cahn; director, Roy Del Ruth; based on a play by George S. Kaufman; screenplay, Roland Kibbee, Devery Freeman; art director, Leo K. Kuter; camera, Carl Guthrie; editor, Owen Marks.

Gordon MacRae (Choir Boy Jones); Jane Powell (Penny Weston); Gene Nelson (Twitch); Jack E. Leonard (Porky); Sam Levene (Joe Woods); George Givot (Rossi); Archer MacDonald (Webster); Raymond Greenleaf (Morrow); Veda Ann Borg (Faye Foss); Burt Lancaster (Marine); Henry Slate (Hank the Sailor); Mickey Simpson (Guard); Elizabeth Flournoy (Secretary); Claire Meade, Dick Simmons, John Parrish, Everett Glass, Bob Carson (Clients); Phil Van Zandt (Garage Owner); Wayne Taylor (Bellhop); Al Hill (Sign Painter); Guy E. Hearn (Workman); Cliff Ferre, Paul Burke (Actors); Grandon Rhodes (George Abbott); David Bond (Moss Hart); Alex Gerry (Ira Gershwin); Frank Scannell (Boxoffice Man); Roy Engel (Walter Kerr, *Herald-Tribune* Critic); Murray Alper, Ed Hinton (Marines); John Crawford, Dennis Dengate (Shore Patrolmen); Merv Griffin, Arthur Walsh, Jack Larson, Michael Pierce, King Donovan (Sailors); Bess Flowers, Harold Miller (Indignant Patrons).

HIS MAJESTY O'KEEFE *(Warner Bros., 1953), C-92 min.*

Producer, Harold Hecht; director, Byron Haskin; based on the novel by Lawrence Klingman, Gerald Green; screenplay, Borden Chase, James Hill; music, Dmitri Tiomkin; costumes, Marjorie Best, Liz Hennings; makeup, Stuart Freeborn; choreography, Daniel Nagrin; assistant director, Richard McWhorter; art directors, Edward S. Haworth, W. Simpson Robinson; set decorator, Jane Roth; sound, Francis J. Scheid; camera, Otto Heller; editor, Manuel Del Campo.

Burt Lancaster (His Majesty O'Keefe); Joan Rice (Dalabo); Andre Morell (Alfred Tetens); Abraham Sofaer (Fatumak); Archie Savage (Boogulroo); Benson Fong (Mr. Chou); Tessa Prendergast (Kakofel); Lloyd Berrell (Inifels); Charles Horvath (Bully Hayes); Philip Ahn (Sein Tang); Guy Doleman (Weber); Grant Taylor (Lieutenant Brenner); and: Alexander Archdale, Harvey Adams, Jim Crawford, Paddy Mulelly, Niranjan Singh, Warren Ray.

APACHE *(United Artists, 1954), C-91 min.*

Producer, Harold Hecht; director, Robert Aldrich; based on the novel *Broncho Apache* by Paul I. Wellman; screenplay, James R. Webb; assistant director, Sid Sidman; production designer, Nicholai Remisoff; set decorator, Joseph Kish; costumes, Norma; makeup, Robert Schiffer, Harry Maret; sound, Jack Solomon; camera, Ernest Laszlo; editor, Alan Crosland, Jr.

Burt Lancaster (Massai); Jean Peters (Nalinle); John McIntire (Al Sieber); Charles Bronson (Hondo); John Dehner (Weddle); Paul Guilfoyle (Santos); Ian MacDonald (Glagg); Walter Sande (Lieutenant Colonel Beck); Morris Ankrum (Dawson); Monte Blue (Geronimo).

VERA CRUZ *(United Artists, 1954), C-94 min.*

Producer, James Hill; co-producers, Harold Hecht, Burt Lancaster; director, Robert Aldrich; story, Borden Chase; screenplay, Roland Kibbee, James R. Webb; music, Hugo Friedhofer; orchestrator-music director, Raul Lavista; song, Hugo Friedhofer and Sammy Cahn; sound, Manuel Topete, Galdino Samperio; camera, Ernest Laszlo; editor, Alan Crosland, Jr.

255

Gary Cooper (Benjamin Trane); Burt Lancaster (Joe Erin); Denise Darcel (Countess Marie Duvarre); Cesar Romero (Marquis de Labordere); Sarita Montiel (Nina); George Macready (Emperor Maximilian); Ernest Borgnine (Donnegan); Henry Brandon (Danette); Charles Bronson (Pittsburgh); Morris Ankrum (General Aguilar); James McCallion (Little-Bit); Jack Lambert (Charlie); Jack Elam (Tex); James Seay (Abilene); Archie Savage (Ballard); Charles Horvath (Reno); Juan Garcia (Pedro).

THE KENTUCKIAN *(United Artists, 1955), C-104 min.*

Producer, Harold Hecht; director, Burt Lancaster; based on the novel *The Gabriel Horn* by Felix Holt; screenplay, A. B. Guthrie, Jr.; screenplay; Guthrie; music, Bernard Herrmann; songs, Irving Gordon; music director, Roy Webb; assistant director, Richard Mayberry; camera, Ernest Laszlo; editor, William B. Murphy.

Burt Lancaster (Big Eli); Dianne Foster (Hannah); Diana Lynn (Susie); John McIntire (Zack); Una Merkel (Sophie); Walter Matthau (Bodine); John Carradine (Fletcher); Donald MacDonald (Little Eli); John Litel (Babson); Rhys Williams (Constable); Edward Norris (Gambler); Lee Erickson (Luke); Clem Bevans (Pilot); Lisa Ferraday (Woman Gambler); Douglas Spencer, Paul Wexler (Fromes Brothers); Whip Wilson (Lancaster's Double).

THE ROSE TATTOO *(Paramount, 1955), 117 min.*

Producer, Hal B. Wallis; director, Daniel Mann; based on the play by Tennessee Williams; adaptor, Hal Kanter; screenplay, Williams; art directors, Hal Pereira, Tambia Larsen; music director, Alex North; costumes, Edith Head; assistant director, Richard McWhorter; camera, James Wong Howe; editor, Warren Low.

Anna Magnani (Serafina Delle Rose); Burt Lancaster (Alvaro Mangiacavallo); Marisa Pavan (Rosa Delle Rose); Ben Cooper (Jack Hunter); Virginia Grey (Estelle Hohengarten); Jo Van Fleet (Bessie); Mimi Aguglia (Assunta); Florence Sundstrom (Flora); Dorrit Kelton (School Teacher); Rossana San Marco (Peppina); Augusta Merighi (Guiseppina); Rosa Rey (Mariella); Georgia Simmons (The Strega); Zolya Talma (Miss Mangiacavallo); George Humbert (Pop Mangiacavallo); Margherita Pasquero (Grandma Mangiacavallo); May Lee (Mamma Shigura the Tattoo Artist); Jean Hart (Violetta); Lewis Charles, Virgil Osborne (Taxi Drivers); Roger Gunderson (Doctor); Roland Vildo (Salvatore); Fred Taylor (Cashier); Natalie Murray (Townswoman); Albert Atkins (Mario); Joe Rogue, Norman Markwell (Bits).

TRAPEZE *(United Artists, 1956), C-105 min.*

Producer, James Hill; director, Sir Carol Reed; based on the novel *The Killing Frost* by Max Catto; adaptor, Liam O'Brien; screenplay, James R. Webb; art director, Rino Mondellini; music, Malcolm Arnold; assistant directors, Richard McWhorter, Michael Romanoff, Robert Gendre; wardrobe, Frank Salvi, Gladys De Segonzac; camera, Robert Krasker; editor, Bert Bates.

Burt Lancaster (Mike Ribble); Tony Curtis (Tino Orsini); Gina Lollobrigida (Lola); Katy Jurado (Rosa); Thomas Gomez (Bouglione); Johnny Puleo (Max the Dwarf); Minor Watson (John Ringling North); Gerard Landry (Chikki); J. P. Kerrien (Otto); Sidney James (Snake Man); Gabrielle Fontan (Old Woman); Pierre Tabard (Paul); Gamil Ratab (Stefan); Michel Thomas (Ringmaster); and: Edward Hagopian, Eddie Ward, Sally Marlowe, Fay Alexander, Willy Krause, Betty Codreano, The Arriolas, Mme. Felco Cipriano, The Codreanos, Simpion Bouglione, The Gimma Boys, Zavatta, Mylos, Lulu and Tonio.

THE RAINMAKER *(Paramount, 1956), C-121 min.*

Producer, Hal B. Wallis; associate producer, Paul Nathan; director, Joseph Anthony; based on the play by N. Richard Nash; screenplay, Nash; art directors, Hal Pereira, Walter Tyler; set decorators, Sam Comer, Arthur Krams; music, Alex North; costumes, Edith Head; assistant director, C. C. Coleman, Jr.; Technicolor consultant, Richard Mueller; makeup, Wally Westmore; sound, Harold Lewis, Winston Leverett; special camera effects, John P. Fulton; camera, Charles Lang, Jr.; editor, Warren Low.

Burt Lancaster (Starbuck); Katharine Hepburn (Lizzie Curry); Wendell Corey (File); Lloyd Bridges (Noah Curry); Earl Holliman (Jim Curry); Cameron Prud'Homme (H. C. Curry); Wallace Ford (Sheriff Thomas); Yvonne Lime (Snookie); Dottie Bee Baker (Belinda); Dan White (Deputy); Stan Jones, John Benson, James Stone, Tony Merrill, Joe Brown (Townsmen); Ken Becker (Phil Mackey).

GUNFIGHT AT THE O.K. CORRAL *(Paramount, 1957), C-122 min.*

Producer, Hal B. Wallis; associate producer, Paul Nathan; director, John Sturges; suggested by the article by George Scullin; screenplay, Leon Uris; assistant director, Michael D. Moore; costumes, Edith Head; music, Dmitri Tiomkin; song, Tiomkin and Ned Washington; art directors, Hal Pereira, Walter Tyler; camera, Charles Lang, Jr.; editor, Warren Low.

Burt Lancaster (Wyatt Earp); Kirk Douglas (Doc Holliday); Rhonda Fleming (Laura Denbow); Jo Van Fleet (Kate Fisher); John Ireland (Ringo); Lyle Bettger (Ike Clanton); Frank Faylen (Cotton Wilson); Earl Holliman (Charles Bassett); Ted De Corsia (Shanghai Pierce); Dennis Hopper (Billy Clanton); Whit Bissell (John P. Clum); George Mathews (John Shanssey); John Hudson (Virgil Earp); DeForrest Kelley (Morgan Earp); Martin Milner (James Earp); Kenneth Tobey (Bat Masterson); Lee Van Cleef (Ed Bailey); Joan Camden (Betty Earp); Olive Carey (Mrs. Clanton); Brian Hutton (Rick); Nelson Leigh (Mayor Kelley); Jack Elam (Tom McLowery); Don Castle (Drunken Cowboy); Dennis Moore, Gregg Martell (Cowboys); Roger Creed, Morgan Lane, Paul Gary (Killers); Dorothy Abbott (Girl); Ethan Laidlaw (Bartender); William Norton Bailey (Merchant); Trude Wyler (Social Hall Guest); Tony Merrill (Barber); Harry Mendoza (Cockeyed Frank Loving); Roger Creed (Deputy); James Davis, Joe Forte, Max Power, Courtland Shepard (Card Players); Paul Bradley (Bartender).

SWEET SMELL OF SUCCESS *(United Artists, 1957), 96 min.*

Executive producer, Harold Hecht; producer, James Hill; director, Alexander MacKendrick; based on the novelette by Ernest Lehman; screenplay, Clifford Odets, Lehman; music and music director, Elmer Bernstein; songs, Chico Hamilton and Fred Katz; art director, Edward Carrere; camera, James Wong Howe.

Burt Lancaster (J. J. Hunsecker); Tony Curtis (Sidney Falco); Susan Harrison (Susan Hunsecker); Marty Milner (Steve Dallas); Sam Levene (Frank D'Angelo); Barbara Nichols (Rita); Jeff Donnell (Sally); Joseph Leon (Robard); Edith Atwater (Mary); Emile Meyer (Harry Kello); Joe Frisco (Herbie Temple); David White (Otis Elwell); Lawrence Dobkin (Leo Bartha); Lurene Tuttle (Mrs. Bartha); Queenie Smith (Mildred Tam); Autumn Russell (Linda); Jay Adler (Manny Davis); Lewis Charles (Al Evans).

RUN SILENT, RUN DEEP *(United Artists, 1958), 93 min.*

Producer, Harold Hecht; associate producer, William Schorr; director, Robert Wise; based on the novel by Captain Edward L. Beach; screenplay, John Gay; art director, Edward Carrere; music, Franz Waxman; camera, Russell Harlan.

Clark Gable (Commander Richardson); Burt Lancaster (Lieutenant Jim Bledsoe); Jack Warden (Mueller); Brad Dexter (Cartwright); Don Rickles (Ruby); Nick Cravat (Russo); Joe Maross (Kohler); Mary LaRoche (Laura); Eddie Foy III (Larto); Rudy Bond (Cullen); H. M. Wynant (Hendrix); John Bryant (Beckman); Ken Lynch (Frank); Joel Fluellen (Bragg); Jimmie Bates (Jessie); John Gibson (Captain Blunt).

SEPARATE TABLES (United Artists, 1958), 98 min.

Producer, Harold Hecht; director, Delbert Mann; based on the play by Terence Rattigan; screenplay, Rattigan, John Gay; production designer, Harry Horner; art director, Edward Carrere; set decorator, Edward G. Boyle; costumes, Mary Grant; makeup, Harry Maret, Frank Prehoda; Miss Hayworth's gowns, Edith Head; assistant director, Thomas F. Shaw; music, David Raksin; title song, Harry Warren and Harold Adamson; sound, Fred Lau; camera, Charles Lang, Jr.; editors, Marjorie Fowler, Charles Ennis.

Rita Hayworth (Ann Shankland); Deborah Kerr (Sibyl Railton-Bell); David Niven (Major Pollock); Burt Lancaster (John Malcolm); Wendy Hiller (Miss Cooper); Gladys Cooper (Mrs. Railton-Bell); Cathleen Nesbitt (Lady Matheson); Felix Aylmer (Mr. Fowler); Rod Taylor (Charles); Audrey Dalton (Jean); May Hallatt (Miss Meacham); Priscilla Morgan (Doreen); Hilda Plowright (Mabel).

THE DEVIL'S DISCIPLE (United Artists, 1959), 82 min.

Producer, Harold Hecht; director, Guy Hamilton; based on the play by George Bernard Shaw; screenplay, John Dighton, Roland Kibbee; art directors, Terence Verity, Edward Carrere; set decorator, Scott Slimon; makeup, Paul Habiger; technical adviser, Alan Binns; music, Richard Rodney Bennett; music conductor, John Hollingsworth; assistant director, Adrian Pryce-Jones; sound, Leslie Hammond; camera, Jack Hildyard; editor, Alan Osbiston.

Burt Lancaster (Anthony Anderson); Kirk Douglas (Richard Dudgeon); Laurence Olivier (General Burgoyne); Janette Scott (Judith Anderson); Eva LeGallienne (Mrs. Dudgeon); Harry Andrews (Major Swindon); Basil Sydney (Lawyer Hawkins); George Rose (British Sergeant); Neil McCallum (Christopher Dudgeon); Mervyn Johns (Reverend Maindeck Parshotter); David Horne (William); Jenny Jones (Essie); Erik Chitty (Titus).

THE UNFORGIVEN (United Artists, 1960), C-120 min.

Producer, James Hill; director, John Huston; based on the novel by Alan Le May; screenplay, Ben Maddow; art director, Stephen Grimes; music and music conductor, Dmitri Tiomkin; wardrobe, Dorothy Jeakins; assistant director, Thomas F. Shaw; makeup, Frank McCoy, Frank Larue; sound, Basil Fenton Smith; camera, Franz Planer; editor, Hugh Russell Lloyd.

Burt Lancaster (Ben Zachary); Audrey Hepburn (Rachel Zachary); Audie Murphy (Cash Zachary); John Saxon (Johnny Portugal); Charles Bickford (Zeb Rawlins); Lillian Gish (Mattilda Zachary); Albert Salmi (Charlie Rawlins); Joseph Wiseman (Abe Kelsey); June Walker (Hagar Rawlins); Kipp Hamilton (Georgia Rawlins); Arnold Merritt (Jude Rawlins); Carlos Rivas (Lost Bird); Doug McClure (Andy Zachary).

ELMER GANTRY (United Artists, 1960), C-146 min.

Producer, Bernard Smith; director, Richard Brooks; based on the novel by Sinclair Lewis; screenplay, Brooks; art director, Edward Carrere; set decorator, Frank Tuttle; assistant directors, Tom Shaw, Rowe Wallerstein, Carl Beringer; costumes, Dorothy Jeakins; music, Andre Previn; sound, Harry Mills; camera, John Alton; editor, Marge Fowler.

Burt Lancaster (Elmer Gantry); Jean Simmons (Sister Sharon Falconer); Dean Jagger (William L. Morgan); Arthur Kennedy (Jim Lefferts); Shirley Jones (Lulu Bains); Patti Page (Sister Rachel); Edward Andrews (George Babbitt); John McIntire (Reverend Pengily); Joe Maross (Pete); Everett Glass (Reverend Brown); Michael Whalen (Reverend Phillips); Hugh Marlowe (Reverend Garrison); Philip Ober (Reverend Planck); Wendell Holmes (Reverend Ulrich); Barry Kelley (Captain Holt); Rex Ingram (Preacher); John Qualen (Sam).

THE YOUNG SAVAGES *(United Artists, 1961), 100 min.*

Executive producer, Harold Hecht; producer, Pat Duggan; director, John Frankenheimer; based on the novel *A Matter of Conviction* by Evan Hunter; screenplay, Edward Anhalt, J. P. Miller; music and music conductor, David Amram; art director, Burr Smidt; set decorator, James Crowe; assistant director, Carter DeHaven, Jr.; makeup, Robert Schiffer; costumes, Jack Angel, Roselle Novello; sound, Harry Mills, Eldon Coutts; camera, Lionel Linden; editor, Eda Warren.

Burt Lancaster (Hank Bell); Dina Merrill (Karen Bell); Shelley Winters (Mary Di Pace); Edward Andrews (Dan Cole); Vivian Nathan (Mrs. Escalante); Larry Gates (Randolph); Telly Savalas (Lieutenant Richard Gunnison); Pilar Seurat (Louisa Escalante); Jody Fair (Angela Rugiello); Roberta Shore (Joenny Bell); Milton Selzer (Walsh); Robert Burton (Judge); David Stewart (Barton); Stanley Kristien (Danny Di Pace); John Davis Chandler (Arthur Reardon); Neil Nephew (Anthony Aposto); Luis Arroya (Zorro); Jose Perez (Roberto Escalante); Richard Velez (Gargantua); William Sargent (Soames); Chris Robinson (Pretty Boy); Stanley Adams (Lieutenant Hardy); Linda Dancil (Maria Amora); Raphael Lopez (Jose); Henry Norell (Pierce); Bob Biheller (Turtleneck); Mario Roccuzzo (Diavalo); Harry Holcombe (Doctor); Tom Conroy (Mr. Abbeney); Helen Kleeb (Mrs. Patton); John Walsh (Lonnie); Clegg Hoyt (Whitey); Irving Steinberg (Officer Wohlman); Joel Fluellen (Court Clerk); Robert Cleaves (Sullivan).

JUDGMENT AT NUREMBERG *(United Artists, 1961), 189 min.*

Producer, Stanley Kramer; associate producer, Philip Langner; director, Kramer; based on the teleplay by Abby Mann; screenplay, Mann; music, Ernest Gold; assistant director, Ivan Volkman; wardrobe, Joe King; art director, Rudolph Sternad; sound, James Speak; camera, Ernest Laszlo; editor, Fred Knudtson.

Spencer Tracy (Judge Dan Haywood); Burt Lancaster (Ernst Janning); Richard Widmark (Colonel Tad Lawson); Marlene Dietrich (Mme. Bertholt); Maximilian Schell (Hans Rolfe); Judy Garland (Irene Hoffman); Montgomery Clift (Rudolf Petersen); William Shatner (Captain Byers); Ed Binns (Senator Burkette); Kenneth MacKenna (Judge Kenneth Norris); Werner Klemperer (Emil Hahn); Torben Meyer (Werner Lammpe); Alan Baxter (General Merrin); Ray Teal (Judge Curtiss Ives); Martin Brandt (Friedrich Hofstetter); Virginia Christine (Mrs. Halbestadt); Ben Wright (Halbestadt); Joseph Bernard (Major Abe Radnitz); John Wengraf (Dr. Wieck); Karl Swenson (Dr. Geuter); Howard Caine (Wailner); Otto Waldis (Phol); Olga Fabian (Mrs. Lindnow); Sheila Bromley (Mrs. Ives); Bernard Kates (Perkins); Jana Taylor (Elsa Scheffler); Paul Busch (Schmidt).

BIRDMAN OF ALCATRAZ *(United Artists, 1962), 147 min.*

Producers, Stuart Miller, Guy Trosper; director, John Frankenheimer; based on the book by Thomas E. Gaddis; screenplay, Trosper; art director, Fernando Carrere; makeup, Robert Schiffer; assistant director, Dave Silver; sound, George Cooper; sound effects, Robert Reich, James Nelson; camera, Burnett Guffey; editor, Edward Mann.

Burt Lancaster (Robert Stroud); Karl Malden (Harvey Shoemaker); Thelma Ritter (Elizabeth Stroud); Betty Field (Stella Johnson); Neville Brand (Bull Ransom); Edmond O'Brien (Tom Gaddis); Hugh Marlowe (Roy Comstock); Telly Savalas (Feto Gomez); Whit Bissell (Dr. Ellis); Crahan Denton (Kramer); Leo Penn (Eddie Kassellis); James Westerfield (Jess Younger); Lewis Charles (Chaplain Wentzel); Art Stewart (Guard Captain); Raymond Greenleaf (Judge); Nick Dennis (Crazed Prisoner); William Hansen (Fred Daw); Harry Holcombe (City Editor); Robert Burton (Senator Ham Lewis); Len Lesser (Burns); Chris Robinson (Logue); George Mitchell (Father Matthieu); Ed Mallory (John Clary); Adrienne Marden (Mrs. Woodrow Wilson); Harry Jackson (Reporter).

A CHILD IS WAITING *(United Artists, 1963), 102 min.*

Producer, Stanley Kramer; associate producer, Phillip Langner; director, John Cassavetes; based on the teleplay by Abby Mann; screenplay, Mann; art director, Rudolph Sternad; music, Ernest Gold; sound, James L. Speak; camera, Joseph La Shelle; editor, Gene Fowler, Jr.

Burt Lancaster (Dr. Matthew Clark); Judy Garland (Jean Hansen); Gena Rowlands (Sophie Widdicombe); Steven Hill (Ted Widdicombe); Bruce Ritchey (Rueben Widdicombe); Gloria McGehee (Mattie); Paul Stewart (Goodman); Elizabeth Wilson (Miss Fogarty); Barbara Pepper (Miss Brown); John Morley (Holland); June Walker (Mrs. McDonald); Mario Gallo (Dr. Lombardi); Frederick Draper (Dr. Sack); Lawrence Tierney (Douglas Benham).

THE LIST OF ADRIAN MESSENGER *(Universal, 1963), 98 min.*

Producer, Edward Lewis; director, John Huston; based on the novel by Philip MacDonald; screenplay, Anthony Veiller; music, Jerry Goldsmith; music supervisor, Joseph Gershenson; assistant directors, Tom Shaw, Terry Morse, Jr.; art directors, Stephen Grimes, George Webb; set decorator, Oliver Emert; second unit director, Ted Scaife; makeup, Bud Westmore; camera, Joseph MacDonald; editors, Terry Morse, Hugh Fowler.

George C. Scott (Anthony Gethryn); Dana Wynter (Lady Jocelyn Bruttenholm); Clive Brook (Marquis of Gleneyre); Herbert Marshall (Sir Wilfred Lucas); Jacques Roux (Raoul Le Borg); Bernard Archard (Inspector Pike); Gladys Cooper (Mrs. Karoudjian); Walter Anthony Huston (Derek); John Merivale (Adrian Messenger); Marcel Dalio (Anton Karoudjian); Anita Sharpe-Bolster (Shopkeeper); Noel Purcell (Farmer); John Huston (Lord Aston the Fox Hunter); Tony Curtis (Harlan); Kirk Douglas (George Brougham); Burt Lancaster (Woman); Robert Mitchum (Jim Slattery); Frank Sinatra (Gypsy Stableman); Joe Lynch (Cyclist); Mona Lilian (Proprietress); Tim Dunant (Hunt Secretary); Richard Peel (Sergeant Flood); Stacy Morgan (Whip Man); Anna Van Der Heide (Stewardess); Roland Long (Carstairs); Bernard Fox (Lynce); Barbara Morrison (Nurse); Jennifer Raine (Student Nurse).

THE LEOPARD *(Twentieth Century-Fox, 1963), C-205 min.**

Executive producer, Pietro Notarianni; producer, Goffredo Lombardo; director, Luchino Visconti; based on the novel by Giuseppe Di Lampedusa; screenplay, Suso Cecchi D'Amico, Pasquale Festa Campanile, Massimo Franciosa, Enrico Medioli, Visconti; art director, Mario Garbuglia; set decorator, Giorgio Pes; costumes, Piero Tosi; makeup, Alberto De Rossi; Mr. Lancaster's makeup, Robert Schiffer; music, Nino Rota; camera, Giuseppe Rotunno.

Burt Lancaster (Prince Don Fabrizio Salinas); Alain Delon (Tancredi); Claudia Cardinale (Angelica Sedara); Rino Morelli (Maria Stella); Paolo Stoppa (Don Calogero Sedara); Romolo Valli (Father Pirrone); Lucilla Morlacchi (Concetta); Serge Reggiani (Don Ciccio Tumeo); Ida Galli (Carolina); Ottavia Piccolo (Caterina); Pierro Clementi (Francesco Paolo); Carlo Valenzano (Paolo); Anna-Marie Bottini (Mlle, Dombreuil); Mario Girotti (Count Cavriaghi); Leslie French (Cavalier Chevally); Olimpia Cavallo (Mariannina); Marino Mase (Tutor); Sandra

Chistolini (Youngest Daughter); Brook Fuller (The Little Prince); Giuliano Gemma (The Garibaldino General); Claudia Cardinale (Bertiana); Giovanni Mesendi (Don Onofrio Rotolo); Howard Nelson-Rubien (Don Diego); Lola Braccini (Donna Margherita); Ivo Garrani (Colonel Pallavicino).

*Partially dubbed, English language version: 165 min.

SEVEN DAYS IN MAY *(Paramount, 1964), 120 min.*

Producer, Edward Lewis; director, John Frankenheimer; based on the novel by Fletcher Knebel, Charles W. Bailey II; screenplay, Rod Serling; art director, Cary Odell; set decorator, Edward Boyle; music, Jerry Goldsmith; assistant director, Hal Polaire; sound, Joe Edmondson; camera, Ellsworth Frederick; editor, Ferris Webster.

Burt Lancaster (General James M. Scott); Kirk Douglas (Colonel Martin "Jiggs" Casey); Fredric March (President Jordan Lyman); Ava Gardner (Eleanor Holbrook); Edmond O'-Brien (Senator Raymond Clark); Martin Balsam (Paul Girard); George Macready (Christopher Todd); Whit Bissell (Senator Prentice); Hugh Marlowe (Harold McPherson); Bart Burns (Arthur Corwin); Richard Anderson (Colonel Murdock); Jack Mullaney (Lieutenant Hough); Andrew Duggan (Colonel "Mutt" Henderson); John Larkin (Colonel Broderick); Malcolm Atterbury (Physician); Helen Kleeb (Esther Townsend); John Houseman (Admiral Barnswell); Colette Jackson (Bar Girl).

THE TRAIN *(United Artists, 1965) 140 min.*

Producer, Jules Bricken; associate producer, Bernard Farrell; director, John Frankenheimer; based on the novel *Le Front de l'Art* by Rose Valland; screenplay, Franklin Coen, Frank Davis, Walter Bernstein (French version, Albert Husson); music, Maurice Jarre; production designer, Willy Holt; sound, Joseph de Bretagne; special effects, Lee Zavitz; camera, Jean Tournier, Walter Wottitz; editors, David Bretherton, Gabriel Rongier.

Burt Lancaster (Labiche); Paul Scofield (Colonel von Waldheim); Jeanne Moreau (Christine); Michel Simon (Papa Boule); Suzanne Flon (Mlle. Villard); Charles Millot (Pesquet); Albert Remy (Didont); Jacques Marin (Stationmaster); Paul Bonifas (Spinet); Wolfgang Preiss (Major Herren); Howard Vernon (Captain Dietrich); Jean-Claude Bercq (Major of Retreating Convoy); Jean-Jacques Lecomte (Lieutenant of Retreating Convoy); Richard Munch (General von Lubitz); Bernard Lajarrige (Bernard); Jean Bouchard (Captain Schmidt); Donald O'-Brien (Sergeant Schwartz); Art Brauss (Lieutenant Pilzer); Richard Baily (Sergeant Grote); Christian Fuin (Robert); Daniel Lecourtois (Priest); Elmo Kindermann (General's Aide); Jacques Blot (Hubert).

THE HALLELUJAH TRAIL *(United Artists, 1965), C-167 min.*

Producer, John Sturges; associate producer, Robert E. Relyea; director, Sturges; based on the novel by Bill Gulick; screenplay, John Gay; assistant director, Jack N. Reddish; art director, Cary Odell; music, Elmer Bernstein; song, Bernstein and Ernie Sheldon; costumes, Edith Head; maps, DePatie-Feleng; sound, Robert Martin; special effects, A. Paul Pollard; camera, Robert Surtees; editor, Ferris Webster.

Burt Lancaster (Colonel Thadeus Gearhart); Lee Remick (Cora Templeton Massingale); Jim Hutton (Captain Paul Slater); Pamela Tiffin (Louise Gearhart); Donald Pleasence (Oracle Jones); Brian Keith (Frank Wallingham); Martin Landau (Chief Walks-Stooped-Over); John Anderson (Sergeant Buell); John Dehner (Narrator); Tom Stern (Kevin O'Flaherty); Robert J. Wilke (Chief Five Barrels); Jerry Gatlin, Larry Duran (Brothers-in-Law); Jim Burk (Elks-

Runner); Dub Taylor (Clayton Howell); John McKee (Rafe Pike); Helen Kleeb (Henrietta); Noam Pitlik (Interpreter); Carl Pitti (Phillips); Bill Williams (Brady); Marshall Reed (Carter); Caroll Adams (Simmons); Ted Markland (Bandmaster).

THE PROFESSIONALS *(Columbia, 1966), C-117 min.*

Producer-director, Richard Brooks; based on the novel *A Mule for the Marquessa* by Frank O'Rourke; screenplay, Brooks; art director, Edward S. Haworth; set decorator, Frank Tuttle; makeup, Robert Schiffer; wardrobe, Jack Martell; assistant director, Tom Shaw; music and music conductor, Maurice Jarre; sound, Charles J. Rice, William Randall, Jr., Jack Haynes; special effects, Willis Cook; camera, Conrad Hall; editor, Peter Zinner.

Burt Lancaster (Bill Dolworth); Lee Marvin (Henry Rico Farden); Robert Ryan (Hans Ehrengard); Jack Palance (Captain Jesus Raza); Claudia Cardinale (Maria Grant); Ralph Bellamy (J. W. Grant); Woody Strode (Jacob Sharp); Joe De Santis (Ortega); Rafael Bertrand (Fierro); Jorge Martinez De Hoyos (Padillia); Maria Gomez (Chiquita); Jose Chavez, Carlos Romero (Revolutionaries); Vaughn Taylor (Banker); Robert Contreras, Don Carlos (Bandits); Elizabeth Campbell (Mexican Girl); John Lopez (Mexican Servant); Darwin Lamb (Hooper); Dirk Evans (Man at Door); John McKee (Sheriff); Eddie Little Sky (The Prisoner); Leigh Chapman (Lady); Phil Parslow (Deputy Sheriff); Foster Hood, Henry O'Brien, Dave Cadiente, Vince Cadiente (Bits).

THE SCALPHUNTERS *(United Artists, 1968), C-103 min.*

Producers, Jules Levy, Arthur Gardner, Arnold Laven; director, Sydney Pollack; story-screenplay, William Norton) music, Elmer Bernstein; art director, Frank Arrigo; costumes, Joe Drury; makeup, Gary D. Liddiard; assistant directors, Charles R. Scott, Jr., Kevin Donnelly; choreography, Alex Ruiz; stunt co-ordinator, Tony Epper; title designer, Phill Norman; sound, Jesus Gonzalez Gancy; camera, Duke Callaghan, Richard Moore; editor, John Woodcock.

Burt Lancaster (Joe Bass); Shelley Winters (Kate); Telly Savalas (Jim Howie); Ossie Davis (Joseph Winfield Lee); Armando Silvestre (Two Crows); Dan Vadis (Yuma); Dabney Coleman (Jed); Paul Picerni (Frank); Nick Cravat (Ramon); John Epper, Jack Williams, Chuck Roberson, Tony Epper, Agapito Roldan, Gregorio Acosta, Marco Antonio Arzate (Scalphunters); Angela Rodriguez, Amelia Rivera, Alicia De Lago (Scalphunters' Women); Nestor Dominguez, Francisco Oliva, Benjamin Ramos, Enrique Tello, Raul Martinez, Jose Martinez, Rodolfo Toldeo, Jose Salas, Cuco Velazquez, Alejandro Lopez, Raul "Pin" Hernandez, Pedro Aguilar (Kiowas).

THE SWIMMER *(Columbia, 1968), C-94 min.*

Producers, Frank Perry, Roger Lewis; directors, Frank Perry, (uncredited) Sydney Pollack; based on the story by John Cheever; screenplay Eleanor Perry; music, Marvin Hamlisch; orchestrators, Jack Hayes, Leo Shuken; art director, Peter Donahue; assistant director, Michael Hertzberg; makeup, John Jiras; wardrobe, Anna Hill Johnstone; sound, William Goodman; camera, David L. Quaid; additional camera, Michael Nebbia; editors, Sidney Katz, Carl Lerner, Pat Somerset.

Burt Lancaster (Ned Merrill); Janice Rule (Shirley Abbott); Janet Landgard (Julianne Hooper); Tom Bickley (Donald Westerhazy); Alva Celauro (Muffie); Marge Champion (Peggy Forsburgh); Nancy Cushman (Mrs. Halloran); Lisa Daniels (Matron at Biswangers' Pool); Charles Drake (Howard Graham); Bill Fiore (Howie Hunsacker); John Garfield, Jr. (Ticket Seller); John Gerstad (Guest at the Bunkers' Pool); Rose Gregorio (Sylvia Finney); Bernie

Hamilton (Chauffeur); Kim Hunter (Betty Graham); House Jameson (Mr. Halloran); Jimmy Joyce (Jack Finney) Michael Kearney (Kevin Gilmartin); Marilyn Langner (Enid Bunker); Ray Mason (Party Guest); Richard McMurray (Stu Forsburgh); Jan Miner (Lillian Hunsacker); Diana Muldaur (Cynthia); Keri Oleson (Vernon); Joan Rivers (Joan); Cornelia Otis Skinner (Mrs. Hammar); Dolph Sweet (Henry Biswanger); Louise Troy (Grace Biswanger); Diana Van Der Vlis (Helen Westerhazy).

CASTLE KEEP *(Columbia, 1969), C-106 min.*

Producers, Martin Ransohoff, John Calley; director, Sydney Pollack; based on the novel by William Eastlake; screenplay, Danile Taradash, David Rayfiel; art directors, Max Douy, Jacques Douy, Morton Rabinowitz; set decorator, Charles Merangel; music and music conductor, Michel Legrand; choreography, Dirk Sanders; makeup, Robert Schiffer; assistant directors, Marc Maurette, Pierre Roubaud; sound, Antoine Petitjean, Yves-Marie Dacquay; special effects, Lee Zavits; camera, Henri Decae; helicopter camera, Nelson Tyler; editor, Malcolm Cooke.

Burt Lancaster (Major Abraham Falconer); Peter Falk (Sergeant Orlando Rossi); Patrick O'Neal (Captain Lionel Beckman); Jean-Pierre Aumont (Comte de Maldorais); Astrid Heeren (Therese); Scott Wilson (Corporal Ralph Clearboy); Tony Bill (Lieutenant Adam B. Amberjack); Michael Conrad (Sergeant Juan De Vaca); Bruce Dern (Lieutenant Billy Byron Bix); Al Freeman, Jr. (Private First Class Alistair Benjamin); James Patterson (Private Henry Three Ears of an Elk); Caterina Boratto (The Red Queen); Karen Blanguernon, Marie Danube, Elizabeth Darius, Merja Allanen, Anne Marie Moscovenko, Elizabeth Teissier, Eya Tuuli (Red Queen Girls); Bisera Vukotic (The Baker's Wife); Jancika Kovac (David); Ernest Clark (British Colonel); Harry Baird (The Dancing Soldier); Jean Gimello (Puerto Rican); Dave Jones (One-eared Soldier).

THE GYPSY MOTHS *(MGM, 1969), C-106 min.*

Executive producer, Edward Lewis; producers, Hal Landers, Bobby Roberts; director, John Frankenheimer; based on the novel by James Drought; screenplay, William Hanley; art directors, George W. Davis, Cary Odell; set decorators, Henry Grace, Jack Mills; wardrobe, Bill Thomas; makeup, William Tuttle; assistant director, Al Jennings; music, Elmer Bernstein; sound, Franklin Milton, Tommy Overton; special visual effects, J. McMillan Johnson, Carroll L. Shepphird; camera, Philip Lathrop; aerial camera, Tyler Camera Systems; special aerial camera, Carl Boenisch; editor, Henry Berman.

Burt Lancaster (Mike Rettig); Deborah Kerr (Elizabeth Brandon); Gene Hackman (Joe Browdy); Scott Wilson (Malcolm Webson); William Windom (V. John Brandon); Bonnie Bedelia (Annie Burke); Sheree North (Mary); Carl Reindel (Pilot); Ford Rainey (Stand Owner); John Napier (Dick Donford).

AIRPORT *(Universal, 1970), C-136 min.*

Producer, Ross Hunter; associate producer, Jacques Mapes; directors, George Seaton, (uncredited) Henry Hathaway; based on the novel by Arthur Hailey; screenplay, Seaton; assistant director, Donald Roberts; art directors, Alexander Golitzen, E. Preston Ames; set decorators, Jack D. Moore, Mickey S. Michaels; music and music director, Alfred Newman; costumes, Edith Head; sound, Waldon O. Watson, David H. Moriarty, Ronald Pierce; special camera effects, Don W. Weed, James B. Gordon; editor, Stuart Gilmore.

Burt Lancaster (Mel Bakersfeld); Dean Martin (Vernon Demerest); Jean Seberg (Tanya Livingston); Jacqueline Bisset (Gwen Meighen); George Kennedy (Joe Patroni); Helen Hayes

(Ada Quonsett); Van Heflin (D. O. Guerrero); Maureen Stapleton (Inez Guerrero); Barry Nelson (Lieutennant Anson Harris); Dana Wynter (Cindy Bakersfeld); Lloyd Nolan (Harry Standish); Barbara Hale (Sarah Demerest); Gary Collins (Cy Jordan); John Findlater (Peter Coakley); Jessie Royce Landis (Mrs. Harriet DuBarry Mossman); Larry Gates (Commissioner Ackerman); Peter Turgeon (Marcus Rathbone); Whit Bissell (Mr. Davidson); Virginia Grey (Mrs. Schultz); Eileen Wesson (Judy); Paul Picerni (Dr. Compagno); Robert Patten (Captain Benson); Clark Howat (Bert Weatherby); Lew Brown (Reynolds); Ilana Dowding (Roberta Bakersfeld); Lisa Gerritson (Libby Bakersfeld); Jim Nolan (Father Steven Lonigan); Patty Poulsen (Joan); Ena Hartman (Ruth); Malila Saint Duval (Maria); Sharon Harvey (Sally); Albert Reed (Lieutenant Ordway); Jodean Russo (Marie Patroni); Nancy Ann Nelson (Bunnie); Dick Winslow (Mr. Schultz); Lou Wagner (Schuyler Schultz); Janis Hansen (Sister Katherine Grace); Mary Jackson (Sister Felice); Shelly Novack (Rollings); Chuck Daniel (Parks); Charles Brewer (Diller).

KING: A FILMED RECORD . . . MONTGOMERY TO MEMPHIS (*Commonwealth United, 1970), 182 min.*

Producer, Ely Landau; associate producer, Richard Kaplan; connecting sequences directed by Sidney Lumet, Joseph L. Mankiewicz; music, Coleridge Perkinson.

VALDEZ IS COMING (*United Artists, 1971), C-90 min.*

Executive producer, Roland Kibbee; associate producer, Sam Manners; producer, Ira Steiner; director, Edwin Sherin; based on the novel by Elmore Leonard; screenplay, Kibbee, David Rayfiel; assistant directors, Tony Ray, Jose Maria Ochoa; art directors, Jose Maria Tapiador, Jose Maria Alarcon; set decorator, Rafael Salazar; music, Charles Gross; costumes, Louis Brown; makeup, Mariano Garcia Rey, Alberto Comenar; sound, Bud Alper; special effects, Chuck Gaspar, Linc Kibbee; camera, Gabor Pogany; editor, James T. Heckert.

Burt Lancaster (Bob Valdez); Susan Clark (Gay Erin); Jon Cypher (Frank Tanner); Barton Heyman (El Segundo); Richard Jordan (R. L. Davis); Frank Silvera (Diego); Hector Elizondo (Mexican Rider); Phil Brown (Malson); Ralph Brown (Beaudry); Juanita Penaloza (Apache Woman); Lex Monson (Rincon); Roberta Haynes (Polly); Maria Montez (Anita); Marta Tuck (Rosa); Jose Garcia (Carlos); James Lemp (Bony Man); Werner Hasselman (Sheriff); Concha Hombria (Inez); Per Barclay (Bartender); Vic Albert, Allan Russell (Ranchers); Michael Hinn (Merchant); Rudy Ugland, Joaquin Parra, Losada (Trackers); Santiago Santos, Losardo Iglesias (Riders); Juan Fernandez (Mexican Buyer); Tony Eppers (Bodyguard); Mario Barros, Raul Castro, Nick Cravat, Santiago Garcia, Jeff Kibbee, Linc Kibbee, Ian Maclean, Tom McFadden, Jose Morales, Mario Sanz, Lee Thaxton, Robin Thaxton, Julian Vidrie, Manolin Vidrie (Gang Members); Sylvia Poggioli (Segundo's Girl).

LAWMAN (*United Artists, 1971), C-99 min.*

Producer-director, Michael Winner; screenplay, Gerald Wilson; assistant directors, Michael Dryhurst, Malcolm Stamp, Jaime Contreras; art director, Herbert Westbrook; set decorator, Ray Moyer; music and music conductor, Jerry Fielding; makeup, Richard Mills; wardrobe, Ron Beck; sound, Terence Rawlings, Manuel Topete Blake, Hugh Strain; special effects, Leon Ortega; camera, Bob Paynter; editor, Freddie Wilson.

Burt Lancaster (Marshal Jered Maddox); Robert Ryan (Marshal Cotton Ryan); Lee J. Cobb (Vincent Bronson); Sheree North (Laura Shelby); Joseph Wiseman (Lucas); Robert Duvall

(Vernon Adams); Albert Salmi (Harvey Stenbaugh); J. D. Cannon (Hurd Price); John Mc-Giver (Mayor Sam Bolden); Richard Jordan (Crowe Wheelwright); John Beck (Jason Bronson); Ralph Waite (Jack Dekker); William Watson (Choctaw Lee); Charles Tyner (Minister); John Hillerman (Totts); Robert Emhardt (Hersham); Richard Bull (Dusaine); Hugh McDermott (Moss); Lou Frizzell (Cobden); Walter Brooke (Harris); Bill Brimley (Marc Corman).

ULZANA'S RAID *(Universal, 1972), C-103 min.*

Producer, Carter DeHaven; associate producer, Alan Sharp; director, Robert Aldrich; screenplay, Sharp; assistant director, Malcolm R. Harding; screenplay, Alan Sharp; art director, James Vance; set decorator, John McCarthy; music, Frank DeVol; sound, Waldon O. Watson, James Alexander; camera, Joseph Biroc; editor, Michael Luciano.

Burt Lancaster (McIntosh); Bruce Davison (Lieutenant Garnett DeBruin); Jorge Luke (Ke-Ni-Tay); Richard Jaeckel (Sergeant); Joaquin Martinez (Ulzana); Lloyd Bochner (Captain Gates); Karl Swenson (Rukeyser); Douglas Watson (Major Cartwright); Dran Hamilton (Mrs. Riordan); John Pearce (Corporal); Gladys Holland (Mrs. Rukeyser); Margaret Fairchild (Mrs. Ginsford); Aimee Eccles (McIntosh's Indian Woman); Richard Bull (Ginsford); Otto Reichow (Steegmeyer); Dean Smith (Horowitz); Larry Randles (Mulkearn).

SCORPIO *(United Artists, 1973), C-114 min.*

Producer, Walter Mirisch; director, Michael Winner; story, David W. Rintels; screenplay, Rintels, Gerald Wilson; music, Jerry Fielding; art director, Herbert Westbrook; assistant director, Michael Dryhust; sound, Brian Marshall; camera, Robert Paynter; editor, Freddie Wilson.

Burt Lancaster (Cross); Alain Delon (Laurier); Paul Scofield (Zharkov); John Colicos (McLeod); Gayle Hunnicutt (Susan); J. D. Cannon (Filchock); Joanne Linville (Sarah); Melvin Stewart (Pick); Vladek Sheybal (Zemetkin); Mary Maude (Anne); Jack Colvin (Thief); James Sikking (Harris); Burke Byrnes (Morrison); William Smithers (Mitchell); Smuel Rodensky (Lang); Howard Morton (Heck Thomas); Celeste Yarnall (Helen Thomas); Sandor Eles (Malkin); Frederick Jaeger (Novins); George Mikell (Dor); Robert Emhardt (Man in Hotel); Morgan Farley (Bellboy).

EXECUTIVE ACTION *(National General, 1973), C-91 min.*

Producer, Edward Lewis; associate producers, Dan Bessie, Gary Horowitz; director, David Miller; story, Donald Freed, Mark Lane; screenplay, Dalton Trumbo; music, Randy Edelman; titles, Bill Brown; art director, Kirk Axtell; technical consultant, Steve Jaffe; research, Robert Polin, Kevin Van Fleet, David Lifton, Lillian Castellano, Penn Jones, Jr., Carol Rosenstein, Eda Hallinan, Barbara Elman; graphics, Ben Nay; sound, Bruce Bisenz, Kirk Fancis, Jock Putnam; camera, Robert Steadman; editors, George Frenville, Irving Lerner; documentary editor, Ivan Dryer.

Burt Lancaster (Farrington); Robert Ryan (Foster); Will Geer (Ferguson); Gilbert Green (Paulitz); John Anderson (Halliday); Paul Carr (Chris); Colby Chester (Tim); Ed Lauter (Operation Chief, Team A); Richard Bull, Lee Delano (Gunmen, Team A); Walter Brooke (Smythe); Sidney Clute (Depository Clerk); Deanna Darrin (Stripper); Lloyd Gough (McCadden); Richard Hurst (Used Car Salesman); Robert Karnes (Man at Rifle Range); James MacColl (Lee Harvey Oswald/Oswald Imposter); Joaquin Martinez (Art Mendoza); Oscar

Oncidi (Jack Ruby); Tom Peters (Sergeant); Paul Sorenson (Officer Brown); Sandy Ward (Policeman); William Watson (Leader, Team B); John Brascia, Dick Miller, Hunter Von Leer (Riflemen, Team B); Ed Kemmer (Reporter).

THE MIDNIGHT MAN *(Universal, 1974), C-177 min.*

Producers-directors, Roland Kibbee, Burt Lancaster; based on the novel *The Midnight Lady and The Mourning Man* by David Anthony; screenplay, Kibbee, Lancaster; music, David Grusin; song, Grusin and Morgan Ames; production designer, James D. Vance; set decorator, Joe Stone; assistant directors, Brad Aronson, Warren Smith; sound, Melvin M. Metcalfe; camera, Jack Priestley; editor, Frank Morriss.

Burt Lancaster (Jim Slade); Susan Clark (Linda); Cameron Mitchell (Quartz); Morgan Woodward (Clayborne); Harris Yulin (Sheriff Casey); Joan Lorring (Quartz' Wife); Richard Winterstein (Deputy Sheriff) William Splawn (Bar Owner); Catherine Bach (Natalie Clayborne); Ed Lauter, Mills Watson, Bill Hicks (Roberry Gang); William Lancaster (Natalie's Boyfriend); Robert Quarry (Psychologist); Charles Tyner (Janitor); Lawrence Dobkin (Professor Mason); Quinn Redeker (Clayborne's Aide); Peter Dane (Artist); Eleanor Ross (Robbers' Friend); Nick Cravat (Bit).

MOSES—THE LAWGIVER *(CBS-TV, 1975), C-360 min.**

Producer, Vincenzo Labella; director, Gianfranco De Bosio; teleplay, Anthony Burgess, Vittorio Bonicello, with Bernardino Zappani, Gianfranco De Bosio; camera, Marcello Gatti; editor, Alberto Galleti.

Burt Lancaster (Moses); Anthony Quayle (Aaron); Irene Papas (Zipporah); Ingrid Thulin (Miriam); Laurent Terzieff (Pharoah); Yousef Shiloah (Dathan); Aharon Ipale (Joshua); William Lancaster (Young Moses); Smuel Rodensky (Hetro); Richard Johnson (Narrator).

*Re-edited for theatrical release; (Avco-Embassy, 1976)

GRUPPO DI FAMIGLIA IN UN INTERNO (CONVERSATION PIECE) *(Gaumont, 1975), C-120 min.*

Executive producer, Giovanni Bertolucci; director, Luchino Visconti; story, Enrico Medioli; screenplay, Visconti, Suso Cecchi D'Amico; art director, Mario Garbuglia; music, Franco Mannino; camera, Pasqualino de Santis; editor, Ruggero Mastroianni.

Burt Lancaster (Professor); Silvana Mangano (Bianca); Helmut Berger (Konrad); Claudia Marsani (Lietta); Stefano Patrizi (Stefano); Elvira Cortese (Erminia); Dominique Sanda (Mother); Claudia Cardinale (Wife).

1900 *(Paramount, 1976), C.*

Producer, Alberto Grimaldi; director, Bernardo Bertolucci; screenplay, Bernardo Bertolucci, Franco Arcalli, Giuseppe Bertolucci; production designer, Ezio Frigerio; costumes, Gitt Magrini; assistant director, Gabriele Polverosi; set decorator, Maria Palo Maino; dialogue director, Peter Shepherd; makeup, Giannetoo De Rossi; camera, Vittorio Storaro; editor, Franco Arcalli.

With Robert De Niro, Gerard Depardlieu, Burt Lancaster, Sterling Hayden, Maria Schneider, Dominique Sanda.

BUFFALO BILL AND THE INDIANS *(United Artists, 1976), C.*

Executive producer, David Susskind; producers, Robert Altman, Paul Newman; director, Altman; suggested by the play *Indians* by Arthur Kopit; screenplay, Alan Rudolph and Altman.

With Paul Newman, Burt Lancaster, Joel Grey, Kevin McCarthy, Geraldine Chaplin, Harvey Keitel.

CASSANDRA CROSSING *(Associated General, 1976) C.*

Producer, Carlo Ponti; director, George Pan Cosmatos; based on the novel by Robert Katz;● screenplay, Tom Mankiewicz.

With Sophia Loren, Richard Harris, Burt Lancaster, Ava Gardner, Martin Sheen, O. J. Simpson, Lee Strasberg, Ingrid Thulin.

TWILIGHT'S LAST GLEAMING *(Lorimer, 1977), C.*

Executive producer, Helmut Jedele; producer, Merv Adelson; director, Robert Aldrich; screenplay, Ronald M. Cohen, Edward Luciano; assistant director, Wolfgang Glattes; productions designer, Rolf Zehetbauer; sound, James Willis; camera, Robert Hauser; editor, Michael Luciano.

With Burt Lancaster, Roscoe Lee Brown, Joe Cotten, Melvyn Douglas, Charles During, Richard Jaeckel, Vera Miles, Gerald S. O'Laughlin, William Marshall, Pippa Scott, Bill Walker, Richard Widmark, Paul Winfield, Burt Young, Charles Aidman, Leif Ericson, Charles Mc-Graw, Bill Smith, Shane Rimmer, Don Fellows.

With Faith Domergue in a publicity pose for *Where Danger Lives* (RKO, 1950)

Robert Mitchum

6'1"
185 pounds
Brown hair
Brown eyes
Leo

He has always been a deceptively simplistic actor. Robert Mitchum's solid beefcake nature has been confused for stolid, and his lackadaisical persona misinterpreted as laziness. In sharp contrast, he is one of the most consummate Hollywood performers, entirely professional and very well respected by his fellow players. He is a sturdy superstar in an age when the term has become almost meaningless.

Throughout the years, before, during, and after he achieved fame, Mitchum refused to play "the game." He remained himself, leery of phoniness and a strict adherent of the let-it-hang-loose philosophy. He has acquired a quiet cult status over the decades, admired for his cool (some claim lethargic) manner, which can make the flattest of roles and films seem far more important and entertaining. His individuality of character and style shines through every performance, making one constantly marvel at how he has salvaged so many trashy projects in his long career.

Robert Charles Mitchum was born on Monday, August 6, 1917, in Bridgeport, Connecticut. His Norwegian-born mother, Ann (Gundarson) Mitchum was the daughter of a sea captain; his father, James Mitchum, was Scotch-Irish with a touch of Blackfoot Indian. Robert had an older sister, Julie, and there would be a younger brother, John. When Robert was eighteen months old, his father, a railroad worker,

269

was killed in a switchyard accident. Thus, he grew up fatherless and in poverty. Mrs. Mitchum was forced to go to work, finding employment as a linotype operator on the *Bridgeport Post-Telegram*. Her meagre income, along with the government's compensation payment for each child (until they each reached the age of eighteen) kept the family from total financial disaster.

When he was old enough, Robert attended the McKinley Grammar School in Bridgeport, where he was known for his rebellious attitude. When he was seven years old he ran away from home, reaching New Haven before he was found. He apparently suffered emotionally from not having a father. "I was always jealous of boys who talked about their dads taking them fishing or camping and teaching them how to play ball. We were pretty poor at times too. My brother and I had to share one suit, so we could never go out together."

As a boy Mitchum wanted to impress his mother and he began writing poetry. Some of the works, such as "A Chreestmus Pome" and "A War Poem," were published in the local newspaper when Robert was nine. "This small spotlight on our material impoverishment inspired in me an introspection ever at odds with my desire for expression," he later commented.

During this period Robert was occasionally sent to live with his grandmother on her farm in Delaware. Then, in 1927, Mrs. Mitchum remarried. By now she was a proofreader on the newspaper, and her new husband was Hugh Cunningham-Moore, feature editor of the *Post-Telegram*. Robert, however, did not take to his stepfather, who had been a World War I hero in the Royal Air Force, and the boy spent as much time as he could with his grandparents. In 1928 Mitchum's mother gave birth to his half-sister, Carol, and the family moved to a farm, although Mr. Moore retained his newspaper post.

By this time the Depression was beginning. In order for the family to have added income, Robert's older sister, Julie, who had become quite an entertainer, obtained a work permit and began working in a New York nightclub. The family, except for Moore, moved to New York City to be with her, and Bob was sent to Haaren High School where he learned to survive with the other residents of Hell's Kitchen. Always impish, he soon joined in the rebellious activities of his peers and was threatened with expulsion for pelting a teacher with a pea shooter.

Eventually the newcomer *was* expelled for dropping a firecracker into a brass horn during a classroom recital. By then the family was moving about wherever Julie's work took her. Moore lost his newspaper job, although he continued in the field as a freelancer with little success. When Julie wed a Navy man and moved to Long Beach, California, the Mitchums-Moores moved to Delaware. Sometimes Robert's step-father had to earn eating money by playing poker. Although Robert's discipline remained a problem during this period, he had his special educational interests. He was an avid reader of poetry, especially of the works of Shakespeare and Wordsworth.

Finally, tired of poverty, Robert, claiming to be eighteen, obtained seaman's papers and became a deck hand on a salvage boat out of Fall River, Massachusetts. After a short trip, however, he was dismissed from the job when his real age of fourteen was discovered.

For the next five years the youth would exist as an apprentice hobo, crossing the United States nine times on trains and trucks. "I rode underneath trains, inside the boxcars and when I heard a guard coming, on the girders. All over! I made a lot of friends—tramps like myself or railroad cops, with whom guys like me had a running war."

After his first trans-continental trip, he returned East to see his family, and for a time he worked in a Pennsylvania coal mine, despite acute claustrophobia. But generally he kept moving, "I seemed to be always moving on. In those days motion itself seemed an adequate philosophy for me. I really had no other choice. Moving around like I did, though, I could be just any place, not high maybe but somehow alone and free."

At sixteen, in Savannah, Georgia, he had his first encounter with the law. Arrested for vagrancy, even though he had money, he was kept in jail for six days without the usual preliminary hearing. A burglary case was trumped up against the Northerner, and the fact he had thirty-eight dollars when he was arrested was used as evidence that he had committed the robbery. When Mitchum proved that he had been in jail when the robbery occurred, the case was dropped but he was given "a nice little indeterminate sentence for vagrancy."

For the next week he worked in the Chatham County Camp number one chain gang in Piemaker Swamp, which did road repair work. He was shackled at the ankles and chained to the men on each side of him. He suffered greatly as the shackles rubbed his ankles raw and he was allowed no relief for the pain. Finally, in desperation, he ran away from the chain gang as the men were being transported and their chains were removed temporarily. Shots were fired at him and he ran for his life, but no actual chase was made by the guards. "In those days they wouldn't spend fifty cents to catch you if they missed you with a rifle. They just went out and rounded up someone else to take your place on the work gang."

Today, Mitchum can look back at the unpleasant episode with some humor. "I worked seven days repairing roads and then I just walked away. I guess I still owe them some time," he has recounted. Another tale he tells is about the overseer on the chain gang. According to Robert, the guard had been in the Spanish-American War and had contracted venereal disease in Cuba; as a result, the man had gone blind. Then, however, he took up religion, and after much prayer his sight had been restored. With a rather sadistic grin on his pudgy face, the fat guard would advise his charges, "If any of you boys thinks I can't see just take off running and find out." Mitchum took up that challenge and lived to relate the story. Years later, Mitchum returned to the vicinity to star in *Cape Fear* (United Artists, 1962). As a joke, the local newspaper ran his mug shot on the front page. Mitchum thought it all very amusing.

After his escape from the Georgia chain gang, he waded through a slimy swamp and slept in ditches outside of small towns. He worked at whatever odd jobs he could find, and when no work was available he stole farm vegetables. During this period his family had moved from their farm to the small town of Rising Sun, Delaware. When Robert reached them, he was in terrible physical condition. His ankles were so badly swollen that the local doctors wanted to amputate one of his legs. His mother would have nothing of this. Instead, she administered hot poultices and fed him home-cooked meals to help him regain his strength. Finally, he was well again but he had to walk with crutches for a while.

Perhaps the boy's philosophy was best summed up by a poem he sent his mother on the back of a postcard when he was fifteen and drifting about the United States:

> Trouble lies in sullen pools along the road I've taken
> Sightless windows stare the empty street
> No love beckons me save that which I've forsaken
> The anguish of my solitude is sweet.

While home for this visit, and regaining his health, Robert was introduced by his brother to one of the latter's schoolmates, Dorothy Spence, who lived in Camden, New Jersey. Robert and fourteen-year-old Dorothy took an immediate liking to each other and began dating. When his health was sufficiently improved, Robert began working for a local branch of the Civilian Conservation Corps (CCC); for several months he dug ditches and planted trees before he finally grew tired of the outdoor job. With some money now saved, he determined to return to California. Before he left, however, he told Dorothy that someday he would return for her. The optimistic girl agreed to wait for him.

On this latest West Coast trek, Mitchum took his brother John with him. Along the way they decided to visit their sister Julie who was still living in Long Beach with her sailor husband.

One of the more outrageous experiences on this cross-country venture occurred down South when the two young men were held captive by a white lightning-drinking family who liked to hear the boys sing and play the guitar. Eventually, the two unwilling guests escaped and made it to California. Once there, Bob again succumbed to wanderlust and took a variety of jobs that kept him on the move. One job included aiding an Indian in the state of Washington who was a dognapper. The man would infiltrate an upper-class neighborhood, coax dogs to follow him, and return a few days later with the pedigree animals to collect a reward.

About this time, Bob's mother, step-father, and half-sister moved to California to live with Julie and her husband. For the first time in years the family was together again. Bob recounted that it was during this phase that he really began to appreciate his step-father. Nevertheless at age eighteen, Bob was back on the road again. He worked for a spell in an auto factory in Toledo, Ohio, and he made a trip back East to see Dorothy Spence, who was then employed as a secretary in an insurance company. For a time in 1936 he was held in custody in a federal transient camp as a vagrant. It was also in this year that restless, experiment-prone Mitchum first tried marijuana.

Having assured himself that Dorothy would still wait for him, Mitchum returned to his roving life out West. In Sparks, Nevada, for a lark, he claimed he was a boxer and was immediately hired to box locally at fifty dollars a bout. He fought a total of twenty-seven fights in the heavyweight division, but he soon had enough of the rough profession. "I want folks to know I was licked-thrashed! I hate fighting. It's too painful. It's not good for me. I much prefer the quiet life." He said one opponent "had my nose all over to one side, gave me the scar on my left eye, had me all messed up. So I quit."

Not long after he returned to California he planned another trip to Toledo. His mother suggested instead that he should join his sister who was in theatre work. He auditioned and was accepted in the community theatre project, where he functioned as a stage hand before he was given supporting actors' roles onstage. He appeared in such fare as *The Day, Rebound,* and *The Petrified Forest.* Within two years, he was writing and directing plays for children. One project, *Trumpet in the Dark,* was quite popular and, later, another one was given an award at the Pittsburgh Festival of Arts for being the best first play written by an amateur.

Looking back on this time, Mitchum says the work was "one of the most enjoyable and satisfying encounters of my life. For the first time I had the acquaintance of young people who shared my ideas and reflections, and though most of us were threadbare poor, we enjoyed the counsel of our mentors and forgot our fears of the future."

Although still working at odd jobs to raise money, Mitchum took an active part in the theatre and even returned to writing poetry and short stories, one of which was published in a local journal, making him "the darling of the Beverly Hills writing set!" He also wrote comedy material for Julie's club act, some of which was risqué and even was purchased by other entertainers, including female impersonator Rae Bourbon. Bob's top accomplishment during this period, which today he recalls as a "vaudeville black-out," was his writing and composing an oratorio for Jewish refugees which was presented at the Hollywood Bowl in 1939 with Orson Welles producing and directing.

The well-known astrologer Carroll Righter then hired Mitchum as his general assistant for a tour of resorts and women's clubs. Bob wrote Righter's speeches, ghosted his syndicated newspaper column, and organized his tours. He found the work to be "a vacation," but after saving $2300, he took a leave of absence to wed Dorothy Spence. Comparing the two horoscopes (Bob is a Leo; Dorothy, a Taurus), Righter advised against the marriage, but Mitchum failed to heed the man's advice.[1]

On Saturday, March 16, 1940, Robert Mitchum wed Dorothy Spence in Dover, Maryland. The two took a cross-country bus trip for their honeymoon, arriving in Long Beach almost dead broke. At this juncture, Bob dissolved his contract with Carroll Righter (who still speaks highly of the actor in his daily columns) and began writing songs and special material for acts performing along the Sunset Strip. It was a precarious existence at best. After failing to receive a promised $1500 for one job, and finding his wife was pregnant, Mitchum decided to aid the war effort, as well as his own, by holding down a factory job. He was hired by the Lockheed aircraft plant after being questioned by the F.B.I. regarding his Georgia chain gang experience.

For the next year Robert was employed as a sheetmetal worker at Lockheed. He considered this the bleakest time of his life. To add to his general problems, his mother, step-father, half-sister, brother, and his sister Julie, who was now divorced, moved into his house. At times, he was supporting them all as well as trying to cope with his growing hatred for his work.

On May 8, 1941, his first son, James, was born, the same evening he was to debut in a local play. His wife was backstage when she went into labor, and Bob rushed her to the hospital. He returned in time for the performance, then rushed back to be with his wife.

Working the day shift at Lockheed,[2] Robert would work evenings with small theatrical productions. But the artistic outlet was not sufficient to make up for his dislike for his main job. On one occasion, volatile Bob flung a wrench at a foreman he did not like because the man had not returned a pencil he borrowed from Mitchum. "Once I didn't get a proper night's sleep for a year. Fifteen minutes in three days, once. That's when I was working at Lockheed. I went to see the doctor. He said the reason I wasn't sleeping was because I knew when I woke up I'd have to go to work. And I hated it. 'Blow your job or blow your mind,' he said. I blew my job."

[1]Ironically, Mitchum has had experiences with the psychic, and in an article in *The National Enquirer* (February 1, 1974), the star recounted how he had purchased two items in an antique shop in New Orleans in 1958, not knowing why he wanted them. Later, he learned that one gift was something his son Chris had been yearning for, while the other was sought by Deborah Kerr. He discovered the latter wish *after* sending Miss Kerr the present.

[2]Working at the next box with Mitchum at Lockheed was James Dougherty, then married to Norma Jean Baker, later to become famous as Marilyn Monroe. Dougherty would frequently show Mitchum pin-up photos of his young wife.

At age eight, with brother Jack   In 1936

With wife Dorothy in Mexico in 1949

Mitchum's emotional situation grew progressively worse. One day when he went "blind" he was rushed to the factory doctor who told him he must quit. He informed the physician he was in a frozen wartime post and could not voluntarily leave his job. However, the doctor agreed to have him discharged on medical grounds. It was Mitchum's mother who suggested another job for Bob once he was freed of the Lockheed syndrome. She proposed that he try his luck in the movies. "I had no burning ambitions to be an actor, and I wasn't much good at reading lines. But I was big and looked like I could handle myself in a brawl. I thought maybe I'd be good enough in professional movies to pick up some work as an extra."

He quit Lockheed and met Paul Wilkins, an artists' manager, who encouraged him, since he was already familiar with Bob's varied theatre work. In the meantime, Dorothy found employment as a part-time secretary, while Bob worked part-time at a shoe shop on Wilshire Boulevard. The couple, with their infant, rented a small apartment. The family's economic situation was so precarious in these days that on one occasion Mitchum had to borrow seventeen cents from his mother to purchase a pound of hamburger and a gallon of gasoline.

Determined to break into the movie business, Robert began making the rounds of auditions for potential screen jobs. Finally, Wilkins took him to meet with producer Harry "Pop" Sherman who was producing the *Hopalong Cassidy* series at United Artists, the new home for the Western properties after the series' seven-year tenure at Paramount. Veteran Sherman thought Mitchum would fit well in the background of the series because he had had experience with horses. "I told them I could ride, so they gave me a mean little pony. I found later he had thrown and killed an actor and I was hired in a hurry to replace him, so as not to hold up production. When I first got on that horse, he threw me forty feet. He threw me three more times in all, before I got the hang of it. After that, I made eight [sic] films in the series. I might have wound up a Western star. You get conditioned, you know. I was their horseshit merchant."

The release dates and the actual production of the *Hopalong Cassidy* entries do not necessarily coincide. *Colt Comrades* (United Artists, 1943) was the first of his series appearances to be issued, seven *Hoppy* installments being distributed to theatres in that year. In these low-budget pictures, Mitchum worked under directors George Archainbaud and Lesley Selander, getting the drift of film-making, especially rough and tough sagebrush quickies. Usually, the fledgling was cast as a villain, and in some of the films he received no billing.[3] In *False Colors* (United Artists, 1943), he was Rip Austin, one of a group of bad guys thwarted by hero Hopalong Cassidy (William Boyd) in a range war over ranchers' water rights. In *Bar 20* (United Artists, 1943), he was billed eighth in the credits and played Richard Adams, a rancher who doubts Hoppy can recover jewels stolen from his girlfriend (Dustine Farnum). For *Border Patrol* (United Artists, 1943), Bob was again unbilled as a member of a crooked mine owner's gang. He also received no billing for *The Leather Burners* (United Artists, 1943), in which he had only a passing bit. In *Riders of the Deadline* (United Artists, 1943), he was billed eighth as Drago, a member of a gang of gun runners, and in *Hoppy Serves a Writ* (United Artists, 1943), he was oncamera as Rigney, a member of gang of rustlers.

Having borrowed fifty-five dollars from his grandmother's "coffin fund" to join

[3]Another regular in the *Hopalong Cassidy* films, which at this point featured Andy Clyde and Jay Kirby as William Boyd's sidekicks, was George Reeves, who gained fame later as television's Superman.

With Jay Kirby, William Boyd, and Andy Clyde in *Hoppy Serves a Writ* (UA, 1943)

the Screen Actors Guild, Mitchum made a total of nineteen film appearances in 1943. This work initially provided him with about one dollar weekly, and eventually "the bread kept getting better, and it sure as hell beat punching a time clock!" The steady income helped to pay for the birth and care of the couple's second child, Christopher, born on October 16, 1943.

Robert's roles as a brief supporting player took him to a number of studios, from the top echelon MGM to the low-class Republic, and kept him active, as well as providing him with a variety of parts. "I was now a character actor, and I played just about everything. . . . I don't know what I was like. I never saw the pictures. But I got overtime, and I'd live on the overtime and save my basic salary."

Mitchum's other 1943 film assignments were a mixed lot. For his first role away from the *Hopalong Cassidy* bread-and-butter series he had a brief bit in *Follow the Band* (Universal), one of those tinsel musicals which that studio was so adept at producing. At MGM, however, he worked with director Clarence Brown on a prestige product, *The Human Comedy*, and had a nice, showy bit as one of three soldiers who meet two smalltown girls (Donna Reed and Dorothy Morris) on a weekend pass. Back at Universal, he was in a message-laden B entry called *We've Never Been Licked*, where he was a student at Texas A & M, the college that provided six thousand men for the war effort. In Columbia's double-bill effort, *Doughboys in Ireland,* he was a commando, and in Universal's *Corvette K-225,* starring Randolph Scott, he had only a brief bit as a member of the ship of the title. But in another Randolph Scott-Universal action film, *Gung Ho ,* Robert had a chance to play a role

With Allen Jung, Paul Dubov, Roland Got, and Richard Quine in *We've Never Been Licked* (Univ., 1943)

With Kenny Baker (on bunk) and George Tyne (with pail) in *Doughboys in Ireland* (Col., 1943)

277

that bore some resemblance to a past job fling of his. As Pig Iron Mathews, he was a boxer from New Jersey, one of the many volunteers to apply for the Second Marine Raider Battalion. Being one of the two hundred ten trained men heading for Makin Island aboard a U.S. submarine, he is later shot in the throat during a battle.

At Twentieth Century-Fox, by contrast, he had one of the rare opportunities in his career to tackle screen comedy when he portrayed his first big city gangster. He had a small, but billed role, as one of two hoodlums who threaten dance-school owners Stan Laurel and Oliver Hardy in *Dancing Masters*. From two William Pine-William Thomas Paramount military service quickies, *Aerial Gunner* and *Minesweeper*, Mitchum returned to the Culver City lot to accept a tiny part in MGM's *Cry Havoc*. Amidst the star-studded female cast he was barely visible, though plainly heard, as a groaning wounded man.

It was in Westerns, however, that Bob made his first important cinematic impression. He was hired to portray one of the lead villains in *Beyond the Last Frontier* (Republic, 1943), an entry in that studio's Texas Ranger series. A reviewer for the *Motion Picture Herald* said his bad-guy performance made him far more appealing than the series' star, Eddie Dew. At Universal, Mitchum appeared with sagebrush star Johnny Mack Brown in *The Lone Star Trail* (1943), where burly Mitchum was again a culprit. The fight between Brown and Mitchum within the plot line was so well handled that several reviewers took the occasion to compliment it and the two lead participants.

It was at the small Monogram studio that Mitchum earned the big break his career needed—a sturdy supporting role in *When Strangers Marry* (1944). Prior to that assignment, however, he had a small role in an amusing wartime comedy which Joe May directed. It was entitled *Johnny Doesn't Live Here Anymore* (Monogram, 1944). In that film, pert Simone Simon sublets an apartment from soldier James Ellison who fails to inform her that eleven other men have keys to the place, including soldier Mitchum, who appears briefly in a well-played feature role.

From this assignment, Monogram next placed Robert in the above-mentioned *When Strangers Marry*, which William Castle directed on loan-out from Columbia. Kim Hunter was cast as a young bride who comes to New York City to meet her new spouse (Dean Jagger) and soon discovers that he may be a murderer. Bob was onscreen as a traveling salesman, the girl's former lover, who tries to help her find her husband as evidence mounts that he is a killer. Also involved is Neil Hamilton as the police detective who collects the necessary evidence against Jagger. At the climax, however, it is Mitchum who turns out to be the murderer. This revelation more than highlights his performance in this taut, unpretentious film. The role of Fred proved to be the turning point in Robert's career. (When the film was reissued in 1947 as *Betrayed*, Mitchum would be given star billing.)

MGM was sufficiently impressed with the showcasing of Bob in *When Strangers Marry* to offer him a solid featured role in *Thirty Seconds Over Tokyo* (1944), directed by Mervyn LeRoy.[4] In elaborate pictorial style the film told of the air raid on Japan by men under the command of Lieutenant Colonel James H. Doolittle (Spencer Tracy). Taken from the bestseller by Captain Ted Lawson and Bob Considine, the motion picture provided Robert with the role of Bob Gray, a crew member of the B-25 that bombed a large Japanese city. *Newsweek* Magazine labeled it "one of Hollywood's finest war films to date."

[4]When he tested Mitchum for the film, LeRoy said, "You're either the lousiest actor in the world or the best. I can't make up my mind which."

With James Ellison and William Terry in *Johnny Doesn't Live Here Anymore* (Mon., 1944)

Just as his performance in *When Strangers Marry* had impressed MGM, so his handsome, masculine presence in *Thirty Seconds over Tokyo* inspired officials at RKO to offer him a long term contract. Although he had already received his draft notice, he signed the studio contract to give his family financial security. Actually, his induction was postponed indefinitely due to a regulation that exempted fathers, but he expected to be called to service at any time. Despite the fact he now was earning often as much as one thousand dollars a week as a freelance actor, he took the RKO contract at $350 a week for the guaranteed income it would provide. As a matter of fact, RKO was so miserly in its fringe benefit terms that Mitchum's agreement didn't even provide for his own dressing room. But iconoclastic Mitchum knew how to remedy that situation. One day he openly took a shower with a water hose. The studio brass took the hint and he was given a private dressing room.

For his initial RKO assignment, Robert was featured in *The Girl Rush* (1944) in a part for which director Gordon Douglas specifically requested him. This comedy-musical was primarily a vehicle for the popular company team of Wally Brown and Alan Carney, as well as for singer Frances Langford, whose screen career was on the skids. The sixty-five-minute entry featured Mitchum as an escort for a vaudeville troupe on the Barbary Coast of 1848. When the gold rush lures audiences away from the theatre, the troupe heads for the rich mine field to entertain the prospectors. Robert's Jimmy Smith is the one who romances the singing Miss Langford.

About this time, producer Frank Ross considered Robert for the plum role of Demetrius the gladiator in RKO's proposed production of Lloyd C. Douglas' *The Robe*. Due to wartime building restrictions, the project which required elaborate sets, was shelved. When Ross did make the film a decade later at Twentieth Century-Fox, it was Victor Mature who was impressive in the same role.

From the potential of a Biblical foray, Mitchum returned to the actuality of the old West where the studio starred him in two Westerns based on the works of Zane Grey, *Nevada* (1944) and *West of the Pecos* (1945).

Both outdoor stories were directed by Edward Killy. In *Nevada,* leading man Robert played the cowboy who escapes being lynched after being unjustly accused of murder. Naturally, he is able to prove that claim jumpers are the true culprits. Guinn "Big Boy" Williams and Richard Martin appeared as Mitchum's sidekicks, and Anne Jeffreys was the very young, pretty leading lady.

Because the closely-budgeted *Nevada* proved to be so boxoffice-worthy, RKO followed it with *West of the Pecos.* The latter film was given a bigger mounting than the first, with Mitchum playing a devil-may-care cowboy who becomes involved with the daughter (Barbara Hale) of a vacationing meat packer (Thurston Hall) after the latter's stagecoach is held up by outlaws. Hard-riding Mitchum and partner Richard Martin eventually round up the villains, allowing enough time for Robert and Miss Hale to fall in love properly. One double-edged sequence had Hale masquerading as a boy to escape the outlaws. She encounters Mitchum who treats her like any other bothersome young lad.

Following the production of the two RKO Westerns, Mitchum was spotted by director William A. Wellman as the actor was sauntering along Sunset Boulevard. The ace director saw to it that Robert was offered a screen test for the role of Lieutenant Bill Walker in *The Story of G. I. Joe* (United Artists, 1945). At first Mitchum was skeptical about even attempting the audition, but astute Wellman assured him he should take the gamble. Wellman's intuition proved correct and the young star-in-the-making was given the second lead in a film that was to become one of the war years' biggest hits.

With Barbara Hale in *West of the Pecos* (RKO, 1945)

With Burgess Meredith (center) in *The Story of G.I. Joe* (UA, 1945)

The Story of G. I. Joe (sometimes called *G. I. Joe*) was conceived by Wellman in a documentary style, with the interpolation of actual newsreel battle scenes. It followed the adventures of forty-three-year-old war correspondent Ernie Pyle (Burgess Meredith) as he joins Company C, 18th Infantry, in the African desert campaign. He becomes involved with the men under the charge of Lieutenant (later Captain) Bill Walker (Robert) as they fight battle after battle, moving on to Italy as the unit is assigned to join in the push up the peninsula from Cassino to Rome. Unlike most 40s films about combat and soldiers, there was little attempt to gloss the production. It detailed the grim and miserable lives of infantrymen, showing the hell of combat as it really was. General Dwight D. Eisenhower is said to have called it the "greatest war film I've ever seen."

By the time *The Story of G. I. Joe* was released (October, 1945) World War II was over and Mitchum had already become a member of the armed forces. Even Hollywood die-hards were amazed at how Robert excelled in the role of the captain who leads his men to death in defeat and victory, hating every minute of it. The part had built-in dramatic appeal, for, near the picture's finale, Robert makes a very memorable exit. Private Dondaro (Wally Cassell) is seen leading a donkey down the road; the animal's cargo is the lifeless body of the much-respected Captain.

The critics were almost extravagant in their praise of the film and Robert's screen work. "It is a movie without a single false note," insisted *Time* Magazine. "A magnificent performance," wrote Rose Pelswick *(New York Journal American)*. According to Alton Cook *(New York World-Telegram)*, "Robert Mitchum as a swaggering captain and Freddie Steele as a grimy sergeant are likely to hit stardom as a result of their glowing achievements in this picture." Thomas M. Pryor *(New York Times)* noted, "The meatiest roles fall to Robert Mitchum, the captain, and Freddie Steele, as the sergeant. Both give excellent characterizations." Kate Cameron *(New York Daily*

281

News), in her four-star tribute to the film, said that Mitchum gave "the best male performance of the year."

Robert's peers, the members of the Academy of Motion Pictures Arts and Sciences, also thought he gave a superlative performance, for he was nominated for a Best Supporting Actor's Oscar. However, the Award that year went to James Dunn of *A Tree Grows in Brooklyn* (Twentieth Century-Fox).

As rosy as Robert's film career seemed to be becoming, the actor was still finding it difficult to adjust his volatile, individualistic nature to the restrictive demands of society. Shortly after the filming of *G.I. Joe*, Mitchum had a brush with the law. It occurred when his sister, who was hostile to his ailing wife, refused to let him talk with weakened Dorothy. Mitchum became rambunctious. When he arrived home he was arrested and "roundly beaten" by policemen and then taken to jail. He was advised to plead guilty to the charge of being in an intoxicated condition on private property and to pay the ten-dollar fine. He did. He was also sentenced to one day in jail. Two days later, he was inducted into the Army and shipped to Camp Roberts, California, for infantry training.

After completing basic training, Mitchum was stationed at Fort MacArthur, where he spent eight months as a drill instructor and later as a medical assistant to an orthopedic examiner. As could be expected, he disliked Army life greatly and resisted any opportunity for promotion. Therefore, he was mustered out of the service as a private first class. He was granted a hardship discharge in the fall of 1945, because he was the sole support of his family including his mother and half-sister. (By this time, Mitchum's stepfather had returned to military service as a captain and took part in the invasions of the Philippines and Okinawa).

Once out of the service, Robert accepted his new industry stature calmly. He was so unmoved, on the surface at least, by his Academy Award nomination that he didn't even attend the ceremonies. When he returned to work at RKO[5] he was cast in *Till the End of Time* (1946) based on Niven Busch's *They Dream of Home*. The "class" production concerns three G.I.s (played by Robert, Guy Madison, and Bill Williams) and how each readjusts to civilian life. "A well-piled shears and some generous snipping might have turned this earnest but overlong and hesitantly paced film into a more absorbing study," was *Variety's* verdict of this lesser imitation of *The Best Years of Our Lives* (RKO, 1946). Robert was Marine veteran William Tabeshaw, who could not return to his life as a New Mexico cowpuncher-rodeo rider due to his head injuries. Robert's tough but tender character becomes involved with the main action of the film, which concerns distraught ex-serviceman Madison coping with neurotic widow Dorothy McGuire. *Newsweek* Magazine thought that it was Mitchum who "lassos top acting honors" in this melee. *Variety* complimented him for lending "the right touch of hard-core gruffness as he fights off hospital treatment." Unassuming Mitchum was rather taken aback by the new leading man status given him in *Till the End of Time*. He much preferred character work.

Next, for his second 1946 film, Robert was loaned to MGM (at a profit to RKO) to co-star with Katharine Hepburn and Robert Taylor in *Undercurrent*. During the filming Mitchum found the equally offbeat Miss Hepburn a bit cold and attempted to humor her with his antics. She was not at all amused. "You can't act," she

[5]Other male players under RKO contract included: Tim Holt, Robert Sterling, Richard Tyler and Bill Williams, as well as fast-rising Robert Ryan and such specially-pacted performers as Pat O'Brien, Dick Powell, George Raft, and Leon Errol.

informed him, "and if you hadn't been good-looking you would never have gotten the picture. I'm tired of playing with people who have nothing to offer." Mitchum found the outburst amusing and to this day he enjoys imitating the divine Kate pouring forth with her tirade.

Perhaps the titian-haired actress should have taken her ire out on the production and not on Mitchum, because it was Robert who garnered the best notices in this largely forgotten, superficial melodrama. The film was the first major foray of both Katharine Hepburn and director Vincente Minnelli into the thriller cinema and neither did too well. The film also marked Robert Taylor's first screen appearance since his war service.

Back at RKO, Robert's trio of 1946 starring vehicles closed out with a poor melodrama, *The Locket. Cue* Magazine rated it "a dull blend of two of Hollywood's hardest-worn current themes: psychiatry and vicious womanhood." Plagued by a weak storyline, the John Brahm-directed feature relied on the unnecessary technique of flashbacks within flashbacks (within flashbacks) to tell its rather dull tale of artist Mitchum being driven to suicide by his love for a psychopathic jewel thief (Laraine Day). The film's biggest asset was its cast, which included Gene Raymond, Ricardo Cortez, and Reginald Denny.

The year almost ended in tragedy for the actor. During October he and publicity man Leonard Shannon, along with stand-in Mel Sternlight, were scouting film locations by plane near Bridgeport, Connecticut, when the plane overshot a mountain landing strip and crashed. The craft was a complete loss and the three men were badly bruised.

Recovery was quick, however, and the star was soon back before the cameras. His first 1947 outing was in *Pursued*, which was issued by Warner Bros. The film was produced and written by Niven Busch and starred the writer's wife, Teresa Wright,

With Brian Aherne in *The Locket* (RKO, 1946)

283

who remembers she and Busch were "pleased" to get popular Robert Mitchum for the project. Raoul Walsh directed the feature which was shot on location in Monument Valley.

Second-billed Robert was cast as Jeb Rand, a young man in turn-of-the-century New Mexico Territory, who is hunted relentlessly for a crime committed by his father. Willowy Miss Wright was cast as the fragile daughter of the woman (Judith Anderson) who caused the crime, and John Rodney was the woman's vengeful son. Filled with extensive psychological overtones and dramatic dialogue, the film finally reaches its violent climax when Mitchum recalls the event in his childhood that has led up to the crime. Regardless of any intrinsic merits the picture might have had, it did not enhance Bob's boxoffice standing.

The extent to which RKO considered Mitchum a boxoffice name could be determined by his star billing for *Crossfire* (1947). He actually had a rather small part, but director Edward Dmytryk knew that Robert's appearance in the film would tremendously enhance the project's chance of success. In *Crossfire,* Bob is merely one of five soldiers under investigation for the murder of a Jewish war veteran (Sam Levene). It turns out the man was murdered by Robert Ryan, the anti-Semitic buddy of Mitchum. In covering Mitchum's career in *Films in Review* (May, 1964), Gene Ringgold observed, "Because they thought *Crossfire* struck a blow at anti-Semitism, many ordinarily honest critics overlooked *Crossfire's* lurid melodrama and implausibilities."

If *Undercurrent* had been a shallow venture, Mitchum's next screen exercise at Metro-Goldwyn-Mayer veered toward disaster. He was hired to join with Greer Garson (whom he upset by calling her "Red") and Robert Montgomery in a project entitled *Desire Me.* The distinguished George Cukor was set as director. Partway through the script-plagued production, Montgomery refused to continue with the venture. He was eventually replaced by newcomer Richard Hart. Then Cukor was removed from the picture and Mervyn LeRoy assumed the directorial reigns.

Mitchum, who was by then being called a "rebel," commented to the press on the film's progress: "It's all being remade, and I think they're going to get a picture that will finally be entertaining. But it was so bad when they first ran it that after the first reel people walked out. So I put my collar up, sneaked out, and pretended I wasn't there. But I'm surprised with what Mervyn LeRoy has been able to do with it. You'd never know it was the same picture. In the original we were made to act like Shakespearean actors. Now there's some comedy in it."

However, the laughs *Desire Me* got were mainly from the critics. "The only remarkable thing about *Desire Me* is the fact that it has dispensed blithely with the services of a director," reported Howard Barnes (*New York Herald-Tribune*). Neither Cukor nor LeRoy was allowed or wanted his name associated with the disaster-prone vehicle. Taken from Leonhard Frank's novel *Karl and Anna,* it was a remake of the German film, *Homecoming.* The story's unworkable premise had Mitchum returning home to his French fishing village after the war to find his wife (Garson) being romanced by a former prison camp buddy (Hart). Mitchum, who appeared only in the opening and closing segments of the feature, and sported a beard, "tries a Gallic gesture now and then but most of the time he just looks sleepy. No audience will blame him for that" (*Time* Magazine). Realistic Howard Barnes of the *Herald-Tribune* judged, "He might well have kept his name off the credits, too, so far as this film will advance his career."

Fortunately, the actor's last 1947 film, made at RKO, was very popular. *Out of the*

284

With Greer Garson in *Desire Me* (MGM, 1947)

Past was a "honey of a thriller" according to the *New York Daily Mirror*. Directed by Jacques Tourneur from Geoffrey Homes' novel *Build My Gallows High,* with beautiful photography by Nicholas Musuraca, the complicated film followed in the tracks of *The Killers* (Universal, 1946) in dealing with a man innocently caught up with low-life characters and an evil woman.[6]

Told in flashback, the story was an eerie account of love, revenge, and greed. New York detective Jeff Bailey (Robert) is hired by underworld figure Kirk Douglas to find his ex-girl (Jane Greer), who has tried to kill him and has departed with $40,000 of stolen funds. The trail leads laconic Mitchum to Mexico City and Acapulco,[7] where he meets and falls in love with the devious Miss Greer. Later, practical but ruthless Greer murders Mitchum's nosey partner (Steve Brodie), which turns Robert sour on their romance. Time passes. Mitchum becomes a small desert town gas station owner. Then he is called to Lake Tahoe by Douglas. He encounters Greer there and she quickly decides to make use of him again. Thereafter, when a wised-up Douglas is shot by Greer, and she threatens to put the blame on Robert unless he runs away with her. Sensing a double-cross, she then shoots him, but is later killed by the police in her getaway bid.

By this point in his career, Robert had gained sufficient prominence in his craft to have become typecast by the critics. Whereas once he had been judged economical and taciturn in his acting style, now scribes such as James Agee (*The Nation*) could mock, "Bob Mitchum is so sleepily self-confident with the women that when he slopes into clinches you expect him to snore in their faces." This slap at Mitchum's brand of acting was easy to justify, so the aisle-sitters thought, because of the

[6]When asked why the plot was so difficult to follow, Mitchum answered, "I think we lost four pages in the mimeo department." •
[7]Malibu Beach was used for the Acapulco sequence.

With William Holden in *Rachel and the Stranger* (RKO, 1948)

contrast between Robert's relaxed performance[8] and the frenetic, dynamic emoting of co-player Kirk Douglas. But for the people who counted, the filmgoers, it was Mitchum who was the boxoffice draw of *Out of the Past*. They appreciated his seemingly honest, non-frilly approach to his characterization. (In mid-1976, producers Jerry Bick and John Ptak hired Jerry Schatzberg to direct a new version of *Build My Gallows High*.)

Fast reaching a boxoffice peak, Mitchum was in two 1948 films. *Rachel and the Stranger*, the first he did that year, was the last film produced by Dore Schary at RKO before he moved over to MGM. Director Norman Foster developed a very interesting motion picture from this story of a frontier farmer (William Holden) who purchases a bond servant (Loretta Young) for his bride. However, the two cannot adapt to each other. Bob plays a thoughtful hunter who is attracted to Young and, through that emotional tie, helps Holden to realize his love for the resourceful woman.

With lovely photography, the well-acted film was highlighted by glowing glimpses of Americana. As the handsome stranger who courted Young with a guitar, Bob had several opportunities to sing oncamera, including "O-He-O-Hi-O-Ho," "Just Like Me," and "Foolish Pride."[9]

Next, Mitchum starred in a likeable Western, *Blood on the Moon* (RKO, 1948), which Robert Wise directed. Again, he played a multi-faceted personality as an earthy gunfighter hired by a rustler-friend (Robert Preston) to force a girl rancher (Barbara Bel Geddes) to either sell her herd cheaply or lose it to outlaws. Eventually, however, Mitchum turns on Preston[10] in defense of Bel Geddes. While the adventure film was a more honest sagebrush venture than many, it hardly lived up to its ads: "Lusty, violent, savage tale of the deadliest range war ever to EXPLODE on the screen!" The fact that the film was so soundstage-bound hindered the project's effectiveness.

These two 1948 films, each good in its own way, might well have come and gone had it not been for a turn of events in Mitchum's personal life. At this period the actor was earning about $250,000 a year and producer David O. Selznick, one of his employers, was charging some $175,000 a picture just to lend his services to other studios. The sudden avalanche of wealth and fame had its effect on the star. As time passed, his ability to cope with his new lifestyle lessened. He tended to rely too heavily on his manager, Paul Behrmann, his secretary, his wife, and an assortment of friends, mostly old wartime buddies. There was an ever-increasing group of

---

[8]Jane Greer recently told this book's author, "Of course no one can underplay Mitchum, and anyone who attempted to do so, quickly found out they were in trouble. Mitchum would start mumbling, and the soundman would stop the take." Miss Greer also admitted, "At twenty-two I was smitten with both [co-stars of *Out of the Past*]. However, Mitchum had a sensitivity which was endearing and extremely comforting to a newcomer."

[9]Two songs sung by Mitchum in the film were issued on a 78 R.P.M. record by Decca Records. The songs, "Rachel" and "O-He-O-Hi-O-Ho," marked the actor's recording debut.

[10]In an interview with Rui Nogueira for *Focus on Films*, Wise recalls, "We tried to do something we thought maybe for the first time in a Western. There have been so many Westerns and so many bar-room fights and it seemed to us that they always seemed to have these big acrobatic fights and when it's all over they're never exhausted or worn out. And we said, why don't we try to do a realistic fight. Let's have these men go at it really all the way, as hard as they can, and let's have them exhausted at the end, which they would be. And I think it worked. Mitchum and Preston liked the idea very much so we developed it that way so that even the winner is almost completely exhausted at the end. I think it's the most distinctive scene in the whole film."

With Barbara Bel Geddes in *Blood on the Moon* (RKO, 1948)

hangers-on who plagued the star. He now was widely known in the film capital as a soft touch.

This period in Mitchum's life showed a startling similarity to the time he worked at Lockheed before becoming a movie actor. Instead of physical reactions to being unhappy, however, Robert appeared to be more mentally upset and hypertense. It was in 1947 that he began to use marijuana occasionally to settle his nerves. Unfortunately, many of the so-called friends and parasites who crowded around the successful actor were "potheads," and they all too quickly accepted him as one of their own, despite his lack of interest in their weed cult.

The first signs of professional trouble came late in 1947 when Robert's "best friend and personal manager," Paul Behrmann, admitted that he could not account for the disappearance of the bulk of Robert's funds. Being philosophical about the matter, Mitchum refused to prosecute. He had just renegotiated his RKO agreement and reasoned he could soon make up the deficit. Later, however, he and his wife were summoned to court to give evidence in a case where Behrmann was charged with defrauding a Burbank housewife, Wanda S. Schoemann. At the trial hearing, the Mitchums had to admit that their manager had only given the actor twenty dollars a week for his personal use, while Dorothy testified she once checked the amount in one of Robert's bank accounts and found it at a low balance of fifty-eight dollars. Another witness, Richard Ellis, then Mitchum's secretary, said Behrmann had once threatened "he would do away with her [Dorothy]" if she "did not stop making trouble for him."

Behrmann pleaded not guilty to defrauding Mrs. Schoemann and was released on bail following the hearing. Later, he went to prison on similar charges. After the courtroom session, according to Mitchum, his ex-manager promised "vengeance." The actor later said the man had tried to turn his mother and sister against him by saying Robert was the one who had taken the money. "Records prove the monstrous falsity of this concept," Mitchum later wrote.

After the legal confrontation, and upon the urging of his mother and sister, Mitchum went to psychiatrist Dr. Frederick Hacker for help. After a brief analysis, the doctor concluded there was nothing mentally wrong with the actor other than the obvious fact that he was too afraid of offending others. The physician suggested the star should be more personally independent and to learn to say no. The best advice he could offer was that Robert should rely more upon his own judgment.

For a holiday, Mitchum took his family east to Delaware. His family remained on the East Coast in June, 1948, when the actor returned to Hollywood to begin work on a film which was eventually canceled. It was no secret that Dorothy preferred the East Coast to Hollywood, but Mitchum began looking around for a new home, and, in the interim, he assisted workmen in turning his present home into a duplex suitable for rental.

The tension of Robert's strained existence finally broke on the warm night of Tuesday, August 31, 1948, when he and three others were arrested at a cottage at 8443 Ridpath Drive in the Laurel Canyon hills. Each was charged with the possession and use of marijuana. There are numerous conflicting stories regarding the arrest and subsequent conviction of the star, but two truths do emerge from the sticky situation. First, Mitchum fully believed that his brief stardom was over due to the bust, and second, the public and his employers rallied behind him in support.

According to police authorities, both state and federal, Mitchum had been under surveillance for over six months because of his alleged use of grass, and that close watch came to a climax the night of the arrest. Also booked in the incident were actress Lila Leeds, her roommate Vicki Evans, and Robin Ford. The latter was a real estate agent and friend of Mitchum's whom the actor had hired to find him a new home. The actor later admitted that Miss Leeds had a romantic interest in him and that they had seen each other a few times, before *he* decided it was best to drop the association.

On the evening of the arrest, Mitchum and Ford, who had been on a hunting trip together, went out to dinner and upon Ford's urging went to see Miss Leeds' new home in Laurel Canyon. Mitchum relates that she offered him a cigarette which he did not have time to smoke since two men came into the house. Robert's first reaction was that it was a "hold-up." The quartet were then placed under arrest by Detective Sergeant Alva M. Barr and Sergeant J. B. McKinnon of the Los Angeles police department. Both policemen said they had witnessed, through a window, both Mitchum and Ford smoking marijuana cigarettes given to them by Miss Leeds. Mitchum and Ford were handcuffed by Barr and escorted to police headquarters where they were booked and charged.

At the police station, Mitchum was asked the nature of his occupation. "Former actor," he replied. He was also quoted as saying, "I'm ruined, I'm all washed up in pictures now, I guess. This is the living end." Ironically, that morning the star had been scheduled to speak at a National Youth Day observance on the steps of the Los Angeles City Hall. Naturally, his appearance was quickly canceled.

While incarcerated, the RKO star was examined by police psychiatrists. "They brought me there in shackles—me and the other peons. I'm sitting there stark naked and the doctor comes in and says, 'How are you?' 'I'm fine,' I said. 'How are you?' Then came the questions: Do you go to parties? Yes, I do. What do you do there? I get drunk, follow pretty broads, make a fool of myself and stagger home.

Do you ever go to parties with men? Yes. What do you do? Talk dirty, play poker, get drunk. Do you like pretty girls? Yeah. Do you go out with them? No. Why not? Because my wife won't let me."

Even before his arrest, Mitchum had been doubtful about his shaky marriage. Now he felt certain the arrest would end the relationship. But then he learned that Dorothy was on her way back to California by car. When asked if her trip was for a reconciliation, Robert replied, "I'd like to believe it might mean reconciliation. But my wife is a very resolute woman."

Having been formally booked, the arrested quartet were each released on $1000 bail pending a *habeas corpus* hearing in a week's time. Mitchum refrained from giving a public statement for a day. When he did, he claimed he had been "framed."

In order to protect their investment in the star, both David O. Selznick and RKO stood by the actor, probably because executives at both studios did not seriously believe Mitchum was a confirmed user. He also had three pictures (*Rachel and the Stranger, Blood on the Moon, The Red Pony*) in the can, and the companies, remembering the earlier 1940s Errol Flynn rape case, intended to make boxoffice gravy from what was predicted would be very highly publicized hearings.

The performer's employers hired attorneys Jerry Giesler and Norman Tyre to defend their star. Giesler had served as advocate for many celebrities, including Errol Flynn. Both Giesler and Tyre issued a statement claiming there were "a number of unexplained facts and peculiar circumstances surrounding the raid" and that eventually the facts would be made clear.

On September third, Dorothy Mitchum and her two sons returned to their home at Oak Glen Drive where she and the actor were soon reconciled. Five days later the grand jury met and Mitchum did not testify, as was his right. At the culmination of the hearing the grand jury returned indictments charging possession of marijuana

With Peter Miles in *The Red Pony* (Rep., 1949)

290

With Lila Leeds and lawyers Grant Cooper and Jerry Giesler (right) at trial sentencing in Los Angeles (February 9, 1949)

and conspiracy to possess marijuana against Miss Leeds, Miss Evans, Ford, and Mitchum.

Standing behind Mitchum, RKO announced he would next star in *The Big Steal,* and during the next several months a series of suits and countersuits[11] were filed which delayed the start of the trial. Finally scheduled to get underway early in 1949, the case was again delayed when Jerry Giesler was injured in a car accident. On January 10, 1949, the trial began with the famed lawyer asking and receiving a trial by court rather than by jury for his clients, Mitchum, Ford, and Miss Leeds. After hearing the testimony—and again, Robert did not testify—Judge Clement D. Nye declared Giesler's clients guilty as charged and all three were again released on bail.

On February ninth, Mitchum and Miss Leeds returned to court for sentencing,[12] and the judge told Mitchum he had "failed to set an example of good citizenship." Both defendants were sentenced to one year in the county jail with the sentence then suspended. The duo were placed on probation for two years and ordered to spend the sixty days of that probation in the county jail with time off for jail time already accumulated. (Mitchum and Miss Leeds had been sentenced on the charge of conspiracy to possess marijuana; the other grand jury indictment, possession of marijuana, was dropped.)

Robert, who was then in the midst of filming *The Big Steal,* was taken into custody by the sheriff's department. Although attorney Giesler submitted a motion to the

[11]One suit, by Nanette Bordeaux, the owner of the house where the arrests were made, demanded $2500 in damages, while Mitchum countersued her for $20,000 for trying to sell a sofa in an ad which read, "Robert Mitchum sat here."
[12]Ford and Miss Evans, the latter having a separate attorney, were sentenced in March. Ford had been arrested on another charge and Miss Evans was detained in New York City.

With Jane Greer in *The Big Steal* (RKO, 1949)

court asking that Mitchum not go to jail until after the completion of the film, due to the high cost to his employers, the motion was denied. The actor was ordered to immediately begin his sentence. In jail he mopped and cleaned cells, and seemingly adapted well to prison life. "I don't like jail, naturally, but they treat us okay," he admitted.

After a few days in jail, and through the influence of Giesler and RKO, Robert was transferred to the Castaic Honor Farm where he worked at the cement plant. During this period the actor still remained fairly happy in jail, although his suit against Nanette Bordeaux was dismissed. He and Miss Leeds were also taken to Vicki Evans' trial, which ended in her eventual release.

While he was in jail Robert was visited by that very private billionaire Howard Hughes, who was assuming control of RKO. The bashful tycoon urged Mitchum to "keep up your strength" and alerted him that he was buying him out of his Selznick contract. Hughes obviously responded to the star's charisma for he promised him more screen work. It was a generous act by the very powerful executive.

On March thirtieth, Robert, along with Miss Leeds, was released from jail after serving fifty days with ten days off for good behavior. Under the terms of their probation, the two were ordered not to associate with one another. The actor informed the press he had received an extension on his income tax payments but noted, "Heck, I've got to work to pay my taxes."

Upon his release from prison Mitchum was queried by a friend what it was like on the "inside." "Just like Palm Springs—without the riff-raff, of course," he responded. He informed the press, "I've been happy because I've had privacy here [in jail]. Nobody envied me. Nobody wanted anything from me. Nobody wanted my bars or the bowl of pudding they shoved at me through the slot. I did my work and they let me alone." He also said he was through with some of his "so-called pals" and promised to spend more time with his family.

In many ways Mitchum's arrest for marijuana helped him personally. As columnist Earl Wilson would later interpret the situation, "Mitchum may even have gained something from his arrest: it was the foundation of his being a Hollywood 'character.'"

Although one of the first stars to be associated with the use of marijuana, Mitchum today does not advocate its legalization. He does, however, foster a sane approach to the problem. "Today you can't get three people together in a room without somebody turning on. All the fuzz manages to do is jack up the price."

Always having claimed that he had been "framed" in the marijuana arrest, Robert was eventually vindicated in the case. In 1950, during the course of another investigation, the Los Angeles District Attorney's office unearthed rumors of a frame[13] against the actor and on January 31, 1951, the court reviewed the case and ordered the guilty verdict against Mitchum set aside. A plea of not guilty was ordered into the record, the complaint dismissed, and the case withdrawn from the official record.

Today, Mitchum is still continually badgered about this "scandalous" period in his hectic life. With his typical humorous cynicism developed in more recent years, he has various comments, all differing on the subject. When one writer asked him about always being stoned Bob responded, "Let them assume what they want. There are all kinds of rumors about me. And they're all true, every one of them. You can make up some if you want. At least the dope users regard me as trustworthy; some of them even lay the stuff on me occasionally. Sometimes I don't even know it till I put my hand in my pocket later. That's all right as long as they don't lay any lemonade on me. The cops? I don't embarrass them and they don't embarrass me."

When Mitchum was released from jail and went back to work, he was obviously headed on a course leading to a straight and lawful existence. "This has been a milestone in my life. . . . a sad lesson. It's the last time anything like this will happen to me. . . . I've learned my lesson. . . . I hope I don't get into any more trouble. . . . But who can say what I might do tomorrow? If I put out some phony reform story and then fall from grace, I'd look like a liar."

After a few days at home with his family, Robert returned to the filming of *The Big Steal*. While he was incarcerated, the studio had used a double for his long shots. In the on-location shooting that remained, he appeared mainly in closeups and a few other vital shots not completed before he was jailed.

During his police difficulties, both *Rachel and the Stranger* and *Blood on the Moon* had been rushed into release to take advantage of the notoriety and did good boxoffice for RKO. So did *The Red Pony*, which he had done on loan-out to Republic. The film was issued early in 1949, and in it he was second-billed to Myrna Loy, the fading ex-leading lady of MGM.

The color version of *The Red Pony* was based on the John Steinbeck novella which was made up of four rather rambling stories centered on a boy and his pony. In the seriously altered and diluted film adaptation, Robert appeared as farmhand Billy Buck, probably the most human of the adults in the screen story. Somewhat of a philosopher, Robert tries to assist a young boy (Peter Miles) when the latter tries to convince his stern father (Shepperd Strudwick) that he should have a pony. When the boy does receive the animal, it eventually becomes ill, wanders away and is

[13]The actor and his attorney had always contended that something "fishy" had been going on, for two reasons. One, the Laurel Canyon home had been bugged with microphones, and two, the press were alerted to Mitchum's arrest almost before the police had seized the suspects.

devoured by vultures. Later, however, his father's mare gives birth to a colt which the boy is permitted to keep as his own. Miss Loy, obviously uneasy in her part, had little pivotal functioning as the boy's loving, devoted mother. It was Louis Calhern who grabbed most of the limelight as her pompous dad, a one-time wagon train master who spouts forth with long-winded tales about bringing settlers across the prairies and fighting rampaging Indians.

Despite the secondary nature of his assignment, Robert brought dignity to his characterization. *Variety* confirmed: "[He] underscores a likeable role with a finely-drawn portrayal of a grownup who understands both kids and horses. Mitchum once again demonstrates his flair for apt characterization without overplaying the faculty for getting at the emotional core of his audience."

The Big Steal was completed and issued in the summer of 1949 to good business. RKO hammered out publicity about the film being "Mitchum's newest picture" and how it re-united him with Jane Greer[14] after the success of *Out of the Past*. Most sources agree that movie mogul Hughes came up with the pedestrian, confused script, based on Richard Wormser's story, *The Road to Carmichael's,* in order to have a legitimate project on tap to show the court that Robert was working and that he was needed out of jail to prevent a huge studio loss. Directing his third feature film, Donald Siegel was put in charge of this chase tale. He had the difficult task of shooting most of the convoluted project while Mitchum, the focal figure, was not closely available. "If you look closely at the film you see that when Mitchum arrives at certain places, there are leaves on the trees and when Bendix arrives moments later, the leaves are gone. I was helped by the fact I had been an editor," Siegel later told cinema historian Stuart Kaminsky.

The rather jumbled film had Mitchum disembarking from a steamer at Vera Cruz and being placed under arrest by police captain William Bendix for the theft of an Army payroll valued at $300,000. Mitchum immediately slugs Bendix, grabs his identity papers, and hastily departs with fellow passenger Jane Greer. She later meets the real crook (Patric Knowles) and demands the two thousand dollars he owes her. Knowles, who is in the employ of hoodlum John Qualen, heads for Thehuacan with Mitchum, Greer, and Bendix (who also works for Qualen) in hot pursuit. Also involved in the merry-go-round proceedings are local police captain Ramon Novarro, who rather cooly observes the situation, and his underling (Don Alvarado).

With a dearth in storyline and most of the emphasis placed on slam-bang action, the picture was played lightly and for laughs. It legitimately could be termed a fun picture. The critics were surprisingly easy on the effort, with *The Commonweal* assessing that it contained "one of the most exciting chase sequences ever put into a movie."

Mitchum was none too happy with the script for *The Big Steal,* but he was glad to be working at his trade and making $3,000 a week. As he rationalized, "When a studio comes up with a musty old script that brings in the shekels, the actor hasn't

[14] Lizabeth Scott had been originally cast for the female lead, but she bowed out of the project when she thought Mitchum's jail escapade might taint her screen reputation. Several other actresses were considered for the lead before Jane Greer was assigned to the role. Although she was pregnant at the time, she agreed to the project. "It was just a gesture to show my fondness for Bob." The scene stealer of the film proved to be William Bendix, who had some unusual habits offcamera. He would gobble up Jane's morning sickness pills on the set, believing that at the mercy of the environs of Mexico, the medication would help prevent dysentery.

got much of an argument. So I don't bother the studio, and it doesn't bother me."

During the Mexican location filming of *The Big Steal*, Robert had his family join him south of the border. If one looks closely, one can spot Dorothy Mitchum as a tourist in a brief sequence within the picture.

While co-RKO worker Robert Ryan was winning new industry and audience respect in *The Set-Up* (RKO, 1949), Mitchum was surprisingly cast in a lightweight entry, *Holiday Affair* (RKO, 1949). At best, it was "a mildly pleasant and generally innocuous tale of a young widow" (*Cue* Magazine). Janet Leigh, one of many actresses to succumb to Howard Hughes' charms, was borrowed from MGM to play the lonely mother of a six-year-old who is just about to wed an old friend (Wendell Corey) when she meets a philosophical department store clerk (Robert). After she causes the toy salesman to lose his job, she is drawn into a romance with him, which finds Mitchum and Corey vying for her hand in marriage. *Holiday Affair* demanded very little from moviegoers, and, in exchange, provided an enjoyable eighty-seven-minute story. It demonstrated that Mitchum, unlike such other tough-guy stars as Kirk Douglas or Burt Lancaster, could handle comedy with a suitable deftness.

However the year 1949 brought another sour note into Mitchum's burgeoning career. This time he treated the event in the rather tongue-in-cheek manner it deserved. He was voted the Least Cooperative Actor "Sour Apple" Award by the Hollywood Women's Press Club, probably because he had refrained from most interviews after his jail term. He made a reply by telegram to the membership at their club luncheon. It read, "Your gracious award becomes a treasured addition to a collection of inverse citations. These include prominent mention in several Ten Worst Dressed Americans lists and a society columnist's Ten Most Undesirable Male

With Wendell Corey, Janet Leigh, Gordon Gebert, Henry "Harry" Morgan, Larry J. Blake, and Charles Sullivan in *Holiday Affair* (RKO, 1949)

Guests list, which happily was published on the date I was made welcome at the County Jail."

Despite his seemingly flippant attitude toward his screen craft, Robert was concerned about the quality of scripts being handed him. He realized the studio thought it could palm off any flimsy property on him and that, with his fan following, it would survive the test at the boxoffice. But occasionally, the script would be so lousy that he would refuse to accept the assignment. On such occasions he would confer with Hughes, or one of the executive's many representatives, and be excused from the unwanted picture. By this time, the actor was referring to his boss as "the phantom," and he told the press, "We get along fine. I told him I'd discuss his problems if he'd discuss mine."

Perhaps the actor should have requested a front office meeting on his next assignment, *Where Danger Lives* (RKO, 1950), a film engendered to showcase Hughes' newest flame Faith Domergue. A dark, moody melodrama, it cast Mitchum as a young intern who only belatedly learns that his romantic interest (Domergue) is not what she seems. The older man (Claude Rains) in her life is not her father, as she insisted, but her husband. When Rains is later killed, Domergue convinces Robert that he murdered the man before suffering a concussion himself. Only in the course of the contrived climax, which finds Mitchum and Domergue fleeing south of the border, does he learn that he is innocent of the crime and that his increasingly disturbed girlfriend is the guilty party. With an eye glued to the dogma that crime does not pay, the script has Domergue gunned down by the border police. The released, unperturbed Mitchum returns to his San Francisco love, Maureen O'Sullivan,[15] (wife of the film's director, John Farrow).

To show how much faith Howard Hughes and RKO had in Mitchum's next entry, *My Forbidden Past,* it was completed on November 16, 1949, but not released until March, 1951. Even at that point it was hardly worth the effort. As directed by Robert Stevenson, it was a dull period piece which had Mitchum as a Northern nineteenth-century doctor working in New Orleans and living in the shadow of his Southern belle wife (Janis Carter). The pivotal role in the film was played by Ava Gardner as a beautiful but fickle young woman who wants Mitchum but cannot have him even after she comes into money. Added to the humbled situation was Dixie gentlemen Melvyn Douglas, who was in love with flirtatious Ava, but was also her cousin. According to the polite *Variety* review, the fiasco hinted "at hidden, spicy secrets which [it] doesn't back up."

Less serious than ever when working with a bad scenario, Mitchum had his own instant remedy for the faulty *My Forbidden Past.* "We didn't have much of a script to start with, so I suggested that the first scene should be about like the climactic one in *Ecstasy.* I figured that if we were going to give the public a shock treatment, we might as well do it up brown."

Although no sparks had flown from the screen teaming of Robert and MGM-borrowed Ava Gardner, Hughes thought there might be some good screen chemistry between Mitchum and his other high-priced studio property, Jane Russell. It was a concept that worked and the public bought it.

Typical of RKO products in this period, *His Kind of Woman* (1951) made little sense. Private detective Dan Milner (Robert) is paid $54,000 by a gambler to come to a small Mexican resort town and await orders on how to earn his hefty salary.

[15] Years later, Miss O'Sullivan would recall to cinema writer Michael R. Pitts of Mitchum, "He is a very casual actor and great care must go into that casualness."

With Ava Gardner and Melvyn Douglas in *My Forbidden Past* (RKO, 1951)

Along the way he meets a sultry, busty singer (Russell), who is going to the same resort on a husband-shopping expedition. If Mitchum's expressionless character believes her ruse—that she is a society gal flitting from one global resort to another —he gives no indication. At the Mexican hotel they encounter Mark Cardigan (Vincent Price), a hammy Hollywood matinee idol who once had "known" Russell and has come here largely to escape his overbearing spouse (Marjorie Reynolds). Once on the premises, Robert soon discovers the purpose for his presence. Deported hoodlum Nick Ferraro (Raymond Burr) plans to have him done away with so he can assume Mitchum's identity and slip back into the U.S. At the climax, Robert is captured by Burr's gang but is rescued by Price and a contingent of Mexican police. The way is now paved for Mitchum and suddenly-turned-honest Russell to make a life together.

Three facets of Mitchum's unique persona distinguish his performance in *His Kind of Woman*. Despite the seeming surface nonchalance, Mitchum has the capacity to bring out the spice in most any leading lady with whom he is working and Russell was no exception. For a change, animalistic Jane was not used as an on-camera freak on display for her mammary wonders. Instead, she played a woman aroused by a virile man.

In past films (such as, *Rachel and the Stranger*) Mitchum's impressive physique had only been used sparingly and subtly. But in *His Kind of Woman* it is thrust at the viewer with all the finesse of a carnival act. Top-heavy Russell might have her beach scene in which her natural assets were enshrined in a form-fitting, black bathing suit, but Robert had his undraped moments, too. As a prisoner on Burr's yacht and about to be given a further working over by the gangster's hoodlums, he is stripped to the waist. It was a beefcake situation that would have made Victor Mature proud.

Thirdly, *His Kind of Woman* demonstrated to those viewers able to divert themselves from the scenic wonders that Mitchum had a cool, casual way of delivering a line. No matter how mundane the lines, he could twist them into something smart, amusing, and sassy:

> RUSSELL: *I hear you killed Ferraro. How does it feel?*
> MITCHUM: *He didn't tell me.*

At another point, Jane confronts Robert:

> RUSSELL: *I've got to tell you something about myself.*
> MITCHUM: *One thing about you. You never talk about others.*

And getting down to the obvious fact, an aspect of his screen attraction that made him as valuable as a Kirk Douglas, a Burt Lancaster, or a Gregory Peck, Mitchum possessed tremendous sexiness. Everything about him suggested a repressed stud itching to kick the traces. Thus, there is a smoldering audience reaction when sleepy-eyed Mitchum drawls to aroused Russell, "You could be a handy thing to have around the house."

It was nothing unexpected that critics despised *His Kind of Woman*. Any intellectual would. The *New York Herald-Tribune* branded it a "nonsensical melodramatic hodgepodge," and the *New York Times* said, "In addition to being one of the worst Hollywood pictures in years, it is probably the only one since the advent of Vitaphone that needs sub-titles."

In 1951, the same year that Mitchum's innocence in the marijuana case was proclaimed, the lawsuits with Naneette Bordeaux were finally settled, and the actor

With William Talman in *The Racket* (RKO, 1951)

paid Miss Bordeaux some $2500 to "cover actual damage" to her cottage where the arrests took place.

With earnings of $4500 a week, a goodly portion of any Mitchum-RKO film in this period went into his salary, rather than into good production values. This fact made it necessary for the studio to deposit additional funds into hefty publicity for the completed product. And if there was any facet of film production that Hughes and his force were good at, it was publicizing anything and everything.

One film that escaped the Hughes "touch" was *The Racket* (RKO, 1951). It was based on Bartlett Cormack's 1927 play which had been a sensational exposé of rackets and had been filmed in 1928 with Hughes as the producer. Unfortunately, the new edition, co-scripted by W. R. Burnett, the author of *Little Caesar* (First National, 1931) and *High Sierra* (Warner Bros., 1941), showed the original story had dated badly.

Mitchum is cast as Captain Thomas McQuigg, an honest big city law enforcer who refuses to accept bribes from a crooked politician (Ray Collins) and assorted hoodlums led by Robert Ryan. The latter is a boyhood chum of the officer. Much of the action is centered around a nightclub where singer Lizabeth Scott falls in love with reporter Robert Hutton. Working with Mitchum is another honest cop (William Talman). Smart cop Mitchum sees an opportunity to corner Ryan, whose political connections have long protected him from arrest. His plan is to fan adroitly the conflict between the gangster and his associates and to induce Miss Scott to confess what she knows about Ryan's business dealings. Eventually, Ryan has to pay the penalty for his crimes. What resulted, however, was just another programmer, which was a shame considering the calibre of the cast and the director (John Cromwell). The *New York Times* said, "As for the film's observations on crooks and politics, they are so generalized and familiar that this is just a case of one more time around."

When *His Kind of Woman* had been released, Hollywood columnist Louella O. Parsons, hoping to have her daughter Harriet reinstated as a producer at RKO, lauded the silly melodrama and referred to Mitchum and Russell as "the hottest combination that ever hit the screen." This statement was an obvious exaggeration by anyone's standards, considering such prior Hollywood love teams as Ronald Colman-Vilma Banky, John Gilbert-Greta Garbo, Clark Gable-Jean Harlow, or Humphrey Bogart-Lauren Bacall. But still, *His Kind of Woman* had earned a nice boxoffice profit, and Howard Hughes determined to re-unite Mitchum and Russell. The vehicle for this was *Macao* (RKO, 1952). The director was Josef von Sternberg, who had done such visual wonders with Marlene Dietrich at Paramount in the early 1930s.

Actually, *Macao* had been lensed in mid-1950, but in typical Hughes fashion it had sat on the shelf for a re-think period. During this time the movie mogul had hired Nicholas Ray (who is not credited onscreen) to reshoot large sections of the picture. As Andrew Sarris would note in his booklet *Josef von Sternberg* (1958), "Sternberg's contribution to *Macao* is exclusively stylistic, and there is no evidence, internal or external, of any deeper involvement than that."

Macao centers around the Oriental city of the title and casts Mitchum as a former Signal Corps lieutenant who has lost his passport. He arrives in the city of intrigue on a steamer, with fellow passengers Julie Benson (Russell) and ostensible salesman Lawrence Trumble (William Bendix). Russell proves to have a considerable past but is soon hired as the chief singer at hoodlum Brad Dexter's club, much to the chagrin

With Jane Russell in *Macao* (RKO, 1952)

of the latter's moll (Gloria Grahame). Dexter and cohort Thomas Gomez, a crooked cop, soon become alerted that one of the three arrivals in town is an undercover agent sent to lure Dexter beyond Macao's three mile limit so that he can be arrested and returned to the United States. For a time Mitchum is mistaken for the officer, but it turns out to be Bendix. When the latter is murdered, Robert takes up the case to avenge his friend's stabbing and eventually tricks Dexter into international waters where the hoodlum is arrested.

Sadly, the only real mood created by *Macao* was apathy. The mixture of newsreel and documentary footage, along with soundstage sets, did not approximate the special allure of Macao, nor was Russell capable of capturing the quixotic qualities necessary for a lady with a shady past. Viewers had only to think how Dietrich, Lauren Bacall, or even Veronica Lake would have handled the assignment. As the American adventurer who cannot return home, Mitchum was asked to step into the shoes of a Humphrey Bogart, a Clark Gable, or even an Alan Ladd. His character is the type of vulnerable man who admits, "I was lonely in Times Square on Christmas Eve," and that his fondest wish now is to retire to some desert island with Russell and forget the rat race of money-grasping civilization. Mitchum seemed unable to cope with the potential subtleties of his character, even when taking into account the confusion that existed in the dialogue delineation of the wandering soul. But Robert was able to pass muster as the virile protector of trouble-prone Jane and gangster-chasing Bendix. He even had another bare-chested scene which was inserted to please one section of the filmgoing audience, as Jane's skin-tight togs were to do for the other portion of ticket buyers.

Mitchum had had good luck with several previous service stories. Such was not the case, however, with *One Minute to Zero* (RKO, 1952), his next feature. Actually, circumstances which occurred during the picture's filming were far more engaging than the melodrama itself. While on location in 1951 in Colorado Springs, the star

With brother John Mallory on the set of *One Minute to Zero* (RKO, 1952)

engaged in a fist fight with soldier Bernard B. Reynolds in the Red Fox Bar at the Alamo Hotel. Reynolds took such a beating from the actor, who was unhurt, that he was sent to the hospital with a suspected skull fracture. What was so improbable about Reynolds' defeat was that he was a rated heavyweight boxer who had knocked out nineteen of twenty-eight opponents in the ring.

Details of how and why the bout of fisticuffs took place are vague and the local police report no complaint was ever filed against Robert in the matter. One witness stated that Mitchum stepped in to protect fellow actor and friend Charles McGraw, while other on-the-spot observers claim Robert kicked Reynolds. Mitchum later said he and the fighter fell to the floor during the scuffle but he denied ever kicking the opponent. "An actor is always a target for the belligerent type of guy who thinks he's tough and movie he-men are softies. I never start a fight, but I assure you I can always finish one if there's no way out. This one was unavoidable and I'm sorry it happened."

One Minute to Zero was a "topical" war picture which offered Robert as an infantry colonel in Korea during the police action in 1950 when multitudes of North Korean soldiers poured through U.S. lines in the guise of refugees. Basically a modest war melodrama, directed by an expert in frou frou romance, Tay Garnett, the film was short on violence and entertainment value. If the relationship between Mitchum's character and Linda Day (Ann Blyth) seemed undeveloped and inconsistent with the storyline, it was because of a sudden change in the original casting. Part way through the location shooting, Claudette Colbert who had the film's female lead, developed pneumonia and was forced out of the cast. Joan Crawford was considered as a replacement, but Hughes instead acquired the services of much younger Ann Blyth, which made the scenario as it was implausible. Hasty rewrites did not properly restructure the characters' interplay.

A *real* romance did develop during the film's production, when Robert and his

301

brother John, who had a part in the picture,[16] met a girl working as an insurance underwriter. John Mitchum and the young lady were married on August 31, 1952, four years to the day after Robert was arrested on the marijuana charges.

Robert had rejected re-teaming with Jane Russell in *The Las Vegas Story* (RKO, 1952), and Victor Mature was substituted. But he did agree to make *The Lusty Men* (RKO, 1952), with Nicholas Ray as director, and Susan Hayward and Arthur Kennedy were his co-stars. The film was a sensible study of a faded bronco buster (Robert) who trains an upcoming champion (Kennedy) with both men competing for gutsy Hayward's love. The production was realistic, filled with an ambience of dust and lost dreams, and balanced with a number of well-staged action sequences. During the picture's filming Mitchum made the gossip columns again, but this time for eating garlic prior to his love scenes with Miss Hayward.[17]

The actor rounded out the year in *Angel Face* (RKO, 1952)[18] which marked his first work with director Otto Preminger. Based on the Beulah Overell murder case in California in 1947, in which Miss Overell and her boyfriend, Bud Gollum, were acquitted of the murder of the woman's parents, the melodramatic film had Robert as the chauffeur of a half-mad heiress (Jean Simmons) who is planning to murder her step-mother (Barbara O'Neil). The title seems to refer to a fluffy love story, but it actually refers to Miss Simmons as the ruthless girl who brings death to those who love her.

The rather unconvincing plot, despite its origin, has Simmons killing both O'Neil and her broken-down novelist dad (Herbert Marshall). Later, when Mitchum spurns her love, she decides to kill herself and him as well, allowing her Jaguar sports car to drop over the same cliff from which her parents fell to their death. "At this point," reported *Time* Magazine, "*Angel Face* comes to an end, having just about run out of both actors and automobiles." Strange as the film was, it was even more uncharacteristic for Robert to play such a passive role, the man who is undone by a conniving woman.

Far more important to Mitchum than any of his 1952 films was the birth of his third child and only daughter, Petrine, on March 3, 1952. The little girl was quickly dubbed Trina. During the summer of that year he prepared a special cabin on the back of a Ford truck and took his two sons and his stand-in, Tim Wallace, on a fishing trip in the High Sierras. Later in the season, he made personal appearances in Colorado Springs to promote *One Minute to Zero*.

By now a seasoned star, Mitchum felt secure enough to pontificate a bit to the press about what he really felt as a movie star. "This is a ridiculous and humiliating profession. I make faces for the silver screen because I just don't have anything better to do at the moment. The silliest part is that most movie stars play it straight. They're so serious. Why doesn't everyone have fun working? What else is there? You don't get to keep much of what you make anyway."

[16]His screen name was then John Mallory.

[17]Jane Greer recalls that during the filming of *The Big Steal*, she noticed "a strange brown circle outlining Bob [Mitchum]'s lips" as they were preparing to rehearse the first love scene. When questioned, the actor admitted it was caused "by my chewing tabaccy." Says Greer, "He removed it before the take, but my stomach was prepared to revolt."

[18]Preminger told Gerald Pratley for *The Cinema of Otto Preminger* (1971) that preparatory to accepting the directing assignment, he conferred with the head of RKO. "We drove around in his [Hughes] little car and he said: 'Otto, you must do this for me because this bitch [meaning Jean Simmons] has cut her hair short, and I hate short hair. She was mad, took the scissors, and we had a fight. I have her only for eighteen days during a six week period, eighteen days to work with her. If you don't like the story, get some other writers. Do anything you want.'"

For the first time in his movie career that now spanned well over a decade, Mitchum went out of North America for location shooting on a picture. The project was *White Witch Doctor* (Twentieth Century-Fox, 1953), and the destination was the Bakuba country of Africa. He was re-teamed with Susan Hayward, who had the title role as a woman who tries to bring medical aids to the natives with the help of Robert, a safari guide. He was also a treasure seeker as was rotund, grasping Walter Slezak. Only the location shooting, the beautiful country, and the animals saved this otherwise vapid spin-off of *Trader Horn* (MGM, 1931). Interestingly enough, Mitchum got along well with give-em-hell director Henry Hathaway, who marveled at the actor's ability to memorize quickly pages of dialogue. The director never seemed to realize the hours of careful study that went into Mitchum's ability to do scenes perfectly on the first take.

Bridling at the fetid productions being turned out at RKO, Mitchum again refused to re-team with Jane Russell, this time in *The French Line* (not released until 1954, and with Gilbert Roland as the substituted co-star). But a contract was a contract, and he was forced to accept *Second Chance* (RKO, 1953). Its virtues were the Mexican locales and the 3-D photography. Robert played a has-been boxer in South America who begins a love affair with a gangster's girl (Linda Darnell) and tries to save her from a stalking hit man, Jack Palance. The highlight of the weak melodrama was the chase scene centered on a cable car suspended seven thousand feet above an Andes valley.

She Couldn't Say No (RKO, 1954) had actually been completed in November, 1951, as part of Jean Simmons' pact with the studio. The picture tried to reinstate screwball comedy into the Hollywood scene with Simmons as an heiress who returns to Progress, Ark., to repay the townsfolk for their kindness during her more humble years. Of this fumbling farce in which Robert was again a clean-cut, moralistic

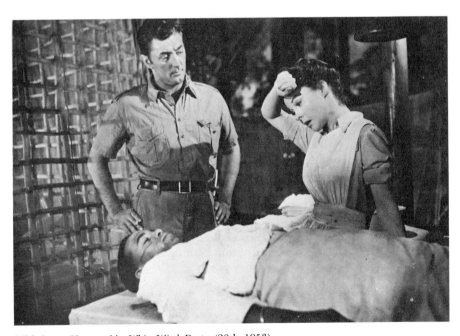

With Susan Hayward in *White Witch Doctor* (20th, 1953)

303

young doctor, *Time* chided, "[It] is a hymn with a sexy title. It is sung in praise of small-town life, but there are rather too many verses and the performers do not seem to know the tune."

Since Howard Hughes was gradually phasing himself and RKO out of actual theatrical production, there was very little trouble about Robert not renewing his studio pact.[19] He chose to freelance, following the common practice of many performers at this time.

On his first freelance job he was teamed with the girl whose near-nude photos he had seen a decade ago. By now, Marilyn Monroe was the queen of Twentieth Century-Fox and the real boxoffice draw of the picture, *River of No Return* (1954), directed by Otto Preminger. Set in the Northwest of 1875, the script offered Robert as a man just released from jail who is heading with his motherless son (Tommy Rettig) to their newly bought farm in the north country. The saloon girl who comes into their life is Monroe, and the antagonist is Rory Calhoun. In the course of the CinemaScope, color production Mitchum and Rettig fight Indians, outlaws, the raging river, and Calhoun. Thanks to the splendid camerawork of Joseph La Shelle, the charisma of Monroe, who "sang" several songs in the course of the feature, and to the masculine presence of Mitchum and Calhoun, *River of No Return* was a substantial moneymaker.

Mitchum next went to Warner Bros. to work again with director William Wellman on an allegorical film, *Track of the Cat*. It was shot in color but utilized a basic spectrum of black and white shades, with occasional bright hues to convey symbolism. Mitchum played Curt, the frontiersman who had fought Indians and outlaws to make his family's mountain home safe but had turned savage himself. When the clan is snowed in at their cabin and tormented by a marauding mountain lion, tempers come to the fore. Before he can take his weak brother's (Tab Hunter) fiancée (Diana Lynn), he is killed by falling off a precipice. The uncommercial *Track of the Cat* was the star's first leading role as a full-fledged villain.

Over the years, industry figures had tended to think of Mitchum in terms of "a leading man" rather than as "an actor." *Not as a Stranger* (United Artists, 1955) changed all that. Produced and directed by Stanley Kramer the film was based on the best selling novel of the same name by Morton Thompson. The screen edition would prove to be a huge moneymaker, grossing $7.1 million in distributors' domestic rentals. It convinced a great many people that, in his quiet way, Robert was an actor of strength. Despite the fact that he looked too old for the role of the young intern who weds an older Swedish nurse (Olivia de Havilland) for her money, he did manage to make the film's soapy hundred thirty-five minutes hold together. The picture depicted, in rather too episodic a fashion, Dr. Lucas Marsh's comradeship with flip fellow doctor Frank Sinatra, his affair with a socialite lush (Gloria Grahame), his causing the death of an elderly physician (Charles Bickford) who inspired him to his profession, and his eventual reconciliation with his patient, too understanding spouse. One of the movie's more powerful scenes took place early in the chronicle when he survives a confrontation with his alcoholic father (Lon Chaney, Jr.) and realizes how far up a cultural path he must travel to surmount his background and accomplish his professional goal.

After the completion of *Not as a Stranger*, which Kramer once described as "ten

[19]Hughes had wanted Mitchum to co-star with Barbara Stanwyck in *Cattle Queen of Montana* (RKO, 1954). When he refused, Ronald Reagan was substituted, and Robert remained on "suspension" until the actual expiration of his contract in early 1954.

With William Hopper, Beulah Bondi, and Tab Hunter in *Track of the Cat* (WB, 1954)

weeks of hell," he gave star Mitchum a leather script cover, inscribed, "To Bob—who possesses within himself the unfortunate power to be whatever he wishes."

Mitchum remained with United Artists for his second 1955 release, *The Night of the Hunter*, set in the mid-South of the 1930s. He was cast as a circuit-riding preacher who believes that anything, stealing or worse, is all right in order to obtain suitable edifices for God. As such, he determines to acquire the money hidden by Shelley Winters' late spouse who had stolen $10,000 in a bank robbery. He is led to marrying, then killing the woman before she has revealed the whereabouts of the loot, which proves to be hidden in one of her children's dolls. The frightened youths are saved from the pursuing Mitchum by spinster Lillian Gish who alerts the police to the whereabouts of the preacher.

James Agee wrote the scenario for *The Night of the Hunter*, which was not a boxoffice winner. In the only film he directed, Charles Laughton[20] used low-key lighting and a storybook quality to the presentation to create a black thriller. The film, which has grown in public esteem over the decades, is one of Mitchum's favorites and he specifically enjoyed playing a "crud." He is the gospel man who has the words "good" and "evil" tattooed on his fingers. At one moment his larger-than-

[20]Not long before he died (1962), Laughton discussed Mitchum with writer Helen Lawrenson. "Bob is one of the best actors in the world. In addition he can imitate any accent there is. . . . He has great talent. He'd make the best Macbeth of any actor living. All his tough talk is a blind, you know. He's a literate, gracious, kind man, with wonderful manners, and he speaks beautifully—when he wants to. He's a very tender man and a very real gentleman. You know he's really terribly shy. I can tell you one thing: he won't thank you for destroying the image he has built up as a defense, . . . He's one of my very favorite people in the whole world. I can't praise him too much." (It was also Laughton, who abhorred working with children, who demanded that Mitchum interpret his direction to the youngsters on the set of *The Night of the Hunter*.)

In *The Night of the Hunter* (UA, 1955)

life character could be charming and in the next become a raving lunatic. Particularly effective is the scene in which the small children are hiding in a barn hayloft. They are awakened before sunrise by the sound of Mitchum singing in the distance on horseback, "Leaning on Jesus, leaning on the everlasting arms." It is an example of the effective underplaying that made his menacing role all the more startling when the character broke out into fits of violence and destructiveness. As *The New Yorker* substantiated, Robert is a "protagonist of surprising ability."

Mitchum concluded his 1955 releases with *Man with the Gun* (United Artists), a pedestrian Western. In the slow, sombre narrative, he is a gunfighter deserted by his wife (Jan Sterling) because he is too ruthless. Later, he is hired to clean up an outlaw-ridden town. The *Hopalong Cassidy* Westerns he had made a decade earlier were a lot more fun.

During his movie career Mitchum has been known to play pranks on the sets of his films, but in 1955 William Wellman, who had twice directed him onscreen, removed him from the lead in *Blood Alley* (Warner Bros., 1955), which was being produced by John Wayne's Batjac Productions. In what the star called a "bit of horseplay" he had pushed the film's transportation manager into San Francisco Bay and Wellman asked that he be fired. At first John Wayne would not agree to the request, but when Mitchum seemed willing to leave the production, Wayne took over the lead in a picture that was a substantial moneymaker for Batjac. The incident did not tarnish Robert's friendship with Wayne, and the two co-starred later in *El Dorado* (Paramount, 1967).

Also in 1955, Mitchum, through his attorney Jerry Giesler, filed a one million-dollar lawsuit against *Confidential* Magazine for a story it printed alleging that Mitchum had become drunk at a party co-hosted by Charles Laughton and producer Paul Gregory and that he had stripped and masqueraded as a hamburger. The exposé also alleged that the star left the party with a young woman who was not his wife. Although Robert never collected any damages on this suit, his action led to the filing of other suits by assorted maligned celebrities and eventually caused the demise of *Confidential*.

In the fall of 1955 Mitchum made one of his few television appearances by guest-starring with hosts Tommy and Jimmy Dorsey on "Stage Show" while appearing in New York City for the premiere of *Man with the Gun*. He sang several songs on the program and was so well-received that he began making plans to do a full-length LP album.

He then went on location to Europe where he starred in *Foreign Intrigue* (United Artists, 1956), based on the popular video series. The film was lensed against the backdrops of Stockholm, Paris, and the south of France. In what the *New York Times* called a "stale melodrama," Robert played the trench-coated investigator who begins to wonder about his employer's past after the man dies "suddenly" on the French Riviera. According to one disgruntled national magazine reviewer this film "is no more intriguing than a deciphered cryptogram reading 'See Europe this year.' " Unmentioned by this critic was that the American release version was missing the specially shot topless scene of a girl that was used for the European distribution prints.

Like many other freelancing stars, Mitchum found working under the United Artists aegis congenial to his career goals. He signed a co-production agreement with the firm, beginning with *Bandido* (1956). Dealing with gun running in 1916 during the Mexican revolution, it was filmed in CinemaScope and color. Gilbert

307

Roland was the rebel leader, Zachary Scott another gunrunner, and Ursula Theiss, the pretty girl in the episode.

In 1957 Mitchum announced that he wished to play the lead in *Battle Hymn* for Universal, the story of Colonel Dean E. Hess who helped to develop the Korean Air Force and who saved the lives of thousands of Korean refugee children. The Colonel, however, had different ideas and publicly stated he did not wish an ex-jailbird playing him on celluloid. The role went to the more acceptable Rock Hudson.

For the first of his trio of 1957 releases, Robert headed to the West Indies where he proceeded to engage in a brawl with three sailors while he was filming *Heaven Knows, Mr. Allison* (Twentieth Century-Fox). John Huston directed this unusual account of a nun (Deborah Kerr), who has not yet taken her final vows, and is stranded on a South Pacific isle with Marine Mitchum during World War II. The two gradually learn to respect each other and even combat a group of Japanese who also become marooned on the island.

During the filming, Robert was injured several times and was almost drowned by the big turtle which figured in the plot. Also during the filming he wrenched an ankle, received a deep cut on one foot, and scraped several layers of skin off his chest by sliding down a palm tree. "You work for John [Huston], you suffer. What else can you expect?" Huston said of his star, "Bob is a wonderful guy . . . amusing, intellectual . . . very much in the Bogart mold."

In this essentially two-character study, both stars offered sterling portrayals. Deborah Kerr was Oscar-nominated, while Mitchum, for a change, won a backhanded compliment from *Time* Magazine. "Even though as usual he does nothing but slob around the screen, [he] has succeeded for once in carrying off his slobbing with significance."

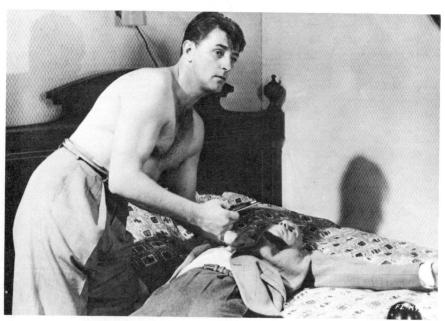

In *Foreign Intrigue* (UA, 1956)

With Deborah Kerr in *Heaven Knows, Mr. Allison* (20th, 1957)

For the first time since playing a bit in *Doughboys in Ireland* in 1943, Robert returned to Columbia to co-star with Rita Hayworth and Jack Lemmon in the drab tropical tale, *Fire Down Below* (1957). Before making the picture, Mitchum is said to have met Columbia boss Harry Cohn and remarked, "You don't seem like such a son of a bitch to me." To which Cohn responded, "That's because you've never worked for me." Perhaps Cohn proved his point by the terrible script for the film which Robert Parrish directed. Mitchum and Lemmon were the operators of a shipping boat who work the waters of the West Indies. They meet shopworn Hayworth, a woman on the lam from the law. About the only real action in the feature resulted from a nightclub sequence where dancers performed the picture's title tune (". . . there's a fire down below, down below in my heart").

Back at Twentieth Century-Fox, Robert rounded out the year with *The Enemy Below* (1957), the first of two pictures he did for former actor Dick Powell. With good special effects, the war melodrama centered on a sea duel between American submarine captain Mitchum and German sub leader Curt Jurgens. While the film lacked the qualified boxoffice appeal of *Run Silent, Run Deep* (United Artists, 1958), which had both Clark Gable and Burt Lancaster, it did prove that Mitchum was a seasoned performer, capable of untheatrical dramatics. *Films in Review* confirmed, "In fact, Mitchum has become an able actor and should no longer be dismissed as merely a dimpled chin."

It was in 1958 that Robert's recording career went into full swing. He signed a five-year contract with Capitol Records. The company issued a single by Mitchum, "What Is This Generation Coming To?" and "Mama Look a Boo Boo," which sold well, and then the firm issued an album of calypso songs by the actor entitled "Robert Mitchum—Calypso Is Like So!"

Continuing his co-production deal with United Artists, Mitchum scripted, pro-

With son James Mitchum on the set of *Thunder Road* (UA, 1958)

duced, wrote the music, and starred in *Thunder Road* (1958), which marked the screen debut of his son Jim.[21] Directed on location in the South by Arthur Ripley, the feature proved to be an immensely popular entry, taken up by the young as a testament to the underdog. In it Robert played a mountain man whose father made illegal booze which he took by car to areas of sale and distribution. The family, which included his admiring younger brother (Jim Mitchum), were at odds with federal revenue agents and big city hoodlums out to corral the moonshine trade. After a brief affair with Keely Smith, Mitchum is killed when his car is run off the road one night by federal agents. *Films in Review* enthused, "Authentic Americana is so rare in American films nowadays that the Little Americana in this 'B' has the force of welcome novelty."

Mitchum wrote two songs for the film, "The Ballad of Thunder Road" and "Poor Whippoorwill." The former was recorded on Capitol Records by Robert and became a big hit, while Keely Smith performed the latter number.

Over at Twentieth Century-Fox, Mitchum joined with Robert Wagner and Richard Egan for the Dick Powell-directed *The Hunters* (1958), a well-executed melodrama dealing with the lives of ex-World War II fighter pilots in war-torn Korea.

Mitchum closed out the decade of the 1950s with two big top grossers, *The Angry Hills* (MGM, 1959) and *The Wonderful Country* (United Artists, 1959). The former was originally scheduled to star Alan Ladd, but he turned down the project and suggested Robert for the lead. Mitchum appeared as Mike Morrison, a journalist who is in Greece during the Nazi invasion and who is asked to turn over a list of

[21]In 1974, Jim Mitchum co-starred in *Moonrunners* (United Artists), dealing with the men who made and transported "corn likker." The ads for the film read, "*Thunder Road* was only a practice run. This is the real thing."

In *Thunder Road*

With May Britt in *The Hunters* (20th, 1958)

With Cary Grant in *The Grass Is Greener* (Univ., 1960)

underground leaders to British Intelligence. In the latter film, the star was cast as a rugged mercenary in the hire of a Mexican dictator who is sent to the U.S. to buy weapons. Along the way he is delayed by a series of incidents, including breaking his leg, having an affair with a soldier's wife (Julie London), and encountering warring Apaches and belligerent Texas Rangers.

Mitchum launched himself into the new decade with *Home from the Hill* (MGM, 1960), a project originally conceived for Clark Gable and Bette Davis. Directed by Vincente Minnelli, the colorful film starred Robert as a wealthy Texas land baron who was no longer living with his wife (Eleanor Parker), and who was hated by his bastard son (George Peppard). In addition, he is sought by a distraught worker (Everett Sloane) who thinks he has seduced his daughter (Luana Patten). The mature star provided strong insights into the complicated character he portrayed. Heavily psychological, the picture also included a great deal of action, tight pacing, and an effective supporting cast.

Although Mitchum had moved his home to a three hundred-acre farm in Maryland, where he hoped to become a horse-raising country squire, he found himself constantly on the move. He went to Ireland to lense *The Night Fighters* (United Artists, 1960), set during the Second World War. Then he crossed the channel to London to co-star with Cary Grant, Deborah Kerr, and Jean Simmons in the very refined *The Grass Is Greener* (Universal, 1960). While it was not unlikely to have found the other three co-stars in such a sophisticated drawing room comedy, it was a surprise to witness Mitchum in such refined celluloid company. But as the American oil millionaire who convinces a well-bred English lady to spend a weekend with him, Robert proved quite adroit. It was not his fault that the Stanley Donen production was so slow-paced or arid of any real humor.

With Deborah Kerr in *The Sundowners* (WB, 1960)

313

Many critics believe Robert Mitchum offered his finest screen performance to date in his next assignment. *The Sundowners* (Warner Bros., 1960). The lead was originally intended for Gary Cooper, who was fatally ill, and Mitchum took the role. He agreed upon second billing, because Deborah Kerr was to be his co-star. The Fred Zinnemann-directed feature provided Robert with another complicated character to portray, this time a sheepherder with wanderlust who must choose between his love of the wide open spaces and his wife (Kerr) and their teenage son (Michael Anderson, Jr.). As a result of his work in *The Sundowners* and *Home from the Hill*, the National Board of Review selected Mitchum for its Best Actor Award of the year. In its journal, *Films in Review,* the board reported, "Robert Mitchum has grown as an actor, and in *The Sundowners* projects a surprising variety of emotions, effortlessly. Mitchum deserves more critical attention than he has received."

Robert turned down the lead in *The Misfits* (United Artists, 1961) and *Town without Pity* (United Artists, 1961),[22] and he was replaced respectively by Clark Gable and Kirk Douglas. Instead, he chose to appear in Jack Webb's *The Last Time I Saw Archie* (United Artists, 1961), for which he was paid $100,000 a week for four weeks of work in late 1960. According to *Cue* Magazine, "This Army comedy is unique: it's the first I can recall in which wit was substituted for the all too familiar G.I. slapstick and typical gags, and in which the perennial khaki goldbricker is exposed, deftly, sharply and memorably." The public disagreed and royally ignored this film in which con artist serviceman Mitchum is ordered to capture a beautiful Japanese spy (France Nuyen).

Reversing this sag in his boxoffice standing, Mitchum enjoyed three sturdy profit-making ventures during the next several years. In *Cape Fear* (Universal, 1962),

[22]The film's producers even agreed to raise the proffered $500,000 salary to $750,000, but Mitchum insisted he found the story's plotline offensive to his tastes.

With Jack Webb and Martha Hyer in *The Last Time I Saw Archie* (UA, 1961)

On the set of *Cape Fear* (Univ., 1962)

filmed in Georgia near where Mitchum had once been on a chain gang, he was second-billed to Gregory Peck. But it was Robert's portrayal of the vicious, psychotic hoodlum that held the thriller together. Unlike his preacher in *The Night of the Hunter,* the character Robert portrayed in *Cape Fear* was not insane but rather a mean person for the sake of meanness. On his release from jail he wants revenge on the lawyer (Peck) who led to his incarceration. The criminal plans to attack Peck through his wife (Polly Bergen) and their teenage daughter (Lori Martin). Eventually, after shooting a local sheriff, Bob is captured and sent back to jail. Throughout the hundred and five minutes of black-and-white film it is Mitchum's cool, evil portrayal that keeps the picture moving. This performance clearly demonstrated that forty-three-year-old Mitchum had the capacity to roll with the times and could readily switch from leading man to character star when the time so demanded.

Never one to stay out of the headlines for too long, Robert made news again in 1961 while in France filming *The Longest Day* (Twentieth Century-Fox, 1962) for producer Darryl F. Zanuck. While talking to the United Press wire service correspondent, the actor commented on the inefficiency of the film's production staff. By the time it reached print, the story had been garbled to insinuate that Mitchum thought the G.I.s used for extras in the film were afraid to do some of the action scenes. The misquote infuriated Robert, who greatly respected the soldiers, if not the military brass. The misquote was to haunt him for a long time to come. In *The Longest Day* which grossed over sixteen million dollars in distributors' domestic rentals, Mitchum portrayed Brigadier General Norman Cota, the man who led the 29th Infantry Division on the Normandy Beaches on D-Day.

For his next assignment, Mitchum reluctantly (he thought he was being miscast) accepted the male lead in *Two for the Seesaw* (United Artists, 1962) for director Robert Wise. The role of the Nebraska lawyer, estranged from his wife, who comes

315

In *The Longest Day* (20th, 1962)

With Shirley MacLaine in *Two for the Seesaw* (UA, 1962)

to New York's Greenwich Village in order to rediscover his values, had already been played on stage by Dana Andrews, Henry Fonda, and Hal March. In the familiar story, Mitchum's character becomes involved with a spaced-out girl, Gittel Mosca (Shirley MacLaine), who thinks she is a modern dancer.[23] She finds Mitchum's Jerry Ryan a strong, if temporarily displaced, person. At the end of their brief affair she does not want to give him up, although he realizes they are better off apart and that he should return to his wife. As uncharacteristic as was his role in this overlong, over-talky, stagey production, so too was his reaction at the critics who panned his work in the film. He insisted that some New York reviewers were "guilty of intellectual snobbery."

As a favor to director John Huston, Robert agreed to perform a cameo in *The List of Adrian Messenger* (Universal, 1963). Along with fellow guest stars Tony Curtis, Kirk Douglas, Burt Lancaster, and Frank Sinatra, he donned a disguise for his brief appearance in this whodunit film starring George C. Scott and Clive Brook. Despite heavy make-up, Mitchum's walk-on was easily recognizable, even before the tacked-on fadeout when the five stars reveal themselves.

Mitchum's next effort was *Rampage* (Warner Bros., 1963), a "shopworn safari meller" (*Variety*) which at least provided him with a location trip to Africa. He played a trapper who ends up at odds with big game hunter Jack Hawkins over the latter's mistress (Elsa Martinelli), whom Mitchum eventually wins. Regarding the likes of *Rampage*, Mitchum has said, "These pictures—I can do them and then walk away from them and forget about them. It's all finished and I never have to see them—I usually never do see them and I'm not *involved*. Furthermore, I don't let anyone down. I don't want that responsibility. I don't want that deep involvement."

[23]Elizabeth Taylor had originally been cast in the part of the girl who has had a brief marriage and hides her fears beneath a facade of bohemia.

Despite his supposed lack of involvement, Mitchum, by this time, had formed Talbot Productions (named for the county in which he lives in Maryland), which produced his next three films. The production company paid the star $400,000 a feature plus ten percent of the movies' gross. The first effort, *Man in the Middle* (Twentieth Century-Fox, 1964), was co-produced with Marlon Brando's Pennbaker Productions and was filmed by director Guy Green in England and India.[24] *Variety* weighed it an "engrossing military courtroom drama" with a "good cast." However, an unenthused public was less generous. Robert was featured as a military attorney in 1945 India who defends Lieutenant Winston (Keenan Wynn) on charges of killing another British soldier. Mitchum was unusually vocal about his attraction to his role. "I think my part as Barney Adams was intriguing because he faces a real dilemma only he can solve. Whichever course he chooses—justice or loyalty—in defense of a self-confessed murderer, will bring him personal unhappiness. It's the sort of decision lots of people have had to face during a war."

Few of Mitchum's recent films could have been termed establishment pap, but there was no other way to describe *What a Way to Go!* (Twentieth Century-Fox, 1964). It had originally been planned for Marilyn Monroe, but after Elizabeth Taylor in turn rejected the property, it was overhauled to suit the mercurial talents of energetic Shirley MacLaine. She plays a wacky, wealthy girl who weds six times, including the world's richest man (Robert). Written by Betty Comden and Adolph Green, this unimportant all-star fluff was one of the better reasons for disbanding

[24]On one occasion he explained, "I like to travel and I travel everywhere to make my pictures, even to Hollywood. I'm not bound to anything or anybody. An actor today can work anywhere in the world, although I sometimes ask myself what I am working for. Certainly not for society. It means nothing to me. You can't say I have given it up by living on a Maryland farm; because I have never taken it up, there was nothing to give up."

With France Nuyen in *Man in the Middle* (20th, 1964)

With Shirley MacLaine in *What a Way to Go* (20th, 1964)

the studio system. One disgruntled critic called it "overopulent; overloaded." As Rod Anderson, Mitchum looked overweight, over-aged, but not overjoyed. Perhaps being back in Hollywood had put him off his mark.[25]

Satisfying his wanderlust, Robert flew back to Africa for *Mister Moses* (United Artists, 1965). This time around he is a diamond-smuggling big game hunter with a tendency toward hard drink. He is persuaded by a missionary's daughter (Carroll Baker) to lead an African tribe to its new home. During the filming of this slowly-paced feature, Mitchum lived in an old trailer in a Masai tribe village. There were rumors that he and Miss Baker, she having replaced Sarah Miles in the project, gave realism to their love scenes on and off camera. Whatever the truth to the stories, Dorothy Mitchum back in Maryland had long ago learned that patience and silence was the best approach for keeping their marriage together.

During this period Mitchum, who still dabbled in writing short stories and poetry, hoped to direct a film and even considered buying a project called *Frankie and Johnny* from John Huston. The film fell through, however, and the actor did not appear before camera for nearly two years, during which time his boxoffice standing eroded badly. He did, however, make a two-week trip to Vietnam to be with servicemen. He exhibited a surprisingly hawkish attitude to the Southeast Asian conflict. "Asking where you stand on Vietnam is like asking where you stand on cancer. It is a declarative motion for survival. Actually I'm an Utopian anarchist—which means nothing. The intellectuals take over and the government crumbles," he said.

[25]Regarding Hollywood, he has said, "This whole place has no relation to real people. Oh, there are real people here, but they're in the oil refineries and the factories, not in movieland. Not here. This is Atlantis."

With Raymond St. Jacques in *Mister Moses* (UA, 1965)

While her husband was overseas, Dorothy Mitchum, who had grown weary of country life, took her spouse's advice literally and sold their Maryland farm, much to Robert's chagrin. When he returned from Vietnam they moved to Hollywood and lived in houses that once belonged to Cole Porter and Ruth Roman before finally settling down in their present Bel Air residence.

After a two-year cinema hiatus, nearly fifty-year-old Mitchum began to make up for lost time, if not lost ground, by appearing in six features in the next two years. His motion picture return was in *The Way West* (United Artists, 1967)[26] directed by Andrew V. McLaglen. Robert was second-billed to Kirk Douglas with Richard Widmark rounding out the trio of the film's male stars. In days of old such an important threesome would have made big financial returns, but *The Way West* grossed only $1.67 million in distributors' domestic rentals. Mitchum was the scout who guides the wagon train to the Oregon country, with Douglas as the wagon master and Widmark as one of the passengers.

If *The Way West* did poorly, Mitchum's second Western of the year, *El Dorado* (Paramount, 1967), reversed the trend by generating distributors' domestic rentals of six million dollars. John Wayne's presence in the Howard Hawks-directed feature had a good deal to do with audience interest in the action story which was a "topnotch oater, with comedy" *(Variety)*. A rather long and complicated, but colorful, saga, *El Dorado* presented Mitchum as the sheriff of a town that is torn apart by a feud over water rights between big rancher Edward Asner and smaller ones (led by R. G. Armstrong). Wayne is the hired gunslinger whom Asner brings in to aid his cause. But since he is a past friend of the sheriff and an ex-lover of Mitchum's girl (Charlene Holt) there are divided loyalties on the mercenary's part. The mixture of rough action with tongue-in-cheek performances was readily appreciated by moviegoers. *El Dorado* made Mitchum an *important* film name again. When director Hawks made *Rio Lobo* (National General, 1970) he tried to re-team Mitchum with Wayne. But Robert said the part offered did not provide him with enough salary. (Son Christopher Mitchum did accept a role in the Western.)

After making the two Westerns, Mitchum made a second trip to Vietnam, and upon his return discovered he was a grandfather for the second time. Son Jim had already presented him with a granddaughter, Carrie, and the new grandchild was a boy, Robert. That year the actor also returned to the recording field. He sang "Little Ole Winedrinker Me," along with eleven other tunes for Monument Records. The LP was entitled "That Man, Robert Mitchum . . . Sings." The record company offered the star a further recording contract, but he rejected it, claiming the edge was now gone from his activity in country music.

It did not require much persuasion to induce global traveler Mitchum to accept a pivotal role in *Anzio* (Columbia, 1968), which was produced in Italy. Robert received solo star billing in a heavily masculine cast. Edward Dmytryk directed this would-be epic which spotlighted Mitchum as a war correspondent who lands at Anzio with the forces of General Mark Clark during World War II. Before beginning the film, Mitchum argued that the script was "violently anti-American" and demanded, and won, some dialogue changes to soften the storyline's intellectual impact. Despite the heavy production mounting by Dino de Laurentis, nothing about *Anzio* jelled. It was historically inaccurate, there were no big battle scenes, and the scenario was as trite in its presentation as were the screen characters clichéd

[26]Mitchum's brother John had a bit in the film.

On the set of *El Dorado* (Par., 1967) with his parents

322

With Arthur Kennedy in *Anzio* (Col., 1968)

in theirs. No way could this mockery of a war film compare to Mitchum's earlier *The Story of G. I. Joe. Anzio* barely managed to gross $1.4 million in distributors' domestic rentals.

Nor was *Villa Rides* (Paramount, 1968) much better. Filmed in Spain by director Buzz Kulik, Yul Brynner had the title role. The film was wedded to the tradition of the recently successful Italian-German-Spanish Westerns that were overly violent with multitudinous scenes of bloody murders, hangings, and wanton sadism. As in his earlier *Bandido*, Mitchum appeared as a gun runner, this time as one caught by Villa's forces, and who joins the famed revolutionary in his rebellion against the Mexican government. Many found that Robert's part had been over-expanded at the expense of a fruitful examination of the legendary bandit leader.

Back in the States, Mitchum was again second-billed in a Western, this time to Dean Martin in *Five Card Stud* (Paramount, 1968). Martin was a sheriff and Mitchum a none-too-religious preacher, the latter replete with a six-shooter and a hollowed out Bible for a holster. The mystery-format plot involved an unknown killer out to murder five poker players who had hanged the sixth player. Everything about the film was predictable, pleasant, and undemanding. It grossed $3.5 million at American and Canadian boxoffices, thus bailing out the star's tepid marquee record.

While he was in Durango, Mexico, making *Five Card Stud,* Mitchum received a phone call from Joseph Losey in Britain, asking him to play the third lead in *Secret Ceremony* (Universal, 1968). It was to be a heavy psychological film, which would hopefully capitalize on the still potent attraction of Elizabeth Taylor, not to mention the presence of Mia Farrow, the star of *Rosemary's Baby* (Paramount, 1968).

Secret Ceremony is set mostly in a gaudy London mansion. Miss Farrow is a girl on the verge of complete insanity, who meets a prostitute (Taylor) on a bus and

323

With Roddy McDowall in *Five Card Stud* (Par., 1968)

"adopts" the woman as the mother. The young woman is plagued by two vulture-like aunts (Pamela Brown and Peggy Ashcroft) who wish to have her committed so they can siphon off her inheritance. Also appearing on the scene is stepfather Mitchum, who had seduced the girl when she was thirteen. After a great deal of morose dialogue, and a then-sensational bathtub scene between Taylor and Farrow, the girl kills herself, Taylor kills Mitchum and the film comes to an end.[27]

Stunningly produced, the film proved to be an enigmatic entry for theatre patrons who were baffled, annoyed, or amused by the portentous nonsense onscreen. Of the three main stars, only Robert emerged with any acting credit. As the lecherous step-father he is pure delight to observe as he eyes his step-daughter, knowing it is only a matter of time before he seduces her again. Mitchum shared some intriguing scenes with Miss Farrow. At one point the girl writes on a blackboard, "I am a virgin," and Mitchum informs her he is one also. He then launches into his theory on why father-daughter incest is normal and concludes by telling her that when he first saw her "slide down the bannister" when she was twelve, he decided "that was for me."

Following the controversial *Secret Ceremony*, which did gross three million dollars in distributors' domestic rentals, Mitchum returned to Hollywood to star in *Blood in the Sun* to be directed by William P. Murphy for Seven Worlds Films. Shortly after the project was begun it was dropped, and the actor then made two Westerns for

[27]When *Secret Ceremony* was later purchased for television screening, fourteen minutes were deleted, and new footage and outtakes added, which transferred the Taylor character from whore to a woman who worked evenings in a wig shop. Most of Mitchum's brief scenes, including any references to incest, were chopped. According to Mitchum, two scenes in which he appeared with Mia Farrow were reshot after he had left London, and Elizabeth Taylor was substituted. One sequence cut was the bathtub bit.

With Mia Farrow in *Secret Ceremony* (Univ., 1968)

Burt Kennedy, *Young Billy Young* (United Artists) and *The Good Guys and the Bad Guys* (Paramount). Both were issued almost simultaneously in the summer of 1969 and neither did good boxoffice.

Since both projects were filmed back to back, it was an exhaustive ordeal for the aging star. *Young Billy Young* was made in Tuscon, Arizona. Mitchum sang the title theme and played a man who comes to a small frontier town and signs on as a deputy in order to bring the title character (Robert Walker, Jr.) to justice for killing his son.

The Good Guys and the Bad Guys was filmed in New Mexico and was intended as a rather tongue-in-cheek study of fading lawlessness in the Old West. Mitchum appeared as Sheriff Flagg who was once famous and who has now been discarded by corrupt mayor Martin Balsam. When Mitchum spots a plan afoot by his old enemy George Kennedy to rob a payroll train, he decides to join with his former opponent to outwit both the mayor and Kennedy's disloyal cohorts. It was a nice and easy production, with salty performances by Douglas Fowley as a grizzled mountaineer and by David Carradine as a cold-blooded outlaw.

After these two unspectacular projects, Robert let it be known that he had "retired." But the mellowed star was dragged out of inactivity by producer Robert Bolt who offered him one of the leads in *Ryan's Daughter* (MGM, 1970), to be filmed in Ireland. The star recalls, "When I arrived in Ireland to play the school teacher in the film, [director David] Lean had second thoughts about me. His first comment was: 'I didn't know he was so large.' I protested that I wasn't 'large.' But he went around putting elevator shoes on everyone else in the film."

Initially, Mitchum had been leery of the project because of the rigorous production schedule involved. But when he was offered over one million dollars in salary, he thought it a too "interesting sum" to ignore. The actor spent over forty weeks

With Lois Nettleton and George Kennedy in *The Good Guys and the Bad Guys* (WB, 1969)

326

With Mrs. Mitchum in 1970

With Sarah Miles in *Ryan's Daughter* (MGM, 1970)

doing the difficult location work on the feature. Because of the perfectionism of meticulous director Lean, the project's shooting schedule was lengthened, and the film finally cost over fourteen million dollars.

Set in 1916 Ireland, Mitchum is Charles Shaughnessy, schoolmaster in the village of Kirrary, who weds local girl Rosy Ryan (Sarah Miles) who is half his age. Because of Shaughnessy's impotency the fickle colleen is drawn into an affair with a wounded British officer, Randolph Doryan (Christopher Jones), who has taken command of the nearby army garrison. Gossip of the affair convinces the locals that the girl is a spy for the British and she and Jones' Doryan are forced to confront the villagers. She is shamed in front of her neighbors, while the soldier later commits suicide. Mitchum's Shaughnessy and Miles' Rosy decide to leave Kirrary, pretending to themselves and to others that their domestic relationship will improve.

Although Mitchum was among the many (producers, distributors, and theatre patrons) who were unhappy and undecided about *Ryan's Daughter* as a viable property, his performance won acclaim and there was even talk of his being Oscarnominated. Several critical sources thought the star had been miscast, echoing the words of Lean who had stated that he had cast the actor in the part because it was against the grain of his usual characterization. But at the same time, there were those critics who agreed with Judith Crist that this was "his finest performance in many years." Through a saturation publicity campaign and constant re-editing of the feature to a shorter running time, the picture was able to gross $13.4 million in distributors' domestic rentals, but in no way could it be termed a substantial hit, particularly considering its original cost. John Mills, as the village idiot Michael, did win a Best Supporting Actor's Academy Award, but Robert was not even nominated.

The star did make headlines late in 1970 when at a film students' screening of

Ryan's Daughter, he distributed marijuana to the youths. He later explained that the grass "was laid on me by some cat and I told the students, 'Now I'll lay it on you.' " He added, "There was tight security around my hotel and I didn't know what to do with it."

Following *Ryan's Daughter,* Mitchum let it again be known that he had retired to "be a bum." His agent, Bullets Durgom, told Earl Wilson, "I don't think he'll work again unless he gets something like *The Birth of a Nation.*" Interestingly enough, the frequently very private star began making a tour of television talk shows to promote *Ryan's Daughter,* an activity he has continued with each successive celluloid venture. Being his usual laconic, calm self, he continually delights video audiences with his long-winded and amusing stories, and his impersonations.

It was not a remake of D. W. Griffith's masterpiece which brought Robert back to films but a "look at my 1971 taxes." He returned to MGM for a very solid melodrama, *Going Home* (1971), which the studio unfortunately was in no position to promote properly. Filmed largely in Wildwood, New Jersey, this feature, produced and directed by Robert B. Leonard, told of a Korean War hero, Harry K. Graham (Mitchum), who is paroled after two decades in prison for killing his unfaithful wife. He returns to a bleak existence at a seashore town and finds a new girlfriend, Jenny (Brenda Vaccaro), and his son Jimmy (Jan-Michael Vincent)[28] who has hated him since the killing of his mother. Regarding this well-intentioned narrative which unfortunately veered too often into lurid melodrama, Roger Ebert (*Chicago Sun-Times*) reported: "[It's] worth seeing primarily for the presence of Robert Mitchum. Not that he's especially good; Mitchum can't be described as good or bad in most of his performances. It's just that he's there, the kind of screen presence that draws your attention. . . . He remains the favorite movie star of a lot of people (myself probably included) and he is able to make a bad movie interesting." Wanda Hale in her three-and-a-half star *New York Daily News* review judged that "Mitchum's extraordinary performance of an ordinary man is one of the best performances of the year." *Going Home* proved to be one of the more-talked-about-than-seen films of the seventies.

While making *Going Home,* Mitchum had injured his shoulder and thus was unhappy about starting work on his next project, *The Wrath of God* (MGM, 1972). Shot in Mexico, this tongue-in-cheek Western offered Robert as a cigar-smoking, hard-drinking, gun-toting (in a Bible) priest mixed up in a Latin American rebellion. Along with comrades Victor Buono and Ken Hutchison, he is opposed to tyrant Frank Langella who has a worried mother (Rita Hayworth).[29]

Mitchum enjoyed a number of good scenes in the picture as the nominal hero. In one bittersweet moment he listlessly reads the last rites to a line of men as they are about to be executed. When the slaughter is over he gingerly walks over the bodies and goes on his way. *Cue* Magazine said the actor gave "one of his customary sincere performances." The sincerity of his acting was a fact moviegoers had known for years.

The Wrath of God made no inroads in the boxoffice, and in 1973 Robert returned

[28]Recently, Vincent said of Mitchum, "He just has the right attitude about himself and the work he does—to not take it so seriously—yet, he always tries to do this fantastic job, taking it with a certain kind of lightness. I think he's a great actor. People say he does walk through a lot of his parts, but he can do more walking through a part than most people can do giving it every bit of juice they've got."

[29]It was Mitchum who convinced his *Fire Down Below* co-star to accept this "comeback" role.

to Paramount for *The Friends of Eddie Coyle*. Shot largely on location in Boston, it detailed the plight of a petty hoodlum, Eddie Coyle (Robert), who is faced with a prison rap in New Hampshire. To appease the police (and possibly to escape conviction), and to keep his wife and two children out of the poorhouse, he agrees to a bout of gun running and informing for the police on the side. Caught in the middle between the law and the lawless, each thinking he has betrayed them, Mitchum's Eddie Coyle is taken for a one way ride by Dillon, one of his "pals" (Peter Boyle).

As the hoodlum known as "Fingers," because he once messed up a job and a gang leader smashed his hand in a drawer, Robert offered a near flawless picture of an aging, small-time punk, a man who is not really evil. He is merely earning money the best way he knows in order to keep his family "off welfare." Any actor of any generation would have been pleased to offer the performance Mitchum did in this Peter Yates-directed venture.

Then the star journeyed to Japan to star in *The Yakuza* (Warner Bros. 1975), which is an attempt to Anglicize a very Oriental genre of picture. The extent of fan reaction to Mitchum's arrival in Japan amazed the easy-going star.

When *The Yakuza* debuted in the spring of 1975, there was much talk about it being the start of a new vogue of Mitchum popularity. Rex Reed in his syndicated column described the star of this film "as ravaged as a bomb site in Hiroshima, as sleepy as a wombat, and as gloriously bigger than life as the Imperial Hotel." *Hollywood Reporter* had greater praise. "A romantic role for Robert Mitchum as a gunman with honor, written by Paul Schrader and Robert Towne (of *Chinatown* Oscar fame) as Hawksian homage to the code of morals of the Japanese gangster, is handsomely realized. Mitchum's role is well-modeled on his own anti-hero 'film noir' origins, with much self-conscious comment on aging. 'Goddamit, I'm getting

In *The Wrath of God* (MGM, 1972)

With Michael McCreery and Peter Boyle in *The Friends of Eddie Coyle* (Par., 1973)

In *The Yakuza* (WB, 1975)

In *Farewell, My Lovely* (Avco Emb, 1975).

too old for this,' Mitchum grudges as he pushes away the woman he had just tried to kiss romantically."

The success of this film made the professional calamities of the past seem bearable. In the spring of 1974 Mitchum had been announced for the lead in *Rosebud* for United Artists, which would have re-united him with director Otto Preminger. In this, their third film together, he was to be cast as an American intelligence agent opposing terrorists who kidnap the five daughters of rich families. After three weeks of production work on Corsica, Mitchum made headlines when he "quit" the film. Rumors spread, claiming that Preminger had found the star drunk for a 6 A.M. shooting call.[30] But the actor retorted: "Otto is the last of the Hollywood dinosaurs. He tends to overact at times. I know his reputation—that he scares hell out of people. But he doesn't frighten me." Peter O'Toole was quickly hired to replace Mitchum.

Later, in Madrid, where Mitchum and his wife were visiting their son Chris, who was making a film there, he told a reporter, "He [Preminger] obviously didn't want me." Then the veteran star added that there was an Italian producer who did want him for an on-going project. However the actor declined the offer, saying there might be a lawsuit over his quick departure from *Rosebud*. "But," reasoned the Rome-based filmmaker, "I just want you for closeups—you only have to breathe hard!"

Following an array of on-again, off-again projects for Mitchum was *Jackpot*, which director Terence Young intended for Robert, Sophia Loren, and Richard Burton. Miss Loren dropped out and Charlotte Rampling replaced her. The ever-active Burton claimed he agreed to remain in the long-delayed project because "I wanted to work with Mitchum. We would be marvelous foils for each other. He's slow dynamite!" But by the time the feature got underway in Rome in January, 1975, Mitchum had become leery of the production. He claimed it was going to interfere with his pending deal to star in a remake of *Farewell, My Lovely* as the famed fictional detective Philip Marlowe. He now wanted "out." By the middle of the month his wish was granted and James Coburn was substituted." *Jackpot*, for lack of finances, was later reshelved permanently.

By this time volatile Otto Preminger had completed *Rosebud* (which proved to be a box-office dud when released by United Artists in 1975) and had now changed his public attitude to Mitchum. "[He] is a lovely man. It was a pity we could not see eye to eye. Maybe we'll do another picture together soon."

The new edition of *Farewell, My Lovely* (Avco Embassy, 1975) is the third screen version of Raymond Chandler's detective thriller. For many it was the best interpretation yet of the near-classic work. As the *New York Times* observed, "The strengths of this movie are in Mr. Chandler and in the high quality of a lot of the acting. The author's lines, tough, funny and baroque, get full value. Robert Mitchum always takes getting to know in a role. He comes on too strongly at first: too stagey, too droopy an eye, an excessively dangling cigarette. But he settles into his part, his performance drops away and he moves through the picture with force, humor and unexpected humility. Inevitably you think of Bogart; he isn't Bogart but he is very

---

[30]In 1973 Mitchum had narrated *America on the Rocks*, which was financed by the National Institute for Alcohol Abuse and Alcoholism. The documentary's project director, Frank Kavanaugh, said of Mitchum's participation, "I don't think he had any overrriding interest in the problem, or had any particular problem with it himself. He was just interested in doing some public service work."

good." Set in the nineteen forties the picture sought to rejuvenate the detective caper, even to having Charlotte Rampling cast as a Lauren Bacall-type doll. Nearly everyone agreed that it was Mitchum's presence, above all, which gave the production stability and boxoffice punch. It proved to be a big moneymaker in the recession-torn 1975.

Today, in the second half of the seventies, only Robert Mitchum and John Wayne remain as vestiges of the male movie stars who are stars of that medium only.[31] Mitchum has since performed in front of the cameras for Paramount's *The Last Tycoon* with Robert De Niro as F. Scott Fitzgerald's film industry "hero." Thereafter Mitchum moved over to Universal for its World War II epic *Midway* (1976), directed by John Guillermin. In a cast which includes Charlton Heston and Henry Fonda, Robert portrays Admiral William F. Halsey.

At this mature period in his career, Mitchum the rebel remains true to his reputation. He is very outspoken on a variety of subjects:

"I don't believe in politics or politicians. In general, politicians are all unsuccessful actors. The only good politician I've ever met—the only honest one—is Barry Goldwater. The Kennedys weren't worth anything, especially poor Bobby who had a child for every election."

Regarding finances: "Not as rich as I could have been. I've given plenty of things to my friends. I'm not a saver and I have no companies in Switzerland. I pay my taxes. What taxes leave me, my horses eat up. In case of necessity, I know a lot of rich women. . . . If I could summon the energy, my idea is to go everywhere, maybe Lake Como, the Bahamas, Switzerland, Africa. I read in the papers how rich I am, why not go?"

On filmmaking: "I have a remarkable resistance to starvation so I work when I have to. It's the heavy loot that interferes with my loafing. I don't think I'd miss the movies. Most of them stink and for my part stardom is meaningless. For God's sake, Rin-Tin-Tin was a star. . . . I am in the freak business. 'That's him, touch him, get him, he's escaped from the zoo.' When people recognize me, it terrifies me. I can't think that many people all headed in your direction can mean you well, they can't be anything but a lynch mob or covering up for a pickpocket. They must have better things to do. . . . I want to sleep. That's my life, trying to sleep. I'll make it someday, too. I'm trying to grow three toes so I can hang by my feet."

About career success: "Essentially [I attribute it] to my skeleton, to my low voice, to my broken nose and to my Bulgarian warrior walk. That's enough. Also, I have an air of being the average guy. I'm not like Brando, who makes guys jealous. When I appear on the screen, guys think: 'If he's become a star, I can hope for anything.' And if their chicks sigh while watching me, they don't let them down. Guys and girls like me."

The other element in his life, his family, is of the utmost importance for Mitchum. He has been exceedingly loyal to his mother, step-father, brother, sister, half-sister, and his wife and children. With pride he states he has been married to the same woman ("I *think* it's the same woman") for over three-and-a-half decades. Columnist Earl Wilson once wrote, "If a wife ever understood a husband, it's Dorothy Mitchum. She's a paragon of patience. She also knows, and says, when the party's over." Mitchum once commented, "My wife is a wonderful woman. She has one fault: she's a bit jealous." Of his offspring, he says, "All our kids are individuals.

[31]He did agree to guest-star on "The Jim Stafford Show" which debuted on ABC-TV July 30, 1975. Mitchum acknowledges himself a "long-standing, self-imposed exile" from the medium.

I was raised an individual and so were they. They're loved and well founded and if they can't think beyond that for themselves, then tough shoes. I hope they learn, decide to contribute, to do something beyond just 'getting.' Maybe you can reach above high C, but if nobody hears you, so what?"

A thoroughgoing professional, Mitchum is above all a thoughtful soul who employs assorted facades to disguise his soft center. "I don't like letting people down because I don't want the responsibility or the involvement. I do my thing and I leave. I guess I must be good at my job because they wouldn't pay me all that money if I weren't. In a movie there's got to be somebody to carry the ball, somebody professional enough to keep things moving. That's me. Everybody can't stop the action to do their own vaudeville act. I'm like a plumber's plumber, a highly paid arrangement, and I'm not glamour-conscious anyway. I try to get the scene finished off in one take, so it'll be cheap and quick and I can go home."

ROBERT MITCHUM

HOPPY SERVES A WRIT *(United Artists, 1943), 67 min.*
    Producer, Harry Sherman; associate producer, Lewis Rachmil; director, George Archainbaud; based on the characters created by Clarence E. Mulford; screenplay, Gerald Geraghty; music director, Irwin Talbot; art director, Ralph Berger; set decorator, Emile Kuri; assistant director, Glenn Cook; sound, William Wilmarth; camera, Russell Harlan; editor, Sherman A. Rose.

    William Boyd (Hopalong Cassidy); Andy Clyde (California Carlson); Jay Kirby (Johnny Travers); Victor Jory (Tom Jordan); George Reeves (Steve Jordan); Jan Christy (Jean Hollister); Hal Taliaferro (Greg Jordan); Forbes Murray (Ben Hollister); Byron Foulger (Storekeeper Danvers); Earle Hodgins (Jim Belnap the Clerk); Roy Barcroft (Tod Colby); Ben Corbett (Card Player); Robert Mitchum (Rigney).

BORDER PATROL *(United Artists, 1943), 64 min.*
    Producer, Harry Sherman; associate producer, Lewis J. Rachmil; director, Lesley Selander; based on characters created by Clarence E. Mulford; screenplay, Michael Wilson; art director, Glenn Cook; set decorator, Emile Kuri; assistant director, Cook; sound, William Wilmarth; camera, Russell Harlan; editor, Sherman A. Rose.

    William Boyd (Hopalong Cassidy); Andy Clyde (California Carlson); Jay Kirby (Johnny Travers); Russell Simpson (Orestes Krebs); Claudia Drake (Inez); Cliff Parkinson (Don Enrique); George Reeves, Duncan Renaldo, Pierce Lyden, Robert Mitchum (Bits).

THE LEATHER BURNERS *(United Artists, 1943), 66 min.*
    Producer, Harry Sherman; associate producer, Lewis J. Rachmil; director, Joseph E. Henabery; based on the characters created by Clarence E. Mulford; story, Bliss Lomax; screenplay, Jo Pagano; music, Samuel Kaylin; music director, Irvin Talbot; art director, Ralph Berger; assistant director, Glenn Cook; sound, William Wilmarth; camera, Russell Harlan; editor, Carroll Lewis.

    William Boyd (Hopalong Cassidy); Andy Clyde (California Carlson); Jay Kirby (Johnny); Victor Jory (Dan Slack); George Givot (Sam Bucktoe); Shelley Spencer (Sharon Longstreet);

Bobby Larson (Bobby Longstreet); George Reeves (Harrison Brooke); Hal Taliaferro (Lafe); Forbes Murray (Bart); Robert Mitchum (Bit).

FOLLOW THE BAND (Universal, 1943), 61 min.

Associate producer, Paul Malvern; director, Jean Yarbrough; based on the story by Richard English; screenplay, Warren Wilson, Dorothy Bennett; art directors, John B. Goodman, Ralph De Lacy; set decorators, Russell A. Gausman, A. J. Gilmore; music director, Charles Previn; choreography, Louis Da Pron; songs, Everett Carter and Milton Rosen; Roc Hillman and Johnny Napton; Harold Adamson and Johnny Noble; Don Raye and Gene DePaul; Robert Crawford; assistant director, Mack Wright; sound, B. Brown, Edwin Wetzel; camera, Elwood Bredell; editor, Milton Carruth.

Eddie Quillan (Marvin Howe); Mary Beth Hughes (Dolly O'Brien); Leon Errol (Mike O'Brien); Anne Rooney (Juanita Turnbull); Samuel S.Hinds (Pop Turnbull); Robert Mitchum (Tate Winters); Russell Hicks (Jeremiah K. Barton); Bennie Bartlett (Cootie); Frank Coghlan, Jr. (Bert); Jean Ames (Lucille Rose); Frances Langford, Leo Carrillo, Ray Eberle, Alvino Rey & The King Sisters, Kings Men & Skinnay Ennis & Groove Boys, Hilo Hattie, The Bombardiers (Themselves); Irving Bacon (Peterson); Isabel Randolph (Mrs. Forbes); Frak Faylen (Brooks); Robert Dudley (Seth Cathcart); Paul Dubov (Alphonse); Frank Mitchell (Charlie); Joe Bernard (Mr. Hawkins); Charles H. Sherlock (Photographer).

COLT COMRADES (United Artists, 1943), 67 min.

Producer, Harry Sherman; associate producer, Lewis J. Rachmil; director, Lesley Selander; based on characters created by Clarence Mulford; screenplay, Michael Wilson; art director, Ralph Berger; assistant director, Glenn Cook; sound, Jack Noyes; camera, Russell Harlan; editor, Sherman A. Rose.

William Boyd (Hopalong Cassidy); Andy Clyde (California Carlson); Jay Kirby (Johnny Nelson); George Reeves (Lin Whitlock); Gayle Lord (Lucy Whitlock); Earle Hodgins (Wildcat Willy); Victor Jory (Jebb Hardin); Douglas Fowley (Joe Brass); Herb Rawlinson (Varney); Robert Mitchum (Henchman).

THE HUMAN COMEDY (MGM, 1943), 118 min.

Producer-director, Clarence Brown; based on the novel by William Saroyan; screenplay, Howard Estabrook; music, Herbert Stothart; choreography, Ernst Matray; art directors, Cedric Gibbons, Paul Groesse; set decorators, Edwin B. Willis, Hugh Hunt; assistant director, Hugh Boswell; sound. W. R. Sparks; camera, Harry Stradling; editor, Conrad A. Nervig.

Mickey Rooney (Homer Macauley); James Craig (Tom Spangler); Frank Morgan (Willie Grogan); Fay Bainter (Mrs. Macauley); Marsha Hunt (Diana Steed); Van Johnson (Marcus Macauley); Donna Reed (Bess Macauley); John Craven (Tobey George); Dorothy Morris (Mary Arena); Jack "Butch" Jenkins (Ulysses Macauley); Mary Nash (Miss Hicks); Katharine Alexander (Mrs. Steed); Ray Collins (Matthew); Henry O'Neill (Charles Steed); Darryl Hickman (Lionel); S. Z. Sakall (Mr. Ara); Alan Baxter (Brad Stickman); Barry Nelson (Fat); Don DeFore (Texas); Robert Mitchum (Horse); Ann Ayars (Mrs. Sandoval); Ernest Whitman (Black Man); Mark Daniels, William Roberts (Soldiers); Rita Quigley (Helen Elliott); David Holt (Hubert Ackley); Byron Foulger (Blenton); Wally Cassell (A Flirt); Carl Switzer (Auggie); Conrad Binyon (Gang Member); Clem Bevans (Henderson); Connie Gilchrist (Dolly); Emory Parnell (Policeman); Frank Jenks (Larry); Robert Emmet O'Connor (Bartender); Gilbson Gowland (Leonine Type Man); Hooper Atchley, Guy D'Ennery (Men on Street); Clancy Cooper (Mess Sergeant); Don Taylor (Soldier at Railroad Station); Sarah Padden (Mother at

Railroad Station); Frank Jenks (Larry), Adeline deWalt Reynolds (Librarian), Hobart Cavanaugh (Drunk at Bar).

WE'VE NEVER BEEN LICKED *(Universal, 1943), 103 min.*
Producer, Walter Wanger; director, John Rawlins; story, Norman Reilly Raine; screenplay, Raine, Nick Grinde; flying scenes director, Vernon Keays; art directors, John B. Goodman, Alexander Golitzen; dialogue director, Gene Lewis; military technical adviser, Colonel J. K. Boles, U.S. Army; music director, Charles Previn; music, Frank Skinner; vocal arranger, Ken Darby; songs, Harry Revel and Paul Francis Webster; technical adviser (battle sequence), Lieutenant Commander John S. Thach, U.S. Navy; assistant director, Fred Frank; sound, Bernard B. Brown, William Fox; camera, Milton Krasner; editor, Philip Cahn.

Richard Quine (Brad Craig); Anne Gwynne (Nina Lambert); Martha O'Driscoll (DeeDee Dunham); Noah Beery, Jr. (Cyanide Jenkins); William Frawley (Traveling Salesman); William Blees (Student); Harry Davenport ("Pop" Lambert); Edgar Barrier (Nishikawa); Samuel S. Hinds (Colonel Jason Craig); Moroni Olsen (Commandant Colonel J. Armstrong); Roland Got (Kazuo Matsui); Allen Jung (Kubo); Robert Mitchum (Panhandle Mitchell); Alfredo DeSa (Fortuno Tavares); Bill Stern (Himself); George Putnam (Army Hour Announcements); Malcolm McTaggart (Chip Goodwin); Paul Dubov, Dick Chandlee, David Street, Michael Moore, Danny Jackson, Roger Daniel, Dick Morris, Herbert Gunn, Henry Rogers, John Forrest, William Lechner, Bob Lowell, Michael Towne, Bill Nash, Jackie Ray, Jack Edwards, Jr., Ward Wood (Students); Gordon Wynne (Hank James); Cliff Robertson (Adams); Mantan Moreland (Willie); Frank Tang (Yoshida); John Frazer (Flight Commander); Students of Texas State College for Women (Girls); Richard Gunn (Officer); Big Wilkie Zapalec (Football Player); Henry Hall (Conductor); Kendall Bryson (Deck Officer); Bruce Wong (Japanese Messenger); Alex Havier (Japanese Sniper); Paul Langton (Naval Officer); Walter Bonn (German Mentor); Franco Corsaro (Italian Mentor); Beal Wong (Japanese Mentor).

BEYOND THE LAST FRONTIER *(Republic, 1943), 57 min.*
Associate producer, Louis Gray; director, Howard Bretherton; screenplay, John K. Butler, Morton Grant; art director, Russell Kimball; set decorator, Charles Thompson; music, Mort Glickman; assistant director, Derwin Abrahams; sound, Ed Borschell; camera, Bud Thackery; editor, Charles Craft.

Eddie Dew (John Paul Revere); Smiley Burnette (Frog Millhouse); Lorraine Miller (Susan Cook); Robert Mitchum (Trigger Dolan); Ernie Adams (Sarge Kincaid); Richard Clarke (Steve Kincaid); Charles Miller (Major Cook); Jack Kirk (Slade); Kermit Maynard (Clyde Barton); Harry Woods (Big Bill Hadley); Curley Dresden (Stage Driver-Ranger); Cactus Mack, Al Taylor (Henchmen); Frank O'Connor (Bartender); Ring-Eye (Frog's Horse); Jack Rockwell (Recruiting Sergeant); Tom Steele (Dew's Double); Henry Willis (Henchman-Driver); Wheaton Chambers (Doc Jessup).

BAR 20 *(United Artists, 1943), 53 min.*
Producer, Harry Sherman; associate producer, Lewis J. Rachmil; director, Lesley Selander; based on characters created by Clarence E. Mulford; screenplay, Morton Grant, Norman Houston, Michael Wilson; music director, Irvin Talbot; art director, Ralph Berger; assistant director, Glenn Cook; sound, Jack Noyes; camera, Russell Harlan; editor, Carroll Lewis.

William Boyd (Hopalong Cassidy); Andy Clyde (California Carlson); George Reeves (Lin Bradley); Dustine Farnum (Marie Stewart); Victor Jory (Mark Jackson); Douglas Fowley (Slash); Betty Blythe (Mrs. Stevens); Robert Mitchum (Richard Adams); Francis McDonald (One Eye); Earle Hodgins (Tom).

337

DOUGHBOYS IN IRELAND *(Columbia, 1943), 61 min.*

Producer, Jack Fier; director, Lew Landers; screenplay, Howard J. Green; additional dialogue, Monte Brice; art directors, Lionel Banks, Paul Murphy; set decorator, Frank Tuttle; music director, Morris W. Stoloff; assistant director, William Mull; sound, Ed Bernds; camera, L. W. O'Connell; editor, Mel Thorsen.

Kenny Baker (Danny O'Keefe); Jeff Donnell (Molly Callahan); Lynn Merrick (Gloria Gold); Guy Bonham (Chuck Mayers); Red Latham (Corny Smith); Wamp Carlson (Tiny Johnson); Robert Mitchum (Ernie Jones); Buddy Yarus (Jimmy Martin); Harry Shannon (Michale Callahan); Dorothy Vaughan (Mrs. Callahan); Larry Thompson (Captain); Syd Saylor (Sergeant); Herbert Rawlinson (Larry Hunt); Neil Reagan (Medical Captain); Constance Purdy (Miss Wood); Harry Anderson (Soldier); James Carpenter (Sentry); Craig Woods (Corporal); Muni Seroff (Nick Broco).

CORVETTE K-225 *(Universal, 1943), 99 min.*

Producer, Howard Hawks; director, Richard Rosson; screenplay, John Rhodes Sturdy, Lieutenant, R.C.N.V.R.; art directors, John B. Goodman, Robert Boyle; set decorators, R. A. Gausman, A. J. Gilmore; music, David Buttolph; music director, Charles Previn; assistant director, William Tummell; sound, Bernard Brown, Edwin Wetzel; special camera effects, John Fulton; camera, Tony Gaudio; convoy camera, Harry Perry; editor, Edward Curtiss.

Randolph Scott (Lieutenant Commander MacClain); James Brown (Lieutenant Paul Cartwright); Ella Raines (Joyce Cartwright); Barry Fitzgerald (Stokey O'Meara); Andy Devine (Walsh): Fuzzy Knight (Cricket); Noah Beery, Jr. (Stone); Richard Lane (Vice Admiral); Thomas Gomez (Smithy); David Bruce (Lieutenant Rawlins); Murray Alper (Jones); James Flavin (Lieutenant Gardner); Walter Sande (Evans); Edmund MacDonald (LeBlanc the Navigator); Matt Willis (Roger); Robert Mitchum (Sheppard); Charles McGraw (E.R.A.); Oscar O'Shea (Captain Smith); Addison Richards (Commander Rowland); Jack Wegman (Naval Captain); James Dodd (Steward); John Diggs (Bailey the Naval Rating Man); Milburn Stone (Canadian Captain); Lester Matthews (British Captain); Ian Wolfe (Paymaster Commander); Holmes Herbert (Commodore Ramsay); Frank Faylen, Charles Cane (Workmen); Oliver Blake (Cook); William Forrest (Commander Manning); John Mylong (Submarine Commander); Guy Kingsford (R.A.F. Pilot); John Frederick, Jack Mulhall, Stewart Garner (Officers); Franklin Parker (Captain); Rod Bacon (Naval Academy Graduate); Peter Lawford (Naval Officer); Frank Coghlan, Jr. (Rating); Eddie Dew (Crewman); Jack Luden (Merchant Marine Officer); Cliff Robertson (Lookout); Richard Crane (Leading Torpedo Man); Michael Kirk (Petty Officer).

AERIAL GUNNER *(Paramount, 1943), 78 min.*

Producers, William Pine, William Thomas; director, Pine; screenplay, Maxwell Shane; art director, F. Paul Sylos; music director, Daniele Amfitheatrof; assistant director, Robert Farfan; sound, Charles Althouse; camera, Fred Jackman, Jr.; editor, William Zeigler.

Chester Morris (Foxy Pattis); Richard Arlen (Ben Davis); Lita Ward (Peggy Lunt); Jimmy Lydon (Sandy Lunt); Dick Purcell (Gadget Blaine); Keith Richards (Sergeant Jones); Billy Benedict (Private Laswell); Ralph Sanford (Barclay); Robert Mitchum (Flyer).

THE LONE STAR TRAIL *(Universal, 1943), 58 min.*

Associate producer, Oliver Drake; director, Ray Taylor; story, Victor Halperin; screenplay, Drake; art director, John Goodman; music director, Hans J. Salter; songs, Milton Rosen and Everett Carter; Drake and Jimmy Wakely; Dick Reinhart and Wakely; camera, William Sickner; editor, Ray Snyder.

Johnny Mack Brown (Blaze Barker); Tex Ritter (Fargo Steele); Fuzzy Knight (Angus Mc-Angus); Jennifer Holt (Joan Winters); Robert Mitchum (Ben Slocum); George Eldredge (Doug Ransom); Michael Vallon (Jonathan Bentley); Harry Strang (Sheriff Waddel); Earle Hodgins (Mayor Cyrus Jenkins); Jack Ingram (Dan Jason); Jimmy Wakely, Johnny Bond, Scotty Harrell (Members of Jimmy Wakely Trio); Billy Engle (Shorty the Stage Passenger); William Desmond (Mike the Bartender/Townsman); Denver Dixon, Carl Mathews (Townsmen); Bob Reeves (Barfly); Tom Steele (Robert Mitchum's Double); Eddie Parker (Lynch); Ethan Laidlaw (Steve Bannister the Cattle Buyer); Henry Roquemore (Bank Teller).

FALSE COLORS *(United Artists, 1943), 65 min.*

Producer, Harry Sherman; associate producer, Lewis J. Rachmil; director, George Archainbaud; based on characters created by Clarence E. Mulford; screenplay, Bennett Cohen; assistant director, Glenn Cook; art director, Ralph Berger; set decorator, Emile Kuri; sound, Jack Noyes; camera, Russell Harlan; editor, Fred Berger.

William Boyd (Hopalong Cassidy) Andy Clyde (California Carlson); Jimmy Rogers (Himself); Tom Seidel (Bud Lawton/Kit Mayer); Claudia Drake (Faith Lawton); Douglass Dumbrille (Mark Foster); Robert Mitchum (Rip Austin); Glenn Strange (Sonora); Pierce Lyden (Lefty); Roy Barcroft (Sheriff Clem Martin); Sam Flint (Judge Stevens); Earle Hodgins (Lawyer Jay Griffin); Elmer Jerome (Jed Stevers); Tom London (Townsman); Dan White (Bar Spectator); George Morrell (Denton the Townsman).

THE DANCING MASTERS *(Twentieth Century-Fox, 1943), 63 min.*

Producer, Lee Marcus; director, Malcolm St. Clair; story, George Bricker; screenplay, W. Scott Darling; art directors, James Basevi, Chester Gore; set decorators, Thomas Little, Al Orenbach; music director, Emil Newman; music, Arthur Lange; assistant director, Sam Schneider; sound, Bernard Freericks, Harry M. Leonard; special effects, Fred Sersen; camera, Norbert Brodine; editor, Norman Colbert.

Stan Laurel, Oliver Hardy (Themselves); Trudy Marshall (Mary Harlan); Robert Bailey (Grant Lawrence); Matt Briggs (Wentworth Harlan); Margaret Dumont (Mrs. Holland); Allan Lane (George Worthing); Nestor Paiva (Silvio); George Lloyd (Jasper); Robert Mitchum (Mickey); Edward Earle (Clerk); Charles Rogers (Butler); Sherry Hall (Dentist); Sam Ash (Pianist); William Haade, Jack Stoney (Truck Drivers); Arthur Space (Director); Daphne Pollard (Mother); Ruthe Brady (Bit); Buddy Yarus (Gangster); Louis Bacigalupi (Patient); Hank Mann (Vegetable Man); Buffalo Bill, Jr. (Stage Driver); Harry Tyler (Man); Florence Shirley (Matron); Emory Parnell (Featherstone); Robert Emmett Keane (Auctioneer); Chick Collins (Bus Driver).

RIDERS OF THE DEADLINE *(United Artists, 1943), 68 min.*

Producer, Harry Sherman; associate producer, Lewis J. Rachmil; director, Lesley Selander; based on characters created by Clarence E. Mulford; screenplay, Bennett Cohen; art director, Ralph Berger; set decorator, Emile Kuri; assistant director, Glenn Cook; sound, Jack Noyes; camera, Russell Harlan; editor, Walter Hannemann.

William Boyd (Hopalong Cassidy); Andy Clyde (California Carlson); Jimmy Rogers (Himself); Richard Crane (Tim Mason); Frances Woodward (Sue); William Halligan (Crandall); Tony Warde (Madigan); Robert Mitchum (Drago); Jim Bannon (Tex); Hugh Prosser (Martin); Herbert Rawlinson (Captain Jennings); Montie Montana (Calhoun); Earle Hodgins (Sourdough); Bill Beckford (Kilroy); Pierce Lyden (Sanders).

GUNG HO! *(Universal, 1943), 88 min.*
Producer, Walter Wanger; director, Ray Enright; based on the story by Lieutenant W. S. Le Francois, M.S.M.C.; screenplay, Lucien Hubbard; additional dialogue, Joseph Hoffman; music, Frank Skinner; music conductor, H. J. Salter; art directors, John B. Goodman, Alexander Golitzen; set decorators, R. A. Gausman, A. J. Gilmore; assistant director, Fred Frank; sound, B. Brown, Ed Wetzel; special camera, John R. Fulton; camera, Milton Krasner; editor, Milton Carruth.

Randolph Scott (Colonel Thorwald); Grace MacDonald (Kathleen Corrigan); Alan Curtis (John Harbison); Noah Beery, Jr. (Kurt Richter); J. Carroll Naish (Lieutenant Christoforos); David Bruce (Larry O'Ryan); Peter Coe (Kozzarowski); Robert Mitchum (Pigiron Matthews); Richard Lane (Captain Dunphy); Rod Cameron (Rube Tedrow); Sam Levene (Transport); Milburn Stone (Commander Blake); Harold Landon (Frankie Montana); John James (Buddy Andrews); Louis Jean Heydt (Lieutenant Roland Browning); Walter Sande (Gunner Mc-Bride); Harry Strang (Sergeant Jim Corrigan); Irving Bacon (Waiter); Joe Haworth (Singing Marine); Carl Varnell (Marine on Submarine); Chet Huntley (Narrator); Robert Kent (Submarine Officer).

MINESWEEPER *(Paramount, 1943), 69 min.*
Producers, William Pine, William Thomas; director, William Berke; screenplay, Edward T. Lowe, Maxwell Shane; art director, F. Paul Sylos; set decorator, Ben Berk; music, Mort Glickman; assistant director, Eddie Mull; sound, Frank Webster; camera, Fred Jackman, Jr.; editor, William Ziegler.

Richard Arlen (Jim Smith); Jean Parker (Mary Smith); Russel Hayden (Elliot); Guinn Williams (Fixit); Emma Dunn (Moms); Charles D. Brown (Commander); Frank Fenton (Lieutenant Gilpin); Chick Chandler (Corney Welch); Douglas Fowley (Lieutenant Wells); Ralph Sanford (Cox); Billy Nelson (Boatswain Helms); Robert Mitchum (Bit).

CRY HAVOC *(MGM, 1943), 97 min.*
Producer, Edwin Knopf; director, Richard Thorpe; based on the play by Allan R. Kenward; screenplay, Paul Osborne; art directors, Cedric Gibbons, Stephen Goosson; set decorators, Edwin B. Willis, Glen Barner; assistant director, Rollie Asher; music, Daniele Amfitheatrof; sound, Frank B. MacKenzie; camera, Karl Freund; editor, Ralph E. Winters.

Margaret Sullavan (Lieutenant Smith); Ann Sothern (Pat); Joan Blondell (Grace); Fay Bainter (Captain Marsh); Marsha Hunt (Flo Norris); Ella Raines (Connie); Connie Gilchrist (Sadie); Heather Angel (Andra); Dorothy Morris (Sue); Gloria Grafton (Steve); Frances Gifford (Helen); Fely Franquelli (Lusita); Diana Lewis (Nydia); Billy Cruz (Philippine Boy); Allan Byron [Jack Randall] (Lieutenant Holt); William Bishop, Victor Kilian, Jr. (Soldiers); James Warren, Richard Crane, Bill Cartledge, Paul Oman (Men); Robert Mitchum (Groaning Man); Lorin Raker (Voice of Japanese Pilot); Bob Lowell (Dying Soldier); Russ Clark (Doctor); Richard Derr (Marine); Anna Q. Nilsson (Nurse); Morris Ankrum (Chaplain); Joy Louie (Frightened Child).

JOHNNY DOESN'T LIVE HERE ANYMORE *(Monogram, 1944), 77 min.*
Producer, Maurice King; associate producer, Franklin King; director, Joe May; story, Alice Means; screenplay, Philip Yordan, John Kafka; art directors, Paul Palmentola, George Moskov; set decorator, Tommy Thompson; music, W. Franke Harling; assistant director, Clarence Bricker; sound, Tom Lambert; special effects, Ray Mercer; camera, Ira Morgan; editor, Martin G. Cohn.

Simone Simon (Kathie); James Ellison (Mike); William Terry (Johnny); Minna Gombell (Mrs. Collins); Chick Chandler (Jack); Alan Dinehart (Judge); Gladys Blake (Sally); Robert Mitchum (Jeff); Dorothy Granger (Irene); Grady Sutton (George); Chester Clute (Mr. Collins); Fern Emmett (Shrew); Jerry Maren (Gremlin); Janet Shaw (Gladys); Joe Devlin (Iceman); Douglas Fowley (Rudy); Charles Williams (Bailiff); Rondo Hatton (Undertaker).

WHEN STRANGERS MARRY (*Monogram, 1944*), *67 min.* (TV title: *And So They Were Married.* Reissue title: *Betrayed.*)

Producers, Maurice King, Franklin King; director, William Castle; story, George V. Moscov; screenplay, Philip Yordan, Dennis Cooper; art director, F. Paul Sylos; assistant director, Clarence Bricker; music, Dmitri Tiomkin; sound, Tom Lambert; camera, Ira Morgan; editor, Martin G. Cohn.

Dean Jagger (Paul); Kim Hunter (Millie); Robert Mitchum (Fred); Neil Hamilton (Blake); Lou Lubin (Houser); Milton Kibbee (Charlie); Dewey Robinson (Newsstand Man); Claire Whitney (Middle-Aged Woman); Edward Keane (Middle-Aged Man); Virginia Sale (Chambermaid); Dick Elliott (Prescott); Lee "Lasses" White (Old Man); Marta Mitrovich (Baby's Mother); Rhonda Fleming (Girl on Train); Minerva Urecal (Landlady).

THIRTY SECONDS OVER TOKYO (*MGM, 1944*), *138 min.*

Producer, Sam Zimbalist; director, Mervyn LeRoy; based on the book by Major Ted W. Lawson, Robert Considine; screenplay, Dalton Trumbo; music, Herbert Strothart; art directors, Cedric Gibbons, Paul Groesse; set decorators, Edwin B. Willis, Ralph S. Hurst; assistant director, Wally Worsley; sound, John F. Dullam; special effects, A. Arnold Gillespie, Warren Newcombe; camera, Harold Rosson, Robert Surtees; editor, Frank Sullivan.

Spencer Tracy (Lieutenant-Colonel James H. Doolittle); Van Johnson (Ted Lawson); Robert Walker (David Thatcher); Phyllis Thaxter (Ellen Lawson); Tim Murdock (Dean Davenport); Scott McKay (Davey Jones); Gordon McDonald (Charles McClure); Robert Mitchum (Bob Gray); John R. Reilly ("Shorty" Manch); Horace "Stephen" McNally ("Doc" White); Donald Curtis (Lieutenant Randall); Louis Jean Heydt (Lieutenant Miller); William "Bill" Phillips (Don Smith); Douglas Cowan ("Brick" Holstrom); Paul Langton (Captain "Ski" York); Leon Ames (Commander Jarrika); Benson Fong (Dr. Chan, Jr.); Dr. Kung Chuan Chi (Dr. Chan, Sr.); Ann Shoemaker (Mrs. Parker); Alan Napier (Mr. Parker); Wah Lee (Foo Ling); Ching Wah Lee (Guerrilla Charlie); Jacqueline White (Emmy York); Dorothy Morris (Jane); Jack McClendon (Dick Joyce); John Kellogg (Pilot); Peter Varney (Spike Henderson); Walter Sande (General); Steve Brodie (M.P.); Eddie Hall (Joe); Edith Leach, Katharine Booth (Girls); Arthur Space (Deck Officer); Mike Kilian, Charles King III, Ralph Brooks, Wally Cassell (Sailors); Selena Royle (Mrs. Jones); Morris Ankrum (Captain Halsey); Blake Edwards (Officer); Luke Chan (Chinese Runner); Mary Chan (School Teacher); Myrna Dell, Lorraine Miller, Lucille Casey, Hazel Brooks, Noreen Nash, Kay Williams (Girls in Officers' Club); Bill Williams (Bud Felton).

GIRL RUSH (*RKO, 1944*), *65 min.*

Director, Gordon Douglas; story, Laszlo Vadnay, Aladar Laszla; screenplay, Robert E. Kent; art directors, Albert D'Agostino, Walter Keller; set decorators, Darrell Silvera, William Stevens; music director, C. Bakaleinikoff; songs, Harry Harris and Lew Pollack; assistant director, James Casey; sound, Richard Van Hessen; special effects, Vernon L. Walker; camera, Nicholas Musuraca; editor, Duncan Mansfield.

Wally Brown (Jerry Miles); Alan Carney (Mike Strager); Frances Langford (Flo Daniels);

Vera Vague (Suzie Banks); Robert Mitchum (Jimmy Smith); Paul Hurst (Muley); Patti Brill (Claire); Sarah Padden (Emma); Cy Kendall (Barlan); John Merton (Scully); Diana King (Martha); Rita Corday, Elaine Riley, Rosemary La Planche, Daun Kennedy, Virginia Belmont (Members of Troupe); Michael Vallon (Prospector); Sherry Hall (Monk); Kernan Cripps (Joe the Bartender); Wheaton Chambers (Dealer); Chili Williams (Bit); Ernie Adams (Dave); Lee Phelps (Mac); Margaret Landry (Girl); Pascal Newlan (Giant Gambler); Dale Van Sickel (Whiskers); Bert Le Baron, Ken Terrell (Heavies); Bud Osborne (Miner); J. L. Palmer (Jack); Byron Foulger (Oscar); Abe Dinovitch (Brewery Wagon Driver); Greta Christensen (Girl in Bustle Bit).

NEVADA *(RKO, 1944), 62 min.*

Executive producer, Sid Rogell; producer, Herman Schlom; director, Edward Killy; based on the novel by Zane Grey; screenplay, Norman Houston; art directors, Albert S. D'Agostino, Lucius Croxton; set decorators, Darrell Silvera, William Stevens; music, Paul Sawtell; music director, C. Bakaleinikoff; sound, Richard Van Hessen; camera, Harry J. Wild; editor, Roland Gross.

Robert Mitchum (Jim Lacy [Nevada]); Anne Jeffreys (Julie Dexter); Guinn "Big Boy" Williams (Dusty); Nancy Gates (Hattie Ide); Richard Martin (Chito Rafferty); Craig Reynolds (Cash Burridge); Harry Woods (Joe Powell); Edmund Glover (Ed Nelson); Alan Ward (William Brewer); Harry McKim (Marvie Ide); Larry Wheat (Ben Ide); Jack Overman (Red Berry); Emmett Lynn (Comstock); Wheaton Chambers (Dr. Darien); Philip Morris (Ed Nolan); Mary Halsey, Patti Brill, Margie Stewart, Virginia Belmont, Bryant Washburn, Bert Moorhouse (Bits); George De Normand, Sammy Blum (Bartenders); Russell Hopton (Henchman).

WEST OF THE PECOS *(RKO, 1945), 66 min.*

Executive producer, Sid Rogell; producer, Herman Schlom; director, Edward Killy; based on the novel by Zane Grey; screenplay, Norman Houston; art directors, Albert S. D'Agostino, Lucius Croxton; set decorators, Darrell Silvera, William Stevens; music, Paul Sawtell; music director, C. Bakaleinikoff; assistant director, Harry Mancke; sound, John E. Tribby, Terry Kellum; camera, Harry J. Wild; editor, Roland Gross.

Robert Mitchum (Pecos Smith); Barbara Hale (Rill Lambeth); Richard Martin (Chito Rafferty); Thurston Hall (Colonel Lambeth); Rita Corday (Suzanne); Russell Hopton (Jeff Stinger); Bill Williams (Tex Evans); Bruce Edwards (Clyde Morgan); Harry Woods (Brad Sawtelle); Perc Launders (Sam Sawtelle); Bryant Washburn (Dr. Howard); Philip Morris (Marshal); Martin Garralaga (Don Manuel); Sammy Blum, Robert Anderson (Gamblers); Italia De Nublia (Dancer); Carmen Granada (Spanish Girl); Ariel Sherry, Virginia Wave (Mexican Girls); Ethan Laidlaw (Lookout); Jack Gargan (Croupier); Allan Lee (Four-Up Driver); Larry Wheat (Butler).

THE STORY OF G. I. JOE *(United Artists, 1945), 109 min.*

Producer, Lester Cowan; associate producer, David Hall; director, William A. Wellman; based on the book by Ernie Pyle; screenplay, Leopold Atlas, Guy Endore, Philip Stevenson; assistant director, Robert Aldrich; music, Ann Ronell, Louis Applebaum; songs, Jack Lawrence and Ronell; art directors, David Hall, James Sullivan, Louis Forbes; set decorator, Edward G. Boyle; sound, Frank McWhorter; camera, Russell Metty; supervising editor, Otho Lovering; editor, Albrecht Joseph.

Technical Guidance: For the Army Ground Forces: Lieutenant Colonel Roy A. Murray, Jr.,

Lieutenant Colonel Edward H. Coffey, Lieutenant Colonel Robert Miller, Major Walter Nye, Captain Milton M. Thornton, Captain Charles Shunstrom. For the combat correspondents: Don Whitehead, George Lait, Chris Cunningham, Hal Boyle, Sergeant Jack Foisie, Bob Landry, Lucien Hubbard, Clete Roberts, Robert Reuben.

Burgess Meredith (Ernie Pyle); Robert Mitchum (Lieutenant/Captain Bill Walker); Freddie Steele (Sergeant Steve Warnick); Wally Cassell (Private Dondaro); Jimmy Lloyd (Private Spencer); Jack Reilly (Private Murphy); Bill Murphy (Private Mew); William Self (Cookie); Dick Rich (Sergeant at Showers); Billy Benedict ("Whitey"); Combat Veterans of the Campaigns of Africa-Sicily-Italy (Themselves); Michael Browne (Sergeant).

TILL THE END OF TIME *(RKO, 1946), 105 min.*

Producer, Dore Schary; director, Edward Dmytryk; based on the novel *They Dream of Home* by Niven Busch; screenplay, Allen Rivkin; art directors, Albert D'Agostino, Jack Okey; set decorators, Darrell Silvera, William Stevens; music, Leigh Harline; music director, C. Bakaleinikoff; songs, Buddy Kaye and Ted Mossman; assistant director, Ruby Rosenberg; sound, Richard Van Hessen, Clem Portman; camera, Harry Wild; editor, Harry Gerstad.

Dorothy McGuire (Pat Ruscomb); Guy Madison (Cliff Harper); Robert Mitchum (William Tabeshaw); Bill Williams (Perry Kincheloe); Tom Tully (C. W. Harper); William Gargan (Sergeant Gunny Watrous); Jean Porter (Helen Ingersoll); Johnny Sands (Tommy); Loren Tindall (Pinky); Ruth Nelson (Amy Harper); Selena Royle (Mrs. Kincheloe); Harry Von Zell (Scuffy); Richard Benedict (The Boy from Idaho); Dickie Tyler (Jimmy); Stan Johnson (Captain Jack Winthrop); Billy Newell (Warrant Officer); Lee Slater (Burton); Robert Lowell (Epstein); Peter Varney (Frank); George Burnett (Gilman); Jack Parker (Collector); Ellen Corby (Mrs. Sumpter); Mary Worth (Mrs. Tompkins); Fred Howard (Zeke Ingersoll); Margaret Wells (Mrs. Ingersoll); Harry Hayden (Ed Tompkins); Tim Ryan (Steve Sumpter); Richard Slattery (Captain); Drew Alan (Marine); John S. Roberts, Anthony Marsh, John Bailey, Michael Kostrick (Interviewers); Blake Edwards (Foreman); Stubby Kruger (Practical Life Guard); Eddie Craven (Waiter); Teddy Infuhr (Freddie Stewart); William Forrest (Detective Lieutenant).

UNDERCURRENT *(MGM, 1946), 114 min.*

Producer, Pandro S. Berman; director, Vincente Minnelli; story, Thelma Strabel; screenplay, Edward Chodorov; art directors, Cedric Gibbons, Randall Duell; set decorators, Edwin B. Willis, Jack D. Moore; music, Herbert Stothart; assistant director, Norman Elzer; sound, Douglas Shearer; camera, Karl Freund; editor, Ferris Webster.

Katharine Hepburn (Ann Hamilton); Robert Taylor (Alan Garroway); Robert Mitchum (Michael Garroway); Edmund Gwenn (Professor "Dink" Hamilton); Marjorie Main (Lucy); Jayne Meadows (Sylvia Burton); Clinton Sundberg (Mr. Warmsley); Dan Tobin (Professor Herbert Bangs); Kathryn Card (Mrs. Foster); Leigh Whipper (George); Charles Trowbridge (Justice Putnam); James Westerfield (Henry Gilson); Billy McLain (Uncle Ben); Milton Kibbee (Minister); Jean Andren (Mrs. Davenport); Forbes Murray (Senator Edwards); Bert Moorhouse (Man); David Cavendish, Ernest Hilliard, Clive Morgan, Reginald Simpson, Oliver Cross, Harold Miller, Frank Leigh, Dick Earle, James Carlisle, Ann Lawrence, Florence Fair, Laura Treadwell, Ella Ethridge, Hazel Keener, Maxine Hudson, Bess Flowers, Hilda Rhoades, Joan Thorsen, Barbara Billingsley (Guests); Sarah Edwards (Manager); Betty Blythe (Saleslady); Eula Guy (Housekeeper); Gordon Richards (Headwaiter); Morris Ankrum (Bit); Hank Worden (Attendant); Robert Emmet O'Connor (Station Master); William Eddritt (Butler); Phil Dunham (Elevator Man); William Cartledge, Jack Murphy (Messengers).

THE LOCKET *(RKO, 1946), 86 min.*

Executive producer, Jack J. Gross; producer, Bert Granet; director, John Brahm; screenplay, Sheridan Gibney; dialogue director, William E. Watts; assistant director, Harry D'Arcy; art directors, Albert D'Agostino, Alfred Herman; set decorator, Darrell Silvera, Harley Miller; music, Roy Webb; sound, John L. Cass, Clem Portman; special effects, Russell Cully; camera, Nicholas Musuraca; editor, J. R. Whittredge.

Laraine Day (Nancy Monks); Brian Aherne (Dr. Blair); Robert Mitchum (Norman Clyde); Gene Raymond (John Willis); Sharyn Moffett (Nancy At Age Ten); Ricardo Cortez (Mr. Bonner); Henry Stephenson (Lord Wyndham); Katherine Emery (Mrs. Willis); Reginald Denny (Mr. Wendell); Fay Helm (Mrs. Bonner); Helene Thimig (Mrs. Monks); Nella Walker (Mrs. Wendell); Queenie Leonard (Woman Singer); Lilian Fontaine (Lady Wyndham); Myrna Dell (Thelma); Johnny Clark (Donald); Vivien Oakland (Mrs. Donovan); Nancy Saunders (Miss Wyatt); George Humbert (Luigi); Trina Varella (Luigi's Wife); Nick Thompson (Waiter); Connie Leon (Bonner's Maid); Cecil Weston (Nurse); Colin Kenny (Chauffeur); Leonard Mudie (Air Raid Warden); Ellen Corby, Jean Ransom (Kitchen Girls); Martha Hyer, Carol Donell, Kay Christopher (Bridesmaids); Broderick O'Farrell (Minister); Dorothy Curtis (Maid).

PURSUED *(Warner Bros., 1947), 100 min.*

Producer, Milton Sperling; director, Raoul Walsh; screenplay, Niven Busch; dialogue director, Maurice Murphy; assistant director, Russell Saunders; art director, Ted Smith; set decorator, Jack McConaghty; music, Max Steiner; music director, Leo F. Forbstein; orchestrator, Murray Cutter; sound, Francis J. Scheid; special effects, William McGann, Willard Van Enger; editor, Christian Nyby.

Teresa Wright (Thorley Callum); Robert Mitchum (Jeb Rand); Judith Anderson (Medora Callum); Dean Jagger (Grant Callum); Alan Hale (Jake Dingle); John Rodney (Adam Callum); Harry Carey, Jr. (Prentice McComber); Clifton Young (The Sergeant); Ernest Severn (Jeb at Age Eleven); Charles Bates (Adam at Age Eleven); Peggy Miller (Thor at Age Ten); Norman Jolley, Lane Chandler, Elmer Ellingwood, Jack Montgomery, Ian MacDonald (The Callums); Kathy Jeanne Johnson (Thor at Age Three); Mickey Little (Jeb at Age Four); Scotty Hugenberg (Adam at Age Four); Ray Teal (Callum); Eddy Waller (Storekeeper); Russ Clark (Drill Master); Jack Davis (Doctor); Crane Whitley (General); Carl Harbaugh (Bartender); Lester Dorr (Dealer); Bill Sundholm, Paul Scardon (Jurymen); Harry Lamont (Ticket Taker); Erville Alderson (Undertaker); Sherman Saunders (Square Dance Caller); Al Kunde (Minister); Ben Corbett (Loafer); Charles Miller (Coachman); Tom Fadden (Preacher); Virginia Brissac (Preacher's Wife); Ervin Richardson (Jeb's Father); Louise Volding (Jeb's Mother); Ian Wolfe (Coroner); Ed Coffey (Man at Hanging).

CROSSFIRE *(RKO, 1947), 86 min.*

Executive producer, Dore Schary; producer, Adrian Scott; director, Edward Dmytryk; based on the novel *The Brick Foxhole* by Richard Brooks; screenplay, John Paxton; art directors, Albert S. D'Agostino, Alfred Herman; set decorators, Darrell Silvera, John Sturtevant; music, Roy Webb; music director, C. Bakaleinikoff; assistant director, Nate Levinson; sound, John E. Tribby, Clem Portman; special camera effects, Russell A. Cully; camera, J. Roy Hunt; editor, Harry Gerstad.

Robert Young (Captain Finlay); Robert Mitchum (Sergeant Peter Kelley); Robert Ryan (Monty Montgomery); Gloria Grahame (Ginny Tremaine); Paul Kelly (The Man); Sam Levene (Joseph Samuels); Jacqueline White (Mary Mitchell); Steve Brodie (Floyd Bowers); George Cooper (Arthur Mitchell); Richard Benedict (Bill Williams); Tom Keene (Detective);

William Phipps (Leroy); Lex Barker (Harry); Marlo Dwyer (Miss Lewis); Harry Harvey (Tenant); Carl Faulkner (Deputy); Jay Norris, Robert Bray, George Turner, Don Cadell (M.P.s); George Meader (Police Surgeon); Bill Nind (Waiter); Allen Ray (Soldier); Kenneth MacDonald (Major); Philip Morris (Police Sergeant).

DESIRE ME (MGM, 1947), 91 min.

Producer, Arthur Hornblow, Jr.; directors, George Cukor, Mervyn LeRoy; based on the novel by Leonhard Frank; adaptor, Casey Robinson; screenplay, Marguerite Roberts, Zoe Akins; art directors, Cedric Gibbons, Urie McCleary; set decorators, Edwin B. Willis, Paul Huldschinsky; music, Herbert Stothart; assistant director, Jack Greenwood; sound, Douglas Shearer, Lowell Kinsall; camera, Joseph Ruttenberg; editor, Joseph Dervin.

Greer Garson (Marise Aubert); Robert Mitchum (Paul Aubert); Richard Hart (Jean Renaud); Florence Bates (Mrs. Lannic ["Joo-Lou"]); Morris Ankrum (Hector Martin); George Zucco (Father Donnard); Max Willenz (Dr. Poulin); David Hoffman (Postman Alex); Clinton Sundberg (Salesman); Cecil Humphreys (Dr. Andre Leclair); Tony Carson (Youth); Mitchell Lewis (Old Man); Fernanda Eliscu (Old Woman); Sid D'Albrook (Assistant); David Leonard (Cobbler); Edward Keane (Baker); Belle Mitchell (Baker's Wife); Hans Schumm, Frederic Brunn (German Voices); John Maxwell Hayes (Church Dignitary); Lew Mason (Sailor); Josephine Victor (Woman); Hans Tanzler (German Guard); Maurice Tauzin (Boy); Stanley Andrews (Emile); Harry Woods (Joseph); Earle Hodgins (Barker); Albert Petit (Tinsel Wreath Vendor); Jack Shafton, Iris Shafton (Puppet Operators); Tom Plank (Clown); Gil Perkins (Soldier to Resemble Robert Mitchum); Bert LeBaron (Bear Trainer); Sam Ash (Master of Ceremonies).

OUT OF THE PAST (RKO, 1947), 97 min.

Executive producer, Robert Sparks; producer, Warren Duff; director, Jacques Tourneur; based on the novel Build My Gallows High by Geoffrey Homes; screenplay, Homes; music, Roy Webb; music director, C. Bakaleinikoff; assistant director, Harry Mancke; art directors, Albert S. D'Agostino, Jack Okey; set decorator, Darrell Silvera; sound, Francis M. Sarver, Clem Portman; special effects, Russell A. Cully; camera, Nicholas Musuraca; editor, Samuel E. Beetley.

Robert Mitchum (Jeff Bailey); Jane Greer (Kathie Moffett); Kirk Douglas (Whit); Rhonda Fleming (Meta Carson); Richard Webb (Jim); Steve Brodie (Fisher); Virginia Huston (Ann); Paul Valentine (Joe); Dickie Moore (The Kid); Ken Niles (Eels); Lee Elson (Cop); Frank Wilcox (Sheriff Douglas); Jose Portugal, Euminio Blanco, Vic Romito (Mexican Waiters); Jess Escobar (Mexican Doorman); Primo Lopez (Mexican Bellhop); Tony Roux (Joe Rodriguez); Sam Warren (Waiter at Harlem Club); Mildred Boy, Ted Collins (People at Harlem Club); Caleb Peterson (Man with Eunice); Theresa Harris (Eunice); James Bush (Doorman); John Kellogg (Baylord); Oliver Blake (Tillotson); Wallace Scott (Petey); Michael Branden (Rafferty); William Van Vleck (Cigar Store Clerk); Phillip Morris (Porter); Charles Regan (Mystery Man); Harry Hayden (Canby Miller); Adda Gleason (Mrs. Miller); Manuel Paris (Croupier).

RACHEL AND THE STRANGER (RKO, 1948), 92 min.

Executive producer, Jack J. Gross; producer, Richard H. Berger; director, Norman Foster; based on the novel Rachel by Howard Fast; screenplay, Waldo Salt; art directors, Albert S. D'Agostino, Jack Okey; set decorators, Darrell Silvera, John Sturtevant; music director, C. Bakaleinikoff; songs, Roy Webb and Salt; assistant director, Harry Mancke; makeup, Gordon Bau; Miss Young's costumes, Edith Head; sound, Earl Wolcott, Terry Kellum; special effects, Russell A. Cully; camera, Maury Gertsman; editor, Les Milbrook.

345

Loretta Young (Rachel); William Holden (Big Davey); Robert Mitchum (Jim); Gary Gray (Davey); Tom Tully (Parson Jackson); Sara Haden (Mrs. Jackson); Frank Ferguson (Mr. Green); Walter Baldwin (Gallus); Regina Wallace (Mrs. Green); Fran Conlan (Jebez).

BLOOD ON THE MOON *(RKO, 1948), 88 min.*

Executive producer, Sid Rogell; producer, Theron Warth; director, Robert Wise; based on the novel *Gunman's Chance* by Luke Short; screenplay, Lillie Hayward; adaptors, Harold Shumate, Short; art directors, Albert S. D'Agostino, Walter E. Keller; set decorators, Darrell Silvera, James Altwies; music, Roy Webb; music director, C. Bakaleinikoff; assistant director, Maxwell Henry; makeup, Gordon Bau; costumes, Edward Stevenson; sound, John Killy; special effects, Russell A. Cully; camera, Nicholas Musuraca; editor, Samuel E. Beetley.

Robert Mitchum (Jim Garry); Barbara Bel Geddes (Amy Lufton); Robert Preston (Tate Riling); Walter Brennan (Kris Barden); Phyllis Thaxter (Carol Lufton); Frank Faylen (Jake Pindalest); Tom Tully (John Lufton); Charles McGraw (Milo Sweet); Clifton Young (Joe Shotten); Tom Tyler (Frank Reardan); George Cooper (Fritz Barden); Tom Keene (Ted Elser); Bud Osborne (Cap Willis); Zon Murray (Nels Titterton); Robert Bray (Bart Daniels); Al Ferguson (Chet Avery); Ben Corbett (Mitch Moten); Joe Devlin (Barney); Erville Alderson (Settlmeir the Liveryman); Robert Malcolm (Sheriff Manker); ChrisPin Martin (Bartender at Commissary); Ruth Brennan (Townswoman); Harry Carey, Jr., Hal Taliaferro, Al Murphy (Cowboys); Iron Eyes Cody (Toma).

THE RED PONY *(Republic, 1949), C-89 min.*

Executive producer, Charles K. Feldman; producer-director, Lewis Milestone; based on the story by John Steinbeck; screenplay, Steinbeck; Technicolor consultants, Natalie Kalmus, Francis Cugat; art director, Victor Green; set decorators, John McCarthy, Jr., Charles Thompson; music, Aaron Copland; assistant director, Robert Aldrich; makeup, Bob Mark; costumes, Adele Palmer; sound, Victor Appel, Howard Wilson; special effects, Howard and Theodore Lydecker; camera, Tony Gaudio; editor, Harry Keller.

Myrna Loy (Alice Tiflin); Robert Mitchum (Billy Buck); Louis Calhern (Grandfather); Shepperd Strudwick (Fred Tiflin); Peter Miles (Tom Tiflin); Margaret Hamilton (Teacher); Patty King (Jinx Ingals); Jackie Jackson (Jackie); Beau Bridges (Beau); Don Kay Reynolds (Little Brown Jug); Nino Tempo (Nino); Wee Willie Davis (Truck Driver); Tommy Sheridan (Dale); George Tyne (Charlie); Poodles Hanneford (Clown); Gracie Hanneford, Eddie Borden (Circus Act); Max Wagner (Bartender); Alvin Hammer (Telegrapher); Dolores Castle (Gert); William Quinan (Ben).

THE BIG STEAL *(RKO, 1949), 71 min.*

Executive producer, Sid Rogell; producer, Jack L. Gross; director, Don Siegel; based on the story *The Road to Carmichael's* by Richard Wormser; screenplay, Geoffrey Homes, Gerald Drayson Adams; music, Leigh Harline; music director, C. Bakaleinikoff; art directors, Albert D'Agostino, Ralph Berger; set decorators, Darrell Silvera, Harley Miller; costumes, Edward Stevenson; makeup, Gordon Bau, Robert Cowan; assistant director, Sam Ruman; camera, Harry J. Wild; editor, Samuel E. Beetley.

Robert Mitchum (Lieutenant Duke Halliday); Jane Greer (Joan "Chiquita" Graham); William Bendix (Captain Vincent Blake); Patric Knowles (Jim Fiske); Ramon Novarro (Inspector General Ortega); Don Alvarado (Lieutenant Ruiz); John Qualen (Julius Seton); Pasqual Garcia Pena (Manuel); Henry Carr (Bellhop); Alfonso Dubois (Police Sergeant); Frank Hagney (Madden the Guard); Ted Jacques (Cole); Virginia Farmer (Woman at Customs); Carl

Sklover, Bing Conley (Dockhands); Nacho Galindo (Pastry Vendor); Tony Roux (Parrot Vendor); Felipe Turich (Guitar Vendor); Don Dillaway, Pat O'Malley (Pursers); Juan Duval, Paul Castellanos, Dimas Sotello, Frank Leyva, Eliso Gamboa (Vendors); Edward Colebrook (Mexican Tourist); Rodolfo Hoyos (Customs Inspector); Salvador Baguez (Morales); Primo Lopez, Gilberto Deval, Josa Loza (Bellhops); Margarito Luna, Jose Aceves, Angel Sequraleyva (Attendants); Beatriz Ramos (Carmencita); Alfredo Soto (Gonzales); Juan Varro (Gonzales); Carlos Reyes (Taxi Driver); Alphonse Sanchez Tello (Basguez); Dorothy Mitchum (Tourist).

HOLIDAY AFFAIR *(RKO, 1949), 87 min.*

Producer-director, Don Hartman; based on the story *Christmas Gift* by John D. Weaver; screenplay, Isobel Lennart; art directors, Albert D'Agostino, Carroll Clark; set decorators, Darrell Silvera, William Stevens; music, Roy Webb; music director, C. Bakaleinikoff; assistant director, Sam Ruman; makeup, James House; costumes, Howard Greer; sound, Frank Sarver, Clem Portman; camera, Milton Krasner; editor, Harry Marker.

Robert Mitchum (Steve); Janet Leigh (Connie); Wendell Corey (Carl); Griff Barnett (Mr. Ennis); Esther Dale (Mrs. Ennis); Henry O'Neill (Mr. Crowley); Henry Morgan (Police Lieutenant); Larry J. Blake (Plainclothesman); Helen Brown (Emily); Gordon Gebert (Timmy); Frances Morris (Mary); Robert Hughes (Joey); Carl Sklover, James Griffith, Joey Ray, Genevieve Kendall, Mame Henderson, Pat Hall (Clerks); Frank Johnson (Santa Claus); Louise Franklin (Elevator Operator); Allen Mathews (Mr. Gow); Al Murphy, Charles Regan, Sam Shack, Theodore Rand, Mike Lally, Mishka Egan (Bits); Jack Chefe (Waiter); George Eldredge (Elevator Starter); Yvonne Crossley (Elevator Operator); Frank Mills (Bum); Phillip Morris (Conductor); Chick Chandler (Joe); Al Rhein (Detective); W. J. O'Brien (Peanut Vendor).

WHERE DANGER LIVES *(RKO, 1950), 84 min.*

Producer, Irving Cummings, Jr.; director, John Farrow; story, Leo Rosten; screenplay, Charles Bennett; art directors, Albert S. D'Agostino, Ralph Berger; music director, C. Bakaleinikoff; camera, Nicholas Musuraca; editor, Eda Warren.

Robert Mitchum (Jeff Cameron); Faith Domergue (Margo); Claude Rains (Mr. Lannington); Maureen O'Sullivan (Julie); Charles Kemper (Police Chief); Ralph Dumke (Klauber); Billy House (Mr. Bogardus); Harry Shannon (Dr. Maynard); Philip Van Zandt (Milo De Long); Jack Kelly (Dr. Mullenbach); Lillian West (Mrs. Bogardus); Ruth Lewis (Nurse Collins); Julia Faye (Nurse Seymour); Dorothy Abbott (Nurse Clark); Steve Gaylord Pendleton, Joey Ray, Jerry James (Cops); Art Dupuis (Interne); Stanley Andrews (Dr. Mathews); Jack Kruschen (Casey); Elaine Riley (Nurse Bates); Gordon Clark (Attendant); Geraldine Wall (Annie); David Stollery (Boy); Sherry Jackson (Girl in Iron Lung); Clifford Brooks (Butler); Jim Dundee (Taxi Driver); Tol Avery (Honest Hal); Robert R. Stevenson (Assistant Clerk); Gene Barnes (Tipsy Youth); Ray Teal (Joe Borden); Lester Dorr (Assistant Police Chief); Duke York (Cowboy Type); Sonny Boyne, Jeraldine Jordan (Women); William Green (Doctor); Gerry Ganzer (Stewardess); Linda Johnson (Airport Announcer); Frank Layva (Mexican); Maxine Gates (Girl in Act); Florence Hamblin, Amilda Cuddy (Hawaiians).

MY FORBIDDEN PAST *(RKO, 1951), 81 min.*

Producers, Robert Sparks, Polan Banks; director, Robert Stevenson; based on the novel *Carriage Entrance* by Banks; adaptor, Leopold Atlas; screenplay, Marion Parsonnet; art directors, Albert D'Agostino, Alfred Herman; music director, C. Bakaleinikoff; camera, Harry J. Wild; editor, George Shrader.

Robert Mitchum (Dr. Mark Lucas); Ava Gardner (Barbara); Melvyn Douglas (Paul Beaureval); Lucile Watson (Aunt Eula); Janis Carter (Corinne); Gordon Oliver (Clay Duchesne); Basil Ruysdael (Dean Cazzley); Clarence Muse (Pompey); Walter Kingsford (Coroner); Jack Briggs (Cousin Phillipe); Will Wright (Luther Toplady); Watson Downs (Hotel Clerk); Cliff Clark (Horse Vendor); John B. Williams (Fishmonger); Louis Payne (Man); Johnny Lee (Toy Vendor); George Douglas (Deputy); Ken MacDonald (Police Lieutenant); Everett Glass (Elderly Doctor); Barry Brooks (Policeman); Daniel DeLaurentis (Candle Boy).

HIS KIND OF WOMAN *(RKO, 1951), 120 min.*

Producers, Howard Hughes, Robert Sparks; director, John Farrow; story, Frank Fenton, Jack Leonard; screenplay, Fenton; art director, Albert S. D'Agostino; music director, C. Bakaleinikoff; songs, Sam Coslow; Harold Adamson and Jimmy McHugh; camera, Harry J. Wild; editor, Eda Warren.

Robert Mitchum (Dan Milner); Jane Russell (Lenore Brent); Vincent Price (Mark Cardigan); Tim Holt (Bill Lusk); Charles McGraw (Thompson); Marjorie Reynolds (Helen Cardigan); Raymond Burr (Nick Ferraro); Leslye Banning (Jennie Stone); Jim Backus (Myron Winton); Philip Van Zandt (Jose Morro); John Mylong (Martin Krafft); Carleton G. Young (Hobson); Erno Verebes (Estaban); Dan White (Tex Kearns); Richard Berggren (Milton Stone); Stacy Harris (Harry); Robert Cornthwaite (Hernandez); Jim Burke (Barkeep); Paul Frees (Corle); Joe Granby (Arnold); Daniel De Laurentis (Mexican Boy); John Sheehan (Husband); Sally Yarnell (Wife); Anthony Caruso (Tony); Robert Rose (Corle's Servant); Tol Avery (The Fat One); Paul Fierro, Mickey Simpson (Hoodlums); Ed Rand, Jerry James (Cops); Barbara Freking, Mamie Van Doren, Joy Windsor, Jerri Jordan, Mary Brewer (Girls); Peter Brocco (Short and Thin); Mariette Elliott (Redhead); Saul Gorss (Viscount); Mike Lally (Henchman); Gerry Ganzer (Countess).

THE RACKET *(RKO, 1951), 89 min.*

Producer, Edmund Grainger; director, John Cromwell; based on the play by Bartlett Cormack; screenplay, William Wister Haines, W. R. Burnett; art directors, Albert S. D'Agostino, Jack Okey; music director, Mischa Bakaleinikoff; camera, George E. Diskant; editor, Sherman Todd.

Robert Mitchum (Captain Thomas McQuigg); Lizabeth Scott (Irene Hayes); Robert Ryan (Nick Scanlon); William Talman (Johnson); Ray Collins (Welch); Joyce MacKenzie (Mary McQuigg); Robert Hutton (Dave Ames); Virginia Huston (Lucy Johnson); William Conrad (Turck); Walter Sande (Delaney); Les Tremayne (Chief Harry Craig); Don Porter (Connolly); Walter Baldwin (Sullivan); Brett King (Joe Scanlon); Richard Karlan (Enright); Tito Vuolo (Tony); Howard Petrie (Governor); William Forrest (Governor's Aide); Howland Chamberlin (Higgins); Ralph Peters (Davis); Iris Adrian (Sadie); Jane Hazzard, Claudia Constant (Girls); Jack Shea (Night Duty Sergeant); Mike Lally (Duty Sergeant); Howard Joslyn (Sergeant Werker); Bret Hamilton, Joey Ray (Reporters); Eric Alden (Day Duty Sergeant); Steve Roberts (Schmidt the Police Guard); Pat Flaherty (Radio Patrolman); Duke Taylor (Cop); Milburn Stone (Foster the Assistant); Max Wagner (Durko); Richard Reeves (Leo the Driver); Johnny Day (Menig); Don Beddoe (Mitchell); Don Dillaway (Harris); Barry Brooks (Cameron); Jack Gargan (Lewis); Harry Lauter, Art Dupuis (Radio Cops); Ed Parker (Hood); Dick Gordon, Allen Mathews, Ralph Montgomery (Pedestrians); Bob Bice, Sally Yarnell, Jane Easton, Kate Belmont (Operators); Harriet Matthews (Librarian).

MACAO *(RKO, 1952), 81 min.*

Executive producer, Samuel Bischoff; producer, Alex Gottlieb; directors, Josef von Sternberg, (uncredited) Nicholas Ray; story, Bob Williams; screenplay, Bernard C. Schoenfeld, Stanley Rubin, (uncredited) Walter Newman; songs, Johnny Mercer and Harold Arlen; Jule Styne and Leo Robin; music, Anthony Collins; art directors, Albert S. D'Agostino, Harley Miller; set decorators, Darrell Silvera, Harley Miller; costumes, Michael Woulfe; makeup, Mel Berns; camera, Harry J. Wild; editor, Samuel E. Beetley.

Robert Mitchum (Nick Cochran); Jane Russell (Julie Benson); William Bendix (Lawrence Trumble); Thomas Gomez (Lieutenant Sebastian); Gloria Grahame (Margie); Brad Dexter (Halloran); Edward Ashley (Martin Stewart); Philip Ahn (Itzumi); Vladimir Sokoloff (Kwam Sun Tang); Don Zelaya (Gimpy); Emory Parnell (Ship Captain); Nacho Galindo (Bus Driver); Philip Van Zandt (Customs Official); George Chan (Chinese Photographer); Sheldon Jett (Dutch Tourist); Genevieve Bell (Woman Passenger); Tommy Lee (Coolie Knifed in Water); Alex Montoya (Coolie Bartender); Spencer Chan (Knifer); Alfredo Santos, James Leong (Hoodlums); Marc Krah (Desk Clerk); May Taksugi (Barber); Lee Tung Foo (Chinese Merchant); Iris Wong, Maria Sen Young (Croupiers); Manuel Paris (Bartender); W. T. Chang (Old Fisherman); Trevor Bardette (Bus Driver); Everett Glass (Garcia); Art Dupuis (Portuguese Pilot).

ONE MINUTE TO ZERO *(RKO, 1952), 106 min.*
Producer, Edmund Grainger; director, Tay Garnett; screenplay, Milton Krims, William Wister Haines; music, Victor Young; English lyrics for Korean-Japanese song, Norman Bennett; art directors, Albert S. D'Agostino, Jack Okey; set decorators, Darrell Silvera, John Sturtevant; music director, C. Bakaleinikoff; camera, William E. Snyder; editor, Sherman Todd.

Robert Mitchum (Colonel Steve Janowski); Ann Blyth (Linda Day); William Talman (Colonel Johnny Parker); Charles McGraw (Sergeant Baker); Margaret Sheridan (Mary Parker); Robert Gist (Major Carter); Richard Egan (Captain Ralston); Eduard Franz (Dr. Gustav Engstrand); Robert Osterloh (Major Davis); Lalo Rios (Chico Mendoza); Roy Roberts (General Thomas); Wally Cassell (Private Means); Larry Stewart (Private Weiss); Alvin Greenman (Private Lane the Cook); Tom Irish (Sergeant Cook); Maurice Marsac (M. F. Villon); Dorothy Granger, Karen Hale (Nurses); Kay Christopher (Mrs. Stuart); Wallace Russell (Pilot Norton); Stuart Whitman (Officer); Hazel Sunny Boyne, Louise Saraydar, Mari Leon (Bystanders); Owen Song (Interpreter); Monya Andre (French U.N. Woman); John Mallory (Bit Soldier).

THE LUSTY MEN *(RKO, 1952), 113 min.*
Producers, Jerry Wald, Norman Krasna; director, Nicholas Ray; story, Claude Stanush; screenplay, Horace McCoy, David Dortort; art directors, Albert S. D'Agostino, Alfred Herman; set decorators, Darrell Silvera, Jack Mills; sound, Phil Brigandi, Clem Portman; camera, Lee Garmes; editor, Ralph Dawson.

Susan Hayward (Louise Merritt); Robert Mitchum (Jeff McCloud); Arthur Kennedy (Wes Merritt); Arthur Hunnicutt (Booker Davis); Frank Faylen (Al Dawson); Walter Coy (Buster Burgess); Carol Nugent (Rusty Davis); Maria Hart (Rosemary Maddox); Loran Thayer (Grace Burgess); Burt Mustin (Jeremiah); Karen King (Ginny Logan); Jimmy Dodd (Red Logan); Eleanor Todd (Babs); Riley Hill (Hoag the Ranch Hand); Bob Bray (Fritz); Sheb Wooley (Slim); Marshall Reed (Jim-Bob); Paul E. Burns (Travis Waite); Dennis Moore (Cashier); George Wallace (Committee Man); Lane Bradford (Jim Bob Tyler); Glenn Strange (Rig Ferris the Foreman); George Sherwood (Vet); Lane Chandler (Announcer); Ralph Volkie (Slicker).

ANGEL FACE *(RKO, 1952), 90 min.*
Producer-director, Otto Preminger; story, Chester Erskine; screenplay, Frank Nugent, Os-

car Millard; music, Dmitri Tiomkin; music coordinator, C. Bakaleinikoff; assistant director, Fred A. Fleck; art directors, Albert S. D'Agostino, Carroll Clark; set decorators, Darrell Silvera, Jack Mills; makeup, Mel Burns; costumes, Michael Woulfe; camera, Harry Stradling; editor, Frederick Knudtson.

Robert Mitchum (Frank Jessup); Jean Simmons (Diane Tremayne); Mona Freeman (Mary Wilson); Herbert Marshall (Charles Tremayne); Leon Ames (Fred Barrett); Barbara O'Neil (Katherine Tremayne); Kenneth Tobey (Bill Crompton); Raymond Greenleaf (Arthur Vance); Griff Barnett (The Judge); Robert Gist (Miller); Morgan Farley (Juror); Jim Backus (District Attorney Judson); Morgan Brown (Harry the Restaurant Owner); Frank Kumagai (Satsuma); Lucille Barkley (Waitress); Herbert Lytton (Doctor); Lewis Martin (Police Sergeant at House); Alex Gerry (Lewis, Frank's Attorney); Bess Flowers (Barrett's Secretary); Mike Lally, Bob Peoples, Clark Curtiss (Reporters); Gertrude Astor (Matron); Larry Blake (Brady the Detective); Theresa Harris (Theresa the Nurse); George Sherwood (Man); Peggy Walker (TV Girl); Charles Tannen (TV Broadcaster).

WHITE WITCH DOCTOR *(Twentieth Century-Fox, 1953), C-96 min.*
Producer, Otto Lang; director, Henry Hathaway; based on the novel by Louise A. Stinetorf; screenplay, Ivan Goff, Ben Roberts; art directors, Lyle Wheeler, Mark-Lee Kirk; camera, Leon Shamroy; editor, James B. Clark.

Susan Hayward (Ellen Burton); Robert Mitchum (Lonni Dougas); Walter Slezak (Huysman); Mashood Ajala (Jacques); Joseph C. Narcisse (Utembo); Elzie Emanuel (Kapuka); Timothy Carey (Jarrett); Otis Greene (Bakuba Boy); Charles Gemora (Gorilla); Paul Thompson, Naaman Brown (Witch Doctors); Myrtle Anderson (Aganza); Everett Brown (Bakuba King); Dorothy Harris (Chief's Wife); Michael Ansara (De Gama); Leo C. Aldridge-Milas (Council Member); Floyd Shackelford (Chief); Gabriel Ukaegbu (Native); Henry Hastings (Man).

SECOND CHANCE *(RKO, 1953), C-82 min.*
Executive producer, Edmund Grainger; producer, Sam Weisenthal; director, Rudolph Mate; story-adaptor, D. M. Marshman, Jr.; screenplay, Oscar Millard, Sydney Boehm; art directors, Albert S. D'Agostino, Carroll Clark; camera, William Snyder; editor, Robert Ford.

Robert Mitchum (Russ Lambert); Linda Darnell (Clare Shepperd); Jack Palance (Cappy); Sandro Giglio (Conductor); Rodolfo Hoyos, Jr. (Vasco); Reginald Sheffield (Mr. Woburn); Margaret Brewster (Mrs. Woburn); Roy Roberts (Malloy); Salvador Baguez (Hernandez); Maurice Jara (Fernando); Judy Walsh (Maria); Dan Seymour (Felipe); Fortunio Bonanova (Manager of La Posada); Milburn Stone (Dawson); Abel Fernandez (Rivera); Michael Tolan (Antonio); Richard Vera (Pablo); Martin Garralaga (Don Pascual); Shirley Patterson, Virginia Linden (Girls); Tony Martinez (Waiter on Balcony); Oresta Seragnoli (Priest); Ricardo Alba (Reporter); Bob Castro (Russ's Handler); David Morales (Spanish Man); Tony Roux (Bartender).

SHE COULDN'T SAY NO *(RKO, 1954), 89 min.*
Producer, Robert Sparks; director, Lloyd Bacon; based on the story *Enough for Happiness* by D. D. Beauchamp; screenplay, Beauchamp, William Powers, Richard Flournoy; art directors, Albert S. D'Agostino, Carroll Clark; camera, Harry J. Wild; editor, George Amy.

Robert Mitchum (Doc); Jean Simmons (Corby); Arthur Hunnicutt (Otey); Edgar Buchanan (Ad Meeker); Wallace Ford (Joe); Raynold Walburn (Judge Holbert); Jimmy Hunt (Digger);

Ralph Dumke (Sheriff); Hope Landin (Mrs. McMurty); Gus Schilling (Ed Gruman); Eleanor Todd (Sally); Pinky Tomlin (Elmer Wooley); Burt Mustin (Amos); Edith Leslie (Nora); Martha Wentworth (Judge's Wife); Gloria Winters (Barbara); Barry Brooks (Clerk); Mary Bayless (Woman); Clarence Muse (Delivery Man); Dabbs Greer (Jordan); Jonathan Hale (Mr. Bentley); Charles Cane (Man at Filling Station); Marjorie Holliday (Emmy Lou); Marlyn Gladstone (Wife in Car); Tony Merrill (Gas Station Attendant);

RIVER OF NO RETURN *(Twentieth Century-Fox, 1954), C-91 min.*

Producer, Stanley Rubin; director, Otto Preminger; story, Louis Lantz; screenplay, Frank Fenton; music, Cyril Mockridge; songs, Ken Darby and Lionel Newman; choreography, Jack Cole; assistant director, Paul Helmick; art directors, Lyle Wheeler, Addison Hehr; special effects, Ray Kellogg; camera, Joseph La Shelle; editor, Louis Loeffler.

Robert Mitchum (Matt Calder); Marilyn Monroe (Kay); Rory Calhoun (Harry Weston); Tommy Rettig (Mark Calder); Murvyn Vye (Dave Colby); Douglas Spencer (Sam Benson); Ed Hinton (Gambler); Don Beddoe (Ben); Claire Andre (Surrey Driver); Jack Mather (Dealer at Crap Table); Edmund Cobb (Barber); Will Wright (Trader); Jarma Lewis (Dancer); Hal Baylor, Mitchell Lawrence, John Veich, Larry Chance (Young Punks); Barbara Nichols, Fay Morley (Dancers); Arthur Shields (Priest); Ralph Sanford (Bartender); Harry Seymour (Man); Jeanne Schaeffer, Anna McCrea, Geneva Gray (Dance Hall Girls); John Cliff (Leering Man); Mitchell Kowal (Roughneck); Paul Newlan (Prospector); John Doucette (Onlooker).

TRACK OF THE CAT *(Warner Bros., 1954), C-102 min.*

Director, William A. Wellman; based on the novel by Walter Van Tilburg Clark; screenplay, A. I. Bezzerides; assistant director, Andrew McLaglen; music, Roy Webb; art director, Al Ybarra; camera, William H. Clothier; editor, Fred MacDowell.

Robert Mitchum (Curt); Teresa Wright (Grace); Diana Lynn (Gwen); Tab Hunter (Harold); Beulah Bondi (Ma Bridges); Philip Tonge (Pa Bridges); William Hopper (Arthur); Carl Switzer (Joe Sam).

NOT AS A STRANGER *(United Artists, 1955), 135 min.*

Producer-director, Stanley Kramer; based on the novel by Morton Thompson; screenplay, Edna and Edward Anhalt; music and music conductor, George Antheil; orchestrator, Ernest Gold; production designer, Rudolph Sternad; art director, Howard Richmond; set decorator, Victor Gangelin; costumes, Joe King; gowns, Don Loper; makeup, Bill Wood; assistant director, Carter De Haven, Jr.; technical advisers, Morton Maxwell, M.D., Josh Fields, M.D., Marjorie Lefevre, R.N.; dialogue director, Anne Kramer; sound, Earl Snyder; camera, Franz Planer; editor, Fred Knudtson.

Olivia de Havilland (Kristina Hedvigson); Robert Mitchum (Lucas Marsh); Frank Sinatra (Alfred Boone); Gloria Grahame (Harriet Lang); Broderick Crawford (Dr. Aarons); Charles Bickford (Dr. Runkleman); Myron McCormick (Dr. Snyder); Lon Chaney (Job Marsh); Jesse White (Ben Cosgrove); Harry Morgan (Oley); Lee Marvin (Brundage); Virginia Christine (Bruni); Whit Bissell (Dr. Dietrich); Jack Raine (Dr. Lettering); Mae Clarke (Miss O'Dell); Jerry Paris (Medical Student); John Dierkes (Treasurer); Will Wright (Patient with Cigar); Nancy Kulp (Hypochondriac Woman); Harry Shannon (Patient); Herbert Vigran (Salesman).

THE NIGHT OF THE HUNTER *(United Artists, 1955), 93 min.*

Producer, Paul Gregory; director, Charles Laughton; based on the novel by Davis Grubb;

screenplay, James Agee; assistant director, Milton Carter; music, Walter Schumann; wardrobe, Jerry Bos; second unit director, Terry Sanders; art director, Hilyard Brown; set decorator, Al Spencer; makeup, Don Cash; sound, Stanford Naughton; camera, Stanley Cortez; editor, Robert Golden.

Robert Mitchum (Preacher Harry Powell); Shelley Winters (Willa Harper); Lillian Gish (Rachel); Evelyn Varden (Icey); Peter Graves (Ben Harper); Billy Chapin (John); Sally Jane Bruce (Pearl); James Gleason (Birdie); Don Beddoe (Walt); Gloria Castillo (Ruby); Mary Ellen Clemons (Clary); Cheryl Callaway (Mary); Corey Allen (Young Man in Town); Paul Bryar (Hangman Bart).

MAN WITH THE GUN *(United Artists, 1955), 83 min.*

Producer, Samuel Goldwyn, Jr.; director, Richard Wilson; screenplay, N. B. Stone, Jr., Wilson; art director, Hilyard Brown; music director, Emil Newman; assistant directors, Sid Sidman, Richard Evans; costumes, Jerry Bos, Evelyn Carruth; camera, Lee Garmes; editor, Gene Milford.

Robert Mitchum (Clint Tollinger); Jan Sterling (Nelly Bain); Karen Sharpe (Stella Atkins); Henry Hull (Marshal Sims); Emile Meyer (Saul Atkins); John Lupton (Jeff Castle); Barbara Lawrence (Ann Wakefield); Ted De Corsia (Rex Stang); Leo Gordon (Ed Pinchot); James Westerfield (Drummer); Florenz Ames (Doc Hughes); Robert Osterloh (Virg Trotter); Jay Adler (Cal); Amzie Strickland (Mary Atkins); Stafford Repp (Arthur Jackson); Thom Conroy (Bill Emory); Maudie Prickett (Mrs. Elderhorn); Mara McAfee (Mabel); Angie Dickinson (Kitty); Norma Calderon (Luz); Joe Barry (Dade Holman).

FOREIGN INTRIGUE *(United Artists, 1956), C-100 min.*

Producer, Sheldon Reynolds; associate producer, Nicole Milinaire; director, Reynolds; story, Reynolds, Harold J. Bloom, Gene Levitt; screenplay, Reynolds; art director, Maurice Petri; music, Paul Durand; assistant directors, Tom Younger, Michel Wyn; costumes, Pierre Balmain; "Foreign Intrigue Concerto" by Charles Norman; camera, Bertil Palmgrem; editor, Leonnart Wallen.

Robert Mitchum (Bishop); Genevieve Page (Dominique); Ingrid Tulean (Brita); Frederick O'Brady (Spring); Gene Deckers (Sandoz); Inga Tidblad (Mrs. Lindquist); John Padovano (Tony); Frederick Schrecker (Mannheim); Lauritz Faulk (Jones); Peter Copley (Brown); Ralph Brown (Smith); George Hubert (Dr. Thibault); Nil Sperber (Baum); Jean Galland (Danemore); and Robert Le Beal, Albert Simmons, Gilbert Robin, John Starck, Jim Gerald.

BANDIDO *(United Artists, 1956), C-92 min.*

Producer, Robert L. Jacks; director, Richard Fleischer; story-screenplay, Earl Felton; music, Max Steiner; assistant director, Virgil Hart; costumes, Oscar Rodirquez and the Costumer; art director, John Martin Smith; camera, Ernest Laszlo; editor, Robert Golden.

Robert Mitchum (Wilson); Ursula Thiess (Lisa); Gilbert Roland (Escobar); Zachary Scott (Kennedy); Rudolfo Acosta (Sebastian); Henry Brandon (Gunther); Douglas Fowley (McGee); Jose I. Torvay (Gonzalez); Victor Junco (Lorenzo); Alfonso Sanchez Tello (G. Brucero); Arturo Manrique (Adolfo); Margarito Luna (Santos); Miguel Inclan (Priest); and: Alberto Pedret, Sanchez Navarro, Antonio Sandoval, Jose Munoz, Jose A. Espinosa.

HEAVEN KNOWS, MR. ALLISON *(Twentieth Century-Fox, 1957), C-107 min.*

Producers, Buddy Adler, Eugene Frenke; director, John Huston; based on the novel by

Charles Shaw; screenplay, John Lee Mahin, Huston; music, Georges Auric; music conductor, Lambert Williamson; costumes, Elizabeth Haffenden; assistant director, Adrian Pryco-Jones; camera, Oswald Morris; editor, Russell Lloyd.

Deborah Kerr (Sister Angela); Robert Mitchum (Mr. Allison); Fusamoto Takasimi, Noboru Yoshida (Japanese Soldiers); Anna Sten (Bit); and The Marines of Trinidad Base.

FIRE DOWN BELOW (Columbia, 1957), C-110 min.

Producers, Irving Allen, Albert R. Broccoli; director, Robert Parrish; based on the novel by Max Catto; screenplay, Irwin Shaw; assistant directors, Gus Agosti, Bluey Hill; music, Arthur Benjamin, Kenneth V. Jones, Douglas Gamley; dance music, Vivian Comma; harmonica theme, Jack Lemmon; music conductor, Muir Mathieson; song, Lester Lee and Ned Washington; choreography, Ken Jones; Miss Hayworth's costumes, Balmain, Bermans; production designer, John Box; art director, Syd Cain; sound, Peter Davies, J. B. Smith; special effects, Cliff Richardson; camera, Desmond Dickinson; editor, Jack Slade.

Rita Hayworth (Irena); Robert Mitchum (Felix Bowers); Jack Lemmon (Tony); Herbert Lom (Harbor Master); Bonar Colleano (Lieutenant Sellers); Bernard Lee (Dr. Sam); Edric Connor (Jimmy-Jean); Peter Illing (Captain of the Ulysses); Joan Miller (Mrs. Canady); Anthony Newley (Miguel); Eric Pohlmann (Hotel Owner); Lionel Murton (The American); Vivian Matalon, Gordon Tanner, Maurice Kaufman (U.S. Sailors); Phillip Baird (Young Man); Stretch Cox, Shirley Rus, Sean Mostyn, Lorna Wood, Brian Blades, Greta Remin, Robert Nelson, Ken Tillson, Barbara Lane, Gina Chare, Roy Evans (Limbo Dancers); Keith Banks (Drunk).

THE ENEMY BELOW (Twentieth Century-Fox, 1957), C-98 min.

Producer-director, Dick Powell; story, Commander D. A. Rayner; screenplay, Wendell Mayes; art directors, Lyle Wheeler, Albert Hogsett; set decorators, Walter Scott, Fay Babcock; music, Leigh Harline; music conductor, Lionel Newman; orchestrator, Edward B. Powell; wardrobe designer, Charles Le Maire; special camera effects, L. B. Abbott; camera, Harold Rosson; editor, Stuart Gilmore.

Robert Mitchum (Captain Murrell); Curt Jurgens (Von Stolberg); David Hedison (Lieutenant Ware); Theodore Bikel (Schwaffer); Russell Collins (Doctor); Kurt Kreuger (Von Holem); Frank Albertson (C.P.O. Crain); Biff Elliott (Quartermaster); Alan Dexter (Mackason); Doug McClure (Ensign Merry); Jeff Daley (Corky); David Bair (Ellis); Joe Di Reda (Robbins); Ralph Manza (Lieutenant Bonelli); Ted Perritt (Messenger); Jimmy Bayes (Quiroga); Arthur La Ral (Kunz); Dan Tana, Dale Cummings, Roger Cornwall, Sasha Harden (German Sailors); Michael McHale, Joe Brooks (German Soldiers); Richard Elmore, Ronnie Rondell, Vincent Deadrick, Dan Nelson, (American Sailors); Peter Dane (Andrews); Werner Reichow (Mueller); Robert Boon (Chief Engineer); Frank Obershall (Braun); David Post (Lewis); Lee J. Winters (Striker); Jack Kramer (Albert, a German Sailor); Robert Whiteside (Torpedo Petty Officer); Maurice Doner (Cook).

THUNDER ROAD (United Artists, 1958), 94 min.

Producer, Robert Mitchum; director, Arthur Ripley; story, Mitchum; screenplay, James Atlee Phillips, Walter Wise; assistant directors, James Casey, Jack Doran; song, Mitchum and Don Raye; makeup, Carly Taylor; sound, Frank Webster; special effects, Jack Lannan, Lester Swartz; camera, Alan Stensvold, David Ettinson; editor, Harry Marker.

Robert Mitchum (Lucas "Luke" Doolin); Gene Barry (Troy Barrett); Jacques Aubuchon (Carl Kogan); Keely Smith (Francie Wymore); Trevor Bardette (Vernon Doolin); Sandra

Knight (Roxanna Ledbetter); Jim Mitchum (Robin Doolin); Betsy Holt (Mary Barrett); Frances Koon (Sarah Doolin); Randy Sparks (Singer-Guitarist); Mitch Ryan (Jed Moultrie); Peter Breck (Stacey Gouge); Peter Hornsby (Lucky); Jerry Hardin (Niles Penland); Robert Porterfield (Preacher).

THE HUNTERS *(Twentieth Century-Fox, 1958), C-108 min.*

Producer-director, Dick Powell; based on the novel by James Salter; screenplay, Wendell Mayes; assistant director, Ad Schaumer; music, Paul Sawtell; second unit director, James C. Haven; art directors, Lyle Wheeler, Maurice Ransford; set decorators, Walter M. Scott, Bertram C. Granger; wardrobe, Charles LeMaire; color consultant, Leonard Doss; technical advisers, Major Robert E. Wayne, USAF, Captain Vernon L. Wright, USAF; makeup, Ben Nye; sound, E. Clayton Ward, Harry M. Leonard; special camera effects, L. B. Abbott; camera, Charles G. Clarke; aerial camera, Tom Tutwiler; editor, Stuart Gilmore.

Robert Mitchum (Major Cleve Saville); Robert Wagner (Lieutenant Ed Pell); Richard Egan (Colonel "Dutch" Imil); May Britt (Kristina Abbott); Lee Philips (Lieutenant Abbott); John Gabriel (Lieutenant Corona); Stacy Harris (Colonel Moncavage); Victor Sen Young (Korean Farmer); Candace Lee (Korean Child); Jay Jostyn (Major Dart); Leon Lontoc (Casey Jones); Nobu McCarthy (Japanese Clerk); and Keye Luke, Captain Hugh Matheson, Ron Ely.

THE ANGRY HILLS *(MGM, 1959), 105 min.*

Producer, Raymond Stross; director, Robert Aldrich; based on the novel by Leon Uris; screenplay, A. I. Bezzerides; music, Richard Bennett; camera, Stephen Dade; editor, Peter Tanner.

Robert Mitchum (Mike Morrison); Stanley Baker (Konrad Heisler); Elisabeth Mueller (Lisa Kryiakides); Gia Scala (Eletheria); Theodore Bikel (Tassos); Sebastian Cabot (Chesney); Peter Illing (Leonides); Leslie Phillips (Ray Taylor); Donald Wolfit (Dr. Stergiou); Marius Goring (Commodore Oberg); Jackie Lane (Maria); Kieron Moore (Andreas); George Pastell (Papa Panos); Patrick Jordan (Bluy); Marita Constantiou (Kleopatra); Stanley Van Beers (Tavern Proprietor); Alec Mango (Papa Phillibos); Tom Chatto (Desk Clerk); and George Eugeniou, Dimitris Nicolaides.

THE WONDERFUL COUNTRY *(United Artists, 1959), C-96 min.*

Producer, Chester Erskine; director, Robert Parrish; based on the novel by Tom Lea; screenplay, Robert Ardrey; music-music conductor, Alex North; art director, Harry Horner; assistant director, Henry Spitz; sound, Del Harris; camera, Floyd Crosby, Alex Philipps; editor, Michael Luciano.

Robert Mitchum (Martin Brady); Julie London (Ellen Colton); Gary Merrill (Major Colton); Pedro Armendariz (Cipriano Castro); Jack Oakie (Travis Hight); Albert Dekker (Captain Rucker); Charles McGraw (Doc Stovall); Leroy "Satchel" Paige (Tobe Sutton); Victor Mendoza (General Castro); Tom Lea (Peebles); Jay Novello (Diego Casas); Mike Kellin (Pancho Gil); Max Slaten (Ludwig Sterner); Joe Haworth (Stoker); Chester Hayes (Rascon); Chuck Roberson (Gallup); Anthony Caruso (Santos); Claudio Brook (Ruelle); Judy Marsh (Entertainer at Fiesta); Mike Luna (Captain Verdugo).

HOME FROM THE HILL *(MGM, 1960), C-150 min.*

Producer, Edmund Grainger; director, Vincente Minnelli; based on the novel by William Humphrey; screenplay, Harriet Frank, Jr., Irving Ravetch; music, Bronislau Kaper; music conductor, Charles Wolcott; art directors, George W. Davis, Preston Ames; set decorators, Henry Grace, Robert Priestley; color consultant, Charles K. Hagedon; assistant director, William McGarry; costumes, Walter Plunkett; makeup, William Tuttle; sound, Franklin Milton; special effects, Robert R. Hoag; camera, Milton Krasner; editor, Harold F. Kress.

Robert Mitchum (Captain Wade Hunnicutt); Eleanor Parker (Hannah Hunnicutt); George Peppard (Rafe Copley); George Hamilton (Theron Hunnicutt); Everett Sloane (Albert Halstead); Luana Patten (Libby Halstead); Anne Seymour (Sarah Halstead); Constance Ford (Opal Bixby); Ken Renard (Chauncey); Ray Teal (Dr. Reuben Carson); Guinn "Big Boy" Williams (Hugh Macauley); Charlie Briggs (Dick Gibbons); Hilda Haynes (Melba); Denver Pyle (Marshal Bradley); Dan Sheridan (Peyton Stiles); Orville Sherman (Ed Dinwoodie); Dub Taylor (Bob Skaggs); Stuart Randall (John Ramsey); Tom Gilson (John Ellis); Reverend Duncan Gray, Jr. (Minister); Joe Ed Russell (Foreman); Burt Mustin (Gas Station Attendant).

THE NIGHT FIGHTERS *(United Artists, 1960), 88 min.*
Producer, Raymond Stross; director, Tay Garnett; based on the book *A Terrible Beauty* by Arthur Roth; screenplay; Robert Wright Campbell; music, Cedric Thorpe Davie; music conductor, Doc Mathieson; art director, John Stoll; set decorator, Josie MacAvin; assistant director, Frank Ernst; wardrobe, John Apperson; makeup, Harold Fletcher; sound, Bill Bulkley; camera, Stephen Dade; second unit camera, Lionel Baines; editor, Peter Tanner.

Robert Mitchum (Dermot O'Neill); Anne Heywood (Neeve Donnelly); Dan O'Herlihy (Don McGinnis); Cyril Cusack (Jimmy Hannafin); Richard Harris (Sean Reilly); Marianne Benet (Bella O'Neill); Niall MacGinnis (Ned O'Neill); Harry Brogan (Patrick O'Neill); Eileen Crowe (Kathleen O'Neill); Geoffrey Golden (Sergeant Crawley); Hilton Edwards (Father McCrory); Wilfrid Downing (Quinn); Christopher Rhodes (Malone); Eddie Golden (Corrigan); Joe Lynch (Tim); Jim Neylan, T. R. McKenna (The McIntyre Brothers).

THE GRASS IS GREENER *(Universal, 1960), C-105 min.*
Producer, Stanley Donen; associate producer, James Ware; director, Donen; based on the play by Hugh and Margaret Williams; screenplay, the Williamses; songs, Noël Coward; music conductor, Muir Mathieson; art director, Paul Sheriff; set decorator, Vernon Dixon; Miss Simmons' clothes, Christian Dior; Miss Kerr's clothes, Hardy Amies; makeup, John O'Gorman, Eric Allwright; assistant director, Roy Stevens; main titles, Maurice Binder; camera, Christopher Challis; editor, James Clarke.

Cary Grant (Victor Rhyall); Deborah Kerr (Hilary Rhyall); Robert Mitchum (Charles Delarcro); Jean Simmons (Hattie Durrant); Moray Watson (Sellers).

THE SUNDOWNERS *(Warner Bros., 1960), C-141 min.*
Producer-director, Fred Zinnemann; based on the novel by Jon Cleary; screenplay, Isobel Lennart; art director, Michael Stringer; set decorators, Frants Folmer, Terrence Morgan; music and music conductor, Dmitri Tiomkin; wardrobe, Elizabeth Haffenden; wardrobe color consultant, Joan Bridge; assistant directors, Peter Bolton, Roy Stevens; second unit director, Lex Halliday; camera, Jack Hildyard; editor, Jack Harris.

Deborah Kerr (Ida Carmody); Robert Mitchum (Paddy Carmody); Peter Ustinov (Venneker); Glynis Johns (Mrs. Firth); Dina Merrill (Jean Halstead); Chips Rafferty (Quinlan); Michael Anderson, Jr. (Sean Carmody); Lola Brooks (Liz); Wylie Watson (Herb Johnson); John Meillon (Bluey); Ronald Fraser (Ocker); Mervyn Johns (Jack Patchogue); Molly Urquhart (Mrs. Bateman); Ewen Solon (Halstead).

THE LAST TIME I SAW ARCHIE *(United Artists, 1961), 98 min.*
Producer-director, Jack Webb; based on actual events; screenplay, William Bowers; music and music conductor, Frank Comstock; makeup, Stanley Campbell; art director, Field Gray; set decorator, John Sturtevant; wardrobe, Jess Munde, Sabine Manela; assistant director, Chico Day; sound, Frank Sarver; special effects, A. P. Pollard; camera, Joseph MacDonald; editor, Robert Leeds.

Robert Mitchum (Archie Hall); Jack Webb (Bill Bowers); Martha Hyer (Peggy Kramer); France Nuyen (Cindy); Joe Flynn (Private Russell Drexel); James Lydon (Private Billy Simpson); Del Moore (Private Frank Ostrow); Louis Nye (Private Sam Beacham); Richard Arlen (Colonel Martin); Don Knotts (Captain Little); Robert Strauss (Master Sergeant Stanley Erlenheim); Harvey Lembeck (Sergeant Malcolm Greenbriar); Claudia Barrett (Lola); Theona Bryant (Daphne); Elaine Davis (Carole); Marilyn Burtis (Patsy Ruth); James Mitchum (Corporal); John Nolan (Lieutenant Oglemeyer); Martin Dean (First Second Lieutenant); Dick Cathcart, Phil Gordon, Bill Kilmer (Soldiers); Robert Clarke (Officer-Aide); Nancy Kulp (Secretary Willoughby); Don Drysdale (Soldier at Mess Hall); Howard McNear (General).

CAPE FEAR *(Universal, 1962), 105 min.*
Producer, Sy Bartlett; director, J. Lee Thompson; based on the novel *The Executioners* by John D. MacDonald; screenplay, James R. Webb; music, Bernard Herrmann; art directors, Alexander Golitzen, Robert Boyle; set decorator, Oliver Emert; costumes, Mary Wills; makeup, Frank Prehoda, Thomas Tuttle; assistant director, Roy Gosnell, Jr.; sound, Waldon O. Watson, Corson Jowett; camera, Sam Leavitt; editor, George Tomasini.
Gregory Peck (Sam Bowden); Robert Mitchum (Max Cady); Polly Bergen (Peggy Bowden); Lori Martin (Nancy Bowden); Martin Balsam (Mark Dutton); Jack Kruschen (Dave Grafton); Telly Savalas (Charles Sievers); Barrie Chase (Diane Taylor); Ward Ramsey (Officer Brown); Edward Platt (Judge); John McKee (Officer Marconi); Page Slattery (Deputy Kersek); Paul Comi (Garner); Will Wright (Dr. Pearsal); Joan Staley (Waitress); Norman Yost (Ticket Clerk); Mack Williams (Dr. Lowney); Thomas Newman (Lieutenant Gervasi); Alan Reynolds (Vernon); Herb Armstrong (Waiter); Paul Levitt (Police Operator); Cindy Carol (Betty); Joseph Smith (Librarian); Jack Elkins, Bob Noble (Passersby); Joseph Jenkins (Janitor); Marion Landers (Cross); Jack Richardson (Deputy); Alan Wells, Allan Ray (Young Blades).

THE LONGEST DAY *(Twentieth Century-Fox, 1962), 180 min.*
Producer, Darryl F. Zanuck; associate producer, Elmo Williams; directors, Andrew Marton, Ken Annakin, Bernhard Wicki, (uncredited) Zanuck; based on the book by Cornelius Ryan; screenplay, Ryan; additional episodes, Romain Gary, James Jones, David Pursall, Jack Seddon; music and music conductor, Maurice Jarre; thematic music, Paul Anka; arranger, Mitch Miller; art directors, Ted Aworth, Vincent Korda, Leon Barsacq; assistant directors, Bernard Farrel, Louis Fitzele, Gerard Renateau, Henri Sokal; sound, Jo De Bretagne, Jacques Maumont, William Sivel; special effects, Karl Baumgartner, Karl Helmer, Augie Lohman, Robert MacDonald, Alex Weldon; camera, Jean Bourgoin, Henri Persin, Walter Wottitz; helicopter shots, Guy Tabary; editor, Samuel E. Beetley.

John Wayne (Colonel Vandervoort); Robert Mitchum (General Norman Cota); Henry Fonda (General Roosevelt); Robert Ryan (General Gavin); Rod Steiger (Commander); Robert Wagner (U.S. Ranger); Richard Beymer (Schultz); Mel Ferrer (General Haines); Jeffrey Hunter (Sergeant Fuller); Paul Anka, Tommy Sands, Fabian (Rangers); Sal Mineo (Private Martini); Roddy McDowall (Private Morris); Stuart Whitman (Lieutenant Sheen); Eddie Albert (Colonel Newton); Edmond O'Brien (General Barton); Red Buttons (Private Steele); Tom Tryon (Lieutenant Wilson); Alexander Knox (General Bedell Smith); Ray Danton (Captain Frank); Henry Grace (General Eisenhower); Mark Damon (Private Harris); Steve Forrest

(Captain Harding); John Crawford (Colonel Caffey); Ron Randell (Williams); Nicholas Stuart (General Bradley); Richard Burton, Donald Houston (R.A.F. Pilots); Kenneth More (Captain Maud); Peter Lawford (Lord Lovat); Richard Todd (Major Howard); Leo Genn (General Parker); John Gregson (Padre); Sean Connery (Private Flanagan); Jack Hedley (Briefing Man); Michael Medwin (Private Watney); Norman Rossington (Private Clough); John Robinson (Admiral Ramsey); Patrick Barr (Captain Stagg); Trevor Reid (General Montgomery); Irina Demich (Janine); Bourvil (Mayor); Jean-Louis Barrault (Father Roulland); Christian Marquand (Kieffer); Arletty (Mme. Barrault); Madeleine Renaud (Mother Superior); Georges Wilson (Renaud); Jean Servais (Admiral Jaujard); Fernand Ledoux (Louis); Curt Jurgens (General Blumentritt); Werner Hinz (Marshal Rommel); Paul Hartmann (Marshal Rundstedt); Peter Van Eyck (Lieutenant Colonel Ocker); Gerd Froebe (Sergeant Kaffeeklatsch); Hans Christian Blech (Major Pluskat); Wolfgang Preiss (General Pensel); Heinz Reincke (Colonel Priller); Richard Munch (General Marcks); Ernst Schroeder (General Salmuth); Christopher Lee, Eugene Deckers (Bits).

TWO FOR THE SEESAW *(United Artists, 1962), 120 min.*
   Producer, Walter Mirisch; director, Robert Wise; based on the play by William Gibson; screenplay, Isobel Lennart; art director, Boris Leven; set decorator, Edward G. Boyle; assistant director, Jerome M. Siegel; costumes, Orry-Kelly; makeup, Frank Westmore; music, Andre Previn; sound, Lambert Day; camera, Ted McCord; editor, Stuart Gilmore.

   Robert Mitchum (Jerry Ryan); Shirley MacLaine (Gittel Mosca); Edmon Ryan (Taubman); Elisabeth Fraser (Sophie); Eddie Firestone (Oscar); Billy Gray (Mr. Jacoby); Vic Lundin (Beat Singer); and: Shirley Cytron, Cia Dave, Virginia Whitmore, Colin Campbell, Mike Enserro, Moira Turner.

THE LIST OF ADRIAN MESSENGER *(Universal, 1963), 98 min.*
   Producer, Edward Lewis; director, John Huston; based on the novel by Philip MacDonald; screenplay, Anthony Veiller; music, Jerry Goldsmith; music supervisor, Joseph Gershenson; assistant directors, Tom Shaw, Terry Morse, Jr.; art directors, Stephen Grimes, George Webb; set decorator, Oliver Emert; second unit director, Ted Scaife; makeup, Bud Westmore; camera, Joseph MacDonald; editors, Terry Morse, Hugh Fowler.

   George C. Scott (Anthony Gethryn); Dana Wynter (Lady Jocelyn Bruttenholm); Clive Brook (Marquis of Gleneyre); Herbert Marshall (Sir Wilfred Lucas); Jacques Roux (Raoul Le Borg); Bernard Archard (Inspector Pike); Gladys Cooper (Mrs. Karoujian); Walter Anthony Huston (Derek); John Merivale (Adrian Messenger); Marcel Dalio (Anton Karoudjian); Anita Sharpe-Bolster (Shopkeeper); Noel Purcell (Farmer); John Huston (Lord Aston the Fox Hunter); Tony Curtis (Harlan); Kirk Douglas (George Brougham); Burt Lancaster (Woman); Robert Mitchum (Jim Slattery); Frank Sinatra (Gypsy Stableman); Joe Lynch (Cyclist); Mona Lilian (Proprietress); Tim Dunant (Hunt Secretary); Richard Peel (Sergeant Flood); Stacy Morgan (Whip Man); Anna Van Der Heide (Stewardess); Roland Long (Carstairs); Bernard Fox (Lynce); Barbara Morrison (Nurse); Jennifer Raine (Student Nurse).

RAMPAGE *(Warner Bros., 1963), C-98 min.*
   Producer, William Fadiman; associate producer, Thomas D. Tannenbaum; Phil Karlson; based on the novel by Alan Caillou; screenplay, Robert I. Holt, Marguerite Roberts; music, Elmer Bernstein; title song, Bernstein and Mack David; art director, Herman Blumenthal; set decorator, George James Hopkins; makeup, Gordon Bau; assistant director, Clark Paylow; Miss Martinelli's clothes, Oleg Cassini; sound, Stanley Jones; camera, Harold Lipstein; editor, Gene Milford.

Robert Mitchum (Harry Stanton); Elsa Martinelli (Anna); Jack Hawkins (Otto Abbot); Sabu (Talib); Cely Carrillo (Chep); Emile Genest (Schelling); Stefan Schnabel (Sakai Chief); David Cadiente (Baka).

MAN IN THE MIDDLE *(Twentieth Century-Fox, 1964), 94 min.*

Executive producer, Max E. Youngstein; producer, Walter Seltzer; director, Guy Hamilton; based on the novel *The Winston Affair* by Howard Fast; screenplay, Keith Waterhouse; theme music, Lionel Bart; orchestral music arranger and conductor, John Barry; art director, John Howell; costumes, Ivy Baker; makeup, Sydney Turner; assistant director, Kip Gowans; sound, Les Hammond, Len Shilton; camera, Wilkie Cooper; editor, John Bloom.

Robert Mitchum (Lieutenant Colonel Barney Adams); France Nuyen (Kate Davray); Barry Sullivan (General Kempton); Trevor Howard (Major Kensington); Keenan Wynn (Lieutenant Winston); Sam Wanamaker (Major Kaufman); Alexander Knox (Colonel Burton); Gary Cockrell (Lieutenant Morse); Robert Nichols (Lieutenant Bender); Michael Goodliffe (Colonel Shaw); Errol John (Sergeant Jackson); Paul Maxwell (Major Smith); Lionel Murton (Captain Gunther); Russell Napier (Colonel Thompson); Jared Allen (Captain Dwyer); David Bauer (Colonel Mayburt); Edward Underdown (Major Wyclift); Howard Marion Crawford (Major Poole); William Mitchell (Staff Sergeant Quinn); Al Waxman (Corporal Zimmerman); Glenn Beck (Corporal Burke); Frank Killibrew (Corporal Baxter); Edward Bishop (Lieutenant at Sikri); Terence Cooper (Major Clement); Graham Skidmore (Major Hennessy); Terry Skelton (Colonel Burnside); Paul Blomley (Colonel Winovich); Alistair Barr (Colonel Kelly); Brian Vaughan (Major McCabe); Julian Burton (Major Cummings).

WHAT A WAY TO GO *(Twentieth Century-Fox, 1964), C-111 min.*

Producer, Arthur P. Jacobs; director, J. Lee Thompson; based on the story by Gwen Davis; screenplay, Betty Comden, Adolph Green; music, Nelson Riddle; songs, Jule Styne, Comden, and Green; orchestrator, Arthur Morton; choreography, Gene Kelly; art directors, Jack Martin Smith, Ted Haworth; set decorators, Walter M. Scott, Stuart A. Reiss; men's wardrobe, Moss Mabry; Miss MacLaine's gowns, Edith Head; assistant director, Fred R. Simpson; makeup, Ben Nye; dialogue coach, Leon Charles; sound, Bernard Freericks, Elmer Raguse; special camera effects, L. B. Abbott, Emil Kosa, Jr.; camera, Leon Shamroy; editor, Marjorie Fowler.

Shirley MacLaine (Louisa); Paul Newman (Larry Flint); Robert Mitchum (Rod Anderson); Dean Martin (Leonard Crawley); Gene Kelly (Jerry Benson); Bob Cummings (Dr. Stephanson); Dick Van Dyke (Edgar Hopper); Reginald Gardiner (Painter); Margaret Dumont (Mrs. Foster); Lou Nova (Trentino); Fifi D'Orsay (Baroness); Maurice Marsac (Rene); Wally Vernon (Agent); Jane Wald (Polly); Lenny Kent (Hollywood Lawyer); Sid Gould (Movie Executive); Army Archerd (TV Announcer); Tracy Butler (Movie Star); Anton Arnold (Mr. Foster); Burt Mustin (Crawleyville Lawyer); Pamelyn Ferdin (Geraldine Crawley at Age Four); Jeff Fithian (Jonathan Crawley at Age Five); Billy Corcoran (Leonard Crawley at Age Seven); Helene F. Winston (Doris); Jack Greening (Chester); Queenie Leonard (Lady Kensington); Tom Conway (Lord Kensington); Barbara Bouchet (Girl on Plane); Marjorie Bennett (Mrs. Freeman); Milton Frome (Lawyer); Marcel Hillaire (French Lawyer); Eugene Borden (Neighbor); Chris Connelly (Ned); and: Lynn Borden, Cleo Ronson, Pat O'Moore, Anthony Eustrel, Justin Smith.

MISTER MOSES *(United Artists, 1965), 113 min.*

Producer, Frank Ross; director, Ronald Neame; based on the novel by Max Catto; screenplay, Charles Beaumont, Monja Danischewsky; music and music conductor, John Barry; art directors, Syd Cain, Robert Liang; title backgrounds painted by Robin Anderson; makeup,

George Frost; sound, John W. Mitchell, Bob Jones, Winston Ryder, James Shields; camera, Oswald Morris; editor, Peter Wetherley.

Robert Mitchum (Joe Moses); Carroll Baker (Julie Anderson); Ian Bannen (Robert); Alexander Knox (Reverend Anderson); Raymond St. Jacques (Ubi); Orlando Martins (Chief); Reginald Beckwith (Parkhurst).

THE WAY WEST (United Artists, 1967), C-122 min.

Producer, Harold Hecht; director, Andrew V. McLaglen; based on the novel by A. B. Guthrie, Jr.; screenplay, Ben Maddow, Mitch Lindemann; music, Bronislau Kaper; music conductor, Andre Previn; title song, Kaper and Mack David; art director, Ted Haworth; set decorator, Robert Priestley; costumes, Norma Koch; makeup, Frank McCoy; assistant directors, Terry Morse, Newt Arnold, Tim Zinnemann; sound, Jack Solomon; special effects, Danny Hays; camera, William H. Clothier; editor, Otho Lovering.

Kirk Douglas (Senator William J. Tadlock); Robert Mitchum (Dick Summers); Richard Widmark (Lije Evans); Lola Albright (Rebecca Evans); Michael Witney (Johnnie Mack); Sally Field (Mercy McBee); Katherine Justice (Amanda Mack); Stubby Kaye (Sam Fairman); William Lundigan (Michael Moynihan); Paul Lukather (Turley); Roy Barcroft (Masters); Jack Elam (Weatherby); Patric Knowles (Colonel Grant); Ken Murray (Hank); John Mitchum (Little Henry); Nick Cravat (Calvelli); Harry Carey, Jr. (Mr. McBee); Roy Glenn (Saunders); Connie Sawyer (Mrs. McBee); Anne Barton (Mrs. Moynihan); Eve McVeagh (Mrs. Masters); Peggy Stewart (Mrs. Turley); Stefan Arngrim (Tadlock, Jr.); Hal Lynch (Big Henry); Gary Morris (Paw-Kee-Mah); Eddie Little Sky, Michael Keep (Sioux Braves); Michael Lane (Sioux Chief); Mitchell Schollars (Indian Boy); Jay Coffer, Everett Creach, Jim Burk, Gary McLarty (Four Drovers).

EL DORADO (Paramount, 1967), C-126 min.

Producer, Howard Hawks; associate producer, Paul Helmick; director, Hawks; based on the novel *The Stars in Their Courses* by Harry Brown; screenplay, Leigh Brackett; music and music conductor, Nelson Riddle; song, Riddle and John Gabriel; orchestrator, Gil Grau; art directors, Hal Pereira, Carl Anderson; set decorators, Robert Benton, Ray Moyer; costumes, Edith Head; makeup, Wally Westmore; assistant director, Andrew J. Durkes; title paintings, Olaf Wieghorst; sound, John Carter, Charles Grenzbach; special effects, David Koehler; special camera effects, Paul K. Lerpae; process camera, Farciot Edouart; camera, Harold Rosson; editor, John Woodcock.

John Wayne (Cole Thorton); Robert Mitchum (Sheriff J. B. Harrah); James Caan (Mississippi); Charlene Holt (Maudie); Paul Fix ("Doc" Miller); Arthur Hunnicutt (Deputy Bull Thomas); Michele Carey (Joey MacDonald); R. G. Armstrong (Kevin MacDonald); Edward Asner (Bart Jason); Christopher George (Nelse McLeod); Marina Ghane (Maria); John Gabriel (Pedro); Robert Rothwell (Saul MacDonald); Robert Donner (Milt); Adam Roarke (Matt MacDonald); Charles Courtney (Jared MacDonald); Victoria George (Jared's Wife); Jim Davis (Jason's Foreman); Anne Newman (Saul's Wife); Diane Strom (Matt's Wife); Johnny Crawford (Luke MacDonald); Olaf Wieghorst (Swedish Gunsmith); Anthony Rogers (Dr. Donovan); Dean Smith (Charlie Hagan); William Albert Henry (Sheriff Bill Moreland); Don Collier (Deputy Joe Braddock).

LO SBARCO DI ANZIO (a.k.a., ANZIO, THE BATTLE OF ANZIO, Columbia, 1968), C-117 min.

Producer, Dino De Laurentiis; director, Edward Dmytryk; based on the book *Anzio* by Wynford Vaughan-Thomas; adaptors, Frank De Felitta, Giuseppe Mangione; English screenplay, Harry A. L. Craig; music, Riz Ortolani; song, Ortolani and Jerome Pomus; art director, Luigi Scaccianoce; set decorators, Francesco Bronz, Emilio D'Andria; costumes, Ugo Pericoli; makeup, Amato Garbini; assistant directors, Giorgio Gentili, Gianni Cozzo; sound, Aldo De Martini; special effects, Walfrido Traversari; camera, Giuseppe Rotunno; editors, Alberto Gallitti, Peter Taylor.

Robert Mitchum (Dick Ennis); Peter Falk (Corporal Rabinoff); Earl Holliman (Sergeant Stimler); Arthur Kennedy (General Lesly); Robert Ryan (General Carson); Mark Damon (Richardson); Reni Santoni (Movie); Joseph Walsh (Doyle); Thomas Hunter (Andy); Giancarlo Giannini (Cellini); Anthony Steel (General Marsh); Patrick Magee (General Starkey); Arthur Franz (General Howard); Elsa Albani (Emilia); Wayde Preston (Colonel Hendricks); Venantino Venatini (Captain Burns); Annabella Andreoli (Anna); Wolfgang Preiss (Marshal Kesselring); Tonio Selwart (General Van MacKensen); Stefanella Giovannini (Diana); Marcella Valeri (Assunta); Enzo Turco (Pepe); Wolf Hillinger (Hans the Sniper).

VILLA RIDES *(Paramount, 1968), C-125 min.*

Producer, Ted Richmond; director, Buzz Kulik; based on the novel *Pancho Villa* by William Douglas Lansford; screenplay, Robert Towne, Sam Peckinpah; music and music conductor, Maurice Jarre; designer, Ted Haworth; conductor, art director, Jose Alguero; set decorator, Roman Calatayud; makeup, Richard Mills; costumes, Eric Seeling; assistant director, Tony Fuentes; sound, Roy Chapman; special effects, Milt Rice; camera, Jack Hildyard; second unit camera, John Cabrera; editor, David Bretherton.

Yul Brynner (Pancho Villa); Robert Mitchum (Lee Arnold); Grazia Buccella (Fina Gonzalez); Charles Bronson (Fierro); Robert Viharo (Urbina); Frank Wolff (Captain Ramirez); Herbert Lom (General Huerta); Alexander Knox (President Madero); Diana Lorys (Emilita); Robert Carricart (Luis Gonzalez); Fernando Rey (Fuentes); Regina De Julian (Lupita Gonzalez); Andres Monreal (Herrera); Antonio Ruiz (Juan Gonzalez); John Ireland (Man in Barber Shop); Jill Ireland (Girl in Restaurant).

FIVE CARD STUD *(Paramount, 1968), C-103 min.*

Producer, Hal B. Wallis; associate producer, Paul Nathan; director, Henry Hathaway; based on the novel by Ray Gaulden; screenplay, Marguerite Roberts; music and music conductor, Maurice Jarre; title song, Jarre and Ned Washington; hymn, W. H. Doane and F. C. Van Alystyne; production designer, Walter Tyler; set decorator, Ray Moyer; makeup, Adelbert Acevedo; assistant director, Fred Gammon; sound, Harold Lewis; camera, Daniel L. Fapp; editor, Warren Low.

Dean Martin (Van Morgan); Robert Mitchum (Reverend Rudd); Inger Stevens (Lily Langsford); Roddy McDowall (Nick Evers); Katherine Justice (Nora Evers); John Anderson (Marshal Dana); Ruth Springford (Mama Malone); Yaphet Kotto (Little George); Denver Pyle (Sig Evers); Bill Fletcher (Joe Hurley); Whit Bissell (Dr. Cooper); Ted De Corsia (Eldon Bates); Don Collier (Rowan); Roy Jenson (Mace Jones); Boyd Morgan (Fred Carson); George Rowbotham (Stoney); Jerry Gatlin (The Stranger); Charles B. Hayward (Stunts); Louise Lorimer (Mrs. Wells); Hope Summers (Woman Customer); Chuck Hayward (O'Hara).

SECRET CEREMONY *(Universal, 1968), C-109 min.* *

Producers, John Heyman, Norman Priggen; director, Joseph Losey; based on a short story by Marco Denevi; screenplay, George Tabori; music, Richard Rodney Bennett; production

*Re-edited for television.

designer, Richard MacDonald; art director, John Clark; set decorator, Jill Oxley; Miss Taylor's wardrobe, Marc Bohan, Christian Dior; makeup, Alex Garfath; costumes, Susan Yelland; assistant director, Richard Dalton; sound, Leslie Hammond; camera, Gerald Fisher; editor, Reginald Beck.

Elizabeth Taylor (Leonora); Mia Farrow (Cenci); Robert Mitchum (Albert); Peggy Ashcroft (Hannah); Pamela Brown (Hilda).

YOUNG BILLY YOUNG *(United Artists, 1969), C-89 min.*

Producer, Max E. Youngstein; associate producer, J. Paul Popkin; director, Burt Kennedy; based on the novel *Who Rides with Wyatt?* by Will Henry; screenplay, Kennedy; music, Shelly Manne; title song, Manne and Ernie Sheldon; art director, Stan Jolley; set decorator, Richard Friedman; wardrobe, Jerry Alpert; makeup, Paul Stanhope, Jr.; assistant director, Maxwell Henry; sound, Al Overton, Glen Glenn Sound; special camera effects, Howard A. Anderson Company; camera, Harry Stradling, Jr.; editor Otho Lovering.

Robert Mitchum (Kane); Angie Dickinson (Lily Belloit); Robert Walker (Billy Young); David Carradine (Jesse Boone); Jack Kelly (John Behan); John Anderson (Frank Boone); Deana Martin (Evvie Cushman); Paul Fix (Charlie); Willis Bouchey (Doc Cushman); Parley Baer (Bell); Bob Anderson (Gambler); Rodolfo Acosta (Mexican Officer); Chris Mitchum (Kane's Son).

THE GOOD GUYS AND THE BAD GUYS *(Warner Bros., 1969), C-90 min.*

Executive producer, Robert Goldstein; producer, Ronald M. Cohen, Dennis Shryack; associate producer, Stan Jolley; director, Burt Kennedy; screenplay, Cohen, Shryack; assistant director, Richard Bennett; music, William Lava; song, Lava and Ned Washington; production designer, Jolley; camera, Harry Stradling, Jr.; editor, Howard Deane.

Robert Mitchum (Flagg); George Kennedy (McKay); David Carradine (Waco); Tina Louise (Carmel); Douglas V. Fowley (Grundy); Lois Nettleton (Mary); Martin Balsam (Mayor Wilker); John Davis Chandler (Deuce); John Carradine (Ticker); Marie Windsor (Polly); Dick Peabody (Boyle); Kathleen Freeman (Mrs. Stone); Jimmy Murphy (Buckshot); Garrett Lewis (Hawkins); Nick Dennis (Engineer).

RYAN'S DAUGHTER *(MGM, 1970), C-206 min.*

Producer, Anthony Havelock-Allan; associate producer, Roy Stevens; director, David Lean; screenplay, Robert Bolt; assistant directors, Pedro Vidal, Michael Stevenson; second unit directors, Roy Stevens, Charles Frend; production designer, Stephen Grimes; art director, Roy Walker; set decorator, Josie MacAvin; costumes, Jocelyn Rickards; music and music director, Maurice Jarre; sound, John Bramall; special effects, Bob MacDonald; camera, Freddie Young; second unit camera, Denys Coop, Bob Huke; editor, Norman Savage.

Sarah Miles (Rosy Ryan); Robert Mitchum (Charles Shaughnessy); Trevor Howard (Father Collins); Christopher Jones (Randolph Doryan); John Mills (Michael); Leo McKern (Tom Ryan); Barry Foster (Tim O'Leary); Archie O'Sullivan (McCardle); Marie Kean (Mrs. McCardle); Yvonne Crowley (Moureen); Barry Jackson (Corporal); Douglas Sheldon (Driver); Philip O'Flynn (Paddy); Ed O'Callaghan (Bernard); Gerald Sim (Captain); Des Keogh (Lanky Private); Niall Toibin (O'Keefe); Donal Meligan (Moureen's Beau); Brian O'Higgins (Constable O'Connor); Niall O'Brien (Joseph); Owen O'Sullivan (Peter); Emmet Bergin (Sean); May Cluskey (Storekeeper); Annie Dalton (Old Woman); Pat Layde (Policeman).

GOING HOME *(MGM, 1971), C-97 min.*

Producer, Herbert B. Leonard; associate producers, Stanley Neufeld, Nicky Blair; director, Leonard; screenplay, Lawrence B. Marcus; action sequences coordinated by Max Kleven; assistant directors, Howard W. Koch, Jr., Don Klune; art director, Peter Wooley; set decorators, Audrey Blais, Hal Watkins; music and music conductor, Bill Walker; wardrobe, Guy Verhille; makeup, Hank Edds; sound, Bob Post, Hal Watkins; camera, Fred Jackman; editor, Sigmund Neufeld.

Robert Mitchum (Harry K. Graham); Brenda Vaccaro (Jenny); Jan-Michael Vincent (Jimmy Graham); Jason Bernard (Jimmy at Age Six); Sally Kirkland (Ann Graham); Joe Attles (Bible Man); Lou Gilbert (Mr. Katz); Josh Mostel (Bonelli); Barbara Brownell (Betsy); Carol Gustafson (Ella); David Wilson, Glenn Walke, Clay Watkins, Bruce Kornbluth (Sailors); Thomas Spratley (Guard); Louis Criscuolo (Angry Man); Richard Goode (Pleasant Man); Vicki Sue Robinson (Hippie Girl); Lawrence E. Bender (Pass Clerk); Tim Wallace, Jules Sicilia (Bowling Alley Drunks); Hope Clarke (Mother at Prison); Hank Luba, Edward Steinfeld, Jack C. Harper, Ginny Heller (Friends on Beach); Robert Rinier (Bowler).

THE WRATH OF GOD *(MGM, 1972), C-111 min.*

Executive producer, Peter Katz; associate producer, William S. Gilmore, Jr.; director, Ralph Nelson; based on the novel by James Graham; screenplay, Nelson; music, Lalo Schifrin; production designer, John S. Poplin, Jr.; set decorator, William Kiernan; wardrobe, Ted Parvin; makeup, Del Armstrong; assistant directors, Mario Cisneros, Jerry Ziesmer; sound, Peter Sutton, Harry W. Tetrick; special effects, Federico Farfan; camera, Alex Phillips; editors, J. Terry Williams, Richard Bracken, Albert Wilson.

Robert Mitchum (Van Horne); Frank Langella (Tomas De La Plata); Rita Hayworth (Senora De La Plata); John Colicos (Colonel Santilla); Victor Buono (Jennings); Ken Hutcheson (Emmet Keogh); Paula Pritchett (Chela); Gregory Sierra (Jurado); Frank Ramirez (Moreno); Enrique Lucero (Nacho); Jorge Russek (Cordona); Chano Urueta (Antonio); Jose Luis Parades (Pablito); Aurora Clavel (Senora Moreno); Victor Eberg (Delgado); Pancho Cordova (Tacho); Guillermo Hernandez (Diaz); Ralph Nelson (Executed Man).

THE FRIENDS OF EDDIE COYLE *(Paramount, 1973), C-102 min.*

Producer, Paul Monash; associate producer, Charles Maguire; director, Peter Yates; based on the novel by George V. Higgins; screenplay, Monash; production designer, Gene Callahan; set decorator, Don Galvin; music, Dave Grusin; titles, Everett Aison; sound, Dick Raguse; camera, Victor J. Kemper; editor, Pat Jaffe.

Robert Mitchum (Eddie Coyle); Peter Boyle (Dillon); Richard Jordan (Dave Foley); Steven Keats (Jackie); Alex Rocco (Scalise); Joe Santos (Artie Van); Mitchell Ryan (Waters); Peter MacLean (Partridge); Kevin O'Morrison (Manager of Second Bank); Marvin Lichterman (Vernon); Carolyn Pickman (Nancy); James Tolkan (The Man's Contact Man); Margaret Ladd (Andrea); Matthew Cowles (Pete); Helena Carroll (Sheila Coyle); Jane House (Wanda); Michael McCleery (The Kid); Alan Koss (Phil); Dennis McMullen (Webber); Judith Ogden Cabot (Mrs. Partridge); Jan Egleson (Pale Kid); Jack Kehoe (The Beard); Robert Anthony (Moran); Gus Johnson (Ames); Ted Maynard (Sauter); Sheldon Feldner (Ferris).

THE YAKUZA *(Warner Bros., 1975), C-112 min.*

Executive producer, Shundo Koji; co-producer, Michael Hamilburg; producer-director, Sydney Pollack; story, Leonard Schrader; screenplay, Paul Schrader, Robert Towne; art director, Ishida Yoshiyuki; costume designer, Dorothy Jeakins; makeup, Garry Morris; assistant directors, D. Michael Moore, Mike Abe; production designer and second unit director, Stephen Grimes; music, Dave Grusin; special effects, Richard Parker, Kasai Tomoo; camera, Okazaki Kozo, Duke Callaghan; editors, Thomas Stanford, Don Guidice.

Robert Mitchum (Harry Kilmer); Takakura Ken (Tanaka Ken); Brian Keith (George Tanner); Herb Edelman (Wheat); Richard Jordan (Dusty); Kishi Keiko (Eiko); Okado Eiji (Tono); James Shigeta (Goro); Kyosuke Mashida (Kato); Christina Kobubo (Hanako); Go Eiji (Spider); Lee Chirillo (Louise); M. Hisaka (Boyfriend); William Ross (Tanner's Guard), Harada (Goro's Doorman).

FAREWELL, MY LOVELY *(Avco Embassy, 1975), C-97 mins.*

Executive producers, Elliott Kastner, Jerry Bick; producers, George Pappas, Jerry Bruckheimer; director, Dick Richards; based on the novel by Raymond Chandler; screenplay, David Zelag Goodman; assistant directors, Henry Lange, David Sonsa; production designer, Dean Tavoularis; art director, Angelo Graham; set decorator, Bob Nelson; costumes, Tony Scarano, Sandy Berke; makeup, Frank Westmore; music, David Shire; camera, John Alonzo; editors, Walter Thompson, Joel Cox.

Robert Mitchum (Philip Marlowe); Charlotte Rampling (Mrs. Grayle [Velma]); John Ireland (Detective Lieutenant Nulty); Sylvia Miles (Mrs. Florian); Jack O'Halloran (Moose Malloy); Anthony Zerbe (Burnette); Harry Dean Stanton (Billy Rolfe); Jim Thompson (Mr. Grayle); John O'Leary (Marriott); Kate Murtagh (Amthor); Walter McGinn (Tommy Ray); Jimmy Archer (Georgie); Joe Spinell (Nick); Sylvester Stallone (Kelly/Jonnie); Burt Gilliam (Cowboy).

THE LAST TYCOON *(Paramount, 1976), C.*

Producer, Sam Spiegel; director, Elia Kazan; based on the novel by F. Scott Fitzgerald; screenplay, Harold Pinter; costumes, Anna Hill Johnstone; production designer, Gene Callahan; set decorator, Jerry Wunderlich; assistant directors, Danny McCauley, Ron Wright; sound, Larry Jost; camera, Victor Kemper.

With Robert De Niro, Tony Curtis, Robert Mitchum, Jeanne Moreau, Jack Nicholson, Donald Pleasence, Ray Milland, Dana Andrews, Ingrid Boulting, Theresa Russell, Anjellica Huston, Peter Strauss, Jeff Corey, Seymour Cassel.

MIDWAY *(Universal, 1976), C.*

Producer, Walter Mirisch; director, John Guillermin; screenplay, Donald S. Sanford; art director, Walter Tyler; set director, John Dwyer; technical advisor, Vice-Admiral Bernard M. Strean, Ret., U.S.N.; assistant director, Jerry Siegel; sound, Bob Martin; camera, Jarry Seradling, Jr.

With Charlton Heston. Robert Mitchum (Admiral William F. Halsey); Henry Fonda (Admiral Chester Nimitz); Glenn Ford (Admiral Raymond Spruance); Toshiro Mifune (Admiral Yamamoto); Cliff Robertson (Admiral Jessop); Ed Nelson (Admiral Pierson); Hal Holbrook (Commander Rochefort); James Coburn (Captain Maddox); and Robert Wagner, Edward Albert, James Shigeta, Robert Webber, Christina Kokobo, Dabney Coleman, Dennis Rucker, Eric Estrade, Kip Niven, Michael Richardson.

Publicity pose for *Hudson's Bay* (20th, 1940)

Paul Muni

5'10"
165 pounds
Brown hair
Brown eyes
Virgo

New generations of film enthusiasts are constantly amazed to rediscover that, in the Thirties, *Mister* Paul Muni was held in such high professional regard. They find it puzzling that the "King of the Character Actors," who instilled such energy into his performances, lacked the subtlety and underplaying that is so admired today.

But in his time, Mr. Muni was King (and his career-directing wife Bella was the power behind the throne). Each in turn—the Yiddish stage, Broadway, and the motion pictures—acclaimed him as a superlative technician. Producers, critics, and the public were enraptured at his uncanny ability to thrust himself so forcibly into his latest characterization. Rumors of his insistence upon draining the most minute detail from a role substantiated his greatness as an "artist."

There were occasional dissenters. Bette Davis who worked with him in *Bordertown* (1935) and *Juarez* (1939) would recall, "Mr. Muni seemed intent on submerging himself so completely that he disappeared." Today, the consensus of opinion is even less kind. His work has been branded as "dated" and his acting as "hammy."

But the intense man who offered such an engaging array of screen roles (from the gangster kingpin *Scarface* to the land-hungry Chinaman in *The Good Earth*) is worthy of fresh reinterpretation. Two full-length biographies have recently been published on his career and a telefeature about *The Actor* is presently in the works. Perhaps the interpreter of *I Am a Fugitive from a Chain Gang* (1932) and *The Story of Louis Pasteur* (1936) will soon find his proper place in cinema history.

Paul Muni was born Muni Weisenfreund in Lemberg, Austria (now part of Poland), on Sunday, September 22, 1895. He was the first-born of three sons of Nachum Favel and Salche (Weisburg) Weisenfreund, who wandered from ghetto to ghetto in Europe in the most basic form of Yiddish theatre. They toured in the most primitive of fashion, their songs, sketches, and dances performed on boards set across two big barrels, usually in the corner of a field, with kerosene lamps for their "footlights." The title tagged onto his father was a "tingle tangle schauspieler"—a combination barker, actor, dancer, and singer whose talents suited the circus as much as the legitimate stage. The family endured a gypsy-like existence, their range of talents maintaining a steady, if dismally modest, income.

As the Weisenfreunds trekked from one haphazard engagement to another, the children were frequently farmed out to obliging relatives or friends. In later years, Muni had little to say on the subject. "I have a rather vague recollection of my background and I've never attempted—for some reason which I can't understand myself—I've never tried to go into the business of checking up on all these things. I never cared very much who I was, where I came from, what my parents were doing."

In 1901, the Weisenfreunds managed to journey to London. Nachum purchased a hovel in Whitechapel that became transformed into a theatre. But soon after that, a gang fight on the theatre steps resulted in a death, causing the authorities to demand the closing of the theatre. Careful thrift during their stay, however, allowed the family to travel to America and New York City in 1902. "We lived downtown, way down on Suffolk Street, I don't remember," Muni would later say. "We moved around from one place to another in those cold-water flats on the fifth or sixth floor, or somewhere." While the parents found steady work in the Lower East Side and in Brooklyn, the children began school. Just when Muni was becoming acclimated to life at P.S. 20, he suffered a bout of rheumatic fever. Then, when the work market for Yiddish performers dried up, his parents were out of a job. When the youth should have been continuing his studies in the fourth grade, he was forced to leave school and join his family as they became vagabonds in search of employment. Thereafter, his education consisted mainly of reading the dictionary during train jaunts.

Having experienced such a precarious livelihood in the theatre, the Weisenfreunds wished no such future for their children. As soon as the boys were old enough to hold a violin, the father began setting aside a portion of his weekly earnings to supply the children with music lessons. When positions opened with a Yiddish company in Cleveland, the Weisenfreunds readily accepted. They subsequently encouraged their sons to master the violin sufficiently to obtain assignments in the group's orchestra.

But fate had other plans for Muni. One evening in 1907, the troupe was presenting a play entitled *Two Corpses for Breakfast*. One of the resident performers fell ill. The company's meagre budget could not supply the ten dollars necessary for a replacement. So, at the last minute, the understudy selected was little Muni. His part was that of a wobbly-kneed lodge president in his late sixties. The fact that young Weisenfreund was only eleven years old and had never acted on stage before was not as important as the fact that his price was right (nothing) and that he was a live body. That evening, Muni made his acting bow, prophetically smothered in make-up. He thoroughly loved the experience. Shortly afterward, the stagestruck boy approached his father who was now in charge of the theatre. He timidly begged to change his prospective vocation. His father, disappointed but understanding, said nothing. He simply took the boy's violin and broke it over his knee. Muni very soon became a regular member of the company, receiving the weekly salary of ten dollars.

The theatre quickly became Muni's entire way of life. "I lived in the theatre ever since I was conscious of the fact that I had to go on the boards and appear before an audience. I lived there from ten in the morning 'til 12 at night every single day. When everybody else was gone, I was acting. I was on the stage doing something, making believe, doing all sorts of things. Whenever anything happened, whenever anything new came along, whether it was American or foreign or whatever, I went to see it."

In Shakespearean times, young would-be actors apprenticed by playing women's roles. The Yiddish theatre gave this practice a twist, casting their young hopefuls as wheezing old codgers. While many adolescents would tire of the yellow pancake, charcoaled age lines, and pasted-on whiskers, Muni reveled in them. "Make-up to me was very much like playing bridge is to somebody. It was a game. When I started in the profession, when I was all of maybe 11 or 12 years old, I used to go into the dressing room, in the theatre that my father ran, at 12 o'clock noon, or 10 o'clock in the morning, buy a pound of grapes or something like that, and some bread, and I'd stay there until the performance, and put it on and take it off, and put it on and just smear my face. And put wigs on, because my father had a lot of wigs, you know, that were changed—we'd put crepe hair on in certain places; we'd take one wig and make four or five different wigs out of it, and I would play around with it and it was a hobby. I enjoyed it, you see, and that ultimately developed. Then I used to buy a lot of greasepaint and I'd fool around with it."

A legend later developed concerning the star's earliest days on the stage. It told of kids fleeing in terror from an alley behind the Cleveland Yiddish theatre as an amber-faced, black-toothed, straggly-haired old man rollerskated toward them in a frenzy of flying beard and ragged clothing. This alley denizen was supposedly none other than Muni, indulging in a little sport between matinee acts.

When Muni was fifteen, his father died. His mother moved the family to Chicago, where she and Muni obtained posts in a Yiddish touring company. Three years later, Mrs. Weisenfreund remarried and retired from the stage at the time her son's career was just really beginning. Over the next eight years, Muni would tour the midwest, work with a Philadelphia burlesque company, and then join Molly Picon's Boston repertory group. During this period, he worked in as many as thirty shows a week, encompassing skits, full length dramas, and song and dance (a format in which he achieved his earliest popularity). The unending routine was a grind and the pay (never exceeding twenty-five dollars a week) was hardly compensatory. But it allowed the future star to learn his profession in the best possible way—acting in front of paying audiences.

The Picon company was a great boon to Muni's burgeoning career, as it allowed him to work with top-flight actors. However, the flu epidemic of 1918 closed down the company. "I was about to sign a contract to go to a legitimate theatre," Muni later recollected, "when Maurice Schwartz, for some reason which I can never understand, sent a chap to Philadelphia, and all of a sudden they signed me up to do the Irving Place Theatre [in New York City], which was at the time the Yiddish Art Theatre . . . the Yiddish Art Theatre was *the* Theatre." Schwartz greatly refined the standards of the Yiddish theatre, promoting performers such as Jacob Ben-Ami

Publicity pose in 1929

and Celia Adler, and playwrights like Chekhov, Gorky, and Sholom Aleichem. It was a wonderful opportunity for Muni, offering him a top salary (forty-five dollars a week). The young man enthusiastically accepted the offer.

Over the next eight years he would not only play to acclaim in New York but also on tours in other parts of America and in Europe. It provided him with the experience necessary to refine his technique.

As Muni's talent took form, so did his personality. He was a painfully shy man. He often daydreamed; he was frequently preoccupied and usually socially awkward. He rarely got along with or befriended fellow actors or employers. (With Schwartz, "we used to converse through a third person.") At this formative time in his life, Muni married. On May 8, 1921, at noon (for there was a matinee that Sunday) he wed Bella Finkel, daughter of the Thomashevsky family, "the Barrymores of the Lower East Side." She was an unusual looking girl whose hollow eyes and slender frame concealed the dominating personality of a female Svengali.

Typical of the married life they were to share was the wedding itself. After the Rabbi intoned the final blessing, Muni shook hands with the bride, threw a quick grin at the guests, and ran out the door. He wished to get to the theatre in order to have sufficient time to prepare for the afternoon's performance. He slept alone for the next two weeks, just to get sufficient rest for the next day's rehearsals. Finally, when Bella became more familiar with her stoical husband fifteen days after the wedding, it was only because they were to go on tour together with a show. The Munis would be childless.

In this period, the actor enjoyed consistent success with Schwartz's company.[1] Among the roles he played were Ivanov in Aleichem's *Hard to Be a Jew*, David

[1]Muni became an American citizen in 1923.

Leizer in Andreyev's *Anathema*, Ossip in Gogol's *The Inspector General*, the father in Gorky's *Middle Class People*, and DuArun, the fop aristocrat, in Romain Rolland's *Wolves*. All of this work was performed in the Yiddish language, in the traditional style of that ethnic theatre. (The actors in the Yiddish theatre were never expected to memorize a play line perfectly but to get "the feel of the part," for there would always be a prompter ready to help out a floundering performer back onto the proper plot path. This custom would be a disservice to Muni the star in later years, for he would find it quite difficult to memorize long passages.

A play entitled *We Americans* was scheduled to open on Broadway on October 12, 1926. It was a comedy about a Jewish family's adjustment to life in the United States and the generation gap brought Muni to the English-speaking stage. And it was the unavailability of another actor, Edward G. Robinson, that resulted in Muni earning his major theatrical break.

Robinson recalls in his memoirs, *All My Yesterdays* (1973), "Waiting for the [Theatre] Guild season to begin, I did a play called *We Americans* in Atlantic City. Because I had already committed myself to the Guild, I could not, unfortunately, continue with it. I tried to get out of the Guild contract [to do *Juarez and Maximilian*], because *We Americans* was bound to be a hit, but the Guild refused to release me." Robinson recalled how his replacement, "a young Yiddish actor named Muni Weisenfreund [whom Guild worker Clara Langsner had suggested]" went on to become his "most potent competition." Muni never acknowledged this fact in his career and the two performers did not warm to one another for years afterward.

Despite Muni's credentials and a top-selling effort by press agent Edward Relkin, he almost lost the part. When he arrived at Sam Harris' office for an audition, the famed producer was out. Max Siegel, who co-authored the comedy with Milton Herbert Gropper, was there and told Muni to be patient. Muni was, for about five minutes. He then announced *he* was leaving. Siegel tried to dissuade him, but Muni retorted with one of his prize sayings, "If a man steals money or property from you, that's one thing, but if he steals time, he steals a piece of your life." Siegel eventually had to strong-arm Muni into remaining. When Harris did appear, the producer was doubly surprised. Greeting him was a young man standing on his head. Harris snapped that he was not interested in acrobats, but Siegel hastened to explain that the acrobat was actually Muni Weisenfreund. Harris was also surprised to see a man so young testing for a role of an old person. Muni retorted that with makeup he could reveal first-hand his ability at suggesting age. Harris relented, and a few hours later Muni had the part.

So eager was Muni to win acceptance on the Broadway stage with this role, that he became nearly fanatical in his preparations for the part. Rather than use a prefabricated beard, he reputedly glued on one hair at a time to make his own. He worked at simulating baggy eyes and wrinkled features until the final effect was uncannily realistic. To test his characterization, he donned the make-up and costume one afternoon and visited his mother-in-law. Mrs. Finkel was of the Thomashevsky clan of famous Yiddish actors and saw Muni every day. Yet when he shuffled to her door, raspily asking for directions and engaging her in conversation, she did not recognize him.

We Americans, under the direction of Sam Forrest, opened on Columbus Day, 1926, at the Sam Harris Theatre with Luther Adler co-starring with Muni. Aside from an unfortunate typographical error in the *New York Times* which listed Muni as "Mimi Weisenfreund" the reviews were most flattering. The best accolades came from several scribes who commented how poetically sad it was that this old man Weisenfreund had to wait all these years to star in a Broadway show

We Americans ran for 120 performances,[2] and during the engagement producer John Golden took notice of Muni. Golden was preparing *Four Walls* by George Abbott and Dana Burnett, concerning a young hoodlum. Bella remembered, "George Abbott called Sam Harris and he said what do you think of—I've got this play with the young gangster, and so forth—and he said what do you think about the fella you have, Muni Weisenfreund, and Sam Harris said, 'Oh no, he only plays old men.'" Once again, Muni had to battle to escape the "typing" that his excellent acting had earned him.

But once again he won. Abbott began directing an excellent cast that included Lee Strasberg and Sanford Meisner. And making her English-speaking stage debut as Muni's sweetheart was Bella. (Ironically, it was during this period that the couple were undergoing a number of separations and reconciliations, Bella being unwilling to adjust to the strange sort of marriage Muni demanded.) *Four Walls* opened on September 19, 1927, at the John Golden Theatre. He played Benny Horowitz, a young ex-convict freshly released from Sing Sing and trying to rehabilitate to civilian life. A tragic ending found him back behind bars after killing his old gang leader. Wrote the *New York Times*, "There is, first and foremost, Mr. Weisenfreund, who, playing his second English speaking part, contributes a sensitive, understanding, and full-rounded portrayal of an East side youth who, caught in the vise-like grip of his environment, manages to evolve a set of home made ideals and remain true to them."

Four Walls required Muni to portray a character approximating his actual age. It was more of an acting and emotional challenge to him than most would imagine, for the lack of excessive make-up made him insecure. As he reminisced, "I opened that door and I was as embarrassed as if I lost my clothes. All of a sudden I was naked, because there wasn't some sort of smear or anything. I didn't have any beard or wigs."

Muni's stage successes occurred at a fortuitous time. Sound pictures were on the horizon, and the motion picture business was undergoing both a transition and a reburgeoning. Albert Lewis, who had co-produced *We Americans,* was one of the Broadway personages lured to California to help the moviemakers make the transition from silents to sound. As an executive assistant to production chief Winfield Sheehan at the Fox Studios, he had to come up with some impressive Broadway star who could be contracted for talking pictures. Lewis persuaded Sheehan and company head William Fox to view a performance of *Four Walls* and to judge Muni's potential.[3] It was agreed that the actor should make a screentest at the company's Manhattan studio.

Treated to a lavish budget and ample time for refinement, Muni's audition was a success. He played scenes from Chekhov's *The Stage Doorman,* bits from Shakespeare's *The Merry Wives of Windsor,* and, among others, segments from O'Neill's *The Hairy Ape.* For each role he created in front of the camera he was allowed to try

[2]When Universal made a silent film version of *We Americans* in 1928, Muni was considered but rejected for the role because he was thought too young (despite his make-up) and too Jewish. George Sidney was cast instead in the part of Mr. Levine.

[3]Once again, when Muni's stage role was created oncamera, another actor played the part; this time it was John Gilbert in MGM's 1928 silent film, and Franchot Tone in *Straight Is the Way* (MGM, 1934), the remake.

a different disguise and a variant voice. Sheehan was sufficiently impressed (he called him the "new Chaney"), as was Fox, that Muni was offered a screen contract. Bella naturally contributed to the document, which bound Muni to a three-year agreement, with options, and which provided for a starting salary of five hundred dollars weekly, to be boosted to fifteen hundred dollars a week in the third year.

The actor's initial film career was doomed from the start. Bella began having second thoughts about the picture deal and infected her husband with her mounting doubts. Producer Albert Lewis said, "Bella insisted that Muni know what scripts he was going to do. She wanted a clause added to the contract that would stipulate what Muni's first film would be. They were afraid that he might go out to Hollywood and get assigned to appear in a Western, or something else beneath his calibre." The clause was not added; Muni would have to wait four years before Warner Bros. would treat him to this rare luxury. Lewis did agree, however, to secure a property worthy of the actor. He and Sheehan decided *Liliom* might suit the new star. Lewis began negotiating with MGM who held the screen rights to the Molnar play.

Meanwhile, the Weisenfreunds reluctantly arrived among the oranges and madmen of Los Angeles. Sheehan's first order of business at the studio was to convince the actor to change his name. Bella saw Sheehan's point; Muni agreed and thereafter became known as Paul Muni. (His acquaintances still always referred to him as Muni.) Neither husband nor wife was delighted when the studio executive next assigned him colorful press agents to promote Paul Muni as a brilliant new discovery recently imported from Russia.

While negotiations for *Liliom* were still in progress, a substitute vehicle was chosen. The property was a one-act play by Holsworthy Hall and Robert M. Middle-

In *The Valiant* (Fox, 1929) with Marguerite Churchill

mass entitled *The Valiant* (Fox, 1929). The premise found a young man denying his identity so that his mother and sister would be freed of his shame.

The director of *The Valiant* was William K. Howard. He found himself not only fighting the complicated technology of the early talkies, battling with a soggy plot, and waging a campaign to tone down the bravura acting of Muni, but also stifling the desire to throttle the film's second director, Bella.

The Valiant was in for even more trouble. William Fox had been away on business when the picture began production. Upon his return, he asked to see the rushes. He was so disappointed in Muni's celluloid charisma that he wanted to shut down the picture. Sheehan argued that the project was thirty-percent complete, that the sets were all built, and that the cast was all contracted. Fox agreed to a compromise. Thus, the movie in completed form ran only sixty-six minutes on four and a half reels, rather than ninety minutes on six reels as originally intended.

Nobody at Fox was too optimistic about the film's fate, but they did decide to release it. In May of 1929, *The Valiant* premiered, winning enthusiastic reviews for Muni and flopping at the boxoffice. The *New York Times* called Muni "splendid." *Variety* reported: "Paul Muni, the former Muni Weisenfreund of the Yiddish stage, brings to his role a wealth of humanity. He registers splendidly with utter natural-ness, and while he will be difficult to cast, he should find an important niche in the talkers. His voice is rich and pleasant, his personality strong and virile, and if he is not pretty, neither is Lon Chaney or Emil Jannings, and Muni has what those fellows have not—dialogue unity. It's going to require much smart showmanship to exploit this young Yiddish-American actor, but directed and handled intelligently, he looks like one of the legits who will survive in the talkers."

For his first picture, Muni appeared to excellent advantage. His facial expressions were very eloquent and rarely exceeded the style requirements of the camera. Muni was nominated for an Academy Award for Best Actor, but lost out to Warner Baxter of *In Old Arizona* (Fox).

Even William Fox had not anticipated the apathetic public reaction to *The Valiant*. Fearing that Muni, whom he now decided was a prestige personality, would flee back to New York, the studio made a concerted effort to avoid letting the star know of his film failure. Instead they rushed him into an ambitious picture entitled *Seven Faces* (Fox, 1929), that proved to be a *tour-de-force* challenge for the actor.

Seven Faces was based on *Friend of Napoleon* by Richard Cornell. It concerned an old caretaker in a Paris Wax Museum who dreams he is, successively, six of the people represented in the museum. The famous characters were Svengali, Don Juan, Franz Schubert, Joe Gans (a black boxer), a Cockney, and Napoleon. The last received the most screen time. The film was somewhat similar to Warner Bros.' *Mystery of the Wax Museum* (1933), though not horrific in scope, but rather central-ized around a lonely man who regards the wax models as his "family." When the museum is later shut down, the caretaker uses his life savings to bid at an auction for the statue of Napoleon, and steals it when he is outbid. A chase through Paris brings the film to a happy finale.

With such a demanding range of characters to portray (all in makeup of one sort or another), Muni was much more intrigued with this, his second, film. He was able to cope with the production's two directors, the official one, Viennese Berthold Viertel (who had language problems communicating with his cast and staff) and Lester Lonergan, the "dialogue director." The unofficial directorial adjunct to the project, Bella, departed halfway through production. In early April, 1929 her mother died and the daughter had to fly back to New York for the funeral. (Muni was refused permission to leave the filming to accompany her.)

Fox decided to publicize Muni's *Seven Faces* appearances as the birth of a new Lon Chaney. But the actor was against such a publicity campaign. He told the press, "Some screen actors have worked up a tremendous reputation as character men by appearing in different make-up in each picture. But they have never rung true to me because I can see the personality behind the disguises. Their foundation isn't right. In order to characterize effectively, it is more important to masquerade the mind than the body. It is possible for a great actor to create the illusion of age, or nationality, or station in life, without once resorting to a beard, false teeth, or whatever. External devices should be used merely to help an audience believe the role, not to help an actor to play it." He did state that he thought Chaney was a superb actor, but that he could not be compared with the master of the horrific. Chaney played grotesques while Muni played "everyday people."

Fox released *Seven Faces* in November, 1929. The unusual film, which had been sloppily edited, earned little public endorsement. But once again, Muni was a critic's darling.

While Muni had been aggressive at the studio with the aid of Bella, the executives discovered just how insecure he was when he made a scheduled personal appearance at the Roxy Theatre in New York for the picture's premiere. He was slated to appear after each show to talk to the audience. However, after the first time in front of the crowd, he refused to follow up the experience. On display before legions of people, he could hardly talk. Devoid of a stage character and makeup, he had no confidence.

Back at Fox, nothing had improved the dismal situation. Muni let it be known that he wanted the lead in *Born Reckless* (1930), a top gangster yarn. The part, however, went to Edmund Lowe. Then the studio decided to proceed with *Liliom* (1930), but with a top boxoffice attraction instead of Muni; the role went to Charles Farrell, in a plan to reteam him with his *Seventh Heaven* co-star, Janet Gaynor. When Fox offered Muni a minor part in the production, it was the final straw. He refused it and told Bella to start packing. The couple drove back to New York City.

When Muni returned to Manhattan in April, 1930, he vowed that he was through with movies forever. Fox seconded the motion, but a number of other producing outfits had taken notice of the actor during his brief but interesting Hollywood stay. One such studio was Universal Pictures. It was preparing to shoot *Dracula* (1931), with Lon Chaney in the lead, but on the eve of production, in August, 1930, Chaney died of throat cancer. Universal expressed interest in Muni's tackling the vampire's role, but he was not enthralled with the idea. The film company finally cast the Broadway Dracula, Bela Lugosi, in the part.

Determined to reacquaint himself with the legitimate stage, Muni agreed to star in Sidney Buchman's play *This One Man*. During the course of the West Coast pre-Broadway tour, the show went through a number of title changes and, before reaching New York in October, 1930, had switched directors. The play, at the Morosco Theatre, cast Muni as a decidedly unsympathetic safecracker who allows his brother to be executed for a murder he had committed. Brooks Atkinson, in the *New York Times,* judged Muni's performance as "overpowering and magnificent." But the play itself was no great piece of entertainment, and the show folded after five weeks. In February, 1931, he starred in another vehicle, *Rock Me, Julie,* as the illegitimate son of a midwestern family. Again, his personal notices were glowing, but the play closed after only seven performances.

Meanwhile, in Hollywood, plans were developing that would change Muni's future career. Armitage Trail had written a brutal and true script, *Scarface,* that exposed the more lethal details of the life of Chicago gangster king Al Capone. It was a fast-paced, exciting story which everybody admired but nobody wanted to produce. The cycle of underworld stories in the talkies had yet to begin. Gangsters were a sore spot in the American conscience; many Americans found themselves shocked by the gang lords' murderous tactics while simultaneously admiring and envying their mode of living. Finally Warner Bros.-First National dared to release a punchy gangster film, *Little Caesar* (1931), which was an enormous success and made Edward G. Robinson a star. Then, in April, 1931, *Public Enemy* (Warner Bros.) followed, again causing tremendous lines to form at the ticket windows, and catapulting James Cagney to stardom. Playing on the success of these ventures, an agent named Al Rosen managed to persuade Howard Hughes to film *Scarface.* Hughes was determined to carry through the production in typical uncompromising style.

He lined up Howard Hawks to direct the film and began pondering which Hollywood actor should play the lead. After some discussion, Al Rosen remembered Muni. The agent had seen him on Broadway in *We Americans* and recalled his Oscar-nominated role of the criminal in *The Valiant.* It was agreed that Hawks, who had seen Muni onstage, too, would go to New York to find the actor. Once there, he tested Muni for the focal part. The director had no doubt that the actor was correct for the role; he wanted to convince Muni of the fact. After viewing his own test, the performer agreed to the part. But then Hughes, on the Coast, demanded that Muni come to California to make additional tests, which if agreeable would lead to a twenty-thousand-dollar salary contract. Muni refused to make further auditions. Either Hughes accepted him on his reputation and the basis of the already-completed run-through, and increase the *Scarface* pay to $27,500, or no deal. Hughes eventually capitulated.

Scarface was filmed at United Artists studios, and later at Metropolitan Studios, during the late spring of 1931. The battles staged between the northside and southside beer barons were filmed with real bullets and technical gadgetry as dangerous as they were realistic. Reportedly, Harold Lloyd's brother lost an eye while visiting the set when he insisted on watching a bullet-flying scene at close range.

The motion picture was loosely based on Al Capone's meteoric career. Capone was represented by Tony Camonte, who is first seen oncamera as a gunman for big shot Johnny Lovo (Osgood Perkins). Muni's Tony is an ambitious punk, quick with a gun and festering with an incestuous desire for his sister, Cesca (Ann Dvorak). The scar-faced Tony gleefully murders hood after hood to consolidate Lovo's status as the district's beer baron. So well does he do his job that his boss, fearing Camonte's growing ambition and resenting his lustful interest in Poppy (Karen Morley), orders him rubbed out. When the fast-rising Camonte learns of the order, he beats Lovo to the punch, slays the squirming beer baron, and takes over the mob. Meanwhile, Camonte promotes Rinaldo (George Raft), who falls in love with Cesca. They marry, but do not tell the erratic Scarface. Camonte learns they are sharing an hotel apartment, but still unaware that the couple is married, rushes to revenge the "honor" of his sister, gunning down Rinaldo. Later, Camonte and the still loyal

With George Raft in *Scarface: Shame of a Nation* (UA, 1932)

Cesca are surrounded by the cops, who are shooting to kill. Cesca is killed in a hail of bullets, while Camonte is shot down in the street.

Muni's vigorous performance hasn't weathered well; there is an inordinate amount of mugging and posturing. Nevertheless, he is impressively evil, with the scar streaking his left cheek, his dark hair greased down, and a wardrobe of loud clothes. Muni does paint an unforgettable character—not attractively cocky like Cagney's *Public Enemy,* not charismatic like Robinson's *Little Caesar*—who is an ambitious monster, lusting for power. His keening delight over his new machine gun, his lecherous leers at women, and his primitive delight when he plugs his rival make for an ugly, chilling experience. Naturally, the ironic ending which finds Scarface dying like a coward makes all that goes before in the photoplay far more effective.

In addition to Muni's work, many of the performances in *Scarface* are near perfect: Osgood Perkins, sporting a bushy moustache and splendid sneer, is an appropriate Lovo; Ann Dvorak is right as Cesca, Scarface's long-suffering sister; and George Raft's greasy, coin-tossing, paper-doll cutting loyal Rinaldo is a classic characterization (a role that would launch his unusual film career). Two perform-ances, however, seem less than suitable. One is Karen Morley as the hard-boiled, well-lacquered Poppy, the moll who services Lovo and later Scarface. In her low-cut sexy costumes, Miss Morley, nevertheless, is still too demure looking. The other very strange characterization in this film is that of Boris Karloff as Gaffney, a Camonte rival, based on the real-life underworld figure of Bugs Moran. As soon as he opens his mouth and his polished English accent rolls out, with a lisp to boot, the effect is thoroughly incongruous.

One of the most potent aspects of Hawks' *Scarface* is the array of death scenes. There are three that rank among the top vignettes in gangster films. The first death

With Henry Armetta in *Scarface*

At his Hollywood home (*c.* 1932)

was Karloff's, machine-gunned down as he hurls a bowling ball. As he gasps his last, the pins fall, and the last one topples as Karloff dies. The second was the famous drilling of Raft. Raft recalled later in life that the realism in the scene was not totally histrionic. "When Muni fired the gun," he says, "I bumped the back of my head against the corner of the set. My eyes rolled upward and I was actually knocked out for a few minutes." The third celluloid demise of note here was Muni's, as the police gun down the cringing weasel. He expires beneath a sign blazing, "The world at your feet."

Scarface was such a magnetic blend of violence, sadism, and sex that the Hays Office refused to pass it. Although Muni obviously played the role as a despicable creature who meets a fitting end, the board believed the motion picture did not sufficiently condemn the character and his counterparts. The Hays Office wanted to insure that anyone who saw the picture would remember that "crime does not pay."

Hughes agreed to make additional changes and lengthened the film's title to *Scarface: Shame of a Nation*. Hawks and Muni, however, were not so inclined to kowtow to the dictates of the ominous censors. Hawks was rightfully proud of the powerful and clever climax of his film, and refused to weaken it by filming the insipid lectures recommended by the board. Muni had returned to New York and refused to participate in any further moves to dilute his performance or the film. Nevertheless, some changes were made. Tully Marshall was given some pompous sermons to deliver as a righteous newspaper editor. Edwin Maxwell, as a chief of detectives, joined in the verbiage against crime. Also, an unknown actor, resembling Muni in silhouette and from the rear, posed in the new scenes while the lectures flowed from the guardians of public morality and Scarface was ultimately tried and hanged. The film was eventually released with both endings, the scrubbed one shown only where local censorship prevailed.

In the meantime, with *Scarface* hamstrung in release problems, Muni returned to Broadway for what would prove to be his greatest stage success to that point, *Counsellor-at-Law*. Written and directed by Elmer Rice, the play cast Paul Muni as a dynamic, self-made attorney, George Simon[4] with scores of unusual clients and a snobbish, cheating wife. The play opened on November 7, 1931, at the Plymouth Theatre and became the hit of the season. Once again, Muni's reviews were exercises in supreme accolades, with the *New York Times* enthusing, "Mr. Muni gives one of those forceful and inventive performances that renew faith in the theatre." The exceedingly worried Muni need not have fretted; Broadway was glad to welcome him back.

Six months after *Counsellor-at-Law* debuted, *Scarface: Shame of a Nation* was finally unleashed and opened in Yonkers, New York, on May 19, 1932. Reviews warned readers that the picture, already notorious due to its nip-and-tuck struggle with the censors, was indeed a wild film, but also a valuable one. "*Scarface* contains more cruelty than any of its predecessors," noted *Variety*, "but there's a squarer for every killing. It uses all the modern artillery tricks ever conceived by imaginative scenario writers who read newspapers and contribute a few of their own. It bumps off more guys and mixes more blood with rum than most of the past gangster offerings combined." The entire cast was praised, but Muni snared the top notices. *Variety* endorsed him with, "Muni, with a scar from his ear to his jaw, *is* Scarface. He's tough enough here to make Capone his errand boy. And convincing along with it, which has as much as anything else to do with the picture's merit." The *New York*

[4]When Universal filmed *Counsellor at Law* (1933), John Barrymore had the lead.

With his wife Bella in Hollywood (1932)

At a radio broadcast from the Warner Bros. lot in 1932, with: Robert Goldstein, Helen Vinson, Joe E. Brown, Lloyd Bacon, Jack L. Warner, Edward G. Robinson, Mervyn LeRoy, Bebe Daniels, Ken Murray, and Glenda Farrell

Times judged that "the picture is dominated by Mr. Muni's virile and vehement acting."

After its release, *Scarface* was condemned from the pulpits, picketed by civic groups, and protested by the Sons of Italy for obvious reasons. It was banned outright by the Nazis when it tried to find distribution in their foreign market in 1934. All this controversy merely served to make the film a bigger hit everywhere that it did play. The film was voted by the *Film Daily* newspaper as one of the best pictures of the year.

On the crest of his *Scarface* triumph, and reaping nightly ovations in *Counsellor-at-Law*, Muni was suddenly on the top of his profession. He had proved himself a tough but sensitive master character actor whose dynamic qualities more than compensated for the lack of "personality" in his work. Hollywood took a long look at his new prestige, and began to believe that it might be possible to turn this very Jewish-oriented talent into a commercial commodity for the mass public.

One person who believed in Muni's future was Jake Wilk, then eastern story editor for Warner Bros. He had purchased a property which Darryl F. Zanuck, then in charge of production at the Burbank studio, agreed to put into production. It required a specific sort of resilient male lead to carry it off at the boxoffice. Wilk approached Muni in New York, offering him a three-film contract at $50,000 a picture. After reading the initial project that Warner Bros. had in mind, *I Am a Fugitive from a Chain Gang* (Warner Bros., 1932), Muni and Bella agreed to the offer. It was decided that the film would be shot in California during the actor's stipulated summer recess from *Counsellor-at-Law*. (Otto Kruger, who was heading the Chicago company of the Rice play, was brought to New York for the duration.)

With Ann Dvorak in *Scarface* (UA, 1932)

The script for *I Am a Fugitive* was based on Robert E. Burns' autobiography, *I Am a Fugitive from a Georgia Chain Gang*, and was quite a story, solidly in the tradition of Jean Valjean from *Les Miserables*. Burns had been sentenced to a Georgia chain gang after a five-dollar hold-up. His sentence was patently unfair—six to ten years of merciless labor on a road gang. Burns' defense was that he was a starving, jobless war veteran who had merely accompanied an acquaintance to a grocery store and stood by while the friend subsequently robbed the clerk. So, in 1922, after taking two months of the horrors of the Georgia penal system, he escaped. He became a writer, and after seven years was a twenty-thousand-dollar-a-year editor on a Chicago magazine. An unfortunate spat with his wife resulted in her disclosing his identity, and despite the pleas of prominent associates, Burns was returned to the Georgia chain gang. A year later, he again escaped, fleeing to New Jersey. There he became a tax consultant and penned his memoirs. The state officials in Georgia were outraged when the book became a bestseller, and demanded his return. Three New Jersey officers, however, refused to extradite him. Finally, in 1945, Burns returned to Georgia after Governor Ellis Arnall volunteered to serve as his lawyer. As a result, the authorities discontinued his sentence and returned his civil rights, although no full pardon was ever granted, due to Burns' admitted participation in the hold-up.

As might be expected, Muni admired the social import of the storyline but was displeased that so "inexperienced" a director as Mervyn LeRoy was selected to helm the project. "Is he the director, that kid?" Muni said to Jack L. Warner. Eventually, the two movie figures developed a rapport. As LeRoy would recollect in his autobiography, *Take One* (1974), "We became friends, a compliment in itself, because Muni had few friends. He was a loner, as opposed to lonely. When he died, the only two people from the film industry who were present at the funeral were his agent and me."

Muni's oncamera character, James Allen, was surrounded by two starlets then being groomed by the studio. There was Glenda Farrell, the breezy, blonde man-chaser from the racier comedy films, and Helen Vinson, an attractive, well-bred sort who was a fine foil to Farrell's surface brassiness. Such expert exponents of oily villainy as Douglass Dumbrille, Berton Churchill, and David Landau represented the least equitable ingredients of the judicial system.

The film, as shot, followed the book quite closely. Allen's original crime is unnecessarily whitewashed, however. Oncamera, Muni is seated in a hamburger shop when a hold-up man (Preston Foster) enters, forcing Muni to pilfer the cash register. The police enter, Foster escapes, and the law finds the cash on Muni and the sentence follows. Thereafter, the events are concurrent. Allen escapes, only to meet up with floozy Farrell. She learns of his background and blackmails him into marrying her, purring lethally, "I wouldn't tell if I had reason to protect you." When Muni's Jim falls for society gal Vinson and asks Farrell for a divorce, the scorned woman informs on him, and he is returned to the chain gang in the Georgia swamps. Muni escapes again, but the film ends tragically. He is a hunted man, forced by society to live by the very means for which he had been punished—stealing.

Director LeRoy spared no pains in depicting the cruelties of the period's southern penal system. The ankle shackles, the disgusting food, the whippings, and the back-breaking work that degraded men's spirits are all soundly displayed, as well as the ignorance of the knuckle-headed authorities. LeRoy would later report, "Of all the actors I've ever worked with, I think Muni threw himself into his parts more

With Allen Jenkins, Jack LaRue, John Wray, Edward Ellis, G. Pat Collins, and Harry Woods in *I Am a Fugitive from a Chain Gang* (WB, 1932)

deeply than any other. He didn't merely act his roles, he lived them. Perhaps he erred too much in that direction."

Although Georgia was never referred to in the film (the locale was called simply "the South"), LeRoy recalls that the state did its best to squash the film at release time. "*Fugitive* caused both myself and Jack Warner plenty of problems," said LeRoy. "The wardens of the Georgia chain gangs weren't too happy for obvious reasons and tried to stop the picture from being shown. It did one thing, however. The chain gangs were taken off the roads in Georgia. But Warner and I were told not to come there again. I don't think that warning still holds, though."

Chain Gang has plenty of excitement, including a thrilling chase scene in which Muni escapes in a stolen dynamite truck. But the most memorable, as it should be, was the final sequence. In tattered clothes, his face a portrait of despair, Muni meets Helen Vinson. After a few lines of desperate dialogue, he says:

MUNI: *I've got to go.*
VINSON: *Can't you tell me where you're going? Will you write? How do you live?*
MUNI: *I steal.*

At this moment, the screen fades out into darkness and Muni is swallowed up into the black air. Pauline Kael (*New Yorker* Magazine), in recalling this film, commented that it contains "one of the great closing scenes in the history of film."

Once again, Muni was excellent. He was likeable, charming, touching, and always believable. For a time he considered the picture his favorite film (he constantly changed his mind about favorites). When the motion picture debuted in November of 1932, the reviews were ecstatic. *Variety* congratulated Warner Bros. on having the "guts" to film it, and the *New York Times* heralded Muni's "convincing and earnest performance." The picture was nominated for an Academy Award for Best Picture, but lost to *Cavalcade* (Fox). Muni won a second Oscar nomination for Best Actor, but was bested by Charles Laughton of *The Private Life of Henry VIII* (United Artists). Nevertheless, the commercial and artistic success of *I Am a Fugitive* convinced Jack L. Warner and Hollywood that Muni was indeed a screen actor of the top rank. At the Burbank studio he would now be considered in the same league with celluloid tough guys James Cagney and Edward G. Robinson. For his part, Muni aspired to fill the shoes of the company's prestige star, the Britisher, Mr. George Arliss.

After completing the strenuous work on *Chain Gang*, Muni returned on September 12, 1932, to *Counsellor-at-Law*.[5] The show closed three months later, and Muni went on tour with the drama, eventually returning to New York (May 15, 1933) for a special two-week limited engagement. While on tour, the star received much attention when an unfortunate event occurred in Boston. One evening, two couples in the first row chatted loudly and ignorantly throughout the first act. Muni struggled to contain his patience (which never had a very high threshold[6]), but the couples' inane chattering continued. Finally, near the end of Act I, Muni stopped the play and lambasted the offenders. When he completed his harangue, the house

[5]Among the supernumerary cast at this point was Jules Garfinkel, who later become Hollywood's John Garfield and even appeared oncamera with Muni.
[6]The star was such a perfectionist about keeping himself immersed within the role that he would refuse to let anyone watch his performance from the wings, feeling it was too much of a distraction.

Publicity pose *c.* 1933

detective briskly escorted the red-faced kibitzers out of the theatre. While Muni's actions are defensible, they forecast the progressively testier temperament that would later handicap his career.

Muni at this time also revealed the "artistic principles" that would severely limit his screen output. Bella was fond of relating the time when Paul received "a wire from DeMille. 'I have a wonderful part for you, just like *Scarface*. Will you do it?' Muni sent back a wire: 'I've already done *Scarface*. Not interested.' " As Muni recalls, "I didn't want to repeat. I've always tried to avoid—I don't know how well I succeeded, I may not have succeeded at all, but at least it was my interest, my desire—to avoid repetition as much as possible."

In mid-1933, Muni and Bella shifted residences to California, paying cash for a ranch in the San Fernando Valley. Hollywood was confused about Muni. His awkwardness and disinterest in social affairs, Bella's authoritarian attitude on the soundstage set, and his exhaustive preparation in tackling screen roles became the talk of the cinema colony. In a branch of the profession where most performers were quick studies, able to adapt to overnight changes in scenarios, Muni was an exception. He would insist upon having a "finished" copy of his script months in advance of production shooting. Then he would record the entire script on a Dictaphone, playing all the parts himself, and then play the recording over and over again. He would also act out his scenes at home, moving furniture to simulate the scene as he pictured it would be filmed. He would completely think out the character's physical appearance, mannerisms, and nuances. If he were to portray a real-life figure, he would read everything he could locate on the subject. Hollywood was not used to such dedication.

Nor was the movie industry used to an actor so dependent on his wife and so lost when not before a camera. His inefficiency in areas not related to acting became the

With Guy Kibbee (with cigar) in *The World Changes* (FN, 1933)

384

inspiration of inside jokes. An oft-told anecdote concerned Muni's move to his new home. Surveying the ranch property, he was delighted to discover sprawling across his property what appeared to him to be flower pots. Touched by what he felt to be a welcoming touch by his real estate agent, he rushed out to purchase some geraniums and spent a pastoral day planting the flowers in the "pots." By sunset, all were planted, and Muni rushed to find Bella to show off his gardening success. Bella was about to explain to her husband that he had planted the blooms in the irrigation standpipes when the system came on and the geraniums flew into the air.

On the Warners' lot, however, Muni was hardly a joke. The script department was kept on its toes trying to create acceptable scripts for him. Soon, he agreed to *The World Changes* (First National, 1933), based on the story *America Kneels* by Sheridan Gibney. It concerned, of all things, a meat-packing king. The project appealed to Muni largely because it allowed him to age from a young man to an elderly soul in his seventies, hence permitting him to dip into the makeup kit that had been neglected in his last two films. Mervyn LeRoy once again directed.

The World Changes had the typical, overly ambitious, complex plot that was so much a part of celluloid sagas of the early thirties. Muni, as Orin Nordholm, Jr., drives cattle for Buffalo Bill (Douglass Dumbrille) to Chicago, where he eventually gets into the meat packing business. Once established and making money rapidly, he meets upper-class Mary Astor,[7] falls in love with the beautiful creature, and weds

[7]In her memoirs, *A Life on Film* (1971), Mary Astor recalls: "Personally I thought Muni was a very attractive man, and as an actor he was very scholarly and as dedicated and hardworking as the character he was playing. . . . I didn't approve of his method of working: his total attention to externals, make-up, hair, clothing, manner of walking, gesturing. Every word of the script memorized and actually recorded and re-recorded before he ever went on the set. And the theory that if your eyes twinkled you conveyed humor, if you shook your fist and shouted and allowed spittle to form on your lips, presto you were an angry man."

With Mary Astor in *The World Changes*

her. The rest of the film finds Miss Astor, sporting a variety of curls, pompadours, and frills, hating the fact that she is a "butcher's wife," trying to drive Muni crazy, going insane herself, and finally dying. Subsequently, Muni sells the business. Apparently, the moral of the film was that butchers, especially tycoons in the field, have tough lives. It was a theme drawn to more conventional standards in Edward G. Robinson's *I Loved a Woman,* also released by First National, also in 1933.

The World Changes was reminiscent of Muni's early films and prophetic of his later ones. He received glowing notices as the focal figure who matures from prairie-life simplicity to big-city opulence, while aging from the youthful son of pioneers to the doddering patriarch. He received glowing notices, but the film was a boxoffice dud. Nevertheless, Jack L. Warner was still impressed with his new prestige attraction and the star treatment kept flowing.

Nineteen hundred thirty-four was a busy year at Warner Bros.-First National. Warren William played leads in six films, Bette Davis and Joan Blondell each did five, James Cagney and Kay Francis starred in four each, while Edward G. Robinson did two, but Muni only one. The script he chose was *Hi, Nellie!* (Warner Bros., 1934),[8] a ridiculous choice explainable only by the selling job director Mervyn LeRoy did on Muni to attempt a comedy. Taking no chances at producing a film without humor, the script copied too closely *Advice to the Lovelorn* (United Artists, 1933), which had been based on Nathaniel West's well-conceived novel, *Miss Lonelyhearts.* Muni was particularly pleased that Bella's brother Abem was allowed to co-adapt the Warners' version for his particular demands.

Supported by Glenda Farrell, expert character players Douglass Dumbrille and Ned Sparks, and the security of LeRoy's direction, Muni had fun playing the part of the newspaper editor who is reduced to writing a lovelorn column. The comic role was a nice relief from the heavy dramatics he had been performing, and his acting was relaxed and likeable. *Variety* opined, "For Paul Muni it represents another film characterization that is as clear cut and fine as it could be." Unfortunately, the public was now accustomed to Muni's heavy dramatics and was not prepared to accept him in a comedy. The offbeat casting was never again repeated.

This was the last picture in which LeRoy directed Muni. In his introduction to Michael Druxman's *Paul Muni—His Life and His Films* (1974), LeRoy commented, "Many people have asked me if he was tough to work with. I guess he was one of the *easiest* actors to work with, because he knew his job and did it well."

When Muni and Bella took a vacation after the lensing of *Hi, Nellie!* they chose to visit Russia and the Moscow Art Theatre. When the couple returned, they took the advice of Muni's West Coast attorney David Tannenbaum, and chose M. C. Levee to be Muni's talent agent, everyone hoping that in the future there would be no more pictures of the calibre of *Hi, Nellie!* Under a new agreement with Warner Bros., the star was now to receive $100,000 a film, with a two-picture-a-year commitment for seven years. It was left to Muni's discretion to grant interviews. Best of all, the studio agreed to avoid making overnight changes in the script, at least so far as Muni's role was concerned.

The next Warner Bros. film Muni accepted was a good one, *Bordertown* (1935),[9] a brisk melodrama sparked by a blonde Bette Davis in one of her earlier neurotic bitch roles. Muni's role was that of Johnny Ramirez, a young Mexican lawyer. Mrs.

[8]Remade with George Brent as *You Can't Escape Forever* (Warner Bros., 1942).
[9]Unofficially remade as *They Drive by Night* (Warner Bros., 1940), with George Raft and Ida Lupino in the Muni-Davis parts.

On the set of Hi, Nellie! (WB, 1934) with Mrs. Muni

In *Hi, Nellie!* with Glenda Farrell

The Munis in Moscow (1934)

With Bette Davis in *Bordertown* (WB, 1935)

Muni would recall, "Before he did *Bordertown* . . . all of a sudden, out of a clear sky, Muni came home with a Mexican flower boy that he had found down in Los Angeles. And he brought him home and put him to work in the garden." Muni himself remembered how "I got his—the feelings of his character, of his accent and general moods."

The special research obviously paid off. Muni's portrayal of Johnny Ramirez, an ambitious young man whose future is nearly ruined by two unbalanced women (Warner Bros.' reliable Margaret Lindsay in the second spot), is one of his best screen performances. He was virile, charming, and sympathetic. When he replies to Davis' flirting with, "I could go for you, lady. I could go for you a lot," there is a hint of sex appeal in the actor's voice and countenance, a quality never before associated with Muni's screen performances.

Within *Bordertown's* eighty-nine minutes, Muni fights to become a lawyer, only to be disbarred when he loses his temper during an early case. To make a living, he takes a job in the bordertown casino of frog-voiced Eugene Pallette, husband of the unscrupulous Marie Roark (Bette Davis, fresh from her triumph in *Of Human Bondage*, RKO, 1934). Margaret Lindsay appears on the scene as a society snip who slums in the bordertown's less than savory establishment. Because Davis yearns for Muni's attentions, she eliminates her rotund spouse by getting him drunk and leaving him in a garage to be poisoned by carbon monoxide. When Muni does not rush to the widow's side, the scorned woman runs to the police and implicates Muni in the crime. But later, Davis' Marie Roark twitches into a breakdown on the witness stand, leaving Muni to return to the casino. When Lindsay scoffs at the comfort-seeking man, Muni forces his attentions on her. She runs away and is hit by a car. As a rather unexpected "happy" finale to all these woes, the film concludes with Muni selling the casino and transferring the proceeds to a school for poor Mexican children.

Director Archie Mayo kept the action rolling at a fast pace, thereby avoiding protracted sections of maudlin interaction. *Bordertown* was a critical and popular hit. The *New York Times* noted how Muni had a new accented part, "permitting him to scrape the nerves in the kind of taut and snarling role at which he is so consummately satisfying." The same paper added, "Mr. Muni brings to the photoplay his great talent for conviction and theatrical honesty, making it seem an impressive account of angry gutter ambitions."

While Muni was able to cope with Davis' equally theatrical and flashy performance, one wonders how one particular sequence with another person on the set was ever approved. It occurs when Muni meets butler Arthur Treacher. When the star turns his back to talk with another character, Treacher indulges in a soliloquy of face-making scene-stealing.

The ever-proletarian conscious Warner Bros. next returned the star to a social consciousness drama, *Black Fury* (First National, 1935). The picture derived from the Henry R. Irving play, *Bohunk,* and the story *Jan Volanik* by Judge M. A. Musmanno. The judge based the narrative on his own experience in bringing three coal company policemen to justice after the murder of an Imperial, Pennsylvania, miner in 1929. To blend the two story sources into a congenial screenplay, Warners agreed to using the services of Abem Finkel once again, who, this time, worked with co-scripter Carl Erickson.

Muni was enthusiastic with the script. To prepare properly for his role of the illiterate, high-spirited miner, Joe Radek, he spent a few weeks in an Eastern coal

With Pedro Regas in *Black Fury* (FN, 1935)

town, investigating the ambience and problems of mining and the dialect of the underground workers.

The studio backed up Muni with a powerful supporting cast under the direction of Michael Curtiz. Karen Morley was assigned to the role of Radek's sweetheart, Anna, who leaves him for law enforcer Slim Johnson (William Gargan), but later returns to him. Ever-sympathetic John Qualen played Radek's friend Mike Shemanski, who is murdered by thugs. The hateful cops, scabs, and strike agitators were played by such expert heavies as Barton MacLane, J. Carrol Naish, and Ward Bond. Vince Barnett injected some comic relief, but Muni's initial objections to his lighthearted scenes almost kept the player out of the picture. Recalls Barnett, "There was nothing personal in his actions, since we had been friends since *Scarface*. He just felt that, in such a serious film as *Black Fury,* there shouldn't be any comic relief. Lucky for me, Mike Curtiz disagreed with him and I stayed. There were no hard feelings on Muni's part and I worked with him again on *The Woman I Love* [RKO, 1937]."

In its day, the heavily laden message of *Black Fury* was greatly praised, and its paean to strikers considered quite controversial and inflammatory. The *New York Times* thought Muni's role was "magnificently performed," and *Variety* termed him "the fulcrum of the film." As the Polish miner ("who likes everybody and everybody likes Joe Radek"), Muni was far closer to the character's reality than he had been as the Mexican in *Bordertown*. With his newly dyed, close-cropped hair, Muni took on the characteristic of the simple-minded, joyous Pole who dances the mazurka, the czardas, and the polka, and sings "Jeniskaya." By the time a Muni characterization reached the screen it was such an integral part of the performer that it hardly seemed acting to many 1930s' filmgoers.

But neither the film nor the star's performance dates well today. In the seventies, an age of civil rights, women's true emancipation and gay liberation, the problems of the oppressed miners appear overly simplified. And, after four decades, Muni's performance, with its thick dialect and even more mugging than usual, resembles more a denigrating caricature than the sincere characterization for which it was originally heralded.

Muni the perfectionist, who could lose sight of commercial practicality, was by no means pleased with the script of *Dr. Socrates* (Warner Bros., 1935) when it was shown to him. However, after having gotten two top properties in a row from the Burbank studio, he temporarily mellowed and accepted the role. Warner warned Muni that if he would not do *Dr. Socrates,* Edward G. Robinson was willing to tackle the part. The threat worked, and Muni agreed to perform in this effort, which was rather mundane, at least by Muni's standards.

In the meantime, the studio and Muni's agent thought it wise that the too-specialized star should tackle the medium of radio. Despite Muni's "actor" standing, the networks were reluctant to hire Muni as a guest star for any big paying radio program. Because of the tremendous publicity generated about Muni the man of makeup, radio executives feared his visual impact was his only asset. Eventually, Muni was signed to guest star on "Lux Radio Theatre" in 1935, with *Counsellor-at-Law* as the chosen property. Muni was exceedingly nervous about performing in front of a live audience, but once the broadcast got underway he relaxed and enjoyed it. Later, on Louella Parsons' "Hollywood Hotel," Muni and Jean Muir re-created scenes from the actor's first feature film, *The Valiant.* After that, he was an occasional performer on "Lux Radio Theatre."[10]

Dr. Socrates was based on a *Liberty* Magazine serial by W. R. Burnett, creator of *Little Caesar.* The film was one of Warners' new variations. Outcry against the glamorizing of celluloid gangsters was becoming quite strong. Therefore, the studio, unwilling to completely abandon the moneymaking genre, simply switched emphasis from the bad guy to the good guy. Earlier that year James Cagney had agreed to the transformation by playing the title role in *G-Man* (Warner Bros., 1935). Thus, *Dr. Socrates* found tough-guy Muni playing a doctor forced by gangsters to become their personal physician.

The rather pedestrian *Dr. Socrates* is interesting in only two aspects: it reunited Muni with Ann Dvorak (Cesca of *Scarface*), and it introduced him to the direction of William Dieterle, who would direct the star in his *Pasteur, Zola,* and *Juarez* portrayals. The film left the rugged emoting to Barton MacLane, who was certainly capable of such a chore, and to such underlings as Marc Lawrence and moll Mayo Methot. The plot of a surgeon forced to treat gangsters was rehashed in a B entry *King of the Underworld* (Warner Bros., 1939) with Muni's role re-tailored for Kay Francis, then being quickly demoted from her formal status as queen on the Warners' lot.

Dr. Socrates ended Muni's 1935 releases on an anticlimactic note. The very pro *New York Times* bent over backward to find some complimentary angle, finally settling on, "Mr. Muni shows himself to be an able critic of drama by resisting any temptation to give the work a false importance in his performance."

After the *Dr. Socrates* compromise, Muni vowed to be more demanding in choosing his scripts. Yet, he was still capable of criticizing those who praised him for doing "message" pictures. He told the *New York Times* that he was "a realist, and in the theatre I am concerned only with the character I am called upon to interpret. I

[10]He was heard on "Lux" in *The Story of Louis Pasteur* (November 23, 1936), and in *The Life of Emile Zola* (May 8, 1939).

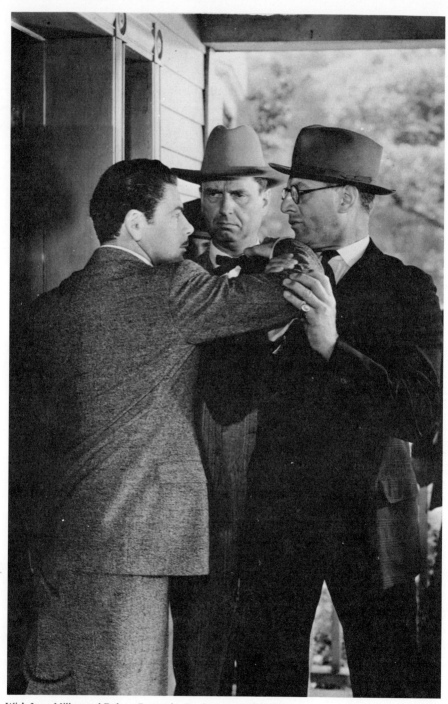

With Ivan Miller and Robert Barrat in *Dr. Socrates* (WB, 1935)

With Carl Stockdale, Ivan Miller, Ann Dvorak, Hobart Cavanaugh, and Helen Lowell in *Dr. Socrates*

have always avoided being brought in as a crusader. My politics is the business of acting. Nothing else matters. It may sound dull, but I'm not really concerned with the depression, or Communism, or capitalism. If Communism comes along, swell If Fascist, that's all right with me. I'll take my chances. My work is the theatre. I work in it like a scientist who works on an invention, not knowing whether his discovery will be constructive or destructive."

About the same time, Muni used the *Los Angeles Times* as a platform to squawk about screen censorship. He claimed that he wanted to star in movie editions of such works as *Looms of Justice* about mercy killing, *The Puritan*, a Liam O'Flaherty piece about religious fanaticism, *Fatherland*, based on a novel about Hitler's Germany, and several other controversial properties. Whenever the interviewers reminded Muni that at least he was starring in films far more socially exciting than any other star, the actor would merely shrug and resume his complaining.

Growing increasingly difficult to please, Muni began refusing anything Warner Bros. brought to him. He explained to the press, "They sent me script after script which were so terrible that I just couldn't accept them." Others claimed Muni had become far too critical; his procedure of grading scenarios like a teacher was making it tougher and tougher for any of them to receive a passing grade.

Muni, the volatile artist, almost vetoed a property that was to win him an Oscar. Sheridan Gibney and Pierre Collins had prepared a screenplay on the life of Louis Pasteur (1822-1895) and approached Muni with the finished product. Hearing what it was about, Muni immediately snapped that he was not at all charmed by the idea of playing "a man with bugs in his beard." However, after being coerced into reading the script, he retracted the remark. He did order six rewrites before he, producer Henry Blanke, and director William Dieterle formed a triumvirate and

With (center) Porter Hall and Fritz Leiber in *The Story of Louis Pasteur* (WB, 1935)

took the project to Jack L. Warner for production approval. The executive said no, especially after polling a few waitresses in the commissary who had never heard of the famed scientist. Warner saw the project as one with no sex, no guns, no laughs, and thus no boxoffice potential.

But Muni insisted on the Pasteur film. He threatened to sit out his contract if Warner did not give approval. According to his contract, if he refused three scripts from the studio and Warners refused three scripts provided as alternatives by Muni, the actor would then be placed on a half-salary situation and do nothing for the duration. But, as the star recalled, "They knew so many studios were out to get me to sign, and all that, so they wanted to keep me there and they gave me leeway, a lot of things that an actor wouldn't be able to get. So, therefore, we practically pushed it down their throats. They just didn't want to do Pasteur."

Jack L. Warner finally relented, but retaliated with his most potent weapon—money. The film was given a paltry $260,000 budget, a five-week shooting schedule, and hand-me-down sets.[11] Nor was any high-priced talent assigned to perform in the picture beyond Muni. The very charming but always underrated actress Josephine Hutchinson played Pasteur's wife; Anita Louise and Donald Woods carried the young love interest; and such expert character actors as Fritz Leiber, Henry O'Neill, Porter Hall, Akim Tamiroff, and Walter Kingsford were the people who aided or handicapped Pasteur's medical progress. In mid-August, 1935, the film began production under the working title *Enemy of Man*.

To fully master his complex characterization, Muni buried himself in a maze of research on Pasteur. "When I was working on *The Story of Louis Pasteur* I read most everything that was in the library—in the studio, where they have their own library

[1]The palace of Napoleon III in the film was actually an overhauled Busby Berkeley set.

—and most everything I could lay my hands on that had to do with Pasteur, with Lister, with his contemporaries. . . . I read everything. I mean, characters like Ehrlich, who had no connection with Pasteur, actually any contact with him, but he also dealt in the same field. I read up everything I could on Ehrlich and others like that."[12]

Blanke, Dieterle, and Muni saw to it that *Pasteur* was completed on schedule in late September. It was an achievement hardly acknowledged by the studio powers. Viewing the completed film, Hal B. Wallis (who felt the film was doomed from Muni's first entrance since, in his opinion, Muni with a beard resembled a rabbi) was still vehemently insistent that the American public could not or would not comprehend the scientific theme. He recommended that a dulcet voice be used as a voice-over for the finale, saying, "And since then, all the mothers are grateful to him because they now have pasteurized milk."

Warner and Wallis decided to exhibit this white elephant as inconspicuously as possible. Bella Muni recalled, "Finally, they sold it at a smaller percentage to the exhibitors because they didn't think they had a picture. And it opened in a second-run theatre in Chicago."

In February of 1936, *The Story of Louis Pasteur* premiered. Thirteen months later, the eighty-five-minute feature nearly won a Best Picture Oscar; the screenplay did win an Academy Award; Jack Warner was recommended for a French government award for his humanitarianism in promoting the picture; and the film became one of the studio's top boxoffice draws of the year. Best of all Muni won the Best Actor Oscar, competing against Gary Cooper (*Mr. Deeds Goes to Town*), Walter Huston (*Dodsworth*), William Powell (*My Man Godfrey*), and Spencer Tracy (*San Francisco*). After Victor McLaglen announced Muni's name as winner, the goateed star exuberantly accepted the trophy. "I have the greatest thrill in my life in getting this," he enthused from the stage of the Biltmore Hotel. Jack Warner wholeheartedly posed with his star on that evening in March, 1937. From that moment on, Warner would end every subsequent argument he had with Muni with: "Muni, for God's sake! Why don't you listen to me? After all, I gave you *Pasteur!*"

Pasteur[13] is actually one of Muni's more refined and quiet interpretations, lacking the fireworks of Scarface or the flamboyance that would mark his Zola. Portraying a humanitarian to whom the world owed a major debt didn't hurt him one bit when he was reviewed. *Variety* said, "Paul Muni in the title role is in his very top form." The *New York Times* respectfully observed, "Brilliantly played by Paul Muni." His solitary Oscar was awarded for what is indeed an a excellent screen performance, but is in no way representative of the full scope of his talents as is a number of his other film parts.

At this time Muni might have been the top dramatic actor of the American cinema, but he certainly did not look the part. He would shuffle about Hollywood in a beret or a narrow-brimmed hat turned up all around so that he looked like a rabbi. Two months after winning the Oscar, he attended a major meeting of the Screen Actors Guild, only to sit with the extras and sneak out the side door. Realizing he was no rancher, he had sold his San Fernando Valley property and bought a mansion in Palos Verdes, a wealthy area some one hour's drive south of Los Ange-

[12]Edward G. Robinson would star in *Dr. Ehrlich's Magic Bullet* (Warner Bros., 1940).
[13]The *Pasteur* role would later haunt Muni. In 1939, while bicycle riding, the actor was bitten by a collie dog. The press jumped on the fact that he refused to undergo the Pasteur rabies shot treatment.

les. There he spent his free time swimming in his pool, playing with his dog, and looking through his telescope at ships sailing the Pacific. Although Muni was scarcely the conventional family man, he insisted upon looking out for the welfare of his family. He supported his mother for years, maneuvered a job as musical arranger for Joseph at Warner Bros., continued to promote screenwriting assignments for Bella's brother Abem, and purchased homes for both his brothers, Joseph and Al, in the San Fernando Valley.

It was in late September, 1935, shortly after the completion of the *Pasteur* film that Irving Thalberg, the MGM executive, invited Muni to a conference. Thalberg was entranced with the possibilities of filming Pearl Buck's novel *The Good Earth,* the story of the Chinese and their land. Thalberg and Louis B. Mayer had been raging over this property at the Culver City lot for years, with Mayer persisting, "Irving, the public won't buy pictures about American farmers. And you want to give them Chinese farmers?" Nevertheless, Thalberg was convinced that the heart of the story, dealing with the life-long love of a man and a woman, was top cinema material. As early as 1934 he had sent director George Hill to China to photograph the country and its artifacts. Hill returned with reels of films, but committed suicide shortly afterward, and the picture was temporarily shut down.

Nevertheless, Thalberg could not be dissuaded from his project. Victor Fleming was assigned to direct and began by ordering rewrites, plaguing Mayer with more delays and costs. Muni had been Thalberg's original choice for Wang Lung and it required a complex trading arrangement for Metro-Goldwyn-Mayer to acquire the services of Muni. As part of the deal, it was agreed that Clark Gable would make a film for Warner Bros., and that the Burbank studio would loan not only Muni to MGM, but also contract star Leslie Howard. To play Muni's oncamera wife, Viennese actress Luise Rainer, who had won an Oscar as Anna Held in *The Great Ziegfeld* (MGM, 1936), was selected. Thus, publicity for *The Good Earth* could proudly note how the film starred two Academy Award winners.

While the cast was being assembled, Metro's technical crews created what became known as "the world's largest set"—five hundred acres of the San Fernando Valley transformed into a complex of Chinese farms. Crops like cabbage and bamboo were planted, and even a Chinese irrigation ditch for rice fields was assembled. The film required sixty-eight English-speaking Chinese, so Metro talent scouts began their difficult search. Mayer saw no need for all this searching, and retaliated with typical misguided irrationality when he ordered contractee James Stewart (6'4", with a midwestern drawl) to test for one of the Oriental roles. Fortunately, Stewart did not win a part. Finally, on the eve of production in late 1935, Fleming required an operation and the directorship passed hands again. This time it was handed to Sidney Franklin, who insisted on additional rewrites before he could begin. Finally, after two years of preparation, *The Good Earth* went before the cameras in February, 1936.

Neither Muni nor Rainer (as O-lan) took any shortcuts in preparing for their roles. Muni spent months in San Francisco's Chinatown, studying Chinese gaits and accents, while Miss Rainer visited the Chinese colonies in both Los Angeles and San Francisco, as well as investigating the moods and nuances of the Chinese actors in the film. Miss Rainer later recalled that while she and Muni prepared in a similar manner for their roles, their acting styles were quite different.

As she explained, "He knew what he wanted to do in each scene. By what door he would enter, how he would make an exit, where each piece of furniture must be.

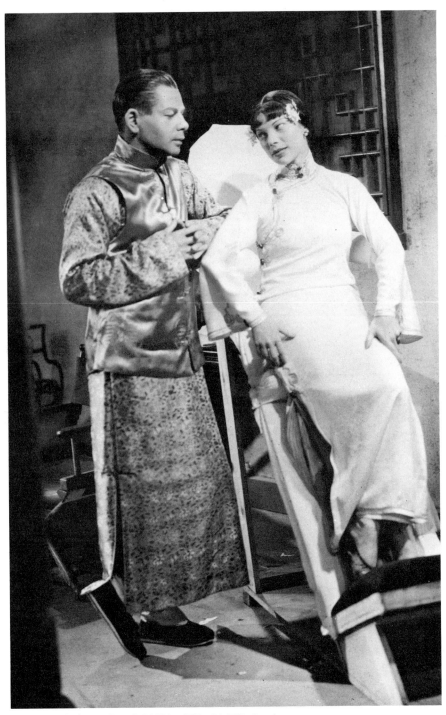

On the set of *The Good Earth* (MGM, 1937) with Tilly Losch

With Walter Connolly in *The Good Earth*

When something was changed, that was difficult for him. He had to change his idea of the scene. But as for me, I didn't care. I never knew how I was going to walk on or off the set, or just what I would do when I got there. . . ."

As a final result, *The Good Earth* emerged as a long (130 minutes), sometimes powerful, but always meaningful film. However, patronizing piety hovers over the presentation from the very start with a prologue which suggests, "The soul of a great nation is expressed in the life of its humble people." At times the parallels between the problems of the land and the lives of the characters get tediously out of hand, but the film exonerated Thalberg's belief in the project. One of the most memorable scenes is during a famine, in which Muni refuses to sell his beloved land, saying, "Before I sell it, I'll feed it to my children!" The next scene finds Muni and Rainer preparing to do just that as they cook earth. The famous locust-attack scene, a masterpiece of trick photography, recutting, and the mixing of Chinese location shooting with closeups of locusts on a miniature soundstage as well as on-celluloid special effects painting, is one of the most famous "epic" scenes of the thirties' cinema. The climax (in which, after Rainer dies, Muni sadly wanders to the peach tree she planted on their wedding day, leans his cheek against the bark and caresses it with his hands, and says "O-lan, you are the earth") can still touch the heart after four decades.

Director Franklin was primarily a "woman's director," which is perhaps why Rainer's performance eclipses Muni's. Her portrayal won her a second Oscar. Muni's performance was a subject of controversy. Some critics agreed with *Variety* that Muni "is a splendid lead for the film." However, others noted that his performance weakened surprisingly as he aged in the storyline. Actually, Muni, then age forty, was so fearful that he would not be able to project the young Wang convincingly that he concentrated mainly on refining his early scenes, hence losing control in the middle and later years. The film wound up as the possession of Miss Rainer. Muni's opinion of the picture was, "*The Good Earth,* while I considered myself very, very badly chosen for that role—I didn't do a good job in it—the film itself was very worthwhile."

The Good Earth was matched only by *Ben Hur* (MGM, 1926) as the most expensive studio picture to that time—$2,816,000. It paid off handsomely, however, reaping a gross of $3,557,000 for a profit of half a million dollars. In addition to the honors afforded Miss Rainer, cameraman Karl Freund won an Oscar, and the film was nominated for Best Picture, but lost to Muni's other blockbuster of 1937, *The Life of Emile Zola.*

Sadly, Thalberg, who had so much faith in Muni and the project, did not live to see the triumph of his ambitious production. He died of pneumonia on September 14, 1936. Diplomatically, Mayer ordered that *The Good Earth* contain an acknowledgment to Thalberg, and as a result, the producer's name appeared on a film for the first and only time:

> To the Memory of
> Irving Grant Thalberg
> We Dedicate This Picture
> His Last Great Achievement

Muni's next picture was as unusual a choice as it was an unfortunate one. RKO's *The Woman I Love* (1937) was an outstanding story as filmed in France by Anatole Litvak as *L'Equipage* (1935). Hollywood decided to remake it, with Litvak again at the helm. It was all a mistake. Charles Boyer, the original choice for the lead, had the sense to refuse the job. However, Muni, to help out his old friend Albert Lewis,

With Josephine Hutchinson in *The Life of Emile Zola* (WB, 1937)

who was producing this story of the Lafayette Escadrille, agreed to step into the starring role. He was cast as a "Jonah" flyer whose wife, Miriam Hopkins, has an affair with a young pilot (Louis Hayward). The film progresses as a tedious triangle picture, relieved on occasion by exciting aerial cinematography. In the convenient finale Hayward is killed, and Muni is wounded sufficiently to win Hopkins' sympathy and reavowal of love.

There was little surprise in the Hollywood community that during the filming of this tangled story of clichéd love temperamental Muni and the even more mercurial Miss Hopkins did not work in harmony. There were many points in the production when it seemed almost inevitable that the filming would have to be abandoned. However, not only was the picture completed, but Miss Hopkins went on to claim her unfriendly director, Mr. Litvak, as her third husband. The *New York Times* was among those who chose to pass off *The Woman I Love* as a mistake. "Mr. Muni's role is strangely unsympathetic. His Pasteur-like beard, his stoop and shambling gait are as unmilitary as they are unromantic."

Fortunately, by the time *The Woman I Love* opened in mid-1937, Muni was represented on the screen by *The Good Earth* and soon thereafter by his next Warners' vehicle, *The Life of Emile Zola* (1937). The screenplay, by Heinz Herald, Geza Herczeg, and Norman Reilly Raine, had originally been offered to Ernst Lubitsch at Paramount. Lubitsch studied the star roster at Paramount (Gary Cooper, George Raft, Bing Crosby) and realized that the splendid scenario would not benefit from the Paramount treatment. He advised the writers to take it, along with his recommendation, to Henry Blanke, the producer who had helped Jack L. Warner to digest *Pasteur*.

This time Warner was more sympathetic to the request of the triumvirate, Blanke, Muni, and director Dieterle. A big budget was arranged, and the studio

With Miriam Hopkins in *The Woman I Love* (RKO, 1937)

brass began coating the production with "class" from the outset in a plot to promote it as the "prestige picture of the year." Muni launched himself into the usual exhaustive research on the novelist (1840-1902), while the studio arranged for a top-grade mounting.

Warner Bros. loaded the picture with top talent. Gale Sondergaard, fresh from her Oscar-winning performance the year before in the studio's *Anthony Adverse*, was cast as Lucie Dreyfus, a character later deleted from the published screenplay for legal reasons. Joseph Schildkraut, mainly familiar to film audiences as a teeth-flashing villain, landed the major role of Dreyfus. Gloria Holden, the tall, stately actress who had just played *Dracula's Daughter* (Universal, 1936), was cast as Zola's fiancée and later wife. Louis Calhern, complete with monocle, and Robert Warwick were splendidly ornate antagonists. Although Bette Davis, fast reaching the pinnacle of her stardom, wanted to play the street tart Nana, upon whom Zola based a novel, the studio refused, fearing it would harm her screen reputation. Erin O'Brien-Moore was cast instead.

The picture traced Zola from his days as a struggling writer to his years as a successful social force, climaxing at the Dreyfus case and concluding with Zola's death. Muni evolved some interesting mannerisms, particularly as the older man, prone to sudden bursts of laughter, angrily twirling his pince-nez, and tapping his belly in contemplation. The role was a dream for such a method performer as Muni.

The high point of the 116-minute black-and-white feature was Zola's address to the French court in his defense of Dreyfus, exiled to rot on Devil's Island due to anti-semitism and government corruption. Almost six hundred words, each one weighed and measured for peak dramatic effect, comprised the very powerful soliloquy. Muni's emotional delivery is one of the classic monologues of the cinema. The speech climaxes with:

> *At this solemn moment, in the presence of this tribunal, which is the representation of human justice, before you, gentlemen of the jury, before France, before the whole world —I swear that Dreyfus is innocent! By my 40 years of work, by all that I have won, by all that I have written to spread the spirit of France, I swear that Dreyfus is innocent! May all that melt away!—may my name perish!—if Dreyfus be not innocent!* He is innocent!

Director Dieterle admitted that this telling scene was not filmed without problems. "We made the J'accuse scene and the address to the court over and over—not because I was dissatisfied, but because he was. The stage was hot. He wore a heavily padded suit and an uncomfortable makeup, and each scene was more than 5 minutes long. Yet not once did he complain. He worked until he was exhausted, and came back the next day to do it all over again."

When the picture was completed, Warner Bros. realized they had a monumental winner in production line-up. In July, 1937, the picture was released with much fanfare and Muni received the famous billing that would become a part of Hollywood folklore: "Warner Bros. takes pride in presenting Mr. Paul Muni . . . in one of the few great pictures of all time." It was the pinnacle of Muni's film career; he had now matched the greatness once bestowed on *Mr. George Arliss*.

On August 16, 1937, Muni's picture appeared on the cover of *Time* Magazine. The journal wrote, "Last week, Warner Bros. released a movie which is probably the outstanding prestige production of the season. It is also one of the best shows. . . . Paul Muni can be considered, at least until March [the next Oscar Awards], the first actor of the U.S. screen." The *New York Times* wrote, "Rich, dignified, honest and strong, it is at once the finest historical film ever made and the greatest screen biography, greater even than *The Story of Louis Pasteur*." The same newspaper said of Muni's work that it was "without a doubt the best thing he has done." *Variety* observed that "the picture is Muni's all the way, even when he is off screen."

Even Muni appeared impressed with *Zola*. To promote the picture, he agreed to interviews with several newspapers. He told the *Los Angeles Times*, "*Zola* is positive proof that Hollywood can produce an intelligent, serious picture that is also a box office success." He informed the *New York Times*, "I found *Zola* tremendously easy to do—one of the easiest films I've ever done, in fact—despite the changes in make-up, long speeches, and everything else. It was the only picture I have ever finished —that and Pasteur—not completely worn out. And the reason is—I liked it. It was close to me. With Zola and Pasteur, I was portraying characters I almost knew." He still dispelled the notion of the "message" aspect of the work. "Yes, there is undoubtedly a great message in the stories of these two men. But when I was doing them, I had no consciousness of delivering a sermon. I simply felt a strong sympathy with my character and—well, I did them."

For his most acclaimed performance, Muni won the New York Film Critics Award as Best Actor. He also won his fourth Oscar nomination. In a less impressive year Muni would have won. His 1937 competition included Charles Boyer for his Napoleon in *Conquest* (MGM), Robert Montgomery for his fetching psychopath in *Night Must Fall* (Columbia), Fredric March for his fading film star in *A Star Is Born* (United Artists), and Spencer Tracy for Manuel the Portuguese fisherman of *Captains Courageous* (MGM). Since Muni had won the year before, the odds-on favorite was March, but it was Tracy who was given the prize.

The Life of Emile Zola did, however, win as Best Picture of the Year, Joseph Schildkraut won the Best Supporting Actor's plaque for his Dreyfus, the screenplay was awarded, and the picture was one of the top-grossing hits of the year. One area where the film was not popular was France, which refused to market it for obvious reasons.

At this time, Muni occupied the most enviable niche in Hollywood. He was the man of disguises who had broken out of his mold as a screen tough to essay important historical figures of great depth and compassion. As a critics' darling, he was a high-priced star who could name his own terms. Yet, with all this, the actor still engaged in moody and unnecessary outbursts of temper. In September, 1937, he was elected to the Jewish Hall of Fame as one of the world's 120 greatest living Jews. He then did an about face. After expressing considerable interest in filming a biography of Haym Solomon, the Jewish banker who helped finance the Continental army in Revolutionary War times, he refused to do the picture. He explained that he felt U.S. citizens would object to the implication that the mastermind behind George Washington was a Jew.

In the face of his enormous success, Muni announced in the fall of 1937 that he and Bella were departing for a trip around the world, skirting the war zones. He sneered to the press, "I'm going away for a while, and stay until I'm sick of it. If I like it better, I may stay permanently."

There were no Muni features released in 1938. Warner Bros. had to content itself with promulgating the career of Edward G. Robinson, ever fearful that with one half of the competition, Muni, away from the lot, Robinson would become too swell-headed to be manageable. As Robinson realistically recalled years later, "The bros. Warner regarded us as two sides of a coin and did not hesitate to exploit the situation." Robinson was even more direct regarding his fellow player. "I disliked Muni and Muni detested me."

When Muni did return from his European tour in March, he wrangled a new studio contract. The agreement called for eight pictures over four to eight years at $100,000 per film, with the usual right to reject any script. He subsequently rejected a version of *The Sea Wolf* that would have cast him as Wolf Larsen. (It was a role that eventually went to Edward G. Robinson in the studio's 1941 edition.) Ultimately, Muni selected *Juarez* (Warner Bros., 1939), the biography of the Mexican Indian (1806-1872) who became president of his country.

Warners had learned that well-mounted biographies could generate good box-office receipts. The company decided to outdo itself on this venture. Bette Davis, now queen of the Warner Bros. lot, and one of the country's most potent marquee attractions, was assigned the role of the Princess Carlota; frequently misused but very talented Brian Aherne was cast as misguided Maximilian; Claude Rains was to be Napoleon, and John Garfield, the latest Warner discovery, was cast as General Porfirio Diaz. William Dieterle again directed, Hal B. Wallis personally served as supervising producer, and Henry Blanke was the associate producer. Erich Wolfgang Korngold scored the picture with his usual majestic style. The $1.75 million *Juarez* went before the cameras in November, 1938 with all the promise of being an epic film. It was actually Muni's arrogance and power that would emasculate the film of much of its potential, transforming it from a sure thing into one of the studio's more expensive misses.

In her biography *The Lonely Life* (1962), Bette Davis, who was a far bigger boxoffice draw than Muni, recalled the project: "The part of the film in which Brian Aherne and I appeared as Maximilian and Carlota was shot and assembled before Mr. Muni as Juarez ever stepped before a camera. He saw our part of the picture in the projection room and his wife, Bella, observed that it was 'a complete picture without ever seeing Juarez.' It was true. Mr. Muni brought with him 50 additional pages of script that he wanted added to his part. He was that powerful and the studio allowed it.

"The length of any picture must be limited. When the Juarez part of the film was finished, we were in trouble lengthwise. Something had to go. Brian's and my part of the film received the cuts. Although it was a good motion picture, the film, before cutting destroyed it in the laboratory, was a great one. Mr. Muni's seniority proved our downfall."

Miss Davis was not the only one put out this time by Muni. The star characteristically insisted on heavy makeup that not only disguised him thoroughly, but also unwittingly froze his face. He wanted to be convincing when he uttered the dialogue line, "I am a poor ugly figure of an Indian indeed." When Jack L. Warner viewed the early rushes of the film, he screamed, "You mean we're paying Muni all this dough and you can't even recognize him?"

While the other cast members would be convivial on the set, Muni would remain in his dressing room, with "assistant" director Bella playing watchdog outside. "Mr. Muni does not communicate with anyone," was her standard rebuff to callers. Muni even aggravated friend Dieterle during the shooting of a scene in which the direc-

With Martin Garalaga in *Juarez* (WB, 1939)

tor wanted him to enter stage left. Muni refused, claiming, "I set the scene at home so that I came in stage right." Producer Blanke finally had to intervene and, to nobody's surprise but to many people's anger, surrendered to Muni. The set was reconstructed and several scenes were reshot to match the new footage.

Juarez premiered in April, 1939, to mixed reviews. Muni's performance was received favorably, but without the drumbeating that critics usually performed in extolling his characterizations for the cinema. Muni's Juarez emerged from the film as a stoic, unsympathetic sort of man, in sorry contrast to the pitiful Maximilian or the understandable Carlota. Part of the problem was Muni's makeup; his face seemed as if it would crack if he registered too much expression. The scene in which he squashes a riot instigated by Alejandro Uradi (Joseph Calleia) finds the liberator marching into the crowd with only his stone face as armor. It was symbolic of the fright his demeanor and look cast over the characterization. The *New York Times* registered a perceptive criticism: "Mr. Muni's performance, however brilliant, is restricted by the range of the character itself and Juarez was a stoic. It is impossible to portray a symbol—as the Zapotecan was—with anything but austerity." (In later years, *Juarez* would suffer lack of exposure for other reasons. By the 1970s the vocal Chicano minority complained that *Juarez* should not be shown on California television for it had non-Mexicans playing Mexicans.)

Muni's next film, *We Are Not Alone* (Warner Bros., 1939), progressed no more smoothly. It was James Hilton's story of a mild-mannered doctor, his shrewish wife (Flora Robson), and his love for a young lady who becomes governess of his child (Raymond Severn). First of all, Muni refused the film, but Bella changed his mind. Then the star declined to make the picture unless James Hilton himself was contracted to write the screenplay. The studio obliged. Production began with Edmund Goulding directing and Dolly Haas as the governess. After a few weeks, Muni

404

With Jane Bryan in *We Are Not Alone* (WB, 1939)

announced that he despised Miss Haas and insisted she be fired. She was, and Jane Bryan, a Warner Bros. starlet and the protegee of Bette Davis, was rushed in to replace her, and the film was completed. But when released in November of 1939, *We Are Not Alone* became a boxoffice disappointment for Muni that year.

We Are Not Alone is actually a rather touching film with its action taking place in a British village. Set in the period before and during the outbreak of World War I (with obvious parallels to the Second World War), it contains a sensitive acting job by Muni. ("A stirring performance," wrote *Variety*.) It is a portrayal free of bombast, very quiet, and intriguingly melancholic. Flora Robson made a fine shrew, and Miss Bryan's performance as the unhappy Austrian girl who is wrongly convicted of murder and goes to her death is finely wrought. The story concludes on the romantic notion that after death, Muni and she will meet in a better world. In the course of the film, Muni rides a bicycle (an art he found difficult to master) and plays the violin (an achievement carried over from his youth).

One distinction of the modest *We Are Not Alone* is that it would be Bella's favorite Muni film, perhaps because of the touching father-son relationship expounded in the storyline. Muni, depending on his mood, usually claimed that he did not have a favorite, and even once insisted he never viewed his own features. "You see, the thing is I haven't seen these films. I can only speak of those things that I enjoyed most while I was working on them."

As if sensing his screen career was coming to a head, Muni impulsively sold his Palos Verdes home, and shopped around for a vehicle that would bring him back to Broadway. He had toyed with performing in a play on the life of Nijinsky, but later rejected that, choosing instead to star in Maxwell Anderson's *Key Largo*.[14] The play

[14]Humphrey Bogart, with Lauren Bacall and Edward G. Robinson, would star in the 1948 Warner Bros. screen version of the play.

opened November 27, 1939, at the Ethel Barrymore Theatre. Muni was the disillusioned soldier King McCloud who opposes a ring of gangsters when they invade a Florida hotel. His reception was, as usual, most complimentary, and he won the Drama League Award for the outstanding performance of the 1939-1940 season. Unfortunately, the too socially conscious play, which included such cast members as Jose Ferrer, Uta Hagen, James Gregory, and Karl Malden, survived only a few months on Broadway. Muni agreed to tour with the show to help the beleaguered producers earn back some of their investment.

During the run of *Key Largo* on Broadway, Muni consented to an interview with *Theatre Arts* Magazine, to discuss something he hated to discuss—his acting technique: "Listen, I'm afraid this sounds precious—knowing much about my job and not wanting to tell about it. But think of it this way. You know how to roller skate, don't you? Well, if someone asks you: how do you do it, what is your answer? You don't know. You just do it! You've learned how. You can become more adept by practicing. But if you try to think about what you are doing, while you are actually rolling along in the park, if you look down at the wheels and attempt to puzzle out what's going on, you fall down. Well, that is a little how I feel."

Muni did reveal that: "If you are listening to music and are suddenly carried away, it is some chemistry within you that responds to the music. It is not the music, but something within you that has been released by the music. Similarly, in the theatre, if you are doing a scene that stimulates some feeling within you, the same kind of chemical reaction takes place. Naturally, it is disciplined. You can't lose yourself in the part but you can, and I think you should, let the part open in you the reservoirs of feeling which are dammed up. I don't think the actor simulates the emotion as much as he draws it out of himself and is stimulated by it."

The actor's summation was, "If I were to use a principle at all in acting, it would be that if the mind, the basic generator, functions alertly and sums up its impulses and conclusions to a correct result, it is possible for the actor to achieve something creative. . . . if his apparatus up here is not functioning, all the technique in the world won't save him; if it is, I'd almost say that the technique would take care of itself."

To the surprise of many, Muni let it be known that he saw nothing inferior in film acting to stage acting. He said that at first films were "disconcerting" to him, with the constant fragmentation of scenes, lack of continuity in shooting, and the absence of an audience. However, these conditions required more effort and imagination than stage playing, which was all to the good. He explained that preparation for a film required picturing other cast members, their reactions, keying his own performance to them, and then "[leaving] it to fate." Perfectionist Muni also liked the cinema bonus of retakes, noting that in the theatre, "a scene played is a scene played."

Muni completed his *Key Largo* tour in Los Angeles. He returned to Warner Bros. to see how his long-cherished Beethoven biography project was progressing. Warner informed him that it was not progressing at all; biographies had run their course and the studio did not plan on making any more major money expenditures in the biography genre. As a consolation, the studio head handed Muni the script of *High Sierra* to read, and told him the picture was his if he wanted it. Muni admitted later that the script by W. R. Burnett was strong stuff. However, he (and Bella) were firm in their refusal—no more gangster pictures. Calling Warner, Muni informed him of his decision and suggested the mogul return his attentions to Beethoven. It was the final straw. Warner exploded and offered Muni an ultimatum: do *High Sierra* and forget Beethoven, or leave the studio. Muni called Warner a bastard. Warner retorted that it was *Mr.* Bastard to Muni. Muni slammed down the receiver, rushed out to find his Warner Bros. contract worth $600,000 and ripped it to pieces. Bella would recall the date (July 19, 1940) of the contract's cremation as a feast of jubilation. "That night he did somersaults in the living room. Believe me. He jumped up and down, yelling 'No one owns me! I'm a free man!'"

While Warner Bros. eventually cast Humphrey Bogart[15] as "Mad Dog" Earle in *High Sierra*, Muni freelanced. He was delighted to contract subsequently with Twentieth Century-Fox to do *Hudson's Bay* (1940). The reasons were more contractual than artistic. It was a one-picture deal for his usual $100,000 fee.

Hudson's Bay was a historical piece about fur-trapping that turned out to be neither entertaining, accurate, nor particularly money-making. The script was verbose and director Irving Pichel allowed Muni (as the bearded trapper Pierre Esprit Radisson) to exude superfluous "cuteness," a pose which would not have been tolerated by "director" Bella, had she been allowed on the set. To make matters worse, Muni, no outdoorsman, fell out of a canoe into the depths of a Fox backlot lake while playing a scene. He nearly developed pneumonia and missed time from the shooting of the picture. Gene Tierney was the love interest (romanced by John Sutton), competing in prettiness with Vincent Price as a curly-wigged, beplumed

[15]After Muni's hasty departure from Warner Bros., the studio offered the role to Edward G. Robinson who refused it on the ground that he did not wish any castoff part from Muni. Then George Raft was asked to take on the project; but he turned it down because he did not wish to star in a film in which his character died onscreen. Eventually the part drifted down to Humphrey Bogart, helping him to become the studio's next big tough-guy star.

With John Sutton, Laird Cregar, Nigel Bruce, Virginia Field, and Vincent Price in *Hudson's Bay*

King Charles II of England. The most solid performance in the black-and-white feature was provided by Laird Cregar with his portrayal of Gooseberry, Muni's hefty sidekick. Said *Variety* of the mini-epic: "[Darryl F.] Zanuck takes another sideswipe at history here and comes off second best again."

It seemed that with the coming of the new decade, Muni's once flourishing screen career was floundering, never to regain its past heights. It was easy enough to blame the fault on his florid acting style, which in World War II times seemed dated. However, the star was his own worst enemy, failing to take proper counsel from wiser, less involved sources than Bella. As a non-contractee, he had the liberty of choosing screen properties as he wished, but did so with an eye to a particular bit in a role that appealed to his actor's instinct, rather than to the over-all scope of his professional standing.

Even Muni would later admit that it was a mistake to refuse the lead in the touring company of Lillian Hellman's *Watch on the Rhine*. He did not want to follow in the footstep of the show's original star, Paul Lukas. Instead, he chose to star in the American premiere of Emlyn Williams' *The Light of Heart*. On London's West End, it had starred Godfrey Tearle and then Williams himself. On Broadway, the study of a declining stage star who abandons the throes of alcoholism to attempt a comeback by starring in *King Lear*[16] was retitled *Yesterday's Magic*. The downbeat title was so close to Muni's real life situation that it should have been a sign to him of impending trouble.

It would be John Anderson (*New York Journal-American*) who would write, "Tempt a star with the part of a broken-down old actor trying to stage a comeback

[16]Ironically, Muni had always avoided playing in a Shakespearean work, fearful that he could not live up to the Bard's best theatre pieces.

With Robert Coote in *Commandos Strike at Dawn* (Col., 1942)

and the chances are that in nine cases out of ten your star will grab the play, plot, lines, and especially sinker." Of the bathos that comprised *Yesterday's Magic* (Theatre Guild Theatre, April 14, 1952), Anderson noted, "For an actor of Mr. Muni's perception and power such stuff must seem hardly more than kindergarten exercises, but he goes through them with scrupulous care." Richard Watts, Jr. (*New York Herald-Tribune*) was more critical of this play by the author of *The Corn Is Green* and *Night Must Fall*: "This is certainly not the type of role that best fits Mr. Muni, since there is little of the required grand manner about him and he must work desperately to simulate it." Jessica Tandy, as Muni's lame daughter Cattrin, received consistently better notices than the star.

Yesterday's Magic limped along for fifty-five performances before it closed. It was a sad defeat for Muni, particularly when he had to contend with the fact that another Emlyn Williams' drama, *The Corn Is Green,* starring the rather imperious Ethel Barrymore, was still running to good houses. On more than one occasion Miss Barrymore took deliberate aim at Muni's failure to woo in ticket buyers as she was doing in her Williams' vehicle.

Anxious to recapture lost ground, Muni hastened back to Hollywood, where he accepted the lead in *Commandos Strike at Dawn* (1942). It was a good war film, but just one of many that was pouring forth from the film industry. He played Eric Toresen, a Norwegian saboteur.[17] Anna Lee, Lillian Gish, and Sir Cedric Hardwicke were in the cast, and John Farrow directed with all the expertise that had made his *Wake Island* (Paramount, 1942) such an all-round success.

Somehow *Commandos Strike at Dawn* never joined the ranks of the other classic-staged accounts of World War II, despite what *The Hollywood Reporter* called "enormously effective portrayals," and what *Variety* termed "a terrific charge of emotion." The death of Muni's Eric Toresen in the last bloody charge against the Axis, as his daughter (Ann Carter) is rescued along with fellow hostages, is a memorable closing to an underrated feature. The picture had been shot on location in Victoria, British Columbia, but with the flinty budget supplied by economy-minded Columbia Pictures, the resulting motion picture had a decided low-budget look to it.

For many, it was a sign of decline that Muni had to return to a former stage success to recoup his sagging reputation. He agreed to a revival of *Counsellor-at-Law* (Royale Theatre, November 24, 1942). During rehearsals, Muni was forced to console Bella whose sister Lucy died that month. As before, Muni captivated audiences with his portrayal of George Simon. The *New York Times* reported, "The evening, of course, is Mr. Muni's. With a soft voice and a loud roar, with quietness, gentleness and fierceness in turn, he dominates the role. . . . He is the *Counsellor-at-Law,* no exception being granted."

During this successful revival, Muni often served as a waiter or bus boy at the Stage Door Canteen. As such, he agreed to join with sixty-four other stars in *Stage Door Canteen* (United Artists, 1943), a musical morale booster, with the proceeds going to charity. He cameoed briefly as himself, congratulating aspiring actress Cheryl Walker on winning a role in what is supposed to be his new play.

Before embarking on a road tour of *Counsellor-at-Law* a considerably pliable Muni agreed to narrate a pageant at Madison Square Garden. Entitled *We Will Never Die,* it focused on Israel's struggle for statehood. Moss Hart directed the

[17]It was a much looser Muni who performed in this film, even indulging in a rather torrid dance scene with Anna Lee (as the young English girl).

With Merle Oberon in *A Song to Remember* (Col., 1945)

show, with dialogue by Ben Hecht and music composed by Kurt Weill. Others in the cast of the program (given on two consecutive Sundays in the spring of 1943) were Edward G. Robinson, John Garfield, George Jessel, Frank Sinatra, and Luther Adler.

After the out-of-town engagement of the Rice play, Muni decided to sell the Long Island home which he had purchased not too long before. He returned to California, with Bella in tow, to make a new picture, *A Song to Remember* (Columbia, 1945). One term of the agreement with Harry Cohn's studio was that Bella could not venture onto the soundstage set of the Charles Vidor-directed project. Muni fumed, but Cohn was adamant. Because Muni greatly desired to play the music teacher who counsels Chopin (Cornel Wilde), he surprisingly acceded to the mogul's dictates. It was another sign that the once great Muni was aware of his diminished status in the movie colony.

As if to compensate for the lack of Bella's guidance and comfort on the set, Muni outrageously overacted and bellowed at fellow players on *A Song to Remember.* When ingenuous Cornel Wilde reverently approached Muni and sincerely asked if he might rehearse with him on the side, the senior actor replied, "Dear boy, I have done considerable research on Chopin and have my own interpretation as to how he should be portrayed. I will play to my conception—not yours."

While all the critics acknowledged the lavishness of this color production and lauded the offcamera piano playing of Jose Iturbi to Wilde's oncamera miming, there were few plaudits for the rather dull storyline. Lovely Merle Oberon as the masculine George Sand received more positive attention than the other co-stars. As for Muni, the usually gentle Kate Cameron (*New York Daily News*) admitted, "Muni's performance is not one of his best. He mugs his way through the role in an elaborate makeup job." The *New York Times* chided the star that "[he] too often

410

plays without restraint. Apparently he didn't receive much direction from Charles Vidor." Otis L. Guernsey, Jr. (*New York Herald-Tribune*) was kinder, with, "Most of the story's brighter moments are contributed by Paul Muni as the amiable, bewhiskered, fussy professor."

Muni had received a percentage deal from Columbia for *A Song to Remember*. He stayed on at the studio for another film, *Counter-Attack* (1945), a sympathetic portrait of the Russian army. Harry Cohn waived Bella's exile from the soundstage set this time, to the dismay of producer-director Zoltan Korda. But it led to the betterment of Muni's performance, which the critics declared was "fine" and "forceful." However, the unremarkable feature met with near apathy from the public. Muni's status slipped down another peg.

Because of his unstable position in the Hollywood hierarchy, Bella advised him to accept a project that would be a sure-fire winner. He did so by contracting for *Angel on My Shoulder* (United Artists, 1946). He was now even willing to play a gangster again if it meant a boost commercially. The fantasy was by Harry Segall who had done so well with *Here Comes Mr. Jordan* (Columbia, 1941). The solid cast included Anne Baxter as the heroine, and Claude Rains as the Devil, with whom Muni makes a pact. Archie Mayo, who eleven years earlier had guided the star through *Bordertown*, directed this project. Miss Baxter would recall that all was not well during the production: "I think he [Muni] was trying to recapture *Scarface*. His career was in a downward slide and he wanted the film to be more than it was. Archie Mayo was not a director in depth, which of course, was an approach completely in contrast to Muni, who had to know the meaning behind every syllable. The two were in constant conflict, which made for a very unhappy set."

Angel on My Shoulder is not bad, but it collapsed at the boxoffice. Muni tried hard, but a little too hard. The *New York Times* said, "Mr. Muni's performance of the

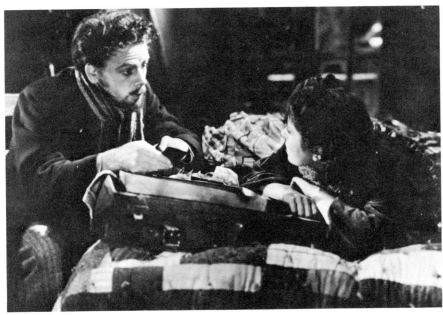

With Charles Wagenheim (left) and Adeline de Walt Reynolds in *Counter-Attack* (Col., 1945)

With Archie Twitchell and Anne Baxter in *Angel on My Shoulder* (UA, 1946)

In *Stranger on the Prowl* (UA, 1953)

gangster is aggressive and versatile, even though he does sometimes make the character look and act like the monster of Frankenstein." Muni became distraught and bitter when the film failed. It would be his last picture in Hollywood for thirteen years.[18]

Although Paul and Bella Muni purchased a new home in California (525 Louise Avenue in Encino), Muni was soon back in New York to appear in *A Flag Is Born.* For this show, which opened on September 6, 1946, he starred as an old Jew en route to Palestine. He worked three months free of charge for the American League for a Free Palestine. The *New York Times* called his work "'one of the great performances of his career." The show later went on tour, with Jacob Ben-Ami replacing Muni, and earned one million dollars for the State of Israel.

After *A Flag Is Born,* Muni's career was a mixed bag. After a summer stock tour in 1947, he again played in *Counsellor-at-Law,* this time (1948) on NBC's "Philco Playhouse." Muni was not pleased with the fast-paced schedule of television. Two plays with which his name was linked, *Sunday Breakfast* and *The Man Who Swindled Goering,* failed to materialize. Arthur Miller offered him the role of Willy Loman in *Death of a Salesman,* but Bella did not care for the project. (Thus, Lee J. Cobb was treated to that Broadway triumph.)

On February 16, 1949, at the Music Box Theatre, Muni, his name advertised in bold type three times the size of the play's title, opened in a revival of *They Knew What They Wanted.* He played Tony, the Italian grape grower who receives a mail-order bride. Said the *New York Daily News,* "Most Italians can't act as Italian as Mr. Muni acts." The play did not run long. Finally, Muni went to England to star in the London version of *Death of a Salesman.* He was breaking his own rule not to take over a role made famous by another. Opening July 28, 1949, at the Phoenix Theatre, Muni was said to play the demanding role with "great feeling," but he had trouble learning his lines, a problem evident in his first night performance. Muni remained with the show until January 28, 1950, leaving when he became "too tired to go on with it."

During this wandering period, the star became increasingly crotchety. Afraid to appear in films, he said that "what they're making out in Hollywood is just plain nonsense." In an angrier moment, he even swore, "I have never liked acting." And his relations with the fans remained on its usual dismal plane: he would rudely brush past autograph seekers, crying, "Don't you have anything better to do?"

For the next six years, Muni would work in various media, without any outstanding success. He traveled to Italy to appear in *Imbarco a Mezzanotte (Stranger on the Prowl),* which was badly edited for American release (United Artists, 1953). On television, he appeared on "Ford Theatre" in *The People vs. Johnson* (NBC, June 25, 1953). It was hoped that he would extend his services and do a series based on the initial program, but Muni had so much trouble learning his lines that he required constant prompting and chose to refuse the series. In late 1953, he again headed for Broadway in *Home at Seven* by R. C. Sheriff, but it closed out of town. It truly appeared that Muni's career was over. The actor hid away in his Encino, California,

---

[18]One of Muni's ambitions was to portray Alfred Nobel oncamera, in a screenplay derived from Herta E. Pauli's book *Alfred Nobel: Dynamite King, Architect of Peace.* The studios rejected the project both for its "dull" subject matter and because Muni was no longer considered boxoffice. In early 1948 there was discussion of boosting the project's appeal by having Greta Garbo co-star in the vehicle.

home, where he passed the time playing with tape recorders, collecting books, and reading.

While vacationing in New York in early 1955, the nearly sixty-year-old performer was asked by Herman Shumlin to read *Inherit the Wind,* a play by Jerome Lawrence and Robert E. Lee, that Shumlin would be producing. The now-classic play dealt with the Scopes Monkey Trial of 1925 in Tennessee, where Clarence Darrow (1857-1938) and William Jennings Bryan (1860-1925) fought a flamboyant battle of tongues. The conflict was also a disguised attack on the recent McCarthy Communist witch-hunt. Muni was enthusiastic and contracted to play the "Darrow role," here called Henry Drummond. Ed Begley was cast as his adversary, Matthew Harrison Brady, and Tony Randall and Bethel Leslie[19] took other major roles.

Age had done nothing to diminish Muni's technique in preparing for a role. For two weeks, the actor worked with makeup alone. The compassionate manner, crisp midwestern accent, and peculiar stomach-extended strut that characterized Darrow were all adapted by Muni to perfection. And, of course, he researched his subject. "I just read up on Darrow as much as I could. I asked people who had any acquaintance with Darrow. I have a very good friend, a judge [Michael A. Musmanno] in Pittsburgh, a Supreme Court justice of the state of Pennsylvania, and he knew that I was working on Darrow, and he'd had personal contact with him and he gave me some information. I have long letters from him."

Muni experienced his usual problems with learning lines and tempering his strident personality during rehearsal. He insisted on frequent line run-throughs with the cast, and had several altercations with producer Shumlin. Muni rationalized, "He's an angry man and I'm an angry man, you see, and we're both very right

[19]Paul and Bella Muni would become exceedingly fond and protective of Miss Leslie after this initial encounter.

With Ed Begley, Tony Randall, and Louis Hector in *Inherit the Wind*

Playbill for *Inherit the Wind* (1955)

With Melvyn Douglas, his successor in *Inherit the Wind*

in our positions. At the rehearsals we weren't getting along. He avoided me, I avoided him. I'm a nice guy, really. I get into trouble with everybody."

On April 21, 1955, *Inherit the Wind* opened at the National Theatre to unanimous praise. Adjectives like "unforgettable," "magnificent," "inspired," "superb," and "brilliant" greeted Muni's performance. He won the Antoinette Perry Tony Award and the Donaldson Award for Best Actor of the season. Bella proudly referred to the play as Muni's "vindication."

Muni's performance was fresh and powerful nightly, with the actor explaining, "If there was a freshness there, then it was because I was not thinking of myself, but always listening to the other fellow. And mine was a reaction—not an action, but a reaction." Every performance also found Muni performing a little ritual in his dressing room. He stared at a picture of Darrow that he had hung over his mirror. "It was sent to me. I had it over my mirror there, my make-up mirror, and invariably—and this is like a superstition, you know, like somebody knocks on wood—I, invariably before I went on stage, I took 5 minutes time, shut the door, nobody was allowed to come in, and I just looked at the picture."

Muni proved he was still a star, but he also demonstrated that he was still very temperamental. Thrown offbase by the color red, he once threatened to have an actor in *Inherit the Wind* fired when the unfortunate player, ignorant of the star's idiosyncrasy, wore red socks one evening onstage. Informed one night by an excited and well-meaning extra that Harry Truman was in the audience, Muni retorted, "I don't give a shit!" Yet, while cantankerous, Muni was never egotistical. After each performance, he would rant in his dressing room about the aspects of his delivery that day which were not up to par. And as he curiously recalled, "When I walked up Sixth Avenue to Broadway, and I saw 'Paul Muni in *Inherit the Wind*,' I got sick to my stomach. And I got nervous and unhappy and I thought—I don't know what I thought at the time, but I was sick. I was unhappy about the whole thing."

After four months in the play, Muni met with a tragedy when a painful, malignant tumor developed in his left eye. The specialists agreed that the eye had to be removed. Muni took three months to adjust emotionally and physically to the aftermath of the operation. He had wanted Karl Malden to replace him in *Inherit the Wind*, but the part of Drummond went to Melvyn Douglas.

Nursed back to health and fitted with an artificial eye, Muni determined to return to *Inherit the Wind*. On the night (December 1, 1955) of his return, Melvyn Douglas stepped before the curtain to the groans and boos of the audience, who recognized this as the announcement of an understudy. Douglas spoke, "According to the rules of Actor's Equity, an announcement must be made if an actor is to be replaced. It is my great honor to announce that tonight the part of Drummond will be played by Paul Muni." The theatre vibrated with applause.

Muni's performance was still powerful, but before long he was forced to admit, "I couldn't take it anymore." He agreed to finish out the season, and even stayed an extra month due to the play's sell-out status. At the end of June, 1956, Muni left the show, his status as one of the great American actors firmly reassured.

Maintaining a New York residence, Muni turned to television. While still in *Inherit the Wind*, he appeared on the CBS "G. E. Theatre," in *A Letter from the Queen* (March 4, 1956). On March 6, 1958, he was in Hollywood to appear on "Playhouse 90" in *The Last Clear Chance*. In the ninety-minute live show, Muni played an old barrister who comes out of retirement to defend his son from disbarment. Although Muni completely failed to learn his lines on time, and because of his poor eyesight was unable to use a teleprompter, director George Roy Hill devised the gambit of providing Muni with a tiny receiver inside a hearing aid. Through this contraption he was able to prompt Muni, line by line, with his part. Audiences were unaware of the device, and Muni was nominated for an Emmy for his acclaimed performance. (The Award went that year to Fred Astaire for his *An Evening with Fred Astaire*.)

There followed Muni's final stage appearance. It was *At the Grand,* a musical rendering of Vicki Baum's *Grand Hotel* which had been a stage success and a bigger money-maker as the all-star MGM film (1932).[20] It opened in the summer of 1958 under the auspices of the Los Angeles and San Francisco Civic Light Opera. Muni had the role of Kringelein, the timid clerk so memorably played by Lionel Barrymore in the 1932 feature. (Bert Lahr had been producer Edwin Lester's original choice for the role.) Said Muni after the opening, "I love the music, and I liked the [Luther] Davis Script. And my part—the little man, Kringelein, delighted me. But I had to know I could do it. They rented a hall and I sang the songs and danced for the composers [Robert Wright and George Forrest] and writer and director Albert Marre and producer Edwin Lester. They said yes, it was right; I could do it. Still, I had to be sure of myself. I recorded my songs on tape. Then I agreed I could do it."

Muni insisted that Kringelein be promoted to the star of the show, and thus was given five song-and-dance numbers, including tunes like "A Table with a View" and "I Waltz Alone," the later a ballroom piece. The play was not well received at all. *Variety* reported that the musical "is many more than 3000 miles from Broadway at the moment. It is, theatrically speaking, light years away." There were discussions as to definitely setting a Broadway opening date, but the play's weaknesses and Muni's constant demands for rewrites and sole star treatment persuaded the producers to let the play die on the Coast.

Muni then began work on his last film, *The Last Angry Man* (Columbia, 1959). Set in 1936, it was the well-known story of a doctor who treats the usually ungrateful, usually empty-pocketed inhabitants of the Brooklyn ghetto where he has always lived. The film was based on the highly regarded Gerald Green novel. Muni managed a contract fit for a tyrant, and one of his stipulations was that Green must not write the scenario (he felt the author would not be objective enough). The cast included David Wayne, Betsy Palmer, and Muni's long-time associate, Luther Adler. Adler recalled that Muni proudly informed him, "They kissed my ass to get me to do *The Last Angry Man.*"

The Last Angry Man is a stark, excellent film. It not only deftly and uncompromisingly illustrates the unsavory side of hellish tenement life, but it attacks with equal fervor the unsavory world of advertising. The film concerns ad man Woodrow Wilson Thrasher's (Wayne) attempt to film a documentary on Dr. Sam Abelman's (Muni) treatment of his neighbors. When Wayne's Thrasher asks Muni's Dr. Abelman why he is so dedicated to a certain black "galoot" (as the old doctor calls him), who is suffering from a possible brain tumor, Dr. Abelman responds, "Because he's my patient!"

Although *The Last Angry Man*[21] met with an undeserved public apathy, Muni won nice notices. The *Hollywood Reporter* cheered, "Paul Muni, who made some of the

[20]Remade by MGM as *Weekend at the Waldorf* (1945).
[21]In 1974, ABC-TV's "Movie of the Week" would offer a telefeature version of *The Last Angry Man* with Pat Hingle starred as Dr. Sam Abelman.

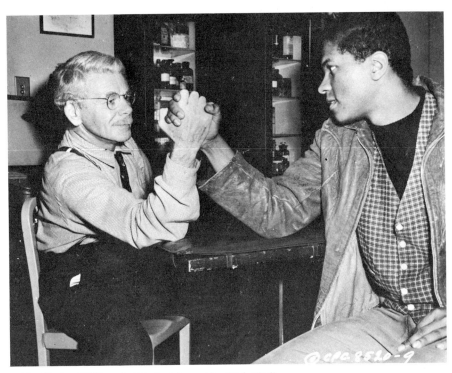

With Billy Dee Williams in *The Last Angry Man* (Col. 1959)

greatest pictures in history . . . has come back, with his remarkable powers undiminished." The performance gained Muni his fifth Oscar nomination, but he lost to Charlton Heston of *Ben Hur* (MGM).

After *The Last Angry Man,* Muni would make no more feature films. First of all, he was just too difficult for modern directors and producers to handle. He took so long in making up his mind about doing *The Last Angry Man* that Harry Cohn had already begun negotiating with Peter Ustinov to tackle the role. Quarreling half a day over direction and demanding additional rewrites just were not allowed in production-cost-controlled Hollywood. Besides his volatile temper, Muni was tired. He was sixty-four years old, his heart was weak, and his always weak ability to memorize lines was deteriorating even more.

In 1962 he and Bella left New York, and bought a home in Montecito, California, near Santa Barbara. He worked for an audience only once more, as a favor to Marc Daniels, who had directed him in his 1947 Massachusetts stock engagement of *Counsellor-at-Law.* Muni appeared on NBC's "Saints and Sinners" (November 26, 1962) as a ninety-three-year-old man who, after seventy-five years of marriage, celebrates his anniversary by planning to divorce his wife (Lili Darvas). Muni was out of sorts and had great difficulty in getting through the show.

Muni lived out his last days in poor health. He was plagued by heart trouble, pneumonia, and weakened eyesight (to the point of near blindness). Bella also began to lose her health. In the spring of 1967, Muni had to have a pacemaker in his heart, but his condition worsened. On August 25, 1967, less than a month before his seventy-second birthday, he died of heart trouble in his home, with Bella at his side.

For a man who had once so dominated the Hollywood scene, the Muni funeral, four days after his death, at Hollywood Memorial Park Cemetery saw only a handful of people present, including Ed Begley and Mervyn LeRoy. But Muni was never able to win the love of his co-workers. As Luther Adler said, "Anybody who says he was close to Paul Muni is a liar."

Muni's estate totaled $1,200,000. Bella was willed it all, save for a $10,000 bequest to Ellis Weisenfreund, his disabled brother. Bella moved to Beverly Hills and began working on Muni's biography, *The Men I've Lived With.* (Her favorite remark to friends was, "I've lived with more men than any other woman," referring to Muni's complete absorption in each new role.) The book was barely started when she died on October 1, 1971, at the age of seventy-three. She left half her estate to the City of Hope Cancer Research Hospital and the other portion to Brandeis University for the establishment of the Paul Muni Theatre Arts and Film Scholarship and Fellowship Fund.

During Muni's last days, the Warner Bros. films of the thirties enjoyed a tremendous revival on television, in art houses, and on the college circuit. Sadly, Muni was bypassed by the cultists and buffs in favor of more flavorful performers like Bette Davis and Humphrey Bogart. Muni was too chameleon-like, too studied an actor for the new breed's taste. Miss Davis herself touched on this in discussing Muni in her memoirs: "There is no question that his technique as an actor was superb. But for me, beneath the exquisite petit point of detail, the loss of his own sovereignty worked conversely to rob some of his character of blood." But as Miss Davis added, "He fought the good fight on his own terms and added greatly to the dignity and respectability of Hollywood."

As an actor and as a man, Muni was indeed unique. As much as he confounded others, often he even confused himself: "Many things I find difficult to explain in myself. I never wanted to be a star. I am still happier in the audience than on the stage. I realize I have always gone against the current; that I am a non-conformist. I know people sometimes call me a 'Male Garbo.' I can sometimes rationalize, but invariably I come up against a stone wall, some sort of enigma."

However, rightly and poetically, it was Bella who perhaps described her husband in the most succinct manner: "If Muni was selling toothpicks," she once said, "he would make it a federal case."

PAUL MUNI

THE VALIANT *(Fox, 1929), 66 min.*
Presenter, William Fox; director, William K. Howard; based on the play by Holsworthy Hall, Robert M. Middlemass; screenplay, John Hunter Booth, Tom Barry; assistant director, Gordon Cooper; sound, Frank MacKenzie; camera, Lucien Andriot, Glen MacWilliams; editor, Jack Dennis.

Paul Muni (James Dyke); John Mack Brown (Robert Ward); Edith Yorke (Mrs. Douglas); Richard Carlyle (Chaplain); Marguerite Churchill (Mary Douglas); De Witt Jennings (Warden); Clifford Dempsey (Police Lieutenant); Henry Kolker (Judge); Don Terry (Cop); George Pearce (Bit).

SEVEN FACES *(Fox, 1929), 78 min.*
Presenter, William Fox; associate producer, George Middleton; director, Berthold Viertel; based on the story *A Friend of Napoleon* by Richard Connell; screenplay, Dana Burnet; dialogue director, Lester Lonergan; sets, William S. Darling; costumes, Sophie Wachner; assistant director, J. Edmund Grainger; sound, Donald Flick; camera, Joseph August, Al Brick; editor, Edwin Robbins.

Paul Muni (Papa Chibou/Diablero/Willie Smith/Franz Schubert/Don Juan/Joe Gans/Napoleon); Marguerite Churchill (Helene Berthelot); Lester Lonergan (Judge Berthelot); Russell Gleason (Georges Dufeyel); Gustav von Seyffertitz (Monsieur Pratouchy); Eugenie Besserer (Madame Vallon); Walter Rogers (Henri Vallon); Walka Stenermann (Catherine of Russia— Waxworks).

SCARFACE: SHAME OF A NATION *(United Artists, 1932), 99 min.*
Producer-supervisor, Howard Hughes; director, Howard Hawks; based on the novel by Armitage Trail; screenplay, Ben Hecht, Seton I. Miller, John Lee Mahin, W. R. Burnett, Fred Palsey; music, Adolph Tandler, Gus Arnheim; assistant director, Richard Rosson; sound, William Snyder; camera, Lee Garmes, L. William O'Connell; editor, Edward D. Curtiss.

Paul Muni (Tony Camonte); Ann Dvorak (Cesca Camonte); Karen Morley (Poppy); Osgood Perkins (Johnny Lovo); Boris Karloff (Gaffney); C. Henry Gordon (Guarino); George Raft (Guido Rinaldo); Purnell Pratt (Publisher); Vince Barnett (Angelo); Inez Palange (Mrs. Camonte); Harry J. Vejar (Costillo); Edwin Maxwell (Chief of Detectives); Tully Marshall (Managing Editor); Henry Armetta (Pietro); Charles Sullivan, Harry Tenbrook (Bottleggers);

Hank Mann (Workers); Paul Fix (Gaffney Hood); Maurice Black (Hood); Bert Starkey (Epstein); Howard Hawks (Man on Bed); Dennis O'Keefe (Dance Extra).

I AM A FUGITIVE FROM A CHAIN GANG *(Warner Bros., 1932), 93 min.*

Director, Mervyn LeRoy; based on the book *I Am a Fugitive from a Georgia Chain Gang* by Robert E. Burns; screenplay, Howard J. Green, Brown Holmes; art director, Jack Okey; technical advisors, S. H. Sullivan, Jack Miller; gowns, Orry-Kelly; camera, Sol Polito; editor, William Holmes.

Paul Muni (James Allen); Glenda Farrell (Marie Woods); Helen Vinson (Helen); Preston Foster (Pete); Allen Jenkins (Barney Sykes); Edward Ellis (Bomber Wells); John Wray (Nordine); Hale Hamilton (Reverend Robert Clinton Allen); Harry Woods (Guard); David Landau, Edward J. McNamara (Wardens); Robert McWade (Ramsey); Willard Robertson (Prison Commissioner); Noel Francis (Linda); Louise Carter (Mrs. Allen); Berton Churchill (The Judge); Sheila Terry (Allen's Secretary); Sally Blane (Alice); James Bell (Red); Edward Le-Saint (Chairman of Chamber of Commerce); Douglass Dumbrille (District Attorney); Robert Warwick (Fuller); Charles Middleton (Train Conductor); Reginald Barlow (Parker); Jack LaRue (Ackerman); Charles Sellon (Owner of Hot Dog Stand); Erville Alderson (Chief of Police); Lew Kelly (Diner Proprietor); William Pawley (Doggy); George Pat Collins (Wilson); Everett Brown (Sebastian T. Yale); William LeMaire (Texas); George Cooper (Vaudevillian); Walter Long (Blacksmith); Wallis Clark (Lawyer); Irvin Bacon (Bill the Barber); Lee Shumway, J. Frank Glendon (Arresting Officers); Frederick Burton (Georgia Prison Official); Dennis O'Keefe (Dance Extra).

THE WORLD CHANGES *(First National, 1933), 90 min.*

Director, Mervyn LeRoy; based on the story *America Kneels* by Sheridan Gibney; screenplay, Edward Chodorov; camera, Tony Gaudio.

Paul Muni (Orin Nordholm, Jr.); Aline MacMahon (Anna Nordholm); Mary Astor (Virginia); Donald Cook (Richard Nordholm); Patricia Ellis (Natalie); Jean Muir (Selma Peterson); Margaret Lindsay (Jennifer); Guy Kibbee (Claflin); Theodore Newton (Paul); Alan Dinehart (Ogden Jarrett); Henry O'Neill (Orin Nordholm, Sr.); Anna Q. Nilsson (Mrs. Peterson); Douglass Dumbrille (Buffalo Bill); Clay Clement (Custer); and Mickey Rooney, Jackie Searle, Marjorie Gateson, Oscar Apfel, Alan Mowbray, William Burress, Wallis Clark, Sidney Toler, Gordon Westcott, Arthur Hohl, William Janney, Philip Faversham.

HI, NELLIE! *(Warner Bros., 1934), 75 min.*

Director, Mervyn LeRoy; story, Roy Chanslor; adaptors, Abem Finkel, Sidney Sutherland; camera, Sol Polito.

Paul Muni (Sam Bradshaw [Nellie Nelson]); Glenda Farrell (Gerry Krale); Douglass Dumbrille (Harvey Dawes); Robert Barrat (Beau Brownell); Ned Sparks (Shammy); Hobart Cavanaugh (Fullerton); Pat Wing (Sue); Edward Ellis (O'Connell); George Meeker (Sheldon); Berton Churchill (J. K. Graham); Sidney Miller (Louie); James Donlan (Evans the Reporter); George Chandler (Danny Sullivan the Cameraman); Milton Kibbee (Dwyer the Reporter); Marjorie Gateson (Mrs. Canfield); Donald Meek (Jimmie Durkin); Kathryn Sergava (Grace); Frank Reicher (Nate Nathan); Dorothy LeBaire (Rosa Marinella); Harold Huber (Leo Moreno); Sidney Skolsky (Himself); Howard Hickman (New York Daily News Reporter/Dr. Wilson); George Humbert (Mike Marinella); John Qualen (Steve the Swedish Janitor); Frank Marlowe (Hood); Paul Kaye (Hellwig); Allen Vincent (Nick Grassi); Antonio Filauri (Head

Waiter); Nena Campana (Italian Woman); Ralph McCullough (Poker Player); Gus Reed (Mac); Harold Miller (Graham's Secretary).

BORDERTOWN *(Warner Bros., 1935), 89 min.*
   Executive producer, Jack L. Warner; director, Archie Mayo; based on the novel by Carroll Graham; adaptor, Robert Lord; screenplay, Laird Doyle, Wallace Smith; music, Bernhard Kaun; art director, Jack Okey; camera, Tony Gaudio; editor, Thomas Richards.

   Paul Muni (Johnny Ramirez); Bette Davis (Marie Roark); Margaret Lindsay (Dale Elwell); Eugene Pallette (Charlie Roark); Soledad Jimenez (Mrs. Ramirez); Robert Barrat (Padre); Gavin Gordon (Brook Mandille); Henry O'Neill (Chase); Arthur Stone (Manuel Diego); Hobart Cavanaugh (Drunk); William B. Davidson (Dr. Carter); Oscar Apfel (Judge at Law School); Samuel S. Hinds (Judge at Trial); Edward McWade (Dean); Wallis Clark (Friend); John Eberts (Alberto); ChrisPin Martin (Jose); Eddie Shubert (Marketman); Carlos Villar (Headwaiter); Marjorie North (Janet); Addie McPhail (Carter's Girl); Frank Puglia (Commissioner); Alphonz Ethier (Banker); Dolores Mandez (Maid); Jack Norton (Customer); Sam Appel (Dealer); Harry Semels, Juan Duval (Waiters); Wade Boteler (Buyer); Fred Malatesta (Foreman); Eddie Lee (Sam); Ed Mortimer, David Newell, Jack Trent (Men); Vivian Tobin, Mary Russell, Elsa Peterson (Women); Alfonso Pedroza, Juan Ortiz (Motor Cops); Arthur Treacher (Butler); Julian Rivero (Prosecuting Attorney); Ralph Navarro (Defense Attorney); Harry J. Vejar (Judge).

BLACK FURY *(First National, 1935), 97 min.*
   Director, Michael Curtiz; based on the story *Jan Volkanik* by Judge M. A. Musmanno, and the play *Bohunk* by Harry R. Irving; screenplay, Abem Finkel, Carl Erickson; dialogue director, Frank McDonald; camera, Byron Haskins.

   Paul Muni (Joe Radek); Karen Morley (Anna Novak); William Gargan (Slim Johnson); Barton MacLane (McGee); John Qualen (Mike Shemanski); Sara Haden (Sophie Shemanski); Henry O'Neill (John W. Hendricks); Willard Robertson (Welch); J. Carrol Naish (Steve Croner); Joseph Crehan (Johnny Farrell); Vince Barnett (Kubanda); Tully Marshall (Tommy Poole); Mae Marsh (Mary Novak); Egon Brecher (Alec Novak); Eddie Shubert (Butch); Effie Ellsler (The Bubitschka); Ward Bond (Mac the Cop); G. Pat Collins (Lefty the Cop); Akim Tamiroff (Sokolsky); Wade Boteler (Mulligan); Purnell Pratt (Henry B. Jenkins); Mike Mazurki, Harry Tenbrook (Cops); Ines Palange (Neighbor); George Offerman, Jr. (Pete Novak); Floyd Shackelford (Mose); Harry Tyler (Johnny); Mitchell Ingraham (Lawyer); Herbert Heywood (Bartender); Samuel S. Hind (Judge); Katherine Claire Ward (Mrs. Clancy); Pedro Regas (Tony); Patrick Moriarity (Bill); Claire McDowell (Nurse); Christian Rub (Miner-Patient); Milton Kibbee (Union Aide); Edith Fellows (Agnes Shemanski); Wally Albright, Jr. (Willie Novak); Addison Richards (Prosecutor); Dick French (Orderly).

DR. SOCRATES *(Warner Bros., 1935), 74 min.*
   Director, William Dieterle; story, W. R. Burnett; adaptor, Mary C. McCall, Jr.; screenplay, Robert Lord; dialogue director, Stanley Logan; camera, Tony Gaudio; editor, Ralph Dawson.

   Paul Muni (Dr. Lee Caldwell); Ann Dvorak (Josephine Gray); Barton MacLane (Red Bastian); Raymond Brown (Ben Suggs); Ralph Remley (Bill Payne); Hal K. Dawson (Mel Towne); Grace Stafford (Caroline Suggs); Mayo Methot (Muggsy); Henry O'Neill (Greer); Robert Barrat (Dr. Ginder); Marc Lawrence (Lefty); Olin Howland (Catlett); Joseph Downing (Cinq Laval); June Travis (Dubin); Gordon (Bill) Elliott (Tom Collins, Greer's Assistant); Sam Wren

(Chuck); John Kelly (Al); Ivan Miller (Ed Doolittle); Otis Harlan (Fisher); Carl Stockdale (Abner Cluett); William Wayne (Dave); Maidel Turner, Vangie Beilby (Women); Grady Sutton (Grocery Clerk); James Donlan, (Salesman); Ralph Lewis (Proprietor); Emerson Treacy (Young Man); June Martel (Young Woman); Jerry Madden (Boy); Lucille Ward (Stout Woman); Alfred P. James (Farmer); Dick Elliott, Harry Harvey, Jack Gardner, Gene Morgan (Photographers); Ben Hendricks (Sentry); Jack Norton, Huey White (Drunks); Al Hill, Robert Perry, James Dundee, Frank McGlynn, Jr., Larry McGrath (Gangsters); Marie Astaire, Lucille Collins (Molls); Milton Kibbee (Bank Teller); Charlie Sullivan, (Henchman); Tom Wilson (Citizen); Helen Lowell (Ma Ganson); John Eldredge (Dr. Burton); Adrian Morris (Beanie).

THE STORY OF LOUIS PASTEUR *(Warner Bros., 1936), 85 min.*

Producer, Henry Blanke; director, William Dieterle; story-screenplay, Sheridan Gibney, Pierre Collins; art director, Robert M. Haas; costumes, Milo Anderson; music director, Leo F. Forbstein; assistant director, Frank Shaw; camera, Tony Gaudio; editor, Ralph Dawson.

Paul Muni (Louis Pasteur); Josephine Hutchinson (Madame Pasteur); Anita Louise (Annette Pasteur); Donald Woods (Jean Martel); Fritz Leiber, Sr. (Dr. Charbonnet); Henry O'Neill (Roux); Porter Hall (Dr. Rosignol); Ray Brown (Dr. Radisse); Akim Tamiroff (Dr. Zaranoff); Walter Kingsford (Napoleon III); Iphigenie Castiglioni (Empress Eugenie); Herbert Heywood (Boncourt); Frank Reicher (Dr. Pheiffer); Halliwell Hobbes (Dr. Lister); Dickie Moore (Phillip Meister); Ruth Robinson (Mrs. Meister); Herbert Corthell (President Thiers); Frank Mayo (President Carnot); William Burress (Doctor); Robert Strange (Magistrate); Mabel Colcord (Lady); Niles Welch (Courier); Leonard Mudie (Coachman); Brenda Fowler (Midwife); Eric Mayne (Lord Chamberlain); Alphonze Ethier (Finance Minister); Edward Van Sloan (Chairman); George Andre Beranger (Assistant); Montague Shaw (British Reporter); Tempe Pigott (Woman); Richard Alexander (Burly Farmer); Wheaton Chambers (Alsatian); Isabelle Lamal (Maid); Gordon "Bill" Elliott, Jack Santoro, Ferdinand Schumann-Heink, Wilfred Lucas (Reporters); Leonid Snegoff (Russian Ambassador); Lottie Williams (Cecile).

THE GOOD EARTH *(MGM, 1937), 138 min. Filmed in Sepia.*

Producer, Irving G. Thalberg; associate producer, Albert Lewin; director, Sidney Franklin; based on the novel by Pearl S. Buck; adapted for the stage by Owen and Donald Davis; screenplay, Talbot Jennings, Tess Schlesinger, Claudine West; art director, Cedric Gibbons; associate art directors, Harry Oliver, Arnold Gillespie, Edwin B. Willis; wardrobe, Dolly Tree; music, Herbert Stohart; montages, Slavko Vorkapich; camera, Karl Freund; editor, Basil Wrangell.

Paul Muni (Wang); Luise Rainer (O-lan); Walter Connolly (Uncle); Tillie Losch (Lotus); Jessie Ralph (Cuckoo); Charley Grapewin (Old Father); Keye Luke (Elder Son); Harold Huber (Cousin); Roland Got (Younger Son); Soo Young (Old Mistress Aunt); Chingwah Lee (Ching); William Law (Gateman); Mary Wong (Little Bride); Charles Middleton (Banker); Suzanna Kim (Little Fool); Caroline Chew (Dancer); Chester Gan (Singer in Tea House); Olaf Hytten (Liu the Grain Merchant); Miki Morita (House Guest of Wang); Philip Ahn (Captain); Sammee Tong (Chinaman); Richard Loo (Rabble-Rouser/Farmer/Peach Seller).

THE WOMAN I LOVE *(RKO, 1937), 85 min.*

Producer, Albert Lewis; director, Anatole Litvak; based on the film *L'Equipage* and the novel (of the same name) by Joseph Kessel; screenplay, Mary Borden; music, Arthur Honneger, Maurice Thiriet; music director, Roy Webb; art director, Van Nest Polglase; special effects, Vernon Walker; camera, Charles Rosher; editor, Henri Rust.

Paul Muni (Lieutenant Claude Maury); Miriam Hopkins (Mme. Helene Maury); Louis Hayward (Lieutenant Jean Herbillion); Colin Clive (Captain Thelis); Minor Watson (Deschamps); Elizabeth Risdon (Mme. Herbillion); Paul Guilfoyle (Berthier); Wally Albright (Georges); Mady Christians (Florence); Alec Craig (Doctor); Owen Davis, Jr. (Mezziores); Sterling Holloway (Duprez); Vince Barnett (Mathieu); Adrian Morris (Marbot); Donald Barry (Michel); Joe Twerp (Narbonne); William Stelling (Pianist); Doodles Weaver (Flyer).

THE LIFE OF EMILE ZOLA *(Warner Bros., 1937), 116 min.*
Executive producer, Jack L. Warner; associate executive in charge of production, Hal B. Wallis; supervisor, Henry Blanke; director, William Dieterle; story, Heinz Herald, Geza Herczeg; screenplay, Herald, Herczeg, Norman Reilly Raine; music, Max Steiner; music director, Leo F. Forbstein; assistant director, Russ Saunders; art director, Anton Grot; set decorator, Albert C. Wilson; gowns, Milo Anderson, Ali Hubert; makeup, Perc Westmore; camera, Tony Gaudio; editor, Warren Lowe.

Paul Muni (Emile Zola); Gale Sondergaard (Lucie Dreyfus); Joseph Schildkraut (Captain Alfred Dreyfus); Gloria Holden (Alexandrine Zola); Donald Crisp (Maitre Labori); Erin O'Brien-Moore (Nana); John Litel (Charpentier); Henry O'Neill (Colonel Picquart); Morris Carnovsky (Anatole France); Louis Calhern (Major Dort); Ralph Morgan (Commander of Paris); Robert Barrat (Major Walsin-Esterhazy); Vladimir Sokoloff (Paul Cezanne); Harry Davenport (Chief of Staff); Robert Warwick (Major Henry); Charles Richman (M. Delagorgue); Gilbert Emery (Minister of War); Walter Kingsford (Colonel Sandherr); Paul Everton (Assistant Chief of Staff); Montagu Love (M. Cavaignac); Frank Sheridan (M. Van Cassell); Lumsden Hare (Mr. Richards); Marcia Mae Jones (Helen Richards); Florence Roberts (Madame Zola); Grant Mitchell (Georges Clemenceau); Moroni Olsen (Captain Guigast); Egon Brecher (Brucker); Frank Reicher (M. Perrenx); Walter Stahl (Senator Scheurer-Kestner); Frank Darien (Albert); Dickie Moore (Pierre Dreyfus); Rolla Gourvitch (Jeanne Dreyfus); Countess Iphigenie Castiglioni (Madame Charpentier); Arthur Aylesworth (Chief Censor); Granville Bates (Waiter); Frank Mayo (Mathieu Dreyfus); Alexander Leftwich (Major D'Aboville); Paul Irving (La Rue); Pierre Watkin (Prefect of Police); Stanley Blystone (Police Officer); Robert Cummings, Sr. (General Gillian); William Von Brincken (Swartzkoppen); Ernie Adams, Joseph De Stefani (Workmen); Myrtle Stedman (Dreyfus Maid); Franklyn Farnum, Edward Biby (Detectives); Edward Dew (Agitator); Herbert Heywood (Prison Guard).

JUAREZ *(Warner Bros., 1939), 132 min.*
Producer, Hal B. Wallis in association with Henry Blanke; director, William Dieterle; based on the play *Juarez and Maximilian* by Franz Werfel, and the book *The Phantom Crown* by Bertita Harding; screenplay, John Huston, Aeneas MacKenzie, Wolfgang Reinhardt; music, Erich Wolfgang Korngold; music director, Leo F. Forbstein; costumes, Orry-Kelly; art director, Anton Grot; camera, Tony Gaudio; editor, Warren Low.

Paul Muni (Benito Pablo Juarez); Bette Davis (Carlota von Habsburg); Brian Aherne (Emperor Maximilian von Habsburg); Claude Rains (Louis Napoleon); John Garfield (Porfirio Diaz); Donald Crisp (Marechal Bazaine); Gale Sondergaard (Empress Eugenie); Joseph Calleia (Alejandro Uradi); Gilbert Roland (Colonel Miguel Lopez); Henry O'Neill (Miguel Miramon); Pedro de Cordoba (Riva Palacio); Montagu Love (Jose de Montares); Harry Davenport (Dr. Samuel Basch); Walter Fenner (Achille Fould); Alex Leftwich (Drouyn de Lhuys); Robert

Warwick (Major DuPont); John Miljan (Mariano Escobedo); Irving Pichel (Carbajal); Walter Kingsford (Prince Metternich); Monte Blue (Lerdo de Tejada); Louis Calhern (LeMarc); Vladimir (Sokoloff (Camilo); Georgia Caine (Countess Battenberg); Hugh Sothern (John Bigelow); Fred Malatesta (Senor Salas); Carlos de Valdez (Tailor); Irving Pichel (Carbajal); Frank Lackteen (Coachman); Gennaro Curci (Senor de Leon); Bill Wilkerson (Tomas Mejia); Walter O. Stahl (Senator del Valle); Frank Reicher (Duc de Morny); Holmes Herbert (Marshall Randon); Egon Brecher (Baron von Magnus); Monte Blue (Lerdo de Tajada); Louis Calhern (LeMarc); Manuel Diaz (Pepe); Mickey Kuhn (Augustin Iturbide); Lillian Nicholson (Josefa Iturbide); Noble Johnson (Regules); Martin Garralaga (Negroin); Grant Mitchell (Mr. Harris); Vladimir Sokoloff (Camilo); Charles Halton (Mr. Roberts).

WE ARE NOT ALONE *(Warner Bros., 1939), 112 min.*

Executive producer, Hal B. Wallis; producer, Henry Blanke; director, Edmund Goulding; based on the novel by James Hilton; screenplay, Hilton, Milton Krims; music, Max Steiner; special effects, Byron Haskin, H. F. Koenekamp; camera, Tony Gaudio; editor, Warren Lowe.

Paul Muni (Dr. David Newcome); Jane Bryan (Leni-Krafft); Flora Robson (Jessica Newcome); Raymond Severn (Gerald Newcome); Una O'Connor (Susan); Alan Napier (Archdeacon); James Stephenson (Sir William Clintock); Montagu Love (Major Millman); Henry Daniell (Sir Ronald Dawson); Stanley Logan (Mr. Guy Lockhead); Cecil Kellaway (Judge); Crauford Kent (Dr. Stacey); E. E. Clive (Major); Eily Malyon (Archdeacon's Wife); Doris Lloyd (Mrs. Jaeggers); May Beatty (Mrs. Patterson); Clarence Derwent (Stage Manager); Billy Bevan (Mr. Jones); Charles Irwin (Working Man); Douglas Scott (Tommy Baker); John Power (Charley); Colin Kenny (George); Joseph Crehan (American); David Clyde (Ticket Collector); Sidney Bracy (The Lamplighter); Viola Moore, Phyllis Barry (Chorus Girls); Lowden Adams, Leyland Hodgson (Detectives); Harry Cording, Cyril Thornton (Men); Douglas Gordon (Mr. Selby); Olaf Hytten (Mr. Clark); Rita Carlyle (Mrs. Deane); Barlowe Borland (Tom Briggs); Egon Brecher (Mr. Schiller); Lillian Kemble-Cooper (Mrs. Stacey); Holmes Herbert (Inspector); Boyd Irwin (Police Officer); Ethel Griffies (Mrs. Raymond); Keith Kenneth (Policeman); Thomas Mills (Judge's Chaplain).

HUDSON'S BAY *(Twentieth Century-Fox, 1940), 95 min.*

Associate producer, Kenneth Macgowan; director, Irving Pichel; screenplay, Lamar Trotti; music, Alfred Newman; art directors, Richard Day, Wiard B. Ihnen; technical advisor, Clifford Wilson; camera, Peverell Marley, George Barnes; editor, Robert Simpson.

Paul Muni (Pierre Esprit Radisson); Gene Tierney (Barbara Hall); Laird Cregar (Gooseberry); John Sutton (Lord Edward Crew); Virginia Field (Nell Gwynn); Vincent Price (King Charles); Nigel Bruce (Prince Rupert); Montagu Love (Governor d'Argenson); Morton Lowry (Gerald Hall); Robert Greig (Sir Robert); Chief Thundercloud (Grimha); Frederick Worlock (English Governor); Ian Wolfe (Mayor); Chief John Big Tree (Chief); Jody Gilbert (Germaine); Jean Del Val (Captain); Eugene Borden, Constant Franke (Sentries); Lilyan Irene (Maid); Keith Hitchcock (Footman); Dorothy Dearing (Girl); John Rogers (Sailor); Reginald Sheffield (Clerk); Robert Cory (Orderly); Eric Wilton, Denis d'Auburn (Councillors).

COMMANDOS STRIKE AT DAWN *(Columbia, 1942), 96 min.*

Producer, Lester Cowan; director, John Farrow; story, C. S. Forester; screenplay, Irwin Shaw; art director, Edward Jewell; music, Louis Gruenberg; music director, Morris W. Stoloff; camera, William C. Mellor; editor, Anne Bauchens.

426

Paul Muni (Eric Toresen); Anna Lee (Judith Bowen); Lillian Gish (Mrs. Bergesen); Sir Cedric Hardwicke (Admiral Bowen); Robert Coote (Robert Bowen); Ray Collins (Bergesen); Rosemary DeCamp (Hilma Arnesen); Alexander Knox (German Captain); Elisabeth Fraser (Anna Korstad); Richard Derr (Gunner Korstad); Erville Alderson (Johan Garmo); Rod Cameron (Pastor); Louis Jean Heydt (Karl Arnesen); George Macready (School Teacher); Barbara Everest (Mrs. Olav); Arthur Margetson (Colonel); Ann Carter (Solveig Toresen); Elsa Janssen (Mrs. Korstad); Ferdinand Munier (Mr. Korstad); John Arthur Stockton (Alfred Korstad); Lloyd Bridges (Young Soldier); Philip Van Zandt (Thirsty Soldier); Walter Sande (Otto); and: Captain V. S. Godfrey, Commander C. M. Cree, Brigadier R. A. Fraser, Commander C. T. Beard, Sergeant-Major L. E. Kemp, Sergeant-Major Mickey Miquelon.

STAGE DOOR CANTEEN *(United Artists, 1943), 132 min.*

Producer, Sol Lesser; associate producer, Barnett Briskin; director, Frank Borzage; screenplay, Delmer Daves; music supervisor, Freddie Rich; music director, C. Bakaleinikoff; songs, Lesser, Al Dubin, and Jimmy Monaco; Lorenz Hart and Richard Rodgers; Al Dubin and Monaco; art director, Hans Peters; assistant director, Lou Borzage; sound, Frank Maher; camera, Harry Wild; editor, Hal Kern.

Cheryl Walker (Eileen); William Terry (Dakota Ed Smith); Marjorie Riordan (Jean); Lon McCallister (California); Margaret Early (Ella Sue); Michael (Sunset Carson) Harrison (Texas); Dorothea Kent (Mamie); Fred Brady (Jersey); Marion Shockley (Lillian); Patrick O'Moore (The Austrialian); Ruth Roman, Francis Pierlot (Bits); Judith Anderson, Henry Armetta, Kenny Baker, Tallulah Bankhead, Ralph Bellamy, Edgar Bergen, Ray Bolger, Helen Broderick, Ina Claire, Katharine Cornell, Lloyd Corrigan, Jane Cowl, Jane Darwell, William Demarest, Virginia Field, Dorothy Fields, Gracie Fields, Arlene Francis, Vinton Freedley, Billy Gilbert, Lucile Gleason, Vera Gordon, Virginia Grey, Helen Hayes, Katharine Hepburn, Hugh Herbert, Jean Hersholt, Sam Jaffe, Allen Jenkins, George Jessel, Roscoe Karns, Virginia Kaye, Tom Kennedy, Otto Kruger, June Lang, Betty Lawford, Gertrude Lawrence, Gypsy Rose Lee, Alfred Lunt and Lynn Fontanne, Bert Lytell, Aline MacMahon, Harpo Marx, Elsa Maxwell, Helen Menken, Yehudi Menuhin, Ethel Merman, Ralph Morgan, Alan Mowbray, Paul Muni, Elliott Nugent, Merle Oberon, Franklin Pangborn, Helen Parrish, Brock Pemberton, George Raft, Lanny Ross, Selena Royle, Martha Scott, Cornelia Otis Skinner, Ned Sparks, Bill Stern, Ethel Waters, Johnny Weissmuller, Arleen Whelan, Dame May Whitty, Ed Wynn. the bands of Count Basie, Xavier Cugat (with Lina Romay), Benny Goodman (with Peggy Lee), Kay Kyser, Guy Lombardo, Freddy Martin (Themselves).

A SONG TO REMEMBER *(Columbia, 1945), C-113 min.*

Producer, Lou Edelman; director, Charles Vidor; story, Ernst Marischka; screenplay, Sidney Buchman; Technicolor director, Natalie Kalmus; art directors, Lionel Banks, Van Nest Polglase; set decorator, Frank Tuttle; assistant director, Abby Berlin; music supervisor, Mario Silva; music director, Morris W. Stoloff; music recordings by William Randall; sound, Lodge Cunningham; camera, Tony Gaudio, Allen M. Davey; editor, Charles Randall.

Paul Muni (Professor Joseph Elsner); Merle Oberon (George Sand); Cornel Wilde (Frederic Chopin); Stephen Bekassy (Franz Liszt); Nina Foch (Constantia); George Coulouris (Louis Pleyel); Sig Arno (Henri Dupont); Howard Freeman (Kalbrenner); George Macready (Alfred DeMusset); Claire Dubrey (Madame Mercier); Frank Puglia (Monsieur Jollet); Fern Emmett (Madame Lambert); Sybil Merritt (Isabelle Chopin); Ivan Triesault (Monsieur Chopin); Fay Helm (Madame Chopin); Dawn Bender (Isabelle Chopin at Age Nine); Maurice Tauzin (Chopin at Age Ten); Roxy Roth (Paganini); Peter Cusanelli (Balzac); William Challee (Titus); William Richardson (Jan); Alfred Paix (Headwaiter); Charles Wagenheim, Paul Zaremba

(Waiters); Charles LaTorre (Postman); Earl Easton (Albert); Gregory Gaye (Young Russian); Walter Bonn (Major Domo); Henry Sharp (Russian Count); Zoia Karabanova (Countess); Michael Visaroff (Russian Governor); John George (Servant); Ian Wolfe (Pleyel's Clerk); Lucy Von Boden (Window Washer); Norma Drury (Duchess of Orleans); Eugene Borden (Duke of Orleans); Alfred Allegro, Cosmo Sardo (Lackeys); Al Luttringer (De La Croux); Darren McGavin (Printer).

COUNTER-ATTACK *(Columbia, 1945), 83 min.*

Producer-director, Zoltan Korda; based on the play by Janet and Philip Stevenson, and the play *Pobyeda* by Ilya Vershinin, Mikhail Ruderman; screenplay, John Howard Lawson; art directors, Stephen Goosson, Edward Jewell; set decorator, Robert Priestley; music, Louis Gruenberg; music director, Morris W. Stoloff; sound, Jack Goodrich; special camera effects, Ray Cory; special effects, Lawrence W. Butler; camera, James Wong Howe; editors, Charles Nelson, Al Clark.

Paul Muni (Alexei Kulkov); Marguerite Chapman (Lisa Elenko); Larry Parks (Kirichenko); Philip Van Zandt (Galkronye); George Macready (Colonel Semenov); Roman Bohnen (Kostyuk); Harro Meller (Ernemann); Erik Rolf (Vassilev); Rudolph Anders (Stillman); Ian Wolfe (Ostrovski); Frederick Giermann (Weiler); Paul Andor (Krafft); Ivan Triesault (Grillparzer); Ludwig Donath (Mueller); Louis Adlon (Huebach); Trevor Bardette (Petrov); Richard Hale (General Kalinev); Adeline DeWalt Reynolds (Old Woman); Virginia Christine (Tanya); Walter Bonn (German Officer); Louis Arco (German Colonel); Arno Frey (German Officer at Telephone); Hugh Beaumont (Russian Lieutenant); Martin Noble, Ted Hecht, Frank Darien (Partisans); Matt Willis, William Challee, John Bagni, Mel Schubert, Alfred Allegro, Darren McGavin, Fred Graff (Paratroopers); Frank Lackteen (Mongolian Partisan); Crane Whitley (Scout); John Vosper (Russian Officer); Otto Reichow, Sven Hugo Borg (German Lieutenants); Alan Ward (Russian Officer); Carl Ekberg, Kurt Neuman (Germans Fighting in Water).

ANGEL ON MY SHOULDER *(United Artists, 1946), 101 min.*

Associate producer, David W. Siegel; director, Archie Mayo; story, Harry Segall; screenplay, Segall, Roland Kibbee; music and music conductor, Dmitri Tiomkin; art director, Bernard Herzbrun; set decorator, Edward G. Boyle; makeup, Ern Westmore; costumes, Maria Donovan; men's wardrobe, Robert Martien; sound, Frank Webster; special effects, Harry Redmond, Jr.; camera, James Van Trees; editors, George Arthur, Asa Boyd Clark.

Paul Muni (Eddie Kagle); Anne Baxter (Barbara Foster); Claude Rains (Nick); Onslow Stevens (Dr. Higgins); George Cleveland (Albert); Erskine Sanford (Minister); Hardie Albright (Smiley); James Flavin (Bellamy); Marion Martin (Mrs. Bentley); Jonathan Hale (Chairman); Murray Alper (Jim); Joan Blair (Brazen Girl); Fritz Leiber (Scientist); Kurt Katch (Warden); Sarah Padden (Agatha); Maurice Cass (Lucius); Addison Richards (Big Harry); Ben Welden (Shaggy); Joel Friedkin (Malvola); George Meeker (Mr. Bentley); Lee Shumway (Bailiff); Russ Whitman (Interne); Noble Johnson (Inferno Guard); James Dundee, Mike Lally, Saul Gross, Duke Taylor (Gangsters); Archie Twitchell (Sergeant); Chester Clute (Kramer); Edward Keane (Prison Yard Captain).

IMBARCO A MEZZANOTTE (a.k.a., STRANGER ON THE PROWL, *United Artists, 1953),* *89 min.*

Producer, Noel Calef; director, Andrea Forzano (Joseph Losey); story, Nissim Calef; screenplay, Ben Barzman; music, G. C. Sonzogno; camera, Henri Alekan; editor, Thelma Connell.

Paul Muni (The Man); Luisa Rossi (Mrs. Fontana); Joan Lorring (Angela); Vittorio Manunta (Giacomo); Aldo Silvani (Peroni); Arnoldo Foa (Inspector); Alfredo Varelli (Castelli).

THE LAST ANGRY MAN *(Columbia, 1959), 93 min.*

Producer, Fred Kohlmar; director, Daniel Mann; based on the novel by Gerald Green; screenplay, Green; adaptor, Richard Murphy; music, George Duning; music conductor, Morris Stoloff; orchestrator, Arthur Morton; art director, Carl Anderson; set decorator, William Kiernan; assistant director, Irving Moore; gowns, Jean Louis; makeup, Clay Campbell; sound, John Livadary. Harry Mills; camera, James Wong Howe; editor, Charles Nelson.

Paul Muni (Dr. Sam Abelman); David Wayne (Woodrow Wilson Thrasher); Betsy Palmer (Anne Thrasher); Luther Adler (Dr. Max Vogel); Joby Baker (Myron Malkin); Joanna Moore (Alice Taggert); Nancy R. Pollock (Sarah Abelman); Billy Dee Williams (Josh Quincy); Claudia McNeil (Mrs. Quincy); Robert F. Simon (Lyman Gattling); Dan Tobin (Ben Loomer); Godfrey Cambridge (Nobody Home); David Winters (Lee Roy); Helen Chapman (Miss Bannahan).

In *Black Tuesday* (UA, 1954)

Edward G. Robinson

5′5″
158 pounds
Black hair
Brown eyes
Sagittarius

There was far more to Edward G. Robinson the man and actor than the enduring stereotype of "Little Caesar," a cigar-chomping, snarling screen gangster.

As a private person he was an intellectual with a cultivated appreciation and knowledge of the art world. As a stage, film, radio, and television performer, he could be joyous, boisterous, sensitive, or disarming as the occasion warranted. Beneath the tough exterior that the public so admired was a complex individual. But whatever his personal problems, he rarely disappointed his audiences. He was a craftsman supreme.

Edward G. Robinson began life as Emanuel Goldenberg in Bucharest, Rumania, on Tuesday, December 12, 1893. The fifth of six sons of Morris and Sarah (Guttman) Goldenberg, he lived in a Jewish area that, while not a ghetto, was "hardly the Ritz," as one of his film characters might have phrased it. His father was a builder. To seek greater opportunities and to overcome the restrictions of Rumanian bigotry, he decided to emigrate to America. By 1903, the whole family was berthed in New York City, soon moving up in the world from a crowded East Side tenement to a home in the Bronx.

While still in Rumania, Emanuel had seen a motion picture; it bored him. He was far more impressed by a staged version of Jules Verne's *Around the World in Eighty Days*. He naively thought the actors were improvising their dialogue as they proceeded, and it seemed like great fun. However, acting would not be his first vocation. After offering the longest Bar Mitzvah speech in the history of the Rivington Street Rumanian Synagogue, he decided to be a Rabbi. "You know, Nietzsche says you have to love your art and religion like you loved your mother and your nurse," said Robinson in his last published interview, for *Touch* Magazine. "And I did, for about six weeks. When I was about 12 I wanted to be a Rabbi, to instill the right sort of ideas into people and make them great influences in the world. But I realized that I'd have to be either a moron or a charlatan to do that to pass as a sacrosanct gent day after day."

There was also a very conventional, typical "American" boy aspect to the young Emanuel. As he would recall in an address to the Philadelphia Museum of Art in 1951, "I remember, as if it were yesterday, the delight I felt as I spread out upon the floor of my bedroom the Edward G. Robinson collection of rare cigar bands. . . . I progressed to cigarette pictures of big league ballplayers . . . then those never forgotten cards depicting the great and beautiful ladies of the stage.

"Long before long pants, I haunted New York's museums and art galleries. How I longed in those days to take home some of the paintings that gave me so much pleasure."

The Goldenberg family was not wealthy, but Morris ran a candy shop with enough success to allow all his children to attend school. Emanuel went to Public School 20. (Paul Muni, then Muni Weisenfreund, was enrolled there about the same time.) Emanuel's good scholastic record led to acceptance at the prestigious Townsend Harris High School and it was there that the acting fever struck him. In 1910 he entered New York's City College, where his dramatic efforts, particularly in Shakespeare, resulted in a scholarship to the American Academy of Dramatic Arts in 1911. It was there that he adopted the name by which he would become internationally known. "Franklin Sargent told me that I had to get an Anglo-Saxon name, whatever that is. I kept the initials E.G. but I don't know to this day why I chose Robinson as a last name. If I had to do it again, I'd take a shorter name. You have no idea how long it takes to write Edward G. Robinson for a flock of autograph-hunters."

Robinson's baptism under fire occurred in 1913. Impressed by Henry Irving's *The Bells,* he wrote a brief dramatization of it called *Bells of Conscience,* playing the leading role of a burgomeister who confesses under hypnotism to a murder he committed many years before. With Edward G. Robinson's name above the title (it would not happen again for fifteen years), it opened professionally at Loew's Plaza Theatre on a night never to be forgotten by the author-star. Shortly afterward, his close friend, rising actor Joseph Schildkraut, managed to talk his illustrious father, Rudolph, into using Edward as a quick replacement in *Number 37* at New York City's West End Theatre. The eighteen-year-old Robinson portrayed a fifty-year-old district attorney, for this was the Yiddish Theatre where young performers often served an apprenticeship playing wrinkled, graying oldsters. It would be Robinson's only actual association with the Yiddish theatre, an ethnic genre that spawned the actor he would later call his "most potent competition," Paul Muni.

Following his graduation from the American Academy (where Mr. George Arliss delivered the commencement address), Robinson practiced his craft in stock assignments. In April, 1913, he appeared in Binghamton, New York in *Paid in Full*; in 1914 he toured the Canadian provinces with *Kismet.* But prospects were bleak for the five-foot, five-inch actor, his face too swarthy and foreign-looking, his voice a bit

432

too sharp. Most New York stage hopefuls were tall, good-looking, and suave. "In those days, I would go for an interview and find myself competing with this other chap who would always be younger and taller and much handsomer than I. I would recognize immediately that the producer wasn't particularly sympathetic and I learned to say, out of intuition, 'I know I'm not much on face value, but when it comes to stage value, I'll deliver for you.'"

Desperate for some future in the theatre, Edward was about to forsake the stage to become a teacher of drama, when he got a break. Strangely enough, his acting ability did not earn it for him as much as his linguistic talent—he could speak nine languages. The play was *Under Fire,* calling for four sets and thirty-one performers. To reduce the overhead, the producers required an actor to double in parts. Robinson did more than that. As he wrote in his autobiography, *All My Yesterdays* (1973), "I got the part. I mean I got the parts, four of them: a Belgian spy, complete with a cutaway coat, goatee, and a Dictaphone he had sneakily hidden in a Belgian inn. He exited and one script page later reentered (I mean, I reentered) as a hysterical Belgian peasant in smock and sabots, crying 'The Germans are coming! The Germans are coming! I then had 5 minutes to change into a German officer, complete with monocle and uniform, and when he exited I came back as a Cockney soldier from the trenches. For that I got $30 a week, but when Klauber and Selwyn [the producers] saw how dandy I was with quick changes and instant dialect, I also replaced some other players (oh, those poor guys), and for $20 more a week I managed to be a soldier of the British army, a member of the English Red Cross, and, off and on, various soldiers in the German army."

After an out-of-town tour, *Under Fire* opened at the Hudson Theatre on Broadway on August 12, 1915. It was a success. The *New York Times* noted: "In minor roles, exceedingly good is done by Robert Fischer, Norman Thorp, E. G. Robinson, and Henry Stephenson." The ice was broken, and, as Robinson said, "After that I never left Broadway."

During World War I, Edward served in the Navy, but a flu epidemic kept him from ever leaving New York Harbor. As he would remember, "The farthest I ever got as a sailor was in a rowboat on Pelham Bay. And when the Armistice was signed, I broke down and cried by myself in a YMCA hut, and I figured, 'Now what have I done to save the world for democracy?'"

Twenty-eight Broadway shows followed for Robinson. Some were successful, others were not, but each helped him to build on his talent. Invariably, he earned good notices. Among the productions he appeared in were *Poldekin* (Park Theatre, September 9, 1920), an anti-Communist play starring George Arliss; *Samson and Delilah* (Greenwich Village Theatre, November 17, 1920), which brought Yiddish Art Theatre star Jacob Ben-Ami to Broadway for the first time; and *Androcles and the Lion* and *Man of Destiny* on a George Bernard Shaw double bill (Klaw Theatre, November 23, 1925), which brought Robinson rave notices from all the major critics.

In early 1926 Edward commenced his association with the celebrated Theatre Guild, playing in *The Goat Song* (Guild Theatre, January 25, 1926) and *The Chief Thing* (Guild Theatre, March 22, 1926). While with the Guild, whose members included the Lunts, Lee Strasberg, Blanche Yurka, Dwight Frye, Zita Johann, and other talented performers, Robinson took a leave of absence to play in Atlantic City in a show called *We Americans.* When he left it, prior to the New York opening (Sam H. Harris Theatre, October 12, 1926) to return to the Guild, his focal role was offered to a Jewish actor who had never played in English before. The performer was Paul Muni.

Although Robinson specialized in playing old men and foreigners on Broadway, roles which utilized his unconventional looks, he attempted to be more dapper offstage. He sported a walking stick, doted on interviews, and thrived on autograph seekers (a liking that would diminish over the years). He was flattered by the girls who dated him, but admitted later, "Certainly they scared the hell out of me, and approaching them to Go All The Way left me sweating and stuttering." His father had always said, "Always live beyond your means. Then you will be forced to succeed." For that reason Robinson always took taxis when comparably salaried players were using the subways. On the road he resided in hotels while the rest of the cast stayed in boarding houses. This love of luxury did not diminish and, along with his love of acting, kept him from retiring at an age when most people call it quits.

It was actually this luxury-loving aspect of Edward that gave him his first film. The film was *The Bright Shawl* (First National, 1923), starring Richard Barthelmess and Dorothy Gish, and featuring Jetta Goudal, William Powell, and Mary Astor. Robinson was cast as an old Spanish Don. The deal "was a trip to Havana where those great cigars were made. That was the only silent part I ever played. I swore off after that because I didn't particularly like it, and I felt that the stage held more of a future for me."

On January 21, 1927, Robinson married. His bride was Gladys Cassell Lloyd, daughter of noted sculptor C. C. Cassell. She was a co-player with Fred and Adele Astaire in *Lady Be Good* on Broadway and was a divorcee with one daughter.[1] Aristocratically attractive and intelligent, she also had a budding mental illness at the time. It was a manic-depressive syndrome that over the years would puzzle and eventually torture her husband. The marriage would last a rocky twenty-nine years.

It was also the year (1927) that Robinson gained Broadway stardom by creating a type of character that would be his constant companion henceforth. The play was *The Racket* (Ambassador Theatre, November 22, 1927), written by Chicago newspaper man Bartlett Cormack. The role was Nick Scarsi, a sneering, monstrous Capone-like character. "It was very documentary and very real," said Robinson to *Touch* Magazine. "We made it in New York about the time Capone was grabbing all the headlines, and it was a big success." The critics were extravagant in their praise. *Theatre* Magazine called Edward's work "a masterly creation of character." The *New York World* assured readers he was "great," and the *New York Herald-Tribune* enthused how he "was quite wicked enough to satisfy the hungriest melodrama fan, and it is reassuring to be able to report that he got 'his' in the end." The "end" was getting gunned down by a vice squad. One night Edward had to indulge in a quick rewrite when the prop crew forgot to fill his co-players' pistols with blanks. "Improvising out of sheer desperation," he wrote in his memoirs, "I changed Bart Cormack's play and died of a heart attack. It was simulated, but it was about real."

The play closed in April, 1928, and, as Robinson told Don Shay in *Conversations* (1969), "We were booked into Chicago about the end of April, but Chicago wouldn't let us in because *The Racket* was much too true. It was documentary, you see. As a result, the season was aborted and disorganized, and some of us were offered a chance to come out for 10 weeks to play it in Los Angeles and San Francisco . . . so I came out and these motion picture tycoons happened to see me in

[1]Her daughter Jeannie grew up with either her father or her maternal grandparents.

434

As *The Kibitzer* (1929)

this particular role. That was my introduction to them. They wanted me to stay and do some pictures then—the pictures had just begun to talk—but I could not divorce myself from the theatre and I went back."[2]

At first, Robinson's loyalty to Broadway was requited. On November 8, 1928, with a colored wig, monocle, and insane smile, he starred in *A Man with Red Hair* (Ambassador Theatre), a chiller in which he played the "maniacal masochist" of Hugh Walpole's novel. The *New York Sun* reported, "Seen last season as the super gangster in *The Racket,* Mr. Robinson proves in his present characterization of a sadistic lunatic that he is without a peer in this particular field on the legitimate stage. His only rival is Lon Chaney!"

Edward then collaborated with playwright Jo Swerling in writing *Kibitzer* (Royale Theatre, February 18, 1929) in which he starred. The *New York Times* wrote, "For Mr. Robinson, it constitutes a minor triumph, another scalp added to his list of histrionic achievements."

But the onthrust of the talking films was becoming more and more difficult for Edward to ignore. While playing in *Red Hair,* he was offered $50,000 by Walter Wanger of Paramount to star in *The Hole in the Wall* (Paramount, 1929) with Claudette Colbert, who was fresh from her Broadway success in *The Barker.* Because the project was to be lensed in New York at the Astoria, Long Island, studios, and because the deal was so lucrative, Robinson accepted what he considered a rotten script and second billing to Miss Colbert. He played a crook named "The Fox," with Miss Colbert cast as an ex-convict. Nobody, particularly Robinson, was enthusiastic about the finished celluloid venture.

But *The Hole in the Wall* did serve to break down Robinson's resistance to the film medium. In late 1929 he traveled West to play in *Night Ride* for Universal, playing an Italian gang leader to Joseph Schildkraut's heroic reporter. Robinson remained in California to accept an offer from MGM to play in *A Lady to Love* (1930), based on Sidney Howard's play *They Knew What They Wanted.* He played Tony, the middle-aged, crippled Italian vineyard owner, with Vilma Banky top-billed as his young, attractive mail-order bride.

While this picture was before the camera, Irving Thalberg, the boy wonder of Culver City, decided Edward G. Robinson should be one of Metro-Goldwyn-Mayer's stars. He invited Robinson to his elaborate beach house during production, where Thalberg's actress wife, Norma Shearer, introduced Edward to such institutions as Louis B. Mayer, Joan Crawford, and Lionel Barrymore. "It was all lavish beyond anything I'd ever known—more butlers, more wine (and Prohibition was still on the books), more caviar, and pate, more diamonds, and more dames on the make." When the picture was released and Robinson garnered the best reviews, Thalberg called the actor to his MGM office to negotiate a long-term contract. The period was to be for three years; the salary would be one million dollars. But Thalberg insisted upon complete control over Robinson's career, refusing to allow the star to take time off from filmmaking each year to appear on Broadway. Thalberg remained adamant, and the negotiations came to naught. As he left Thalberg's office, the relization of what he had done so overwhelmed Edward that he vomited in front of Thalberg's office building. It would be several years before Edward returned to MGM to make a film, and by that time, 1937, Thalberg was dead.

[2]When Howard Hughes filmed *The Racket* (Paramount, 1928) Louis Wolheim had the Robinson role; in Hughes' 1951 remake (RKO), Robert Ryan assumed the part.

With Claudette Colbert in *The Hole in the Wall* (Par., 1929)

With Harry Stubbs in *Night Ride* (Univ., 1930)

With Vilma Banky in *A Lady to Love* (MGM, 1930)

If Robinson had lost out on the MGM pact and seen roles that were "meant" for him go to the likes of Wallace Beery, there were still other offers from other studios. While Fox Pictures was attempting to mold Robinson's contemporary, Paul Muni, into the leading competitor of Lon Chaney, Universal made use of Edward's talents. In *Outside the Law* (1930) he was stereotyped as a gang leader named Cobra Collins. In *East Is West* (Universal, 1930), which derived its title but little else from a 1923 Lon Chaney film, Robinson was billed third, under Lupe Velez and Lew Ayres, as a likeable Chop Suey king. Miss Velez was well known in the film colony for her hot-blooded affection for her leading men (especially Gary Cooper), and Edward G. Robinson was no exception. However, he welcomed her offcamera hugs and fondlings with more trepidation than most of her male co-stars. "Because she was a hot tomato and I was not a rock, it was not easy," attested the married man in his autobiography.

Finally, the star received an enticing offer to return to New York for a play called *Mr. Samuel* (Little Theatre, November 10, 1930). The show was adapted from the Comedie-Francaise's *The Merchant of Tours*. It lasted one week on Broadway. Robinson was bitter, later telling the *New York Post:* "That disaster decided me. I thought, 'What's the good of being true to the theatre when in eighteen years, one hasn't built up a following big enough to support one in even his lesser efforts?'" Robinson berated himself as the closing notices were posted and the nightmare of Thalberg's elusive one-million-dollar offer haunted him. While he was in this frame of mind Hal B. Wallis of Warner Bros. found Robinson when he came backstage after a performance of *Mr. Samuel* to offer him a screen contract.

In *East Is West* (Univ., 1930)

With Alice White in *The Widow from Chicago* (FN, 1930)

The Warner Bros.-First National contract was not comparable to the MGM offer; it gave the actor four months off a year for theatre work,[3] but started him at the salary of one thousand dollars per week, with escalation clauses for pay raises. Encouraged by his wife Gladys, who was attracted to the idea of playing in movies herself and upset by the fickleness of the theatre, Robinson signed the pact, setting up residence at Hollywood's Chateau Elysee Apartments (now an old-age home) and retaining his New York apartment on Eleventh Street.

Robinson's first feature at the Burbank studio was an ordinary entry, *The Widow from Chicago* (First National, 1930), a run-of-the-mill underwold entry in which he was cast as a hood named Dominic. He was billed under Alice White and Neil Hamilton. *Variety* noted, "Edward G. Robinson's gang leader is the poorest such characterization he has turned in," and there was other skepticism about his chances for steady success in pictures.

In his next film, thirty-seven-year-old Robinson would definitely prove them wrong.

In the late summer of 1930, Edward answered a call of Hal B. Wallis, meeting the Warner Bros. potentate at the Burbank headquarters. Wallis handed the actor his next picture assignment. It was based on a W. R. Burnett novel, *Little Caesar*. The actor was distinctly unimpressed with the project. For one thing, he was not set for the title role; he was to play a minor part, Otexo, one of Little Caesar's underlings. After reading the script in his dressing room, Robinson, curious about how much weight he had with his bosses in the new medium, returned to Wallis' office. His response was, "If you're going to have me in *Little Caesar* as Otexo, you will completely imbalance the picture. The only part I will consider playing is Little Caesar." There was more to follow: "I had the advantage of reading the book by Burnett, and when the script was first submitted to me, it was just another gangster story— the East side taking over the West side, and all that," said Robinson. There would have to be more than a recasting, there would have to be a serious rewrite.

Wallis was amused rather than angered by this haughty response. He reminded Robinson that according to his contract, he had no script approval, and that suspension could very easily be the result of this demand. Yet Wallis was impressed by Edward's reasons for the script revisions. The producer announced coolly that he would speak to Jack L. Warner, the head of the studio, about the picture and Robinson's reaction to it.

Warner was by no means a father confessor to problem actors: his tolerance threshold was sorely tried by the likes of Al Jolson, George Arliss, and John Barrymore. His first impulse was to suspend Robinson for several months. But, as he recalls in his memoirs, *My First 100 Years in Hollywood* (1965), Robinson had earlier been recommended to him by a Warner Bros. agent who had seen the actor in *The Racket*. Besides, Mervyn LeRoy, who was to direct *Little Caesar,* had persuaded Warner to test another actor for the title role and he had proven unsuitable. As Warner recollected:

> *I told Mervyn LeRoy that we owned* Little Caesar, *and he exclaimed: "Great, Jack! And I know just the guy to play the lead."*
> *"Eddie Robinson?"*

[3]He did not return to the stage for twenty years.

441

"No, that young fellow who's here in the road show of The Last Mile. *Clark Gable."*

"You mean the guy with the big ears?"

"Let me test him, Jack."

"All right. But I doubt that he's right for the part."

Mervyn brought Gable to the studio for the test, and when I looked at it in the projection room I was more adamant than ever. Gable's ears stuck out like a couple of wind socks and I told Mervyn I didn't want him.

"Okay, Jack," Mervyn said, "but I'm going to use him in a couple of pictures anyway. I've already signed him."

"Make the picture and then get rid of him," I said.

LeRoy followed suit.[4] Warner did not regret his 1930 action, or so he would claim. "I always liked and admired Gable," he says, "but after seeing Edward G. Robinson in *Little Caesar* I knew I had not made a mistake. He turned into a great star overnight, and has been my good friend all these years."

Changes were made in *Little Caesar*. Francis Edward Faragoh remodeled the scenario. Robinson was far more pleased with draft number two. As he said in retrospect, "Finally I was given a version that made some difference, reading more or less like a Greek tragedy. It's a man with a perverted mind, ambitious of a kind, who sets a goal more important than himself—that's what makes him a highly moral character in his perverted way. He is a man who defies society, and in the end is

[4]According to his autobiography, *Take One* (1974), as told to Dick Kleiner, LeRoy insists that he wanted Gable to play the secondary lead, that of Joe Massara, a part later given to Douglas Fairbanks, Jr.

With (center) Ben Hendricks, Jr., Noel Madison, Stanley Fields, and George E. Stone in *Little Caesar* (FN, 1930)

mowed down by the gods and society, and doesn't even know what happened. If Rico had expended his energies in another way, he would have been a great, great fellow. In his own mind, he thought he was doing the right thing, and that's the way you color him. You, as an actor, comment on him—subjectively and objectively. Rico in his way was like Macbeth and Othello and Richard—all of those great characters—and it was like a Greek tragedy or one by Shakespeare."

Actually, Robinson was not initially pleased that LeRoy was to direct the project. The actor saw LeRoy as a good-humored, surface director of mediocre intelligence. Later, he realized that LeRoy had a sensitivity that was a very accurate gauge in making his pictures. Actor and director would develop a great respect for one another that would mount over the years.

Meanwhile, the cast of players was rounded out. Douglas Fairbanks, Jr., his career just beginning to build after a lead in the Greta Garbo-John Gilbert *Woman of Affairs* (MGM, 1929), was cast as Joe Massara, Little Caesar's one-time friend and eventual nemesis. Glenda Farrell, a delightfully wise-cracking blonde whom Warner Bros. would work like a horse, sparking scores of the studio's products of the Depression era, was Olga Stassoff, Fairbanks' dance partner and another figure behind Caesar's downfall. Sidney Blackmer was the "Big Boy," city crime czar, Maurice Black was Arnie Lorch, and Ralph Ince appeared as "Diamond" Pete Montana. The latter two were shifty-eyed rivals whose territory Little Caesar eventually gains. Thin, bouncy George E. Stone played Little Caesar's faithful flunky Otero, the role originally set for Robinson. With Tony Gaudio as the cinematographer, production began in the Indian summer of 1930.

Throughout the filming of the punchy picture, Robinson tried very hard to hate Hollywood, a fashionable sentiment for a stage actor to hold toward the bastard art, in which actors rose early, worked long hours, and made such ridiculously big money. "Those of us in *Little Caesar* who had come from the stage—Sidney Blackmer, Glenda Farrell, William Collier Jr., and George E. Stone (for whom I felt a special affection because he was playing Otero, the role originally intended for me) —banded together. We were, I think, insufferable. Our conversation was a constant put-down of Hollywood, and our plans for our return to Mother Earth—Broadway. We were, I must admit, quite sickening." Several times, Robinson dined with co-star Fairbanks, then wed to MGM star Joan Crawford. He found their dinner parties overly ostentatious and their conversation insipid (he admitted that both stars progressed by leap and bounds as both artists and people as the years passed). All in all, Robinson hated Hollywood, and his hostility doubtlessly aided his onscreen performance.

LeRoy kept things moving on the *Little Caesar* set.[5] There was little excess footage to trim from the production, no score to record (background music had yet to be introduced as a standard ingredient), and the premiere was soon ready. Robinson was not thrilled with the final results, though his performance satisfied him. His own lack of enthusiasm about the medium itself led him to believe that the film would find a limited, sensation-seeking audience.

Culture-bent intellectual that he was, Edward could never understand how the picture, despite its deep but basically ordinary gangster film trappings, made him a star and itself became a cinema milestone. When the *New York Times* reviewed the

[5]LeRoy would later recall that to keep a sense of levity on the set, he would play practical jokes on Robinson, such as nailing his ever-present cigar to any wood prop at hand. The star eventually entered into the humorous mood.

film in mid-January, 1931, the paper said, "The production is ordinary and would rank as just one more gangster film but for two things. One is the excellence of Mr. Burnett's credible and compact story. The other is Edward G. Robinson's wonderfully effective performance. Little Caesar becomes at Mr. Robinson's hands a figure out of Greek epic tragedy, a cold, ignorant, merciless killer, driven on and by an insatiable lust for power, the plaything of a force greater than himself."

Over the years, accredited film scholars would laud the film and its effectiveness. Lewis Jacobs, in *The Rise of the American Film* (1939), would write, "It was shocking, it was hard, it was not pleasant, but it was real. Lack of sentiment, brutal assault on the viewer with gunplay, violence, chases, tense struggles over big stakes, callousness toward human feelings, appealed to a public suddenly insecure in their own lives."

In retrospect (always a dangerous way to look at a film), one has doubts whether *Little Caesar* really merits all the ballyhoo it has generated over the years. There is no question that Edward G. Robinson's performance is a classic and that LeRoy's direction is well-paced. However, the plot tries too hard to become a good old Greek tragedy, and it is just a bit too predictable.

The narrative opens with Cesare Bandello, alias Rico, leaving the sticks to seek fame, fortune, and power in the big city. He finds a spot with Sam Vettori's (Stanley Fields) gang, working under the direct control of Pete Montana (Ralph Ince), who in turn is the chief lieutenant to the "Big Boy" (Blackmer). Robinson's Rico rises rapidly in the gang hierarchy, taking over territories of rivals. Soon, Rico himself is the "Big Boy's" favorite son and is even planning on filling the chair of the "Big Boy" himself.

Rico's tragic flaw is his friendship for handsome, more genteel Jose Massara (Fairbanks, Jr.). More precisely, Joe's love affair with Olga (Farrell), his dance partner, is the fly in the ointment. Olga wants Joe to leave the gang; Rico wants Joe to leave Olga. Rico threatens to kill Olga, which only convinces Joe to turn state's evidence to save them both. Rico retorts by aiming his pistol at Joe, but he cannot pull the trigger. In the meantime, assassination attempts are plaguing him, and he soon decides to turn himself in, a pauper with only his braggadocio remaining. Soon, even that is gone; the police reply to his surrender bid with bullets. Soon, the once-successful gangster is dead in the streets.

The movie does not have the pace of *The Public Enemy* (Warner Bros., 1931), the glossiness of *The Secret Six* (MGM, 1931), or the fireworks of *Scarface* (United Artists, 1932). But its title character does match those of the other motion pictures due to Robinson's significant interpretation. Not a roughhouse kid gone wrong like Cagney's Public Enemy, or a sadistic, leering monster like Muni's Scarface, Robinson's Rico is an entertaining but also a very believable blend of all the traits that can lead a man to become a "Little Caesar." He is showy (flashy suits, jaunty derbies, snug spats), loves attention and notoriety, yet is stoical and careful of his position. At the banquet he throws for his "teammates" after reaching the heights, a banner reading "Loyalty and Friendship" looms, Rico receives a stolen watch as a gift, and he smirks, "The liquor is good. I don't drink it myself. . . . Good to see you gents with your molls." He has no moll, for his philosophy is "Women . . . dancin' . . . where do they get you?" Like most of the great screen gangsters, his most intense feelings are for his gun. "That's all I got between me and them," he broods, "between me and the whole world."

Of all Rico's faults, the most mortal is his friendship with Joe, too easily interpretable as latent homosexuality. It is on Joe that he dotes; it is Joe's Olga that infuriates Rico and precipitates his demise. When Robinson's Rico aims his gun at Fairbanks,

Jr. to wreak a hearty revenge, he cannot pull the trigger. His bitter delivery of the line, "That's what I get for liking a guy too much," is about as memorable as the famous closing line of the film, "Mother of Mercy . . . is this the end of Rico?"[6]

When *Little Caesar* went into general release in January, 1931, Robinson was not billed above the title. "When I did *Little Caesar* they wanted to star me, put me above the title, but I said to Warners that despite the fact that I had been starred in many plays on Broadway, this is another field. I suggested that they try another picture, and if the public really accepts me as such, then they could put my name above the title. But once you do, I told them, since I am signing,a long term contract with you, you will continue to do it so long as I am working for you."

It was a stipulation for which the actor would not have to fight very hard. *Little Caesar* would make Robinson one of the most popular stars of the Depression, a bantam dynamo. His small size and lack of good looks, supplying him with a somewhat "underdog" cast, would actually help him become accepted by thirties' audiences who were mostly underdogs themselves. The domineering personality exploding out of the diminutive, un-handsome body gave Edward G. Robinson a distinctive trademark. Conversely, for many years ahead, he would be dogged by the public's identification of him as Little Caesar, or Little Caesar being Edward G. Robinson. It was a state that was perpetuated by unthinking critics as much as by audiences.

It took Warner Bros. five months to develop a suitable new vehicle for Robinson, who, along with George Arliss, ex-Paramount contractee William Powell, Richard Barthelmess, Ben Lyon, and comedian Joe E. Brown, was now considered one of the company's top male assets. In the interim, the actor's fan mail and the wildfire success of James Cagney in *The Public Enemy* suggested a novel idea to the studio: pair the two pint-sized stars in an underworld film. The result was *Smart Money* (Warner Bros., 1931) the only teaming of the celebrated screen gangsters, and a rather unsatisfying one at that.

In the ninety-minute feature, Robinson's role of Nick (the Barber) Venizelos (a gambler who goes to the big city, is fleeced, and returns to become a hot-shot done in by his weakness for blondes) was far too dominant over Cagney's henchman Jack. There are a few good scenes between them: the pantomime between the duo in which Cagney announces a blonde's visit via a repertoire of expressions and hand movements, and a climactic brawl in which Robinson kills loyal Cagney, unaware he has been duped by the district attorney's contact (Evalyn Knapp). Since the acting assignments are not balanced between these two powerhouse performers, the film loses something. This is not to deny *Smart Money*'s virtues, for it is a fine little picture. Robinson is in excellent shape as a sympathetic gambler, trying hard to be impressive, passing out cigars with the boast that "a fella in Havana makes them up for me." Cagney is relaxed and far less cocky than in his later-developed screen persona. Miss Knapp, Noel Francis, and Margaret Livingston provide an engaging parade of blondes. Boris Karloff creeps in briefly as a gambler with whom Robinson does not like to play. ("I don't like the way he parts his hair.") And even Mrs. Edward G. Robinson, billed as Gladys Lloyd, appears briefly as a cigar stand clerk.[7] The *New York Times* observed, "Mr. Robinson gets all that is humanly possible out of the part of Nick the Barber."

Robinson would later remark of his co-star, Cagney, "One of the most extraordi-

[6]Also shot as "Mother of God . . ." but pruned by the Hays censorship board who refused to have the Deity being "namedropped" in pictures.

[7]She would also have small roles in Robinson's *Five Star Final*, *The Hatchet Man*, and *Two Seconds*.

With Noel Francis (left) in *Smart Money* (WB, 1931)

nary talents—that curious quality of pugnaciousness. Maybe if you took that away from him, he'd be an ordinary Nick."

Warner Bros.-First National next supplied Edward with one of his best roles in one of his finest (and favorite) feature films—as editor Joe Randall in *Five Star Final* (First National, 1931),[8] the expose of the muckraking tabloids and the human flotsam and jetsam that produce them. Mervyn LeRoy directed this frenetically paced, spicy drama based on the Louis Weitzenkorn play of 1930 in which Arthur Byron was Randall. As a volcanic attack on sensationalism it matches *The Front Page* (United Artists, 1931).

This story concerns the managing editor of the scurrilous *New York Evening Gazette,* who agrees to dig up a twenty-year-old scandal to lure prurient readers. The survivor of the scandal is Nancy Voorhees (Frances Starr), who shot her lover and later bore his child, who is now grown (Marian Marsh) and engaged to be married. Nancy's husband (H. B. Warner) is so decent a man that the girl, whom he had adopted, has been raised without knowing the truth about her parents. On the eve of the marriage the story breaks in the tabloid and the shamed parents kill themselves. The daughter nearly kills Randall, who is tormented by what he did and quits his job. He explodes at his former bosses and co-workers, telling off everybody concerned in as strong a language as the 1931 censors would permit. Robinson's Randall, who once believed "ideals won't put a patch on your pants,"

[8]Remade as *Two Against the World* (First National, 1936), with Humphrey Bogart in the Robinson role.

With Oscar Apfel in *Five Star Final* (FN, 1931)

447

concludes his tirade by throwing a telephone through the plate glass window of his superior's office.

Some four-and-a-half decades after its release, *Five Star Final* still packs a wallop, due mainly to its crackling dialogue and a wonderful rogue's gallery of performers. There is Aline MacMahon as Miss Taylor, Robinson's flip secretary, who snidely quips about the paper's dirt-digging, "I think you can always get people interested in the crucifixion of a woman." Ona Munson, in fishnet hoisery, a streetwalker's makeup and outfits, delivers a delicious floozy interpretation of Kitty Carmody, who doubles as a reporter and a concubine for the lecherous brass. And there is Boris Karloff, not yet having worn the Frankenstein monster guise, as T. Vernon Isopod, a slimy degenerate of whom Robinson says, "You're the most blasphemous thing I've ever seen—it's a miracle you've not been struck dead!"

But it is Edward G. Robinson who makes the film sparkle. He plays the editor who must answer Miss Marsh when she invades his office, screaming, "Why did you kill my mother?" Washing his hands throughout the film in the vein of a Pontius Pilate, he is especially effective in the climax of the film when he weans himself away from the rag. "I'm not working here anymore. No, Hinchecliffe [Oscar Apfel] has to get himself a new head butcher. I've had ten years of filth and blood, I'm splashed with it, drenched with it! I've had all I can stand! Plenty of it! Take your . . . killings to Hinchecliffe with my compliments! And tell him to shove it up his . . . "

Almost needless to say, *Five Star Final* was a bit hit in the U.S. and abroad. The *Times* of London wrote, "As Randall, Edward G. Robinson succeeds in the best way an actor can—he succeeds, that is, in endowing the character he is playing with definite personality." It wrapped up the year for Robinson on a note of triumph.

During this eventful year, a season in which onscreen Clark Gable roughed up Norma Shearer, Lugosi played Dracula and Karloff the Monster, Cagney achieved cinema stardom, and the Marx Brothers created *Monkey Business* on film—Robinson realized that he was really a movie star. When Warner Bros. sent him to New York to attend the premiere of *Smart Money,* mobs pursued him, the Winter Garden Theatre spread his name across the marquee in twelve-foot-high letters, and mounted policemen were used to keep the crowds in control. "I'd never known anything like it," he later admitted. "I was frightened, and deep inside, a little excited."

When *Five Star Final* opened at the Warner Theatre in New York in September, Edward not only came to town, but teamed at the Palace Theatre (a block and a half away) in a miniature vaudeville act. Sharing the marquee with him was Miss Kate Smith. *Variety* noted that in the "Robinson number, which doesn't bear too much repetition, he gives little speeches between screen showings of scenes from *Little Caesar* and *Smart Money."* Had Robinson realized the shadow of *Little Caesar* that would pursue him afterward, he probably would have passed up this two-a-day engagement.

When Robinson returned to California it was with some expectation that he would take over the mantle from George Arliss as the studio's new class performer. If Edward expected to have this post with little competition, it was a short-lived wish, for soon Paul Muni would become a Warner Bros. contract star and snare the number one post at the studio. Not until Muni's stormy departure from the company seven years later would Robinson regain his spot; by that time, Humphrey Bogart (and to a lesser extent, George Raft) would be his most fierce competition.

448

In *Two Seconds* (FN, 1932)

For a variety of reasons, including their ethnic and temperamental differences, physically similar Robinson and Cagney always remained contrasting screen types, though not essentially in competition with one another.

After the sterling successes of 1931, the following year's output for Robinson was remarkable more for its quantity than for its quality. *The Hatchet Man* (First National, 1932), directed by William A. Wellman, was a hoary tale of Chinatown tong wars in San Francisco, with Robinson as the title character. Rumanian Jew Robinson as Oriental Wong Low Get is an entertaining sight, though he carries off the masquerade far better than a still unpolished Loretta Young (as Toya San). Next, Mervyn LeRoy directed the compact star in *Two Seconds* (First National, 1932), one of the most bizarre stories in the actor's long career. The film's title refers to the last seconds of a man's life before his execution. The narrative concerns a man's murder of his bitchy wife (Vivienne Osborne) because of her affair with a dance hall punk (J. Carrol Naish). Robinson's John Allen goes to the chair protesting that the murder was no crime, and that if he should be punished it should have been for his accidental participation in events leading up to the demise of his pal (Preston Foster).

Much more resilient was *Tiger Shark* (First National, 1932), which has earned its own reputation over the years, thanks largely to the feature having been directed by Howard Hawks. Once again, the director used the favorite theme of a woman coming between two friends, here played by Robinson and Richard Arlen. Edward was cast as Mike Mascarena, the accented, poor man's Captain Ahab, with a hook where his hand used to be. It was one of those underdog roles, with Robinson's Mascarena losing Quita (Zita Johann) to Arlen's Pipes Boley and eventually being chewed alive by a shark. (Even his death was borrowed from *Moby Dick*, with

With Richard Arlen in *Tiger Shark* (FN, 1932)

Robinson's character being yanked from the boat when a harpoon coil is caught around his foot.) Although the actor enjoyed making *Tiger Shark* under the liberal direction of Hawks, the location shooting off Catalina Island was unattractive to him. In the sequences requiring Mike Mascarena to plunge through the waves, a stuntman was used, because Robinson was frightened of the water and could not swim.

The cinematic year was salvaged somewhat for Robinson with *Silver Dollar* (First National, 1932), a biographic film in which he played H. A. W. Tabor (called Yates Martin in the film), the Colorado silver-mining senator. Bebe Daniels and Aline MacMahon flanked on the distaff side. Robinson enjoyed a meaty role, one that allowed him to age and to suffer through an expansive death scene. "The picture provides Edward G. Robinson with one of the most vibrant of all the lively parts he has portrayed," said the *New York American,* with the *New York Sunday Times* adding, "Whatever Mr. Robinson did in *Little Caesar* is even more convincing here." The top accolade came from ex-New York governor Alfred E. Smith, who wired Warner Bros., "Robinson is more Haw Tabor than Tabor himself could have been." The interesting aspect of Robinson's chronicle performance here, in contrast to similar roles undertaken by Paul Muni or George Arliss, is that the star goes through his paces with little pretention, no display that suggests to the audience: "Look how hard I am working." It is all very relaxed, yet still intense, very similar in execution to the less deft, but still underrated performance of Edward Arnold in *Sutter's Gold* (Universal, 1936).

Meanwhile, Robinson was trying still to acclimate himself to the Hollywood type of life. It was fashionable for all Broadway defectors to despise the clean air, the

450

beaches, the easy living, and the big money. However, despite himself, Edward was still wide-eyed. As he told *Touch* Magazine, "Well, it certainly was a glamorous era. . . . All these magnificent personalities here—the great producers, directors, writers, people from all over the world. These pictures that were being beautifully mounted, talents from all over the world, artisans, and technicians. It was the mecca of the world as a matter of fact."

Robinson and his family would commute between New York and Hollywood. In 1932, Gladys became pregnant, and March 19, 1933, a baby boy was born at Doctors Hospital in Manhattan. He was named Emanuel, and, like the father himself, grew up being called Manny. The birth of his son impressed upon Robinson the importance of being financially secure. Soon, he rented a home on Arden Drive in Beverly Hills, where he, Gladys, the baby, a nurse, and Edward's mother moved. By this time he had become a compulsive art collector, and his new home became a gallery for his growing collection.[9]

Although Robinson had dreams about being free artistically by breaking his Warner Bros. contract, he was astute enough to realize the impossibility. So the parade of studio pictures continued. *The Little Giant* (First National, 1933) allowed Edward a chance to play comedy when he created the role of "Bugs" Ahearn, beer baron bursting into polite society. The *New York Times* reported, "Edward G. Rob-

[9] Robinson would later admit, "[Art] becomes like a drug habit; you cannot live without it. Your walls may be bulging with paintings, business may be bad and prospects none too good, baby needs a pair of shoes, and you've sworn off buying. But honest, it's just this once and there's nothing you can do about it. There's no cure for it. Fact is, you don't want to be cured."

With Aline MacMahon in *Silver Dollar* (FN, 1932)

With his mother and his wife at a Hollywood premiere (September, 1933)

With Kay Francis in a publicity pose for *I Loved a Woman* (FN, 1933)

inson, as the prime player, reveals himself as no mean comedian, and yesterday afternoon, the audience roared when the gangster tackled a French menu and when he turned up at an informal afternoon party in full regalia."

Once again, to compensate for Robinson's lack of obvious sex appeal, the studio cast two leading ladies to pretty up the scene: Helen Vinson and Mary Astor. In her book, *A Life on Film* (1971), the latter recalled, "*Little Giant* with that little giant of an actor, Eddie Robinson, the two of us rather sadly doing a bad picture together, knowing it, telling each other, 'It might be funny.' It was. Sort of. But there was something wrong about Edward G. Robinson taking pratfalls from a polo pony."

I Loved a Woman (First National, 1933) was another two-leading-lady picture, though Genevieve Tobin hardly garnered closeups or shading afforded top-billed Kay Francis. The film revolved around an exploitive meat packer—a curious subject made even more curious since Paul Muni also played a meat magnate that year for the same studio in *The World Changes*. Even Miss Tobin's role, as Robinson's shrewish wife, was similar to Mary Astor's in *The World Changes*, a society bitch who laughs at her husband's idealism regarding quality meat and humane working conditions. Miss Francis was cast as Laura McDonald, a beautiful opera singer who enchants Robinson. Within the ninety-minute feature, Edward had the opportunity to age from an enthusiastic young businessman to a broken old man. He carried out his character change with far less fanfare, makeup, or display of method acting than Muni did in *The World Changes*.

453

In 1933 Warner Bros. had intended to star Robinson in *The Kingfish,* a biography of Huey Long, scripted by William Rankin. Plans were scrapped when politician Long read the script and forbade the studio to produce the picture, claiming it was a defamation of his character. The next year, plans to have Robert Florey direct Robinson in a celluloid reconstruction of the life of Napoleon fell apart when the star rejected the proposed scenario. Bette Davis would have been Josephine with Reginald Owen as Tallyrand.

Instead, tough-guy Robinson went back to the old pattern of breezy program pictures. *Dark Hazard* (First National, 1934) reunited him with Genevieve Tobin and Glenda Farrell in a work by W. R. Burnett. He played a gambler; the title character was a racing dog. Much more melodramatic was *The Man with Two Faces* (First National, 1934), based on a play by George Kaufman and Alexander Woollcott, and called *The Dark Tower.* With genuine flair, Edward portrayed Damon Welles, an actor who had the opportunity to masquerade behind a beard and a French accent. "A suave bit of acting, done in the best tradition of good actors impersonating good actors," said the *New York World-Telegram.* Mary Astor and Mae Clarke (James Cagney's grapefruit target) provided the "looks" in this entry, with Ricardo Cortez injecting swarthy polish as a determined detective.

Despite his growing unhappiness with his career, Robinson "went Hollywood" about this time and purchased a large Tudor mansion, at 910 North Rexford Drive in Beverly Hills. It was a sprawling, French-windowed home, without a swimming pool (due to his fear of water). There was also a badminton court that would soon

With Margaret Dale, Emily Fitzroy, and Louis Calhern in *The Man with Two Faces* (FN, 1934)

be taken out by Robinson (who loathed exercise) and replaced by an art gallery addition designed by the Chicago Art Institute. The remodeling of the house was extensive, and eventually the home resembled more an elegant art museum than a private residence. Except for a brief period in the late 1950s when he had to sell the house for needed divorce funds (he later bought it back), the house was his residence for forty years. Over the decades, Rexford Drive neighbors included such celebrities as Marlene Dietrich, Mickey Rooney, Jane Wyman, Clifton Webb, and Boris Karloff.

While the continual refurbishing of the house would be a satisfactory diversion from Robinson's unsatisfactory marital situation, it also provided another aspect of torment in his love/hate relationship with Hollywood. He now had a mortgage as well as a family. Stardom had escalated his expenses; he needed the kind of money that only an ongoing movie-star contract could provide. Yet, his most recent screen efforts had been far from memorable. As he would observe in his autobiography: "You couldn't exactly say the Brothers Warner were turning handsprings either. You'd think they'd have said, 'That's it, brother. Good-bye. Good luck! Let's forget the rest of the contract.' I personally would have danced the Big Apple.

"The point, of course, was that they'd run out of ideas for this creature they'd invented. My gangster was getting to be a bore. God knows, he was boring me."

Trouble eventually did erupt. On November 19, 1933, The *Hollywood Reporter* published, "Warners latest star battle is with Edward G. Robinson, who turned down his next assignment, *Upper World,* and absolutely refuses to make that picture, with Warners flying off the handle over his refusal and trying to force the star to accept the story. The battle has reached the stage where both Warners' and Robinson's attorneys have gotten together and are trying to straighten out the trouble."[10]

Many of the star's studio problems resulted from his frustrated wish to be loaned out to other film lots. "They [Warner Bros.] never personally explained this position to me," he said later, "but I've come to understand the mentality of the studio system as it was practiced by all of them—I was under contract to them. If they lent me to another of the factories and the ensuing picture was a hit, it could mean that Warners were not as bright and clever as the new guy. This was common reflex behavior on the part of all the studios as far as their contract players were concerned; on the other hand, each one wanted the others' contract players."

Finally, Jack Warner did see things Edward's way and loaned him to Columbia for *The Whole Town's Talking* (1935). As directed by John Ford, the film was a crackly comedy about a timid hardware clerk, Arthur Ferguson, who happens to be a look-alike for Killer Mannion, a gangster freshly escaped from prison. The two, of course, cross paths. Killer tries to use Arthur in his schemes, but seeming Milquetoast Arthur turns the tables. He not only wins the reward money, but earns self-respect, and the girl (in this case, Jean Arthur). Robinson found working with crusty Ford a wonderful experience. "If I argued a line of dialogue with him or objected to a bit of business, I can now assure you that it was more to assert my ego than it was to attack him. Almost entirely throughout the film, when we clashed, it turned out he was right and I was wrong. The main point to be made is that he would sit me down and *show* me where I was wrong. He is a totally remarkable director and one of the few deserving a place in the pantheon."

When *The Whole Town's Talking* premiered in New York (Edward's first film at

[10]Warren William took the assignment in this 1934 feature.

Radio City Music Hall and the first time his photograph illustrated a *New York Times* review), it was a smash hit. The *New York Times* exclaimed that the film "may be handsomely recommended as the best of the new year's screen comedies," adding about the star, "With a splendid narrative like this, he returns with a rush to the front line of film players." The *New York Herald-Tribune* amplified, "The work manages to supply a one-man carnival for its star, and, with Mr. Robinson taking every advantage of its side show possibilities, you have the opportunity to enjoy good acting and to have the soul satisfying pleasure of watching the shrewd and resourceful performer on one of the happiest times of his life." Many people agreed with the *New York American* reviewer, "The best thing Mr. Robinson has done since the unforgettable *Little Caesar.*" Speculations of an Oscar nomination were not fulfilled, but the picture gave Robinson's stock an impressive boost at the home lot.

When Warner Bros. discovered that it did not hurt one bit, Robinson was permitted to be loaned out again, this time to the Goldwyn Studios for *Barbary Coast* (1935).[11] With a script by Ben Hecht and Charles MacArthur, the Howard Hawks-directed feature was a boisterous yarn of 1849 San Francisco, loaded with a barrage of fun performances. Walter Brennan was a larcenous coot named Old Atrocity, while Frank Craven portrayed a grandly verbose, gallant newspaperman. A young Brian Donlevy, in his first major film appearance, was a black-clad henchman known as Knuckles, and Joel McCrea was likeable, if not very believable, as a poetry-spouting vagabond earning survival money by cleaning out spittoons. As Louis Chamalis, Robinson gave a zesty account of the corrupt big boss of wild San Francisco in the gold rush days. However, for the first time since being starred in *Little Caesar,* Robinson lost top billing to Miriam Hopkins. The matronly ingenue played a lady with an eye on gold. She becomes Robinson's mistress until McCrea's aesthetic whimsies win her away.

Hopkins' early dialogue in *Barbary Coast* sets the stage for the rowdy proceedings:

ROBINSON: *Miss, how do you like San Francisco?*
HOPKINS: *(flirting) I think I'm going to like it very much.*
ROBINSON: *That's fine. I own it!*

Miriam Hopkins is better remembered in Hollywood as a temperamental impossibility than as a unique actress (Bette Davis dubbed her a "pig" recently in an interview with Dick Cavett). She usually sparred with co-stars, and Edward was no exception. They rapidly came to despise one another. Robinson would recall, "What was really too much was that Miss Hopkins, in period costume and headdress, was taller than I. When we did a scene together, Miss Hopkins wanted me to stand on a box. I refused, not only because it was undignified and made me self-conscious, but because I was unable to play with any sincerity high on an insecure perch. My suggestion was that Miss Hopkins take off her shoes. When I think of it now, I suspect she could not play with any sincerity standing in her stockings."

These problems are evident in the expensively mounted, occasionally ponderous feature.[12] Robinson and haughty Miss Hopkins share many scenes together, but

[11]The loan-out took longer than Warner Bros. expected. There was a four-week false start filming, with Gary Cooper and Anna Sten under William Wyler's direction. Production then stopped, with McCrea replacing Cooper and Miriam Hopkins replacing Sten.

[12]At one point during the production of *Barbary Coast,* Robinson lost all patience and blistered

456

With Miriam Hopkins and Joel McCrea in *Barbary Coast* (UA, 1935)

they just as well might have been on different sound stages. Throughout the ninety-one minutes, it is a battle between Edward's extravagant acting and Hopkins' extravagant posing (with poor, simplistic McCrea looking bemused).

Robinson's vindication occurred when *Barbary Coast* debuted and he received the best of the reviews. Interestingly enough, this film and the experience with Miss Hopkins marked a change in Robinson's attitude toward picture making. After years of regarding the movies as a bastard art, Edward had encountered an exaggeration of his own high-handedness via his blonde co-star. "Even though I didn't know it then," he would later reason, "it was clear (in the words I spoke over and over again on the screen) that I could dish it out, but I couldn't take it."

With two back-to-back loan-outs, Warner Bros. did not manage to release one Robinson feature in 1935. For a time, they had attempted to interest him in *Dr. Socrates* (1935), but he was unimpressed by this tale of a doctor embroiled in underworld goings-on. The studio finally persuaded Edward's rival, Paul Muni, to tackle the role by convincing him that Robinson had "his heart set" on playing the pedestrian part.

Determined to find some property for Robinson, the studio thought of *The Petrified Forest* as an ideal vehicle for their important star. Leslie Howard, who had starred in the Robert Sherwood vehicle on Broadway, was under contract to the studio, and it was agreed that he would repeat his role as the wandering intellectual, with Bette Davis to be the dreamy cafe waitress. Edward seemed perfect to assume the rule of Duke Mantee, the gang leader who bursts upon the scene, causes

---

his leading lady verbally before the entire cast and crew. The set grew deadly quiet. Then, the next scene was shot. It called for Robinson's pugnacious character to smack Miss Hopkins in the face. When he did so—solidly—the soundstage erupted in applause.

457

Howard's death and brings about Davis' cultural redemption. However, Robinson never got to tackle the role that was performed on the stage by Humphrey Bogart. There were two different explanations for this loss of a plum role. He himself claimed, "I didn't want to go along and keep playing gangster parts. . . . I kept insisting that I wanted to get away from the gangster category. And it was nice, because it brought Humphrey Bogart back into pictures and then eventually he became a very important star." Bogart, however, always claimed that Leslie Howard had wired Warner Bros. when he learned of Robinson's casting in the project, threatening to drop out of the film unless Bogart was reinstated to his original role. "It's not for nothing my daughter's name is Leslie," Bogart later mused.

Despite this setback in his status, it was not long before Robinson was definitely back into harness with *Bullets or Ballots* (First National, 1936), loosely based on the career of New York detective Johnny Broderick. Edward was not delighted with the script, nor was Broderick. Rewrites were ordered and made. These days *Bullets or Ballots* is one of the favorites of the Warner Bros. package circulating on television's late late show, and with good cause. It has a crackerjack cast with some of the studio's favorite faces: saucy Joan Blondell as a moll who reforms, Barton MacLane (once described as "never speaking when shouting would do") as a hefty sourpuss numbers racket leader, Frank McHugh supplying his usual giggly comic relief, and Bogart, in his first film since *The Petrified Forest*, as Bugs Fenner, the trigger-happy gang member who supplies the picture with its more violent moments.

Bullets or Ballots, turned out with extreme competence by company director William Keighley, put Robinson in the position of playing a refined celluloid cop, the kind that puffs on a pipe. The last shoot-out finds him killing the sinister Bogart, but only after being fatally wounded himself by the underworld figure. It was the first of the celebrated Robinson-Bogart bullet swappings, and the studio, knowing a good thing when it saw one, would rehash the situation many times. "In those days," said Robinson in later years, "I would play the leading role, and he would be opposite me, and we would shoot at each other perhaps a reel before the picture finished. Since I happened to be the so-called 'star,' he would die a reel ahead of me, and I would go on with a bullet in me right up to the last scene. In *Key Largo,* the last time we did a picture together, the situation was reversed. He was then their star and I was just a visitor, and we had our shootout as usual, but I died first and he went on for another reel." (In 1936, Robinson was earning $5,000 weekly from Warner Bros.; Bogart was making $650. At the same time, Kay Francis was earning $6,000 weekly—on a forty-week yearly salary—from Warner Bros.)

During the thirties there had been several erosions of the Warners' star stable. When Darryl F. Zanuck had left in 1933 to form Twentieth Century Pictures (later merged into Twentieth Century-Fox), he had taken George Arliss and Loretta Young, among others, with him. In 1934, dapper William Powell moved over from Warners to MGM; in 1935 Warren William left the Burbank fold. In 1936, Jack L. Warner and James Cagney feuded, with the star moving on to Grand National for two independent productions. (He would later return to the fold for the 1938 season.) Bette Davis would run off to Europe to escape her fate on the studio production line-up, and Paul Muni would fume and fuss with his employers because his cherished project—a biography of Beethoven—was being shelved once again. Of all the company's heavily dramatic stars, Robinson remained most tractable to the studio system. He had become so addicted to art buying, that he feared he might perish financially without the security of a film factory contract.

458

Then too, the studio had a less than subtle way of letting a star know he was "replaceable." Not only was there the "threat" system of pitting Robinson against Muni (at one point Edward was considered for Muni's cherished Beethoven property), but now there was Humphrey Bogart to toss into a lesser picture if Edward proved unmanageable. Another ploy was to loan out the star to a lesser studio for a decidedly off-the-cuff project. It may have been a case of the company cutting off its nose to spite its face (lessening the player's marquee value), but it worked. So Robinson was shunted over to Columbia for *Thunder in the City* (1937). It did provide the star with a trip to London to perform in a script by Robert Sherwood, and it did allow him another chance to emote in a comedy. But it was all filmed on the cheap, under the too-heavy-handed guidance of ex-Paramount director Marion Gering, who once had specialized in Sylvia Sidney screen tearjerkers. However, Robinson rose to the occasion, offering one of his most razzle-dazzle performances and even managing to instill a bit of romanticism into his characterization. The story employed a favorite gambit of Hollywood: an American caught in the grips of British titled society. The supporting cast included Nigel Bruce, Constance Collier, and Ralph Richardson, with a very pert Luli Deste as Robinson's vis-à-vis.

It was during this period that Edward's acquisitions for his art collection reached the greatest heights. They had been escalating for the past few years, especially after a Philadelphia art patron sold Edward a Pissarro, a Degas, and a Monet. "They appealed to my emotions," he later told *The Saturday Evening Post.* "They weren't intellectual puzzle pictures. I liked them all. Gladys liked them too, and since the price was very reasonable, she didn't kick. That's what really got me started. It was fun buying those pictures and more fun owning them, having them where I could

With Luli Deste in *Thunder in the City* (Col., 1937)

459

look at them whenever I wanted. We loved these paintings and they led to other spoils." In London, Robinson visited the galleries of Reed and LeFevre, which led to the Wildenstein Paris Gallery, which in turn led to the acquisition of a number of paintings and the assumption of a substantial debt. "I mortgaged my earnings for the next year. I couldn't afford to be a failure when I came back home. I had a fabulous appetite to support."

At this strategic point Robinson and Warner Bros. negotiated a new contract. With one film left to his original commitment, and with debts from purchases of paintings and house furnishings, he bargained with Warner with only a fraction of the bluffing he would have employed had his bank account been more healthy. Then too, at age forty-six he anticipated the approaching career dilemma—that of the aging leading man—which would have frightened almost any top echelon performer into accepting the security of a term pact.

Under the agreement Robinson had script approval, a promise to cast his features with other "names," and a weekly salary of $7,000. Both producer and star referred to it as "the million-dollar contract." Jack Warner left Robinson's new project, *Kid Galahad,* with the star for his perusal. Neither the movie mogul nor accommodating contractee mentioned the Beethoven biography that was still "in the works" for either Robinson or Muni, depending upon whom Warner was talking to at the moment.

By now, Robinson's hate-Hollywood days were largely behind him. His contract renewal did not torture him as had his former one seven years ealier. More and more, his life was being integrated into the the varied Los Angeles scene. His close friends from New York, Sam Jaffe and Joseph Schildkraut, were spending more and more time on the soundstage, and he had a whole new set of close friends from the acting, writing, and directing ranks of Hollywood. (Curiously, few of his cronies were under contract to Warner Bros.) He discovered that he enjoyed the socializing and parties; he had grown dependent on the high yearly income, and as he would later admit when he finally returned to the theatre, he began to doubt if he could ever readjust to the demands of stage acting.

After his European hiatus, Robinson reported back to Burbank for *Kid Galahad* (1937). It was a basic fight story: a hard-nosed promoter discovers a boxer by accident; the boxer tumbles romantically for the promoter's sister; the promoter raises obstacles for the union; and the promoter deserts the boxer before violence ushers in a bittersweet fade-out. Thankfully, *Kid Galahad* was packaged in an extremely entertaining fashion. With Michael Curtiz directing, Robinson played the Italian fight manager Nick Donati; Bette Davis was his mistress, "Fluff" Phillips; Wayne Morris was the ex-bellhop-turned-boxer; Humphrey Bogart appeared as Robinson's unspeakable rival; and comely starlet Jane Bryan performed as the ingenue. Others in the proceedings included Harry Carey as a loyal trainer, William Haade as Morris' opponent in the ring, and such character faces as Veda Ann Borg, Frank Faylen, Joyce Compton, and Horace McMahon.

Acquiring Bette Davis as the film's leading lady (of sorts) was a concession to Robinson's recent contractual demand for a big name to be paired with his in forthcoming productions. Despite her recent Oscar, he retained top billing. Robinson did not particularly admire his co-star, recalling her as "not a very gifted amateur." Yet neither performer was the type to walk through a role, and in *Kid Galahad* they were in a tussle to squeeze as much as possible from their juicy characterizations, with Edward reveling in his dialect routines during his interlude with his old country mama (Soledad Jiminez).

Interestingly enough, when Edward G. Robinson's name is mentioned to Bette Davis, the first thing that comes to her mind is the death scene in this film. "I remember a very powerful actor [she is usually careful not to divulge his name] who was doing a death scene. I was crying, and Janie Bryan was crying. I still remember his plaintive complaint to the director, 'Don't you think the girls are crying too much?'"

The death of Robinson in *Kid Galahad* was caused by Bogart's Turkey Morgan, who swapped bullets, of course, with Robinson's Nick Donati:

> TURKEY: *I've been achin' to fill you fulla slugs!*
> NICK: *Come on. Use your head, Turkey. You can't get away with it in here! There's cops all over the place! Come on, I'll square it with you—*
> TURKEY: *—Yeah—like you always have. It's starting to crawl, eh?*
> NICK: *Anything you say. I'll settle it with ya anyway ya wanta, but leave these two [indicating Morris and Carey] alone.*
> TURKEY: *So they can put the tag on me?*
> NICK: *You're too used to a machine gun, Turkey! You might miss somebody with that peashooter! We wanta rush you . . .*
> TURKEY: *I'll settle with you, ya double crosser . . .*
> [GUNFIRE as Nick pulls a pistol; Turkey crumbles, dead.]
> NICK *(fatally wounded, to Turkey's corpse): You shouldn't have thrown away that machine gun.*

Kid Galahad was deservedly another hit, making blond, wholesome Wayne Morris an important screen name, bolstering Davis' career, and strengthing Robinson's cinema status.[13] This time it was the *New York Journal-American* that insisted upon dredging up the past by reporting, "Robinson has his best role since the Little Caesar days."

Like most other established screen stars, Edward was not averse to capitalizing upon his film name by starring on radio, for it not only won him new fans, but also brought added revenue. Over the years he would be heard in a number of radio renditions of his screen hits, starting with *Bullets or Ballots* broadcast on "Hollywood Hotel" (CBS, May 8, 1936). In 1937, he leaped out of the guest star status by starting his own radio series. On October nineteenth he began a five-year run as Steve Wilson, crusading newspaper editor of the CBS radio program, "Big Town." Besides being the star, Robinson was also producer, director, casting authority, and, as he put it, "Final Word." Assisting Edward every week was Claire Trevor, as Lorelei Kilbourne, the snappy reporter. She was later replaced by Ona Munson, still later by Fran Carlon. Frequently, "Big Town" was rated the number two show in the country, following closely the exceedingly popular "Jack Benny Show."

There was another 1937 film for Robinson. *The Last Gangster* sounds as if it were a Warner Bros. concoction, but the blender was actually Metro-Goldwyn-Mayer. Warners had a multitude of projects to offer Edward at this time, but the star felt obliged to exercise his script approval clause. As he wrote in his book, "I know now

[13]In 1962, United Artists remade *Kid Galahad* with Elvis Presley and Gig Young (in the Robinson role), with the result that on television, the 1937 edition is called *The Battling Bellhop*.

461

that the decision to accept the Metro offer was made out of bad temper, anxiety, and the ever mounting costs of the remodeling of the house. Money was the overriding consideration, not art."

For an actor trying to buck his gangster image, Robinson hardly solved things by choosing *The Last Gangster,* and for a star who wanted to make movies with *other* stars, this was an even stranger choice. His co-lead was Rose Stradner, an Austrian acquisition by Louis B. Mayer made during a talent-seeking junket to Europe. She could barely speak a word of English. Also in the cast was twenty-nine-year-old James Stewart. Robinson's role was that of the familiar gang boss, though the script (based on a story co-authored by William A. Wellman) provided considerable punch and some sympathy for the title character. What made Robinson's return to Metro feasible was that his old professional adversary, Irving Thalberg, had died, and unlike the late boy genius, Mayer had never held any grudge against Robinson for the 1930 misunderstanding.

As glossy underworld stories go, *The Last Gangster* is slick and entertaining. Robinson was in safe territory as a Capone-like czar who, like Big Al himself, is finally sent to Alcatraz on an income tax rap. His wife (Stradner) bears him a son while he is in prison, eventually divorcing him, and remarrying. Her new spouse (Stewart) is a highly moral newspaperman. Worked into the main plot was a touching secondary theme, which finds Robinson, upon his getting out of prison, discovering that he's become a has-been. The "boys" have a new leader and want to retire Robinson, permanently, with a pension of lead-jacketed slugs. Had this aspect of the film been more thoroughly explored, it might have given the entire project a good deal more substance. As it happened, with Robinson offering a sympathetic portrayal of a crook-turned-doting-papa, he was commended for "keeping the thug human, recognizable, and pathological" (*New York Herald-Tribune*). Naturally, Robinson was doomed, and he gets his, courtesy of Alan Baxter in a rain-drenched alley.

Just as Warner Bros. had redirected Jimmy Cagney's tough guy-screen career with *G-Men* (1935), so the studio determined to give Robinson another crack at lampooning his lucrative gangster image.[14] Unlike *The Little Giant* attempt at comedy, *A Slight Case of Murder* (Warner Bros., 1938) went all the way to become a full-fledged farce. For its source material, the studio refashioned a Damon Runyon-Howard Lindsay play into a tailor-made vehicle for Robinson. It was the typical Runyon comedy, loaded with amusing toughs, and supplying the star with another beer baron role. Robinson thoroughly approved of the script and had no qualms about burlesquing his standard cinema image. But Warners was taking no chances with a potentially fickle public. It promoted the film with posters that claimed, "Edward G. Robinson in Damon Runyon's blazing story of the mobster who murdered and laughed!" Also, despite Robinson's contract stipulation, the feature was peopled with such players of minor (if sterling) status as Jane Bryan, Willard Parker, Ruth Donnelly, and Allen Jenkins. The studio would remake this superior comedy in 1952 as *Stop, You're Killing Me!,* with Broderick Crawford inheriting Robinson's role.

By purchasing the rights to the stage success, *The Amazing Dr. Clitterhouse,* Warner Bros. insured a solid storyline with built-in marquee lure. It provided the basis for Edward's second of three 1938 releases. Robinson portrayed the title character

---

[14] *Bullets or Ballots,* on a far more modest scale, had offered Robinson in a heroic-type role within the framework of a gangster tale.

Advertisement for *The Amazing Dr. Clitterhouse* (WB, 1938)

who becomes involved with a gang of thieves in order to study their criminal behavior. Along the way he discovers that he enjoys being a hood. Anatole Litvak, who had just married Miriam Hopkins, directed and Claire "Big Town" Trevor was the attractive fence who becomes Robinson's "in" with the mob. Humphrey Bogart, outfitted with another ridiculous character name (Rocks Valentine), was the gang leader.[15]

Unfortunately for Robinson's well-being with the fourth estate, Dr. Clitterhouse had been played on stage by Cedric Hardwicke, who had essayed the role so smoothly that the major critics were biased against Edward and made critical comparisons between the movie star and the stage star. For example, the *New York Herald-Tribune* carped that Robinson "has trouble in underlining the Jekyll and Hyde quality which Sir Cedric Hardwicke accomplished so suavely in the drama."

Critical comments would be a handicap to the star in other ways, for it seemed that the important, well-circulated reviewers so enjoyed him in nasty, nail-chewing parts that they griped in print whenever the familiar formula was changed. In his next film, *I Am the Law* (1938), which he did on loan-out to Columbia, he played a professor-turned-rackets-buster, performing the chore as well or better than any other actor in movies could. Nevertheless, Howard Barnes *(New York Herald-Tribune)* felt obliged to write, "It's still hard for me to keep in mind that he is a cleaner-upper rather than *Little Caesar*."

To Warner Bros.' credit, the studio was not as myopic as many of the critics, and a very interesting project awaited him upon his return from Columbia. This was *Confessions of a Nazi Spy* (1939), a semi-documentary account of German espionage based on Leon G. Turrow's controversial book, *The Nazi Spy Conspiracy in America*.

[15]By this time Bogart was sick of Warner Bros. casting him as hood after hood and broodingly referred to this project as *The Amazing Dr. Clitoris*.

With Lucien Littlefield in *I Am the Law* (Col., 1938)

Again working with director Anatole Litvak, Robinson played a conscientious G-man who determinedly cracks the spy ring. With such expert villains as Paul Lukas, Francis Lederer, and George Sanders (the latter complete with a Hun haircut) as the Teutons, an effectively strong production was planned.

Nazi Spy, which began shooting late in 1938, was very controversial stuff, geared to be in the studio's tradition of a film "yanked from the headlines." At the time, America was not yet completely sold against Hitler's Third Reich and there were pro-Nazi groups flourishing all over America, many of them hardly subtle in their praise of Hitler. Jack L. Warner saw the feature as a necessary jab at the Axis war machine. The German Consul in Los Angeles wrote to the Film Code Administrator, Joseph Breen, and demanded that the film, if completed, be banned, threatening "serious reprisals by the German government." The German-American Bund openly protested the making of the film. As Warner would recall in *My First 100 Years in Hollywood,* "Even some of our powerful Hollywood executives were furious with me for going ahead on the film. 'Look, Jack,' one studio owner told me, 'a lot of us are still booking pictures in Germany, and taking money out of there. We're not at war with Germany and you're going to hurt some of our own people here.'"

Warner, who had a representative in Germany who was killed when he opposed government policy, was not to be dissuaded. Not only did he complete the feature film against strong opposition, he also took pains to provide it with a class A production mounting. But the threats continued. As he would recall:

> *On the eve of the premiere, Ann [Warner] got a letter in the mail with a detailed*

464

With his wife and son, Edward, Jr. (September, 1939)

floor plan of our Beverly Hills home, the grounds around it, and all the roads leading to the gate. "If this picture opens," the letter read, "the whole Warner family will be wiped out, and the theatre will be bombed."

For three days before the premiere of Confessions of a Nazi Spy *we stationed policemen on the theatre roof in case some screwball wanted to plant a bomb in the chimneys or air vents. On opening night there were almost more cops and special agents in the house than paying customers.*

Ann was scared to the point of hysteria. I was shaky myself. But fortunately nothing happened, and the film was a global sensation.

While Robinson was at work on *Confessions of a Nazi Spy,* the studio placed the star under guard, and Edward himself hired protection to keep his son under surveillance. Frightening phone calls and letters promising death to the Robinson clan invaded his Rexford Drive home. When he visited England some years later in the midst of the war, the authorities there provided him with heavier protection than necessary, specifically because he had starred in that film.

The graphic picture was a hit, justifying Warner's determination to produce it in the face of threats. The *New York Journal-American* noted, "It is one of Robinson's finest roles, one which he plays with neither bluster nor ranting heroics, but with a quiet and authoritative conviction." His very believable performance in this explosive picture was a big step forward out of the shadow of Little Caesar.

However, it was back to the cells-and-stripes a few months later, with Robinson back at MGM for *Blackmail* (1939). A good cast, including Ruth Hussey and a vibrantly hateful Gene Lockhart, told this story of an innocent man bounced in and out of prison. The story smacked of *I Am a Fugitive from a Chain Gang* (Warner Bros., 1932), which had done so much for Paul Muni's career. But by now the formula had pretty much run its course. Even movie critic dean Bosley Crowther *(New York Times)* jumped on the keep-Robinson-hateful bandwagon after viewing this film. He wrote: "In his day, Edward G. Robinson has been one of the screen's greatest criminals. There was a time in fact, during the height of the vogue, when he was said to be widely imitated in the underworld. What a sad thing it is, then, to see this distinguished inhabitant of the Rogues' Gallery, this Napoleon of crime, this indomitably amoral spirit who belongs with the Borgias, feebly trying to go straight in *Blackmail.*"

Fortune stepped in at this point to aid Robinson in escaping similar attacks. Paul Muni, the most indulged star on the Burbank lot, was leaving Warner Bros. His demands were considered unreasonable; his personality and his wife's Svengali-like influence over him made him indigestible to executives and co-workers alike. At this stage, his films were no longer profitable enough to warrant the high salary and special treatment his contract demanded. With Muni gone, the studio required another actor to handle the "class" biographies and "actor's actor" roles. Robinson was a natural successor.

A great heritage left by Muni was a script-writing department that had been long pressured into producing work of 110 percent quality. Historical figures had been thoroughly researched to determine if they would meld into a good film. Famous novels were adapted with much care to cinema effectiveness. And even current social and political problems were fashioned into topical film possibilities. Since Muni had been so unreasonably perfectionistic in choosing vehicles, many of these excellently researched dramatizations had been left sitting on the script department shelf. Now, with Robinson making demands but not being overly critical, some of these products would be saved from permanent, undeserved discard.[16]

As a result, Robinson created a role that became his personal favorite, and which *Variety* would label "one of the most distinguished performances in the star's lengthy screen career." It was the characterization of Paul Ehrlich (1845-1915), the German bacteriologist who pioneered modern immunology and chemotherapy. The film was entitled *Dr. Ehrlich's Magic Bullet* (Warner Bros., 1940), and told of an extremely dedicated doctor determined to tell patients the unfashionable truth. More importantly it was Dr. Ehrlich who experimented with "606," a specific cure for syphilis, a very hushed-up disease in 1909. Under William Dieterle's direction, it evolved as one of the great medical films as well as one of the most distinguished of all cinema biographies.

Robinson found playing the role a revelation. "While doing *Ehrlich* the world outside seemed to vanish, or at least diminish in importance. During the filming I kept to myself, studied the script, practiced gestures before the mirror, read about his life and times, studied pictures of the man, tried to put myself in his mental state, tried to *be* him." Apparently, the Muni dominance had infected the script, as this was the same sort of exhaustive preparation with which Muni always tortured himself in playing a role.

Edward realized that this feature was an opportunity that came to a screen actor very infrequently. Rarely had he worked on a motion picture alongside such talent.

[16]Robinson did reject Muni's cast-off role of "Mad Dog" Earle in *High Sierra* (Warner Bros., 1941), a part eventually played by Humphrey Bogart. Another project that never came to fruition was *The Gamblers* with Bette Davis, Errol Flynn, and Basil Rathbone.

In *Dr. Ehrlich's Magic Bullet* (WB, 1940)

At the White House with Mrs. Pat O'Brien, Gloria Jean, Brenda Joyce, Dorothy Lamour, William Boyd, Mrs. Franklin Delano Roosevelt, Mrs. William Boyd, Mrs. Edward G. Robinson, Olivia de Havilland, Ona Munson, and James Cagney (January, 1940)

Dieterle (Muni's mentor in most of his extravangazas) was helming, expert cameraman James Wong Howe was the cinematographer, Max Steiner was scoring the film, John Huston, Heinz Herald, and Norman Burnside wrote the screenplay, and the cast was overloaded with incisive performers. Ruth Gordon, in a rare screen appearance, played Ehrlich's wife; Otto Kruger was Dr. Emil Von Behring, the physician who supports Ehrlich when established medicine shuns him; Maria Ouspenskaya portrayed the elderly philanthropist who sponsors his research; and such character actors as Donald Crisp, Henry O'Neill, Sig Rumann, Harry Davenport, and Louis Jean Heydt gave the project substance and life. The expert surroundings brought out the best in the bearded Robinson, inspiring him to develop his portrayal with even greater expertise than usual.

Public response was very enthusiastic, especially to Robinson's dominating performance. It looked as if *Dr. Ehrlich's Magic Bullet* would certainly garner some Academy Award consideration. But the film was not nominated for a single major award.

Robinson had reason to be bitter, but he was not. The role had been its own reward. "You can't imagine the pleasure I got out of playing Dr. Ehrlich," he told the *New York Post.* "So far, most of the rats, detectives, prosecutors, and editors I've played were two-dimensional characters, and it was up to me to round them out, to give them flesh and blood and qualities of human beings. But Ehrlich is a different matter altogether. The character is there—and a great character it is—and all an actor has to do is play it honestly and simply." The friendship that the film initiated between Edward and Ehrlich's daughter and son-in-law, and a correspondence with the doctor's widow (who sent him a personal letter of her husband's), truly meant more to the star than the gilded Oscar statue would have.

Of course, as with most fulfilling things, *Dr. Ehrlich* had a catch to it. To play the role, Robinson had to promise the studio to accept another gangster part. Thankfully, it was a vehicle with a twist to it. In *Brother Orchid* (Warner Bros., 1940), Robinson played Little John Sarto and somehow managed to change believably from a self-promoting sly crook to a flower-growing monk. As the *New York Times* observed, "Obviously, this is a story that was destined for no one but Mr. Robinson, and he plays it with all the egotistical but vaguely cautious push that one would expect from a gangster who found himself in such a spot." Ann Sothern was a perfect floozie girlfriend for Robinson, Ralph Bellamy was dependable as the rancher who refines her and ultimately takes Robinson's place in her love life, Donald Crisp was the benign Brother Superior, and Humphrey Bogart, closing out his dog days as a heavy, was Jack Buck, who takes Robinson's Little John for the "ride" that initiates his monastery visit. Lloyd Bacon directed with dispatch.

Edward was not perfectly delighted with *Brother Orchid*. Although he enjoyed making the film, happily chatting between takes with Bogart and Ralph Bellamy ("the kind of star that made it possible to make pictures"), he felt he was slumming. As he was now the classiest, if non-Oscar winning, star of the Burbank lot, it was an unfortunate drawback that he believed his own publicity and sometimes took his ample talent too seriously. Yet, incensed as he became at his gangster screen image, he would never desert the snarling delineation that the public liked best, lest his home, art collection, and reputation as a top contributor to worthy causes suffer in the bargain.

To appease Robinson, Warner Bros. offered him *A Dispatch from Reuters* (1940), and to keep him happy, the studio populated the picture with much of the same talent from *Ehrlich:* director Dieterle, cameraman Howe, actors Albert Bassermann, Montagu Love, and Otto Kruger. Both the company and Robinson looked forward to another artistic and commercial success.

However, the response was mixed this time. *Variety* hailed Robinson's "excellent characterization," but the *New York Times* determined that he "gives a sincere though not always convincing performance in the leading role." His main problem in portraying Julius Reuter (1816-1899), the German pioneer newsgatherer, was the makeup. His face received a curly moustache each morning that made the actor resemble an organ grinder more than a trailblazer for press freedom. He was less surprised than before when the film received no Oscar nomination, but he nevertheless rated *Reuters* as his second favorite role.

Another Muni hand-me-down followed, *The Sea Wolf* (Warner Bros., 1941), in which Robinson grappled with the characterization of Wolf Larsen in Jack London's exciting tale of a sadistic captain of a fog-drenched, scum-sailored boat. So picturesque was this seafaring story that several previous versions had already been filmed.[17] The script contained good bloody stuff, and Warner Bros. entrusted direction to flamboyant Michael Curtiz, with top co-starring roles going to John Garfield as the young sailor George Leach and Ida Lupino as a mysterious stowaway. Alexander Knox was cast as the thoughtful, rather than tough, hero.

The Sea Wolf was a character actor's delight. Gene Lockhart shone as the ship's alcoholic doctor who is inspired to decency by Lupino. He was also treated to one of the most dramatic suicide scenes on film, climbing to the crow's nest and, after a wild-eyed recital, plummeting to the deck. Barry Fitzgerald is so detestable a hyena

[17]Among the actors to play the lead role have been Hobart Bosworth (1913), Noah Beery, Sr. (1920), Ralph Ince (1925), Milton Sills (1930), Raymond Massey (in *Barricade,* 1950), Barry Sullivan (1958), and Chuck Connors (1975).

as Cooky, the ship's most rotten apple, that it is hard to believe it is the same man who warmed hearts in Oscar-winning style in *Going My Way* (Paramount, 1944). Character actors like Stanley Ridges, Francis McDonald, and Howard da Silva lent credibility to a very compelling, eerie production.

The Robert Rossen script was geared to make Wolf Larsen a three-dimensional figure, not just a man-you-love-to-hate heavy. Robinson's portrayal took full advantage of this acting possibility, and the result is a most rewarding character study. Larsen perceives mercy as weakness, reads John Milton's *Paradise Lost,* exulting on the line, "Better to reign in Hell than serve in Heaven," and, ultimately, begins to go blind. The scenes in which Edward's Larsen forces Knox's character to read to him in his cabin are powerful, indeed. Robinson's characterization is one of those few exceptional villainous portrayals that simultaneously inspire audience hatred and sympathy. The *New York Times* summed it up quite well. "We don't recall that he [Larsen] has ever been presented with such scrupulous psychological respect as he is in [this] version of *The Sea Wolf.* . . . This time his monstrous sadism is explored, and the mind of Wolf is exposed as just a bundle of psychoses. With Edward G. Robinson playing him, the expose is vivid indeed."

The Sea Wolf was destined to be big a boxoffice hit. To strengthen the publicity campaign, the studio held a press preview on an ocean liner in the Pacific between Los Angeles and San Francisco. The picture's starring trio was aboard, as was Hobart Bosworth, the original Wolf of the 1913 version.

The Burbank lot again shuffled Robinson with two top stars for his next outing, *Manpower* (1941). Edward and George Raft flanked Marlene Dietrich in a lusty story of two linemen brawling over a sultry cafe hostess. A reworking of the studio's 1937 *Slim* (with Henry Fonda, Pat O'Brien and Margaret Lindsay), it was a predictable

With Barry Fitzgerald, John Garfield, and Gene Lockhart in *The Sea Wolf* (WB, 1941)

story with Dietrich attracted to sulky, brooding Raft but marrying good-natured Robinson. The ensuing jealousy leads to the latter toppling to his death from a line while trying to kill Raft.

The already legendary Dietrich had never worked with Robinson before, and a friendship developed. "God, she was beautiful," Robinson would recall. "One of the things that astonished me most was her knowledge of the technical side of motion pictures. She seemed to know everything. She constantly watched the camera and the lighting. And she would politely superintend, make suggestions to the camera-men so subtly and so sexily that no one was offended, and she got precisely what she wanted. (I didn't mind; what possible difference could it make which side of my face was photographed? Both sides were equally homely.) She is rough and tough—and absolutely and uniquely and gloriously herself."

Robinson was less taken with George Raft. As with Dietrich this was the first time the stars worked together, and it was not the most pleasant association. The ex-Paramount rough guy, Raft, along with Robinson, James Cagney, and Humphrey Bogart were considered the top quartet of screen hoodlums, all of which precipi-tated an unspoken rivalry between some of the contenders. Raft was notorious for settling problems with his fists, a heritage from his underworld-tinged days back East (and in Hollywood). During the filming of this picture, the differences reached a climax on April 26, 1941, during a "take" when Raft was to grab Robinson's arm. Raft grabbed mightily and, swinging his co-star around, nearly threw him off bal-ance. Robinson retorted, "Not so rough, George!" Raft told Robinson to keep his directing to himself, and fisticuffs erupted, while director Raoul Walsh looked on, amazed. Fortunately, Ward Bond and Alan Hale, huge stocky men in the cast, were nearby and rushed to separate the sparring 5'5" Robinson and 5'7" Raft.

Robinson, who could be just as difficult as the professionally insecure but cocky Raft, told executive producer Hal B. Wallis that he was walking off the picture. Wallis managed to calm him down, and Edward's inbred professionalism saw him through. Shortly after this incident, which was well-publicized in national journals, Raft fell from a soundstage pole, cracking several ribs. Robinson was not on the pole at the time. Fortunately for *Manpower,* the co-players' animosity was dissipated in offcamera moments; oncamera they were dynamite together. As the *New York Times* announced, "To say that Mr. Raft and Mr. Robinson make excellent 'squir-rels' is like saying two and two make four. . . . Take it from us, *Manpower* is a tough picture, awfully tough." (The three stars reprised *Manpower* on "Lux Radio Theatre" on March 16, 1942.)

To round out the year, Edward made another junket to MGM for *Unholy Partners* (1941). It was a newspaper story of the twenties, when "death and emotions were cheap." Mervyn LeRoy, of *Little Caesar,* was director, and the excellent Edward Arnold was a good co-star, but the film turned out to be only passable snarls-and-sneers entertainment. *Larceny, Inc.* (1942), which Edward did upon returning to Warner Bros., was not much better. The picture was supposed to be a spoof with Edward and Broderick Crawford trying to resist temptation to rob banks and mugging superfluously to vitalize the picture. Jack Carson, Edward Brophy, and Jackie Gleason supplied the low comedy touch that director Lloyd Bacon felt the audience required to get the salient points of the script.

With this unsuccessful fare, Edward completed his last film under the million-dollar Warner Bros. contract. There was to have been an all-star war picture, *Heroes without Uniforms,* with parts for Robinson, Raft, Humphrey Bogart, and Sydney

Greenstreet, By the time it was released, as *Action in the North Atlantic* (1943), only Bogart was included, with the only featured co-star being Raymond Massey. There were no contract negotiations between Robinson and the studio. Warner Bros. now had Humphrey Bogart fast on the rise; Edward G. Robinson had status and unbridled possibilities as a freelancer.

The departure from the Burbank lot was the beginning of many changes in Robinson's life, not all of them good. His relationship with Gladys was deteriorating even more. As the star candidly related in his memoirs, Gladys was, to be blunt, mentally ill, a manic-depressive. "I lied about Gladys' illness as long as she was alive," he wrote. "I was worried, fearful, and deeply heartsick about it; I was also, in my heart, ashamed." Robinson was informed by specialists that his wife must check into a sanitarium for shock treatments. At first, she refused to go, threatening divorce in harsh, bitter terms. She finally relented. Initial treatment at Las Encinas in Pasadena, California, brought Gladys some improvement emotionally. However, her personality would waver between pleasant and horrid for the remainder of their marriage. As Robinson phrased it, "When she was manic I was Jesus Christ; when she was depressed, I was the meanest son of a bitch that ever lived." In the meantime, the star's relationship with his moody son Manny grew increasingly poor. As such, Edward's home life left much to be desired.

Robinson's first post-Warners picture was *Tales of Manhattan* (Twentieth Century-Fox, 1942). It was a five-sequence (originally six; a W. C. Fields episode was deleted), all-star picture that used the history of a tail coat to tie together the various segments. Charles Boyer, Rita Hayworth, Ginger Rogers, Henry Fonda, Charles Laughton, George Sanders, and Paul Robeson were among the celebrities that were featured. Robinson played with Sanders, James Gleason, and Harry Davenport in the fourth part. He was the poverty-stricken attorney who acquires the coat in question in a pawn shop to wear to his twenty-fifth college reunion. Fox tried to super-sell the well-mounted production, with limited success.

On July 2, 1942, Edward broadcast the last of his "Big Town" radio shows. As he told Don Shay in *Conversations*, "Then the war came on, and they still confined me to cleaning up the rackets, and I said, 'Now this is an enterprising and alive editor. There's a war going on and I'd like to concern myself with some of the day's big questions.' And they said, 'Well, no, we can't do that. We can't have anything factual or fictional about the war because it becomes controversial and they won't buy our soap' and that kind of thing. And so I got dropped off it after 5 years." Before leaving the air, Edward received from the American Legion of California a citation of honor for "his outstanding contributions to Americanism through his patriotic appeals on the program." (It was an unusual award indeed for an individual who in five years would be labeled a Communist during the witch-hunt days.)

There was also an off-the-record reason for Robinson leaving the radio program. With the ever-increasing problems at home, he was anxious for a change of scenery. At forty-nine, he was too old for the military service, but he hoped to find some way in which he could work and travel for the war effort. Finally, Robert Sherwood let him know that Washington, D.C., was interested in recruiting his services. He was assigned to making morale speeches to the British, and to broadcast in his various foreign languages to occupied areas of Europe. Edward found the patriotic work invigorating, but was saddened that in making speeches to servicemen, "what they

With Ona Munson on radio's "Big Town" (CBS, 1941)

wanted was not Edward G. Robinson but Little Caesar. . . . I remember the opening of one of my earlier speeches at an Air Force base in the north of England. I began by saying, 'I am happy to be here, the most privileged moment of my life to see the men who are defeating Hitler.' I have never laid so big a bomb in my life. I could sense the audience despising me. So that crazy actor instinct took over, and to stop the buzzing of their boos and Bronx cheers, I ad-libbed, 'Pipe down, you mugs, or I'll let you have it. Whaddaya hear from the mob?' There was an instant burst of high laughter and applause. What they didn't know was that I wasn't laughing; I was crying."

When Edward returned to Hollywood in January, 1943, he joined Gladys in opening their home to luncheons and dinner parties, for visiting servicemen. Before the war ended, Robinson had given $100,000 to the U.S.O. and to other wartime groups.

As far as movie roles were concerned, he had reached a delicate position. At fifty, he was at the point where most male stars (and certainly most female stars) face professional survival decisions. Even though Robinson was always a "character" star, age and public taste were in a position to handicap him. For a brief time, his film career floundered as he struggled to adjust properly to the new career facts of life.

For Columbia, he starred in *Destroyer* (1943), a sloppy mixture of comedy and wartime propaganda. Edward was not the "type" to play a petty officer with any notice. Universal's elaborate *Flesh and Fantasy* (1943) was much better. It was a group of three short playlets woven into an attractive comment on the supernatural. Robinson was cast as Marshall Tyler, an attorney who is told by palmist Thomas Mitchell that he will commit murder. The prediction so tortures him that he does just that, with Mitchell the ultimate victim. *Tampico* (Twentieth Century-Fox, 1944) was another propaganda entry, with second-string Lynn Bari serving as leading lady and Victor McLaglen, past his prime, as a sparring partner. Edward was a ship captain cracking a Nazi spy ring. A fiasco followed with *Mr. Winkle Goes to War* (Columbia, 1944). It was the tale of an over-age inductee who overcomes his meekness to become a great war hero. The *New York Herald-Tribune* analyzed, "Columbia has made the grave error of casting Edward G. Robinson in the Mr. Winkle part. He never succeeds in being either meekly amusing or properly courageous."

During this spotty period, Robinson was a regular guest on radio programs, being especially now in demand since so many name performers were in the service. He was heard on such programs as "Cavalcade of America," "Radio Reader's Digest," and "U.S. Rubber Hour." One particularly invigorating credit was an engagement on "Lux Radio Theatre" (February 8, 1943) as Sam Spade in *The Maltese Falcon*. It was the property that had done so much for Humphrey Bogart oncamera some fourteen months earlier. Gail Patrick took Mary Astor's treacherous role with Laird Cregar intoning the giggling villainy of insidious Casper Gutman.

Robinson returned very briefly to the stage on March 9, 1943. He joined Paul Muni, Frank Sinatra, Ralph Bellamy, George Jessel, John Garfield, Luther and Stella Adler, Jacob Ben-Ami, and fifty Orthodox rabbis in a mammoth memorial to Nazi-executed Jews called *We Shall Never Die*. It featured Ben Hecht's words, Kurt Weill's music, and Moss Hart's direction. It was held at New York's Madison Square Garden where forty thousand people jammed the hall during two performances, while an additional twenty thousand supporters listened outside over loudspeakers.

With Richard Gaines and Ruth Warrick in *Mr. Winkle Goes to War* (Col., 1944)

Muni and Robinson appeared together professionally for the only time, forgetting differences to read the history of the Jewish people. They stood on the stage on which there were two enormous stone tablets representing the Ten Commandments.

His next film salvaged his self-respect and his career, even if he had to succumb to third billing. This was *Double Indemnity* (Paramount, 1944), the famous chiller based on the 1927 New York slaying of Albert Snyder by his wife Ruth and her lover Judd Gray for his insurance stipend. Billy Wilder, who also directed, and Raymond Chandler originally fashioned so tawdry a script (based on a James M. Cain novel) that they had a very difficult time enlisting a name cast to play in it. George Raft was originally considered to play the lover, Walter Neff, but his old demand that he could not die in a picture led him to refuse. Brian Donlevy was next considered for the role, but it was Fred MacMurray, then about to leave Paramount (and thus not afraid to change his comedian's image), who accepted the part. The opportunity to affect a blonde wig aided Barbara Stanwyck in agreeing to play the murderess. Ever anxious to improve his wavering industry standing, Robinson was attracted by the revamped script and agreed to play the insurance investigator—MacMurray's colleague, in fact—who uncovers the crime. The project was a decided gamble for all concerned; fortunately it paid off in rich dividends.

The scenario had been churned out in seven weeks, and the film was shot at Paramount in forty days, between September and November, 1943. Because of Wilder's insistence on elaborate rehearsals, there were few if any retakes required. Most of the alterations occurred in the editing, when it was decided to delete a twenty-minute sequence detailing MacMurray's trial and gas-chamber execution.

475

Despite splendid jobs by Stanwyck and MacMurray as the criminal lovers, Robinson provided the best performance, "The only one you care two hoots for in the film," said the staid *New York Times.* Considering that Edward's best scenes—the courtroom-gas chamber sequences—had been deleted from the final print, it said a great deal for his performance as the man who must bring his trusting prey to justice.

A J. H. Wallis novel, *Once Off Guard,* provided the story for Robinson's next task, *The Woman in the Window* (RKO, 1944), directed by Fritz Lang. Once more, Edward took a Milquetoast role, that cf psychology professor Richard Wanley,[18] who is seduced into murder by a beautiful model whose portrait hangs in a gallery window near his club. Originally, Merle Oberon had been set for the role of the siren, but she was replaced by Joan Bennett. Raymond Massey joined in the adult proceedings as district attorney Frank Lalor. It was pretty grisly and mature stuff, with Robinson's character being caught in an innocent visit to Bennett's apartment by her keeper (Arthur Loft). Robinson stabs Loft with a pair of scissors. There is a blackmail attempt by slimy Dan Duryea, leading to a life of crime by Robinson and his later near suicide. But the most ghastly thing about the black-and-white film is that it turned out to be a shaggy dog tale—a dream! Explained Robinson, "They were thinking, I suppose, of box office. Why kill him since he was a sympathetic character. Perhaps they thought that would be too morbid—like *Double Indemnity.*"

The *New York Herald-Tribune* lauded Edward's performance, saying he "has seldom, if ever, been better." Unfortunately, the star did not enjoy making the

[18]In the 1931 *La Chienne,* Michel Simon had starred as "Legrand," the middle-aged man. This Jean Renoir-directed feature was the basis for the American film.

In *The Woman in the Window* (RKO, 1944)

picture. "Among the cast—guess their names—there was violent and accusatory anti-Communist talk. At first I defended my Russian War Relief friends, the believers in Uncle Joe, the defenders of Stalingrad, the strength and will of the Russian people. Then, having failed to convince anybody of anything, except that I was a Communist manqué, I retreated to my dressing room and kept my mouth shut.

"I do not like keeping my mouth shut."

Trouble was brewing.

The war was near the end. Before it was over, Edward managed to tour Europe with the U.S.O., safely delivering his speeches a la Little Caesar. Besides his multilingual propaganda broadcasts for the Voice of America, he spoke the commentary for *Moscow Strikes Back,* a 1942 Soviet documentary, and a 1943 short subject called *The Red Cross at War.* He appeared gratis in *Journey Together,* a semi-documentary, produced by the British Ministry of Information. He was Dean McWilliams, a U.S. flight instructor with the R.A.F. The picture was not shown in America until 1946.

Besides his flow of professional and patriotic work, Robinson kept his home open to servicemen on a continual basis, thrilled at the opportunity to display his art collection to this meritorious segment of the public. Sometimes there would be five hundred soldiers in the house at a time; Edward, Gladys, or their butler, John Reeves, would provide a running commentary on the artwork. Eventually it became a nightmare. "They wanted to see the inside of an actor's home, and if possible, the actor," Robinson confided to *The Saturday Evening Post* in 1944, relating how his autograph usually rated more guest interest than any of the paintings. "Life for me was something like being a bear behind the bars at the zoo." Nevertheless, Edward kept the home open, sometimes sneaking in the back way to avoid the mob stomping through at the moment.

At Metro-Goldwyn-Mayer, Edward starred with Margaret O'Brien in the effectively sentimental *Our Vines Have Tender Grapes* (1945). Behind a full moustache, and with a Scandinavian accent and soiled farmer clothes, he effectively portrayed a soft, warm character, one who rises in the middle of the night to take O'Brien to the train stop to see the circus (particularly the elephant) rest-stopping at the junction. It was a role that, thankfully, Metro's resident character star, Wallace Beery, had rejected. Of Robinson's interpretation of Norwegian Martinius Jacobson, the *New York Times* said, "One of the finest performances in a long and varied career." However, the picture would ultimately do him more harm than good. During production of the Roy Rowland-directed family picture,[19] he befriended scenarist Dalton Trumbo, soon to become one of the Hollywood Ten. Trumbo's friendship would be remembered when Hollywood was under investigation.

Bright Journey, his next scheduled film, was to deal with boxing, but did not survive pre-production. Instead, he honored another Fritz Lang production to join with *Woman in the Window* co-players Joan Bennett and Dan Duryea in a new love triangle, *Scarlet Street* (Universal, 1945). It proved to be one of the forties' most sensationalistic features, so much so that no major studio at first wanted to handle the project. So, Lang, Walter Wanger, and his wife (Miss Bennett) formed their own Diana Productions to do the film.

Once again, Edward played a gentle middle-aged man with a weakness for mysterious, low-moraled Bennett, and an abhorrence of his shrewish wife (Rosalind Ivan). Dan Duryea, in straw boater and striped suit, was a fine and rotten pimp,

[19] *Parents'* Magazine awarded the feature a silver medal for being the most wholesome entertainment of the year for the entire family.

With Joan Bennett in *Scarlet Street* (Univ., 1945)

blowing smoke in Bennett's face. The whole sordid plotline winds up with Robinson ice-picking Bennett to death and with Duryea sentenced to the electric chair for the murder.

Scarlet Street is filled with strangely picturesque touches: Robinson painting Bennett's toenails as she languishes on a bed in a negligee; Robinson climbing a telephone pole to hear the high voltage hum en route to the electric chair where Duryea sits; and, of course, the highly controversial ice pick scene (which may seem tame by today's *Death Wish* standards). When the New York Board of Censors banned the film some six weeks before its opening, it inadvertently resulted in wonderful publicity for the picture. The censors demanded that six of the seven pick stabs be snipped, along with isolated pieces of dialogue.

Actually, *Scarlet Street* does not match *The Woman in the Window* in quality. Although the former does not use the "cheat" ending of the latter, there is a distinct quality of *déjà vu* about the proceedings. Robinson was completely unmoved by the carbon-copy film and its racy publicity. He recalled, "[I] hastened to finish it, so monotonous was the story and the character I played. So monotonous was I as an actor." One might have thought he would have derived some satisfaction from portraying the clothing concern cashier who has an enormous talent for painting, turning out canvases that are rated sensational.

One of Edward's most underrated performances in films followed, in *The Stranger* (RKO, 1946), Orson Welles' flamboyant post-World War II melodrama of a notorious Nazi killer of Jews. It called for three powerful performances: the Nazi posing as a genteel college professor at a small New England college, the girl who

478

unknowingly marries him, and the war crimes commissioner who eventually tracks him down. Welles played the Nazi in addition to directing the film, and Loretta Young was cast as his adoring wife. The war crimes agent was originally intended for Welles' Mercury Theatre friend Agnes Moorehead. However, for boxoffice value, she was replaced by Edward. As much of the investigator's scheme in snaring the criminal involves psychologically torturing the wife with films and evidence, some of the role's effectiveness—a woman telling another woman that her husband is a monster—was lost in the marquee shuffle. At the same time, the fact that Robinson in real life was a Jew helped the role to take on a new kind of dimension and excitement.

Welles pulled out all stops in directing this feature: his work is both clever (as in the scene where, in a phone booth, he casually graffitis a swastika on the booth wall) and grandiose (featuring one of the wildest finales ever shot). In *The Stranger* Robinson poses as an art collector who wrangles his way into Welles' confidence. At a dinner conversation, the latter gives himself away by remarking, "[Karl] Marx wasn't a German, Marx was a Jew." The climax is theatrical, exciting, and totally representative of the director's flair for the dramatic. The three protagonists gather high in the steeple of a church while the townspeople mill outside in a vigilante style. "I was only following orders!" pleads a terrified Welles. "You *gave* the orders!" snarls Robinson. As the investigator corners him, Welles escapes from the steeple on to the face of a clock he has recently repaired. The chimes sound, and two metal figures, a devil and an angel, proceed to make their mechanical rounds. Welles falls to the base of the sword-brandishing angel, and he is pierced by the "avenging" automaton. Both statue and villain topple to the ground as the townspeople scream and the bells ring madly.

Robinson plays his part with a determined, mordant humor. When a dazed Miss Young is escorted from the church in the denouement of the picture, after learning that her husband was a Third Reich executioner and that he had intended to kill her, Robinson calls after her to "have pleasant dreams."

Next, Edward tried his hand, reluctantly, at producing. Sol Lesser, former RKO executive, approached the star with a script by Delmar Daves called *The Red House*. It was a substantial thriller with a meaty role for Robinson, that of a crippled farmer. As Pete Morgan, who has murdered Allene Roberts' parents in the house of the title, he keeps anybody from going there. Later, he commits suicide by driving his truck into a mud bank where he has interred his victims. Edward admired the script sufficiently to produce the project, but he did not enjoy the experience. The Film Guild Corporation, which he formed, was quickly disbanded. *The Red House,* with the aid of a capable performance by Judith (*Rebecca*) Anderson, won good reviews. The *New York Herald-Tribune* acknowledged it as "a taut and steady item of menacing make-believe." Ironically the film's title was to be prophetic of the tragedy about to befall Robinson.

Since becoming a substantially wealthy man, Edward's activities to aid various causes had been exhaustive. While his political leanings had always been liberal, his U.S.O. work, radio broadcasts, and opening of his home to soldiers left no doubt as to his patriotism. Nevertheless, when the House Un-American Activities Committee began its famous hearings in 1947, Edward G. Robinson was entangled.

There was, in fact, considerable leftist thinking in the movie colony. The first stars to be attacked had little recourse when their backgrounds were publicized. Howard da Silva, a Paramount character lead, was an alumnus of the Group

Theatre, whose politics were unquestionably far left; Karen Morley, former MGM starlet and Paul Muni's moll in *Scarface,* had little defense either for her Communist sympathies. However, as the Committee became heady with its own power, the list of names grew, names being added in many cases for ridiculous reasons. Edward's name was among them.

On August 31, 1947, the *New York Times* printed a story entitled "Civil Rights Groups Called Red Front," claiming Edward G. Robinson was on the "initiating committee." *Newsweek* Magazine flatly claimed, "Edward G. Robinson is persistently found in Communist fronts." And, in 1950, Oliver Carlson wrote in a pamphlet entitled *Red Star over Hollywood* that Robinson was "a notorious example of an actor who has sponsored literally dozens of red undertakings and organizations." Robinson's response was harsh and led his persecutors to believe that he was protesting too much, especially when he stated, "These accusations . . . emanate from sick and diseased minds." In a less intense moment, he reasoned, "If I lent my name, I am sure it was in behalf of the best American ideals. I don't believe in Communism and I never lent my name to any organization that smacks of Communism."

Fortunately for Robinson, as hate mail came forth and his reputation was besmirched, some top cinema projects were in the works.

All My Sons (Universal, 1948) was a fine film version of Arthur Miller's play, in which Edward was Joe Keller, guiltily manufacturing defective airplane parts and selling them to the government, resulting in the death of twenty-one World War II flyers (including his son). "It was a part I played with such passion and intensity that the director, Irving Reis, told me constantly to take it easy. He also called me One-Take Eddie because rarely did I ever have to repeat a scene. And my passion imbued the whole cast." Mady Christians as the wife and Burt Lancaster as the other son were particularly impressive in this hard-hitting production.

Key Largo (Warner Bros., 1948) is one of Hollywood's superior gangster films, and Robinson's Johnny Rocco is one of the great celluloid gangsters. John Huston directed what was originally a Maxwell Anderson play (the Broadway version, several years earlier, had starred Paul Muni). During the years between the stage version and the film edition, Humphrey Bogart, Edward's old bullet target, had become a major star and was undisputed king of the Warner Bros. lot. Bogart was cast as the film's hero, with his wife and frequent co-star Lauren Bacall in the female lead. The result was a complicated billing arrangement in which Edward's name appeared slightly above Bogart's and Bacall's.

In a seemingly perfect cast that included ever-roaring Lionel Barrymore, Oscar-winning Claire Trevor as Robinson's alcoholic floozy Gaye, and such oily underlings as Thomas Gomez, Dan Seymour, Harry Lewis, and Marc Lawrence, Robinson's performance as Johnny Rocco was the standout. The scene in which Rocco promises strung-out Gaye Dawn (Trevor) a drink only if she sings him a chorus of his favorite song, "Moanin' Low," and then sadistically refuses to give it to her, is a classic. And for the last time oncamera, Robinson and Bogart shot it out. This time there was no exchange of biting dialogue. Bogart's cool hero Frank McCloud silently stares toward his plumpish prey while Robinson's Rocco sweats through a tense monologue, hiding under the deck of a boat:

Soldier . . . listen to me. It's just me and you. From now on we'll be partners, everything will be fifty-fifty. Whatta ya say? Can you hear me? Whatta ya say? Is it a deal? I know what you're thinking. You'd get rid of me and have all the money for yourself. Is that

With Walter Soderling (standing), Jerry Hausner, Burt Lancaster, Charles Meredith, and Herbert Vigran (with hat) in *All My Sons* (Univ., 1948)

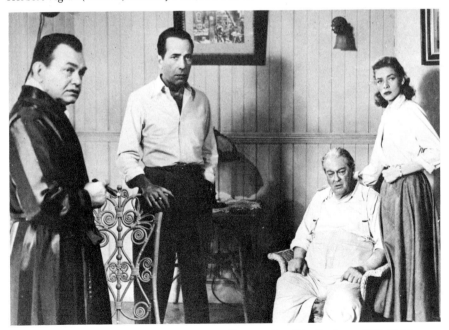

With Humphrey Bogart, Lionel Barrymore, and Lauren Bacall in *Key Largo* (WB, 1948)

With Susan Hayward in *House of Strangers* (20th, 1949)

it? Is it? Answer me! I'll tell ya what. 'Spose I say the money is yours. Yah! Look, it's yours, all yours, Soldier. Plenty more when we get to Cuba. O.K., Soldier, do you hear me? I'll make you rich! Soldier! SOLDIER! You're not big enough to do this to Rocco . . . I'll kill you. You'll never bring me in! NEVER! Look, Soldier, I know what it is. You figure I got a gun so you can't trust me. Right? O.K. Look . . . see, I'm leveling with you. O.K., Soldier. I'm coming out . . . O.K., Soldier. I got no gun and I'm comin' out. SOLDIER!

But Rocco's tossing out a pistol does not fool McCloud, who knows he has another one. And without a word, Bogart's Frank McCloud shoots the cowering ex-gangland kingpin.

Bogart might have been the star in this film, but Robinson recalled, years later, "Let me tell you something about Bogie. On that set *he* gave it all to me. Second billing or no, I got the star treatment because he insisted upon it—not in words but in actions. When asked to come on the set, he would ask: 'Is Mr. Robinson ready?' He'd come to my trailer dressing room to get me."

House of Strangers (Twentieth Century-Fox, 1949) reaped Robinson his only major acting award prior to his posthumous Oscar. He received the Cannes Film Festival Best Actor Award for his portrayal of Gino Monetti, barber-turned-banker with three rotten sons and a vengeful fourth one. The film was directed by Joseph L. Mankiewicz, with a Philip Yordan scenario based on the well-distributed Jerome Weidman novel. So successful was the completed film that Fox reworked it in 1954 as a Western, *Broken Lance,* starring Spencer Tracy, and in 1961 as a circus tale, *The Big Show,* with Nehemiah Persoff handling a considerably revised version of the Robinson part.

These powerhouse roles were quickly becoming few and far between for Robinson. As the HUAC pressure increased, Robinson found good film assignments increasingly rare. *Night Has a Thousand Eyes* (Paramount, 1948), in which he was a vaudeville mentalist, was "unadultered hokum" (*New York Times*). He was merely one of fourteen guest stars in *It's a Great Feeling* (Warner Bros., 1949), a Jack Carson-Dennis Morgan-Doris Day comedy. In *My Daughter Joy,* made in England and released in the U.S. by Columbia in 1950 as *Operation X,* he was cast as a megalomaniac banker. Such jobs as these were hurting his status in the industry. Therefore, Robinson demanded and received a chance to testify personally before HUAC. He would testify three times.

On October 27, 1950, Edward appeared in Washington, D.C., supplying the Committee with a twelve-page list of the three hundred organizations to which he had contributed over a ten-year period. He also fully detailed his war activities. Two months later on December 21, he appeared again, with the statement, "You are the only tribunal in the United States where an American citizen can come and ask for this kind of relief." He added diplomatically, and some thought too conciliatorily, "I am sorry if I have become a little bit emotional . . . because I think I have not only been a good citizen, I think I have been an extraordinarily good citizen, and I value this above everything else! . . . I think I may have taken money under false pretenses in my own business, and I may not have been as good a husband or father or friend as I should have been, but I know my Americanism is unblemished and fine and wonderful, and I am proud of it, and I don't feel it is conceit on my part to say this, and I stand on my record or fall on it."

With Richard Greene, Nora Swinburne, and Peggy Cummins in *My Daughter Joy* (Col., 1950)

It was not until April 30, 1952, that Robinson was finally cleared by HUAC. Again, Edward showcased his contribution files and his war record. Congressman Francis Walter of Pennsylvania, Chairman of the Committee, finally said, "Well, this committee has never had any evidence presented to indicate that you were anything more than a very choice sucker. I think you are number 1 on the sucker list in the country." The official statement was dusted off to read, "According to the evidence to this committee, you are a good, loyal, and intensely patriotic American citizen."

Robinson would have the final laugh on Mr. Walter. In 1954, the latter was dismissed from his post. The official reason was "intense struggles between factions of the committee." The unofficial reason was that the congressman had borrowed three hundred dollars from Robinson during the actor's Washington stay.

Although Edward was finished with the HUAC, he was hardly redeemed in Hollywood. He was caught between two factions: the right-of-center, who stubbornly insisted that where there had been smoke there must have been fire; and the left-of-center, who resented Edward's "friendly" co-operation with the Committee, feeling he should have taken the Fifth Amendment as had John Garfield, Howard da Silva, J. Edward Bromberg, and the Hollywood Ten, among many others. As friend Jo Swerling said, Edward would now find trouble getting "the type of parts he was accustomed to getting." Since he had spent about $100,000 to clear himself, it was imperative that he work.

In the midst of the controversy, he had returned to the stage in his first play in twenty years, *Darkness at Noon* by Sidney Kingsley and Arthur Koestler and based upon the latter's book of the same title. The plot was strongly anti-Communist, forecasting how Stalin would soon be turned upon by his people as the bestial nature of Communism became more apparent. Edward refused to do the role on Broadway. He feared the Broadway critics would regard him as a movie star on leave and pan him accordingly. Moreover, the role was very exhausting. Instead, Claude Rains handled the pivotal role in New York. However, when *Darkness at Noon* toured, Edward accepted the part, touring in it from September 28, 1951, to April 26, 1952. Opening night in Princeton, New Jersey, was almost a disaster. Nervous Edward was inaudible and so shaky for the first ten minutes that he himself finally stopped the play and he and the cast started all over again. The remainder of the tour went well. "Sure," wrote Robinson later on, "there were crank letters accusing me of being a Communist—and even an occasional 'Boo.' But during the whole tour, do you know who I was? Edward G. Robinson, movie star, that's who I was. I was a ranking celebrity, an entertainer, adored, given adulation and deference, and it seemed to me that nobody had ever heard of the House Committee on Un-American Activities."

But life in Hollywood was not so pleasant. *Actors and Sin* (United Artists, 1952) was produced, directed, and scripted by Ben Hecht. It was middling screen fare. Edward played in one of the two stories as a Shakespearean star who tries to make his daughter's (Marsha Hunt)[20] suicide look like murder. *Vice Squad* (United Artists, 1953) cast him as a police captain, though aging Paulette Goddard was far more exciting as a mink-clad "escort business" manager in this very routine cops picture. *Big Leaguer* (MGM, 1953) was nothing more than a double-bill entry in which Robinson was a baseball manager. *The Glass Web* (Universal, 1953) was a crime story with such an involved plotline that the histrionics were nearly sidetracked.

Although *Black Tuesday* (United Artists, 1954) was produced on the cheap, moviegoers were happy to see Robinson in a meaty criminal role as "his old, savage,

[20]Miss Hunt was also a victim of the Red probes.

With Robert Carson in *Actors and Sin* (UA, 1952)

485

With Harlan Warde, Adam Williams, and K. T. Stevens in *Vice Squad* (Col., 1953)

In *Big Leaguer* (MGM, 1953)

With Kathleen Hughes in *The Glass Web* (Univ., 1953)

With Brian Keith and Ginger Rogers in *Tight Spot* (Col., 1955)

snarling self" (*New York Times*). Ever anxious to work, Edward tried his hand at a Western ("Little Caesar in buckskin," said the *New York Herald-Tribune*), joining with Barbara Stanwyck, Glenn Ford, and Brian Keith in *The Violent Men* (Columbia, 1955). The very underrated *Tight Spot* (Columbia, 1955) offered Edward in competition with a figure-expanding Ginger Rogers. It seemed to be a split contest to determine which thirties' star was aging the worst, with Edward coming in a close second.

To keep busy and solvent, Robinson moved into the realm of television. In 1954 he made his debut on *For the Defense,* a thirty-minute pilot for a proposed weekly series that did not sell. Later that year he appeared on CBS-TV's "Climax," and in 1955 played on two episodes of "Ford Theatre." Far more interesting and publicity-gathering were his matches on the "$64,000 Question," competing with fellow culture vulture Vincent Price on the field of art. When the rumors ran high that Robinson and Price were among the quiz show guests to have been tutored on their answers, both celebrities denied any such cram sessions. Above and beyond this repercussion to his most watched video appearances, Edward did not really take to the medium. "Television is much too hard a game," he told cinema historian Don Shay. "I think it's very good for the young people, but it's a matter of compromise after compromise after compromise. When I came from the theatre and went into pictures, I already compromised; when I came from pictures into radio, I compromised. You see, every new idea takes its pound of flesh." Robinson's major dislike of television was the lack of proper rehearsal time.

The parade of mundane pictures continued, at least assuring that new generations of filmgoers would be aware of the once great star. There was *A Bullet for Joey*

488

(United Artists, 1955), reuniting him with old sparring partner George Raft.[21] Edward was a police inspector, Raft an exiled gangster in this low-budget feature. Times had changed; Raft was willing to die oncamera in the picture, and there were no flare-ups between the two stars of the sort that had erupted on *Manpower*. There was not as much audience interest, either. "These are the things Mr. Raft and Mr. Robinson can act with their eyes shut—and sometimes do," cracked the *New York Times*. *Illegal* (Warner Bros., 1955), a remake of *The Mouthpiece* (Warner Bros., 1921), with Warren William, and of *The Man Who Talked Too Much* (Warner Bros., 1940), with George Brent, had little to recommend it beyond an early but distinctive appearance by buxom Jayne Mansfield. *Hell on Frisco Bay* (Warner Bros., 1956) bears some attention as it teamed Robinson as a crime lord of the San Francisco docks with Alan Ladd as a bitter ex-cop. At the climax Ladd battles Edward aboard a boat, providing some degree of excitement, a factor largely lacking in Robinson's other vehicles of the time, such as *Nightmare* (United Artists, 1956).

Things looked bad for the veteran star. As he wrote in his memoirs, "It was obvious that while I was forgiven my premature anti-fascism, I was doomed, both by age and former political leanings, to a slow graveyard. The top directors and producers wouldn't have me and while I'm grateful to those who did in the period and bow low to them for their guts, what I needed was recognition again by a top figure in the industry . . . the name of that top figure—Cecil B. DeMille."

DeMille, conservative, right-wing, and a very fair man (on most matters), was preparing his remake of *The Ten Commandments* (Paramount, 1956), and trying to insure that the costly production would be the epic of epics. Enlisting an all-star

[21]Late in life during a hospital stay, Robinson was not surprised when a flower arrangement arrived with the card. "Get well, Your pal, George Raft." The once-tough Raft had definitely mellowed in later years.

With Hugh Marlowe and Nina Foch in *Illegal* (WB, 1955)

With Debra Paget and Vincent Price in *The Ten Commandments* (Par., 1956)

cast, the producer asked his advisors who they felt would be a good Dathan, the evil overlord who defies Moses and convinces the people to worship the golden calf. His associates recommended Robinson, hastily adding that his political problems made him unsuitable. DeMille, believing Robinson did not warrant such ostracism, decided that he was the correct man for the part, and as a result he was billed fourth in the big-name production.

Undoubtedly, Edward was ecstatic to land the role, and he played the potentially one-dimensional villain with ebullience. He is splendidly decadent, especially in the orgy scene as the followers worship the animal idol. Robinson's Dathan can be seen dancing about, waving and leering at the wild spectacle. As everyone expected, *The Ten Commandments* was a smash with the public (gathering $43 million in distributors' domestic rentals), and even some of the highbrow critics were favorable. "Mr. DeMille has worked photographic wonders," reported the *New York Times*. "And his large cast of characters is very good, from Sir Cedric Hardwicke as a droll and urbane Pharaoh to Edward G. Robinson as a treacherous overlord." More important, as Robinson would himself admit, "Cecil B. DeMille returned my self-respect."

Nevertheless, there would be more than two years before he would do another film. Much of the time would be filled with performances on stage. On February 8, 1956, at the ANTA Theatre on Broadway, he opened in *Middle of the Night*. He was the manufacturer, a middle-aged man in love with a much younger girl, played by Gena Rowlands. The playwright was Paddy Chayevsky; the director was Joshua Logan. The rehearsal period was rampant with battles among author, director, and star. The play somehow survived the rehearsal skirmishes and ran for 479 performances, with Robinson regaining the respect of the Broadway community. *Life* Magazine wrote, "*Middle of the Night* is long on human understanding and a little short on content. But forcefully directed by producer Joshua Logan and given status by Robinson's acting, it adds up to a rewarding display of theatrical skill."

Also playing on Broadway at the time was Paul Muni, giving an almost legendary performance in *Inherit the Wind*. Although the two celebrities never liked one another, Robinson was gentlemanly enough to Muni to invite his old rival to visit him during the early months of *Middle of the Night*. Muni accepted but was livid when he saw the lavish apartment, limousine, and various other fringe benefits that Robinson had written into his contract. With the battle cry, "I remember Robinson when he was a spear carrier," Muni rushed back to the *Inherit the Wind* management to vehemently demand the same treatment.

On February 25, 1956, seventeen days after his Broadway opening, Robinson was brought back to earth when Gladys sued for divorce. This was not the first time such an action had been taken. Never permanently cured of her mental illness, she had been threatening such a suit over the years, and in 1949 had announced her decision *en route* to sanitarium treatment. Edward had had to "explain" to the press. Determined to reap an enormous settlement, Gladys Lloyd Robinson's lawyers demanded an equitable arrangement, dividing the $3.5 million estate and at least twenty-five percent of her ex-husband-to-be's future earnings. To obtain what she wished, Gladys was prepared to name as co-respondent Jane Adler, her former fashion agent, who had developed a strong rapport with the actor. Robinson agreed to Gladys' demands, but as all his money was in paintings, it meant parting with his beloved art collection.

Robinson refused to dredge up his only defense, the unhappiness Gladys' mental condition had caused him. Gladys told the press that she "was tired of being a curator of an art museum" and was happy to see them sold. Robinson sadly watched the works of art go on sale at M. Knoedler and Co. Among the famous works that were auctioned were Gauguin's "Horseman on Beach" (worth $200,000), Renoir's "After the Ball" ($60,000), Matisse's "Dinner Table" ($75,000), Corot's "Italian Woman" ($200,000), Seurat's "Le Crotoy" ($185,000), and what used to hold a place of honor in Robinson's house—Cezanne's "Black Clock" ($200,000). In total, fifty-eight of the actor's seventy-two paintings were sold, bringing in $3.25 million. When the press asked the star which one had been his favorite, he replied sadly, "My favorite? They are all my favorite."

The home in Beverly Hills was also lost in the divorce settlement, sold to insure that the assets could be divided equally. Robinson would eventually repurchase it, and, as he regained solvency, he began to re-acquire some of his lost art. (Many had been sold to Greek shipping tycoon Starvos Niarchos, who, although he "allowed" Edward to visit his former paintings, always left town whenever the actor arrived. Eventually he sold fourteen of the masterpieces back to Robinson at a tidy profit.) It was a costly end to a hazardous marriage,[22] and the notoriety surrounding the event did nothing to solve matters between Robinson and his son, who was floundering in his attempts to break from his father.

[22]Following the lucrative divorce, Gladys spent a great deal of time in Europe, sponsoring young artists and painting canvases herself. Later, she set up headquarters in Los Angeles' expensively elegant Century City Towers. She died on June 6, 1971, after a coma-inducing stroke suffered at her granddaughter Francesca's commencement activities from Marymount in Palos Verdes, California. Robinson and his new wife, Jane, were in attendance on that occasion. Edward was present at Gladys' funeral.

With Jane Adler in Washington, D.C., on their wedding day (January 16, 1958)

After the lengthy Broadway run, Robinson toured with *Middle of the Night* from October, 1957, to March, 1958. During the Washington, D.C. run, on January 16, 1958, the sixty-four-year-old star married thirty-eight-year-old Jane Bodenheimer Adler, who was then working on the production staff of the show. She had been a pillar of strength during the divorce fracas and would share his interests, especially in art, throughout the rest of his life.

Edward returned to Hollywood, where his new wife began refurnishing his home to make it less pretentious and more liveable. In October, 1958, he appeared in an impressive performance on "Playhouse 90," and a month later played a "Zane Grey Theatre," appearing with his son, and thereby concluding a long, well-publicized estrangement. While his personal life became happier, his career as a high-priced, well-billed, in-demand character actor continued. Even though he lost out to Fredric March the chance to play *Middle of the Night* (Columbia, 1959) oncamera, he did have the opportunity to score a big success in *A Hole in the Head* (United Artists, 1959). As Mario Manetta, wed to Thelma Ritter and the parent of not-so-bright Jerry Komack, Robinson shone brightly in this flavorful comedy largely set in Miami Beach. Edward's zesty performance almost made one forget that he was inappropriately cast as the dreadfully dull brother of Frank Sinatra. Director Frank Capra recalled in his memoirs, *The Name Above the Title* (1971):

Sinatra plays his best scenes without *rehearsing, and Robinson plays his best scenes after an hour of rehearsing. If I rehearse them together they'll wreck each other. So I rehearse Robinson with someone else playing Sinatra's lines. Robinson says "No!" Sinatra must rehearse with him. I say, I'll tell Sinatra what to do, not Robinson. So Eddie ups and runs and says he'll quit. If he does, he's a damn fool. He's great in the picture.*

With Frank Sinatra, Eleanor Parker, and Thelma Ritter in *A Hole in the Head* (UA, 1959)

493

With Edward G. Robinson, Jr. on "The Zane Grey Theatre" (CBS-TV, 1962)

With Alexander Scourby (rear), Sebastian Cabot, and Eli Wallach (prone) in *Seven Thieves* (20th, 1960)

With Shirley MacLaine, Yves Montand, and Yoko Tani in *My Geisha* (Par., 1962)

With David Wayne and Tim O'Connor in *The Devil and Daniel Webster* (CBS-TV, 1962)

After conferring with Robinson's agent, Capra was summoned to the actor's dressing room:

> *I opened the door. Eddie is sobbing like a child. He runs to me, embraces me roughly, and plants warm wet kisses all over my face. The heart and maleness of this sentimental man were something to experience. "How could I do this to you, Frank. My old, dear friend. Me! Who's been in the theatre since before I could blow my own nose— How could I do this to you?"*

Capra concluded the episode with:

> *It was a happy picture from then on, so happy that I think neither Sinatra nor Robinson—nor Thelma Ritter for that matter—ever gave warmer or better performances.*

Throughout the sixties, Edward, unlike contemporaries James Cagney or George Raft, kept very active in show business. There were solid film roles, such as *The Prize* (MGM, 1963), a lavishly mounted espionage thriller with the star in a double role as a kidnapped physician and his defecting brother. In *Two Weeks in Another Town* (MGM, 1962) he was cast as a distraught movie director (with old associate Claire Trevor as his shrewish but efficient wife); and, most impressively, *The Cincinnati Kid* (MGM, 1965), the Steve McQueen-Tuesday Weld starring vehicle which reunited Robinson with Joan Blondell (she as Lady Fingers). Edward appeared as Lancy Howard, the impeccably groomed card shark, in a part originally intended for Spencer Tracy (as had been Edward's role of the Secretary of the Interior in John Ford's *Cheyenne Autumn* [Warner Bros., 1964]). Much of Robinson's screen work in the 1960s showed him sporting a very flattering goatee. He did a great

With George Hamilton in *Two Weeks in Another Town* (MGM, 1962)

With Francesco Mule, Raquel Welch, and Robert Wagner in *The Biggest Bundle of Them All* (MGM, 1968)

many television guest spots, though the aging trouper found it exhausting. He appeared on shows like "G.E. Theatre," "Project 20," and "Bracken's World." In the latter show, televised in 1970, son Edward, Jr. had a bit role. He even did video commercials for Maxwell House Coffee, growling in Little Caesar style to the television audiences, "Now do it my way, see?" then dissolving into a chuckled, "You'll like it." He also advertised razor blades, following through on his earlier endorsement of an Edward G. Robinson brand of pipe tobacco, which is still being marketed with a 1930's portrait of the star on the package.

There were also plenty of film cameos which Edward defined as "the small parts you play for a fancy price and still retain your position." These international productions took him on many location trips. There was *The Biggest Bundle of Them All* (MGM, 1968), in which he performed a hot dance number with Raquel Welch, *MacKenna's Gold* (Columbia, 1969), an all-star flop Western, and *Mad Checkmate* (1968), in which he planned yet another bank robbery, and a number of others that took him about the globe.

During his last years, age was handicapping the venerable star. In 1962, on location in Africa for *A Boy Ten Feet Tall* (Paramount), he suffered a heart attack but recuperated sufficiently to complete his pivotal role in the film. In June, 1966, he was seriously hurt when he apparently fell asleep while driving his car and smashed into a tree a few blocks from his home. He was also becoming quite deaf, and the rehearsals he always insisted upon now took on another purpose—to accustom him to reading the lips of his co-workers. Yet he heartily continued, defying the odds against him, once laughing to the press, "I'm a lucky son of a bitch."

Publicity shot for *A Boy Ten Feet Tall* (Par., 1965)

After playing a well-disposed piano dealer in *Song of Norway* (Cinerama, 1970) a big-budget musical that never found its proper market, he co-starred with close friend Sam Jaffe on an ABC "Movie of the Week," *The Man Who Cried Wolf* (1970). He was then in Israel to star in *Neither by Day or Night,* a 1972 film that has yet to play in America. He was cast as a New York furrier who flies to Israel to visit his American expatriate son who has been injured in a bomb attack while picking oranges on a kibbutz. (When the film was shown in England in 1975, the British *Monthly Film Bulletin* reported, "Edward G. Robinson's neatly etched cameo provides a morsel of pleasure.")

Then he accepted what proved to be his last major film role. It was *Soylent Green* (MGM, 1973), a pessimistic science fiction entry in which he was teamed with Charlton Heston. In an interview with *Touch* Magazine, Robinson described his role of Sol Roth with feeling and understanding. "He's kind of an anachronism. He happens to be a hangover from the old days, who knew the richness of life, the richness of the soil, the richness of our waters, the wonderful plant life and the animal life, in short the richness of living as it *had* been. He saw all this [desolation] coming on and there's a certain sense of guilt that he feels, that perhaps he hadn't shouted enough, and he hadn't tried hard enough in his own particular way to stop it." He added, "The story takes place in the year 2022, which I hope will never be, even though I'm not going to be around."

It was also about this time that he began writing his memoirs with the aid of Leonard Spigelgass, the well-known playwright and scripter. But cancer struck and the seventy-nine-year-old actor was forced to check into Mount Sinai Hospital on Beverly Boulevard.

With Charlton Heston in *Soylent Green* (MGM, 1973)

As he told reporter William Otterburn-Hall before entering the hospital, "When I go out, I want it to be quiet and painless. I'm not frightened of death. I can face it without fear. I've had a good life, and I've spent my last years surrounded by beautiful things. What more can a man ask. . . . Death comes to all of us, doesn't it? The moment you're destined to live, you're destined to die. I'm not worried about it too much. I'm worried about the indignities and pains that might go with it. . . . I think you're so conditioned for it, that you're ready when the time comes. I've gone through crisis after crisis in my time, and survived. My paintings have sort of immunized me against many of the horrible things in the world, and they'll go on helping me."

Soon it was well known in the film community that Robinson's condition was critical. Rightly feeling shame that Robinson had never even been nominated for an Oscar, the Academy of Motion Picture Arts and Sciences quickly decided, on December 31, 1972, to award him with an honorary Oscar that coming March. The Academy sent a morbid but necessary query to find out if the actor would be around to receive it; when the response was that the doctors weren't sure, they sent the actor an unengraved Oscar. Robinson welcomed the news with disbelief; only after seeing the Oscar itself did he allow emotion to overtake him, embracing the statue and weeping. There was talk of Sir Laurence Olivier presenting the award, and a delighted Robinson hoped so much to live long enough to receive it, even preparing his personal thank you to Olivier and resolving to accept the award in a wheel chair, if necessary. But he did not survive. In the late afternoon of January 26, 1973, cancer took his life.

The following Sunday, January 28, funeral services were conducted at Los Ange-

Funeral services at Temple Israel in Hollywood (January 28, 1973)

les' Temple Israel, where Charlton Heston delivered the eulogy. Burial took place in New York the following day.[23]

On March 27, 1973, Edward G. Robinson was posthumously awarded the Oscar that he had deserved so many times before. It was the high point of a classless show where an "Indian" refused Marlon Brando's *The Godfather* Oscar. Mrs. Jane Robinson, wearing a light, sleeveless dress (Robinson, in a moment of morbid levity, had asked her not to wear black to the ceremony), received the award. It was engraved:

TO EDWARD G. ROBINSON, WHO ACHIEVED GREATNESS AS A PLAYER, A PATRON OF THE ARTS, AND A DEDICATED CITIZEN . . . IN SUM, A RENAISSANCE MAN. FROM HIS FRIENDS IN THE INDUSTRY HE LOVES.

She quietly read the words that Robinson wanted read on this so-deserving night:

It couldn't have come at a better time in a man's life. Had it come earlier, it would have aroused deep feelings in me. Still, not so deep as now. I am so very grateful to my

[23]When Robinson's estate was settled, Dr. Armand Hammer, president of Occidental Petroleum Corp., paid a reported five million dollars for Robinson's famous art collection. This sum, along with other assets, were to supply a trust fund (up to one-fourth the value of the estate) for his son, on the condition that he behave reasonably.

Edward G. Robinson, Jr., who had chronicled his trouble-plagued life in *My Father, My Son* (1958), had not inherited anything from his mother's $756,000 estate, beyond a baby chair, a baby picture, and a tea set, because of "his unbearable conduct toward me." Throughout the years he had tried to start up an acting career, but with little success.

Shortly after midnight on February 26, 1974, his second wife, Nan, discovered him retching uncontrollably and he was rushed to the hospital. He died en route. The coroner listed the death as "a possible heart attack," initially, later stating simply that the death was due to "natural causes." Services were held at Hollywood Memorial Cemetary. Ironically, Edward G. Robinson had written in his memoirs, "All of us Goldenbergs live to our eighties. You've got 41 years more. Enjoy yourself, but make it work for you." Edward G. Robinson, Jr. was forty when he died.

Perhaps the most bitter testament to his tormented life appeared in Robinson, Jr.'s autobiography, where he wrote:

"It must be so easy and wonderful if your parents are a couple of slobs. If you dad is a drunk, all you have to do is stay sober and you're a hero. Get a regular milk route and stick with it, and you're a success.

"If your dad is a poor immigrant who never got a formal education, you bring home a decent report card and make it to the 8th grade and you're a celebrity in the family. If you finish high school you're an intellectual. If you manage a little night-school work in college, you're a regular professor around the poolroom.

"If your dad is a nobody, and you get the lead in the school play, you're a big actor. Everybody begins seeing your name in lights. If you get a small part in a play, or even get your face on TV or in the movies, you're the biggest man in town.

"If you're any of these things, you can hate your parents, you can be ashamed of them, you can live them down, and everybody thinks you're understanding, so great. And then one day when you're 22, you can go see them and forgive them for being slobs and discover they're real one-hundred-carat, salt-of-the-earth characters, and everything's fine. You can sit for a portrait together, and there you are, one big, happy family.

"But if your father is a poor immigrant boy who turns hardship into triumph, physical limitations into movie stardom, cheap celebrity status into durable fame, a fabulous person who marries another fabulous person, a pair who've gathered laurels in every grove where you could hope to go, how about that. Go ahead, try their son's clothes on for size. Try being somebody in that kind of shade."

501

rich, warm, creative, talented, intimate colleagues who have been my life's associates. How much richer can you be?

Perhaps the finest tribute occurred when *Soylent Green* debuted later in 1973. Of this modestly received entry, The *Hollywood Reporter* wrote that this film claims "the only pleasant experience [is] Death, a perverse idea which provides Edward G. Robinson with as moving a screen farewell as any actor has ever had."

EDWARD G. ROBINSON

THE BRIGHT SHAWL *(Associated First National, 1923), 80 min.*
Presenter, Charles H. Duell; director, John S. Robertson; based on the novel by Joseph Hergesheimer; adaptor, Edmund Goulding; art director, Everett Shinn; camera, George Folsey; editor, William Hamilton.

Richard Barthelmess (Charles Abbott); André Beranger (Andrés Escobar); Edward G. Robinson (Domingo Escobar); Margaret Seddon (Carmenita Escobar); Mary Astor (Narcissa Escobar); Luis Alberni (Vincente Escobar); Anders Randolf (Cesar y Santacilla); William Powell (Gaspar de Vaca); Dorothy Gish (La Clavel); Jetta Goudal (La Pilar); George Humbert (Jaime Quintara).

THE HOLE IN THE WALL *(Paramount, 1929), 73 min.*
Supervisor, Monta Bell; director, Robert Florey; based on the play by Fred Jackson; adaptor-dialogue, Pierre Collings; camera, George Folsey; editor, Morton Blumenstock.

Claudette Colbert (Jean Oliver); Edward G. Robinson (The Fox); David Newell (Gordon Grant); Nellie Savage (Madame Mystera); Donald Meek (Goofy); Alan Brooks (Jim); Louise Closser Hale (Mrs. Ramsey); Katherine Emmett (Mrs. Carslake); Marcia Kango (Marcia); Barry Macollum (Dogface); George MacQuarrie (Inspector); Helen Crane (Mrs. Lyons); Gamby-Hall Girls (Themselves).

NIGHT RIDE *(Universal, 1930), 5,418 feet.*
Presenter, Carl Laemmle; director, John S. Robertson; based on the story by Henry La Cossitt; dialogue, Tom Reed, Edward T. Lowe, Jr.; adaptor, Lowe, Jr.; titles, Charles Logue; sound, C. Roy Hunter; camera, Alvin Wyckoff; editors, Milton Carruth, A. Ross.

Joseph Schildkraut (Joe Rooker); Barbara Kent (Ruth Kearns); Edward G. Robinson (Tony Garotta); Harry Stubbs (Bob O'Leary); De Witt Jennings (Police Captain); Ralph Welles (Blondie); Hal Price (Mac); George Ovey (Ed).

A LADY TO LOVE *(MGM, 1930), 92 min.*
Director, Victor Seastrom; based on the play *They Knew What They Wanted* by Sidney Howard; screenplay, Howard; art director, Cedric Gibbons; gowns, Adrian; sound, J. K. Brock, Douglas Shearer; camera, Merritt B. Gerstad; editors, Conrad A. Nervig, Leslie F. Wilder.

Vilma Banky (Lena Schultz); Edward G. Robinson (Tony); Robert Ames (Buck); Richard Carle (Postman); Lloyd Ingraham (Father McKee); Anderson Lawler (Doctor); Gum Chim (Ah Gee); Henry Armetta (Angelo); George Davis (Giorgio).

OUTSIDE THE LAW *(Universal, 1930), 76 min.*
Presenter, Carl Laemmle; associate producer, E. M. Asher; director, Tod Browning; screenplay, Browning, Garrett Fort; art director, William R. Schmidt; sound, C. Roy Hunter; camera, Roy Overbaugh; editor, Milton Carruth.

503

Mary Nolan (Connie); Edward G. Robinson (Cobra Collins); Owen Moore ("Fingers" O'Dell); Edwin Sturgis (Jake); John George (Humpy); Delmar Watson (The Kid); De Witt Jennings (Police Captain); Rockcliffe Fellowes (Officer O'Reilly); Frank Burke (District Attorney); Sidney Bracy (Assistant); Rose Plummer (Woman at Bank).

EAST IS WEST (Universal, 1930), 75 min.

Presenter, Carl Laemmle; associate producer, E. M. Asher; director, Monta Bell; based on the play by Samuel Shipman, John B. Hymer; adaptor, Winifred Eaton; screenplay, additional dialogue, Tom Reed; sound, C. Roy Hunter; special effects, Frank H. Booth; camera, Jerry Ash; editor, Harry Marker.

Lupe Velez (Ming Toy); Lew Ayres (Billy Benson); Edward G. Robinson (Charlie Yong); Mary Forbes (Mrs. Benson); E. Alyn Warren (Lo Sang Kee); Henry Kolker (Mr. Benson); Tetsu Komai (Hop Toy); Edgar Norton (Thomas); Charles Middleton (Dr. Fredericks).

THE WIDOW FROM CHICAGO (First National, 1930), 64 min.

Director, Edward Cline; story-screenplay, Earl Baldwin; sound, Clifford A. Ruberg; camera, Sol Polito; editor, Edward Schroeder.

Alice White (Polly Henderson); Neil Hamilton (Swifty Dorgan); Edward G. Robinson (Dominic); Frank McHugh (Slug O'Donnell); Lee Shumway (Chris Johnston); Brooks Benedict (Mullins); John Elliott (Detective Lieutenant Finnegan); Dorothy Mathews (Cora); Ann Cornwall (Mazie); E. H. Calvert (Captain Davis); Betty Francisco (Helen); Harold Goodwin (Jimmy Henderson); Mike Donlin (Desk Man); Robert Homans (Patrolman); Al Hill (Johnston's Henchman); Mary Foy (Neighbor Woman); Allan Cavan (Sergeant Dunn).

LITTLE CAESAR (First National, 1930), 80 min.

Director, Mervyn LeRoy; based on the novel by William R. Burnett; screenplay, Francis E. Faragoh; camera, Tony Gaudio.

Edward G. Robinson (Cesar "Little Rico" Bandello); Douglas Fairbanks, Jr. (Joe Massara); Glenda Farrell (Olga Strassoff); Sidney Blackmer (Big Boy); Thomas Jackson (Police Sergeant Flaherty); Ralph Ince (Pete Montana); William Collier, Jr. (Tony Passa); Maurice Black (Arnie Lorch); Stanley Fields (Sam Vettori); George E. Stone (Otero).

SMART MONEY (Warner Bros., 1931), 90 min.

Director, Alfred E. Green; story, Lucien Hubbard, Joseph Jackson; screenplay, Kubec Glasmon, John Bright; additional dialogue, Hubbard, Jackson; music director, Leo F. Forbstein; makeup, Perc Westmore; camera, Robert Kurrle; editor, Jack Killifer.

Edward G. Robinson (Nick "The Barber" Venizelos); James Cagney (Jack); Evalyn Knapp (Irene Graham); Ralf Harolde (Sleepy Sam); Noel Francis (Marie); Margaret Livingston (District Attorney's Girl); Maurice Black (The Greek Barber); Boris Karloff (Sport Williams); Morgan Wallace (District Attorney Black); Billy House (Salesman-Gambler); Paul Porcasi (Alexander Amenoppopolus); Polly Walters (Lola); Gladys Lloyd (Cigar Stand Clerk); Clark Burroughs (Back-to-Back Schultz); Edwin Argus (Two-Time Phil); John Larkin (Snake Eyes); Walter Percival (Dealer Barnes); Mae Madison (Small Town Girl); Eulalie Jensen (Matron);

Charles Lane (Desk Clerk); Edward Hearn (Reporter); Clinton Rosemond (George the Porter); John George (Dwarf on Train).

FIVE STAR FINAL *(First National, 1931), 89 min.*
Director, Mervyn LeRoy; based on the play by Louis Weitzenkorn; screenplay, Byron Morgan; camera, Sol Polito; editor, Frank Ware.

Edward G. Robinson (Joseph Randall); H. B. Warner (Michael Townsend); Marian Marsh (Jenny Townsend); Anthony Bushell (Phillip Weeks); Frances Starr (Nancy [Vorhees] Townsend); Ona Munson (Kitty Carmody); George E. Stone (Ziggie Feinstein); Oscar Apfel (Bernard Hinchecliffe); Purnell Pratt (Robert French); Aline MacMahon (Miss Taylor); Boris Karloff (T. Vernon Isopod); Robert Elliott (Brannegan); Gladys Lloyd (Miss Edwards); Harold Waldridge (Goldberg); Evelyn Hall (Mrs. Weeks); David Torrence (Mr. Weeks); Polly Walters (Telephone Operator); Franklin Parker (Reporter); Frank Darien (Schwartz).

THE HATCHET MAN *(First National, 1932), 74 min.*
Director, William A. Wellman; based on the play *The Honorable Mr. Wong* by Achmed Abdullah, David Belasco; screenplay, J. Grubb Alexander; camera, Sid Hickox; editor, Owen Marks.

Edward G. Robinson (Wong Low Get); Loretta Young (Toya San); Dudley Digges (Nag Hong Fah); Leslie Fenton (Harry En Hai); Edmund Breese (Yu Chang); Tully Marshall (Long Sen Yat); Noel Madison (Charley Kee); Blanche Frederici (Madame Si-Si); J. Carrol Naish (Sun Yat Ming); Toshia Mori (Miss Ling); Charles Middleton (Li Hop Fat); Ralph Ince (Malone); Otto Yamaoka (Chung Ho); Evelyn Selbie (Wah Li); E. Allyn Warren (Soo Lat); Eddie Piel (Foo Ming); Willie Fung (Fung Loo); Gladys Lloyd (Fan Yi); Anna Chang (Sing Girl); James Leong (Tong Member).

TWO SECONDS *(First National, 1932), 68 min.*
Director, Mervyn LeRoy; based on the play by Elliott Lester; screenplay, Harvey Thew; camera, Sol Polito; editor, Terrill Morse.

Edward G. Robinson (John Allen); Preston Foster (Bud Clark); Vivienne Osborne (Shirley Day); J. Carrol Naish (Tony); Guy Kibbee (Bookie); Adrienne Dore (Annie); Frederick Burton (Judge); Dorothea Wolbert (Lizzie); Edward McWade (The Doctor); Berton Churchill (The Warden); William Janney (A College Boy); Lew Brice, Franklin Parker, Frederick Howard (Reporters); Helena Phillips (Mrs. Smith); June Gittleson (Fat Girl); Jill Bennett, Luana Walters (Tarts); Otto Hoffman (Justice of the Peace); Harry Woods (Executioner); Gladys Lloyd (Woman); John Kelly, Matt McHugh (Mashers).

TIGER SHARK *(First National, 1932), 80 min.*
Director, Howard Hawks; based on the story *Tuna* by Houston Branch; screenplay, Wells Root; assistant director, Richard Rosson; camera, Tony Gaudio; editor, Thomas Pratt.

Edward G. Robinson (Mike Mascarena); Zita Johann (Quita); Richard Arlen (Pipes Boley); Leila Bennett (Lady Barber); Vince Barnett (Engineer); J. Carrol Naish (The Man); William Ricciardi (Manuel).

SILVER DOLLAR *(First National, 1932), 84 min.*
Director, Alfred E. Green; based on the biography of H. A. W. Tabor by David Karsner; screenplay, Carl Erickson, Harvey Thew; camera, James Van Trees; editor, George Marks.

Edward G. Robinson (Yates Martin); Bebe Daniels (Lily Owens); Aline MacMahon (Sarah Martin); Jobyna Howland (Poker Annie); De Witt Jennings (Mine Foreman); Robert Warwick (Colonel Stanton); Russell Simpson (Hamlin); Harry Holman (Adams); Charles Middleton (Jenkins); John Marston (Gelsey); Marjorie Gateson (Mrs. Adams); Emmett Corrigan (President Chester A. Arthur); Wade Boteler, William Le Maire, David Durand (Miners); Lee Kohlmar (Rische); Theresa Conover (Mrs. Hamlin); Leon Ames (Secretary); Virginia Edwards (Emma Abbott); Christian Rub (Hook); Walter Rogers (General Grant); Niles Welch (William Jennings Bryan); and Wilfred Lukas, Herman Bing, Bonita Granville, Walter Long, Alice Wetherfield, Charles Coleman, Frederick Burton, Willard Robertson.

THE LITTLE GIANT *(First National, 1933), 74 min.*
Director, Roy Del Ruth; story, Robert Lord; screenplay, Lord, Wilson Mizner; music conductor, Leo F. Forbstein; art director, Robert Haas; camera, Sid Hickox; editor, George Marks.

Edward G. Robinson (James Francis "Bugs" Ahearn); Helen Vinson (Polly Cass); Mary Astor (Ruth Wayburn); Kenneth Thomson (John Stanley); Russell Hopton (Al Daniels); Shirley Grey (Edith Merriam); Donald Dillaway (Gordon Cass); Louise Mackintosh (Mrs. Cass); Berton Churchill (Donald Hadley Cass); Helen Mann (Frankie); Selmer Jackson (Voice of Radio Announcer); Dewey Robinson (Butch Zanwutoski); John Kelly (Ed [Tim]); Sidney Bracy (Butler); Bob Perry, Adrian Morris (Joe Milano's Hoods); Rolfe Sedan (Waiter); Charles Coleman (Charteris); Gordon "Bill" Elliott (Guest); John Marston (D.A.); Guy Usher (Detective); Nora Cecil (Maid).

I LOVED A WOMAN *(First National, 1933), 90 min.*
Director, Alfred E. Green; based on the book by David Karsner; screenplay, Charles Kenyon, Sidney Sutherland; camera, James Van Trees; editor, Bert Levy.

Kay Francis (Laura McDonald); Edward G. Robinson (John Hayden); Genevieve Tobin (Martha Lane Hayden); J. Farrell MacDonald (Shuster); Henry Kolker (Sanborn); Robert Barrat (Charles Lane); George Blackwood (Henry); Murray Kinnell (Davenport); Robert McWade (Larkin); Walter Walker (Oliver); Henry O'Neill (Farrell); Lorena Layson (Maid); Sam Godfrey (Warren); E. J. Ratcliffe (Theodore Roosevelt); Paul Porcasi (Hotel Proprietor); William V. Mong (Bowen).

DARK HAZARD *(First National, 1934), 72 min.*
Director, Alfred E. Green; based on the novel by William R. Burnett; screenplay, Ralph Block, Brown Holmes; camera, Sol Polito; editor, Herbert Levy.

Edward G. Robinson (Jim "Buck" Turner); Genevieve Tobin (Marge Mayhew); Glenda Farrell (Valerie); Robert Barrat (Tex); Gordon Westcott (Joe); Hobart Cavanaugh (George Mayhew); George Meeker (Pres Barrow); Henry B. Walthall (Schultz); Sidney Toler (Bright); Emma Dunn (Mrs. Mayhew); Willard Robertson (Fallen); Barbara Rogers (Miss Dolby); William V. Mong (Plummer).

THE MAN WITH TWO FACES *(First National, 1934), 72 min.*
Director, Archie Mayo; based on the play *The Dark Tower* by George S. Kaufman, Alexander Woollcott; screenplay, Tom Reed, Niven Busch; camera, Tony Gaudio; editor, William Holmes.

Edward G. Robinson (Damon Wells); Mary Astor (Jessica Wells); Ricardo Cortez (Ben Weston); Mae Clarke (Daphne Martin); Louis Calhern (Stanley Vance); John Eldredge (Barry Jones); Arthur Byron (Dr. Kendall); Henry O'Neill (Inspector Crane); David Landau (William Curtis); Emily Fitzroy (Hattie); Margaret Dale (Martha Temple); Dorothy Tree (Patsy Dowling); Arthur Aylesworth (Morgue Keeper); Virginia Sale (Peabody); Mary Russell (Debutante); Mrs. Wilfred North (Matron); Howard Hickman (Mr. Jones); Maude Turner Gordon (Mrs. Jones); Dick Winslow (Call Boy); Frank Darien (Doorman); Bert Moorhouse (Driver); Ray Cooke (Bellboy); Jack McHugh (Newsboy); Douglas Cosgrove (Lieutenant of Detectives); Wade Boteler (Detective); Guy Usher (Weeks); Milton Kibbee (Rewrite Man); Joseph Crehan (Editor).

THE WHOLE TOWN'S TALKING *(Columbia, 1935), 93 min.*
Producer, Lester Cowan; director, John Ford; based on the novel by William R. Burnett; screenplay, Jo Swerling; dialogue, Robert Riskin; assistant director, Wilbur McGaugh; camera, Joseph August; editor, Viola Lawrence.

Edward G. Robinson (Arthur Ferguson Jones/Killer Mannion); Jean Arthur (Wilhelmina "Bill" Clark); Arthur Hohl (Detective Sergeant Mike Boyle); Wallace Ford (Healy); Arthur Byron (District Attorney Spencer); Donald Meek (Hoyt); Paul Harvey (J. G. Carpenter); Edward Brophy (Bugs Martin); Etienne Girardot (Seaver); James Donlan (Detective Sergeant Pat Howe); J. Farrell MacDonald (Warden); Effie Ellsler (Aunt Agatha); Robert Emmet O'Connor (Police Lieutenant Mac); John Wray, Joe Sawyer (Mannion's Henchmen); Frank Sheridan (Russell); Clarence Hummel Wilson (President of the Chamber of Commerce); Ralph M. Remley (Ribber); Virginia Pine (Seavers' Private Secretary); Ferdinand Munier (Mayor); Cornelius Keefe (Radio Man); Francis Ford (Reporter at Dock); Lucille Ball (Girl); Robert E. Homans (Detective); Grace Hayle (Sob Sister); Walter Long (Convict); Ben Taggart (Traffic Cop); Al Hill (Gangster); Gordon DeMain, Charles King (Men); Tom London (Guard); Mary Gordon (Landlady); Bess Flowers (Secretary); Emmett Vogan (Reporter).

BARBARY COAST *(United Artists, 1935), 91 min.*
Producer, Samuel Goldwyn; director, Howard Hawks; screenplay, Ben Hecht, Charles MacArthur; music director, Alfred Newman; camera, Ray June; editor, Edward Curtiss.

Miriam Hopkins (Mary Rutledge [Swan]); Edward G. Robinson (Louis Chamalis); Joel McCrea (Jim Carmichael); Walter Brennan (Old Atrocity); Frank Craven (Colonel Marcus Aurelius Cobb); Brian Donlevy (Knuckles Jacoby); Otto Hoffman (Peebles); Rollo Lloyd (Wigham); Donald Meek (Sawbuck McTavish); Roger Gray (Sandy Ferguson); Clyde Cook (Oakie); Harry Carey (Jed Slocum); J. M. Kerrigan (Judge Harper); Matt McHugh (Bronco); Wong Chung (Ah Wing); Russ Powell (Sheriff); Frederik Vogeding (Ship's Captain); Dave Wengren (First Mate); Anders Van Haden (McCready the Second Mate); Jules Cowles (Pilot); Cyril Thornton (Steward); Clarence Wertz (Drunk); David Niven (Sailor Thrown out of Saloon); Edward Gargan (Bill); Herman Bing (Fish Peddler); Tom London (Ringsider); Heinie Conklin, Charles West, Constantine Romanoff, Art Miles, Sammy Finn (Gamblers); Bert Sprotte, Claude Payton, Frank Benson, Bob Stevenson (Passengers); George Simpson (Lead Line Sailor).

BULLETS OR BALLOTS *(First National, 1936), 81 min.*
Associate producer, Louis F. Edelman; director, William Keighley; story, Martin Mooney, Seton I. Miller; screenplay, Miller; assistant director, Chuck Hansen; art director, Carl Jules Weyl; music, Heinz Roemheld; sound, Oliver S. Garretson; special effects, Fred Jackman, Jr., Warren E. Lynch; camera, Hal Mohr; editor, Jack Killifer.

Edward G. Robinson (Johnny Blake); Joan Blondell (Lee Morgan); Barton MacLane (Al Kruger); Humphrey Bogart (Nick "Bugs" Fenner); Frank McHugh (Herman); Joseph King (Captain Dan McLaren); Richard Purcell (Ed Driscoll); George E. Stone (Wires); Louise Beavers (Nellie LaFleur); Joseph Crehan (Grand Jury Spokesman); Henry O'Neill (Bryant); Gilbert Emery (Thorndyke); Henry Kolker (Hollister); Herbert Rawlinson (Caldwell); Rosalind Marquis (Specialty); Norman Willis (Vinci); Frank Faylen (Gatley); Addison Richards (Announcer's Voice); Harry Watson, Jerry Madden (Kids); Herman Marks, Al Hill, Dutch Schlickenmeyer, Jack Gardner, Saul Gorss (Men); Anne Nagel, Gordon "Bill" Elliott (Bank Secretaries); Milton Kibbee (Jury Foreman); William Pawley (Crail); Carlyle Moore, Jr. (Kruger's Secretary); Virginia Dabney (Mary).

THUNDER IN THE CITY *(Columbia, 1937), 76 min.*
Producer, Alexander Esway; director, Marion Gering; screenplay, Robert Sherwood, Aben Kandel; camera, Al Eilks; editor, Arthur Hilton.

Edward G. Robinson (Dan Armstrong); Luli Deste (Lady Patricia); Nigel Bruce (The Duke of Glenavon); Constance Collier (The Duchess of Glenavon); Ralph Richardson (Henry Graham Manningdale); Annie Esmond (Lady Challoner); Arthur Wontner (Sir Peter Challoner); Elizabeth Inglis (Dolly); Cyril Raymond (James); Nancy Burne (Edna); Billy Bray (Bill); James Carew (Snyderling); Everley Gregg (Millie); Roland Drew (Frank); Elliott Nugent (Casey); Terence De Marney (Reporter).

KID GALAHAD *(Warner Bros., 1937), 101 min.*
Associate producer, Samuel Bischoff; director, Michael Curtiz; based on the novel by Francis Wallace; screenplay, Seton I. Miller; assistant director, Jack Sullivan; music, Heinz Roemheld, Max Steiner; art director, Carl Jules Weyl; sound, Charles Lang; special effects, James Gibbons, Edwin B. DuPar; camera, Tony Gaudio; editor, George Amy.

Edward G. Robinson (Nick Donati); Bette Davis (Louise "Fluff" Phillips); Humphrey Bogart (Turkey Morgan); Wayne Morris (Kid Galahad/Ward Guisenberry); Jane Bryan (Marie Donati); Harry Carey (Silver Jackson); William Haade (Chuck McGraw); Soledad Jiminez (Mrs. Donati); Joe Cunningham (Joe Taylor); Ben Welden (Buzz Stevens); Joseph Crehan (Editor Brady); Veda Ann Borg (Redhead at Party); Frank Faylen (Barney); Harland Tucker (Gunman); Bob Evans (Sam McGraw); Hank Hankinson (Jim Burke); Bob Nestell (Tim O'Brien); Jack Kranz (Denbaugh); George Blake (Referee); Charlie Sullivan (Second); Joyce Compton (Girl on Phone); Emmett Vogan (Ring Announcer); Stanford Jolley, Don DeFore (Ringsiders); Milton Kibbee, Horace McMahon (Reporters); Eddie Chandler (Title Fight Announcer).

THE LAST GANGSTER *(MGM, 1937), 81 min.*
Director, Edward Ludwig; story, William A. Wellman, Robert Carson; screenplay, John Lee Mahin; art directors, Cedric Gibbons, Daniel Cathcart; set decorator, Edwin Willis; montage effects, Slavko Vorkapich; camera, William Daniels; editor, Ben Lewis.

Edward G. Robinson (Joe Krozac); James Stewart (Paul North, Sr.); Rose Stradner (Talya Krozac); Lionel Stander (Curly); Douglas Scott (Paul North, Jr.); John Carradine (Casper); Sidney Blackmer (San Francisco Editor); Edward Brophy (Fats Garvey); Alan Baxter (Frankie "Acey" Kile); Grant Mitchell (Warden); Frank Conroy (Sid Gorman); Moroni Olsen (Shea); Ivan Miller (Wilson); Willard Robertson (Broderick); Louise Beavers (Gloria); Donald Barry (Billy Ernst); Ben Welden (Bottles Bailey); Horace McMahon (Limpy); Edward Pawley (Brockett); John Kelly (Red); David Leo Tillotson, Jim Kehner, Billy Smith, Reggie Streeter, Dick Holland (Boys); William Benedict (Office Boy), Lee Phelps (Train Guard); Pierre Watkin, Cy Kendall (Editors); Ernest Wood, Phillip Terry (Reporters); Walter Miller (Mike Kile); Wade Boteler (Turnkey); Larry Simms (Jo Krozac).

A SLIGHT CASE OF MURDER *(Warner Bros., 1938), 85 min.*

Producer, Hal B. Wallis; associate producer, Sam Bischoff; director, Lloyd Bacon; based on the play by Damon Runyon, Howard Lindsay; screenplay, Earl Baldwin, Joseph Schrank; art director, Max Parker; songs, M. K. Jerome and Jack Scholl; camera, Sid Hickox; editor, James Gibbons.

Edward G. Robinson (Remy Marco); Jane Bryan (Mary Marco); Willard Parker (Dick Whitewood); Ruth Donnelly (Mora Marco); Allen Jenkins (Mike); John Litel (Post); Eric Stanley (Ritter); Harold Huber (Giuseppe); Edward Brophy (Lefty); Paul Harvey (Mr. Whitewood); Bobby Jordan (Douglas Fairbanks Rosenbloom); Joseph Downing (Innocence); Margaret Hamilton (Mrs. Cagle); George E. Stone (Ex-Jockey Kirk); Bert Hamilton (Sad Sam); Jean Benedict (Remy's Secretary); Harry Seymour (The Singer); Betty Compson (Loretta); Joe Caits (No Nose Cohen); John Harmon (Blackhead Gallagher); George Lloyd (Little Butch); Harry Tenbrook (A Stranger); Duke York (The Champ); Pat Daly (The Champ's Manager); Bert Roach (Speakeasy Proprietor); Harry Cody (Pessimistic patron); Ben Hendricks, Ralph Dunn, Wade Boteler (Policemen); Myrtle Stedman, Loia Cheaney (Nurses).

THE AMAZING DR. CLITTERHOUSE *(Warner Bros., 1938), 87 min.*

Associate producer, Robert Lord; director, Anatole Litvak; based on the play by Barre Lyndon; screenplay, John Wexley, John Huston; assistant director, Jack Sullivan; art director, Carl Jules Weyl; music, Max Steiner; sound, C. A. Riggs; camera, Tony Gaudio; editor, Warren Low.

Edward G. Robinson (Dr. Clitterhouse); Claire Trevor (Jo Keller); Humphrey Bogart (Rocks Valentine); Gale Page (Nurse Randolph); Donald Crisp (Inspector Lane); Allen Jenkins (Okay); Thurston Hall (Grant); John Litel (Prosecuting Attorney); Henry O'Neill (Judge); Maxie Rosenbloom (Butch); Curt Bois (Rabbit); Bert Hanlon (Pal); Ward Bond (Tug); Vladimir Sokoloff (Popus); Billy Wayne (Candy); Robert Homans (Lieutenant Johnson); William Worthington, Larry Steers, Ed Mortimer (Guests); William Haade (Watchman); Thomas Jackson (Connors); Edward Gargan (Sergeant); Ray Dawe, Bob Reeves (Policemen); Winifred Harris (Mrs. Ganwoort); Eric Stanley (Dr. Ames); Loia Cheaney (Nurse Donor); Wade Boteler (Captain MacLevy); Libby Taylor (Mrs. Jefferson); Edgar Dearing (Patrolman); Sidney Bracy (Chemist); Irving Bacon (Jury Foreman); Vera Lewis (Woman Juror).

I AM THE LAW *(Columbia, 1938), 83 min.*

Producer, Everett Riskin; director, Alexander Hall; based on the magazine articles by Fred Allhoff; screenplay, Jo Swerling; music director, Morris Stoloff; camera, Henry Freulich; editor, Viola Lawrence.

Edward G. Robinson (John Lindsay); Barbara O'Neil (Jerry Lindsay); John Beal (Paul Ferguson); Wendy Barrie (Frankie Ballou); Otto Kruger (Eugene Ferguson); Arthur Loft (Tom Ross); Marc Lawrence (Eddie Girard); Douglas Wood (Berry); Robert Middlemass (Moss Kitchell); Ivan Miller (Inspector Gleason); Charles Halton (Leander); Louis Jean Heydt (J. W. Butler); Emory Parnell (Brophy); Joseph Downing (Cronin); Theodor Von Eltz (Martin); Horace McMahon (Prisoner); Frederick Burton (Governor); Lucien Littlefield (Roberts); Ed Kearne, Robert Cummings, Sr., Harvey Clark, Harry Bradley, James Flavin (Witnesses); Kane Richmond, James Bush, Robert McWade, Jr., Anthony Nace (Students); Fay Helm (Mrs. Butler); Lee Shumway (Police Sergeant); Bess Flowers (Secretary); Reginald Simpson, Cyril Ring (Photographers); Scott Colton, "Steve" Gaylord Pendleton (Graduate Law Students); Bud Wiser, Lane Chandler (Policemen); Susan Hayward (Patient); Ronald Reagan (Announcer's Voice).

CONFESSIONS OF A NAZI SPY (Warner Bros., 1939), 102 min.
Director, Anatole Litvak; based on the book *The Nazi Spy Conspiracy in America* by Leon G. Turrou; screenplay, Milton Krim, John Wexley; camera, Sol Polito; editor, Owen Marks.

Edward G. Robinson (Ed Renard); Francis Lederer (Schneider); George Sanders (Schlanger); Paul Lukas (Dr. Kassel); Henry O'Neill (District Attorney Kellogg); Lya Lys (Erika Wolff); Grace Stafford (Mrs. Schneider); James Stephenson (Scotland Yard Man); Sig Rumann (Krogman); Fred Tozere (Phillips); Dorothy Tree (Hilda); Celia Sibelius (Mrs. Kassel); Joe Sawyer (Renz); Lionel Royce (Hintze); Hans Von Twardowsky (Wildebrandt); Henry Victor (Helldorf); Frederik Vogeding (Captain Richter); George Rosener (Klauber); Robert Davis (Straubel); John Voigt (Westphal); Willy Kaufman (Gruetzwald); William Vaughn (Von Brincken); Willy Kaufman (Captain Von Eichen); Jack Mower (McDonald); Robert Emmett Keane (Harrison); Eily Malyon (Mrs. MacLaughlin); Frank Mayo (Staunton); Alec Craig (Postman); Jean Brook (Kassel's Nurse); Lucien Prival (Kranz); Frederick Burton (U.S. District Court Judge); Ward Bond (American Legionnaire); Charles Trowbridge (U.S. Intelligence); John Ridgely (Army Hospital Clerk); Emmett Vogan (Hotel Clerk); Edward Keane (F.B.I. Man); Martin Kosleck (Goebbels); Selmer Jackson (Customs Official); Egon Brecher (Nazi Agent); John Deering (Narrator).

BLACKMAIL (MGM, 1939), 81 min.
Producer, John Considine, Jr.; director, H. C. Potter; based on the story by Andre Bohem, Dorothy Yost; screenplay, David Hertz, William Ludwig; camera, Clyde De Vinna; editor, Howard O'Neill.

Edward G. Robinson (John Ingram); Ruth Hussey (Helen Ingram); Gene Lockhart (William Ramey); Bobs Watson (Hank Ingram); Guinn Williams (Moose McCarthy); John Wray (Diggs); Arthur Hohl (Rawlins); Esther Dale (Sarah); Joe Whitehead (Anderson); Joseph Crehan (Blaine); Victor Kilian (Warden Miller); Gil Perkins (Kearney); Mitchell Lewis, Lew Harvey (Workmen); Willie Best (Sunny); Art Miles (Driver); Robert Middlemass (Desk Sergeant); Ivan Miller (Weber); Hal K. Dawson (Desk Clerk); Phillip Morris (Local Trooper); Charles Middleton, Trevor Bardette (Deputies); Joe Dominguez (Pedro); Ed Montoya (Juan); Cy Kendall (Sheriff); Harry Fleischmann (Oil Worker); Eddy Chandler (Boss Brown); Lee Phelps (Guard); Wade Boteler (Police Sergeant).

DR. EHRLICH'S MAGIC BULLET (Warner Bros., 1940), 103 min.
Producers, Jack L. Warner, Hal B. Wallis; associate producer, Wolfgang Reinhardt; director, William Dieterle; story, Norman Burnside; screenplay, John Huston, Heinz Herald,

Burnside; art director, Carl Jules Weyl; music, Max Steiner; sound, Robert E. Lee; special microscopic effects, Robert Burks; camera, James Wong Howe; editor, Warren Low.

Edward G. Robinson (Dr. Paul Ehrlich); Ruth Gordon (Heidi Ehrlich); Otto Kruger (Dr. Emil Von Behring); Donald Crisp (Minister Althoff); Sig Rumann (Dr. Hans Wolfert); Maria Ouspenskaya (Franziska Spever); Henry O'Neill (Dr. Lantz); Edward Norris (Dr. Morgenroth); Harry Davenport (Judge); Montagu Love (Professor Hartman); Albert Bassermann (Dr. Robert Koch); Louis Jean Heydt (Dr. Kunze); Donald Meek (Mittelmeyer); Douglas Wood (Speidler); Irving Bacon (Becker); Charles Halton (Sensenbrenner); Hermine Sterler (Miss Marquardt); Louis Calhern (Brockdorf); John Hamilton (Hirsch); Paul Harvey (Defense Attorney); Frank Reicher (Old Doctor); Torben Meyer (Kadereit); Theodor Von Eltz (Dr. Kraus); Louis Arco (Dr. Bertheim); Wilfred Hari (Dr. Hata); John Hendrick (Dr. Bucher); Ann Todd (Marianne); Rolla Stewart (Steffi); Ernst Hausman (Hans Weisgart); Stuart Holmes (Male Nurse); Egon Brecher (Martl); Herbert Anderson (Assistant); Robert Strange (Koerner); Cliff Clark (Haupt).

BROTHER ORCHID *(Warner Bros., 1940), 91 min.*
Executive producer, Hal B. Wallis; associate producer, Mark Hellinger; director, Lloyd Bacon; story, Richard Connell; screenplay, Earl Baldwin; assistant director, Dick Mayberry; art director, Max Parker; music, Heinz Roemheld; special effects, Byron Haskin, Willard Van Enger; camera, Tony Gaudio; editor, Willliam Holmes.

Edward G. Robinson (Little John Sarto); Ann Sothern (Flo Addams); Humphrey Bogart (Jack Buck); Ralph Bellamy (Clarence Fletcher); Donald Crisp (Brother Superior); Allen Jenkins (Willie "The Knife" Corson); Charles D. Brown (Brother Wren); Cecil Kellaway (Brother Goodwin); Joseph Crehan (Brother MacEwen); Wilfred Lucas (Brother MacDonald); Morgan Conway (Philadelphia Powell); Richard Lane (Mugsy O'Day); John Ridgely (Texas Pearson); Dick Wessel (Buffalo Burns); Tom Tyler (Curtley Matthews); Paul Phillips (French Frank); Don Rowan (Al Muller); Granville Bates (Pattonsville Superintendent); Nanette Vallon (Fifi); Paul Guilfoyle (Red Martin); Tim Ryan (Turkey Malone); Joe Caits (Handsome Harry Edwards); Pat Gleason (Dopey Perkins); Tommy Baker (Joseph); G. Pat Collins (Tim O'Hara); John Qualen (Mr. Pigeon); Leonard Mudie, Charles Coleman (Englishmen); Edgar Norton (Meadows); Jean Del Val, Armand Kaliz (Frenchmen); Charles de Ravenne (Stable Boy); Paul Porcasi (Warehouse Manager); William Hopper, George Haywood, Creighton Hale (Reporters); James Flavin (Parking Attendant); Sam McDaniel (Janitor); Lee Phelps (Policeman); Frank Faylen (Superintendent of Service); Mary Gordon (Mrs. Sweeney); Georges Renavent (Cable Office Clerk).

A DISPATCH FROM REUTERS *(Warner Bros., 1940), 89 min.*
Producer, Hal B. Wallis; associate producer, Henry Blanke; director, William Dieterle; story, Valentine Williams, Wolfgang Wilhelm; screenplay, Milton Krims; art director, Anton Grot; music director, Leo F. Forbstein; sound, C. A. Riggs; special effects, Byron Haskin; camera, James Wong Howe; editor, Warren Low.

Edward G. Robinson (Julius Reuter); Edna Best (Ida Reuter); Eddie Albert (Max Stargardt); Albert Bassermann (Franz Geller); Nigel Bruce (Sir Randolph Persham); Gene Lockhart (Herr Bauer); Montagu Love (Delane); Otto Kruger (Magnus); James Stephenson (Carew); Walter Kingsford (Napoleon III); David Bruce (Bruce); Alec Craig (Geant); Dickie Moore (Julius Reuter as a Boy); Billy Dawson (Max Stargardt as a Boy); Richard Nicholas (Herbert); Lumsden Hare (Chairman of the Anglo-Irish Telephone Company); Hugh Sothern (American Ambassador); Egon Brecher (Reingold); Frank Jaquer (Stein); Walter O. Stahl

(Von Danstadt); Paul Irving (Josephat Benfey); Edward McWade (Chemist); Gilbert Emery (Lord Palmerston); Robert Warwick (Opposition Speaker); Ellis Irving (Speaker); Henry Roquemore (Otto); Paul Weigel (Gauss); Joseph Stefani (Assistant); Mary Anderson (Girl); Wolfgang Zilzer (Post Office Clerk); Stuart Holmes (Attendant); Grace Stafford (Young Woman); Theodor Von Eltz (Actor); Holmes Herbert, Leonard Mudie, Lawrence Grant, Kenneth Herbert (Parliament Members); Cyril Delevanti, Bobby Hale, Norman Ainsley (News Vendors); Pat O'Malley (Workman).

THE SEA WOLF *(Warner Bros., 1941), 100 min.*

Producers, Jack L. Warner, Hal B. Wallis; associate producer, Henry Blanke; director, Michael Curtiz; based on the novel by Jack London; screenplay, Robert Rossen; art director, Anton Grot; music, Erich Wolfgang Korngold; special effects, Byron Haskin, H. F. Koenekamp; camera, Sol Polito; editor, George Amy.

Edward G. Robinson (Wolf Larsen); John Garfield (George Leach); Ida Lupino (Ruth Webster); Alexander Knox (Humphrey Van Weyden); Gene Lockhart (Dr. Louie Prescott); Barry Fitzgerald (Cooky); Stanley Ridges (Johnson); Francis McDonald (Svenson); David Bruce (Young Sailor); Howard da Silva (Harrison); Frank Lackteen (Smoke); Ralf Harolde (Agent); Louis Mason, Dutch Hendrian (Crew Members); Cliff Clark, William Gould (Detectives); Charles Sullivan (First Mate); Ernie Adams (Pickpocket); Wilfred Lucas (Helmsman); Jeane Cowan (Singer).

MANPOWER *(Warner Bros., 1941), 105 min.*

Executive producer, Hal B. Wallis; producer, Mark Hellinger; director, Raoul Walsh; screenplay, Richard Macaulay, Jerry Wald; music, Adolph Deutsch; art director, Max Parker; sound, Dolph Thomas; special effects, Byron Haskin, H. F. Koenekamp; camera, Ernest Haller; editor, Ralph Dawson.

Edward G. Robinson (Hank McHenry); Marlene Dietrich (Fay Duval); George Raft (Johnny Marshall); Alan Hale (Jumbo Wells); Frank McHugh (Omaha); Eve Arden (Dolly); Barton MacLane (Smiley Quinn); Walter Catlett (Sidney Whipple); Joyce Compton (Scarlett); Lucia Carroll (Flo); Ward Bond (Eddie Adams); Egon Brecher (Pop Duval); Cliff Clark (Cully); Joseph Crehan (Sweeney); Ben Welden (Al Hurst); Carl Harbaugh (Noisy Nash); Barbara Land (Marilyn); Barbara Pepper (Polly); Dorothy Appleby (Wilma); Roland Drew, Eddie Fetherston, Charles Sherlock, Jeffrey Sayre, William Hopper, Al Herman (Men); Ralph Dunn (Man at Phone); Harry Strang (Foreman); Joan Winfield, Faye Emerson (Nurses); Isabel Withers (Floor Nurse); James Flavin (Orderly); Chester Clute (Clerk); Nella Walker (Floorlady); Harry Holman (Justice of the Peace); Dorothy Vaughan (Mrs. Boyle); Eddy Chandler, Lee Phelps (Detectives); Beal Wong (Chinese Singer); Murray Alper, Dick Wessel (Linemen); Robert Strange (Bondsman).

UNHOLY PARTNERS *(MGM, 1941) 94 min.*

Producer, Samuel Marx; director, Mervyn LeRoy; screenplay, Earl Baldwin, Bartlett Cormack, Lesser Samuels; art director, Cedric Gibbons; music, David Snell; sound, Douglas Shearer; camera, George Barnes; editor, Harold F. Kress.

Edward G. Robinson (Bruce Corey); Laraine Day (Miss Cronin); Edward Arnold (Merrill Lambert); Marsha Hunt (Gail Fenton); William T. Orr (Tommy Jarvis); Don Beddoe (Mike Reynolds); Charles Dingle (Clyde Fenton); Charles Cane (Inspector Brody); Walter Kingsford (Managing Editor); Charles Halton (Kaper); Clyde Fillmore (Jason Grant); Marcel Dalio (Molyneaux); Frank Faylen (Roger Ordway); Joseph Downing (Jerry); William Benedict

(Boy); Charles B. Smith (Copy Boy); Frank Dawson (Old Man); Tom Seidel (Reporter); Tom O'Rourke (Young Man); George Ovey (Old Timer); Emory Parnell (Colonel Mason); Al Hill (Rector); Jay Novello (Stick Man); John Dilson (Circulation Man); Billy Mann (Barber); Lorraine Kreuger, Natalie Thompson (Girls at Party); Ann Pennington (Operator); Lee Phelps (Mechanic); Lester Dorr (Circulation Manager); Gertrude Bennett, Estelle Etterre (Newspaper Women); Milton Kibbee (Drunk).

LARCENY, INC. *(Warner Bros., 1942), 95 min.*
Producer, Hal B. Wallis; associate producers, Jack Saper, Jerry Wald; director, Lloyd Bacon; based on the play *The Night Before Christmas* by Laura and S. J. Perelman; screenplay, Everett Freeman, Edwin Gilbert; camera, Tony Gaudio; editor, Ralph Dawson.

Edward G. Robinson (Pressure Maxwell); Jane Wyman (Denny Costello); Broderick Crawford (Jug Martin); Jack Carson (Jeff Randolph); Anthony Quinn (Leo Dexter); Edward Brophy (Weepy Davis); Harry Davenport (Homer Bigelow); John Qualen (Sam Bachrach); Barbara Jo Allen [Vera Vague] (Mademoiselle Gloria); Grant Mitchell (Aspinwall); Jackie Gleason (Hobart); Andrew Tombes (Oscar Engelhart); Joseph Downing (Smitty); George Meeker (Mr. Jackson); Fortunio Bonanova (Anton Copoulos); Joseph Crehan (Warden); Jean Ames (Florence); William Davidson (McCarthy); Chester Clute (Buchanan); Creighton Hale (Mr. Carmichael); Emory Parnell (Officer O'Casey); Joe Devlin (Umpire); Jimmy O'Gatty, Jack Kenney (Convicts); John Kelly (Batter); Eddy Chandler, James Flavin (Guards); Bill Phillips (Muggsy); Hank Mann, Eddie Foster, Cliff Saum, Charles Sullivan (Players); Charles Drake (Auto Driver); William Hopper, Lucien Littlefield (Customers); Pat O'Malley (Cop); Roland Drew (Man); Grace Stafford (Secretary); Vera Lewis (Woman); Ray Montgomery (Young Man).

TALES OF MANHATTAN *(Twentieth Century-Fox, 1942), 118 min.*
Producers, Boris Morrois, S. P. Eagle; director, Julien Duvivier; stories-screenplay, Ben Hecht, Ferenc Molnar, Donald Ogden Stewart, Samuel Hoffenstein, Alan Campbell, Ladislas Fodor, Laslo Fodor, Laslo Vadnay, Laszlo Gorog, Lamar Trotti, Henry Blankfort; assistant director, Robert Stillman; music, Sol Kaplan; art directors, Richard Day, Boris Leven; sound, W. D. Fleck, Robert Heman; camera, Joseph Walker; editor, Robert Bischoff.

Sequence A: Charles Boyer (Orman); Rita Hayworth (Ethel); Thomas Mitchell (Halloway); Eugene Pallette (Luther); Helene Reynolds (Actress); Robert Greig (Lazar); William Halligan (Webb); Charles Williams (Agent); Jack Chefe (Tailor); Eric Wilton (Holloway Butler).
Sequence B: Ginger Rogers (Diane); Henry Fonda (George); Cesar Romero (Harry); Gail Patrick (Ellen); Roland Young (Edgar the Butler); Marian Martin (Squirrel); Frank Orth (Second Hand Dealer); Connie Leon (Mary).
Sequence C: Charles Laughton (Charles Smith); Elsa Lanchester (Mrs. Smith); Victor Francen (Arturo); Christian Rub (Wilson); Adeline deWalt Reynolds (Grandmother); Sig Arno (Piccolo Player); Forbes Murray (Dignified Man); Buster Brodie (Call Boy); Frank Jaquet (Musician); Will Wright (Skeptic); Dewey Robinson (Proprietor); Frank Darien (Grandpa); Rene Austin (Susan).
Sequence D: Edward G. Robinson (Browne); George Sanders (William); James Gleason (Father Joe); Harry Davenport (Professor); James Rennie (Hank Bronson); Harry Hayden (Davis); Morris Ankrum (Judge); Don Douglas (Henderson); Mae Marsh (Molly); Barbara Lynn (Mary); Alex Pollard (Waiter); Don Brodie (Whistler); Ted Stanhope (Chauffeur); Joseph Bernard (Postman).
Sequence E: Paul Robeson (Luke); Ethel Waters (Esther); Eddie Anderson (Lazarus); J. Carrol Naish (Costello); Hall Johnson Choir (Themselves); Clarence Muse (Grandpa); George Reed (Christopher); Cordell Hickman (Nicodemus); Alberta Gary (Girl); Charles Tannen (Pilot); Phillip Hurlic (Jeff); Charles Gray (Rod); Lonnie Nichols (Brad); John Kelly (Monk).

DESTROYER *(Columbia, 1943), 99 min.*

Producer, Louis F. Edelman; director, William A. Seiter; story, Frank Wead; screenplay, Wead, Lewis Melzer, Borden Chase; art director, Lionel Banks; music, Anthony Collins; camera, Franz F. Planer; editor, Gene Havlick.

Edward G. Robinson (Steve Boleslavski); Glenn Ford (Mickey Donohue); Marguerite Chapman (Mary Boleslavski); Edgar Buchanan (Kansas Jackson); Leo Gorcey (Sarecky); Regis Toomey (Lieutenant Commander Clark); Ed Brophy (Casey); Warren Ashe (Lieutenant Morton); Craig Woods (Bigbee); Curt Bois (Yasha); Pierre Watkin (Admiral); Al Hill (Knife Eating Sailor); Bobby Jordan (Sobbing Sailor); Roger Clark (Chief Engineer); Dean Benton (Fireman Moore); David Alison (Fireman Thomas); Paul Perry (Doctor); John Merton (Chief Quartermaster); Don Peters (Helmsman); Virginia Sale (Spinster); Eleanor Counts (Sarecky's Girl); Dale Van Sickel (Sailor); Addison Richards (Ferguson); Lester Dorr, Bud Geary (Ship's Fitters); Eddie Drew (Survivor); Tristram Coffin (Doctor); Larry Parks (Ensign Johnson); Eddy Chandler (Chief Gunner's Mate); Lloyd Bridges (Fireman); Dennis Moore (Communications Officer); Charles McGraw (Assistant Chief Engineer); Edmund Cobb (Workman); Eddy Waller (Riveter).

FLESH AND FANTASY *(Universal, 1943), 93 min.*

Producers, Charles Boyer, Julien Duvivier; director, Duvivier; based on the story *Lord Arthur Saville's Crime* by Oscar Wilde, and stories by Laslo Vadnay, Ellis St. Joseph; screenplay, Ernest Pascal, Samuel Hoffenstein, St. Joseph; art directors, John B. Goodman, Richard Riedel, Robert Boyle; set decorators, R. A. Gausman, E. R. Robinson; music, Alexandre Tansman; music director, Charles Previn; assistant directors, Seward Webb, Joseph A. McDonough; sound, Bernard Brown, Edwin Wetzel; camera, Paul Ivano, Stanley Cortez; editor, Arthur Hilton.

Edward G. Robinson (Marshall Tyler); Charles Boyer (Paul Gaspar); Barbara Stanwyck (Joan Stanley); Betty Field (Henrietta); Robert Cummings (Michael); Thomas Mitchell (Septimus Podgers); Charles Winninger (King Lamarr); Anna Lee (Rowena); Dame May Whitty (Lady Pamela Hardwick); C. Aubrey Smith (Dean of Chichester); Robert Benchley (Doakes); Edgar Barrier (Stranger); David Hoffman (Davis); Mary Forbes (Lady Thomas); Ian Wolfe (Librarian); Doris Lloyd (Mrs. Caxton); June Lang, Jacqueline Dalya (Angels); Grace McDonald (Equestrienne); Joseph Crehan (Acrobat); Arthur Loft, Lee Phelps (Detectives); James Craven (Radio Announcer); Clinton Rosemond (Old Black); Charles Halton (Old Man Prospector); Paul Bryar, George Lewis (Harlequins); Gil Patrick (Death); Lane Chandler (Satan); Peter Lawford (Pierrot); Marjorie Lord (Justine); Eddie Acuff (Policeman).

TAMPICO *(Twentieth Century-Fox, 1944), 75 min.*

Producer, Robert Bassler; director, Lothar Mendes; story-adaptor, Ladislas Fodor; screenplay, Kenneth Gamet, Fred Niblo, Jr., Richard Macaulay; choreography, Geneva Sawyer; music, David Raksin; music director, Emil Newman; art directors, James Basevi, Albert Hogsett; set decorators, Thomas Little, Al Orenbach; assistant director, Jasper Blystone; sound, W. D. Flick; special camera effects, Fred Sersen; camera, Charles Clarke; editor, Robert Fritsch.

Edward G. Robinson (Captain Bart Manson); Lynn Bari (Kathie Ball); Victor McLaglen (Fred Adamson); Robert Bailey (Watson); Marc Lawrence (Valdez); E. J. Ballantine (Silhouette Man); Mona Maris (Dolores); Tonio Selwart (Kruger); Carl Ekberg (Mueller); Roy Roberts (Crawford); George Sorel (Stranger); Charles Lang (Gun Crew Naval Officer); Ralph

Byrd (Quartermaster O'Brien); Daniel Ocko (Immigration Inspector); Nestor Paiva (Naval Commander); David Cota (Messenger Boy); Muni Seroff (Rodriguez); Juan Varro (Photographer); Antonio Moreno (Justice of Peace); Ben Erway (Dr. Brown); Helen Brown (Mrs. Kelly); Martin Garralaga (Serra); Martin Black (Steward); Chris-Pin Martin (Waiter); Margaret Martin (Proprietor); Trevor Bardette (Waiter); Virgil Johanson (Seaman); Jean Del Val (Pilot); Arno Frey (Navigator).

MR. WINKLE GOES TO WAR *(Columbia, 1944), 80 min.*

Producer, Jack Moss; director, Alfred E. Green; based on the novel by Theodore Pratt; screenplay, Waldo Salt, George Corey, Louis Solomon; art directors, Lionel Banks, Rudolph Sternad; set decorator, George Montgomery; Army technical adviser, Lieutenant Robert Albaugh; music, Carmen Dragon, Paul Sawtell; assistant director, Earl Bellamy; sound, Lambert Day; camera, Joseph Walker; editor, Richard Fantl.

Edward G. Robinson (Wilbert Winkle); Ruth Warrick (Amy Winkle); Ted Donaldson (Barry); Bob Haymes (Jack Pettigrew); Richard Lane (Sergeant "Alphabet"); Robert Armstrong (Joe Tinker); Richard Gaines (Ralph Wescott); Walter Baldwin (Plummer); Art Smith (McDavid); Ann Shoemaker (Martha Pettigrew); Paul Stanton (A. B. Simkins); Buddy Yarus (Johnson); William Forrest, Warren Ashe (Captains); Bernardine Hayes (Gladys); Jeff Donnell (Hostess); Howard Freeman (Mayor); Nancy Evans, Ann Loos (Girls); Larry Thompson (M.P.); James Flavin, Fred Kohler, Jr. (Sergeants); Robert Mitchum (Corporal); Fred Lord, Cecil Ballerino, Ted Holley (Draftees); Ben Taggart, Sam Flint, Nelson Leigh, Forbes Murray, Ernest Hilliard, Herbert Heyes (Doctors); Emmett Vogan (Barbert); Tommy Cook (Kid); Hugh Beaumont (Range Officer).

DOUBLE INDEMNITY *(Paramount, 1944), 106 min.*

Associate producer, Joseph Sistrom; director, Billy Wilder; based on the novel by James M. Cain; screenplay, Wilder, Raymond Chandler; art directors, Hans Dreier, Hal Pereira; set decorator, Bertram Granger; music, Miklos Rozsa; assistant director, C. C. Coleman; sound, Stanley Cooley; camera, John Seitz; editor, Doane Harrison.

Fred MacMurray (Walter Neff); Barbara Stanwyck (Phyllis Dietrichson); Edward G. Robinson (Barton Keyes); Porter Hall (Jackson); Jean Heather (Lola Dietrichson); Tom Powers (Mr. Dietrichson); Byron Barr (Nino Zachette); Richard Gaines (Mr. Norton); Fortunio Bonanova (Sam Gorlopis); John Philliber (Joe Pete); George Magrill (Bit); Bess Flowers (Norton's Secretary); Kernan Cripps (Conductor); Harold Garrison (Redcap); Oscar Smith, Frank Billy Mitchell, Floyd Shackelford, James Adamson (Pullman Porters); Dick Rush (Pullman Conductor); Edmund Cobb (Train Conductor); Constance Purdy (Woman); Clarence Muse (Black Man); Miriam Franklin (Keyes' Secretary); Sam McDaniel (Garage Attendant); Judith Gibson (Pacific All-Risk Telephone Operator).

THE WOMAN IN THE WINDOW *(RKO, 1944), 99 min.*

Producer, Nunnally Johnson; director, Fritz Lang; based on the novel *Once Off Guard* by J. H. Wallis; screenplay, Johnson; art director, Duncan Cramer; set decorator, Julie Heron; music, Arthur Lang; assistant director, Richard Harlan; sound, Frank McWhorter; special effects, Vernon Walker; camera, Milton Krasner; editor, Gene Fowler, Jr.

Edward G. Robinson (Professor Richard Wanley); Raymond Massey (Frank Lalor); Joan Bennett (Alice Reed); Edmond Breon (Dr. Barkstone); Dan Duryea (Heidt); Dorothy Peterson (Mrs. Wanley); Spanky MacFarland (Boy Scout); Arthur Space (Captain Kennedy); Claire Carleton (Blonde); Arthur Loft (Claude Mazard); Frank Dawson (Steward); Carol Camerson (Elsie); Thomas E. Jackson (Inspector Jackson); Bobby Blake (Dickie).

OUR VINES HAVE TENDER GRAPES *(MGM, 1945), 105 min.*

Producer, Robert Sisk; director, Roy Rowland; based on the book by George Victor Martin; screenplay, Dalton Trumbo; music, Bronislau Kaper; art directors, Cedric Gibbons, Edward Carfagno; set decorators, Edwin B. Willis, Hugh Hunt; assistant director, Horace Hough; sound, Douglas Shearer; special effects, A. Arnold Gillespie, Danny Hall; camera, Robert Surtees; editor, Ralph E. Winters.

Edward G. Robinson (Martinius Jacobson); Margaret O'Brien (Selma Jacobson); James Craig (Nels Halverson); Agnes Moorehead (Bruna Jacobson); Jackie "Butch" Jenkins (Arnold Hanson); Morris Carnovsky (Bjorn Bjornson); Frances Gifford (Viola Johnson); Sara Haden (Mrs. Bjornson); Louis Jean Heydt (Mr. Faraasen); Arthur Space (Mr. Pete Hanson); Elizabeth Russell (Kola Hanson); Charles Middleton (Kurt Jensen); Dorothy Morris (Ingborg Jensen); Arthur Hohl (Dvar Svenson); Abigail Adams (Girl); Johnny Berkes (Driver); Rhoda Williams (Marguerite Larsen).

SCARLET STREET *(Universal, 1945), 103 min.*

Executive producer, Walter Wanger; producer-director, Fritz Lang; based on the novel and play *La Chienne* by Georges de la Fouchardiére; screenplay, Dudley Nichols; assistant director, Melville Shyer; art director, Alexander Golitzen; set directors, Russell A. Gausman, Carl Lawrence; music, H. J. Salter; special camera, John Fulton; camera, Milton Krasner; editor, Arthur Hilton.

Edward G. Robinson (Christopher Cross); Joan Bennett (Kitty March); Dan Duryea (Johnny Prince); Jess Barker (Janeway); Margaret Lindsay (Millie); Rosalind Ivan (Adele Cross); Samuel S. Hinds (Charles Pringle); Arthur Loft (Dellarowe); Vladimir Sokoloff (Pop Lejon); Charles Kemper (Patcheye); Russell Hicks (Hogarth); Anita Bolster (Mrs. Michaels); Cyrus Kendall (Nick); Fred Essler (Marchetti); Edgar Dearing, Tom Dillon (Policemen); Chuck Hamilton (Chauffeur); Gus Glassmire, Ralph Littlefield, Sherry Hall, Howard Mitchell, Jack Statham (Employees); Rodney Bell (Barney); Henri de Soto (Waiter); Milton Kibbee (Saunders); Tom Daly (Penny); George Meader (Holliday); Lou Lubin (Tiny); Clarence Muse (Ben); Emmett Vogan (Prosecuting Attorney); Will Wright (Loan Officer Manager); Syd Saylor (Crocker); Dewey Robinson (Derelict); Dick Wessell, Dick Curtis (Detectives); Byron Foulger (Jones); Fritz Leiber (Evangelist).

JOURNEY TOGETHER *(English Films, 1946), 80 min.*

Producer, Royal Air Force Film Unit; director, John Boulting; story, Terence Rattigan; screenplay, Boulting; music, Gordon Jacob; production designer, John Howell; special effects, Ray Morse; camera, Harry Waxman.

Sergeant Richard Attenborough (David Wilton); Aircraftsman Jack Watling (John Aynesworth); Flying Officer David Tomlinson (Smith); Warrant Office Sid Rider (A Fitter); Squadron Leader Stuart Latham (A Flight Sergeant Fitter); Squadron Leader Hugh Wakefield (An Acting Lieutenant); Leading Aircraftsman Bromley Challenor (A. C. 2 Jay); Flying Officer Z. Peromowski (An Anson Pilot); Edward G. Robinson (Dean McWilliams); Patrick Waddington (Flight Lieutenant Mander); Flight Lieutenant Sebastian Shaw (Squadron Leader Marshall); Wing Commander Ronald Adam (The Commanding Officer); Bessie Love (Mary McWilliams); Sergeant Norvell Crutcher (A Driver); and Personnel of the Royal Air Force, Royal Canadian Air Force, United States Army.

THE STRANGER *(RKO, 1946), 94 min.*
Producer, S. P. Eagle; director, Orson Welles; based on the story by Victor Trivas, Decla Dunning; screenplay, Anthony Veiller; adaptors-dialogue, Veiller, John Huston, Welles; assistant director, Jack Voglin; music, Bronislaw Kaper; art director, Perry Ferguson; camera, Russell Metty; editor, Ernest Nims.

Edward G. Robinson (Wilson); Loretta Young (Mary Longstreet); Orson Welles (Professor Charles Rankin); Philip Merivale (Judge Longstreet); Richard Long (Noah Longstreet); Byron Keith (Dr. Jeff Lawrence); Billy House (Potter); Konstantin Shayne (Konrad Meinike); Martha Wentworth (Sara); Isabel O'Madigan (Mrs. Lawrence); Pietro Sosso (Mr. Peabody).

THE RED HOUSE *(United Artists, 1947), 100 min.*
Producer, Sol Lesser; director, Delmer Daves; based on the novel by George Agnew Chamberlain; screenplay, Daves; art director, McClure Capps; set decorator, Dorcy Howard; music and music director, Miklos Rozsa; assistant director, Robert Stillman; sound, Frank McWhorter; camera, Bert Glennon; editor, Merrill White.

Edward G Robinson (Pete Morgan); Lon McCallister (Nath Storm); Judith Anderson (Ellen Morgan); Allene Roberts (Meg Morgan); Julie London (Tibby); Rory Calhoun (Teller); Ona Munson (Mrs. Storm); Harry Shannon (Dr. Byrne); Arthur Space (Officer); Walter Sande (Don Brent); Pat Flaherty (Cop).

ALL MY SONS *(Universal, 1948), 94 min.*
Producer, Chester Erskine; director, Irving Reis; based on the play by Arthur Miller; screenplay, Erskine; assistant director, Frank Shaw; art directors, Bernard Herzbrun, Hilyard Brown; set decorators, Russell A. Gausman, Al Fields; music, Leith Stevens; orchestrator, David Tamkin; makeup, Bud Westmore; costumes, Grace Houston; sound, Leslie I. Carey, Corson Jowett; special effects, David S. Horsley; camera, Russell Metty; editor, Ralph Dawson.

Edward G. Robinson (Joe Keller); Burt Lancaster (Chris Keller); Mady Christians (Kate Keller); Louisa Horton (Ann Deever); Howard Duff (George Deever); Frank Conroy (Herbert Deever); Lloyd Gough (Jim Bayliss); Arlene Francis (Sue Bayliss); Henry "Harry" Morgan (Frank Lubey); Elisabeth Fraser (Lydia Lubey); Walter Soderling (Charlie); Therese Lyon (Minnie); Charles Meredith (Ellsworth); William Johnstone (Attorney); Herbert Vigran (Wertheimer); Harry Harvey (Judge); Pat Flaherty (Bartender); George Sorel (Headwaiter); Helen Brown (Mrs. Hamilton); Joseph Kerr (Norton); Walter Bonn (Jorgenson); Victor Zimmerman, George Slocum (Attendants).

KEY LARGO *(Warner Bros., 1948), 101 min.*
Producer, Jerry Wald; director, John Huston; based on the play by Maxwell Anderson; screenplay, Richard Brooks, Huston; art director, Leo K. Kuter; set decorator, Fred M. MacLean; music, Max Steiner; orchestrator, Murray Cutter; assistant director, Art Lueker; sound, Dolph Thomas; special effects, William McGann, Robert Burks; camera, Karl Freund; editor, Rudi Fehr.

Humphrey Bogart (Frank McCloud); Edward G. Robinson (Johnny Rocco); Lauren Bacall (Nora Temple); Lionel Barrymore (James Temple); Claire Trevor (Gaye Dawn); Thomas Gomez (Curley Hoff); Harry Lewis (Toots Bass); John Rodney (Deputy Clyde Sawyer); Marc Lawrence (Ziggy); Dan Seymour (Angel Garcia); Monte Blue (Sheriff Ben Wade); William Haade (Ralph Feeney); Jay Silverheels (Tom Osceola); Rodric Redwing (John Osceola); Joe P. Smith (Bus Driver); Alberto Morin (Skipper); Pat Flaherty (Man); Jerry Jerome, John Phillips, Lute Crockett (Ziggy's Henchmen); Felipa Gomez (Old Indian Woman).

NIGHT HAS A THOUSAND EYES *(Paramount, 1948), 80 min.*
Producer, Endre Bohem; director, John Farrow; based on the novel by Cornell Woolrich; screenplay, Barre Lyndon, Jonathan Latimer; art directors, Hans Dreier, Franz Bachelin; set decorators, Sam Comer, Ray Moyer; music and music director, Victor Young; assistant director, William Coleman; makeup, Wally Westmore; costumes, Edith Head; sound, Hugo Grenzbach, Gene Garvin; process camera, Farciot Edouart; camera, John F. Seitz; editor, Eda Warren.

Edward G. Robinson (John Triton); Gail Russell (Jean Courtland); John Lund (Elliott Carson); Virginia Bruce (Jenny); William Demarest (Lieutenant Shawn); Richard Webb (Peter Vinson); Jerome Cowan (Whitney Courtland); Onslow Stevens (Dr. Walters); John Alexander (Mr. Gilman); Roman Bohnen (Melville Weston); Luis Van Rooten (Mr. Myers); Henry Guttman (Butler); Mary Adams (Miss Hendricks); Philip Van Zandt (Chauffeur); Douglas Spencer (Dr. Ramsdell); Jean King (Edna the Maid); Dorothy Abbott (Maid); Bob Stephenson (Gowan); William Haade (Bertelli); Stuart Holmes (Scientist); Jean Wong, Anna Tom (Chinese Women); Weaver Levy (Chinese Man); Edward Earle (Man); Lester Dorr (Mr. Byers); Renee Randall, Marilyn Gray, Betty Hannon (Secretaries); Julia Faye (Companion); Minerva Urecal (Italian Woman); Eleanore Vogel (Scrubwoman); Joey Ray (Radio Announcer); Harland Tucker (Husband of Frantic Mother); Violet Goulet (Deb's Mother); Major Sam Harris (Deb's Father).

HOUSE OF STRANGERS *(Twentieth Century-Fox, 1949), 101 min.*
Producer, Sol C. Siegel; director, Joseph L. Mankiewicz; based on the novel by Jerome Weidman; screenplay, Philip Yordan; music, Daniele Amfitheatrof; orchestrator, Maurice de Packh; art directors, Lyle Wheeler, George W. Davis; set decorators, Thomas Little, Walter M. Scott; assistant director, William Eckhart; makeup, Ben Nye, Dick Smith; costumes, Charles Le Maire; sound, W. D. Flick, Roger Heman; special effects, Fred Sersen; camera, Milton Krasner; editor, Harmon Jones.

Edward G. Robinson (Gino Monetti); Susan Hayward (Irene Bennett); Richard Conte (Max Monetti); Luther Adler (Joe Monetti); Paul Valentine (Pietro Monetti); Efrem Zimbalist, Jr. (Tony Monetti); Debra Paget (Maria Domenico); Esther Minciotti (Theresa Monetti); Hope Emerson (Helena Domenico); Diana Douglas (Elaine Monetti); Tito Vuolo (Lucca); Alberto Morin (Victoro); Sid Tomack (Waiter); Thomas Browne Henry (Judge); David Wolfe (Prosecutor); John Kellogg (Danny); Dolores Parker (Nightclub Singer); Tommy Garland (Pietro's Opponent); Charles F. Flynn (Guard); Joseph Mazzuca (Bat Boy); Argentina Brunetti (Applicant); Maurice Samuels, Mario Siletti (Men); John Pedrini, George Magrill (Cops); George Spaulding (Doorman); Scott Landers, Fred Hildebrand (Detectives); Mushy Callahan (Referee); Mike Stark, Herbert Vigran (Neighbors).

IT'S A GREAT FEELING *(Warner Bros., 1949), C-84 min.*
Producer, Alex Gottlieb; director, David Butler; story, I. A. L. Diamond; screenplay, Jack Rose, Melville Shavelson; art director, Stanley Fleischer; set decorator, Lyle B. Reifsnider; assistant director, Phil Quinn; music numbers staged by LeRoy Prinz; music director, Ray Heindorf; music, Jule Styne; songs, Styne and Sammy Cahn; makeup, Perc Westmore, Mickey Marcellino; costumes, Milo Anderson; sound, Dolf Thomas, David Forrest; Technicolor consultants, Natalie Kalmus, Mitchell Kovaleski; special effects, William McGann, H. F. Koenekamp; camera, Wilfred M. Cline; editor, Irene Morra.

Dennis Morgan (Himself); Doris Day (Judy Adams); Jack Carson (Himself); Bill Goodwin

(Arthur Trent); Irving Bacon (Information Clerk); Claire Carleton (Grace); Harlan Warde (Publicity Man); Jacqueline de Wit (Trent's Secretary); David Butler, Michael Curtiz, King Vidor, Raoul Walsh, Gary Cooper, Joan Crawford, Errol Flynn, Sydney Greenstreet, Danny Kaye, Patricia Neal, Eleanor Parker, Ronald Reagan, Edward G. Robinson, Jane Wyman, Maureen Regan (Themselves); Errol Flynn (Jeffrey Bushdinkel).

MY DAUGHTER JOY (a.k.a., OPERATION X, Columbia, 1950), 79 min.

Producer, Gregory Ratoff; associate producer, Phil Brandon; director, Ratoff; based on the novel *David Golder* by Irene Nemirowsky; screenplay, Robert Thoeren, William Rose; set director, Andre Andrejew; assistant director, Cliff Brandon; sound, Jack Drake; camera, Georges Perinal; editor, Raymond Poulton.

Edward G. Robinson (George Constantin); Nora Swinburne (Ava Constantin); Peggy Cummins (Georgette); Richard Greene (Larry Boyd); Finlay Currie (Sir Thomas MacTavish); Gregory Ratoff (Marcos); Ronald Adam (Colonel Fogarty); Walter Rilla (Andreas); James Robertson Justice (Professor Karol); David Hutcheson (Annix); Dod Nehan (Polato); Peter Illing (Sultan); Ronald Ward (Dr. Schindler); Roberto Villa (Prince Alzar); Harry Lane (Barboza).

ACTORS AND SIN (United Artists, 1952), 85 min.

Producer-director-screenplay, Ben Hecht; co-director, Lee Garmes; set director, Howard Bristol; music, George Antheil; camera, Garmes; editor, Otto Ludwig.

Actor's Blood: Edward G. Robinson (Maurice Tillayou); Marsha Hunt (Marcia Tillayou); Dan O'Herlihy (Alfred O'Shea); Rudolph Anders (Otto Lachsley); Alice Key (Tommy); Rick Roman (Clyde Veering).

Woman of Sin: Eddie Albert (Orlando Higgens); Alan Reed (J. B. Cobb); Tracey Roberts (Miss Flannigan); Paul Guilfoyle (Mr. Blue); Doug Evans (Mr. Devlin); Jenny Hecht (Daisy Marcher); Jody Gilbert (Mrs. Egelhofer); John Crawford (Movie Hero).

VICE SQUAD (United Artists, 1953), 88 min.

Producers, Jules Levey, Arthur Gardner; director, Arnold Laven; based on the novel *Harness Bull* by Leslie T. White; screenplay, Lawrence Roman; art director, Carroll Clark; music, Herschel Burke Gilbert; camera, Joseph C. Biroc; editor, Arthur H. Nadel.

Edward G. Robinson (Captain Barnaby); Paulette Goddard (Mona); K. T. Stevens (Ginny); Porter Hall (Jack Hartrampf); Adam Williams (Mary Kusalich); Edward Binns (Al Barkis); Lee Van Cleef (Pete); Jay Adler (Frankie); Joan Vohs (Vickie); Dan Riss (Lieutenant Imlay); Mary Ellen Kay (Carol).

BIG LEAGUER (MGM, 1953) 73 min.

Producer, Matthew Rapf; director, Robert Aldrich; story, John McNulty, Louis Morheim; screenplay, Herbert Baker; art directors, Cedric Gibbons, Edde Imazu; music director, Alberto Colombo; sound, Douglas Shearer; camera, William Mellor; editor, Ben Lewis.

Edward G. Robinson (John B. "Hans" Lobert); Vera-Ellen (Christy); Jeff Richards (Adam Polachuk); Richard Jaeckel (Bobby Bronson); William Campbell (Julie Davis); Carl Hubbell, Al Campanis, Bob Trocolor, Tony Ravish (Themselves); Paul Langton (Brian McLennan);

Lalo Rios (Chuy Aguilar); Bill Crandall (Tippy Mitchell); Frank Ferguson (Wally Mitchell); John McKee (Dale Alexander); Mario Siletti (Mr. Polachuk); Robert Caldwell (Pomfret); Donald "Chippie" Hastings (Little Joe)

THE GLASS WEB *(Universal, 1953), 81 min.*

Producer, Albert J. Cohen; director, Jack Arnold; based on the novel by Max S. Ehrlich; screenplay, Robert Blees, Leonard Lee; art directors, Bernard Herzbrun, Eric Orbon; music director, Joseph Gershenson; camera, Maury Gertsman; editor, Ted J. Kent.

Edward G. Robinson (Henry Hayes); John Forsythe (Don Newell); Marcia Henderson (Louise Newell); Kathleen Hughes (Paula Ranier); Richard Denning (Dave Markson); Hugh Sanders (Lieutenant Stevens); Jean Willes (Sonia); Harry O. Tyler (Jake); Clark Howat (Bob Warren); Paul Dubov (Other Man); John Hiestand (Announcer); Bob Nelson (Plainclothesman); Dick Stewart (Everett); Jeri Lou James (Barbara Newell); Duncan Richardson (Jimmy Newell); Jack Kelly (Engineer); Alice Kelley (Waitress); Lance Fuller (Bit); Brett Halsey (Lew); Kathleen Freeman (Mrs. O'Halloran); Eve McVeagh (Viv); Beverly Garland (Sally); Jack Lomas (Cliffie); Helen Wallace (Mrs. Doyle); Howard Wright (Weaver); Herbert C. Lytton (Attorney Gilbert); James Stone (Mr. Weatherby); John Verros (Fred Abbott); Benny Rubin (Tramp Comic); Donald Kerr (Paper Man); Tom Greenway (District Attorney).

BLACK TUESDAY *(United Artists, 1954), 80 min.*

Producer, Robert Goldstein; director, Hugo Fregonese; story-screenplay, Sydney Boehm; assistant director Sam Wurtzel; art director, Hilyard Brown; set director, Al Spencer; music, Paul Dunlap; sound, Tom Lambert; camera, Stanley Cortez; editor, Robert Golden.

Edward G. Robinson (Vincent Canelli); Peter Graves (Peter Manning); Jean Parker (Hatti Combest); Milburn Stone (Father Slocum); Warren Stevens (Joey Stewart); Jack Kelly (Frank Carson); Sylvia Findley (Ellen Norris); James Bell (John Norris); Victor Perrin (Dr. Hart).

THE VIOLENT MEN *(Columbia, 1955), C-96 min.*

Producer, Lewis J. Rackmil; director, Rudolph Mate; based on the novel by Donald Hamilton; screenplay, Harry Kleiner; music, Max Steiner; assistant director, Sam Nelson; gowns, Jean Louis; camera, Burnett Guffey, W. Howard Greene; editor Jerome Thoms.

Glenn Ford (John Parrish); Barbara Stanwyck (Martha Wilkison); Edward G. Robinson (Lew Wilkison); Dianne Foster (Judith Wilkison); Brian Keith (Cole Wilkison); May Wynn (Caroline Vail); Warner Anderson (Jim McCloud); Basil Ruysdael (Tex Hinkleman); Lita Milan (Elena); Richard Jeckel (Wade Matlock); James Westerfield (Magruder); Jack Kelly (Derosa); Willis Bouchey (Sheriff Martin Kenner); Harry Shannon (Purdue); Peter Hanson (George Menefee); Don C. Harvey (Jackson); Robo Bechi (Tony); Carl Andre (Dryer); James Anderson (Hank Perdue); Katharine Warren, Tom Browne Henry (Mr. & Mrs. Vail); Frank Ferguson (Mahoney); Raymond Greenleaf (Dr. Henry Crowell); Edmund Cobb (Anchor Rider); Bill Phipps (Bud Hinkleman).

TIGHT SPOT *(Columbia, 1955), 97 min.*

Producer, Lewis J. Rackmil; director, Phil Karlson; based on the novel *Dead Pigeon* by Leonard Kantor; screenplay, William Bowers; art director, Carl Anderson; music director, Morris Stoloff; assistant director, Milton Feldman; gowns, Jean Louis; camera, Burnett Guffey; editor, Viola Lawrence.

Ginger Rogers (Sherry Conley); Edward G. Robinson (Lloyd Hallett); Brian Keith (Vince Striker); Lucy Marlow (Prison Girl); Lorne Greene (Benjamin Costain); Katherine Anderson (Mrs. Willoughby); Allen Nourse (Marvin Rickles); Peter Leeds (Fred Packer); Doye O'Dell (Mississippi Mac); Eve McVeagh (Clara Moran); Helen Wallace (Warden); Frank Gerstle (Jim Hornsby); Gloria Ann Simpson (Miss Masters); Robert Shield (Carlyle); Norman Keats (Arny); Kathryn Grant (Honeymooner); Ed "Skipper" McNally (Harris); Erik Page, Tom Greenway, Kevin Enright (Men); John Larch, John Marshall, Ed Hinton (Detectives); Tom de Graffenried (Doctor); Will J. White (Plainclothesman); Alfred Linder (Tonelli).

A BULLET FOR JOEY *(United Artists, 1955), 85 min.*

Producers, Samuel Bischoff, David Diamond; director, Lewis Allen; story, James Benson Nablo; screenplay, Geoffrey Homes, A. I. Bezzerides; music, Harry Sukman; assistant director, Bert Glazer; camera, Harry Neumann; editor, Leon Barsha.

Edward G. Robinson (Inspector Raoul Leduc); George Raft (Joe Victor); Audrey Totter (Joyce Geary); George Dolenz (Carl Macklin); Peter Hanson (Fred); Peter Van Eyck (Eric Hartman); Karen Verne (Mrs. Hartman); Ralph Smiley (Paola); Henri Letondal (Dubois); John Cliff (Morrie); Joseph Vitale (Nick); Bill Bryant (Jack Allen); Stan Malotte (Paul); Toni Gerry (Yvonne Temblay); Sally Blane (Marie); Steven Geray (Garcia); John Alvin (Percy); Bill Henry (Artist).

ILLEGAL *(Warner Bros., 1955), 88 min.*

Producer, Frank P. Rosenberg; director, Lewis Allen; based on the play *The Mouthpiece* by Frank J. Collins; screenplay, W. R. Burnett, James R. Webb; art director, Stanley Fleischer; music, Max Steiner; wardrobe, Moss Mabry; assistant director, Phil Quinn; camera, Peverell Marley; editor, Thomas Reilly.

Edward G. Robinson (Victor Scott); Nina Foch (Ellen Miles); Hugh Marlowe (Ray Borden); Robert Ellenstein (Joe Knight); De Forrest Kelley (Edward Clary); Jay Adler (Joseph Carter); James McCallion (Allen Parker); Edward Platt (Ralph Ford); Albert Dekker (Frank Garland); Jan Merlin (Andy Garth); Ellen Corby (Miss Hinkel); Jayne Mansfield (Angel O'Hara); Clark Howat (George Graves); Henry Kulky (Taylor); Howard St. John (E. A. Smith); Addison Richards (Steve Harper); Lawrence Dobkin (Al Carol); John McKee, Barry Hudson (Detectives); Kathy Marlowe (Blonde Girl); Ted Stanhope (Bailiff); Charles Evans (Judge); Jonathan Hale (Doctor); Marjorie Stapp (Night Orderly); Fred Coby (Guard); Max Wagner (Bartender); John Cliff (Barfly); Henry Rowland (Jailer); Julie Bennett (Miss Worth); Herb Vigran, Chris Alcaide (Policemen); Archie Twitchell (Mr. Manning); Stewart Nedd (Phillips); Roxanne Arlen (Miss Hathaway); Pauline Drake (Woman).

HELL ON FRISCO BAY *(Warner Bros., 1956), C-98 min.*

Associate producer, George Bertholon; director, Frank Tuttle; based on a novel by William P. McGivern; screenplay, Sydney Boehm, Martin Rackin; art director, John Beckman; music, Max Steiner; assistant director, William Kissel; costumes, Moss Mabry; sound, Charles B. Lang; camera, John Seitz; editor, Folmar Blangsted.

Alan Ladd (Steve Rollins); Edward G. Robinson (Victor Amato); Joanne Dru (Marcia Rollins); William Demarest (Lieutenant Dan Bianco); Paul Stewart (Joe Lye); Fay Wray (Kay Stanley); Perry Lopez (Mario Amato); Renata Vanni (Anna Amato); Nestor Paiva (Lou Fiaschetti); Stanley Adams (Hammy); Willis Bouchey (Lieutenant Neville); Peter Hanson (Detective Connors); Tina Carver (Bessie); Rodney Taylor (Brody Evans); Anthony Caruso (Sebastian Pasmonick); Peter Votrian (George Pasmonick); George J. Lewis (Father Larocca); Jayne Mansfield (Blonde.)

NIGHTMARE *(United Artists, 1956), 89 min.*
Producers, William Thomas, Howard Pine; director, Maxwell Shane; based on the novel by Cornell Woolrich; screenplay, Shane; art director, Frank Sylos; wardrobe, Frank Beetson, Fay Moore; sound, Jack Solomon, Paul Wolff; camera, Joseph Biroc; editor, George Gittens.

Edward G. Robinson (Rene); Kevin McCarthy (Stan Grayson); Connie Russell (Gina); Virginia Christine (Sue); Rhys Williams (Torrence); Gage Clarke (Belnap); Barry Atwater (Warner); Marian Carr (Madge); Billy May (Louie Simes).

THE TEN COMMANDMENTS *(Paramount, 1956), C-221 min.*
Producer, Cecil B. DeMille; associate producer, Herbert Wilcoxon; director, DeMille; based on the novels *Prince of Egypt* by Dorothy Clarke Wilson, *Pillar of Fire* by Reverend J. H. Ingraham, *On Eagle's Wings* by Reverend G. E. Southon, in accordance with The Holy Scripture, the ancient texts of Josephus, Eusebius, Philo, The Midrash; screenplay, Aeneas Mac-Kenzie, Jesse L. Lasky, Jr., Jack Gariss, Fredric M. Frank; music, Elmer Bernstein; costumes, Edith Head, Ralph Jester, John Jensen, Dorothy Jenkins, Arnold Friberg; assistant directors, Francisco Day, Michael Moore, Edward Salven, Daniel McCauley, Fouard Aref; choreography, LeRoy Prinz, Ruth Godfrey; camera, Loyal Griggs; editor, Anne Bauchens.

Charlton Heston (Moses); Yul Brynner (Rameses); Anne Baxter (Nefretiri); Edward G. Robinson (Dathan); Yvonne De Carlo (Sephora); Debra Paget (Lilia); John Derek (Joshua); Sir Cedric Harwicke (Sethi); Nina Foch (Bithiah); Martha Scott (Yochabel); Judith Anderson (Memnet); Vincent Price (Baka); John Carradine (Aaron); Eduard Franz (Jethro); Olive Deering (Miriam); Donald Curtis (Mered); Douglass Dumbrille (Jannes); Lawrence Dobkin (Hur Ben Caleb); Frank DeKova (Abiram); H. B. Warner (Amminadab); Henry Wilcoxon (Pentaur); Julia Faye (Elisheba); Lisa Mitchell (Jethro's Daughter); Joan Woodbury (Korah's Wife); Francis J. McDonald (Simon); Ian Keith (The Blind One); John Miljan (Rameses I); Woody Strode (King of Ethiopia); Dorothy Adams (Slave Woman); Henry Brandon (Commander of the Hosts); Mike Connors (Amalekite Herder); Gail Kobe (Pretty Slave Girl); Fred Kohler, Jr. (Foreman); Addison Richards (Fanbearer); Kenneth MacDonald, Frankie Darro, Carl Switzer (Slaves); Onslow Stevens (Lugal); Clint Walker (Sardinian Captain); Michael Ansara (Taskmaster); Zeev Bufman (Hebrew at Golden Calf); Herb Albert (Drum Player); Katy Garver (Child Slave); Luis Alberni (Old Hebrew at Moses' House); Frank Wilcox (Wazir); Frank Lackteen (Old Man Praying); John Hart (Cretan Ambassador); Robert Vaughn (Hebrew at Golden Calif.).

A HOLE IN THE HEAD *(United Artists, 1959), C-120 min.*
Producer, Frank Capra; co-producer, Frank Sinatra; director, Capra; based on the play *The Heart Is a Forgotten Hotel* by Arnold Schulman; screenplay, Schulman; music, Nelson Riddle; songs, Sammy Cahn and James Van Heusen; makeup, Bernard Ponedel; art director, Edward Imazu; assistant directors, Arthur S. Black, Jr., Jack R. Berne; costumes, Edith Head; sound, Fred Lau; camera, William H. Daniels; editor, William Hornbeck.

Frank Sinatra (Tony Manetta); Edward G. Robinson (Mario Manetta); Eddie Hodges (Ally Manetta); Eleanor Parker (Eloise Rogers); Carolyn Jones (Shirl); Thelma Ritter (Sophie Manetta); Keenan Wynn (Jerry Marks); Joi Lansing (Dorine); George De Witt (Mendy); Jimmy Komack (Julius Manetta); Dub Taylor (Fred); Connie Sawyer (Miss Wexler); Benny Rubin (Mr. Diamond); Ruby Dandridge (Sally); B. S. Pully (Hood); Pupi Campo (Master of Ceremonies).

SEVEN THIEVES *(Twentieth Century-Fox, 1960), 120 min.*

Producer, Sydney Boehm; director, Henry Hathaway; based on the novel *Lions at the Kill* by Max Catto; screenplay, Boehm; music, Dominic Frontiere; art directors, Lyle Wheeler, John De Cuir; set decorators, Walter M. Scott, Stuart A. Reiss; costumes, Bill Thomas; makeup, Ben Nye; assistant director, Ad Schaumer; sound, Charles Peck, Harry M. Leonard; camera, Sam Leavitt; editor, Dorothy Spencer.

Edward G. Robinson (Theo Wilkins); Rod Steiger (Paul Mason); Joan Collins (Melanie); Eli Wallach (Pancho); Alexander Scourby (Raymond Le May); Michael Dante (Louis); Berry Kroeger (Hugo Baumer); Sebastian Cabot (Monte Carlo Director); Marcel Hillaire (Duc di Salins); John Berardino (Chief of Detectives); Alphonse Martell (Governor); Jonathan Kidd (Seymour); Marga Ann Deighton (Governor's Wife).

PEPE *(Columbia, 1960), C-195 min.*

Producer, George Sidney; associate producer, Jacques Gelman; director, Sidney; based on a play by Ladislas Bush-Fekete; screen story, Leonard Spigelgass, Sonya Levien; screenplay, Dorothy Kingsley, Claude Binyon; art director, Ted Haworth; set decorator, William Kiernan; assistant director, David Silver; makeup, Ben Lane; gowns, Edith Head; background music and music supervisor, Johnny Green; special musical material, Sammy Cahn, Roger Edens; songs, Andre Previn and Dory Langdon; Hans Wittstatt and Dory Langdon; Previn; Augustin Lara and Langdon; choreography, Eugene Loring, Alex Romero; camera, Joe MacDonald; editors, Viola Lawrence, Al Clark.

Cantinflas (Pepe); Dan Dailey (Ted Holt); Shirley Jones (Suzie Murphy); Carlos Montalban (Auctioneer); Vicki Trickett (Lupita); Matt Mattox (Dancer); Hank Henry (Manager); Suzanne Lloyd (Carmen); Carlos Rivas (Carlos); Stephen Bekassy (Jewelry Salesman); Carol Douglas (Waitress); Francisco Reguerra (Priest); Joe Hyams (Charro); and Joey Bishop, Michael Callan, Maurice Chevalier, Charles Coburn, Richard Conte, Bing Crosby, Tony Curtis, Bobby Darin, Sammy Davis, Jr., Jimmy Durante, Zsa Zsa Gabor, the voice of Judy Garland, Greer Garson, Hedda Hopper, Ernie Kovacs, Peter Lawford, Janet Leigh, Jack Lemmon, Dean Martin, Jay North, Kim Novak, Andre Previn, Donna Reed, Debbie Reynolds, Edward G. Robinson, Cesar Romero, Frank Sinatra, Billie Burke, Ann B. Davis, William Demarest, Jack Entratter, Colonel E. E. Fogelson, Jane Robinson, Bunny Waters (Themselves).

MY GEISHA *(Paramount, 1962), C-120 min.*

Producer, Steve Parker; director, Jack Cardiff; screenplay, Norman Krasna; assistant director, Harry Kratz; music, Franz Waxman; song, Waxman and Hal Davis; art directors, Hal Pereira, Arthur Lonegan, Makoto Kikuchi; costumes, Edith Head; sound, Harold Lewis, Charles Grenzbach; camera, Shunichiro Nakao; second unit camera, Stanley Sayer; editor, Archie Marshek.

Shirley MacLaine (Lucy Dell [Yoko Mori]); Yves Montand (Paul Robaix); Edward G. Robinson (Sam Lewis); Bob Cummings (Bob Moore); Yoko Tani (Kazumi Ito); Tatsuo Saito (Kenichi Takata); Alex Gerry (Leonard Lewis); Nobuo Chiba (Shig); Ichiro Hayakawa (Hisako Amatsu); George Furness (George).

TWO WEEKS IN ANOTHER TOWN *(MGM, 1962), C-107 min.*

Producer, John Houseman; associate producer, Ethel Winant; director, Vincente Minnelli; based on the novel by Irwin Shaw; screenplay, Charles Schnee; music, David Raksin; assistant director, Erich Von Stroheim, Jr.; art directors, George W. Davis, Urie McCleary; set decorators, Henry Grace, Keogh Gleason; color consultant, Charles K. Hagedon; Miss Charisse's gowns, Pierre Balmain; wardrobe, Walter Plunkett; makeup, William Tuttle; sound, Franklin

Milton; special visual effects, Robert R. Hoag; camera, Milton Krasner; editors, Adrienne Fazan, Robert J. Kern.

Kirk Douglas (Jack Andrus); Edward G. Robinson (Maurice Kruger); Cyd Charisse (Carlotta); George Hamilton (David Drew); Dahlia Lavi (Veronica); Claire Trevor (Clara Kruger); Rosanna Schiaffino (Barzelli); James Gregory (Brad Byrd); Joanna Roos (Janet Bark); George Macready (Lew Jordan); Mino Doro (Tucino); Stefan Schnabel (Zeno); Vito Scotti (Assistant Director); Tom Palmer (Dr. Cold Eyes); Erich Von Stroheim, Jr. (Ravinski); Leslie Uggams (Chanteuse).

THE PRIZE *(MGM, 1963), C-135 min.*
Producer, Pandro S. Berman; associate producer, Kathryn Hereford; director, Mark Robson; based on the novel by Irving Wallace; screenplay, Ernest Lehman; art directors, George W. Davis, Urie McCleary; set decorators, Henry Grace, Dick Pefferle; wardrobe, Bill Thomas; music, Jerry Goldsmith; makeup, William Tuttle; assistant director, Hank Moonjean; sound, Franklin Milton; special visual effects, J. McMillan Johnson, A. Arnold Gillespie, Robert R. Hoag; camera, William H. Daniels; editor, Adrienne Fazan.

Paul Newman (Andrew Craig); Edward G. Robinson (Dr. Max Stratman); Elke Sommer (Inger Lisa Anderson); Diane Baker (Emily Stratman); Micheline Presle (Dr. Denise Marceau); Gerard Oury (Dr. Claude Marceau); Sergio Fantoni (Dr. Carlo Farelli); Kevin McCarthy (Dr. John Garrett); Leo G. Carroll (Count Bertil Jacobsson); Sacha Pitoeff (Daranyi); Jacqueline Beer (Monique Souvir); John Wengraf (Hans Eckart); Don Dubbins (Ivar Cramer); Virginia Christine (Mrs. Bergh); Rudolph Anders (Mr. Bergh); Martine Bartlett (Saralee Garrett); Karl Swenson (Hilding); John Qualen (Oscar); Ned Wever (Clark Wilson).

GOOD NEIGHBOR SAM *(Columbia, 1964), C-130 min.*
Producer, David Swift; associate producer, Marvin Miller; director, Swift; based on the novel by Jack Finney; screenplay, James Fritzell, Everett Greenbaum, Swift; production designer, Dale Hennesy; costumes, Micheline and Jacqueline; set decorator, Ray Moyer; assistant director, R. Robert Rosenbaum; music, DeVol; makeup, Ben Lane; choreography, Miriam Nelson; sound, James Z. Flaster; camera, Burnett Guffey; editor, Charles Nelson.

Jack Lemmon (Sam Bissel); Romy Schneider (Janet Lagerlof); Dorothy Provine (Min Bissel); Edward G. Robinson (Mr. Nurdlinger); Michael Connors (Howard Ebbets); Edward Andrews (Burke); Louis Nye (Shiffner); Robert Q. Lewis (Earl); Anne Seymour (Irene Krupp); Charles Lane (Jack Bailey); Joyce Jameson (Elsie Hooker); Linda Watkins (Edna); Peter Hobbs (Phil Reisner); Tris Coffin (Sonny Blatchford); Neil Hamilton (Larry Boling); Riza Royce (Miss Halverson); The Hi-Los (Themselves); Gil Lamb (Drunk); David Swift (TV Director); Vicki Cos, Kym Karath (Bissel Children); Barbara Bouchet (Receptionist); William Forrest (Millard Mellner).

ROBIN AND THE SEVEN HOODS *(Warner Bros., 1964), C-123 min.*
Executive producer, Howard W. Koch; producer, Frank Sinatra; associate producer, William H. Daniels; director, Gordon Douglas; screenplay, David R. Schwartz; art director, Leroy Deane; set decorator, Ralph Bretton; assistant directors, David Salven, Lee White; music and music conductor, Nelson Riddle; songs, Sammy Cahn and James Van Heusen; orchestrator, Gil C. Grau; costumes, Don Feld; dialogue supervisor, Thom Conroy; makeup, Gordon Bau; sound, Everett Hughes, Vinton Vernon; camera, Daniels; editor, Sam O'Steen.

Frank Sinatra (Robbo); Dean Martin (John); Sammy Davis, Jr. (Will); Bing Crosby (Allen A.

Dale); Edward G. Robinson (Big Jim); Peter Falk (Guy Gisborne); Barbara Rush (Marian); Victor Buono (Sheriff Potts); Hank Henry (Six Seconds); Allen Jenkins (Vermin); Jack LaRue (Tomatoes); Robert Foulk (Sheriff Glick); Phil Crosby, Harry Wilson, Richard Bakalyan, Sonny King (Hoods); Robert Carricart (Blue Jaw); Phil Arnold (Hatrack); Bill Zuckert (Prosecutor); Bernard Fein (Bananas); Joseph Ruskin (Twitch).

THE OUTRAGE *(MGM, 1964), 97 min.*

Producer, A. Ronald Lubin; associate producer, Michael Kanin; director, Martin Ritt; based on the film *Rashomon,* from stories by Ryunosuke Akutagawa and the play by Fay and Michael Kanin; screenplay, Michael Kanin; music-music conductor, Alex North; art directors, George W. Davis, Tambi Larsen; set decorators, Henry Grace, Robert R. Benton; assistant director, Daniel J. McCauley; costumes, Don Feld; makeup, William Tuttle; special visual effects, J. McMillan Johnson, Robert R. Hoag; camera, James Wong Howe; editor, Frank Santillo.

Paul Newman (Juan Carrasco); Laurence Harvey (Husband); Claire Bloom (Wife); Edward G. Robinson (Con Man); William Shatner (Preacher); Howard da Silva (Prospector); Albert Salmi (Sheriff); Thomas Chalmers (Judge); Paul Fix (Indian).

CHEYENNE AUTUMN *(Warner Bros., 1964), C-156 min.*

Producer, Bernard Smith; director, John Ford; associate director, Ray Kellogg; based on the novel by Mari Sandoz; screenplay, James R. Webb; art director, Richard Day; set decorator, Darryl Silvera; assistant directors, Wingate Smith, Russ Saunders; music-music conductor, Alex North; sound, Francis E. Stahl; camera, William H. Clothier; editor, Otho Lovering.

Richard Widmark (Captain Thomas Archer); Carroll Baker (Deborah Wright); Karl Malden (Captain Wessels); James Stewart (Wyatt Earp); Edward G. Robinson (Secretary of the Interior Carl Schurz); Sal Mineo (Red Shirt); Dolores Del Rio (Spanish Woman); Ricardo Montalban (Little Wolf); Gilbert Roland (Dull Knife); Arthur Kennedy (Doc Holliday); Patrick Wayne (Second Lieutenant Scott); Elizabeth Allen (Miss Plantagenet); John Carradine (Jeff Blair); Victor Jory (Tall Tree); Mike Mazurki (Senior First Sergeant); George O'Brien (Major Braden); Sean McClory (Dr. O'Carberry); Judson Pratt (Mayor Dog Kelly); Carmen D'Antonio (Pawnee Woman); Ken Curtis (Joe); John Qualen (Svenson); Shug Fisher (Trail Boss); Nancy Hsueh (Little Bird); Harry Carey, Jr. (Trooper Smith); Ben Johnson (Trooper Plumtree); Major Sam Harris (Townsman); Denver Pyle (Senator Henry); Louise Montana (Woman); William Henry (Infantry Captain); Carleton Young (Secretary to Schurz).

WHO HAS SEEN THE WIND *(ABC-TV, 1965), C-90 min.*

Producer-director, George Sidney; story, Tad Mosel; teleplay, Don Mankiewicz.

Edward G. Robinson (Captain); Stanley Baker (Janos); Maria Schell (The Mother); Veronica Cartwright (Kirk); Gypsy Rose Lee (Proprietress); Lilia Skala (Nun); Simon Oakland (Inspector); Paul Richards (Father Ashton); Victor Jory (Peralton).

A BOY TEN FEET TALL *(Paramount, 1965), C-88 min.*

Producer, Hal Mason; director, Alexander MacKendrick; based on the novel *Sammy Going South* by W. H. Canaway; screenplay, Denis Cannan; art director, Edward Tester; set decorator, Scott Slimon; camera, Erwin Hillier; editor, Jack Harris.

Edward G. Robinson (Cocky Wainwright); Fergus McClelland (Sammy Hartland); Constance Cummings (Gloria Van Imhoff); Harry H. Corbett (Lem); Paul Stassino (Spyros Dra-condopolous); Zia Mohyeddin (The Syrian); Orlando Martins (Abu Lubaba); John Turner (Heneker); Zena Walker (Aunt Jane); Jack Gwillim (District Commissioner); Patricia Donahue (Cathie); Jared Allen (Bob); Guy Deghy (Doctor); Marne Maitland (Hassan); Steven Scott (Egyptian Policeman); Frederick Schiller (Head Porter).

THE CINCINNATI KID *(MGM, 1965), C-113 min.*
Producer, Martin Ransohoff; associate producer, John Calley; director, Norman Jewison; based on the novel by Richard Jessup; screenplay, Ring Lardner, Jr., Terry Southern; assistant director, Kurt Neumann; art directors, George W. Davis, Edward Carfagno; set decorators, Henry Grace, Hugh Hunt; music, Lalo Schifrin; camera, Philip H. Lathrop; editor, Hal Ashby.

Steve McQueen (The Cincinnati Kid); Edward G. Robinson (Lancey Howard); Ann-Margret (Melba); Karl Malden (Shooter); Tuesday Weld (Christian); Joan Blondell (Lady Fingers); Rip Torn (Slade); Jack Weston (Pig); Cab Calloway (Yeller); Jeff Corey (Hoban); Theo Marcuse (Felix); Milton Selzer (Sokal); Karl Swenson (Mr. Rudd); Emile Genest (Cajun); Ron Soble (Danny); Irene Tedrow (Mrs. Rudd); Midge Ware (Mrs. Slade); Dub Taylor (Dealer); Joyce Perry (Hoban's Wife); Claude Hall (Gambler); Olan Soule (Desk Clerk); Barry O'Hara (Eddie); Pat McCaffrie, Bill Zuckert, John Hart, Sandy Kevin (Poker Players); Howard Wendell (Charlie the Poker Player); Hal Taggart (Bettor); Andy Albin (Referee); Robert Do Qui (Philly).

LA BLONDE DE PEKIN *(a.k.a., THE BLONDE FROM PEKING, Paramount, 1968), C-80 min.*
Director, Nicolas Gessner; based on the novel by James Hadley Chase; adaptor, Jacques Vilfrid; screenplay, Gessner, Mark Behm; music, Francois de Roubaix; art director, Georges Petitot; camera, Claude Lecomte; editor, Jean-Michel Gauthier.

Mireille Darc (Christine); Claudio Brook (Gandler); Edward G. Robinson (Douglas); Pascale Roberts (Secretary); Francoise Brion (Erika); Joe Warfield (Doctor); and Giorgia Moll, Karl Studer, Yves Eliot, Valery Inkijinoff, Tiny Young, Aime de March, Jean-Jacques Delbo.

THE BIGGEST BUNDLE OF THEM ALL *(MGM, 1968), C-110 min.*
Producer, Josef Shaftel; associate producer, Sy Stewart; director, Ken Annakin; story, Shaftel; screenplay, Shaftel, Sy Salkowitz, Riccardo Aragno; music, Riz Ortolani, The Counts; assistant director, Victor Merenda; art director, Arrigo Equini; camera, Piero Portalupa; editor, Ralph Sheldon.

Robert Wagner (Harry Price); Raquel Welch (Juliana); Vittorio De Sica (Cesare Celli); Edward G. Robinson (Professor Samuels); Godfrey Cambridge (Benjamin Brownstead); Davy Kaye (Davey Collins); Francesco Mule (Antonio Tozzi); Victor Spinetti (Captain Giglio); Yvonne Sanson (Teresa); Femi Benussi (Carlotta); Paola Borboni (Rosa); Andrea Aureli (Carabiniere); Aldo Bufi Landi (Del Signore); Carlo Croccolo (Franco the Fence); Roberto De Simone (Carlo Celli); Giulio Marchetti (Naldi); Lex Monson (Percy Peckinpaugh); Carlo Rizzi (Maitre d'); Nino Musco (Chef); The Counts (Themselves); Calisto Calisti (Inspector Bordoni); Gianna Dauro (Signora Clara); Massimo Sarchielli (Paqueletto).

AD OGNI COSTO *(a.k.a., GRAND SLAM, Paramount, 1968), C-121 min.*

Producers, Harry Colombo, George Papi; director, Giuliano Montaldo; screenplay, Mino Roli, Marcello Fondato, Antonio De La Loma, Caminito; music, Ennio Morricone; music conductor, Bruno Nicolai; art directors, Alberto Boccianti, Juan Alberto Soler; assistant directors, Mauro Sacripanti, Carlos Luiz Corito, Federico Canudas; sound, Umberto Picistrelli; camera, Antonio Macasoli; editor, Nino Baragli.

Janet Leigh (Mary Ann); Robert Hoffman (Jean-Paul Audry); Edward G. Robinson (Professor James Anders); Adolfo Celi (Mark Muilford); Klaus Kinski (Erich Weiss), Georges Rigaud (Gregg); Riccardo Cucciolla (Agostini Rossi); Jussara (Setuaka); Miguel Del Castillo (Manager).

UNO SCACCO TUTTO MATTO *(a.k.a., MAD CHECKMATE, Kinesis/Miniter/Tecisa, 1968), C-89 min.* (T.V. title: *It's Your Move.*)

Producer, Franco Porro; director, Robert Riz; screenplay, Fiz, Massimilliano Capriccoli, Ennio De Concini, Jose G. Maesso, Leonardo Martin, Juan Cesarabea; music, Manuel Asins Arbo; set decorator, Rafael Ferri; camera, Antonio Macasoli; editor, Mario Morra.

Edward G. Robinson (MacDowell); Terry-Thomas (Jerome); Maria Grazi Buccella (Monique); and Adolfo Celi, Manuel Zarzo, Jorge Rigaud, Jose Bodalo, Louis Bazzocchi, Rossella Como.

OPERATION ST. PETER'S *(Paramount, 1968), C-88 min.*

Producer, Turi Vasile; director, Lucio Fulci; screenplay, Ennio De Concini, Adriano Baracco, Roberto Gianviti, Fulci; assistant director, Francesco Massaro; art director, Giorgio Giovannini; camera, Erico Menczer.

Lando Buzzanca (Napoleon); Edward G. Robinson (Joe); Heinz Ruhmann (Cardinal Braun); Jean-Claude Brialy (Cajella); Pinuccio Ardia (The Baron); Dante Maggio (The Captain); Ugo Fancareggi (Agonia); Marie-Christine Barclay (Marisa); Uta Levka (Samantha); Antonella Delle Porti (Cesira).

NEVER A DULL MOMENT *(Buena Vista, 1968), C-100 min.*

Producer, Ron Miller; director, Jerry Paris; based on the novel *Thrill a Minute* by John Godey; screenplay, A. J. Carothers; art directors, Carroll Clark, John B. Mansbridge; set decorators, Emile Kuri, Frank R. McKelvy; matte artist, Alan Maley; costumes, Bill Thomas; assistant director, John C. Chulay; music, Robert F. Brunner; orchestrator, Cecil A. Crandall; makeup, Gordon Hubbard; special effects, Eustace Lycett, Robert A. Mattey; camera, William Snyder; editor, Marsh Hendry.

Dick Van Dyke (Jack Albany); Edward G. Robinson (Leo Joseph Smooth); Dorothy Provine (Sally Inwood); Henry Silva (Frank Boley); Joanna Moore (Melanie Smooth); Tony Bill (Florian); Slim Pickens (Cowboy Schaeffer); Jack Elam (Ace Williams); Ned Glass (Rinzy Tobreski); Richard Bakalyan (Bobby Macoon); Mickey Shaughnessy (Francis); Philip Coolidge (Fingers Felton); James Millhollin (Museum Director); Johnny Silver (Prop Man); Anthony Caruso (Tony Preston); Paul Condylis (Lenny); Dick Winslow (TV Actor); Bob Homel (TV Actor Playing Police Captain Jacoby); Jackie Russell (Sexy Girl); Rex Dominick (Sam); Ken

Lynch (Police Lieutenant); John Cliff, John Dennis (Museum Guards); Tyler McVey (Police Chief Grayson); Jerry Paris (Police Photographer).

U.M.C. *(CBS-TV, 1969), C-120 min.*
Producer, Frank Glicksman; director, Boris Sagal; creators, Glicksman, Al C. Ward; teleplay, Ward; camera, Joseph Lashelle; editor, Henry Batista.

Richard Bradford (Dr. Joseph M. Gannon); Edward G. Robinson (Dr. Lee Forestman); James Daly (Dr. Paul Lochner); Kim Stanley (Joanna Hanson); Maurice Evans (Dr. George Barger); Kevin McCarthy (Coswell); J. D. Cannon (Jarris); William Windom (Janson); Don Quine (Martin); Shelley Fabares (Mike); James Shigeta (Chief Resident); William Marshall (Dr. Tawn); Alfred Ryder (Dr. Corlane); Robert Emhardt (Judge).

MacKENNA'S GOLD *(Columbia, 1969), C-128 min.*
Producers, Carl Foreman, Dmitri Tiomkin; director, J. Lee Thompson; based on the novel by Will Henry; screenplay, Foreman; second unit director, Tom Shaw; assistant director, David Salven; music, Quincy Jones; orchestrators, Leo Shuken, Jack Hayes; song, Jones and Freddie Douglass; production designer, Geoffrey Drake; art directors, Drake, Cary Odell; set decorator, Alfred E. Spencer; stunt co-ordinator, Buzz Henry; costumes, Norma Koch; sound, Derek Frye, William Randall, Jr.; special effects, Geoffrey Drake, Abacus Productions (John Mackey, Bob Cuff), Willis Cook, Larry Butler; camera, Joseph MacDonald; second unit camera, Harold Wellman; additional camera, John Mackey, Don Glouner, Farciot Edouart, Richard Moore; editor, Bill Lenny.

Gregory Peck (MacKenna); Omar Sharif (Colorado); Telly Savalas (Sergeant Tibbs); Camilla Sparv (Inga); Keenan Wynn (Sanchez); Julie Newmar (Hesh-Ke); Ted Cassidy (Hachita); Lee J. Cobb (The Editor); Raymond Massey (The Preacher); Burgess Meredith (The Storekeeper); Anthony Quayle (Older Englishman); Edward G. Robinson (Old Adams); Eduardo Ciannelli (Prairie Dog); Dick Peabody (Avila); Rudy Diaz (Besh); Robert Phillips (Monkey); Shelley Morrison (Pima Squaw); J. Robert Porter (Young Englishman); John Garfield, Jr. (Adams' Boy); Pepe Callahan (Laguna); Madeleine Taylor Holmes (Old Apache Woman); Duke Hobbie (Lieutenant); Victor Jory (Narrator).

SONG OF NORWAY *(Cinerama, 1970), C-142 min.*
Producers, Andrew L. and Virginia Stone; director, Andrew L. Stone; suggested by the stage play by Milton Lazarus (music and lyrics [based on the works of Edvard Grieg] by Robert Wright, George Forrest) from a play by Homer Curran; screenplay, Stone; choreography, Lee Theodore; assistant director, John O'Connor; second unit director, Yakima Canutt; musical supervisor, orchestrator and conductor, Roland Shaw; live animation sequence director, Kinney-Wolf; camera, Davis Boulton; editor, Virginia Stone.

Toralv Maurstad (Edvard Grieg); Florence Henderson (Nina Grieg); Christina Schollin (Therese Berg); Frank Poretta (Rikard Nordraak); Harry Secombe (Björnsterne Björnson); Robert Morley (Berg); Edward G. Robinson (Krogstad); Elizabeth Larner (Mrs. Björnson); Oscar Homolka (Engstrand); Frederick Jaeger (Henrik Ibsen); Henry Gilbert (Franz Liszt); Richard Wordsworth (Hans Christian Andersen); Bernard Archard (George Nordraak); Susan Richards (Aunt Aline); John Barrie (Hagerup); Wenke Foss (Mrs. Hagerup); Ronald Adam (Gade); Carl Rigg (Captain Hansen); Aline Towne (Mrs. Thoresen); Nan Munro (Irate Woman); James Hayter (Berg's Butler); Erik Chitty (Helsted); Maoug Parikian (Violinist); Richard Vernon, Ernest Clark (Councilmen); Eli Lindtner (Björnson's Secretary).

THE OLD MAN WHO CRIED WOLF *(ABC-TV, 1970), C-90 min.*

Executive producer, Aaron Spelling; producer-director, Walter Grauman; story, Arnold Horwitt; teleplay, Luther Davis; music, Robert Drasnin; art director, Paul Sylos; assistant director, Max Stein; camera, Arch R. Dalzell; editor, Art Seid.

Edward G. Robinson (Emile Pulska); Martin Balsam (Stanley Pulska); Diane Baker (Peggy Pulska); Percy Rodrigues (Frank Jones); Ruth Roman (Lois); Edward Asner (Dr. Morheim); Martin E. Brooks (Hudson Ewing); Paul Picerni (Detective Green); Sam Jaffe (Abe Stillman); Robert Yuro (Detective Seroly); Bill Elliott (Carl); James A. Watson (Leon); Naomi Stevens (Mrs. Raspili); Virginia Christine (Miss Cummings); Jay C. Flippen (Pawnbroker).

SOYLENT GREEN *(MGM, 1973), C-97 min.*

Producers, Walter Seltzer, Russell Thacher; director, Richard Fleischer; based on the novel *Make Room! Make Room!* by Harry Harrison; screenplay, Stanley R. Greenberg; assistant directors, Daniel S. McCauley, Gene Marum; art director, Edward C. Carfagno; set decorator, Robert Benton; music, Fred Myrow; symphony music director, Gerald Fried; costumes, Pat Barto; technical consultant, Frank A. Bowerman; action scenes co-ordinator, Joe Canutt; sound, Charles M. Wilborn, Harry W. Tetrick; special camera effects, Robert R. Hoag, Matthew Yuricich; special camera sequences, Braverman, Productions; camera, Richard H Kline; editor, Samuel E. Beetley.

Charlton Heston (Detective Thorn); Leigh Taylor-Young (Shirl); Edward G. Robinson (Sol Roth); Chuck Connors (Tab Fielding); Joseph Cotten (William Simonson); Brock Peters (Hatcher); Paula Kelly (Martha); Stephen Young (Gilbert); Mike Henry (Kulozik); Lincoln Kilpatrick (Priest); Roy Jenson (Donovan); Leonard Stone (Charles); Whit Bissell (Governor Santini); Celia Lovsky (Exchange Leader); Dick Van Patten (Usher); Morgan Farley, John Barclay, Belle Mitchell, Cyril Delevanti (Books); Forrest Wood, Faith Quabius (Attendants); Jane Dulo (Mrs. Santini); Carlos Romero (New Tenant); Pat Houtchens (Fat Guard).

NEITHER BY DAY OR NIGHT *(Monarch, 1973), 95 min.*

Producer, Mordechai Slonim; associate producer, Mischa Asherov; director, Steven Hilliard Stern; based on the play by Avraham Raz; screenplay, Stern, Gisa W. Slonim; music/music director, Vladimir Cosma; songs, Cosma and Stern; set decorator, Gidi Levi; camera, Ammon Salomon; editor, Alain Jakubowicz.

Zalman King (Adam); Miriam Bernstein Cohen (Hannah Sokolova); Dalia Friedland (Yael); Edward G. Robinson (Father); Mischa Asheroff (Doctor); Chaim Anitar (Akira); Eli Cohen (Reuver); and: Jetta Luka, Zicha Gold, David Smadar.

Publicity pose for *Act of Violence* (MGM, 1948)

Robert Ryan

6′ 3″
190 pounds
Black hair
Brown eyes
Scorpio

Rugged, tough, and handsome Robert Ryan proved that you cannot judge a person merely on appearance. On the surface he seemed surly, but was actually invariably kind and considerate. He played screen skunks with a two-fisted virtuosity, but once admitted, "I have been in films pretty well everything I am dedicated to fighting against." In private life he was a most dedicated public-spirited citizen, with an intelligent concern for the welfare of his fellow man.

In short, Ryan was a Hollywood professional who was such a consummate actor that he made every performance seem only a lark of self-indulgence. His face, with dark squinting eyes, always appeared frozen into a sneer on film. He was ideally cast as the evil, sinister, sick person, a man forever the outsider and brimming over with cunning malice. One has only to recall his cruel bigot in *Crossfire* (1947) or *Odds Against Tomorrow* (1959) to savor his capacity for etching the obsessed rough guy.

Few who saw Ryan performing in forties films would have guessed that in the fifties he would have emerged as a sterling Shakespearean stage actor or that in his final film offering, *The Iceman Cometh* (1973), he would steal the limelight as the focal force of the Eugene O'Neill drama.

The son of a Chicago building contractor, Robert Bushnell Ryan was born on Thursday, November 11, 1909, in Chicago. His paternal grandfather had come from Ireland to live in Lockport, Illinois, where he constructed boats, an occupation that later led to the building of his Chicago business. Robert's father, Timothy, carried on the family tradition and established the Ryan Contracting Company, which he owned with two brothers. Robert's mother, Mabel (Bushnell) Ryan, was of English descent. Five years after Robert's birth, the Ryans had another child, John, who died when Robert was eight.

Ryan's early life was influenced by his family's background and his immediate environment. His father's family were Roman Catholic, and his mother was an Episcopalian. He attended both churches but joined neither. His father was an avid Democrat. "They were all Democrats, in fact, all the Irish Catholics of the Chicago of those days were Democrats. Any who weren't were shunned," he later said. The boy, however, had none of the vigor of his father and basically was a shy lad, overpampered by his mother after the death of his small brother.

Although he was a good student, Robert was a socially backward child, and his mother determined to give him violin lessons to build his self-confidence. His father, however, decided that boxing lessons would be of more use to the lad. Young Robert began to excel in the sport, far eclipsing any desire he might have had for the violin.

After grammar school, Ryan attended Chicago's Loyola Academy, run by Jesuits, and there his interest in acting began in his junior year. One of his instructors spent an entire semester on *Hamlet*. "I got hooked. I read all of Shakespeare's plays as well as Shaw and Chekhov." It was also during these years that he became an avid movie fan. "I idolized Douglas Fairbanks and later Jimmy Cagney."

In 1928 he entered Dartmouth College, and majored in dramatic literature. He also began to write, but continued his boxing and became the heavyweight champion of the school during his four years there.[1] "Athletic prowess did a lot for my ego and my acceptance in school. The ability to defend yourself lessens the chance you'll ever have to use it."

Writing and boxing were the two most important things in life for the young Ryan, and when he was not fighting he was writing and working for the college newspaper. "First I wanted to be a reporter because in movies they were always running up and down the back stairs. Then I wanted to be a writer and have my picture taken with a pipe. Dartmouth was so goddamned isolated—it took five hours just to get to Smith—we were forced to develop other interests. The college there was among the best so for me it became [a decision to become a] playwright."

During his junior year Robert wrote a one-act play about death called *The Visitor*, which won a prize. A rebel at heart even then, he also participated in the burgeoning anti-Prohibition movement at the college, even to the point of distilling bathtub gin. Mainly, however, the young Robert was preparing himself for a career in journalism. It was a career that would never see fruition mainly because, by the time he graduated from the Ivy League school in 1932, the Depression had swept the country. By this time Ryan had realized fully that he was not emotionally suited to a businessman's career. As Ryan said years later, "It would have been my father's business, if any, though Dad was wiped out in the Crash."

With the Ryan Contracting Company floundering badly, Mr. Ryan did not insist

[1]He was the first freshman to win the Dartmouth heavyweight crown; he was never defeated during his four years of intercollegiate boxing.

With his father (*c.* 1925)

that Robert return to Chicago to work in the firm. Instead, the college graduate went to New York City where he beat the pavement from one newspaper to another with no success. "There were no newspaper jobs—there were no jobs, period." Living with two fraternity brothers he decided to take any type of work to keep body and soul together. One day, while on the Brooklyn waterfront with a friend, he asked for a job on one of the docked freighters. He was quickly hired as the engine room janitor and sailed with the ship to Africa and back.

Upon his return to New York, he received news from his mother that his father had been seriously injured in an accident, and Robert went back to Chicago. When his father's condition seemed to improve, Robert and a pal headed for Montana to work a gold claim, but when this did not pan out, they ended up working on a ranch near Missoula. Their weekly salary was room, board, and eight dollars.

Shortly after that, Robert's father died, and he returned home to support his mother, taking any job he could get. This was in 1936, and his first job was selling cemetery plots but he soon graduated to salesman for a steel company. At one point, for two weeks, he was a collector for a loan company. "That really brought me face to face with reality. . . . Here I was collecting money from families who hadn't eaten in days. It was too much. I was bugged by it and quit after two weeks. Hell, this country must have been near revolution, near as we'll ever get."

In his entry in *Who's Who in the American Theatre* (1967), Ryan listed numerous jobs in his pre-theatre days: sandhog, seaman, salesman, miner, cowboy, gold prospector, photographer's model, WPA laborer, paving supervisor, loan collector, and school supplies superintendent. During these years, however, Robert continued to write plays.

Now over six feet tall, the slim, handsome, curly-haired young man was quite popular with the girls, and, through a girl friend (whose name in later years he could not remember), he won several modeling jobs. She also talked him into joining her amateur theatre group. There he was given a small role in a play to be given for a women's club. "Suddenly it hit me—I loved being on stage." When he told his patient mother of his career choice, the practical woman replied, "But you can't act."

Although writing plays and acting in amateur theatre offerings satisfied the young man's cultural cravings, these time-consuming activities did not put bread on the table. According to Ryan, Chicago's Mayor Kelly, a childhood friend of his mother, "felt sorry for her because she was a widow stuck with an overgrown 27-year-old college graduate prepared for absolutely nothing, and he got me a job in the office of the Chicago Board of Education's superintendent of supplies. All the people who worked there were political appointees and didn't have any worries about *their* jobs, so nobody paid attention to me. I remember spending much of my time in that office writing up notes for Dartmouth's alumni magazine."

Through a young reporter friend, Edith Dixon, he was introduced to the drama group run by Edward Boyle, a stock company actor turned teacher. Boyle taught theatre for five dollars a week and Ryan joined his troupe. Boyle told the young actor, "You have all the faults of a young actor but you are positive. You don't know anything, but you always act as if you did." During this fledgling period, Ryan decided to make a stab at movie stardom sometime in the future. He mapped out a schedule which called for him to study for two years and then make an assault on the movies.

Sometimes fate can help a career more than all the hard work and determination in the world. Look at Ryan's case. He had invested three hundred dollars as a favor to a friend who had engineered an oil well deal. A gusher came in. Ryan's share in the bonanza was two thousand dollars. It would be enough to keep him alive and well for a year, so he determined to head for California then and there. In the summer of 1938 Robert traveled to California, where he registered for the fall term at the Pasadena Playhouse. He never matriculated at that training ground, however, because he spoke to an actor named Jack Smart, a friend of a girl Robert knew in Chicago. Smart suggested that Robert enroll in Max Reinhardt's new school. Ryan was so impressed by the continental Reinhardt and his training center that he abandoned the idea of acting at the Pasadena Playhouse. It was also during this test-and-trial period that Ryan made a screen test at Paramount Picutres, but was informed that he was "not the type for pictures."

Reinhardt and one of his teachers, veteran actor Vladimir Sokoloff, both liked Ryan. "You do things with gusto—you are never shy!," the school owner informed him. Robert began to obtain a number of good roles in the school's productions, such as the father in *Six Characters in Search of an Author,* Bottom in *A Midsummer Night's Dream,* and Prince Beladore in *Sister Beatrice,* where a young actress, Jessica Cadwalader, played the Madonna. She and Ryan fell in love, and within three months, on Saturday, March 11, 1939, they were married in St. Thomas' Episcopal Church in Los Angeles. She was twenty-four; he was twenty-nine.[2]

After graduating from the Max Reinhardt Workshop in 1939, Ryan believed he was ready to set the world on fire as an actor. "In those days I thought everything I did was good since I had no experience that told me otherwise." He made his professional debut that year at the Belasco Theatre in Los Angeles in a musical version of *Too Many Husbands* by W. Somerset Maugham. In it, he both sang and danced, two disciplines he had studied at the Reinhardt school. He was successful in the production and was spotted by a Paramount talent scout. The Marathon Street studio, which had previously thought him unsuitable for motion pictures, now offered him a seventy-five-dollar-a-week movie contract which he quickly accepted.

In 1939 Paramount was quite an exciting film factory. Not only did the company have its share of marquee blockbusters (Claudette Colbert, Dorothy Lamour, Bing Crosby, Paulette Goddard, Bob Hope, Martha Raye, Ray Milland, Gary Cooper, Fred MacMurray and Madeleine Carroll) but it had a strong stable of supporting lead players for its array of economy B pictures. These up-and-coming performers included Lloyd Nolan, Robert Preston, William Henry, Akim Tamiroff, J. Carrol Naish, Anthony Quinn, Robert Paige, Broderick Crawford, John Howard, Buster Crabbe, young Donald O'Connor, and, now, Robert Ryan.

It is interesting to note that Robert's screen debut was as a boxer in a B melodrama, *Golden Gloves* (Paramount, 1940), obviously created to accrue to it some of the success of *Golden Boy* (Columbia, 1939). In this Richard Denning-Jeanne Cagney-J. Carrol Naish programmer, Ryan had but one line of dialogue. To crooked fight manager Naish he says, "I thought you could get me more." Ryan did his own

[2] Jessica was a Quaker on her father's side and an Episcopalian on her maternal side. Despite a great yearning to be an actress when she met Ryan, in later years her interest leaned toward writing, and she was author of such juvenile and mystery books as *The Smoking Mountain* and *The Crack in the Ring.* During the early years of their marriage, she often supplemented the Ryan's income by acting and modeling jobs.

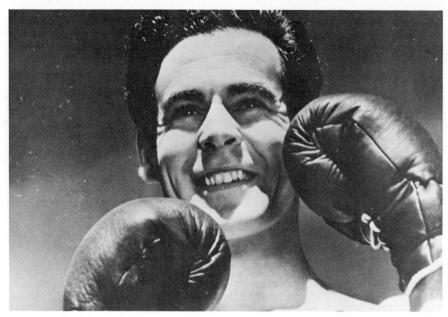

In *Golden Gloves* (Par., 1940)

oncamera boxing and was noticed in the film. Edward Dmytryk directed the feature. The latter, who had risen from the ranks as a studio editor, would have a great effect on Ryan's later career.

Next, contract player Ryan was tossed into another B, *Queen of the Mob* (Paramount, 1940), one of four films the studio would adapt from J. Edgar Hoover's book, *Persons in Hiding*. Directed by James Hogan, the sixty-one-minute feature was based on the Ma Barker case and cast Broadway veteran Blanche Yurka in the title role as the leader of a clan of homicidal sons (Paul Kelly, Richard Denning, and Jack Carson—William Henry was the good son) who go on a robbery spree which nets them some $400,000. Their crimes are to no avail, however, as they are eventually captured by G-Man Ralph Bellamy. Ryan was merely cast as an office worker for agent Bellamy and had one scene, although he could be spotted standing behind Bellamy when he captured Yurka and her cohorts. Of this unsung film, Howard Barnes (*New York Herald-Tribune*) would report, "At this late date it is difficult for the screen to work a new angle on the Federals-and-gunmen theme."

After two speaking roles on celluloid, Paramount then put Ryan into Cecil B. DeMille's epic *Northwest Mounted Police* (1940), in which he had not a word to utter in the 125 minutes of color screen fare. In a huge cast he was surprisingly given seventeenth billing as a character named Constable Dumont, one of the Mounties in this expansive account of Texas Ranger Gary Cooper searching for renegade killer George Bancroft in the great north, and becoming involved with Indians-versus-British tactics, aristocratic Madeleine Carroll and fiery half-breed Paulette Goddard. As Howard Barnes (*New York Herald-Tribune*) assessed it, "You've got to see the mounties in Technicolor's brightest red, fighting their way out of a half-breed ambush, or keeping the Indians from revolting, to realize how much sheer spectacle can amount to in terms of screen melodrama." The film did serve overlooked Ryan with his first color film appearance as well as his initial screen role as a Mountie, a part he would do again in 1961 in *The Canadians* (Twentieth Century-Fox), this time as a star.

Robert's final film under his Paramount contract, *The Texas Rangers Ride Again,* was issued in January, 1941, and again he worked with director James Hogan. He had only an unbilled bit in this lower-case entry that starred John Howard, Ellen Drew, Akim Tamiroff, and May Robson (as the elderly rancher bothered by cattle rustlers). By the time this unremarkable entry was issued, Paramount had decided not to pick up Ryan's contract option.

Rationalizing that if he could not make a go of his acting career on the screen, then perhaps the stage was his true medium, Robert and his wife went across country to the East Coast hoping to find jobs in the then blooming summer stock field. During the warm months of 1940 they worked in the straw hat circuit in Arden, Delaware, before settling down at the Mill Playhouse in Roslyn, Long Island, where they worked for two dollars a week plus room and board. At the time, Ryan was still receiving tiny dividends from his oil well investment, which, however, soon ran dry. The couple often had to subsist on the additional income earned by Jessica as a fashion model. The high spot of the summer occurred when Robert was hired to play the rugged looking big fellow in Luise Rainer's edition of *A Kiss for Cinderella* at the Cape Playhouse in Dennis, Massachusetts.

Viennese Oscar-winner Miss Rainer, whom Robert later described as "everything a temperamental European actress is supposed to be," apparently took a liking to the young actor because she suggested him for a small role in her ex-husband's (Clifford Odets) new play, *Clash by Night,* which was about to be produced on Broadway by Billy Rose with Tallulah Bankhead starring. Both Odets and Miss Bankhead saw Robert in *A Kiss for Cinderella* when the Rainer production moved to Maplewood, New Jersey. Always a good judge of masculine presence, Tallulah agreed to the casting of Ryan in the forthcoming show.

After rather labored tryouts in Detroit and Philadelphia, *Clash by Night* stumbled into Manhattan on Monday, December 29, 1941, at New York's Belasco Theatre. In rather stark terms the play told of a Staten Island girl (Bankhead) who marries a slow thinking man (Lee J. Cobb) and soon begins carrying on with a psychotic (Joseph Schildkraut). The character portrayed by Schildkraut was also sought by a nice young girl (Katherine Locke) who, in turn, is loved by Joe W. Doyle (Ryan). Robert's main speech occurs in the third act when he proposes marriage to Locke. Brooks Atkinson, in the *New York Times,* thought his acting was "manly and clear-headed." Another critic judged him "a handsome, capable performer," while Arthur Pollack (*Brooklyn Daily Eagle*) reported that Ryan "is the only one in the play who seems to know what it really is." There were some dissenting votes regarding Ryan's appearance, with one aisle sitter insisting that Robert was the weakest link in the production.

"I was so full of myself then, I was impossible," Ryan later recalled. "I remember going into Tallulah's dressing room—*swaggering* might be a better description—and demanding to know how long it was going to take before I was a really great actor. I expected her to say a year or so. But instead she said very quietly, 'In 15 or 20 years you may be a good actor, Bob—if you're lucky.' She was right."

Unfortunately for Miss Bankhead, not to mention the cast or backers, who was hoping for another success to follow her work in *The Little Foxes, Clash by Night* did little more for her than reestablish her sex appeal. Due to poor boxoffice response and her on-again-off-again ailments, the show folded after only forty-nine performances.

For Ryan, *Clash by Night* was a positive venture. It brought him another film contract, because producer Pare Lorentz saw him during the show's brief run and offered him a six-hundred-dollar-a-week agreement to work at RKO Radio. He wanted Robert to star in a production to be called *Name, Age and Occupation,* in which Frances Dee and Erford Gage had already been cast.

Besides leading Ryan to a studio contract, *Clash by Night* had another effect on the actor's life. According to some circles, because of his association with leftist Clifford Odets, he came into direct contact with the playwright's Marxist interpretation of the Depression. Writing about Ryan in *Films in Review* in 1968, Jeanne Stein commented obliquely, "Those who know Ryan better say he knew the Depression with a realism Odets did not possess."

Arriving back in Hollywood in 1942, Ryan found his RKO debut in *Name, Age and Occupation* had been canceled with America's entrance into World War II. The project, which was supposed to be Lorentz' first non-documentary, was to have starred Robert as a young man involved in the trials and tribulations of the Depression.

RKO was then adjusting itself to the debacle of having Orson Welles and his Mercury Players on their payroll, and the studio was not very excited about their new contractee, a man with some film bits and a Broadway flop to his credits. With such unmonumental credentials to go on, the studio grudgingly gave him sixth billing as Joe Connor, a student in a bombardier school, in a film aptly titled *Bombardier* (1943). It was to be the first of six films for the actor in 1943.

Produced by Robert Fellows and directed by Richard Wallace from John Twist's screenplay, *Bombardier* was made at the suggestion of the Air Force, and it gained for RKO needed concessions regarding restricted building materials. A "cheap, fictitious film" (*New York Times*), it starred Pat O'Brien (also recently signed by RKO) as Colonel Paddy Ryan, the man who perfected the modern bombsight. The regulation plot had him constantly at odds with rival Randolph Scott, who thought more highly of pilots than bombardiers. Anne Shirley had the leading lady spot as the girl friend of soldier Walter Reed, with Eddie Albert (her real-life beau) as her younger brother killed in combat. Before the ninety-nine-minute plot spins dry, Scott meets his demise in a raid over Japan that is led by O'Brien. On the whole, *Bombardier* did little for anyone, especially Ryan.

Next, Ryan popped up in *The Sky's The Limit* (RKO, 1943), which starred Fred Astaire as a war-hero Flying Tiger on an eight-day leave in Manhattan. Doing the town in civilian garb he meets and falls in love with Joan Leslie who, not knowing he is a flyer, wants him to get a job. Robert was on tap as Reg, the fourth-billed Air Force buddy of Astaire. No one in the cast had very good material to work with, and, despite the Harold Arlen score, it remained a minor musical.

Behind the Rising Sun (RKO, 1943) reunited Ryan with director Edward Dmytryk, and again for the director, as in *Golden Gloves,* he played a boxer. Based on the inflammatory book by James R. Young, the film focused on Tom Neal as a Cornell University-educated Japanese who returns home to become engrossed in the Axis war machine. Neal goes so overboard in his military enthusiasm that his publisher father (J. Carrol Naish) feels obliged to commit hara-kiri. Eventually, Neal is shot down during a raid. Ryan was cast as Lefty, an American boxer in Japan who engages in a well-staged, but brutal, fight with a jujitsu artist (Mike Mazurki).

Variety called the film a "good drama of inside information on the Japanese indoctrination and thinking." For a change, in this drama Robert was noticed by critics. The *Brooklyn Daily Eagle* noted Ryan as one of "the capable members of the cast."

Sometimes it is the smaller films, the ones that almost sneak into distribution and often fail to garner the attention of major critics, which offer the most insight into the development of a star in the making. Such was the case with Ryan and *Gangway for Tomorrow* (RKO, 1943). Written by Arch Oboler from Aldar Laszlo's story, this sixty-nine-minute economy offering centered around five persons (Margo, John Carradine, Robert, Amelita Ward, and James Bell) who work in a defense plant and are driven to work daily by a minor executive. The latter invites them to Sunday dinner, hoping to learn about their individual backgrounds. Ryan is Joe Dunham, a retired race driver who had smashed up his car in the big race. In the course of his scenes he demonstrated the quiet resourcefulness that would become such a firm part of the Robert Ryan acting method.

Following this assignment Robert was in *The Iron Major* (RKO, 1943), directed by Ray Enright, and he was third-billed behind Pat O'Brien and Ruth Warrick. The film told the supposedly true story of Major Frank Cavanaugh, the football coach of Dartmouth, Boston College, and Fordham who became a hero in World War I and died from war injuries in 1933. RKO executives had two things clearly in mind when they tackled this project: one, O'Brien had scored heavily with *Knute Rockne— All American* (Warner Bros., 1940) and RKO hoped to take advantage of casting O'Brien in a similar role, and, two, the film's scripters were ordered to emphasize the parallels between Cavanaugh's World War I heroics and those of soldiers in the Second World War. Warrick was cast as O'Brien's patient, sweet wife, and Robert was impressive as Father Donovan of Notre Dame, the only priest in Cavanaugh's colorful life. Obviously made in a patriotic fervor, *The Iron Major* went astray along

With Ginger Rogers in *Tender Comrade* (RKO, 1943)

the way. The *New York Times* referred to it as "a quite bad picture in its own right."

If none of Robert's RKO efforts to this date had won him plaudits from the critics or the public, he had attracted the attention of the lot's number one female star, Ginger Rogers. It was she who insisted that he play the role of her husband in one of the all-time tearjerkers of World War II, *Tender Comrade* (RKO, 1943). The film would mark Ryan's first lead in an A-budgeted production.

Tender Comrade was directed by. Edward Dmytryk, who Ryan always said "brought him luck." In maudlin terms the film told of four girls (Rogers, Ruth Hussey, Patricia Collinge, and Kim Hunter) who work in a defense plant and who band together to share a house and hire a maid, refugee Mady Christians. The girls then relate their individual stories—shown in flashbacks—with Rogers relating how she wed Ryan who goes off to war after they have had only one night together as man and wife. She later has his baby but then learns he has been killed in combat. The film concludes in a sticky, lachrymose scene with a teary Rogers telling her infant son that his father died fighting for freedom.

The production of *Tender Comrade* was plagued with several problems. An alternative ending, with Ginger bravely going to work after hearing of her hubby's demise, was shot but not used. Then Ginger, prompted by her ever-present mama, Lela, demanded and won her point that the front office have a number of lines of Dalton Trumbo's anti-American dialogue removed from her character's speeches (some were transposed for other players to mouth). Years later, congressional probers would point to this film as an example of Reds at work in Hollywood, especially in the light of both Dmytryk's and Trumbo's political backgrounds.

Despite all these behind-the-scenes hassles, *Tender Comrade* did prove to have a winning way at the boxoffice, thanks largely to Ginger's name on the marquee. *Time* Magazine, no champion of schmaltz of any variety, labeled the film a "kind of *Little Women* of World War II," while the *Brooklyn Daily Eagle* asserted that this picture "has garnered some of the finest corn that was ever written." However, Robert did attract some positive critical notices. Leo Mishkin *(New York Morning Telegram)* evaluated, "Robert Ryan, a heretofore secondary player, is elevated to the male lead for Miss Rogers in the role of her husband, turning in a quiet, sure job of work that will have him long remembered."

Marine Raiders (RKO, 1944) was just what the title promised, another service action feature. Ryan was Captain Dan Craig, a marine paratrooper in Australia recuperating from jungle fighting. He meets and falls in love with Ruth Hussey. The romance is interrupted when he is called back to the United States to teach others the techniques of tropical warfare. Returning to the war in Southeast Asia, however, he stops off in Australia where he and languid-eyed Hussey renew their love affair. The *New York Times* said, "Robert Ryan is particularly well cast as the case-hardened Paramarine." Top-billed Pat O'Brien was on hand as Ryan's commanding officer, and it had been O'Brien who insisted that the studio give Ryan equal billing with him.

Realizing he would soon be drafted, Ryan joined the Marine Corps in 1943. He worked as drill instructor at Camp Pendleton until he was discharged late in 1945 to resume his film career. At the Separation Center where he was being mustered out of the service, Robert met novelist Richard Brooks, who had served as a Marine combat-cameraman during the war. Brooks also told Ryan about a book he had written. The tome was *The Brick Foxhole*, which told of three soldiers who murder a homosexual. Ryan read the novel and told Brooks he would like to play the part of

With Joan Bennett in *The Woman on the Beach* (RKO, 1947)

the leader of the murderous trio if the project ever reached the screen. Brooks agreed.

Robert returned to work at RKO in 1946, finding himself in quite a different career bracket than when he had entered military service. Like fellow contract player Robert Mitchum, Ryan would enter the armed forces with only a few large roles to his credit, yet upon his military discharge he would reappear at the studio as a star. In the next six years, the period of Ryan's remaining tenure at RKO, he would develop into a genuine boxoffice figure.

Robert's first post-war feature, *Trail Street,* was released by RKO in the spring of 1947. Directed by Ray Enright, who had helmed him in *The Iron Major,* this Western was based on William Corcoran's novel, *Golden Horizon.* Set in Liberal, Kansas, it dealt with Bat Masterson (Randolph Scott), who teams with land agent Allen Harper (Ryan) to combat rustlers plaguing the local farmers. Ryan was even allowed a love interest in this shoot-'em-up film, a love affair with local girl Madge Meredith. Leading lady Anne Jeffreys had an eye on Scott, and George "Gabby" Hayes was present to provide comedy relief. *Variety* justifiably labeled the film as "rough, tough westerned entertainment." In his way, Robert proved that he was a man with whom to reckon on the range as much as he had been in the fight ring in past films.

If the action-packed *Trail Street* was one step forward in his career, *The Woman on the Beach* (RKO, 1947) was the reverse. French refugee Jean Renoir was still marking time in Hollywood until he could return home. He directed this bizarre concoction derived from Michael Wilson's novel, *None So Blind.* Ryan was unhappily cast as a coast guardsman with mental problems who falls in love with the fetching, but decidedly evil wife (Joan Bennett) of a blind and aging painter (Charles Bickford). This modern siren wants her spouse murdered and hopes Robert will be up to the

541

task. Eventually, Ryan escapes her clutches and returns to marry his sensible fiancée (Nan Leslie). The film may have been a commercial nonentity, but it was a rewarding experience for co-star Ryan. He considered director Renoir "a dear friend" and "one of the most remarkable men I've ever met. Working with him opened my eyes to aspects of character that were subtler than those I was accustomed to."

By this point, Dore Schary was an important fixture at RKO. He had approved the filming of Richard Brooks' novel, *The Brick Foxhole.* To assuage the censors and to appease Schary's dedications to causes, the homosexual victim was changed to a Jew, thus converting the film into an attack on anti-Semitism. The project was retitled *Crossfire* (RKO, 1947) and brought Ryan his greatest screen acclaim, although it would forever typecast him as a psychotic sort. The film reunited Robert with director Edward Dmytryk for the fourth time. To insure the anti-Semitism attack gambit would have the proper boxoffice influence, the film was rushed into release before *Gentleman's Agreement* (Twentieth Century-Fox, 1947), the latter a more viable exposé of the subject.

In *Crossfire,* five soldiers are under investigation for the murder of Joseph Samuels (Sam Levene). They include the commanding officer (Robert Mitchum, highbilled for box-office purposes but in a smallish role) and braggart Monty Montgomery (Ryan), the latter proving to be the uneducated, Jewish-hating soldier who killed Samuels. For dramatic balance there was Robert Young as the patient, sensitive district attorney assigned to this vile case, and Gloria Grahame as a tawdry girl of the streets. *Crossfire* was well promoted and made money as well as being named to the National Board of Review's list of the top ten films of the year.

For Ryan, the film solidified his stardom (the *New York Times* called him "frighteningly real") but it also cast him in the mold of screen characters who are

With Robert Mitchum and Robert Young in *Crossfire* (RKO, 1947)

mentally unhinged. In his later years, the star acknowledged his indebtedness to *Crossfire* but still wished he had never agreed to being cast in the feature. He was never able to comprehend "the bone-chilling evil I presumably projected," and he felt, or so he insisted, that the film was just a good mystery instead of a social and moral critique.

Crossfire, along with *Tender Comrade,* came under heavy fire from the House Un-American Activities Committee hearings a few years later. In fact, in 1969, Ryan said *Crossfire* "helped trigger the McCarthy era." Both director Dmytryk (who later repudiated Communism) and producer Adrian Scott were named as members of the Hollywood Ten. "How did I escape? Because I hadn't joined anything—or even thought about much. I was too busy trying to be a movie star. But during the blacklisting days I started asking myself some questions."[3]

Robert, who had become a father (Timothy, born on April 13, 1946), had something else to boast of in his early-post-World War II days. In the 1947 Oscar sweepstakes he was nominated for a Best Supporting Actor's Award. He lost, however, to Edmund Gwenn of *Miracle on Thirty-Fourth Street* (Twentieth Century-Fox).

The villainous angle of Robert's movie career was not immediately evident, as his first 1948 film was a spy melodrama, *Berlin Express* (RKO), directed by Jacques Tourneur. Filmed mostly in Europe, with much good footage of bombed-out Frankfurt and Berlin, this espionage entry was about several passengers on the train of the title, going from Paris to Berlin. During the trip a government officer is murdered. Ryan was cast as U.S. agricultural expert Robert Lindley who is a prime suspect, along with anti-Nazi Perrot (Charles Korvin) and his secretary (Merle Oberon). Eventually, Robert helps the local police locate a kidnapped world peace leader (Paul Lukas) who was also one of the passengers on the train. Of this stark potboiler, the *New York Herald-Tribune* offered, "The whole of the picture is much better than the sum of its parts."

In the summer of 1948, Ryan was reunited with Randolph Scott, Anne Jeffreys, George "Gabby" Hayes, and director Ray Enright, all of whom had been in *Trail Street,* for a new sagebrush effort, *Return of the Bad Men* (RKO). "Ten times the thrills of *Badman's Territory* [RKO, 1946] . . . when the bloodiest band in history, led by the angel-faced gun-girl of the Badlands, plunder and blast frontier Oklahoma!" Such ran the ads for this amalgam account of the who's who of desperadoes. Set in Oklahoma during the 1889 land rush, Robert appeared as the colorful Sundance Kid, a vicious killer, who is at odds with the one-time retired sheriff (Randolph Scott). Miss Jeffreys volleyed forth as the gun-toting gunslinger's daughter, with Jacqueline White as the heroine's counterpart. Said the *New York Times,* "Robert Ryan has managed to come through unscathed with a cool, expert performance as a prairie sadist."

In 1948, the Ryans, who were now occupying a rambling Spanish style home at 301 North Carolwood Drive in Holmby Hills, became the parents of a second child, son Cheyney. Also during this year, Robert appeared in two other features.

He was in *Act of Violence* (1948) on loan-out to MGM. Directed by Fred Zinne-

[3]On one occasion, Ryan mused, "When [Senator Joseph] McCarthy started, I expected to be a target simply because I was involved in things he was throwing rocks at. I never was a target. Now, looking back, I suspect my Irish name, my being a Catholic and an ex-Marine sort of softened the blow." On January 21, 1964, when Robert was delivering a speech to the student body at Dartmouth College, he denounced the House Un-American Activities Committee and said, "I'm not a Communist, or a historian, but only trying to tell you that my own experiences and involvement lead me to think the way I do."

With Fritz Kortner and Charles Korvin in *Berlin Express* (RKO, 1948)

With Dean Stockwell in *The Boy with Green Hair* (RKO, 1948)

mann from a story by Collier Young, the feature offered Robert as Joe Parkson, a World War II veteran. He is a limping, whining neurotic who sets out to "get even" with his former officer (Van Heflin) who, he believes, betrayed him during the war. "It is strong meat for the heavy drama addicts, tellingly produced and played to develop tight excitement," said *Variety*. The well-wrought feature is essentially a cat-and-mouse chase through a California town but it contains a twist ending with Heflin turning out to be the bad guy. Janet Leigh was present as Heflin's worried wife, and Mary Astor offered a theatrical but very effective appearance as an aging prostitute to whom Heflin confides his problems. Underrated Phyllis Thaxter was seen as Ryan's girl. Within this "terrifyingly realistic and almost unbearably tense" (*Cue* Magazine) thriller, Ryan was rated by the *New York Times* as being "infernally taut."

Issued at about the same time as *Act of Violence* was *The Boy with Green Hair* (RKO, 1948) which had a long and varied production history. Basically an anti-war film, it was originally budgeted at nearly $900,000 and was director Joseph Losey's first feature film assignment. When Adrian Scott resigned as the film's producer after being named a member of the Hollywood Ten, Dore Schary took over the production. Then Howard Hughes acquired RKO Radio Pictures, and one of the orders of his new regime was that certain scenes within *The Boy with the Green Hair* be reshot to eliminate overly obvious sequences of pacificism and possible Red tints.

This mishmash, of which no one was proud, had Ryan second-billed as Dr. Evans, who appears briefly at the beginning and end of this allegory. The substance of the picture deals with a young boy (Dean Stockwell), a wartime refugee, who lives with his grandfather (Pat O'Brien) and who awakes one morning to find his hair has turned green. The youth tells his story to police psychiatrist Ryan. It seems that after his parents died in an air raid, and his hair had turned green, the boy was ostracized by his peers and ran away into a woods where he had visions of orphaned children. These European youths tell him his hair has turned green to symbolize their plight. When his hair is later shaved off, Stockwell tells Ryan he hopes it will grow back green and that he will be able to fight against war when he is an adult. In this "bright notion gone wrong" (*New York Times*), Ryan was relegated to the sidelines, a situation which proved to have in it a blessing in this instance.

No one could deny that Ryan was not having his share of arty, offbeat film assignments. *Caught* (MGM, 1949) was no exception. Directed by Max Ophuls, it was adapted by Arthur Laurents from Libbie Block's novel. Producer Wolfgang Reinhardt did not have to use much imagination to cast Robert as the psychotic millionaire who, to spite his psychiatrist, weds a poor girl (Barbara Bel Geddes) and proceeds to make her life miserable. Eventually, the girl falls in love with a hard-working doctor (James Mason), but Ryan will not free her to marry the man. A quirk of fate eventually has Robert's Smith Ohlrig succumbing to a fatal heart attack. Few disagree with *Cue* Magazine, which determined that Ryan "plays with tremendous power the role of the Napoleonic multi-millionaire with a demonical hatred of the wife who hooked him." *Caught,* one of the last productions of the defunct Enterprises Studios, failed to gain a foothold with the public. *Time* reasoned, "*Caught's* real shocker lies in its callous assumption that paranoia is a specific form of villainy to be exploited at the box office."

In Ryan's next film that year, *The Set-Up,* (RKO, 1949), he was in the top-billed role of Stoker Thompson; it proved to be his favorite film role. Directed by Robert Wise, the picture cast Robert as a former heavyweight boxing contender who is now thirty-five-years-old and over the hill.[4] But the pugilist believes he still has enough

[4]In an interview with Rui Nogueira *(Focus on Film,* #12, 1972), Wise said, about *The Set-Up,* "I thought *The Set-Up* was such a marvelous concept and look at the boxing game. For once it

With Barbara Bel Geddes in *Caught* (MGM, 1949)

spunk left to win the title. His loyal wife (Audrey Totter) wants him to quit the ring, but he is pushed on by his money-grubbing manager (George Tobias), who uses him for what small purses he can still command. The crux of the seventy-two-minute film has Tobias promising a hoodlum (Alan Baxter) that Ryan will take a dive against an up-and-coming opponent. But the aging fighter, in the dark about the set up, pulls an upset and kayoes the younger man. As a result of his win, the fighter is beaten by gangsters, and one hand is mangled so he will never be able to fight again.

Robert's portrayal of the has-been fighter was a deft piece of acting. His boxing scenes were well-staged, heightened by Director Wise who frequently cut to the arena crowd watching the punching, to make a film comment on the type of persons who come to small, sleazy arenas to watch second-raters do battle for a few dollars.

The star always loved the film. "My favorite movie is *The Set-Up,* about a third-rate boxer—it's the best picture about boxing that was ever made."

The *New York Times* called the movie "a sizzling melodrama." There was also a lot of sizzling action behind the scenes on this feature. RKO brought suit against the producers of the film *Champion* (United Artists, 1949) because the original title of that Kirk Douglas-starring entry was *The Set-Up,* which RKO's management insisted infringed upon the Ryan production.[5] In July, 1950, the two companies reached an out-of-court agreement, with the RKO suit being dismissed.

After the release of *The Set-Up* in March, 1949, Ryan was technically off the screen for fourteen months, since his next film, *The Woman on Pier 13,* was a revamped and retitled issue of the project *I Married a Communist* (RKO, 1949). This Robert Stevenson-directed melodrama was the actor's first financial failure for RKO. In it, he was cast as an executive in a San Francisco waterfront shipping company who is being blackmailed by Communists who wish to instigate a labor strike. Years before, Ryan's Brad Collins had been led into the Communist fold by

wasn't Madison Square Garden, it wasn't the championship bout, it was the dirty, nitty-gritty day-in-day-out grind of the tank-town fighter, and that interested me very much. It was a look at the seaminess of the fight game and the cheapness of it, the dirtiness, the gambling involved in the whole thing. The other thing that obviously I liked very much was that Robert Ryan had been a fighter himself. He knew how to box and handle himself. Usually the good guys win and the bad guys lose—in *The Set-Up* the hero loses but in a sense he wins because he's going to give up boxing which he should have done anyway. He will face up to the reality which his wife already understands."

[5]In *Hollywood in the Forties* (1968), authors Charles Higham and Joel Greenberg discuss the trio of boxing films that are, in their way, landmarks of the forties' cinema. "In *The Set-Up* (1949) and to a lesser extent in *Champion* (1949) and *Body and Soul* [United Artists] (1947) boxing was cleverly exploited as a theme. Robert Wise's *The Set-Up* was the most impressive film of the three. . . . The boxing scenes have a harshness, a sure feeling for cruelty and mob hysteria, that have seldom been surpassed. . . . The carefully orchestrated use of natural sound and of speech is a notable feature, and Milton Krasner's photography, flashy and sombre, creates a massive canvas of this inferno, moving out only to take in the scarcely less claustrophobic atmosphere of cafes, streets filled with searching people and neons late at night.

"Less concentrated—the action of *The Set-Up* carefully preserves the unities—*Champion,* directed by Mark Robson, suffers from a rather too involved and flash-back ridden script. Moreover, for the agony and despair of Robert Ryan's great performance, Kirk Douglas substitutes a cold implacability. . . . And *Body and Soul,* despite John Garfield's intensity as another boxer, is crippled by Robert Rossen's stiff and artificially posy handling, the kitschy quality of the central love affair between Garfield and Lilli Palmer; the film's technical accomplishment and the mannered, quasi-idiomatic script of Abraham Polonsky have a fatal softness at the centre."

With Audrey Totter in *The Set-Up* (RKO, 1949)

pretty Christine (Janis Carter), but during the war he forgot the cause and took up with Nan Collins (Laraine Day), having changed his name and prepared to begin a new life. Jealous, however, Christine plots her revenge and alerts the Reds to his whereabouts. At the finale, Ryan's Brad is killed as a retribution for his past. As with *I Married a Communist,* the episodic action entry had a brief release, but then the Howard Hughes-RKO regime withdrew it, demanding extensive cuts and alterations to lessen the impact of the film's intended message. In its vitiated form it dragged into release in mid-1950s, a deficit in all capacities.

Even worse than *The Woman on Pier 13* was Ryan's second 1950 release, *The Secret Fury.* Helmed by fledgling director and sometime actor Mel Ferrer, this weak melodrama found Ryan as David, an architect who is engaged to accomplished pianist Ellen (Claudette Colbert). It develops that his ultimate purpose is to drive the pretty matron mad. On their wedding day he accuses her of being legally wed to another man and when that individual is murdered she ends up being committed to a mental institution. Ellen must endure a lengthy, arduous court battle before she is finally vindicated and David's evil is disclosed to the public. Bosley Crowther (*New York Times*) called the unimaginative venture "cheap and lurid twaddle." The one redeeming factor of this presentation was that it offered the very professional Jane Cowl in a rare latter day screen appearance.

One project that Robert did not make at RKO was *The Johnny Broderick Story,* which would have dealt with the life of a retired New York City cop. Instead, he was encased in another twisted woman's story, this time *Born to Be Bad* (RKO, 1950). Nicholas Ray indulged his penchant for showcasing neurotic, erotic femininity in this study of Joan Fontaine's Cristabel, a contemporary vamp. The young lady steals the wealthy Curtis (Zachary Scott) away from sweet Donna (Joan Leslie) and weds him, even though she longs for the writer Nick (Ryan). Later, she dabbles in an

With Richard Rober and Thomas Gomez in *The Woman on Pier 13* (RKO, 1949)

With Clifford Brooke, Paul Kelly, Claudette Colbert, and Jane Cowl in *The Secret Fury* (RKO, 1950)

affair with Ryan's Nick, who insists that she divorce Curtis. She refuses, and by the finale she has lost both men. The film did little for Ryan's stagnating career, although it did cast him in his first-loved profession, that of a journalist.

After *Born to Be Bad,* Robert was thrown back into the film genre he hated most, Westerns. In the Technicolor epic, *Best of the Badmen* (RKO, 1951) Ryan played Jeff Clanton, a Union officer who takes the Younger Brothers (Jack Buetel and Bruce Cabot), the Ringo Kid (John Archer), and Jesse James (Lawrence Tierney) into protective custody and then is framed on a murder charge by a corrupt detective (Robert Preston). Ryan's Clanton then escapes from jail and joins the outlaw gang, but a girl, Lily (Claire Trevor), the wife of Preston's detective, persuades him to give up the lawless life, and together they gather sufficient evidence against the crooked detective. As had become typical of dependable Robert, he lived up to all the requirements of the outdoor role.

A much more viable project was *Flying Leathernecks* (RKO, 1951), which featured the studio's pride and joy, John "Money-Earner" Wayne. The film was Ryan's second teaming with director Nicholas Ray, the latter a favorite with the Howard Hughes regime. The color feature was a 102-minute essay into the first rule of warfare: discipline. Wayne portrayed a major who is disliked by his men as he leads a Marine fighter squadron in the South Pacific of World War II. The major is also disliked by his fellow officer, Captain Carl Griffin (Ryan), for his overly strict and rigid orders. When the men go into actual combat, however, they soon learn that what their major taught them was necessary in order to stay alive. The action scenes more than compensated for the rather production-line romantic interludes and the stereotyped array of military men. Not to be overlooked was the effectiveness with which Ryan matched Wayne in a good example of magnetic screen chemistry.

With Joan Fontaine in *Born to Be Bad* (RKO, 1950)

Ryan's next 1951 release, *The Racket* (RKO), re-teamed the actor with Robert Mitchum, both of whom had been in *Crossfire*. This time, however, it was burly Mitchum who had the decidedly larger part, with Ryan co-starred as a hoodlum. It was all a remake of executive producer Howard Hughes' 1928 silent film of the same title which the eccentric billionaire had produced and Lewis Milestone had directed for Paramount, with Thomas Meighan, Marie Prevost, and Louis Wolheim, the featured stars.

The new version was also derived from Bartlett Cormack's sensational 1927 play, which had been an exposé of the rackets. The melodrama, churned out in low-key fifties style, told of political corruption in a big city, with Mitchum as an honest policeman who refuses to take bribes from corrupt politician Ray Collins and hoodlum leader Ryan. The film focuses on the club where singer Lizabeth Scott falls in love with reporter Robert Hutton. In the film's torpid final scene, crime kingpin Ryan is arrested by his boyhood pal, Mitchum. (Shades of MGM's 1934 entry, *Manhattan Melodrama*.) The *New York Times* summed up this rather unpropitious entry with, "As for the film's observations on crooks and politics they are so generalized and familiar that this is just a case of one more time around." It would be one of the peculiarities of Hollywood—despite its penchant for typecasting performers —that Robert, who so ably deported himself as an underworld figure here, would so rarely be cast in the mobster mold after that film.

Robert's third film for director Nicholas Ray, *On Dangerous Ground* (RKO, 1951), had actually been completed in May, 1950. Due to the vagaries of the Hughes' regime, it did not see release for eighteen months. In it, Ryan was the hard-nosed, but honest cop, Jim Wilson who is ordered out of the big city to take over the investigation of the murder of a mentally retarded girl in the country. (Wilson's

551

superiors hope the change of scenery will reduce his neurotic anxieties about hating lawbreakers.) There, Ryan's Jim Wilson not only finds the culprit but is humanized by the murdered girl's blind sister (played by Ida Lupino), and learns that hate is a disease. Good photography contrasted the shabbiness of the city compared with the clean, clear country life. The *New York Times*' Bosley Crowther noted that, although "the story is a shallow, uneven affair, Robert Ryan does a straight coldeyed, stout muscled job."

There are cycles to almost everyone's life, but it must have caused Ryan some pause when he was cast in the film version of *Clash by Night* (RKO, 1952), not in the role he had created on Broadway (that was now played by the younger Keith Andes), but as Earl Pfeiffer, the part once interpreted on the stage by Joseph Schildkraut.

The scene of this Clifford Odets' melodrama was changed from Staten Island to a West Coast fishing village. Barbara Stanwyck was cast as Mae, a cynical woman who returns to her hometown after being away for several years. Her younger brother, Joe (Andes), is not pleased with her return, fearing that she will have an adverse influence on his girl Peggy (Marilyn Monroe), who works in a local fish cannery. Mae meets and marries Jerry (Paul Douglas), a dense fishing boat captain, and they have a child. But earthy Mae is a restless soul. "If I loved a man again I could bear anything. . . . He could have my teeth for watch fobs." Movie theatre projectionist Earl Pfeiffer (Ryan), a violent sort, takes Mae's fancy. When Mae and Pfeiffer have an affair, Jerry's uncle (J. Carrol Naish) tries to tell the boat captain about the situation, but he refuses to listen. Eventually, Mae taunts Jerry with the truth and he seeks out Ryan's Pfeiffer, planning to kill him. Somehow, Mae stops him. Then, Pfeiffer tries to persuade her to leave Jerry and her baby but she refuses. She

With Charles Kemper and Anthony Ross in *On Dangerous Ground* (RKO, 1951)

With Paul Douglas and Barbara Stanwyck in *Clash by Night* (RKO, 1952)

realizes now that she loves her family and returns to Jerry, begging his forgiveness, which he gives her freely.

As interpreted by director Fritz Lang, *Clash by Night* seethes with offbeat tensions that heighten the melodrama. The crisp dialogue accentuates the passions building within these ordinary persons. Ryan's Earl Pfeiffer is a man not yet middle-aged, but already defeated by life. Considering the fiery nature of his role, even in contrast to the smoldering characterizations offered by Stanwyck and Douglas, it is to Ryan's consummate credit that he made his part so believable. Bosley Crowther (*New York Times*) confirmed, "As the lover, Robert Ryan is natural in his depiction of a man groping for a way out of a lonely existence." By his performance in *Clash by Night,* tough guy Robert proved that he had another very vulnerable side to his screen persona: on the screen he could portray a man who is human and craving some substantiation of purpose in his life. It was an extension of the personality at which he had hinted in *Tender Comrade* and expanded upon in the closing sections of *On Dangerous Ground.*

From a production point of view, *Clash by Night* had several unique factors. It was produced by Harriet Parsons, daughter of the inestimable gossip columnist Louella. More important, for the sake of the film's potential revenue, it offered Marilyn Monroe in her first major dramatic screen role.

Next, Robert was reunited with Ida Lupino for another neurotic merry-go-round adventure. This time, he was cast as the half-crazed handyman in *Beware My Lovely* (RKO, 1952), which Miss Lupino's ex-husband, Collier Young, produced and which Harry Horner directed. With a simplistic plotline, the film concerns a lonely widow (Lupino) who hires a handyman (Robert) to look after her large house. The man's character develops strange twists: one minute he is the ultimate in kindness, the next he is bizarre. Soon, she realizes that he is bent on killing her. With its low-key

553

but brooding tensions, *Beware My Lovely* had a good deal of entertainment value to offer, but neither the critics nor the public were impressed with the economy production values. Regarding Ryan's appearance, Bosley Crowther *(New York Times)* weighed, "As the psychopath, Robert Ryan does a competent, conventional 'menace' job, running through all the exercises of a tabloid-type fiend on the loose."

Beware My Lovely was not exactly a propitious swan song for Ryan's tenure at RKO. In the television-oriented fifties, Hughes was losing interest in theatrical film production and distribution, and saw no reason not to cut back on his contract stable. Robert Mitchum and Jane Russell were still on the payroll, along with a few other players, including Vincent Price and William Bendix, but commodities such as Robert Ryan were considered dispensable. From all evidence, the always self-sufficient Robert did not seem to mind the termination of his contract.

Not doubting his abilities to survive on the freelance market (after all, he was not just another "pretty face")[6] Ryan faced the future with a good deal of confidence.

His third child Liza was born in 1952, and during that same year he continued his outside activities in the community. As he would reflect in 1963, "My marriage . . . had a lot to do with my changing ideas. My wife is a Quaker. They're very sincere and persuasive people. Then too, even though I was just a Marine drill instructor during the war, I began to feel that war was an insane way out." Following through on his convictions, Robert became involved with the Hollywood Ten American Veterans Committee and the American Friends Service Committee, participated in the early UN movement, later joining the American Civil Liberties group (as a militant dove), and at one time becoming president of the Southern California Branch of the United World Federalists.

Now away from RKO, Ryan went to Universal, where he appeared in *Horizons West* (1952), the first of two films he would do with director Budd Boetticher. This Technicolor action tale gave Robert top billing as Dan Hammond, the psychotic brother of Neal Hammond (Rock Hudson, then the fair haired young hope of the studio). Both men had just returned from the Civil War; with Hudson's Neal becomes a rancher while Ryan's Dan starts a gang of cattle rustlers, composed of service veterans. Dan becomes enamored of Lorna Hardin (Julia Adams), who stimulates his vengefulness and eventually he is killed (with his boots on). For Robert, *Horizons West* was just another job. Unlike many other aging leading men, he was not particularly grateful for the sagebrush genre simply because it offered him steady employment.[7]

Robert remained at Universal to star in *City Beneath the Sea* (1953), a color deep-sea epic, which was directed by Boetticher from Harry F. Reisberg's novel, *Port Royal, the Ghost City Beneath the Sea.* Highlighted by effective underwater photography, the film was shot on location in the West Indies, with Ryan and Anthony

[6]In an interview with *Films and Filming* (March, 1971) Ryan discussed his "long, seamy face": "Generally, I'm fated to work in faraway, desolate places. As I said to Cary Grant one time—I told him how much I envied him because as the suave, charming, gifted man he is, he makes all his pictures in places like Monte Carlo, London, Paris, the French Riviera, and I make mine in deserts with a dirty shirt and a two day growth of beard and bad food. But that's an act of birth. As I said, I get all the worst locations because of the way I look."

[7]In 1971, Ryan admitted, "There's a whole body of Americans, at least, who think I've never made anything but Westerns. The reasons they think that is because they only go to see Westerns. . . . But I *am* an urban character. I was born in the big city. I also have a long seamy face which adapts itself to Westerns—but I don't for one moment consider myself a Western actor essentially."

With Julia Adams in *Horizons West* (Univ., 1952)

Quinn as deep sea divers who salvage a gold shipment at the sunken city of Port Royal. They nearly lose the money to the mercenary Trevor (Karel Stepanek). Shackled by a poor plot and tacky dialogue, the film had little to offer. ("About as banal and uninspired as they come," stated the *New York Times*).

Issued at about the same time as *City Beneath the Sea* was *The Naked Spur* (MGM, 1953). Robert joined star James Stewart and director Anthony Mann on this lusty Western, in which Stewart portrayed Civil War veteran Howard Kemp, who sets out to hunt down a convict, Ben Vandergroat (Robert), with a price of $5,000 on his head. Stewart's Kemp intends to use the reward to buy back land he lost in Texas during the Civil War. While searching for the escapee, Kemp encounters an aging miner (Millard Mitchell) and a dishonorably discharged Union soldier (Ralph Meeker). They join in the search, thinking he is a marshal. The trio locate and capture Ryan's Ben, but find he is traveling with a young girl (Janet Leigh), who knows him only as a friend of her family. Realizing his only chance for survival is to make his captors fight among themselves, Ben turns the three men against each other. Adding to the action of this adult study is a rousing Indian attack on the whites. Although *The Naked Spur* may seem tame to today's viewer, in the early fifties it was considered rough screen fare. *Variety* insisted that the plotline was "probably too raw and brutal for some theatregoers."

"[A] picture nobody ever heard of" proved to be one of Ryan's favorite screen assignments. It was *Inferno* (Twentieth Century-Fox, 1953), shot in 3-D and color and directed by Roy Baker. As Carson, he is left to die in the Mojave Desert by his wife, Geraldine (Rhonda Fleming), and her lover Joseph (William Lundigan). With a broken leg and no food or water, Ryan's flinty Carson manages to get back to civilization, to take revenge on the selfish couple. Acclaimed the *New York Times*, "Mr. Ryan's portrayal of the gritty, determined protagonist is, of course, a natural."

In *Inferno* (20th, 1953)

Unlike such tough guy contemporaries as Burt Lancaster and Kirk Douglas, Robert Ryan saw no need to enmesh himself in the problems and ego glorification involved in establishing his own production company. He was content to accept the array of roles that came along, occasionally being blessed with a part that appealed to his actor's instinct, but always giving his performances a controlled presentation. It was a visual dependability that belied an inner turmoil. By this point in his career, Robert had become a heavy drinker. Unlike Wendell Corey, who developed into a nearly hopeless alcoholic, destroying his looks and professional capabilities, Ryan's offcamera problems never interfered with the tangible, final results onscreen.

For Paramount, Robert appeared in *Alaska Seas* (1954), a rather inept remake of that studio's 1938 outdoors saga, *Spawn of the North,* which had starred Henry Fonda, George Raft, and Dorothy Lamour. The film was the tale of a salmon fisherman (top-billed Robert as Matt Kelly) who is out to steal a buddy's (Brian Keith) fleet as well as his girl (Jan Sterling). But he has a change of heart before the final scene. The film sported a lot of action but a barely credible plot. The *New York Times* noted of this entertainment miscarriage, "Mr. Ryan leers sheepishly from start to finish."

Ryan's second professional break with Hollywood (after leaving the film capital for summer stock in 1941) came in 1954. An old friend, director John Houseman, whom Ryan had known since they worked together with Max Reinhardt, asked him to do the title role in *Coriolanus* at New York City's Phoenix Theatre, which was just beginning operations. The actor agreed to do the off-Broadway show for eighty-five dollars a week, because "in common with just about every actor from comic to heavy, I've wanted to play Shakespeare ever since I applied my first quota of grease-paint." Robert had just made *About Mrs. Leslie* (Paramount, 1954) in Hollywood, and "I was free to enjoy what turned out to be among the happiest and most rewarding months of my history."

Coriolanus opened October 1, 1954, and Robert had the title role in this morality drama dealing with the age-old conflict between the rulers and the ruled. The cast included Will Geer (Sicinius), Mildred Natwick (Volumnia), John Emery (Tulius Aufidius), Jack Klugman, Jerry Stiller, Gene Sacks (Volsian servants), and Lori March—daughter of Joseph Moncure March who wrote *The Set-Up*—played Coriolanus' wife. The critics' feelings about *Coriolanus* were as mixed as they were about Ryan's performance. Walter Kerr *(New York Herald-Tribune)* wrote, "Robert Ryan, tackling his first Shakespeare role, is a virile, headstrong, commanding Coriolanus" who makes the character "amusingly fatuous." He added, "Because his voice is patently untrained for verse, he finds himself rasping his best speeches, and studiously sneering his way through some which are filled with far more menace than he makes them. The result is a performance which is visually handsome but vocally harsh, and the incessant snarl takes from his haughty intellectual any real suggestion of integrity." On the other hand, Robert Colman *(New York Daily Mirror)* offered, "He [Ryan] brings a lot of heart and feeling to his characterization." And John McLain *(New York Journal-American)* decided, "I have the greatest regard for Mr. Ryan's talent as an actor but I feel the festivities would have improved immeasurably with a different player in the part."

When he went to the East Coast to appear in the play, Ryan took his family with him, as his wife was "not . . . the kind of wife who stays behind." In leaving the West Coast, Robert and his wife had left behind a now-thriving business they had started in 1953, the Oakwood School Corporation, a private school that had classes from kindergarten through junior high school. When their two boys were approaching school age, the Ryans had become disturbed at the quality of education in the public schools, so they had joined with producer Sydney Harmon and geologist Ross Gabeen in setting up the school. Located in the San Fernando Valley, this non-sectarian private school for children began with twelve pupils and still operates today with over 250 students.

Beginning the school, according to Ryan "was a foolhardy thing to do, but we did it. We were dissatisfied with the education system where we lived in North Holly-wood. The public schools were too crowded, the private schools were too full of rich kids. We held our first class in our living room with a dozen students. Later, we moved into an abandoned synagogue. A year later we bought some property with a friend, got a bank loan and built a building. In the beginning, we didn't have a clear-cut educational philosophy, it was watered-down progressive. We did want our kids to have a good grounding in history, literature and the sciences but we didn't want them to feel stifled. For a while we had trouble with the more conserva-tive element in the community. When we ran up the UN flag, they threw eggs in the windows and at night they painted crosses on the building. My wife and I were actively involved with Oakwood for eleven years, until our kids all graduated. Now it's considered one of the top elementary schools in Southern California. Other teachers come over to watch the way the classes are run. See what a little effort can do?"

Following his work in *Coriolanus,* which lasted forty-seven performances, Robert returned to Hollywood to co-star in *Her Twelve Men* (MGM, 1954) with Greer Garson. In the meantime, *About Mrs. Leslie,* directed by Daniel Mann, went into release. The film primarily belonged to Oscar-winning star Shirley Booth. How-ever, for a change, Ryan was cast in a wholly sympathetic role. Miss Booth por-

With Shirley Booth in *About Mrs. Leslie* (Par., 1954)

558

trayed a boarding house operator who continually functions as a surrogate mother for her tenants. Through it all, in flashbacks, she has memories of her happier young years, when she spent six weeks a year at a resort with an unhappily married airplane tycoon whom she knows simply as George Leslie. (Actually, as she learns from seeing a newsreel, he is George L. Hendersall, the head of a vital government bureau upon which rests the future of allied air power.) Content to be his mistress and companion for this brief period each year, she lives for these times to bring him "peace and contentment." There was no denying that the whole celluloid affair was soap from start to finish, a project that would have done Fannie Hurst credit. (*Time* Magazine insisted that it was "the kind of suds that leaves sticky rings around the mind.") However, the offbeat casting of both stars (she in particular as a Greenwich Village club pianist-vocalist who become the "old bag" old maid) gave the project a high entertainment quotient. Today it is one of the actor's most popular (or at least most frequently shown) films on television.

Ryan had pleasant memories of working with Miss Booth, who, he said, "was uncomfortable working in pictures. She is a very timid woman and walked part of the way to work for a week before someone told her she could park her car on the Paramount lot. In fact, *I* told her. I picked her up in my car about a quarter of a mile from the studio on three consecutive days, and on the third day I finally asked her why she walked. She said she parked her car where she did because it was the only parking lot she could find—and she paid $3 a day to do it. So I informed her that, as the star of the picture, she had the right to park on Paramount's lot."

Her Twelve Men did little for the fading career of MGM's "Mrs. Miniver," but Greer Garson did make a valiant try to instill some life into this synthetic account of a good-hearted woman teacher at a private boys' school who is romanced by teacher Joe Hargrave (Ryan) as well as rich widower Richard Y. Oliver, Sr. (Barry Sullivan).

With Rex Thompson and Greer Garson in *Her Twelve Men* (MGM, 1954)

John Houseman produced this entertainment disappointment which found both Ryan and Sullivan "drowned in the goo" *(New York Times)*.

In September, 1954, *Parents* Magazine ran a feature by Robert Ryan called "Backstage with Us Ryans." In it, the actor detailed his very happy family life. He explained the methods he and his wife used to rear their three children, the psychological benefits reaped by their kids, and his work with the Oakwood School.

> *It's a conglomeration of all creeds (we celebrate Chanukah as well as Christmas) and shades of color (there are scholarships of Negro and Mexican pupils whose parents can't afford private school tuition). This is important to Jessica and me for we want to shield our children from the more common kinds of bias that often make an unhappy impression in formative years. The school itself is a product of community cooperation, started by parents with stars in their eyes.*

The effect of this public relations piece was to make the actor seem to be quite contented in his role as a concerned citizen and doting parent.

Back in Hollywood, Robert overworked himself with four film releases in a row, along with a television debut. Late in 1954, *Bad Day at Black Rock* (MGM) was issued, which reunited him with producer Dore Schary. John Sturges directed this now-classic modern Western, which returned Ryan to the villain mold. Spencer Tracy (for whom Ryan had great admiration) starred as John Macreedy, a one-armed man who comes to the tiny southwestern settlement of Black Rock to give a Japanese farmer his son's posthumous war medal. Wherever he turns, however, his search for the man is hampered. He eventually learns that the farmer had been burned out of his dwelling and killed. Angered by this mass ignorant hostility, Tracy's Macreedy brings vengeance upon the killers. Naturally, Ryan (as Reno Smith) was the leader of the bad guys. He with the other locals (Lee Marvin and Ernest Borgnine) work to run Tracy out of town. Of this CinemaScope, color production, John O'Hara (*Colliers* Magazine) assessed, "This is one of the finest motion pictures ever made." Robert Hatch, of *The Nation,* added, "It is a tight, economical work, directed and acted with conviction, and it enlarges the stature of everyone connected with it."

From that classic film, Ryan next appeared in *Escape to Burma* (RKO), in which he again worked with sterling Barbara Stanwyck. Made in SuperScope but shot on a cheaply constructed studio jungle set, the sleazy venture had Stanwyck running a Burmese plantation and marrying one of her workmen (Robert). He is a wanted fugitive whose innocence of a murder charge is proven at the finale of the film.

Robert returned to the gangster genre in his third 1955 release, *House of Bamboo* (Twentieth Century-Fox, 1948). In adapting the storyline to a Japanese setting, Samuel Fuller not only directed the feature but also added dialogue to Harry Kleiner's original screenplay and played a bit part as a policeman. In this melodrama, Sandy Dawson's (Robert) gang plans to rob an army munitions train outside of Tokyo. In the course of the theft, an American soldier is killed. The Japanese police and the U.S. military police agree to pool their resources to solve the case, with a policeman sergeant Eddie Spanier (Robert Stack) posing as an AWOL soldier to infiltrate the mob. Ryan's Dawson eventually discovers Spanier's identity, but at the shoot-out Stack's Spanier kills him, and the gang is disbanded. Despite the good wide-screen cinematography, *House of Bamboo* was not a commercial winner. Bosley Crowther (*New York Times*), however, did admit, "Ryan's faint hint of psychopathic

560

With David Farrar and Barbara Stanwyck in *Escape to Burma* (RKO, 1955)

tension introduces a fine uncertainty, and his skill at subdued underplaying provides a sense of dread." Many years later, when Fuller had become a cult figure, this film could come in for its fair share of recognition.

Ryan's fourth and final picture of the year was *The Tall Men* (Twentieth Century-Fox, 1955), and it was a big money earner,[8] due mainly to the teaming of Clark Gable and Jane Russell. Directed by Raoul Walsh and shot partially on location in Durango, New Mexico,[9] this lusty Western had Gable and Cameron Mitchell as Ben and Clint Allison, Texas brothers who head westward after the Civil War. They hold up a wealthy businessman, Nathan Stark (Robert), who later convinces them to help him lead a large cattle herd from Texas to Montana. On the way back to Texas they rescue the shapely Nella Turner (Miss Russell) from Indians, and she tumbles for Gable's Ben Allison. Snowed in, in a cabin during a blizzard, Russell's Nella and Gable's Ben have a falling out, and Nella eventually takes up with Ryan's Nathan Stark in Texas. He insists she accompany the group back to Montana with the cattle herd, and in the final stages of the trek they penetrate hostile Indian country. Nathan Stark is prepared to abandon the drive, but Ben Allison refuses, even after

---

[8]It pulled in five million dollars in distributors' domestic rentals.

[9]Years later, when Ryan returned to Durango to undertake location filming for *Lawman* (United Artists, 1971), he would crisply reflect, "The place hasn't changed much, though I don't remember it any too well. I've given up booze now, but in those days I was drinking a hell of a lot. Finally I got hepatitis—down here in Durango, as a matter of fact. I couldn't take a drink for a year, not even a glass of beer. I damn near died when I heard that. I thought: 'I'll never get through this year.' But I got through the first two weeks and I never had the same urge again.

"But in those days I went through the location in a haze. I've hardly any recollections of Durango—Gable and Jane and I would sit around and get swacked. I can't even remember where I lived!"

561

With Shirley Yamaguchi in *House of Bamboo* (20th, 1955)

his brother is killed. Gable's Ben runs the herd through a narrow canyon, defeats the Indians, and out-maneuvers Ryan's Stark, who still attempts to double-cross him. Quite naturally, it is Gable who rewins comely Jane at the finale. As had been the case when Ryan acted in tandem with John Wayne, or, more recently, with Spencer Tracy, he rose to the occasion, offering a fine balance and counterpoint to the performance of the male lead (in this case, Gable).

The Tall Men was issued in October, and on December 14, 1955, Ryan made his dramatic debut on television in NBC's "Screen Directors Playhouse" in a segment called *Lincoln's Doctor's Bag*.

Robert stayed with Twentieth Century-Fox (a studio pushing such younger players as Robert Wagner and Jeffrey Hunter) for his first 1956 release, *The Proud Ones*. He was top-billed as Cass, a marshal whose killing of a man has engendered a revenge hunt by the man's son (Jeffrey Hunter). The law enforcer is also hunted by two mercenaries and a saloon keeper, who arrive in his small Kansas town with a trail herd and also vow vengeance for a past offense against them. The main thrust of the story, however, was the mental growing-up of the Hunter character. Walter Brennan stole the show with his delightful performance as Ryan's eventual jailer.

Next, Robert returned to the moribund RKO to star in *Back from Eternity* (1956), a remake of *Five Came Back,* which the studio had issued in 1939. Directed by John Farrow (who had helmed the original), Ryan was spotlighted as the heavily drinking pilot Bill (played in the original by Chester Morris) who is in charge of a plane which crashes in the South American jungle with an odd assortment of passengers. Among the travelers are Rena (Anita Ekberg), a prostitute, and Vasquez, a condemned hoodlum (Rod Steiger). A fairly exciting and well-made melodrama, even if it was not up to the less pretentious thirties' edition. The Ryan character was

With George Mathews and Robert Middleton (right) in *The Proud Ones* (20th, 1956)

563

forced to forsake the bottle in order to help organize a plan for the salvation of his dozen passengers.

It was also in 1956 that forty-six-year-old Robert Ryan made the first of five appearances on CBS-TV's "Zane Grey Theatre." On the initial outing he starred in an episode entitled *You Only Run Once* (October 5, 1956).

That same year he also joined with friend John Houseman in forming The Group Theatre at UCLA, for which he served as president. During the presidential election that year he actively campaigned for Democrat Adlai E. Stevenson. One of Ryan's prized possessions was a picture of the White House candidate which was inscribed, "To my dear friends, Robert and Jessica Ryan."

The actor's sole 1957 feature film release was *Men in War* (United Artists), directed by Anthony Mann who had handled the star in *The Naked Spur*. This was the first of a number of pictures that Ryan was to make which were written by Philip Yordan. For *Men in War,* the screenwriter took his plot from the Van Van Pragg book, *Combat.* The black-and-white feature also marked the first of three movies Ryan made with Aldo Ray. In the action entry, Robert was Lieutenant Benson, the commander of an isolated platoon in Korea which is struggling to make its way back to the main line. The soldiers in the platoon are troubled with battle fatigue and fright. Ryan is bothered by a colonel (Robert Keith) who has gone mad and by a brutal sergeant (Ray) who accompanies him. Certainly not a top-flight production, *Men in War* did manage to bring forth some of the hell that does exist on the battle-front and highlight in particular the plight of the foot soldier.

The year 1958 also saw only one film appearance for Robert, but in *God's Little Acre* (United Artists), he had one of his favorite (and most acclaimed) parts, that of uneducated philosopher and Georgia farmer Ty Ty Walden.[10] It is he who spends his time looking for gold supposedly buried on his farm and who continually moves the location of a plot of land he has set aside for the Lord. Again directed by Anthony Mann in a scenario by Philip Yordan, Robert performed in a weakened version of Caldwell's explosive study of raw Americana. No one was more adept than Caldwell (who had also created that classic *Tobacco Road*) in depicting the plight of the poor whites in the Depression-ridden South. This melodrama of passion and violence was set against the sometimes comical Walden family and their friends and an attempt by Ty Ty's son-in-law (Aldo Ray) to re-open a cotton mill to bring work to a small town.

God's Little Acre, which had its premiere in Augusta, Georgia, on May 12, 1958, omitted most of the earthy language and situations of the book. (Thus, it received a B, not a C, rating from the National Legion of Decency.) Thankfully, however, the 118-minute black-and-white feature retained a good deal of the flavor of the visceral Ty Ty, who, with his sons, continues to dig hole after hole in his rich farm land while his black tenants nearly starve. His youngest daughter (Gloria Talbott) is promiscuous, although she is also carrying on a romance with rotund sheriff Pluto Squint (Buddy Hackett). And Ty Ty's daughter-in-law (Tina Louise) is seduced by another daughter's husband (Ray). The latter dies attempting to reopen the mill.

Much of the philosophy of Ty Ty Walden's character was kept in the scenario, which led Ryan to claim on more than one occasion that he enjoyed tremendously the salty part. Ironically, most highbrow critics passed up an appreciation of the film (as they did with most of Caldwell's works). *Variety,* however, reported, in very

---

[10]By 1958 Erskine Caldwell's novel (1933) had sold over nine million copies.

With Fay Spain and Jack Lord in *God's Little Acre* (UA, 1958)

heady language, that Ryan gave "the performance of his career . . . he opens a whole vista of roles for himself by this portrayal, as remarkable perhaps, as Walter Huston's performance in *The Treasure of Sierra Madre*."

In 1958, Robert increased his television appearances to eight (he performed in five television outings in 1957). For those of the newer generations who automatically connect the role of Jay Gatsby with Robert Redford (from the 1974 Paramount film), it needs to be restated that Robert Ryan tackled the title role of F. Scott Fitzgerald's *The Great Gatsby*[11] in a television version on CBS' "Playhouse 90" (June 26, 1958). Franklin Schaffner directed the David Shaw adaptation, with Jeanne Crain cast as the beautiful, willful Daisy. Unfortunately, the well-intentioned rendition won few plaudits. John Crosby (*New York Herald-Tribune*) reported, "[It] was so disorganized that a good part of the meaning of the novel got misplaced. . . . Robert Ryan's Gatsby was a puzzlement but then I don't know any other actor who could have made it less so." Marie Torre, reviewing for the same newspaper, was less kind in her attack: "Robert Ryan assumed a wooden manner which failed to give life to the character."

In the realm of theatre that year, Ryan performed in a stock production of Jean Girandoux's *Tiger at the Gates* in Los Angeles, under the direction of Harold J. Kennedy. For the chance to play in this showcase, the star accepted the minimum stock salary of forty dollars a week.

The following year, 1959, the star jumped further into politics by becoming one of the founders of the Committee on Sane Nuclear Policy, serving as a board member of SANE until his death. He began making appearances around the country with impassioned speeches "because nobody understood that the new bomb was

[11]In earlier motion picture versions, Warner Baxter (Paramount, 1926) and Alan Ladd (Paramount, 1949) portrayed the mysterious bootlegger-playboy of the Roaring Twenties.

With Myrna Loy in *Lonelyhearts* (UA, 1958)

no ordinary damn bomb. We wanted people to know what nuclear holocaust could mean."

Always anxious to experiment further with legitimate theatre, Ryan eagerly appeared in his and John Houseman's Group Theatre production of T. S. Eliot's *Murder in the Cathedral.* He undertook the focal role of Thomas à Becket.

On the film front, the mature Ryan had three 1959 releases. *Lonelyhearts* was issued in March by United Artists and was adapted by Dore Schary from Nathaniel West's novel, *Miss Lonelyhearts,* written in 1933. (It had been filmed in 1933 by United Artists as *Advice to the Lovelorn,* starring Lee Tracy and Sally Blane.) The new film edition cast Ryan as a sadistic newspaper editor who assigns a bright-eyed cub reporter (misplayed by Montgomery Clift) to the task of running a daily love-lorn column in his large Midwest newspaper. A strident Myrna Loy appeared as Ryan's long-suffering wife. *Time* Magazine was among those who found Robert's emoting unsatisfactory. "[He does] an incredible stylized caricature of hard-bitten editors."

Then, working again with scripter Philip Yordan, Ryan was spotlighted in *Day of the Outlaw* (United Artists, 1959). Following the trend of taking a percentage interest in a starring vehicle, the star had a $250,000 interest in the $1.1 million production, which was directed by Andre De Toth. Overlooked by critics and the public alike, this pedestrian outdoor adventure offered Ryan as cowboy Blaise Starrett who lusts after the wife (Tina Louise) of a rancher (Alan Marshal), she having once rejected him. The bulk of the plot, however, focused on a gang of outlaws who ride into a small town with their injured leader and terrorize the community. The town is inundated by a blizzard, and eventually the lawbreakers are confronted by the cavalry, leading to the anticipated shootout.

On one occasion outspoken Ryan admitted, "I have been in films pretty well

With Shelley Winters in *Odds against Tomorrow* (UA, 1959)

everything I am dedicated to fighting against." Such was the case with his role of Earle Slater in *Odds Against Tomorrow,* issued in October, 1959, by United Artists. Robert Wise, who had led Robert through his paces in *The Set-Up,* was the director on this project. In *Crossfire* Ryan had hated Jews, and in this effort he detested blacks.[12] The sharply etched melodrama related the story of a man (Harry Belafonte) who owes a bookie $75,000. Hoping to get out of the financial bind he joins with an ex-con (Ed Begley) and an Oklahoma drifter (Robert) in an "easy" bank robbery job. Due to the anti-black attitudes of Ryan's character, the robbery plan is foiled. For distraction from the grimness of the main plot, there was vivacious Shelley Winters as Ryan's crude girl and Gloria Grahame as the sex-hungry next-door neighbor.

Robert owned twenty percent of *Odds Against Tomorrow,* but unfortunately his investment turned out badly (commercially, if not artistically), as the picture was a financial disappointment.

On the other hand, the specious *Ice Palace* (Warner Bros., 1960) was a modest moneymaker despite being a very mediocre adaptation of Edna Ferber's book. As directed by Vincent Sherman, Ryan portrayed an Alaskan fisherman who goes into politics and loses the two women he loves in his fight to obtain statehood for Alaska. Richard Burton, Carolyn Jones, Martha Hyer, and a supporting cast of studio

[12]Recently, director Wise has admitted to Rui Nogueira in a *Focus on Films* interview, "The original end of the script and the novel had the black and white getting together. *The Defiant Ones* had just come out before this and I said to Harry [Belafonte] and others around, 'Gee, it's too similar, we can't make our point or do the same as the other film, it would be a repetition even though this is a different story.' It was my suggestion that we try to make the same point in an opposite way by saying hate destroys, so we should get along. So that's how we decided to end the film. . . . We made it all in New York, on location at a little, old town upstate, and in the old Gold Medal Studios up on the Bronx. . . . New York crew entirely.

With Carolyn Jones, Richard Burton, and Martha Hyer in *Ice Palace* (WB, 1960)

568

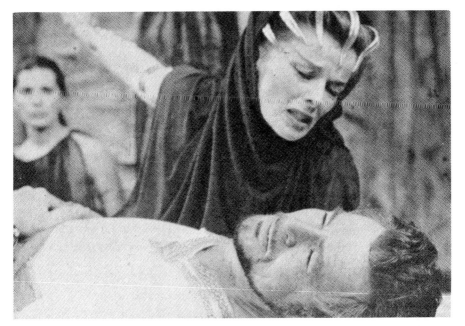

With Katharine Hepburn in *Antony and Cleopatra* (1960)

contract players suffered with audiences through the 143 minutes of multi-hued trash. Despite the pans the film and most of its cast received, it should be noted that a good number of critics found positive things to say of Ryan's screen interpretation. "[He] is persuasive enough in a conventionally dedicated role" (Britain's *Monthly Film Bulletin*).

On March 25, 1960, Ryan appeared in his most prestigious television appearance to date, "Buick Electra TV Playhouse's" special, *The Snows of Kilimanjaro*, based on the Ernest Hemingway novel.[13] This ninety-minute version, broadcast live with some taped segments, was produced by Gordon Duff, adapted by A. E. Hotchner, and directed by John Frankenheimer. Robert portrayed Harry Walters, a writer injured on an African hunting trip, who is dying. He is on a plain beneath the shadow of Mount Kilimanjaro, being attended by his wife (Ann Todd), when he has bitter memories of his past: his writing career, world adventures, and the women in his life. The star's salty interpretation gave a great deal of credence to the telescoped video version. Others in the cast were Janice Rule, Jean Hagen, Mary Astor, James Gregory, and Brock Peters.

Also in 1960, the still very energetic Ryan returned to Shakespearean drama. He was billed as "Guest Co-star" to Katharine Hepburn's "Guest Star" in a production of *Antony and Cleopatra* at the American Shakespeare Festival Theatre in Stratford, Connecticut. As staged by Jack Landau, the two stars played the title characters and they worked for minimum wages. Also in the cast were Morris Carnovsky, Will Geer, Clifton James, and Sada Thompson. Reporting on this August, 1960, theatre event, Frank Aston *(New York World-Telegram)* wrote of Robert's Roman emperor: "[He] established a striking characterization. He looked like a dissolute bruiser,

[13]In the 1952 Twentieth Century-Fox film version, Gregory Peck, Susan Hayward, and Ava Gardner were top-billed.

With Brigid Bazlen in *King of Kings* (MGM, 1961)

talked like a poet, and behaved like a spoiled fellow whose ideals were acceptable, whose judgment was erratic, whose will was no stronger than a prowling dame would want it to be. Mr. Ryan started with a tendency to slur words at high speed; but by the time he got to telling Egypt he was dying he was parting his syllables right down the middle."

By this time in his eventful career, Ryan was looking for "the one motivating factor" in the parts he played rather than just monetary compensation. By now he had no illusions about the film capital. "When I first went to Hollywood, I thought all I wanted to be was a movie star. Then, when I became one, I realized it wasn't all it was cracked up to be."

For the remaining fourteen years of his life, Robert would concentrate his life and career on doing the things he liked most. Occasionally, just to replenish his bank account, he would work in unworthy vehicles, both on television and in film. Then he would turn around and ply his craft on stage for minimum wages because he believed in what he was doing. Politically, Ryan increasingly voiced his opinions for liberal causes, such as Artists Help All Blacks (AHAB), which he formed with Bill Cosby, Robert Culp, and Sidney Poitier. A friend of the actor once observed he was "a square in the heat of action." Robert once termed himself "not a do-gooder—I hate that word," but "just a guy who believes deeply in the better instinct of man."

In 1961 the actor appeared as a member of the Canadian Mounted Police in *The Canadians* (Twentieth Century-Fox), which provided the directorial debut for scripter Burt Kennedy. Featured in this tepid melodrama was opera singer Teresa Stratas who paraded about as The White Squaw.

Next, Ryan took special billing, as John the Baptist[14] and $50,000 for one week's work in *King of Kings* (MGM, 1961), which reunited him with director Nicholas Ray and scriptor Philip Yordan. The Samuel Bronston production presented Jesus Christ (Jeffrey Hunter) in a rather offbeat fashion for that time. Not surprisingly, it de-emphasized the many miracles mentioned in the Bible. *Time* Magazine declared the film's "imitation of Christ is little better than blasphemy." Nearly all critics voted thumbs down on the production. Robert's interpretation of John the Baptist drew many negative reactions from film appraisers; they just could not picture him in such a role because of his many previous villainous screen parts.

By the early 1960s it was necessary for even such an easily employable performer as Ryan to spend a good deal of time in Europe if he wished to find film roles. He was among those who performed cameo duty in *The Longest Day* (Twentieth Century-Fox, 1962). He was cast as General James Gavin in this lengthy but dutiful presentation of the events leading up to and including the D-Day invasion of Europe.

From a career standpoint, the biggest event for Robert in 1962 was being chosen by the producers of the expensive Broadway musical *Mr. President* for the title role. Katharine Hepburn had suggested Ryan to Howard Lindsay, who wrote the book with Russel Crouse (Irving Berlin created the score). When requested to audition for the show, Ryan said to Hepburn, "Kate, if they take me, they're really dragging the bottom of the barrel." Nevertheless, he agreed to test for the part, singing

[14]Of this unusual project for such a typed figure as Ryan, the star later reflected, "I think if a guy starts out making something about Christ rather than Madame Pompadour, he's already on a higher plane. Besides, a producer must consider a profit. But I would look at the end product—not the motive. . . . When they called me in for this Bible picture, I was sure they'd ask me to play Judas. I almost fell down when they offered me John the Baptist."

With Nanette Fabray and Jerry Strickler in *Mr. President* (1963)

"Always" and "Blue Skies," and talking his way through a version of "September Song." As Ryan recalled the ordeal, Berlin at the audition asked if he had any singing experience. "I told him I used to sing pretty well around bars in my drinking days, but that I hadn't had a drink in five years. So I took a few belts of scotch and sang. Berlin liked it."

The large-scale musical concerned President of the United States Stephen Decatur Henderson and his wife (Nanette Fabray) and daughter (Anita Gillette) doing a good will tour. Although the trek is canceled, the presidential group decides to head for the Soviet Union anyway, where Ryan's character espouses the virtues of the American way of life. Having made the desired impression, the group continues on its way.

As produced by Leland Hayward, the musical opened in Boston on August 27, 1962, to mixed reviews and then moved to Washington, D.C., on September twenty-fifth for a three-week stand. On October twentieth, the show opened at the St. James Theatre with advance sales of $2.4 million. "On *Mr. President*'s opening night," remembered its star, "everybody but me was in a state of absolute hysteria. I knew I'm not a singer and hence wasn't worrying." The aisle-sitters, like most discriminating playgoers, were unimpressed by the lavish venture. "Regarded in minimal entertainment terms, *Mr. President* is mechanical in an old-fashioned way. . . . Robert Ryan . . . plays Mr. President as uninflectedly as written" (Howard Taubman, *New York Times*). "Ryan never deems his role, nor does he let himself be tempted by theatrics. Except that he doesn't sing well [as in the number "This Is a Great Country"], he makes a good musical comedy President. His greatest political and stage assets are personality, warmth, and dignity" (Norman Nadel, *New York World-Telegram*).

The show, which Ryan later termed "disastrous," had a Broadway run of 262

With Peter Ustinov in *Billy Budd* (AA, 1962)

performances. (As is often the case with short-lived shows, the original cast album, as recorded by Columbia Records, is now a collector's item.)

Also in 1962, the actor made the first of two appearances on ABC's "Wagon Train." Telecast on November 21, 1962, he starred in *The John Bernard Story*. The same year also saw Ryan featured in Peter Ustinov's production of *Billy Budd* (Allied Artists). Multi-talented Ustinov not only collaborated on the screenplay derived from Herman Melville's novel, but he directed the feature as well as starring as Captain Vere. Following the novel closely, the black-and-white picture (set in the eighteenth century) retold the story of a young man (Terence Stamp) who ventures onto the high seas for the first time. Aboard ship, he is taunted by the sadistic master-at-arms John Claggart (Robert). Unable to defend himself against the unjust accusations leveled at him by Claggart, and in a fit of the moment, the young man kills his taunter. It is then up to Captain Vere to administer "justice." As Jeanne Stein wrote in her *Films in Review* career study of Ryan, "This role is an apotheosis of screen villainy, and is probably the best single piece of work in his [Ryan's] acting career. He suggested 'depravity according to nature,' as Herman Melville intended. If ever the 'typing' of an actor paid off it was here."

Billy Budd marked Robert's final screen appearance for three years. During his absence from the movies he moved from Hollywood to New York City, where he and his family took up residence at the old-fashioned but very prestigious The Dakota, the exclusive apartment building on Central Park West. During this time his wife continued to write and they both stayed active in various political and civic movements. Son Timothy was studying theatre arts at Pomona College while Cheyney was enrolled at Harvard and Lisa attended the Bamford-Nightingale School.

Ryan continued to keep his name in front of the public by appearing in an assortment of prime-time video fare. Much more important to him was his participation in such projects as *The Inheritance* (Amalgamated Clothing Workers of America—Harold Mayer, 1964). Combining old motion picture footage with vintage still photographs, the sixty-minute documentary depicted the influx of workers into America since 1900. The union-oriented production benefited from the "crisp narration" (*Cue* Magazine) by Ryan. Later in that year, Robert's sonorous, distinctive voice could be heard narrating *The City of Ships* (NBC-TV, December 17, 1964), a study of New York Harbor.

In the mid-sixties, Ryan accepted a series of nondescript roles in equally nondescript features. He was third-billed in *Battle of the Bulge* (Warner Bros., 1965), made in Spain and directed by Ken Annakin, as produced-written by Milton Sperling and Philip Yordan. Another "epic," showing a phase of World War II, Ryan was General Grey, who, at Ambelve, scoffs at the rumor of a massive German attack. Projected in Cinerama, the film was a near entertainment bust. (Judith Crist would label the film "an unspectacular spectacle.")

Despite its derivation from a Morris L. West novel, *The Crooked Road* (Seven Arts, 1965) had only the marquee names of Ryan and top-billed Stewart Granger to give it any boxoffice thrust. It was shot on location in a small island villa in Yugoslavia. One of the less blistering reviews of this miniature potboiler exclaimed that Ryan was "playing the kind of adventurous newspaperman role he has clearly outgrown."

Robert remained in Europe for his first 1966 film feature, *La Guerra Secrete*, issued in the U.S. by American-International as *The Dirty Game*. Originally produced as a television pilot which did not sell, the feature was strung together with footage directed by Terence Young, Christian-Jacque, and Carlo Lizzani. Ryan was second-billed as dour-faced General Bruce, who announces at the film's finale, "This is a hell of a way to make a living." The words rather fit the plight of stars Henry Fonda, Peter Van Eyck, Robert Hossein, Annie Girardot, and Ryan as they waded through this espionage junk film.

After his lengthy sabbatical, Ryan returned to Hollywood. It was an auspicious return, for he co-starred in *The Professionals* (Columbia, 1966). In this Richard Brooks' produced-director-scripted Western, Ryan was third-billed as Ehrengard, one of four mercenaries (along with Burt Lancaster, Lee Marvin and Woody Strode) hired by wealthy Ralph Bellamy. Bellamy wants the group to retrieve his wife (Claudia Cardinale), who seems to prefer staying with the Mexican bandit (Jack Palance) who had kidnapped her. The *New York Journal-Tribune* rightly labeled this tough outdoors feature "a sleek, slam bang adventure-suspense film." A good deal of the picture's stability came from the taut performance of leathery Ryan.

On March 9, 1966, Ryan starred in the *Guilty or Not Guilty* segment of the "Bob Hope Chrysler Theatre" on NBC-TV. Like *The Dirty Game,* it was a pilot for a proposed video series that did not sell. Ryan had the focal role of a New York assistant district attorney.

"You say Shakespeare and I'll play it in the men's room at Grand Central." So spoke Robert Ryan who went to England in March, 1967, to tackle the title role of *Othello*. Asked why he couldn't have done this venture on home soil, the star explained, "Suppose I searched this country and found a place here to do this kind of work. It would take eight lawyers, five accountants, six tax men and who knows who else and we'd talk and talk. All I needed there was a work permit—no lawyers, no accountants, no tax men." Besides performing with the Nottingham Repertory Theatre in the Shakespearean tragedy, Ryan also performed for the same group as James Tyrone in Eugene O'Neill's *Long Day's Journey into Night*. The critics were

574

With Stewart Granger in *The Crooked Road* (7 Arts, 1965)

With Henry Fonda in *The Dirty Game* (AIP, 1966)

With Lee Marvin, Claudia Cardinale, and Woody Strode in *The Professionals* (Col., 1966)

With Bill Dana and Sid Caesar in *The Busy Body* (Par., 1967)

more than kind to the actor, who worked in the two arduous productions for $180 a week.

While many name players of Ryan's age were finding it difficult to obtain any film work, Robert was represented with four films released in 1967.

The entry with the least in value came first. *The Busy Body* (Paramount, 1967), was a spoof of the gangster genre. William Castle produced and directed this well-meaning, if fumbling, take-off on the underworld melodramas. Sid Caesar starred as a man accused of murder by a scatter-brained mob, and Ryan appeared as Charlie Barker, the leader of the hoodlums.

Next, Robert accepted a role in *The Dirty Dozen* (MGM, 1967), the film which helped to launch the new wave of screen violence in the mid-sixties. Robert Aldrich directed this 149-minute thriller which concerned twelve convicts trained by an army major (Lee Marvin) to go on a "suicide raid" behind Nazi lines before D-Day. Containing a great deal of action, this masculine film told of the training of the seemingly incorrigible men into a well-knit group for the raid which led to a great deal of slaughter. Ryan was featured as stern Colonel Breed, the conscientious officer who was opposed to the raid. Appearing in a feature that grossed $20,067 million in distributors' domestic rentals gave Robert renewed status in the Hollywood community.

There are very few positive things to say of *Hour of the Gun* (United Artists, 1967), which producer-director John Sturges created as a sequel to his 1957 film *Gunfight at the O.K. Corral*. This entry took up where the previous study of the legendary Wyatt Earp, Doc Holliday, and the Clanton Brothers left off. This version had Ike Clanton (Robert)[15] escaping with two henchmen, while Doc Holliday (Jason Robards) and Wyatt Earp (James Garner) set out to take revenge on vicious Clanton.

The actor's final 1967 release, which was issued in the U.S. in July, 1968, was another Cinerama-process film, *Custer of the West* (Cinerama) directed by Robert Siodmak and co-produced by Philip Yordan. Filmed in Spain, *Variety* reported of this hacked-together feature, "Visual values hold up [its] disappointing story line." As the title indicates the film details the career of George Armstrong Custer (Robert Shaw), from his Civil War days to the massacre at the Little Big Horn. Ryan was featured as Mulligan, an alcoholic calvary sergeant and a deserter.

Both of Robert's 1968 pictures were made abroad. He was third-billed in *A Minute to Pray, A Second to Die* (Cinerama), a routine Italian-produced Western. Alex Cord was featured in the lacklustre production, with Robert making a virtual cameo appearance as Governor Carter.

He remained in Rome for *Lo Sbarco Di Anzio,* which reunited him with Robert Mitchum for the third occasion. It also marked the final time Ryan would work with director Edward Dmytrik. Robert was featured as headline-hungry General Mark Clark in this "dull story" (*Variety*) that traces the course of the famed Allied landing in Italy during World War II. Presented almost as a documentary, the picture failed to engross sophisticated filmgoers.[16] It produced only $1.6 million in distributors' domestic rentals, which caused a hefty deficit to its producing-releasing company, Columbia. Ryan's undemanding assignment in this film would have been called "doing boxoffice duty" in the old days.

Robert's reaction to this string of stereotyped rough-guy roles that required little

[15]In the 1957 Western, Lyle Bettger played Ike Clanton.
[16]"Do we really need another war film that mixes action, GI humor, and a mere pretense of having something to say?" (William Wolf, *Cue* Magazine).

projection of character on his part was reflected by a conversation he had with Wanda Hale, then the doyenne of the *New York Daily News* reviewing corps. "My mother, bless her, is offended by my tough roles. She wants me to play a shaved fellow in a business suit, white shirt, tie and the gold cuff links. I did have a role like that; she loved it, I didn't. . . . But she doesn't object to the money I make."

In September, 1968, Robert proved once again that he had never really "gone Hollywood." He joined the Mineola Theatre in Long Island for *Our Town,* a production of the American National Theatre established by Martha Scott, in which major stars could appear in worthwhile revivals. Directed by Edward Hastings, this production of Thornton Wilder's Americana play featured Henry Fonda, Ryan, Estelle Parsons, Jo Van Fleet, and John Beal. Critic Clive Barnes *(New York Times)* judged that Robert "showed great authority" in the role of Mr. Webb.

Ryan had appeared at the Democratic convention in Chicago the previous month as an alternate Democratic delegate from New York for the presidential candidacy of Eugene McCarthy.[17]

After the brief run of *Our Town,* Robert recommended a revival of *The Front Page,* the 1928 political satire by Ben Hecht and Charles MacArthur. The comedy opened at the Mineola Theatre on October 20, 1968, and was staged by Leo Brady. Besides Ryan as Walter Burns, the cast included Henry Fonda, John Beal, Anthony George, Anne Jackson, Estelle Parsons, and John McIntire. Said Clive Barnes (of the *New York Times),* "With a pencil-thin mustache and a manner suggesting that he kept a spittoon in his dressing room, Mr. Ryan very clearly would have run virtually any other paper out of town."

On May 12, 1969, *The Front Page* was reopened at the Ethel Barrymore Theatre on Broadway, and in it Ryan achieved probably his greatest stage success. Set in the press room in Chicago's City Hall, the new edition recaptured the deft satire on both politics and the news media. Restaged by Harold J. Kennedy, the show featured Bert Convy as ace reporter Hildy Johnson, Ryan as arrogant managing editor Burns, and a cast which included Helen Hayes, Doro Merande, Peggy Cass, Katharine Houghton, Julia Meade, John McGiver, and Arnold Stang. *The Wall Street Journal* stated Ryan played "crisply and cynically," and John Bartholomew Tucker (WABC-TV) said the play was "topped by that wonderful actor, Mr. Robert Ryan. I think he was born to play the lead in *The Front Page."*

Ryan appeared in the comedy at the Equity minimum salary of $167.50 a week, and out of it he paid his dresser $120 a week. After being a thespian for over three decades, Robert announced, "Now I enjoy acting more and more all the time."

Harold J. Kennedy, who helmed and played a part in *The Front Page,* later wrote in the *New York Times* of Ryan:

> *He was the spark plug of* The Front Page. *He never came to the theatre without the urgent desire that that night's performance be the best.* The Front Page *was a joyous experience for all of us. I recall only one disagreement during the entire run: a violent argument between Robert Ryan and Helen Hayes over the star dressing room. Not the*

[17]While stumping in New Hampshire, Ryan said, "McCarthy did a courageous thing to come out unendorsed. I'm for him because I'm against the war in Vietnam, and I'm against our country being run by IBM machines and Gallup polls. What we need is more of an individual view—unaffected by these things. If we are to operate by consensus we will never get anything done."

kind of argument you would expect but typical of the two people involved. Neither one of them would touch it.

Miss Hayes maintained that Mr. Ryan was the star of the play and she was not about to usurp his dressing room. Mr. Ryan contended that he wasn't going to loll around in a ground-floor dressing room while the first lady of the theatre climbed the stairs. A hastily made, rather flimsy set of drapes solved it. We hung them across the middle of the room and Mr. Ryan and Miss Hayes shared the star dressing room with the same grace that they shared the stage.

As Walter Burns in The Front Page, *Mr. Ryan delivered one of the most famous curtain lines in the American theater: "The son of a bitch stole my watch."*

When he finally left the play, the company gave him a party in the basement of the Ethel Barrymore Theatre. There in the room where we shared his 59th birthday and Thanksgiving and Christmas, we hung a huge banner, paid for and signed by the entire company. It said simply: "Robert Ryan—The son of a bitch stole our hearts."

Asked how he enjoyed his successful Broadway return. Ryan admitted: "It's great to be back on Broadway—even though a lot of Broadway right now is damn dull. I'm for any theatre that keeps theatre existing in New York; what bothers me about some of this new stuff is it doesn't give young actors the kind of training they should have. Hell! *Anybody* can stand naked in front of an audience and shout holy! holy! But *anybody* can't perform Shakespeare or Shaw or Neil Simon. And in the new, non-verbal theatre, who gives a damn about young playwrights, huh? And where are they?"

If culture in the theatre concerned Ryan, it did not appear to matter much to the actor cinematically. His sole 1969 release was Sam Peckinpah's R-rated *The Wild Bunch* (Warner Bros.-Seven Arts). Made on location in Mexico, the violent film told of a bounty hunter (Robert) who is hired by executives of a Texas railroad in 1913. His job is to track down his former partner (William Holden) and his gang who have pulled their "last big job" and have headed south after provoking a town massacre.

Viewers may have lost track of the number of oncamera killings in this gratuitously bloody Western, but the producers were well aware of each of the 5.25 million dollars that the picture grossed in distributors' domestic rentals.

In 1970, after appearing in a syndicated video version of *The Front Page*, sponsored by Xerox Corporation and telecast over the Howard Hughes network. Ryan surprised some of his more artistic associates by appearing in *Captain Nemo and the Underwater City* (MGM, 1970). The sixty-year-old leading man had his own rationalization for participating in such uninspired low-jinks. "I'm not wealthy, but I don't think I'll ever go hungry again. It's important to continue working in films to keep your image warm. You can have six million dollars, but if you insist on turning down bad pictures, people are going to say, 'What ever happened to Robert Ryan?'" James Hill directed this Jules Verne-inspired film which was noteworthy largely for its good special effects. The underwater scenes were filmed in the Mediterranean near Malta. Unfortunately, there was too little use of the underwater city set and of the battle with the sea monster. Then, too, despite the array of actors who had tackled the role of the urbane, nefarious, mysterious Captain Nemo over the years, the part had become synonymous with James Mason's interpretation for *20,000 Leagues under the Sea* (Buena Vista, 1954). Of this venture and Ryan's performance, *Cinefantastique* reviewed, "The film lacks originality. . . . Robert Ryan, a very competent actor, convincingly portrays Nemo, but is restrained by lack of forceful dialogue."

The tranquility that the Ryans hoped for in the 1970s (they had built a house in New Hampshire) did not come, for it was discovered that the actor had cancer. He spent the next three years combating the disease.

Apparently undaunted by his personal problems, Robert determined to tackle once again the exhausting role of James Tyrone in Eugene O'Neill's *Long Day's Journey into Night*. This time it was an off-Broadway mounting of the production, which opened at the Promenade Theatre on upper Broadway on April 21, 1971, and lasted through a theatre change (to the Cherry Lane in Greenwich Village) until August 21, 1971. Ryan was in fine fettle as the faded matinee idol, with Geraldine Fitzgerald as his drug-addicted wife, Stacy Keach as son James, James Naughton as the other offspring Edmund Tyrone, and Paddy Croft as the maid Cathleen. Reporting of this "authentic, heartfelt, and thrilling" staging, Clive Barnes *(New York Times)* added, regarding Ryan, "It is a great part, and Robert Ryan moves into it with care, love and understanding. He shows us the character, little by little, and finally creates a picture of a man, neither good nor bad, but understandable." Like many tough-guy actors, Ryan was proving again that his movie stereotype was only the top of the iceberg of his true acting range.

That same year the respected actor made two additional film appearances. In *Lawman* (United Artists, 1971) which Michael Winner produced-directed, he was reunited with Burt Lancaster. He was the weak-willed sheriff of a small town which is invaded by marshal Lancaster, who has arrived there to arrest bigtime rancher Lee J. Cobb for the accidental slaying of an old man. The *New York Times* labeled the film "a potent but curiously exasperating Western," but it did earn $2.7 million in distributors' domestic rentals.

Next, Robert's talent was badly wasted as a television executive kingpin in *The Love Machine* (Columbia, 1971). The slick but unmoving bit of claptrap was based on Jacqueline Susann's bestseller. Jack Haley, Jr. directed this X-rated melodrama which pretended to delve into the behind-the-scenes aspects of big-league video production. As the harassed executive who must cope with corporate politicking and his sexually itchy wife (Dyan Cannon), Ryan somehow survived this celluloid mess. (Before he was signed for the role, Irving Mansfield, husband-promoter of author Miss Susann, conferred with Ryan to determine his actual health. "Look," said Ryan, "there is one thing about cancer: you don't die quickly. I'll be able to make the picture." Ironically, Ryan was not aware that Jacqueline herself was then unsuccessfully battling a ten year-old fight against the dread disease.

In the last years of his life, Robert remained extremely active. Although plans for him to co-star with Telly Savalas in *Pancho Villa* did not work out, and although other plans were abandoned to have Ryan head an independent production of *Don Quixote,* he did appear in Rene Clement's Canadian-filmed . . . *And Hope to Die* (Twentieth Century-Fox, 1972). As Charlie, the leader of a group of hoodlums and mental defectives, Ryan's taciturn character is planning a million-dollar robbery. Set in the Montreal area, Jean-Louis Trintignant had the lead as a man on the lam who is being hunted by a clan of gypsies because he once accidentally killed some of their children when he crashlanded his plane on a beach. The interaction of Trintignant and Ryan provided an intriguing contrast of acting styles. Sadly, this sturdy gangster film never found its proper level with the critics or the public.

Ironically, for the Ryans who had been so concerned about Robert's malignancy,

With Lea Massari in *And Hope to Die* (20th, 1972)

it was Jessica Ryan, age fifty-seven, who suddenly developed cancer symptoms. On May 22, 1972, she died. Shortly afterward, Ryan transferred his Manhattan home to 135 Central Park West, down the street from The Dakota. It was just too painful for Ryan to continue living in the couple's Dakota dwelling.

Although it would not be revealed until after his death, later in 1972 the sixty-two-year-old Ryan became romantically involved with actress Maureen O'Sullivan,[18] who was also then residing on Central Park West. She would disclose to the press, "I loved Robert very dearly. The love we had for each other was something very special. He was a man of tremendous courage and great feeling. His death was so awful. We hadn't planned a marriage but we would have been very happy to find out if it would have worked."

While undergoing treatment for his cancer condition, Ryan continued to perform oncamera. He made his final television appearance on April 24, 1973, for the ninety-minute ABC-TV special *The Man Without a Country*. Cliff Robertson starred in the title role as Philip Nolan, with Ryan as Vaughan, a naval officer who reports on Robertson's case at the start of the program.

Most of Robert's remaining four features would be released posthumously. Each performance revealed that the actor had carefully selected roles in projects which were meaningful to him for their subject matter, and because, in a few cases, it offered him a new acting challenge.

On the surface *Lolly-Madonna XXX* (MGM, 1973) resembles a blend of *L'il Abner* and *The Grissom Gang*. Set in the Tennessee mountains, it traces the feud between the Feather family (headed by Rod Steiger) and the more recently arrived Gutshalls (led by Robert) over the rights to an adjacent meadow. As the director's program notes for the fiasco detailed, he considered the project an allegory of the bellicose conditions of the present day. In reviewing this here-today-gone-tomorrow film, the Britain's *Monthly Film Bulletin* decided, "[It] slides into a sickly and sickening cautionary tale" with "everything . . . plainly manipulated towards the climactic moment of apocalyptic violence, with every shade of pacifist and war-mongering opinion distributed through each of the families." At the very best, one could only conceive of Ryan's grisly characterization as a wasted extension of his well-meaning but cantankerous Ty Ty of the earlier *God's Little Acre*.

It was even more obvious why Ryan so readily accepted a role in *Executive Action* (National General, 1973). Dalton Trumbo had adapted a scenario from a story by Donald Freed and Mark Lane. (The latter was Lee Harvey Oswald's posthumous attorney and the 1968 Peace and Freedom Party's candidate for vice-president.) The gist of this rather complicated thriller, which combined newly-shot sequences with newsreel footage and restaged reality, was that the American right wing was responsible for the assassination of President John F. Kennedy in Dallas, Texas on November 22, 1963. The film was very hazy regarding Oswald, claiming an imposter (James MacColl) pretended to be Oswald to throw suspicion onto him and his relationship with Jack Ruby (Oscar Oncidi). Actually, the film relied more on sensationalism than cinematic effort for success, and the result was "grim stuff for these times" *(Variety)*. Regarding *Executive Action, Films in Review* analyzed, "As chief conspirators, Burt Lancaster, Robert Ryan and Will Geer give thoroughly professional, low-key performances in what are half-dimensional roles." Unfortunately, Robert, as he sometimes did in his effort for "causes," let the producers use him to

[18]Tisa Farrow, the daughter of Miss O'Sullivan and John Farrow (the director who died in 1963), had a role in Ryan's . . . *And Hope to Die*.

mouth dialogue which espouses their political themes. In one poorly conceived and politically blatant scene Ryan talks about killing blacks, Jews, the poor, Orientals and social undesirables in order to reduce the planet's population. Proving that you can fool some of the people some of the time, *Executive Action* grossed $2.5 million distributors' domestic rentals, thanks largely to a heavy television exploitation campaign.

Released only a few days after *Executive Action* was MGM's *The Outfit* (1973), which was Ryan's last work in the gangster film genre. Following the completion of the film in early 1973 in Los Angeles, that city presented the actor with an official plaque noting his contributions over the years to the art of the cinema.

The Outfit was an old-fashioned thriller which brought together a good number of screen veterans, including genre specialist, Elisha Cook, Jr. Robert was fourth-billed as Mailer, a gangland chief and head of the organization of the title. In *New York* Magazine, Judith Crist noted, "Ryan's syndicate-head is a piece of cake, but, as was his wont throughout his career, he gives dimension and complexity to the smallest and stalest of scenes." While no great shakes as entertainment, the film tried to hurdle a further obstacle when MGM, in its death throes, assigned its remaining products to United Artists to release. *The Outfit* nearly got lost in the distribution shuffle.

Late in October, 1973, Robert's greatest single screen performance was offered. *The Iceman Cometh* was the first of a series of prestigious filmed theatre pieces offered to the public by the American Film Theatre via subscription sales. In its 239-minute version, the motion picture was extremely faithful to the Eugene O'Neill play. Three men (Robert, Jeff Bridges, Bradford Dillman) who frequented Fredric March's bar are impatiently awaiting the arrival of Hickey (Lee Marvin) on his bi-annual drunk. The latter arrives and psychologically tears the men apart so they will give up their "lyin' pipe dreams and hopes" and find peace of mind. Although the bulk of the footage belong to Marvin's loquacious character, all five male stars turned in excellent performances. Most of the critical acclaim was leveled at Ryan, who appeared as Larry Slade, a mentally defeated political activist.

Variety commented, "The late Robert Ryan is amazing. He has enlarged the role of Larry, too frequently played as a glib, whining cynic, and invested him with something close to heroism. The doomed detached anarchist is less a copout in this interpretation than one fearful of exercising a huge power to affect other lives. His strength and dignity have almost created a new Larry." According to Jack Cocks (*Time* Magazine), "The movie belongs most securely to Robert Ryan, and it is an eloquent memorial to his talent. . . . It would be easy to sentimentalize his perform-ance. But such a gesture would diminish its greatness. With the kind of power and intensity that is seldom risked, much less realized, it has its own pride and stature." Charles Champlin summed it all up in the *Los Angeles Times*: "The performance of Robert Ryan is also his monument . . . his finest hour as a superb craftsman." As a result of his acting achievement in this film, the National Board of Review posthu-mously awarded the star the Best Actor of the Year citation for his performance.

According to those who worked with Ryan in his last films, if he was aware that death was so near, he kept it a close secret.[19] In fact, in May, 1973, doctors told Ryan

[19]At one point, near the end, Ryan admitted, "At first it's a shock, then you become reconciled. I am much more tolerant now that I know I'm on borrowed time. I see trees and flowers and pretty girls. I see beauty that I used to be oblivious to. Actually life is much better enjoying it day to day."

In *Executive Action* (National General, 1973)

he was sufficiently recovered from his bouts with cancer that it would be safe for him to sign to play the lead in *Shenandoah*, a musical based on the 1965 James Stewart film which was to open on Broadway the following spring.[20] However, on July 3, the actor was admitted to New York Hospital with a recurrence of the disease which took his life on July 11. During the last days of his life, Maureen O'Sullivan was constantly at his bedside.

After his death, Ryan's body was taken to the Walter B. Cooke Funeral Chapel at 72nd Street and Broadway. There was no viewing, and in place of flowers, the family requested that contributions be made to the Cancer Center. The funeral was held on Monday afternoon, July 17, at the Blessed Sacrament Roman Catholic Church on West 71st Street. It was a completely private service, with the burial taking place in Chicago. The star was survived by his three children: Timothy who lives in California, Cheyney, a lecturer at Boston University, and Lisa, who resides in New York City.

Columnist Pete Hammil offered a fitting tribute to the late actor: "There should be a poem of farewell for Robert Ryan who was a good man in a bad time. . . . The poem should express his quiet presence through so many lonely years when few people were struggling to bring decency to the world.

"Life, death, loneliness, loss: these were some of the things we learned from the quiet art of Robert Ryan, who was a good man in a bad time. It will be a while before we find anything to put in its place."

It was the late Ryan's close friend Harold J. Kennedy who recorded: "[He] was a beautiful actor and an even more beautiful human being. Though his fame was as a film actor, his real love was the legitimate stage and he would do a good part in a good play anytime, anywhere, and for nothing—which he usually did."

[20]After Ryan was forced to drop plans for the *Shenandoah* venture, Jack Palance was mentioned as a replacement. When the musical opened on Broadway in January, 1975, it was John Cullum who played the lead role.

ROBERT RYAN

GOLDEN GLOVES *(Paramount, 1940), 69 min.*
Associate producer, William C. Thomas; director, Edward Dmytryk; story, Maxwell Shane; screenplay, Shane, Lewis R. Foster; art directors, Hans Dreier, William Flannery; music director, Sigmund Krumgold; camera, Henry Sharp; editor, Doane Harrison.

Richard Denning (Bill Crane); Jeanne Cagney (Mary Parker); J. Carrol Naish (Joe Taggerty); Robert Paige (Wally Matson); William Frawley (Emory Balzer); Robert Ryan (Pete Wells); George Ernest (Joey Parker); David Durand (Gumdrop Wilbur); James Seay (Jimmy); Sidney Miller (Sammy Sachs); Johnny Morris (Jerry Kolker); Frank Coghlan, Jr. (Kid Lester); Alec Craig (McDonald); Thomas E. Jackson (Sergeant Piersall); Lorraine Kreuger (Jenny); Leona Roberts (Mrs. Parker); John Gallaudet (Folger); Pierre Watkin (A. P. Berton); Philip Warren (Hank); Norman Phillips (Gordon); Matty Kemp (Lefty); Abner Biberman (Torsovitch); Joe Devlin (Cloudy Maple); Edward Earle (Mr. Lester); Harold Minjir (Willoughby); Byron Foulger (Hemingway); Frank Bruno (Gimble); James Millican (Bob); John Laird (Employee); Rolfe Sedan (Pepper Customer); George Anderson (Doctor); Jimmy Butler (Willie

Burke); Pop Byron, Harry Bailey (Customers); Lee Phelps (Announcer); Jack North (Jake); John "Skins" Miller (Carpenter).

QUEEN OF THE MOB *(Paramount, 1940), 61 min.*

Director, James Hogan; based on the book *Persons in Hiding* by J. Edgar Hoover; screenplay, Horace McCoy, William R. Lipman; art directors, Hans Dreier, Ernst Fegte; camera, Theodor Sparkuhl; editor, Arthur Schmidt.

Ralph Bellamy (Scott Langham); Jack Carson (Ross Waring); Blanche Yurka (Ma Webster); Richard Denning (Charles Webster); James Seay (Eddie Webster); Paul Kelly (Tom Webster); William Henry (Bert Webster); Jeanne Cagney (Ethel Webster); J. Carrol Naish (George Frost); Hedda Hopper (Mrs. Emily Sturgis); Pierre Watkin (Stitch Torey); Billy Gilbert (Caterer); John Harmon (Pinky); John Miljan (Pan); Russell Hicks (Judge); William Duncan (District Attorney); Raymond Hatton (Auto Camp Proprietor); Betty McLaughlin (Girl); Leona Roberts (Mrs. Greenough); Charles Lane (Horace Grimley); Charlotte Wynters (Mrs. Grimley); Neil Hamilton (Murdock); Robert Ryan (Jim); Tommy Conley (Billy Webster); Lloyd Corrigan (Photographer); Edward Gargan (Policeman in Bank); Mary Treen (Billy's Nurse); Harry Bradley (Lawyer); May Beatty (Ellen); Selmer Jackson (Bank Manager); William Pawley (Man with Pan); John "Skins" Miller (Man in Hideout); Edgar Dearing (Motorcycle Cop); Donald Douglas (F.B.I. Director); James Flavin (F.B.I. Chief); Mary Gordon (Janitress); Paul Fix, Brooks Benedict (Men); Charles McMurphy (Bailiff); Ethan Laidlaw (Court Officer); Alec Craig (Proprietor).

NORTHWEST MOUNTED POLICE *(Paramount, 1940), C-125 min.*

Producer, Cecil B. DeMille; associate producer, William H. Pine; director, DeMille; based on the book *Royal Canadian Mounted Police* by R. C. Fetherston-Haugh; screenplay, Alan LeMay, Jesse Lasky, Jr., C. Gardner Sullivan; art directors, Hans Dreier, Roland Anderson; set decorators, Dan Sayre Groesbeck, Joe De Yong; assistant director, Arthur Rosson; costumes, Natalie Visart, De Yong; makeup, Wally Westmore; dialogue supervisor, Edwin Maxwell; Technicolor consultants, Natalie Kalmus, Henri Jaffa; technical advisors, Major G. F. Griffin, R.C.M.P., Sergeant George A. Pringle, N.W.M.P.; music, Victor Young; sound, Harry M. Lindgren, John Cope; special effects, Gordon Jennings, Farciot Edouart; camera, Victor Milner, W. Howard Greene; editor, Anne Bauchens.

Gary Cooper (Dusty Rivers); Madeleine Carroll (April Logan); Paulette Goddard (Louvette Corbeau); Preston Foster (Sergeant Jim Brett); Robert Preston (Constable Ronnie Logan); George Bancroft (Jacques Corbeau); Lynn Overman (Tod Croft); Akim Tamiroff (Dan Duroc); Walter Hampden (Chief Big Bear); Lon Chaney, Jr. (Shorty); Montagu Love (Inspector Cabot); Francis McDonald (Louis Riel); George E. Stone (Johnny Pelang); Willard Robertson (Superintendent Harrington); Regis Toomey (Constable Jerry Moore); Richard Denning (Constable Thornton); Robert Ryan (Constable Dumont); Douglas Kennedy (Constable Carter); Clara Blandick (Mrs. Burns); Ralph Byrd (Constable Ackroyd); Lane Chandler (Constable Fyffe); Julia Faye (Wapiskan); Jack Pennick (Sergeant Field); Rod Cameron (Corporal Underhill); James Seay (Constable Fenton); Jack Chapin (Bugler); Eric Alden (Constable Kent); Wallace Reid, Jr. (Constable Rankin); Bud Geary (Constable Herrick); Evan Thomas (Captain Gower); Jack Pennick (Sergeant Field); Chief Thundercloud (Wandering Spirit); Harry Burns (The Crow); Lou Merrill (Lesur); Ynez Seabury (Mrs. Shorty); Eva Puig (Ekawo); Julia Faye (Wapiskau); Norma Nelson (Niska); John Hart (Constable Norman); Phillip Terry (Constable Judson); Ethan Laidlaw (Constable Adams); Kermit Maynard (Constable Porter); Emory Parnell (George Higgins); Jim Pierce, John Laird (Corporals); James Flavin, Colin Tapley (Mounties); Sid D'Albrook (Anton); Ray Mala, Chief Yowlachie, Chief Thunderbird (Indians); Franklyn Farnum (Townsman).

TEXAS RANGERS RIDE AGAIN *(Paramount, 1941), 68 min.*
Director, James Hogan; screenplay, William R. Lipman, Horace McCoy; camera, Archie Stout; editor, Arthur Schmidt.

Ellen Drew (Ellen "Slats" Dangerfield); John Howard (Jim Kingston); Akim Tamiroff (Mio Pio); May Robson (Cecilia Dangerfield); Broderick Crawford (Mase Townsley); Charley Grapewin (Ben Caldwalder); John Miljan (Carter Dangerfield); William Duncan (Captain Inglis); Anthony Quinn (Joe Yuma); Harvey Stephens (Blair); Eva Puig (Maria); Harold Goodwin (Comstock); Edward Pawley (Palo Pete); Eddie Foy, Jr. (Mandelin); Joseph Crehan (Johnson); Jim Pierce (Highboots); Monte Blue (Slide Along); Stanley Price (Nevers); Tom Tyler (Gilpin); Donald Curtis (Stafford); Franklin Parker (Gas Station Attendant); Chuck Hamilton (Truck Driver); Charles Lane (Train Passenger); Eddie Acuff (Stenographer); Henry Roquemore (Conductor); Paul Kruger (Laborer); Robert Ryan (Eddie—Boy in Car); Ruth Rogers (Girl in Car); Gordon Jones (Announcer); Jack Perrin (Radio Technician); John "Skins" Miller (Station Attendant).

BOMBARDIER *(RKO, 1943), 99 min.*
Producer, Robert Fellows; director, Richard Wallace; story, John Twist, Martin Rackin; screenplay, Twist; music director, C. Bakaleinikoff; music, Roy Webb; songs, M. K. Jerome and Jack Scholl; art directors, Albert D'Agostino, Al Herman; set decorators, Darrell Silvera, Claude Carpenter; assistant director, Edward Killy; montage, Douglas Travers; sound, Bailey Fesler, James G. Stewart; special effects, Vernon L. Walker; camera, Nicholas Musuraca; editor, Robert Wise.

Pat O'Brien (Major Chick Davis); Randolph Scott (Captain Buck Oliver); Anne Shirley (Burt Hughes); Eddie Albert (Tom Hughes); Walter Reed (Jim Carter); Robert Ryan (Joe Connor); Barton MacLane (Sergeant Dixon); Richard Martin (Chito Rafferty); Russell Wade (Paul Harris); James Newill (Captain Rand); Bruce Edwards (Lieutenant Ellis); John Miljan (Chaplain Craig); Harold Landon (Pete Jordon); Margie Stewart (Mamie); Joe King (General Barnes); Leonard Strong (Jap Officer); Abner Biberman (Jap Sergeant); Russell Hoyt (Photographer); Wayne McCoy, Charles Russell (Instructors); Bud Geary (Sergeant); Warren Mace, George Ford, Mike Lally (Co-Pilots); Neil Hamilton, Lloyd Ingraham (Colonels); James Craven (Major Harris); Cy Ring (Captain Randall); Joan Barclay, Marty Faust (Bits); John Calvert (Illusionist); Eddie Dew, Kirby Grant (Pilots); Hugh Beaumont (Soldier); Dick Winslow (Navigator); Bert Moorhouse (Congressman).

THE SKY'S THE LIMIT *(RKO, 1943), 89 min.*
Producer, David Hempstead; associate producer, Sherman Todd; director, Edward H. Griffith; based on the story *A Handful of Heaven* by Frank Fenton, Lynn Root; screenplay, Fenton, Root; songs, Johnny Mercer and Harold Arlen; choreography-stager, Fred Astaire; music director, Leigh Harline; art directors, Albert S. D'Agostino, Carroll Clark; set decorators, Darrell Silvera, Claude Carpenter; assistant director, Ruby Rosenberg; sound, Terry Kellum, James Stewart; special effects, Vernon L. Walker; camera, Russell Metty; editor, Roland Gross.

Fred Astaire (Fred Atwell [Fred Burton]); Joan Leslie (Joan Manion); Robert Benchley (Phil Harriman); Robert Ryan (Reg Fenton); Elizabeth Patterson (Mrs. Fisher); Marjorie Gateson (Canteen Hostess); Richard Davies (Lieutenant Dick Merlin); Clarence Kolb (Harvey J. Sloan); Freddie Slack & His Orchestra (Colonial Club Orchestra); Eric Blore (Jackson); Henri DeSoto (Headwaiter); Dorothy Kelly (Harriman's Secretary); Norma Drury (Mrs. Roskowski); Jerry Mandy (Italian Waiter); Clarence Muse (Doorman); Ida Shoemaker (Flower Woman); Paul Hurst (Stevedore Foreman); Amelita Ward (San Francisco Girl); Rhoda Reese (Powers

Model); Neil Hamilton (Naval Commander); Dick Rush (Railway Conductor); Georgia Caine (Charwoman); Ann Summers, Rita Maritt (Bits); Buck Bucko, Roy Buco, Clint Sharp (Cowboys); Ed McNamara (Barman); Joe Bernard, Al Murphy (Bartenders); Jack Carr (Customer); Ferris Taylor (Keifer the Chef); Peter Lawford (USAF Officer); Olin Howland (4-F Man); Victor Potel (Joe the Bartender).

BEHIND THE RISING SUN *(RKO, 1943), 89 min.*

Director, Edward Dmytryk; based on the book by James R. Young; screenplay, Emmet Lavery; assistant director, Ruby Rosenberg; art directors, Albert S. D'Agostino, Al Herman; set decorators, Darrell Silvera, Claude Carpenter; music, Roy Webb; music director, C. Bakaleinikoff; sound, Terry Kellum, James G. Stewart; special effects, Vernon L. Walker; camera, Russell Metty; editor, Joseph Noriega.

Margo (Tama); Tom Neal (Taro); J. Carrol Naish (Publisher); Robert Ryan (Lefty); Gloria Holden (Sara); Don Douglas (O'Hara); George Givot (Boris); Adeline deWalt Reynolds (Grandmother); Leonard Strong (Tama's Father); Iris Wong (Secretary); Wolfgang Zilzer (Max); Shirley Lew (Servant); Benson Fong, Philip Ahn, Richard Loo, William Yip (Japanese Officers); Lee Tung Foo (Dinner Guest); Mike Mazurki (Japanese Wrestler); Paul Hilton (Japanese School Boy); George Lee (Japanese Soldier); Paul Fung, James Leong, Spencer Chan, Stanley Wong (Japanese Swordsmen); Preston Don Lee (Japanese Boy); H. T. Tsiang (Policeman); Nancy Gates (Sister); Connie Leon (Tama's Mother); Abner Biberman (Inspector); Allan Jung (Captain Matsuda); Robert Katcher (Professor Namachi); Charles Lung (Broker); Beal Wong (Japanese Major).

GANGWAY FOR TOMORROW *(RKO, 1943), 69 min.*

Producer-director, John H. Auer; story, Aladar Laszlo, Arch Oboler; screenplay, Oboler; music, Roy Webb; music director, C. Bakaleinikoff; art directors, Albert S. D'Agostino, Al Herman; set decorators, Darrell Silvera, William Stevens; assistant director, Lloyd Richards; sound, Terry Kellum, James G. Stewart; special effects, Vernon L. Walker; camera, Nicholas Musuraca; editor, George Crone.

Margo (Lisette); John Carradine (Wellington); Robert Ryan (Joe Dunham); Amelita Ward (Mary Jones); William Terry (Bob Nolan); Harry Davenport (Fred Taylor); James Bell (Burke); Charles Arnt (Jim Benson); Alan Carney (Swallow); Wally Brown (Sam); Erford Gage (Dan Barton); Richard Ryen (Colonel Mueller); Warren Hymer (Pete); Michael St. Angel, Don Dillaway (Drivers); Bruce Edwards (Rogan); Carole Gallagher (Peanuts); Wheaton Chambers (Priest); Hope Landin (Emma); Earle Hodgins (Constable); Anne Kundee (Sara Henry); Al Kundee (Sam Kowalski); Al Ferguson (Ed Gilroy); Angelos Desfis (Worker); Richard Martin (Jules); Ida Shoemaker (Grandma); Harro Meller (Officer); Sam McDaniel (Hank); John Wald (Radio Announcer); Dave Thursby (Fogarty); Edythe Elliott (Mary's Mother); Noelle DeLorme (French Girl in Truck); Chester Carlisle, Brandon Beach (Judges); Robert Bice (Stooge); Frederick Brunn (General Sergeant); Hooper Atchley (Desk Clerk); John Sheehan (Producer Bell).

THE IRON MAJOR *(RKO, 1943), 85 min.*

Producer, Robert Fellows; director, Ray Enright; based on the story by Florence S. Cavanaugh; screenplay, Aben Kandel, Warren Duff; art directors, Albert S. D'Agostino, Carroll Clark; set decorators, Darrell Silvera, Al Fields; technical advisers, William "Hiker" Joy, Ernest E. La Blanche; music, Roy Webb; music director, C. Bakaleinikoff; assistant director, Edward Killy; sound, Terry Kellum, James G. Stewart; camera, Robert de Grasse; editors, Robert Wise, Philip Martin, Jr.

Pat O'Brien (Frank Cavanaugh); Ruth Warrick (Florence "Mike" Ayres Cavanaugh); Robert Ryan (Father Tim Donovan); Leon Ames (Robert Stewart); Russell Wade (Private Manning); Bruce Edwards (Lieutenant Jones); Richard Martin (Davie Cavanaugh); Robert Bice (Coach); Virginia Brissac (Mrs. Ayres); Robert Anderson, Mike Lally, Lee Phelps, Craig Flanagan, Michael Road (Bits); Arnold Stanford, Bob Thom (Soldiers); Lew Harvey (Lieutenant); Bud Geary (Sergeant); Walter Brooke (Lieutenant Stone); Louis Jean Heydt (Recruiting Sergeant); Frank Puglia (Nurse); Pierre Watkin (Colonel White); Walter Fenner (Doctor); Louis Borell (French Officer); Billy Roy (Bob as a Boy); Robert Winkler (Frank as a Boy); Cy Ring (Ross); Wheaton Chambers (Army Doctor); Dean Benton (William Cavanaugh); Myron Healey (Paul Cavanaugh); Kirk Alyn (John Cavanaugh); James Jordan (Philip Cavanaugh); Victor Kilian (Francis Cavanaugh); Margaret Landry (Sis Cavanaugh); Ian Wolfe (Professor Runnymead); Harry Tyler, Eddie Woods (Friends); Pat O'Malley (Charlie); Gloria Duran, Ramon Ros (Dancers); Bonnie Braunger (Baby); Sada Simmons, Mary Currier (Nurses); Joe Crehan (Judge); Joe King (Defense Attorney); Eddie Hart (Bailiff); Milton Kibbee (Watkins); Paul LePere (Court Clerk); Joe O'Connor (Second Defense Attorney); Harold Landon, James Courtney, Buddy Yarus, Mel Schubert, Greg McClure (Boston College Players); Sam McDaniel (Pete); John Miljan (Oregon Coach); John Dilson (Doctor); Dorothy Vaughan (Ma Cavanaugh); Frank Shannon (Pa Cavanaugh); Richard Davies (Chuck, a Player); Brooks Benedict, Brandon Beach (Alumni); Florence Hansen (Bob's Girl Friend); Fred Kohler, Jr. (Boston College Captain).

TENDER COMRADE *(RKO, 1943), 101 min.*

Producer, David Hempstead; associate producer, Sherman Todd; director, Edward Dmytryk; story-screenplay, Dalton Trumbo; art directors, Albert S. D'Agostino, Carroll Clark; set decorators, Darrell Silvera, Al Fields; music director, C. Bakaleinikoff; music, Leigh Harline; sound, Roy Meadows; special effects, Vernon L. Walker; camera, Russell Metty; editor, Roland Gross.

Ginger Rogers (Jo); Robert Ryan (Chris); Ruth Hussey (Barbara); Patricia Collinge (Helen Stacey); Mady Christians (Manya); Kim Hunter (Doris); Jane Darwell (Mrs. Henderson); Mary Forbes (Jo's Mother); Richard Martin (Mike); Richard Gaines (Waldo Pierson); Patti Brill (Western Union Girl); Euline Martin (Baby); Edward Fielding (Doctor); Claire Whitney (Nurse); Donald Davis, Robert Anderson (Boys).

MARINE RAIDERS *(RKO, 1944), 91 min.*

Producer, Robert Fellows; director, Harold Schuster; story, Warren Duff, Martin Rackin; screenplay, Duff; assistant director, Edward Killy; art directors, Albert S. D'Agostino, Walter E. Keller; set decorators, Darrell Silvera, Harley Miller; music, Roy Webb; music director, C. Bakaleinikoff; sound, James S. Thomson; special effects, Vernon L. Walker; camera, Nicholas Musuraca; editor, Philip Martin, Jr.

Pat O'Brien (Major Steve Lockhard); Robert Ryan (Captain Dan Craig); Ruth Hussey (Ellen Foster); Frank McHugh (Sergeant Louis Leary); Barton MacLane (Sergeant Maguire); Richard Martin (Jimmy); Edmund Glover (Miller); Russell Wade (Tony Hewitt); Robert Andersen (Lieutenant Harrigan); Michael St. Angel (Lieutenant Sherwood); Martha Vickers (Sally); Harry Brown (Cook); Sammy Stein (Sergeant); Edward Fielding (General Slayton); William Forrest (Colonel Carter); Richard Davies (Instructor); Jimmy Jordan (Jackson); Chris Drake (Orderly); Mike Kilian (Shoe Gag Soldier); Patrick O'Moore (Doctor); Patricia Cameron (Nurse); Robert Dane (Lieutenant, j.g.); Selmer Jackson (Colonel Douglas); James Leong (Japanese Officer); Bert Moorhouse (Ship's Captain); James Hamilton, Jack Reeves, Melvin Mix, James Damore, Glenn Vernon, Blake Edwards, Carl Kent, Don Dillaway (Marines); Eddie Acuff (Marine Veteran); Laurie Shermoen (Communications Corp.); George Ford

(Flyer); Barry Macollum (Inn Keeper); Daun Kennedy (Model); Mike Lally (Conductor); Isabel O'Madigan (Newswoman).

TRAIL STREET *(RKO, 1947), 84 min.*

Executive producer, Jack Gross; producer, Nat Holt; director, Ray Enright; based on the novel *Golden Horizons* by William Corcoran; screenplay, Norman Houston, Gene Lewis; art directors, Albert S. D'Agostino, Ralph Berger; set decorators, Darrell Silvera, John Sturtevant; music, Paul Sawtell; assistant director, Grayson Rogers; sound, John L. Speak; montage, Harold Palmer; special effects, Russell A. Cully; camera, J. Roy Hunt; editor, Lyle Boyer.

Randolph Scott (Bat Masterson); Robert Ryan (Allen Harper); Anne Jeffreys (Ruby Stone); George "Gabby" Hayes (Billy and Brandyhead Jones); Madge Meredith (Susan Pritchett); Steve Brodie (Logan Maury); Billy House (Carmody); Virginia Sale (Hannah); Harry Woods (Lance Larkin); Phil Warren (Slim); Harry Harvey (Mayor); Jason Robards (Jason); Elena Warren (Mrs. Brown); Betty Hill (Dance Hall Girl); Al Murphy (Dealer); Larry McGrath, Warren Jackson, Billy Vincent, Howard McCrorey, Glen McCarthy (Henchmen); Ernie Adams (Eben Bowen); Lew Harvey (Heavy); Kit Guard (Drunk); Roy Butler, Frank Austin, Carl Wester, Sam Lufkin, Joe Brockman (Farmers); Guy Beach (Doc Evans); Jessie Arnold (Jason's Wife); Paul Dunn, Donald Olson, Eugene Perrson (Boys); Willowbird (Indian); Frank McGlynn (McKeon); Sarah Padden (Mrs. Ferguson); Stanley Andrews (Ferguson); Forrest Taylor (Dave).

THE WOMAN ON THE BEACH *(RKO, 1947), 71 min.*

Executive producer, Jack J. Gross; associate producer, Will Price; director, Jean Renoir; based on the novel *None So Blind* by Mitchell Wilson; adaptor, Michael Hogan; screenplay, Frank Davis, Renoir; art directors, Albert S. D'Agostino, Walter E. Keller; set decorators, Darrell Silvera, John Sturtevant; technical adviser, Charles H. Gardiner, Lt. Comdr. USCGR; music, Hanns Eisler; music director, C. Bakaleinikoff; orchestrator, Gil Grau; dialogue director, Paula Walling; assistant director, James Casey; sound, Jean L. Speak, Clem Portman; montage, Harold Palmer; special effects, Russell A. Cully; camera, Leo Tover, Harry Wild; editor, Roland Gross, Lyle Boyer.

Joan Bennett (Peggy); Robert Ryan (Scott); Charles Bickford (Tod); Nan Leslie (Eve); Walter Sande (Otto Wernecke); Irene Ryan (Mrs. Wernecke); Glenn Vernon (Kirk); Frank Darien (Lars); Jay Norris (Jimmy); Hugh Chapman (Young Fisherman); Carl Faulkner (Old Fisherman); Marie Dodd (Nurse); Harry Harvey (Dr. Smith); Charles Pawley (Barton); Robert Andersen, Drew Miller, Robert Manning (Coast Guardsmen); Martha Hyer (Mrs. Barton); Bonnie Blair, Carol Donell, Kay Christopher, Nancy Saunders (Girls at Party); John Elliott (Old Workman); Jackie Jackson (Johnnie); Donald Gordon (Donnie); Harry Tyler (Carter); Bill Shannon (Blacksmith).

CROSSFIRE *(RKO, 1947), 86 min.*

Executive producer, Dore Schary; producer, Adrian Scott; director, Edward Dmytryk; based on the novel *The Brick Foxhole* by Richard Brooks; screenplay, John Paxton; art directors, Albert S. D'Agostino, Alfred Herman; set decorators, Darrell Silvera, John Sturtevant; music, Roy Webb; music director, C. Bakaleinikoff; assistant director, Nate Levinson; sound, John E. Tribby, Clem Portman; special camera effects, Russell A. Cully; camera, J. Roy Hunt; editor, Harry Gerstad.

Robert Young (Captain Finlay); Robert Mitchum (Sergeant Peter Keeley); Robert Ryan

(Monty Montgomery); Gloria Grahame (Ginny Tremaine); Paul Kelly (The Man); Sam Levene (Joseph Samuels); Jacqueline White (Mary Mitchell); Steve Brodie (Floyd Bowers); George Cooper (Arthur Mitchell); Richard Benedict (Bill Williams); Tom Keene (Detective); William Phipps (Leroy); Lex Barker (Harry); Marlo Dwyer (Miss Lewis); Harry Harvey (Tenant); Carl Faulkner (Deputy); Jay Norris, Robert Bray, George Turner, Don Cadell (M.P.s); George Meader (Police Surgeon); Bill Nind (Waiter); Allen Ray (Soldier); Kenneth MacDonald (Major); Philip Morris (Police Sergeant).

BERLIN EXPRESS *(RKO, 1948), 86 min.*

Executive producer, Dore Schary; producer, Bert Granet; assistant producer, William Dorfman; director, Jacques Tourneur; story, Curt Siodmak; screenplay, Harold Medford; art directors, Albert S. D'Agostino, Alfred Herman; set decorators, Darrell Silvera, William Stevens; music, Frederick Hollander; music director, C. Bakaleinikoff; assistant director, Nate Levinson; makeup, Gordon Bau; costumes, Orry-Kelly; sound, Jack Grubb, Clem Portman; special effects, Harry Perry, Russell A. Cully, Harold Stine; camera, Lucien Ballard; editor, Sherman Todd.

Merle Oberon (Lucienne); Robert Ryan (Robert Lindley); Charles Korvin (Perrot); Paul Lukas (Dr. Bernhardt); Robert Coote (Sterling); Reinhold Schunzel (Walther); Roman Toporow (Lieutenant Maxim); Peter Von Zerneck (Hans Schmidt); Otto Waldis (Kessler); Fritz Kortner (Franzen); Michael Harvey (Sergeant Barnes); Tom Keene (Major); Jim Nolan (Train Captain); Arthur Dulac (Dining Car Steward); Ray Spiker, Bruce Cameron (Huskies); Charles McGraw (Colonel Johns); Buddy Roosevelt (M.P. Sergeant); David Clarke (Army Technician); Roger Creed (M.P.); William Yetter, Jr. Robert Boon (German Youths); David Wold, Taylor Allen, George Holt, Bill Raisch, Carl Ekberg, Hans Hopf (Germans); Willy Wickerhauser (Frederich); Will Allister (Richard); Richard Flato (Master of Ceremonies); Jack Serailian (Cigarette Maker); Norbert Schiller (Saxophone Player); Bert Goodrich, George Redpath (Acrobatic Team); Marle Hayden (Maja); Eric Wyland (Clown); Gene Evans (Train Sergeant); Robert Shaw (R.O.T. Sergeant); Hermine Sterler (Frau Borne); Curt Furburg (German Bystander); Fred Datig, Jr. (American Jeep Driver); Leonid Snegoff (Russian Colonel); James Craven (British Major).

RETURN OF THE BAD MEN *(RKO, 1948), 89 min.*

Executive producer, Jack J. Gross; producer, Nat Holt; director, Ray Enright; story, Jack Natteford, Luci Ward; screenplay, Charles O'Neal, Natteford, Luci Ward; art directors, Albert S. D'Agostino, Ralph Berger; set decorators, Darrell Silvera, James Altwies; music, Paul Sawtell; music director, C. Bakaleinikoff; assistant director, Grayson Rogers; makeup, Gordon Bau; costumes, Renie; sound, Jean L. Speak, Terry Kellum; special effects, Russell A. Cully; camera, J. Roy Hunt; editor, Samuel E. Beetley.

Randolph Scott (Vance); Robert Ryan (Sundance Kid); Anne Jeffreys (Cheyenne); George "Gabby" Hayes (John Pettit); Jacqueline White (Madge Allen); Steve Brodie (Cole Younger); Tom Keene (Jim Younger); Robert Bray (John Younger); Lex Barker (Emmett Dalton); Walter Reed (Bob Dalton); Michael Harvey (Grat Dalton); Dean White (Billy the Kid); Robert Armstrong (Wild Bill Doolin); Tom Tyler (Wild Bill Yeager); Lew Harvey (Arkansas Kid); Gary Gray (Johnny); Walter Baldwin (Muley Wilson); Minna Gombell (Emily); Warren Jackson (George Mason); Robert Clarke (Dave); Jason Robards (Judge Harper); Harry Shannon (Wade Templeton); Charles McAvoy (Elmer); Larry McGrath (Scout); Ernie Adams (Leslie the Townsman); Billy Vincent, Howard McCrorey (Deputies); George Nokes (Donald Webster); Ronnie Ralph (Tim Webster); Polly Bailey (Mrs. Webster); Forrest Taylor (Farmer); Lane Chandler (Ed the Posse Leader); Bud Osborne (Steve the Stagecoach Driver); Brandon

Beach (Conductor); Charles Stevens (Grey Eagle); Kenneth McDonald (Colonel Markham); Ida Moore (Mrs. Moore); Dan Foster (Outlaw); Richard Thorne (Soldier); John Hamilton (Doc Peters); Cy Ring (Bank Clerk); Earle Hodgins (Auctioneer).

ACT OF VIOLENCE *(MGM, 1948), 82 min.*
Producer, William H. Wright; director, Fred Zinnemann; story, Collier Young; screenplay, Robert L. Richards; art directors, Cedric Gibbons, Hans Peters; set decorators, Edwin B. Willis, Henry W. Grace; music, Bronislau Kaper; music director, Andre Previn; assistant director, Marvin Stuart; makeup, Jack Dawn; sound, Douglas Shearer, Charles E. Wallace; camera, Robert Surtees; editor, Conrad A. Nervig.

Van Heflin (Frank Enley); Robert Ryan (Joe Parkson); Janet Leigh (Edith Enley); Mary Astor (Pat); Phyllis Thaxter (Ann Sturges); Berry Kroeger (Johnny); Nicholas Joy (Mr. Gavery); Harry Antrim (Fred Finney); Connie Gilchrist (Martha Finney); Will Wright (Pop); Tom Hanlon (Radio Voice); Phil Tead (Clerk); Eddie Waglin (Bellboy); William "Bill" Phillips (Vet); Larry and Leslie Holt (Georgie Enley); Garry Owen (Attendant); Fred Santley (Drunk); Johnny Albright (Bellboy); Dick Elliott (Pompous Man); Irene Seidner (Old Woman); Ralph Peters (Tim the Bartender); Douglas Carter (Heavy Jowled Man); Frank Scannell (Bell Captain); Rocco Lanzo, Rex Downing, Mickey Martin (Teenage Boys); Dick Simmons (Vet); Don Haggerty, Paul Kruger (Cops); William Bailey, Phil Dunham, Wilbur Mack (Drunks); Howard Mitchell (Bartender); Walter Merrill, Ralph Montgomery, Cameron Grant (Men at Bar); George Ovey, Jimmie Kelly, David Newell, Fred Datig, Jr., Margaret Bert, Mary Jo Ellis, Ann Lawrence (Bystanders at Accident); Robert Skelton (Cab Driver); Andre Pola, Rudolph Anders, Ann Lawrence (German Voices); Florita Romero (Girl in Church).

THE BOY WITH GREEN HAIR *(RKO, 1948), C-82 min.*
Executive producer, Dore Schary; producer, Stephen Ames; director, Joseph Losey; based on the story by Betsy Beaton; screenplay, Ben Barzman, Alfred Lewis Levitt; art directors, Albert S. D'Agostino, Ralph Berger; set decorators, Darrell Silvera, William Stevens; music, Leigh Harline; orchestra, Gil Grau; music director, C. Bakaleinikoff; Technicolor consultants, Natalie Kalmus, Morgan Padelford; makeup, Gordon Bau; costumes, Adele Balkan; assistant director, James Lane; sound, Earl Wolcott, Clem Portman; camera, George Barnes; editor, Frank Doyle

Pat O'Brien (Gramp); Robert Ryan (Dr. Evans); Barbara Hale (Miss Brand); Dean Stockwell (Peter); Richard Lyon (Michael); Walter Catlett ("The King"); Samuel S. Hinds (Dr. Knudson); Regis Toomey (Mr. Davis); Charles Meredith (Mr. Piper); David Clarke (Barber); Billy Sheffield (Red); John Calkins (Danny); Teddy Infuhr (Timmy); Dwayne Hickman (Joey); Eilene Janssen (Peggy); Curtis Jackson (Classmate); Charles Arnt (Mr. Hammond); Don Pietro (Newsboy); Patricia Byrnes, Carol Coombs, Cynthia Robichaux, Georgette Crooks, Donna Jo Gribble (Girls); Billy White, Rusty Tamblyn, Baron White, Spear Martin (Boys); Peter Brocco (Mr. Hammond); Max Rose (Man); Al Murphy (Janitor); Anna Q. Nilsson, Lynn Whitney (Townswomen); Eula Guy (Mrs. Fisher); Brick Sullivan, Kenneth Patterson, Dale Robertson (Cops); Ann Carter (Eva); Howard Brody (Eva's Brother); Ray Burkett, Warren Shannon (Short Old Men); Wendy Oser (Frail Girl).

CAUGHT *(MGM, 1949), 88 min.*
Producer, Wolfgang Reinhardt; director, Max Opuls; based on the novel *Wild Calendar* by Libbie Block; screenplay, Arthur Laurents; art director, Frank Sylos; set decorator, Edward G. Boyle; music, Frederick Hollander; music director, Rudolph Polk; assistant director, Albert van Schmus; makeup, Gus Norin; wardrobe, Louise Wilson; technical adviser, Dr. Leo Mor-

ton Schulman; sound, Max Hutchinson; montage, Michael Luciano; process camera, Mario Castegnaro; camera, Lee Garmes; editor, Robert Parrish.

James Mason (Larry Quinada); Barbara Bel Geddes (Leonora Eames); Robert Ryan (Smith Ohlrig); Ruth Brady (Maxine); Curt Bois (Franzi); Frank Ferguson (Dr. Hoffman); Natalie Schaefer (Dorothy Dale); Art Smith (Psychiatrist); Sonia Darrin (Miss Chambers); Bernadene Hayes (Mrs. Rudecki); Ann Morrison (Miss Murray); Wilton Graff (Gentry); Jim Hawkins (Kevin); Vicki Raw Stiener (Lorraine).

THE SET-UP *(RKO, 1949), 72 min.*
Producer, Richard Goldstone; director, Robert Wise; based on the poem by Joseph Moncure Marsh; screenplay, Art Cohn; art directors, Albert S. D'Agostino, Jack Okey; set decorators, Darrell Silvera, James Altwies; music and music director, C. Bakaleinikoff; technical adviser, John Indrisano; makeup, Gordon Bau; sound, Phil Brigandi, Clem Portman; assistant director, Edward Killy; camera, Milton Krasner; editor, Roland Gross.

Robert Ryan (Stoker); Audrey Totter (Julie); George Tobias (Tiny); Alan Baxter (Little Boy); Wallace Ford (Gus); Percy Helton (Red); Hal Baylor (Tiger Nelson); Darryl Hickman (Shanley); Kenny O'Morrison (Moore); James Edwards (Luther Hawkins); David Clarke (Gunboat Johnson); Phillip Pine (Souza); Edwin Max (Danny); Dave Fresco (Mickey); William E. Green (Doctor); Abe Dinovitch (Ring Caller); Jack Chase (Hawkins' Second); Mike Lally, Arthur Sullivan, William McCarter (Handlers); Herbert Anderson, Jack Raymonds, Helen Brown, Constance Worth (Married Couples); Archie Leonard (Blind Man); Ralph Volkie, Tony Merrill, Lillian Castle, Frances Mack, Sam Shack, Carl Sklover (Bits); Larry Anzalone (Mexican Fighter); Jess Kirkpatrick, Paul Dubov (Gamblers); Jack Stoney (Nelson's Second); John Butler (Blind Man's Companion); Walter Ridge (Manager); Bernard Gorcey (Tobacco Man); Donald Kerr (Vendor).

THE WOMAN ON PIER 13 *(a.k.a., I MARRIED A COMMUNIST, RKO, 1949), 73 min.*
Executive producer, Sid Rogell; producer, Jack J. Gross; director, Robert Stevenson; story, George W. George, George F. Slavin; screenplay, Charles Grayson, Robert Hardy Andrews; art directors, Albert S. D'Agostino, Walter E. Keller; set decorators, Darrell Silvera, James Altwies; music, Leigh Harline; music director, C. Bakaleinikoff; assistant director, William Dorfman; makeup, W. H. Phillips; costumes, Michael Woulfe; sound, Phil Brigandi, Clem Portman; camera, Nicholas Musuraca; editor, Roland Gross.

Laraine Day (Nan Collins); Robert Ryan (Brad Collins); John Agar (Don Lowry); Thomas Gomez (Vanning); Janis Carter (Christine); Richard Rober (Jim Travis); William Talman (Bailey); Paul E. Burns (Arnold); Paul Guilfoyle (Ralston); G. Pat Collins (Charles Dover); Fred Graham (Grip Wilson); Harry Cheshire (Mr. Cornwell); Jack Stoney (Garth); Lester Mathews (Dr. Dixon); Marlo Dwyer (Evelyn); Erskine Sanford (Clerk); Bess Flowers (Secretary); Charles Cane (Hagen); Dick Ryan (Waiter at Cocktail Bar); Barry Brooks (Burke); William Haade (Cahill); John Duncan (Bellhop); Iris Adrian (Waitress); Don Brodie (Drunk); Al Murphy (Jeb); Evelyn Ceder (Girlfriend); Marie Voe (Striptease Dancer); Jim Nolan (Cop).

THE SECRET FURY *(RKO, 1950), 86 min.*
Producer, Jack Skirball; director, Mel Ferrer; story, Jack R. Leonard, James O'Hanlon; screenplay, Lionel House; art directors, Albert S. D'Agostino, Carroll Clark; music director, C. Bakaleinikoff; camera, Leo Tover; editor, Harry Marker.

Claudette Colbert (Ellen); Robert Ryan (David); Jane Cowl (Aunt Clara); Paul Kelly (Eric

Lowell); Philip Ober (Kent); Elisabeth Risdon (Dr. Twining); Doris Dudley (Pearl); Dave Barbour (Lucian Randall); Vivian Vance (Leah); Percy Helton (Justice of Peace); Dick Ryan (Postman); Ann Codee (Tessa); Joseph Forte (Martin); Edit Angold (Flora); Adela Rowland (Mrs. Palmer); Aileen Babs Cox (Woman); Howard Quinn (Bellhop); John Mantley (Hotel Clerk); Herbert Evans (Butler); Marjorie Babe Kane (Maid); Ralph Dunn (McCafferty); Ruth Robinson (Mrs. Updyke); Pat Barton (Louise); Charmienne Harker (Ethel); Eddie Dunn (Mike); Willard Parker (Smith); Abe Dinovitch (Man); Wheaton Chambers (District Attorney); Bert Moorhouse (Deputy Assistant Attorney); Hazel Boyne, Gail Bonney, Vangie Beilby, June Benbow, Connie Van (Patients); Joel Friedkin (Cavendish); Frank Scannell (Wilson); Bert Kennedy (Fisherman).

BORN TO BE BAD *(RKO, 1950), 94 min.*
Producer, Robert Sparks; director, Nicholas Ray; based on the novel *All Kneeling* by Anne Parrish; screenplay, Edith Sommer, art directors, Albert S. D'Agostino, Jack Okey; music director, C. Bakaleinikoff; camera, Nicholas Musuraca; editor, Frederick Knudtson.

Joan Fontaine (Christabel); Robert Ryan (Nick); Zachary Scott (Curtis); Joan Leslie (Donna); Mel Ferrer (Gobby); Harold Vermilyea (John Caine); Virginia Farmer (Aunt Clara); Kathleen Howard (Mrs. Bolton); Dick Ryan (Arthur); Bess Flowers (Mrs. Worthington); Joy Hallward (Mrs. Porter); Hazel Boyne (Committee Woman); Irving Bacon (Jewelry Salesman); Gordon Oliver (The Lawyer); Sam Lufkin (Taxi Driver); Helen Crozier (Ann); Bobby Johnson (Kenneth); Tim Taylor (Messenger Boy); Ray Johnson, John Mitchum, Evelyn Underwood (Guests); Georgianna Wulff, Ann Burr (School Girls); Avery Graves (Curtis' Friend); Don Dillaway (Photographer).

BEST OF THE BADMEN *(RKO, 1951), C-84 min.*
Producer, Herman Schlom; director, William D. Russell; story, Robert Hardy Andrews; screenplay, Andrews, John Twist; art directors, Albert S. D'Agostino, Carroll Clark; music director, C. Bakaleinikoff; camera, Edward Cronjager; editor, Desmond Marquette.

Robert Ryan (Jeff Clanton); Claire Trevor (Lily Fowler); Jack Buetel (Bob Younger); Robert Preston (Matthew Fowler); Walter Brennan ("Doc" Butcher); Bruce Cabot (Cole Younger); John Archer (Curley Ringo); Lawrence Tierney (Jesse James); Barton MacLane (Joad); Tom Tyler (Frank James); Bob Wilke (Jim Younger); John Cliff (John Younger); Lee MacGregor (Lieutenant); Emmett Lynn (Oscar); Carleton Young (Wilson); Byron Foulger (Judge); Larry Johns (Jury Foreman); Harry Woods (Proprietor of Trading Post); William Tannen (Adjutant); Ed Max (Hawkins); David McMahon (Perk); Everett Glass (Doctor).

FLYING LEATHERNECKS *(RKO, 1951), C-102 min.*
Producer, Edmund Grainger; director, Nicholas Ray; story, Kenneth Gamet; screenplay, James Edward Grant; art directors, Albert S. D'Agostino, James W. Sullivan; music director, C. Bakaleinikoff; camera, William E. Snyder; editor, Sherman Todd.

John Wayne (Dan); Robert Ryan (Griff); Don Taylor (Cowboy); Janis Carter (Joan Kirby); Jay C. Flippen (Clancy); William Harrigan (Dr. Curan); James Bell (Colonel); Barry Kelley (General); Maurice Jara (Shorty Vogay); Adam Williams (Lieutenant Malotke); James Dobson (Pudge McCabe); Carleton Young (Captain McAllister); Steve Flagg (Lieutenant Jorgenson); Brett King (Lieutenant Ernie Stark); Gordon Gebert (Tommy); Lynn Stalmaster (Lieutenant Castle); Brit Norton (Lieutenant Tanner); John Mallory (Lieutenant Black); Douglas Henderson (Lieutenant Foster); Ralph Cook (Lieutenant Kelvin); Frank Fiumara (Lieutenant Hawkins); Michael Devry (Lieutenant Hoagland); Adam York (Lieutenant Simmons); Don Rockland (Lieutenant Stuart); Hal Bokar (Lieutenant Deal); Tony Layng (Lieutenant Woods); Hugh Sanders (General); Mack Williams (Colonel); Leslie O'Pace (Peter); Milton Kibbee (Clark); Bernard Szold (Papa Malotke); Eda Reis Merin (Mama Malotke); Pat Prest (Greta Malotke); Shela Fritz, Charles Bruner (Old Indians); Fred Graham (Marine); Gail Davis (Virginia); Inez Cooper (Nurse); Rollin Moriyama, Frank Iwanaga (Japanese Pilots).

THE RACKET *(RKO, 1951), 89 min.*

Producer, Edmund Grainger; director, John Cromwell; based on the play by Bartlett Cormack; screenplay, William Wister Haines, W. R. Burnett; art directors, Albert S. D'Agostino, Jack Okey; music director, Mischa Bakaleinikoff; camera, George E. Diskant; editor, Sherman Todd.

Robert Mitchum (Captain Thomas McQuigg); Lizabeth Scott (Irene Hayes); Robert Ryan (Nick Scanlon); William Talman (Johnson); Ray Collins (Welch); Joyce MacKenzie (Mary McQuigg); Robert Hutton (Dave Ames); Virginia Huston (Lucy Johnson); William Conrad (Turck); Walter Sande (Delaney); Les Tremayne (Chief Harry Craig); Don Porter (Connolly); Walter Baldwin (Sullivan); Brett King (Joe Scanlon); Richard Karlan (Enright); Tito Vuolo (Tony); Howard Petrie (Governor); William Forrest (Governor's Aide); Howland Chamberlin (Higgins); Ralph Peters (Davis); Iris Adrian (Sadie); Jane Hazzard, Claudia Constant (Girls); Jack Shea (Night Duty Sergeant); Mike Lally (Duty Sergeant); Howard Joslyn (Sergeant Werker); Bret Hamilton, Joey Ray (Reporters); Eric Alden (Day Duty Sergeant); Steve Roberts (Schmidt the Police Guard); Pat Flaherty (Radio Patrolman); Duke Taylor (Cop); Milburn Stone (Foster the Assistant); Max Wagner (Durko); Richard Reeves (Leo the Driver); Johnny Day (Menig); Don Beddoe (Mitchell); Don Dillaway (Harris); Barry Brooks (Cameron); Jack Gargan (Lewis); Harry Lauter, Art Dupuis (Radio Cops); Ed Parker (Hood); Dick Gordon, Allen Mathews, Ralph Montgomery (Pedestrians); Bob Bice, Sally Yarnell, Jane Easton, Kate Belmont (Operators); Harriet Matthews (Librarian).

ON DANGEROUS GROUND *(RKO, 1951), 82 min.*

Producer, John Houseman; director, Nicholas Ray; based on the novel *Mad with Much Heart* by Gerald Butler; adaptors, A. I. Bezzerides, Ray; screenplay, Bezzerides; art directors, Albert S. D'Agostino, Ralph Berger; music director, C. Bakaleinikoff; camera, George E. Diskant; editor, Roland Gross.

Ida Lupino (Mary Malden); Robert Ryan (Jim Wilson); Ward Bond (Walter Brent); Charles Kemper (Bill Daly); Anthony Ross (Pete Santos); Ed Begley (Captain Brawley); Ian Wolfe (Carrey); Sumner Williams (Danny Malden); Gus Schilling (Lucky); Frank Ferguson (Willows); Cleo Moore (Myrna); Olive Carey (Mrs. Brent); Richard Irving (Bernie); Pat Prest (Julie); Bill Hammond (Fred); Gene Persson (Boy); Tommy Gosser (Crying Boy); Ruth Lee (Helen Daly); Kate Lawson, Esther Zeitlin (Women); Vera Stokes (Mother); Steve Roberts (Running Man); Vince Barnett (Waiter); G. Pat Collins (Sergeant Wendell); Jimmy Conlin (Doc Hyman); Joan Taylor (Hazel); Nestor Paiva (Gabbanierri); A. I. Bezzerides (Gates); Nita Talbot (B-Girl).

CLASH BY NIGHT *(RKO, 1952), 105 min.*

Executive producers, Jerry Wald, Norman Krasna; producer, Harriet Parsons; director, Fritz Lang; based on the play by Clifford Odets; screenplay, Alfred Hayes; art directors, Albert S. D'Agostino, Carroll Clark; set decorators, Darrell Silvera, Jack Mills; costumes, Michael Woulfe; music, Roy Webb; music director, C. Bakaleinikoff; song, Dick Gasparre, Jack Baker, and George Fragos; special effects, Harold Wellman; camera, Nicholas Musuraca; editor, George J. Amy.

Barbara Stanwyck (Mae Doyle); Paul Douglas (Jerry D'Amato); Robert Ryan (Earl Pfeiffer); Marilyn Monroe (Peggy); J. Carroll Naish (Uncle Vince); Keith Andes (Joe Doyle); Silvio Minciotti (Papa D'Amato); Diana Stewart and Deborah Stewart (Twin Babies); Gilbert Frye (Man); Al Cavens (Guest); Mario Siletti (Bartender); Frank Kreig (Art); Tony Dante (Fisherman at Pier).

BEWARE MY LOVELY *RKO, 1952), 77 min.*

Producer, Collier Young; director, Harry Horner; based on the story and the play *The Man* by Mel Dinelli; screenplay, Dinelli; art directors, Albert S. D'Agostino, Alfred Herman; set decorators, Darrell Silvera, Al Oremback; music, Leith Stevens; music director, C. Bakaleinikoff; camera, George E. Diskant; editor, Paul Weatherwax.

Ida Lupino (Mrs. Gordon); Robert Ryan (Howard); Taylor Holmes (Mr. Armstrong); Barbara Whiting (Ruth Williams); James Willmas (Mr. Stevens); O. Z. Whitehead (Mr. Franks); Dee Pollack (Grocery Boy); Brad Morrow, Jimmy Mobley, Shelly Lynn Anderson, Ronnie Patterson, Jeanne Eggenweiler (Children).

HORIZONS WEST *(Universal, 1952), C-81 min.*

Producer, Albert J. Cohen; director, Budd Boetticher; story-screenplay, Louis Stevens; art directors, Bernard Herzbrun, Robert Clatworthy; set decorators, Russell A. Gausman, Joe Kish; music director, Joseph Gershenson; sound, Leslie I. Carey, Herbert Pritchard; camera, Charles P. Boyle; editor, Ted J. Kent.

Robert Ryan (Don Hammond); Julia Adams (Lorna Hardin); Rock Hudson (Neil Hammond); John McIntire (Ira Hammond); Judith Braun (Sally); Raymond Burr (Cord Hardin); James Arness (Tiny); Frances Bavier (Martha Hammond); Dennis Weaver (Dandy Taylor); Tom Powers (Frank Tarleton); Rodolfo Acosta (General Eccobar); John Hubbard (Sam Hunter); Douglas Fowley (Tompkins); Walter Reed (Layton); Raymond Greenleaf (Eli Dodson); Tom Monroe (Jim Clawson); Lillian Molieri (Teresa); Dan White (Dennis); Edward Coch, Jr. (Juan); Paulette Turner (Celeste); John Harmon (Deputy Sheriff Johnson); Robert Bice (Righteous Citizen); Dan Poore (Henchman); Frank Chase (Borden); Tom Riste (Al); Mae Clarke (Mrs. Tarleton); Peter Mamakos (Lieutenant Salazar); Alberto Morin (M. Auriel); Edwin Parker (Northerner); Monte Montague (Doctor); Forbes Murray (Player); Buddy Roosevelt, Claude Dunkin (Bits).

CITY BENEATH THE SEA *(Universal, 1953), C-87 min.*

Producer, Albert J. Cohen; director, Budd Boetticher; based on the book *Port Royal, the Ghost City Beneath the Sea* by Harry E. Reisberg; screenplay, Jack Harvey, Ramon Romero; art directors, Alexander Golitzen, Emrich Nicholson; camera, Charles P. Boyle; editor, Edward Curtiss.

Robert Ryan (Brad Carlton); Mala Powers (Terry McBride); Anthony Quinn (Tony Bartlett); Suzann Ball (Venita); George Mathews (Captain Meade); Karel Stepanek (Dwight Trevor); Hilo Hattie (Mama Mary); Lalo Rios (Calypso); Woody Strode (Kjion); Tommy Garland (Martin); Michael Dale (Kirk); Leon Lontoc (Kip); Bernie Gozie (Maru); John Warburton (Captain Clive); Barbara Morrison (Mme. Cecile); Peter Mamakos (Mendoza); LeRoi Antoine (Calypso Singer); Elizabeth Root, Sherry Moreland (Girls); George Hamilton (High Priest); Bruce Riley (Passenger); Marya Marco (Half-caste Woman); Gerado De Cordovier (Waiter); Michael Ferris (Ship's Steward); Joe Keane (Stuart the Secretary); Peter Similuk (Radio Operator).

THE NAKED SPUR *(MGM, 1953), C-91 min.*

Producer, William H. Wright; director, Anthony Mann; screenplay, Sam Rolfe, Harold Jack Bloom; art directors, Cedric Gibbons, Malcolm Brown; music, Bronislau Kaper; camera, Willaim Mellor; editor, George White.

James Stewart (Howard Kemp); Robert Ryan (Ben Vandergroat); Janet Leigh (Lina Patch); Ralph Meeker (Roy Anderson); Millard Mitchell (Jesse Tate).

INFERNO *(Twentieth Century-Fox, 1953), C-83 min.*

Producer, William Bloom; director, Roy Baker; screenplay, Francis Cockrell; art directors, Lyle Wheeler, Lewis Creber; camera, Lucien Ballard; editor, Robert Simpson.

Robert Ryan (Carson); Rhonda Fleming (Geraldine Carson); William Lundigan (Joseph Duncan); Larry Keating (Emory); Henry Hull (Sam Elby); Carl Betz (Lieutenant Mike Platt); Robert Burton (Sheriff); Everett Glass (Detective Mason); Adrienne Marden (Secretary); Barbara Pepper (Waitress); Dan White (Lee); Harry Carter (Fred Parks); Robert Adler (Ken); Charles Conrad (Man);

ALASKA SEAS *(Paramount, 1954), 78 min.*

Producer, Mel Epstein; director, Jerry Hopper; based on the story *Spawn of the North* by Barrett Willoughby; screenplay, Geoffrey Homes, Walter Doniger; assistant director, C. C. Coleman, Jr.; camera, William Mellor; editor, Artie Marshek.

Robert Ryan (Matt Kelly); Jan Sterling (Nicky); Brian Keith (Jim Kimmerly); Gene Barry (Verne Williams); Richard Shannon (Tom Erickson); Ralph Dumke (Jackson); Ross Bagdasarian (Joe); Fay Roope (Walt Davis); Timothy Carey (Wycoff); Peter Coe (Greco); Jim Hayward (Jailer); Aaron Spelling (Knifer); William Fawcett (Silversmith); Earl Holliman (Indian Boy); Richard Kipling (Croupier); Laura Mason (Girl at Gaming Table); Pearl S. Cooper (Woman); Eugene Roth (Dan); Ed Hinton (Baker); Abel Fernandez (Rechie); Albert D'Arno (Paxton); Michael Moore (Roy).

ABOUT MRS. LESLIE *(Paramount, 1954), 104 min.*

Producer, Hal B. Wallis; director, Daniel Mann; based on the novel by Vina Delmar; screenplay, Ketti Frings, Hal Kanter; art directors, Hal Pereira, Earl Hedrick; set decorators, Sam Comer, Arthur Kram; music, Victor Young; costumes, Edith Head; special camera effects, John P. Fulton; process camera, Farciot Edouart; camera, Ernest Laszlo; editor, Warren Low.

Shirley Booth (Mrs. Vivien Leslie); Robert Ryan (George Leslie); Marjie Millar (Nadine Roland); Alex Nicol (Ian McKay); Sammy White (Harry Willey); James Bell (Mr. Poole); Eilene Janssen (Pixie); Philip Ober (Mort Finley); Henry Harry Morgan (Fred Blue); Gale Page (Marion King); Virginia Brissac (Mrs. Poole); Ian Wolfe (Mr. Pope); Ellen Corby (Mrs. Croffman); Ray Teal (Barney); Isaac Jones (Jim); Maidie Norman (Camilla); Laura Elliot (Felice); Amanda Blake (Gilly); Percy Helton (Hackley); Ric Roman (Rick); Mabel Albertson (Mrs. Sims); Edith Evanson (Mrs. Fine); Nana Bryant (Mrs. McKay); Pierre Watkin (Lewis); Joan Shawlee, Anne McCrea (Girls at Nightclub); Benny Rubin (TV Director); Jane Novak (Mrs. Stell, a Customer); Jeanne Gail (Diana); Steve Rowland (Boy in Hot Rod); Jerry Paris (Mr. Harkness).

HER TWELVE MEN *(MGM, 1954), C-91 min.*
Producer, John Houseman; director, Robert Z. Leonard; screenplay, William Roberts, Laura Z. Hobson; art directors, Cedric Gibbons, Daniel B. Cathcart; music, Bronislau Kaper; assistant director, Al Jennings; camera, Joseph Ruttenberg; editor, George Boemler.

Greer Garson (Jan Stewart); Robert Ryan (Joe Hargrave); Barry Sullivan (Richard Y. Oliver, Sr.); Richard Haydn (Dr. Avord Barrett); Barbara Lawrence (Barbara Dunning); James Arness (Ralph Munsey); Rex Thompson (Homer Cùrtis); Tim Considine (Richard Y. Oliver, Jr.); David Stollery (Jeff Carlin); Frances Bergen (Sylvia Carlin); Ian Wolfe (Roger Frane); Donald MacDonald (Bobby Lennox); Dale Hartleben (Kevin Clark); Ivan Triesault (Erik Haldeman); Stuffy Singer (Jimmy Travers); Peter Votrian (Alan Saunders); Dee Aaker (Michael); Peter Roman (Tim Johnson); Timothy Marxer (Tommy); Patrick Miller (Pat); Aurelio Celli (Tony); Peter Dane (Pete); Robert Clarke (Prince); Larry Olsen (Edgar); Gary Stewart (Stanley); Kate Lawson (Maid); Sarah Spencer (Mrs. Travers); Vernon Rich (Mr. Travers); Peter Adams (Mr. Saunders); Sandy Descher (Little Sister); John Dodsworth (Mr. Curtis); Jean Dante (Mrs. Saunders); Phyllis Stanley (Mrs. Curtis); Norman Ollestad (Attendant); Edgar Dearing (Fire Chief); Ron Rondell (Older Boy); A. Cameron Grant (Teacher).

BAD DAY AT BLACK ROCK *(MGM, 1954), C-81 min.*
Producer, Dore Schary; assistant producer, Herman Hoffman; director, John Sturges; story, Howard Breslin; screenplay, Millard Kaufman; assistant director, Joel Freeman; music, Andre Previn; art directors, Cedric Gibbons, Malcolm Brown; set decorators, Edwin B. Willis, Fred MacLean; color consultant, Alvord Eiseman; camera, William C. Mellor; editor, Newell P. Kimlin.

Spencer Tracy (John J. Macreedy); Robert Ryan (Reno Smith); Anne Francis (Liz Wirth); Dean Jagger (Tim Horn); Walter Brennan (Doc Velie); John Ericson (Pete Wirth); Ernest Borgnine (Coley Trimble); Lee Marvin (Hector David); Russell Collins (Mr. Hastings); Walter Sande (Sam).

ESCAPE TO BURMA *(RKO, 1955), C-88 min.*
Producer, Benedict Bogeaus; director, Allan Dwan; based on the story *Bow Tamely to Me* by Kenneth Perkins; screenplay, Talbot Jennings, Hobart Donavan; art director, Van Nest Polglase; set decorator, Fay Babcock; assistant directors, Nate Watt, Lew Borzage; costumes, Gwen Wakeling; music, Louis Forbes; camera, John Alton; editor, James Leicester.

Barbara Stanwyck (Gwen Moore); Robert Ryan (Jim Brecan); David Farrar (Cardigan); Murvyn Vye (Malesh); Lisa Montell (Andora); Robert Warwick (Sawbwa); Reginald Denny (Commissioner); Peter Coe (Captain of the Guard); Alex Montoya (Dacoit); Robert Cabal (Kumat); Anthony Numkema (Kasha); Lal Chand Mehra (Poo Kan).

HOUSE OF BAMBOO *(Twentieth Century-Fox, 1955), C-102 min.*
Producer, Buddy Adler; director, Samuel Fuller; screenplay, Harry Kleiner; additional dialogue, Fuller; art directors, Lyle Wheeler, Addison Hehr; set decorators, Walter M. Scott, Stuart A. Reiss; music, Leigh Harline; assistant director, David Silver; camera, Joe MacDonald; editor, James B. Clark.

Robert Ryan (Sandy Dawson); Robert Stack (Eddie Spanier) Shirley Yamaguchi (Mariko); Cameron Mitchell (Griff); Brad Dexter (Captain Hanson); Sessue Hayakawa (Inspector Kito); Biff Elliot (Webber); Sandro Giglio (Ceram); Elko Hanabuss (Japanese Screaming Woman);

Harry Carey, Jr. (John); Peter Gray (Willy); Robert Quarry (Phil); DeForrest Kelley (Charlie); John Doucette (Skipper); Teru Shimada (Nagaya); Robert Hosai (Doctor); Jack Maeshiro (Bartender); May Takasugi (Bath Attendant); Robert Okazaki (Mr. Hommaru); Neyle Morrow (Army Corporal); Kazue Ikeda, Clifford Arashiro (Policemen); Fred Dale (Man); Kinuko Ann Ito (Servant); Samuel Fuller (Cop).

THE TALL MEN *(Twentieth Century-Fox, 1955), C-122 min.*

Producer, William A. Bacher, William·B. Hawks; director, Raoul Walsh; based on the novel by Clay Fisher; screenplay, Sydney Boehm, Frank Nugent); music, Victor Young; songs, Ken Darby and Jose Lopez Alaves; costumes, Travilla; assistant director, Stanley Hough; art director, Lyle R. Wheeler, Mark-Lee Kirk; camera, Leo Tover; editor, Louis Loeffler.

Clark Gable (Ben Allison); Jane Russell (Nella Turner); Robert Ryan (Nathan Stark); Cameron Mitchell (Clint Allison); Juan Garcia (Luis); Harry Shannon (Sam); Emile Meyer (Chickasaw); Steven Darrell (Colonel); Will Wright (Gus the Bartender); Robert Adler (Wrangler); Russell Simpson (Emigrant Man); Tom Wilson (Miner); Tom Fadden (Stable Owner); Dan White (Hotel Clerk); Argentina Brunetti (Maria); Doris Kemper (Mrs. Robbins); Carl Harbaugh (Salesman); Post Park (Stagecoach Driver); Gabriel Del Valle (Man); Gilda Fontana, Meyito Pulito (Spanish Girls); Frank Leyva (Waiter); Jack Mather (Cavalry Lieutenant).

THE PROUD ONES *(Twentieth Century-Fox, 1956), C-94 min.*

Producer, Robert L. Jacks; director, Robert D. Webb; based on the novel by Verne Athanas; screenplay, Edmund North, Joseph Petracca; music, Lionel Newman; orchestrator, Maurice de Packh; costumes, Travilla; assistant director, Ad Schaumer; art directors, Lyle Wheeler, Leland Fuller; camera, Lucien Ballard; editor, Hugh S. Fowler.

Robert Ryan (Cass); Virginia Mayo (Sally); Jeffrey Hunter (Thad); Robert Middleton (Honest John Barrett); Walter Brennan (Jake); Arthur O'Connell (Jim Dexter); Ken Clark (Pike); Rodolfo Acosta (Chico); George Mathews (Dillon); Fay Roope (Markham); Edward Platt (Dr. Barlow); Whit Bissell (Mr. Bolton); Paul Burns (Billy Smith); Richard Deacon (Barber); Lois Ray (Belle); Jack Low (Guard); Ken Terrell (The Weasel); Don Brodie (Hotel Clerk); Jackie Coogan (Man on Make); Juanita Close (Helen); Stanford Jolley (Crooked Card Player); Jack Mather (Cattle Buyer); Steve Darrell (Trail Boss).

BACK FROM ETERNITY *(RKO, 1956), 97 min.*

Producer-director, John Farrow; screenplay, Jonathan Latimer; art directors, Albert S. D'Agostino, Gene Allen; assistant director, Emmett Emerson; music, Franz Waxman; costumes, Ann Peck; camera, William Mellor; editor, Eda Warren.

Robert Ryan (Bill); Anita Ekberg (Rena); Rod Steiger (Vasquez); Phyllis Kirk (Louise); Keith Andes (Joe); Gene Barry (Ellis); Fred Clark (Crimp); Beulah Bondi (Martha); Cameron Prud'Homme (Henry); Jesse White (Pete); Adele Mara (Maria); Jon Provost (Tommy); Tris Coffin (Grimsby); Daniel Bernaduccio (Bartender); Rex Lease (Airport Representative); Kay English (Dowager); Joan Tyler, Sandra Werner (Girls); Charles Meredith (Dean); Alex Montoya (Police Sergeant); Felipe Turich (Sinister Peddler).

MEN IN WAR *(United Artists, 1957), 104 min.*

Producer, Sidney Harmon; director, Anthony Mann; based on the novel *Combat* by Van Van Praag; screenplay, Philip Yordan; assistant director, Leon Chooluck; music, Elmer Bernstein; art director, Frank Sylos; camera, Ernest Haller; editor, Richard C. Meyer.

Robert Ryan (Lieutenant Benson); Aldo Ray (Montana); Robert Keith (Colonel); Philip Pine (Riordan); Vic Morrow (Zwickley); Nehemiah Persoff (Lewis); James Edwards (Killian); L. Q. Jones (Sam Davis); Adam Kennedy (Maslow); Scott Marlowe (Meredith); Walter Kelley (Ackerman); Race Gentry (Haines); Robert Normand (Christensen); Anthony Ray (Penelli); Michael Miller (Lynch); Victor Sen Yung (Korean Sniper).

GOD'S LITTLE ACRE *(United Artists, 1958), 118 min.*
Producer, Sidney Harmon; director, Anthony Mann; based on the novel by Erskine Caldwell; screenplay, Philip Yordan; music and music conductor, Elmer Bernstein; assistant director, Louis Brandt; makeup, Maurice Seiderman; production designer, John S. Poplin, Jr.; set decorator, Lyle B. Reifsnider; dialogue coach, Janet Brandt; costumes, Sophia Stutz; sound, Jack Solomon; special camera effects, Jack Rabin, Louis DeWitt; camera, Ernest Haller; editor, Richard C. Meyer.

Robert Ryan (Ty Ty Walden); Aldo Ray (Bill Thompson); Tina Louise (Griselda); Buddy Hackett (Pluto Swint); Jack Lord (Buck Walden); Fay Spain (Darlin' Jill); Vic Morrow (Shaw Walden); Helen Westcott (Rosamund); Lance Fuller (Jim Leslie); Rex Ingram (Uncle Felix); Michael Landon (Dave Dawson the Albino); Russell Collins (Watchman).

LONELYHEARTS *(United Artists, 1958), 102 min.*
Producer, Dore Schary; associate producer, Walter Reilly; director, Vincent J. Donehue; based on the book *Miss Lonelyhearts* by Nathanael West, and the play by Howard Teichmann; screenplay, Schary; art director, Serge Krizman; set decorator, Darrell Silvera; assistant director, Clarence Eurist; wardrobe, Chuck Arrico, Angela Alexander; makeup, Abe Haberman, Frank Laure; music, Conrad Salinger; camera, John Alton; editor, Aaron Stell.

Montgomery Clift (Adam White); Robert Ryan (William Shrike); Myrna Loy (Florence Shrike); Dolores Hart (Justy Sargent); Maureen Stapleton (Fay Doyle); Frank Maxwell (Pat Doyle); Jackie Coogan (Gates); Mike Kellin (Goldsmith); Frank Overton (Mr. Sargent); Don Washbrook (Older Brother); John Washbrook (Younger Brother); Onslow Stevens (Adam's Father); Mary Alan Hokanson (Edna); John Gallaudet (Bartender); Lee Zimmer (Jerry).

DAY OF THE OUTLAW *(United Artists, 1959), 90 min.*
Producer, Sidney Harmon; associate producer, Leon Chooluck; director, Andre De Toth; screenplay, Philip Yordan; set designer, Jack Polin; set decorator, Lyle B. Reifsnider; music, Alexander Courage; makeup, Jack Dusick; wardrobe, Bob Martien, Elva H. Martien; sound, Ben Winkler; special effects, Daniel Hays; camera, Russell Harlan; editor, Robert Lawrence.

Robert Ryan (Blaise Starrett); Burl Ives (Jack Bruhn); Tina Louise (Helen Crane); Alan Marshal (Hal Crane); Nehemiah Persoff (Dan); David Nelson (Gene); Venetia Stevenson (Ernine); Donald Elson (Vic); Helen Westcott (Vivian); Robert Cornthwaite (Tommy); Jack Lambert (Tex); Lance Fuller (Pace); Frank De Kova (Denver); Paul Wexler (Vause); Jack Woody (Shorty); William Schallert (Preston); Arthur Space (Clay); Michael McGreevey (Bobby); Betsy Jones Moreland (Mrs. Preston); Elisha Cook (Larry); George Ross (Clagett).

ODDS AGAINST TOMORROW *(United Artists, 1959), 95 min.*
Producer, Robert Wise; associate producer, Phil Stein; director, Wise; based on the novel by William P. McGivern; screenplay, John O. Killens, Nelson Gidding; art director, Leo Kerz; set decorator, Fred Ballmeyer; assistant director, Charles Maguire; makeup, Robert Jiras; costumes, Anna Hill Johnstone; music and music conductor, John Lewis; sound, Edward Johnstone, Richard Voriseck; camera, Joseph Brun; editor, Dede Allen.

Harry Belafonte (Johnny Ingram); Robert Ryan (Earle Slater); Shelley Winters (Lorry); Ed Begley (Dave Burke); Gloria Grahame (Helen); Will Kuluva (Bacco); Kim Hamilton (Ruth Ingram); Mae Barnes (Annie); Carmen De Lavallade (Kitty); Richard Bright (Coco); Lou Gallo (Moriarity); Fred J. Scollay (Cannoy); Lois Thorne (Eadie); Zohra Lampert (Girl in Bar); Burtt Harris (Man in Bar); William Zuckert (Bartender); Mil Stewart (Elevator Operator); Paul Hoffman (Garry); Cicely Tyson (Fra); William Adams (Bank Guard); Allen Nourse (Police Chief of Melton); John Garden (Clerk in Bus Station).

ICE PALACE *(Warner Bros., 1960), C-143 min.*
Producer, Henry Blanke; director, Vincent Sherman; based on the novel by Edna Ferber; screenplay, Harry Kleiner; music, Max Steiner; orchestrator, Murray Cutter; art director, Malcolm Bert; set decorator, George James Hopkins; assistant directors, Russell Llewellyn, Gil Kissel; costumes, Howard Shoup; makeup, Gordon Bau; sound, Stanley Jones; camera, Joseph Biroc; editor, William Ziegler.

Richard Burton (Zeb Kennedy); Robert Ryan (Thor Storm); Carolyn Jones (Bridie Ballantyne); Martha Hyer (Dorothy Wendt); Ray Danton (Bay Husack); Diane McBain (Christine Storm); Karl Swenson (Scotty Ballantyne); Shirley Knight (Grace Kennedy at Age Sixteen); Barry Kelley (Einer Wendt); Sheridan Comerate (Pilot Ross); George Takei (Wang); Steve Harris (Christopher Storm at Age Sixteen); Dorcas Brower (Thor's Eskimo Wife); Sam McDaniel (Porter); Lennie Bremen, Charles Hicks, James Hope (Doughboys); Saul Gorss (White Checkers); John Pedrini (Foreman); Serge Mauriet, Carl Ratcliff (Fishermen-Kazatzka Dancers); William Yip (Chinese Maitre d'); Helen Seveck (Old Eskimo Woman); I. Stanford Jolley (Mr. Lawson); Robert Griffin (Engineer); John Bliefer, David McMahon (Fishermen); Judd Holdren (Muriel's Escort); Carol Nicholson (Grace at Age Seven); Alan Roberts (Christopher at Age Seven).

THE CANADIANS *(Twentieth Century-Fox, 1961), C-85 min.*
Producer, Herman E. Webber; director and screenplay, Burt Kennedy; wardrobe, Jim Dunlevy; sound, Arthur Bradburn; camera, Arthur Ibbetson; editor, Douglas Robertson.

Robert Ryan (Inspector William Gannon); John Dehner (Frank Boone); Torin Thatcher (Master Sergeant McGregor); Teresa Stratas (The White Squaw); Burt Metcalfe (Constable Springer); John Sutton (Superintendent Walker); Jack Creley (Greer); Scott Peters (Ben); Richard Alden (Billy); Michael Pate (Chief Four Horns).

KING OF KINGS *(MGM, 1961), C-165 min.*
Producer, Samuel Bronston; associate producers, Noel Howard, Sumner Williams; director, Nicholas Ray; screenplay, Philip Yordan; narration written by Ray Bradbury; music, Miklos Rozsa; assistant directors, Carlo Lastricati, Jose Maria Ochoa, Jose Lopez Rodero; choreography, Betty Utey; sets and costumes, Georges Wakhevitch; set decorator, Enrique Alarcon; sound, Franklin Milton, Basil Fenton Smith; second unit directors, Noel Howard, Sumner Williams; special camera effects, Lee Le Blanc; special effects, Alex C. Weldon; camera, Franz F. Planer, Milton Krasner, Manuel Berenguer; editor, Harold Kress.

Jeffrey Hunter (Jesus Christ); Siobhan McKenna (Mary); Robert Ryan (John the Baptist); Hurd Hatfield (Pontius Pilate); Ron Randell (Lucius the Centurion); Viveca Lindfors (Claudia); Rita Gam (Herodias); Carmen Sevilla (Mary Magdalene); Brigid Bazlen (Salome); Harry Guardino (Barabbas); Orson Welles (Narrator); Rip Torn (Judas); Frank Thring (Herod Antipas); Guy Rolfe (Caiaphas); Maurice Marsac (Nicodemus); Gregoire Aslan (Herold); Royal Dano (Peter); Edric Connor (Balthazar); George Couloris (Camel Driver); Conrado San Martin (General Pompey); Gerard Tichy (Joseph); Jose Antonio (Young John);

601

Luis Prendes (The Good Thief); David Davies (The Burly Man); Jose Nieto (Caspar); Ruben Rojo (Matthew); Fernando Sancho (The Madman); Michael Wager (Thomas); Felix De Pomes (Joseph of Arimathea); Barry Keegan (The Bad Thief); Tino Barrero (Andrew); Rafael Luis Calvo (Simon of Cyrene).

THE LONGEST DAY *(Twentieth Century-Fox, 1962), 180 min.*

Producer, Darryl F. Zanuck; associate producer, Elmo Williams; directors, Andrew Marton, Ken Annakin, Bernhard Wicki, (uncredited) Zanuck; based on the book by Cornelius Ryan; screenplay, Ryan; additional episodes, Romain Gary, James Jones, David Pursall, Jack Seddon; music and music conductor, Maurice Jarre; thematic music, Paul Anka; arranger, Mitch Miller; art directors, Ted Haworth, Vincent Korda, Leon Barsacq; assistant directors, Bernard Farrel, Louis Fitzele, Gerard Renateau, Henri Sokal; sound, Jo De Bretagne, Jacques Maumont, William Sivel; special effects, Karl Baumgartner, Karl Helmer, Augie Lohman, Robert MacDonald, Alex Weldon; camera, Jean Bourgoin, Henri Persin, Walter Wottitz; helicopter shots, Guy Tabary; editor, Samuel E. Beetley.

John Wayne (Colonel Vandervoort); Robert Mitchum (General Cota); Henry Fonda (General Roosevelt); Robert Ryan (General Gavin); Rod Steiger (Commander); Robert Wagner (U.S. Ranger); Richard Beymer (Schultz); Mel Ferrer (General Haines); Jeffrey Hunter (Sergeant Fuller); Paul Anka, Tommy Sands, Fabian (Rangers); Sal Mineo (Private Martini); Roddy McDowall (Private Morris); Stuart Whitman (Lieutenant Sheen); Eddie Albert (Colonel Newton); Edmond O'Brien (General Barton); Red Buttons (Private Steele); Tom Tryon (Lieutenant Wilson); Alexander Knox (General Bedell Smith); Ray Danton (Captain Frank); Henry Grace (General Eisenhower); Mark Damon (Private Harris); Steve Forrest (Captain Harding); John Crawford (Colonel Caffey); Ron Randell (Williams); Nicholas Stuart (General Bradley); Richard Burton, Donald Houston (R.A.F. Pilots); Kenneth More (Captain Maud); Peter Lawford (Lord Lovat); Richard Todd (Major Howard); Leo Genn (General Parker); John Gregson (Padre); Sean Connery (Private Flanagan); Jack Hedley (Briefing Man); Michael Medwin (Private Watney); Norman Rossington (Private Clough); John Robinson (Admiral Ramsey); Patrick Barr (Captain Stagg); Trevor Reid (General Montgomery); Irina Demich (Janine); Bourvil (Mayor); Jean-Louis Barrault (Father Roulland); Christian Marquand (Kieffer); Arletty (Mme. Barrault); Madeleine Renaud (Mother Superior); Georges Wilson (Renaud); Jean Servais (Admiral Jaujard); Fernand Ledoux (Louis); Curt Jurgens (General Blumentritt); Werner Hinz (Marshal Rommel); Paul Hartmann (Marshal Rundstedt); Peter Van Eyck (Lieutenant Colonel Ocker); Gerd Froebe (Sergeant Kaffeeklatsch); Hans Christian Blech (Major Pluskat); Wolfgang Preiss (General Pensel); Heinz Reincke (Colonel Priller); Richard Munch (General Marcks); Ernst Schroeder (General Salmuth); Christopher Lee, Eugene Deckers (Bits).

BILLY BUDD *(Allied Artists, 1962), 123 min.*

Executive producer, A. Ronald Lubin; producer-director, Peter Ustinov; based on the novel *Billy Budd, Foretopman* by Herman Melville, and the play by Louis O. Coxe, Robert H. Chapman; screenplay, Ustinov, Robert Rossen, DeWitt Bodeen; music and music conductor, Anthony Hopkins; production designer, Don Ashton; art director, Peter Murton; costumes, Anthony Mendelson; makeup, Bob Lawrence; assistant director, Michael Birkett; sound, Charles Crafford, Charles Poulton, Len Shilton; camera, Robert Krasker; editor, Jack Harris.

Terence Stamp (Billy Budd); Peter Ustinov (Captain Edward Vere); Robert Ryan (Master at Arms John Claggart); Melvyn Douglas (The Dansker); Ronald Lewis (Jenkins); David McCallum (Lieutenant Wyatt); John Neville (Lieutenant Ratcliffe); Paul Rogers (Lieutenant Seymour); Lee Montague (Squeak); Thomas Heathcote (Payne); Ray McAnally (O'Daniel); Robert Brown (Talbot); John Meillon (Kincaid); Cyril Luckham (Hallam); Niall MacGinnis (Captain Graveling).

THE INHERITANCE *(Amalgamated Clothing Workers of America-Harold Mayer, 1964), 60 min.*
Producer-director, Harold Mayer; screenplay, Millard Lampell; music-music conductor, George Kleinsinger; song, Kleinsinger and Lampell; camera, Mayer; editor, Lawrence Silk.

Robert Ryan (Narrator).

THE BATTLE OF THE BULGE *(Warner Bros., 1965), C-187 min.*
Producers, Milton Sperling, Philip Yordan; director, Ken Annakin; screenplay, Yordan, Sperling, John Nelson; music, Benjamin Frankel; song, Frankel and Kurl Wiehle; art director, Eugene Lourie; assistant directors, Jose Lopez Rodero, Martin Sacristan, Luis Garcia; technical advisers, General Meinred von Lauchert, Colonel Sherman Jolle, Major Edward King; sound, David Hildyard, Gordon McCallum; camera, Jack Hildyard; editor, Derek Parsons.

Henry Fonda' (Lieutenant Colonel Kiley); Robert Shaw (Colonel Hessler); Robert Ryan (General Grey); Dana Andrews (Colonel Pritchard); George Montgomery (Sergeant Duquesne); Ty Hardin (Schumacher); Pier Angeli (Louise); Barbar Werle (Elena); Charles Bronson (Wolenski); Werner Peters (General Kohler); Hans Christian Blech (Conrad); James MacArthur (Lieutenant Weaver); Telly Savalas (Guffy).

THE CROOKED ROAD *(Seven Arts, 1965), 90 min.*
Executive producer, Jack O. Lamont; producer, David Henley; director, Don Chaffey; based on the novel by Morris L. West; screenplay, J. Garrison; music, Bojan Adamic.

Robert Ryan (Richard Ashley); Stewart Granger (Duke of Orgagna); Nadia Gray (Cosima); Marius Goring (Harlequin); George Coulouris (Carlo).

LA GUERRE SECRETE *(a.k.a., THE DIRTY GAME, and THE DIRTY AGENTS, American International, 1966), 91 min.*
Executive producer, Richard Hellman; associate producer, Eugene Tucherer; directors, Terence Young, Christian-Jacque, Carlo Lizzani; screenplay, Jo Eisinger; music, Robert Mellin; art directors, Robert Gabriti, H. Weideman; sound, G. Mardiguian; camera, Pierre Petit, Richard Angst, Enrico Menczer; editors, Borys Leurn, Alan Osbiston.

Henry Fonda (Kourlov); Robert Ryan (General Bruce); Vittorio Gassman (Perego); Annie Girardot (Nanette); Bourvil (Laland); Robert Hossein (Dupont); Peter Van Eyck (Berlin C.M.); Maria Grazia Buccela (Natalia).

THE PROFESSIONALS *(Columbia, 1966), C-117 min.*
Producer-director, Richard Brooks; based on the novel *A Mule for the Marquesa* by Frank O'Rourke; screenplay, Brooks; art director, Edward S. Haworth; set decorator, Frank Tuttle; makeup, Robert Schiffer; wardrobe, Jack Martell; assistant director, Tom Shaw; music and music conductor, Maurice Jarre; sound, Charles J. Rice, William Randall, Jr., Jack Haynes; special effects, Willis Cook; camera, Conrad Hall; editor, Peter Zinner.

Burt Lancaster (Bill Dolworth); Lee Marvin (Henry Rico Farden); Robert Ryan (Hans Ehrengard); Jack Palance (Captain Jesus Raza); Claudia Cardinale (Maria Grant); Ralph Bellamy (J. W. Grant); Woody Strode (Jacob Sharp); Joe De Santis (Ortega); Rafael Bertrand (Fierro); Jorge Martinez De Hoyos (Padillia); Maria Gomez (Chiquita); Jose Chavez, Carlos Romero (Revolutionaries); Vaughn Taylor (Banker); Robert Contreras, Don Carlos (Bandits);

Elizabeth Cambell (Mexican Girl); John Lopez (Mexican Servant); Darwin Lamb (Hooper); Dirk Evans (Man at Door); John McKee (Sheriff); Eddie Little Sky (The Prisoner); Leigh Chapman (Lady); Phil Parslow (Deputy Sheriff); Foster Hood, Henry O'Brien, Dave Cadiente, Vince Cadiente (Bits).

THE BUSY BODY *(Paramount, 1967), C-101 min.*

Producer, William Castle; associate producer, Dona Holloway; director, Castle; based on the novel by Donald E. Westlake; screenplay, Ben Starr; music, Vic Mizzy; song, Edward Heyman and Johnny Green; art directors, Hal Pereira, Roland Anderson, Al Roelofs; set decorators, Robert Benton, Jack Mills; assistant director, Andrew J. Durkus; makeup, Wally Westmore; sound, Harold Lewis, John Wilkin; special camera effects, Paul K. Lerpae; process camera, Farciot Edouart; camera, Hal Stine; editor, Edwin H. Bryant.

Sid Caesar (George Norton); Robert Ryan (Charley Barker); Anne Baxter (Margo Foster); Kay Medford (Ma Norton); Jan Murray (Murray Foster); Richard Pryor (Whittaker); Arlene Golonka (Bobbi Brody); Charles McGraw (Fred Harwell); Ben Blue (Felix Rose); Dom De Luise (Kurt Brock); Bill Dana (Archie Brody); Godfrey Cambridge (Mike); Marty Ingels (Willie); George Jessel (Mr. Fessel); Audrie Magee (Mrs. Fessel); Mickey Deems (Cop); Choo Choo Collins (Woman); Paul Wexler (Mr. Merriwether); Marina Koshetz (Marcia Woshikowski); Norman Bartold, Mike Wagner, Larry Gelman, Don Brodie (Board Members).

THE DIRTY DOZEN *(MGM, 1967), C-149 min.*

Producer, Kenneth Hyman; associate producer, Raymond Anzarut; director, Robert Aldrich; based on the novel by E. M. Nathanson; screenplay, Nunnally Johnson, Lukas Heller; music, Frank De Vol; songs, De Vol and Mack David; De Vol and Sibylle Siegfried; title design, Walter Blake; art director, W. E. Hutchinson; assistant director, Bert Batt; sound, Franklin Milton, Claude Hitchcock; special effects, Cliff Richardson; camera, Edward Scaife; editor, Michael Luciano.

Lee Marvin (Major Reisman); Ernest Borgnine (General Worden); Charles Bronson (Joseph Wiadislaw); Jim Brown (Robert Jefferson); John Cassavetes (Victor Franko); Richard Jaeckel (Sergeant Bowren; George Kennedy (Major Max Armbruster); Trini Lopez (Pedro Jiminez); Ralph Meeker (Captain Stuart Kinder); Robert Ryan (Colonel Everett Dasher-Breed); Telly Savalas (Archer Maggott); Donald Sutherland (Vernon Pinkley); Clint Walker (Samson Posey); Robert Webber (General Denton); Tom Busby (Milo Vladek); Ben Carruthers (Glenn Gilpin); Stuart Cooper (Roscoe Lever); Colin Maitland (Seth Sawyer); Thick Wilson (General Worden's Aide); Dora Reisser (German Officer's Girl).

HOUR OF THE GUN *(United Artists, 1967), C-101 min.*

Producer-director, John Sturges; based on the novel *Tombstone's Epitaph* by Douglas D. Martin; screenplay, Edward Anhalt; music, Jerry Goldsmith; art director, Alfred C. Ybarra; set decorator, Victor Gangelin; wardrobe, Gordon Dawson; makeup, Charles Blackman; assistant directors, Thomas Schmidt, Robert Jones; sound, Jesus Gonzalez Gancy; special effects, Sass Bedig; camera, Lucien Ballard; editor, Ferris Webster.

James Garner (Wyatt Earp); Jason Robards (Doc Holliday); Robert Ryan (Ike Clanton); Albert Salmi (Octavius Roy); Charles Aidman (Horace Sullivan); Steve Ihnat (Andy Warshaw); Michael Tolan (Pete Spence); Frank Converse (Virgil Earp); Sam Melville (Morgan Earp); Austin Willis (Anson Safford); Richard Bull (Thomas Fitch); Larry Gates (John P. Clum); Karo Swenson (Dr. Goodfellow); Bill Fletcher (Jimmy Ryan); Robert Phillips (Frank Stillwell); John Voight (Bill Brocius); William Schallert (Herman Spicer); Lonnie Chapman

(Turkey Creek Johnson); Monte Markham (Sherman McMasters); William Windom (Texas Jack Vermillion); Edward Anhalt (Sanitarium Doctor); Walter Gregg (Billy Clanton); David Perna (Frank McLowery); Jim Sheppard (Tom McLowery); Jorge Russek (Latigo).

CUSTER OF THE WEST *(Cinerama, 1968), C-146 min.* *

Producers, Philip Yordan, Louis Dolivet; director, Robert Siodmak; producer-director of Civil War sequence, Irving Lerner; screenplay, Bernard Gordon, Julian Halevy; music and music conductor, Bernardo Segall; songs, Segall and Will Holt; Segall and Robert Shaw; art directors, Jean-Pierre D'Eaubonne, Eugene Lourie, Julio Molina; set decorators, Antonio Mateos; makeup, Julian Ruiz; assistant director, Jose Maria Ochoa; sound, Kurt Herrnfeld, Alban Streeter; camera, Cecilio Paniagua; editor, Maurice Rootes.

Robert Shaw (General George Armstrong Custer); Mary Ure (Elizabeth Custer); Jeffrey Hunter (Lieutenant Benteen); Ty Hardin (Major Marcus Reno); Charles Stalnaker (Lieutenant Howells); Robert Hall (Sergeant Buckley); Lawrence Tierney (General Philip Sheridan); Kieron Moore (Chief Dull Knife); Marc Lawrence (The Goldminer); Robert Ryan (Sergeant Mulligan).

*Cut to 120 min.

ESCONDIDO *(a.k.a., A MINUTE TO PRAY, A SECOND TO DIE, Cinerama, 1968), C-103 min.* *

Executive producer, Selig J. Seligman; producer, Alfredo Antonini; director, Franco Giraldi; story, Albert Band, Ugo Liberatore; screenplay, Liberatore, Louis Garfinkle; art director, Massimo Capriccioli; set decorator, Guido Josia; costumes, Luciana Fortini; makeup, Michele Trimarchi; assistant director, Franco Cirno; music, Carlo Rustichelli; sound, Fernando Prescetelli; camera, Alace Parolin; editor, Alberto Gillitti.

Alex Cord (Clay McCord); Arthur Kennedy (Roy Colby); Robert Ryan (Governor Lem Carter); Nicoletta Machiavelli (Laurinda); Mario Brega (Kraut); Renato Romano (Cheap Charley); Gianpiero Albertini (Fred Duskin); Daniel Martin (Father Santana); Enzo Fiermonte (Dr. Chase); Pedro Canalejas (Seminole); Franco Lantieri (Butler); Osiride Peverello (Fuzzy); Jose Manuel Martin (El Bailarin); Antonio Molina Rojo (Sein); Rosa Palomar (Ruby); Paco Sanz (Barber); Paolo Magalotti (Sid); Massimo Sarchielli (Zack); Ottaviano Dell'Acqua (Clay as a Boy); Antonio Vico (Jonas); Alberto Dell'Acqua (Ruby's Son).

*English dubbed version: 97 min.

LO SBARCO DI ANZIO *(a.k.a., ANZIO/THE BATTLE OF ANZIO, Columbia, 1968), C-117 min.*

Producer, Dino De Laurentiis; director, Edward Dmytryk; based on the book *Anzio* by Wynford Vaughan-Thomas; adaptors, Frank De Felitta, Giuseppe Mangione; English screenplay, Harry A. L. Craig; music, Riz Ortolani; song, Ortolani and Jerome Pomus; art director, Luigi Scaccianoce; set decorators, Francesco Bronz, Emilio D'Andria; costumes, Ugo Pericoli; makeup, Amato Garbini; assistant directors, Giorgio Gentili, Gianni Cozzo; sound, Aldo De Martini; special effects, Walfrido Traversari; camera, Giuseppe Rotunno; editors, Alberto Gallitti, Peter Taylor.

Robert Mitchum (Dick Ennis); Peter Falk (Corporal Rabinoff); Earl Holliman (Sergeant Stimler); Arthur Kennedy (General Lesly); Robert Ryan (General Carson); Mark Damon (Richardson); Reni Santoni (Movie); Moseph Walsh (Doyle); Thomas Hunter (Andy); Giancarlo Giannini (Cellini); Anthony Steel (General Marsh); Patrick Magee (General Starkey); Arthur Franz (General Howard); Elsa Albani (Emilia); Wayde Preston (Colonel Hendricks); Venantino Venatini (Captain Burns); Annabella Andreoli (Anna); Wolfgang Preiss (Marshal Kesselring); Tonio Selwart (General Van MacKensen); Stefanella Giovannini (Diana); Marcella Valeri (Assunta); Enzo Turco (Pepe); Wolf Hillinger (Hans the Sniper).

THE WILD BUNCH *(Warner Bros.-Seven Arts, 1969), C-140 min.*

Producer, Phil Feldman; associate producer, Roy N. Sickner; director, Sam Peckinpah; story, Walon Green, Sickner; screenplay, Green, Peckinpah; second unit director, Buzz Henry; assistant director, Cliff Coleman, Fred Gammon; music, Jerry Fielding; music supervisor, Sonny Burke; art director, Edward Carrere; wardrobe, Gordon Dawson; makeup, Al Greenway; sound, Robert J. Miller; special effects, Bud Hulburd; camera, Lucien Ballard; editor, Louis Lombardo.

William Holden (Pike Bishop); Ernest Borgnine (Dutch Engstrom); Robert Ryan (Deke Thornton); Edmond O'Brien (Sykes); Warren Oates (Lyle Gorch); Jaime Sanchez (Angel); Ben Johnson (Tector Gorch); Emilio Fernandez (Mapache); Strother Martin (Coffer); L. Q. Jones (T. C.); Albert Dekker (Pat 'Harrigan); Bo Hopkins (Crazy Lee); Dub Taylor (Mayor Wainscoat); Jorge Russek (Lieutenant Zamorra); Alfonso Arau (Herrera); Chano Urueta (Don Jose); Sonia Amelio (Teresa); Aurora Clavel (Aurora); Elsa Cardenas (Elsa); Fernando Wagner (German Army Officer); and Paul Harper, Constance White, Lilia Richards.

CAPTAIN NEMO AND THE UNDERWATER CITY *(MGM, 1970), C-106 min.*

Executive producer, Steven Pallos; producer, Bertram Ostrer; director, James Hill; inspired by the character created by Jules Verne; screenplay, Pip Baker, Jane Baker, R. Wright Campbell; art director, Bill Andrews; costumes, Olga Lehmann; assistant director, Ted Lewis; music, Walter Scott; sound, A. W. Watkins; camera, Alan Hume; underwater camera, Egil S. Woxholt; editor, Bill Lewthwaite.

Robert Ryan (Captain Nemo); Chuck Connors (Senator Robert Fraser); Nanette Newman (Helena); John Turner (Joab); Luciana Paluzzi (Mala); Bill Fraser (Barnaby); Kenneth Connor (Swallow); Allan Cuthbertson (Lomax); Christopher Hartstone (Philip); Vincent Harding (Mate/Navigator); Ralph Nosseck (Engineer).

LAWMAN *(United Artists, 1971), C-99 min.*

Producer-director, Michael Winner; screenplay, Gerald Wilson; assistant directors, Michael Dryhurst, Malcolm Stamp, Jaime Contreras; art director, Herbert Westbrook; set decorator, Ray Moyer; music and music conductor, Jerry Fielding; makeup, Richard Mills; wardrobe, Ron Beck; sound, Terence Rawlings, Manuel Topete Blake, Hugh Strain; special effects, Leon Ortega; camera, Bob Paynter; editor, Freddie Wilson.

Burt Lancaster (Marshal Jered Maddox); Robert Ryan (Marshal Cotton Ryan); Lee J. Cobb (Vincent Bronson); Sheree North (Laura Shelby); Joseph Wiseman (Lucas); Robert Duvall (Vernon Adams); Albert Salmi (Harvey Stenbaugh); J. D. Cannon (Hurd Price); John McGiver (Mayor Sam Bolden); Richard Jordan (Crowe Wheelwright); John Beck (Jason Bronson); Ralph Waite (Jack Dekker); William Watson (Choctaw Lee); Charles Tyner (Minister); John Hillerman (Totts); Robert Emhardt (Hersham); Richard Bull (Dusaine); Hugh McDermott (Moss); Lou Frizzell (Cobden); Walter Brooke (Harris); Bill Bramley (Marc Corman).

THE LOVE MACHINE *(Columbia, 1971), C-108 min.*

Executive producer, Irving Mansfield; producer, M. J. Frankovich; director, Jack Haley,

Jr.; based on the novel by Jacqueline Susann; screenplay, Samuel Taylor; music and music arranger, Artie Butler; songs, Brian Wells and Ruth Batchelor; Butler and Mark Lindsay; production designer, Lyle R. Wheeler; set decorator, George Hopkins; titles, Maury Nemoy; dialogue coach, Kathleen Freeman; costumes, Moss Mabry; makeup, Hank Edds; assistant director, Philip P. Parslow; sound, Les Fresholtz, Arthur Piantodosi; camera effects, Butler-Glouner; camera, Charles B. Lang; second unit camera, Frederick L. Guarino; editor, David Blewitt.

John Phillip Law (Robin Stone); Dyan Cannon (Judith Austin); Robert Ryan (Gregory Austin); Jackie Cooper (Danton Miller); David Hemmings (Jerry Nelson); Jodi Wexler (Amanda); William Roerick (Cliff Dorne); Maureen Arthur (Ethel Evans); Shecky Greene (Christie Lane); Clinton Greyn (Alfie Knight); Sharon Farrell (Maggie Stewart); Alexandra Hay (Tina St. Claire); Eve Bruce (Amazon Woman); Greg Mullavey (Bob Summers); Edith Atwater (Mary); Gene Baylos (Eddie Flynn); Ben Lessy (Kenny Ditto); Elizabeth St. Clair (Susie); Claudia Jennings (Darlene); Mary Collinson (Debbie); Madeline Collinson (Sandy); Ann Ford (Model); Gayle Hunnicutt (Astrological Girl at Party); Jerry Dunphy, Michael Jackson, Ted Meyers (Newscasters).

LE COURSE DU LIEVRE A TRAVERS LES CHAMPS (a.k.a., ... AND HOPE TO DIE, Twentieth Century-Fox, 1972), C-140 min.

Producer, Serge Silberman; director, Rene Clement; based on the novel *Black Friday* by David Goodis; screenplay, Sebastian Japrisot; music, Francis Lai; camera, Edmond Richard; editor, Roger Dwyre.

Robert Ryan (Charley); Jean-Louis Trintignant (Tony); Aldo Ray (Mattone); Tisa Farrow (Pepper); Lea Massari (Sugar); Jean Gaven (Rizzio); Nadine Nabokov (Majorette); Andre Lawrence (Gypsy); Daniel Breton (Paul).

LOLLY-MADONNA XXX (MGM, 1973), C-105 min.

Producer, Rodney Carr-Smith; director, Richard C. Sarafian; based on the novel by Sue Grafton; screenplay, Carr-Smith; art director, Herman Blumenthal; set decorator, Jim Payne; music, Fred Myrow; song, Kim Carnes and David Ellingson; assistant directors, Mike Moder, Terry Carr; sound, Charles W. Wilborn, Hal Watkins; special camera effects, Tim Smyth; camera, Philip Lathrop; editor, Tom Rolf.

Rod Steiger (Laban Feather); Robert Ryan (Pap Gutshall); Scott Wilson (Thrush Feather); Jeff Bridges (Zack Feather); Season Hubley (Roonie Gill); Katherine Squire (Chickie Feather); Timothy Scott (Skylar Feather); Ed Lauter (Hawk Feather); Randy Quaid (Finch Feather); Tresa Hughes (Elspeth Gutshall); Paul Koslo (Villum Gutshall); Kiel Martin (Ludie Gutshall); Gary Busey (Seb Gutshall); Joan Goodfellow (Sister E. Gutshall).

EXECUTIVE ACTION (National General, 1973), C-91 min.

Producer, Edward Lewis; associate producers, Dan Bessie, Gary Horowitz; director, David Miller; story, Donald Freed, Mark Lane; screenplay, Dalton Trumbo; music, Randy Edelman; titles, Bill Brown; art director, Kirk Axtell; technical consultant, Steve Jaffe; research, Robert Polin, Kevin Van Fleet, David Lifton, Lillian Castellano, Penn Jones, Jr., Carol Rosenstein, Eda Hallinan, Barbara Elman; graphics, Ben Nay; sound, Bruce Bisenz, Kirk Francis, Jock Putnam; camera, Robert Steadman; editors, George Frenville, Irving Lerner; documentary editor, Ivan Dryer.

Burt Lancaster (Farrington); Robert Ryan (Foster); Will Geer (Ferguson); Gilbert Green (Paulitz); John Anderson (Halliday); Paul Carr (Chris); Colby Chester (Tim); Ed Lauter

(Operation Chief, Team A); Richard Bull, Lee Delano (Gunmen, Team A); Walter Brooke (Smythe); Sidney Clute (Depository Clerk); Deanna Darrin (Stripper); Lloyd Gough (Mc-Cadden); Richard Hurst (Used Car Salesman); Robert Karnes (Man at Rifle Range); James MacColl (Lee Harvey Oswald/Oswald Imposter); Joaquin Martinez (Art Mendoza); Oscar Orcini (Jack Ruby); Tom Peters (Sergeant); Paul Sorenson (Officer Brown); Sandy Ward (Policeman); William Watson (Leader, Team B); John Brascia, Dick Miller, Hunter Von Leer (Riflemen, Team B); Ed Kemmer (Reporter).

THE OUTFIT *(MGM, 1973), C-102 min.*

Producer, Carter De Haven; director, John Flynn; based on the novel by Richard Stark; screenplay, Flynn; music, Jerry Fielding; art director, Tambi Larsen; set decorator, James I. Berkey; assistant director, William McGarry; sound, Richard Raguse, Jall Watkins; camera, Bruce Surtees; editor, Ralph E. Winters.

Robert Duvall (Macklin); Karen Black (Bett Harrow); Joe Don Baker (Cody); Robert Ryan (Mailer); Timothy Carey (Menner); Richard Jaeckel (Chemey); Sheree North (Buck's Wife); Felice Orlandi (Frank Stern); Marie Windsor (Madge Coyle); Jane Greer (Alma); Henry Jones (Doctor); Joanna Cassidy (Rita); Tom Reese (Man); Elisha Cook (Carl); Bill McKinney (Buck); Anita O'Day (Herself); Archie Moore (Packard); Tony Young (Accountant); Roland LaStarza (Hit Man); Roy Roberts (Bob Caswell); Edward Ness (Ed Macklin); Tony Andersen (Parking Attendant); Emile Meyer (Amos); Roy Jenson (Al); Philip Kenneally (Bartender); Bern Hoffman (Jim Sinclair); John Steadman (Gas Station Attendant); Paul Genge (Pay-Off Man); Francis De Sales (Jim); James Bacon (Bookie); Army Archerd (Butler); Tony Trabert (Himself); Jeannine Riley (Prostitute); Charles Knapp (Motel Owner).

THE ICEMAN COMETH *(American Film Theatre, 1973), 239 min.*

Producer, Ely Landau; director, John Frankenheimer; based on the play by Eugene O'-Neill; text edited by Thomas Quinn Curtiss; camera, Ralph Woolsey; editor, Harold Kress.

Lee Marvin (Hickey); Fredric March (Harry Hope); Robert Ryan (Larry Slade); Jeff Bridges (Don Parritt); Martyn Green (The Captain); George Voskovec (The General); Moses Gunn (Joe Mott); Tom Pedi (Rocky Pioggi); Evans Evans (Cora); Bradford Dillman (Willie Oban); Sorrell Booke (Hugo Kalmar); John McLiam (Jimmy Tomorrow).

About the Author and Researchers:

JAMES ROBERT PARISH, California-based biographer, was born in Cambridge, Massachusetts. He attended the University of Pennsylvania and graduated as a Phi Beta Kappa with a degree in English. A graduate of the University of Pennsylvania Law School, he is a member of the New York Bar. As president of Entertainment Copyright Research Co., Inc., he headed a major researching facility for the film and television industries. Later he was a film interviewer-reviewer for *Motion Picture Daily* and *Variety*. He is the author of *The Fox Girls*, *The RKO Gals*, *Actors' Television Credits*, *Hollywood's Great Love Teams*, and *Elvis!* He is co-author of *The MGM Stock Company*, *The Glamour Girls*, *The Great Gangster Pictures*, *Liza!*, and others. Mr. Parish is also a film commentator for national magazines.

GREGORY MANK is a graduate of Mount St. Mary's College, with a B.A. in English. He has written for *Films in Review* and *Film Fan Monthly* and has been associated with Mr. Parish on *The Hollywood Players: The Forties*, *The Great Screen Heroes*, *Great Child Stars*, and others. Mr. Mank lives with his wife Barbara in Maryland where he is active in theatre as a performer and a teacher.

MICHAEL R. PITTS is a journalist and free-lance writer. A graduate of Ball State University with a B.S. in history and a Master's Degree in journalism, he is the former entertainment editor of the *Anderson* (Ind.) *Daily Bulletin*. Besides writing, Mr. Pitts currently works as a researcher for the Madison County Council of Governments, a local planning advisory agency, and he is film reviewer for Channel 7 in Anderson where he resides. Besides contributing to cinema journals here and abroad, with Mr. Parish he has prepared *The Great Spy Pictures*, *Film Directors: A Guide to Their American Films*, and *The Great Western Pictures*.

DON E. STANKE was born in St. Paul, Minnesota, but has spent most of his adult life in or near San Francisco where he worked for several years for the *San Francisco Examiner*. Don started interviewing screen personalities for movie magazines in 1971. To date he has interviewed some forty celebrities. He is employed as office manager by the CGR Medical Corporation in the San Leandro, California, district office. Besides his film magazine pieces, he has co-authored with Mr. Parish *The Glamour Girls*, *The Debonairs*, and *The Swashbucklers*.

T. ALLAN TAYLOR, godson of the late Margaret Mitchell, has long been active in book publishing and is currently production manager of one of the largest abstracting-technical indexing services in the U.S. He has served as editor of such volumes as *The Fox Girls*, *The MGM Stock Company*, *Good Dames*, *Vincent Price Unmasked*, *Hollywood's Great Love Teams*, *Liza!*, *The Glamour Girls*, and *Hollywood Players: The Forties*.

JOHN ROBERT COCCHI has been viewing and collecting data on motion pictures since childhood and is now considered one of the most thorough film researchers in the United States. He is the New York editor of *Boxoffice* Magazine. He was research associate on *The American Movies Reference Book, The Fox Girls,* and many others, and has written cinema history articles for such journals as *Film Fan Monthly* and *Screen Facts.* He recently authored a book on *The Westerns.* He is the co-founder of one of Manhattan's leading film societies.

New York-born FLORENCE SOLOMON attended Hunter College and then joined Ligon Johnson's copyright research office. Later she was director of research at Entertainment Copyright Research Co., Inc., and she is currently a reference supervisor at ASCAP's Index Division. Ms. Solomon has collaborated on such works as *The American Movies Reference Book, TV Movies, Film Directors Guide: Western Europe,* and others. She is the niece of the noted sculptor, the late Sir Jacob Epstein.

Index

Gabin, Jean, 188
Gable, Clark, 25, 28, 38, 44, 69, 190, 218-9, 299-300, 309, 313-5, 396, 442, 448, 561, 563
Gage, Erford, 538
Gaines, Richard, 475
Gallant Hours, The, 68-9, 95
Gangway for Tomorrow, 539, 588
Garalaga, Martin, 404
Garbo, Greta, 299, 443
Gardner, Ava, 144, 146, 188, 190, 247, 297
Garfield, John, 47, 194, 196, 403, 410, 469-70, 474, 484
Gargan, William, 54, 390
Garland, Judy, 55, 226, 229-30
Garland, Robert, 187
Garner, James, 577
Garnett, Tay, 301
Garson, Greer, 54, 158, 225, 284-5, 558-9
Gaudio, Tony, 443
Gavin, John, 138
Gaynor, Janet, 373
Gaynor, Mitzi, 144
Gebert, Gordon, 295
Geer, Will, 242, 557, 569, 582
Genn, Leo, 105
Gentleman's Agreement, 542
George, Anthony, 578
George, Gladys, 47-8
George, Grace, 54-5, 101
Gering, Marion, 459
Gibney, Sheridan, 385, 393
Gibson, Wynne, 15
Giesler, Jerry, 290-2, 307
Gigi, 220
Gilbert, John, 299, 443
Gilchrist, Connie, 109
Gillette, Anita, 572
Girandoux, Jean, 566
Girardot, Annie, 574
Girl Rush, 279, 341
Girosi, Marcello, 123
Gish, Dorothy, 434
Gish, Lillian, 305, 409
Glasmon, Kuber, 20
Glass Menagerie, The, 113, 165
Glass Web, The, 485-6, 520
Gleason, Jackie, 471
Gleason, James, 472
Gloria Jean, 468
G-Men, 37, 80, 391, 462
Goat Song, The, 433
Goddard, Paulette, 485, 535-6

Godfather, The, 153, 501
God's Little Acre, 564, 582, 600
Goff, Ivan, 58
Going Home, 329, 362
Going My Way, 470
Golden Boy, 535
Golden Gloves, 535-6, 538, 585
Golden Horizon, 541
Golden, John, 370
Goldstein, Robert, 379
Goldwyn, Sam, 39, 40, 42
Gomez, Thomas, 300, 480, 549
Good Earth, The, 365, 396-400, 424
Good Guys and the Bad Guys, The, 326, 361
Good Neighbor Sam, 524
Gordon, Mary, 37
Gordon, Ruth, 101, 468
Gorky, 368-9
Gorshin, Frank, 71-2, 151
Got, Roland, 277
Goudal, Jetta, 434
Goulding, Edmund, 404
Gow, Gordon, 130, 223
Grahame, Gloria, 119, 125, 300, 304, 542, 568
Graham, Martha, 187
Graham, Sheilah, 99, 111
Grand Hotel, 418
Grand Slam, 527
Grand Street Follies of 1928, 16
Grand Street Follies of 1929, 16
Granger, Stewart, 574-5
Grant, Cary, 109, 111, 146, 219, 312-3
Grass Is Greener, The, 312-3, 355
Greatest Show on Earth, The, 114, 196, 203
Great Expectations, 202
Great Gatsby, The, 566
Great Guy, 42-3, 82
Great Sinner, The, 109
Great Ziegfeld, The, 396
Green, Adolph, 318
Green, Gerald, 418
Green, Guy, 318
Greene, Richard, 484
Greenstreet, Sidney, 472
Greer, Jane, 65, 105, 285, 292, 294
Gregory, James, 406, 569
Gregory, Paul, 307
Grey, Zane, 280
Griffith, D.W., 329
Grisson Gang, The, 582
Gropper, Herbert, 369
Guernsey, Otto L., Jr., 188, 411

Puzo, Mario, 153
Pygmalion, 45

Qualen, John, 294, 390
Queen of the Mob, 536, 586
Quine, Richard, 126, 277
Quinlavan, Lager-hard, 72
Quinn, Anthony, 49, 130, 535, 555

Racers, The, 125, 169
Rachel and the Stranger, 286–7, 290, 293, 297, 345
Rachevasky, Zina, 212
Racket, The, 298–9, 348, 434, 436, 441, 551, 595
Raffin, Deborah, 160–1
Raft, George, 28, 42, 45–7, 71, 247, 374–5, 377, 400, 448, 470–1, 475, 489, 496, 557
Raine, Norman Reilly, 400
Rainer, Luise, 396, 398–9, 537
Raines, Ella, 189
Rainmaker, The, 214–5, 257
Rains, Claude, 197, 296, 403, 411, 485
Rampage, 317, 357
Rampling, Charlotte, 333–4
Randall, Tony, 414
Random Harvest, 54
Ranieri, Massino, 156
Rankin, William, 454
Rathbone, Basil, 37
Rattigan, Terence, 219
Ray, Aldo, 564
Raye, Martha, 535
Raymond, Gene, 283
Ray, Nicholas, 299, 302, 549–51, 571
Reagan, Ronald, 70–1
Reagan, Nancy, 70
Red Cross at War, The, 477
Redgrave, Michael, 68, 105
Red House, The, 479, 517
Red Pony, The, 290, 293, 346
Red Star Over Hollywood, 480
Reed, Carol, 212
Reed, Donna, 276
Reed, Rex, 330
Reed, Walter, 538
Reeves, John, 477
Regas, Pedro, 390
Reinhardt, Max, 38–9, 535, 557
Reinhardt, Wolfgang, 546
Reisberg, Harry F., 554

Reis, Irving, 480
Relkin, Edward, 315
Remick, Lee, 235
Remy, Albert, 234
Renoir, Jean, 541
Retreat, Hell, 116
Rettig, Tommy, 304
Return of the Bad Men, 543, 591
Rey, Fernando, 156
Reynolds, Adeline de Walt, 411
Reynolds, Bernard B., 301
Reynolds, Marjorie, 297
Riccio, Pete, 99
Rice, Elmer, 377, 379, 410
Rice, Joan, 206
Richard III, 38
Richards, Ann, 193
Richardson, Ralph, 459
Riddle, Nelson, 71
Riders of the Deadline, 275, 339
Ridges, Stanley, 470
Riffi, 196
Righter, Carroll, 273
Ringgold, Gene, 284
Rin Tin Tin, 17, 334
Rio Lobo, 321
Ripley, Arthur, 310
Ritchey, Bruce, 229
Ritter, Thelma, 14, 144, 493, 496
River of No Return, 304, 351
Road to Carmichael's, The, 294
Roaring Twenties, The, 47–8, 84
Robards, Jason, 577
Rober, Richard, 549
Roberts, Ben, 58
Robertson, Cliff, 582
Robeson, Paul, 472
Robe, The, 279
Robin and the Seven Hoods, 524
Robin, Dany, 121
Robinson, Dewey, 38
Robinson, Edward G., 11–2, 23–5, 30, 39, 40, 45, 50, 58–9, 140–1, 191, 193, 369, 374–5, 379, 382, 386, 391, 403, 410, 431–529
Robinson, Edward G., Jr., 465, 472, 494
Robinson, Jane Adler, 491–3, 501
Robson, Flora, 404–5
Robson, Mark, 110, 196
Robson, May, 537
Rock Me, Julie, 374
Rodann, Ziva, 135
Rodney, John, 284
Roerick, William, 151

Roger, Gregory, 37
Rogers, Ginger, 472, 488, 539–40
Roland, Gilbert, 303, 308
Rolland, Romain, 369
Roman, Ruth, 109–10, 321
Romero, Cesar, 209
Romeo and Juliet, 16, 38
Rooney, Mickey, 38–9, 455
Rope of Sand, 197, 251
Rose, Billy, 537
Rosebud, 333
Rosen, Al, 374
Rosemary's Baby, 323
Rose Tattoo, The, 211, 256
Ross, Anthony, 552
Rossen, Robert, 103, 470
Ross, Frank, 197, 279
Rowland, Roy, 477
Rowlands, Gena, 139–40, 229, 490
Rozsa, Miklos, 128
Rubin, Daniel N., 16
Rule, Janice, 236, 569
Rumann, Sig, 468
Run for Cover, 62–3, 91
Run Silent, Run Deep, 218–9, 257, 309
Runyon, Damon, 462
Rush, Barbara, 136
Russell, Jane, 296, 298–300, 302–3, 554, 561, 563
Russell, Rosalind, 105, 160
Ryan's Daughter, 326, 328–9, 361
Ryan, Robert, 110, 210, 235, 241–3, 284, 295, 299, 530–608

Sacks, Gene, 557
Sagal, Boris, 162
St. Clair, Lydia, 101
St. Columba and the River, 196
St. Louis Kid, The, 36, 79
Samson and Delilah, 433
Sanders, George, 464, 472
Sands, Dorothy, 16
San Francisco, 395
Sargent, Franklin, 432
Saroyan, William, 58
Sarris, Andrew, 299
Savalas, Telly, 236, 580
Sawyer, Joe, 39
Scalawag, 156, 180
Scalphunters, The, 236, 262
Scarface: Shame of a Nation, 28–9, 365, 374–7, 379–80, 384, 390–1, 411, 421, 444, 480

Scarlet Street, 477–8, 516
Schaffner, Franklin, 566
Schary, Dory, 542, 545, 560, 567
Schatzberg, Jerry, 287
Schell, Maximilian, 226
Schildkraut, Joseph, 401–2, 432, 436, 460, 537, 552
Schoemann, Wanda S., 288
Schorr, William, 115
Schrader, Paul, 330
Schwartz, Maurice, 367–8
Scofield, Paul, 234, 241
Scorpio, 241–2, 265
Scott, Adrian, 543, 545
Scott, George C., 71, 142, 150, 317
Scott, Janette, 135
Scott, Lizabeth, 103, 106–7, 187, 189–91, 198, 206, 299, 551
Scott, Martha, 578
Scott, Randolph, 116, 276, 538, 541, 543
Scott, Zachary, 308, 549
Scourby, Alexander, 495
Seaton, George, 141, 239
Sea Wolf, The, 403, 469–70, 512
Seberg, Jean, 158
Second Chance, 303, 350
Second Gun, The, 245
Second to Die, A, 577
Secret Ceremony, 323–4, 360
Secret Fury, The, 549–50, 593
Secret Six, The, 444
Segall, Harry, 411
Selander, Lesley, 275
Selznick, David O., 287, 290, 292
Selznick, Myron, 29
Separate Tables, 219–20, 258
Serling, Rod, 144
Set-Up, The, 110, 295, 546–8, 557, 593
Seven Days in May, 144–6, 175, 233, 242, 261
Seven Faces, 372–3, 421
Seven Little Foys, The, 65, 92
Seventh Heaven, 373
Seven Thieves, 495, 523
Severn, Raymond, 404
Seymour, Dan, 480
Shadow, The, 119
Shake Hands with the Devil, 68, 94
Shannon, Harry, 109
Shannon, Leonard, 283
Shanty Town, 30
Shaw, David, 566
Shaw, George Bernard, 135, 220, 433